The Penn Commentary on Piers Plowman
Volume 1

The Penn Commentary on Piers Plowman

VOLUME 1

C Prologue–Passus 4; B Prologue–Passus 4;
A Prologue–Passus 4

Andrew Galloway

PENN

University of Pennsylvania Press
Philadelphia

Copyright © 2006 University of Pennsylvania Press
All rights reserved
Printed in the United States of America on acid-free paper

10   9   8   7   6   5   4   3   2   1

Published by
University of Pennsylvania Press
Philadelphia, Pennsylvania 19104–4112

A cataloging-in-publication record is available from the Library of Congress

Contents

Note to the Reader

The text of *Piers* quoted here is that of the Athlone edition, under the general editorship of George Kane. The commentary is keyed first of all to the C Version of the poem, then in reverse chronology to the B and A versions. Latin quotations in the poem are cited by adding the letter "a" to the end of the line number. The editions of Schmidt and Pearsall differ little in their lineation from the Athlone edition, and the quotation of the beginning and ending words of each passage commented upon will make reference to those editions easy. Skeats line-numbering differs somewhat more; in the C Version, add one to the Athlone passus number to arrive at Skeats passus number. References to lines of the A and B versions are specifically labeled with the letters A and B; references to C lines are generally not labeled. When reference is made to lines that fall in parallel passages of the versions, the references to parallel passages are enclosed within parentheses. Hence the notation "see 11.116–33 (B.10.176–221, A.11.128–64)" refers to passages that are closely parallel in the three versions; a notation like "see C.1.146–58 (B.1.148–62; cp. A.1.135–38)" indicates a substantive difference in the version prefaced by "cp." Each passus of the poem in this installment is supplied with an introductory "Headnote," which summarizes the main features of the passus and treats matters relevant to the passus (or groups of passūs) as a whole. We have been careful to provide divisions of the text as we understand the movement of the poem. These are usually preceded by a more general, summary note; such *summulae* are followed by notes on particular passages. The discussion repeatedly encompasses larger units first, then devolves to smaller ones, in a nested structure.

Translations from the Vulgate Bible are taken from the Douay-Rheims text (Challoner revision) in modernized spelling (New York: P.J. Kenedy & Sons, 1914), with slight adjustments when necessary. Douay references to 1 and 2 Kings correspond to 1 and 2 Samuel in the Authorized Version, 3 and 4 Kings to AV's 1 and 2 Kings, and Psalms 10–145 to AV's Psalms 11–146. Quotations from the Latin Vulgate generally follow the modern (Clementine) text, as represented in the edition printed by Typis Societatis S. Joannis Evangelistae (Rome, 1956).

Except where otherwise noted, translations are our own.
The following special abbreviations are used:

Alford, *Gloss.*: John Alford, *Piers Plowman: A Glossary of Legal Diction*. Cambridge: D. S. Brewer, 1988.

Alford, *Quot.*: John Alford, *Piers Plowman: A Guide to the Quotations*. Binghamton, N.Y.: Medieval and Renaissance Texts and Studies, 1992.

A-ND: *The Anglo-Norman Dictionary*. Ed. William Rothwell et al. London: Modern Humanities Association, 1981–92.

L: Langland.

MED: *The Middle English Dictionary*. Ed. Hans Kurath et al. Ann Arbor: University of Michigan Press, 1956–2001.

OED: *The Oxford English Dictionary*. 2nd ed. Oxford and New York: Oxford University Press, 1989.

PL: *Patrologiae Cursus Completus . . . Series Latina*. Ed. J.-P. Migne et al. 221 vols. Paris, 1844–64.

PP: *Piers Plowman.*

Rot. Parl.: *Rotuli Parliamentorum*. Ed. J. Strachey et al. 6 vols. London: Stationery Office, 1767–77.

SR: *The statutes of the realm. Printed by command of His Majesty King George the Third. In pursuance of an address of the House of Commons of Great Britain. From original records and authentic manuscripts*. 11 vols. London: George Eyre and Andrew Strahan, 1810–1828.

Citations of primary works are indicated by editor and year of publication, and so listed in the Works Cited; all citations of Chaucer are from Larry D. Benson, gen. ed., *The Riverside Chaucer* (Boston: Houghton Mifflin, 1987). The major editions of *Piers Plowman*, with their prefaces and notes, are abbreviated as follows:

K-A: George Kane, ed., *Piers Plowman: The A Version: Wills Visions of Piers Plowman and Do-Well*. London: Athlone, 1960. Cited is the Revised Edition (Athlone and University of California Press, 1988), with only slight revisions.

KD-B: George Kane and E. Talbot Donaldson, eds., *Piers Plowman: The B Version: Wills Visions of PIers Plowman, Do-Well, Do-Better and Do-Best*. London: Athlone, 1975. Similarly, Revised Edition, 1988.

RK-C: George Russell and George Kane, eds., *Piers Plowman: The C Version: Wills Visions of Piers Plowman, Do-Well, Do-Better and Do-Best*. London: Athlone; Berkeley: University of California Press, 1997.

Bnt: J. A. W. Bennett, ed., *Langland: Piers Plowman: The Prologue and Passus I-VII of the B Text as found in Bodleian MS. Laud 581*. Oxford: Clarendon Press, 1972.

Prsl: Derek Pearsall, ed., *William Langland: Piers Plowman, The C-Text*. London: Edward Arnold, 1978. Cited is the Corrected Edition, Exeter: Exeter University Press, 1994.

Schm: A. V. C. Schmidt, ed., Text cited from A Parallel-Text Edition. Volume I: *Text*.

London and New York: Longman, 1995. Schmidts comments are cited from *William Langland: The Vision of Piers Plowman: A Critical Edition of the B-Text* (whose text is identical to the B text in the *Parallel Text Edition*). 2nd ed. Everyman, London: Dent; Vermont: Tuttle, 1995.

Skt: Walter W. Skeat, ed., *The Vision of William concerning Piers the Plowman in Three Parallel Texts*. 2 vols. London: Oxford University Press, 1886; with addition of Bibliography, 1954. Other editions or works by Skeat are cited by their year of publication and included in the Works Cited.

Preface

After some fifteen years of study of this poem, it seems to me more than ever that a new extended commentary on *Piers Plowman* in all of its versions has a range of useful purposes that are difficult to aim at by other means: to sum up, absorb, and assess the most useful work to date and make that available to a wide range of readers (with the assumption that these know at least enough Middle English to be picking up this poem in the first place); to solve as many unsolved puzzles as possible and ferret out a range of unexplored meanings with original research and ideas; and to find terms to appreciate the whole expanse of a work whose fine detail, existence in a set of more or less separate "versions," and long process of poetic development are all extraordinarily complex and potent with meaning. The center of these purposes is to investigate with new ambition a work that seems to demand a wider range of literary history and perhaps literary sensibility than any other in the language, yet which situates itself far beyond what we narrowly define as "literature" by its profound and witty involvement in fields that we distinguish as theology, law, politics, economics, and many other domains of culture.

Each volume of this Commentary proceeds under similar assumptions and formats, but presents an individual scholar's attention to and understanding of the poem, in a scope and with a degree of detail that have been less often pursued in treating *Piers Plowman* than other major medieval English poems, and in relation to a range of critical, literary, and other cultural contexts that each commentator deems pertinent. The Commentary is not a variorum, nor does it proceed within impersonally fixed boundaries of what aspects of these three versions and their contexts to cover; rather, it unfolds from the individual commentator's knowledge, sensitivity, and judgment, and from a commitment to explicate in fine detail and more broadly one of the most important and challenging works of the later Middle Ages. The volumes of this Commentary do not withhold the individual commentator's interpretive thought or opinions, but they are guided by a desire to present a range of observations, materials, and reasoning as fairly, rigorously, and evocatively as possible, sustained by the hope of generating further attention, investigations, and interpretations by others.

The Note to the Reader sets forth the main formal assumptions of the commentary. It is worth reemphasizing that the commentary's use of the C text as its first point of reference, turning then to B and A, treats the poetic project of *Piers Plowman* in archaeological terms, allowing consideration of each version in its own integrity as well as investigation of the complex succession of the three. The Z text, whose differences from A are shrewdly indicated in the edition by A. G. Rigg and Charlotte Brewer (1983), is not considered in close detail here or assumed to be part of the same author's work, nor is the afterlife of *Piers Plowman* pursued beyond some isolated indications, but these omissions are not constraints on this project so much as practical boundaries that others may well use this Commentary to press beyond.

The unity of this Commentary is by its nature less important than its parts, but it is hoped that it can foster a new sense of the comprehensive achievement of the poem. Beginning with the Headnotes of each section, an effort is made to link developing larger issues through the versions where possible and helpful, but to do so with sensitivity to the immediate passage and version. The attention to detail and to the individual versions of such a project means that readers of any one version can consult this as readily as those considering all three versions; the quotation of substantial portions at the beginning and ending of each lemma being commented on allows users of any edition of the poem to use this Commentary in spite of minor differences in line numbers. Two indexes provide further means of tracing the materials, issues, and passages treated in the Commentary.

The preface to the last volume of the Commentary by Stephen Barney explains the genesis of this collaborative but not impersonal endeavor. My role in this project began as a graduate student assistant to an intimidating group of *Piers Plowman* scholars gathered at the University of California Humanities Research Institute at the University of California, Irvine, in 1990, who were planning a full commentary on the poem. I remain deeply grateful to the staff at HRI and its then director, Professor Mark Rose, for their warm support of a research student, as I casually entered a path whose length and interest for me I could not then imagine. I owe a fundamental debt to John Alford, not simply because of the centrally useful guides to the poem that he produced and on which I, like all scholars of it, have continuously depended, but because he functioned as a mentor in countless ways in my early career, and especially in the development of my role in *Piers Plowman* studies. To the collaborators in this project, each of whom is responsible for a volume, I owe inestimable debts: Stephen A. Barney, Ralph Hanna, Traugott Lawler, and Anne Middleton. In particular, the repeated and scrupulous attention to this volume by Traugott Lawler and especially Stephen Barney, the instigator of the project and the first to complete his volume, cannot be sufficiently thanked. I am indebted also to three other remarkable scholars, Derek Pearsall, James Simpson, and Robert N. Swanson, who provided searching and learned comments on this work at several stages, and to David Benson as one of the two splendidly helpful and careful readers for the Press.

I have learned much from co-teachers of *Piers* in three very different kinds of classroom settings at Cornell, who have helped make this the most intellectually and humanly generous academic setting I can imagine: Tom Hill, Pete Wetherbee, and Paul Hyams, as well as all the present and former students who in those or other settings who have offered reactions to the poem or papers that have assisted my understanding of it. It is a pleasure to thank particularly Diane Cady, Cynthia Camp, Nicole Clifton, Kara Doyle, Pam Hammons, Tricia Har, Leigh Harrison, Mark Hazard, Curtis Jirsa, Johanna Kramer, Roscoe Leasure, Nicole Marafioti, John Sebastian, Sachi Shimomura, Fiona Somerset, Jacqueline Stuhmiller, Katherine Terrell, Misty Urban, and Kim Zarins for all their ideas and reactions to *Piers* in my seminars, and Bryan Lowrance for his insightful suggestions when he read a draft of this commentary as part of his undergraduate Presidential Research Scholar work. At a late stage, Diane Cady and Curtis Jirsa checked a passus each and offered important questions and suggestions as well as rigorous proofreaders' eyes; in producing the final product the energetic and shrewd labors that the Press has applied to the whole volume have been exemplary. I am moreover generally grateful to the good people of Malvern, particularly Pat Neve and Dorothy and David Sharp, for allowing my reasons to visit there to serve as delightful opportunities for warm hospitality and witty and informative correspondence.

To my wife Ellen, who has patiently supported this project throughout its seemingly endless and pervasive presence, and my son Aidan, who has endured its claims for only half of its existence but all his life so far, remain my greatest thanks and debts.

C Prologue; B Prologue; A Prologue

Headnote

Readers and especially rereaders of PP in any version have long perceived the general unity of the first two dream-visions. The pronounced division between these dreams and the rest of the poem has contributed to a long-held tradition of identifying and distinguishing "the *Visio*," taken to end with these initial two visions in which the narrator is often merely an observer, and "the *Vita*," the further stretches defined by the narrator's search for Dowel, Dobet, and Dobest (on these titles see below, *Rubrics and Passus Headings*). The first two visions are, in their general boundaries, the most stable across all revisions; only the final three visions are equally stable (C.20–22/B.18–20), and those perhaps because they are almost untouched by revision (a circumstance that continues to elicit the hypothesis that the author died before completing the C revision [RK-C 82–88]).

Among modern scholars, John M. Manly—whose 1908 polemical essay on the multiple authorship of PP began the modern tradition of trenchant speculation and critical argument about most aspects of this poem—first drew emphatic attention to the unity of the first two visions: he argued that those visions in A were the work of the first writer, whose work ceased there, to be followed by various continuators and revisers (1908:17; see Huppé 1947 for an example of the many vigorous rejections that this view elicited). Although from the mid-twentieth century on there has been little interest in pursuing claims of multiple authorship for the original poem in at least the A, B, and C versions, the stability of the first vision in particular remains sufficiently notable that it suggests another prospect: the poet originally conceived the poem to go through Meed's and Conscience's debate only, as "a single-vision satire of contemporary conditions" (Hanna 1996:232).

Even in the first version of the first vision, however, a range of widely developing genres and forms can be seen as more or less dominant contributions and parallels to the poem, as they can for PP as a whole. Morton Bloomfield (1962:3–43) first sought to survey these broadly in a discussion that remains essential for situating the work's formal properties within a very large historical expanse. Bloomfield saw it as based on three "literary" genres and three "religious" ones: allegorical dream narrative, dialogue, and encyclopedic satire, in the first category; and complaint, commentary, and sermon in the second (1962:10–43). Affiliations with other genres, such as travel literature, lyric *aventure*, and chivalric romance have since been added to Bloomfield's influential and capacious list (see below, 1–13n, 4n, B 6n). The poem in sum constituted for Bloomfield an "apocalypse," although he noted that this was not "an established genre," and that "the particular shifting organization of *Piers* can be understood only in terms of other and more common high medieval literary forms" (1962:10).

In the simplest narrative conceits, the poem establishes itself and continues as visionary experience. This "type of psychic experience" is, as Paul Piehler notes, "by no means confined to the Middle Ages, though it attained at that time its most sophisticated literary expression" (1971:1). From Boethius' early sixth-century *De consolatione Philosophiae* through the late fourteenth-century *Pearl* and beyond, visionary literature presents some recognizable similarities: a dreamer (or at least human narrator granted a vision) is faced with an alarming problem that exceeds his ability to solve or understand it, then finds in a vision or dream an authority or series of authorities (often female) who instruct him or show him allegorically a means to resolve his crisis. The visionary literature in Latin transmitted to the later Middle Ages (often in school-room contexts) is often continuously allegorical and often lacks an explicit dream-frame, presenting itself as directly and authoritatively visionary and instructive: from Martianus Capella's fourth-century *De Nuptiis Philologiae et Mercurii*, so widely known in medieval academic settings (see Wetherbee 1972:83–92), to Boethius' continuously influential *De consolatione Philosophiae*, through the great twelfth-century visionary allegories, Bernardus Silvestris' *Cosmographia*, and Alan of Lille's *Anticlaudianus* and *De Planctu Naturae* (see Piehler 1971; Wetherbee 1972; Lynch 1988; Spearing 1976:18–24). All of these are single visions, and some have been proposed as direct models for PP, but their influence is more likely general and variously mediated, especially through French allegorical poetry (see Barney 1988; for claims to direct knowledge of some works by Alan of Lille, see Schmidt 1987:22; for Boethius, see also below 199–219n, and passus 1 Headnote).

Early thirteenth-century French didactic allegorical dream-visions mix satire with allegory and thereby present a closer parallel to the general mode of PP, although their specific influence remains debated (see Owen 1912; Barney 1988:126). Raoul de Houdenc's *Songe d'Enfer* (c. 1215; ed. Mihm 1984) presents the author's journey in a dream to the city of Hell (whose denizens turn out to have some close relations in Poitou, and whose king, after an infernal banquet, rewards Raoul for entertaining him with stories of sinful minstrels); Huon de Méri's *Le Torneiment Anticrist* (c. 1235; ed. Bender 1976) recounts that author's journey in a vision to a battle of the Virtues and Vices and the respective castles of their lords, Christ and Antichrist (see Barney 1988:126–28, and notes to passūs 20–22). The dream-frame that is important in most later medieval vernacular dream-vision poetry and is especially elaborated between the linked visions of PP was more securely established, however, by French visionary love literature than by didactic literature, especially by the mid- to late thirteenth-century French *Roman de la Rose*, written (successively) by Guillaume de Lorris (c. 1230–45) and Jean de Meun (c. 1270–85; see Lynch 1988:120 for the novelty of the *Rose*'s dream-frame).

The immense popularity, literary authority, and ethical controversy of the *Rose* are unquestionable (see Badel 1980, Huot 1993), but its relation to PP has rarely been considered. If the *Rose* were one of the major works L knew, and it is hard to imagine that he did not in some measure, it would stand as a challenge to be answered rather than a model to be followed for his own ambition in creating a monumental work of vernacular ethical poetry. As the *Rose* in its sprawling, allegorical, and dialectical style attempts a full-ranging consideration of "all the art of love" (ed. Poirion 1974, line 38; trans. Dahlberg 1986; see below 10n), so PP endeavors to probe and encompass all the principles of the Christian social life, that is, of both of the "two cities" that St. Augustine set forth in the *De civitate Dei*: the City of God and the earthly city or community of humanity in its mixture of uncertain sin and virtue. Some details support the view of PP as in some sense a response, from a more overtly Christian, more socially capacious, and in some measure anti-courtly perspective, to this monument of intellectually ambitious, courtly, vernacular dream-vision poetry: like Holy Church, Reason in the *Rose* initially comes down from a tower; like Holy Church, she begins by explaining the meaning of what the dreamer has just seen (see 1.4n, 1.6–9n, and below, Prol.15n). Meed resembles Richesse in some precise as well as general ways, although Meed's moral valence and social implications are fundamentally different (see 2.10–15n, 2.10n, 2.12–15n, A.2.12n). Even Piers' map for the path to "St. Truth," in a very different style from what precedes or follows it, may be said to nod toward but fundamentally dismiss the purposes of the erotic pursuit of the Rose, in the movement from the garden to the tower in the French poem; see 7.206–82 (B.5.560–29, A.6.48–114). Not Oiseuse (Idleness), as in the *Rose*, but a faithful laborer shows the way into this garden. In turn, the arrows of Love in the *Rose* may be the arrows of Lechery in PP (see 22.111–20n). At the end of the *Roman de la Rose*, when that narrator is at the point of sexual consummation with the Rose, he reflects on the need to try all things and to know good foods by knowing bad ones, expanding the claim into a general principle: "il fait bon de tout essaier / Por soi miex es biens esgaier. . . . Qui mal essaié n'avra / Ja du bien guieres ne savra" ("it is good to try everything in order to take greater pleasure in one's good fortune . . . he who has not tried evil will hardly ever know anything of the good"; ed. Poirion 1974, lines 21550–74; trans. Dahlberg 1986). At the climactic moment of the Crucifixion and the Harrowing of Hell in PP, Peace asserts the same principle to account for all human understanding of goodness, fulfillment, and peace—"no with woet what wele is þat neuere wo suffrede / Ne what is hoet hunger þat hadde neuere defaute" (20.211–12 [B.18.206–7]), and even to account for God's Incarnation and Crucifixion: he "soffrede hym synne sorwe to fele / To wyte what wele was, kyndeliche to knowe hit" (20.229–30 [B.18.220–21]). Indeed, the principle of knowing "the true" by encountering "the false" is offered as the narrator's own principle of learning from as early as his meeting with Meed and False (2.1–4n), and the idea of "trying all things," first summed up in Holy Church's sermon and later in Conscience's and other figures' use of the tag *omnia probate* from Thessalonians 5:21 (1.77–78n; 1.81–204n; 3.489–500n), is relevant to the concept of "trial" throughout the first vision and beyond (see passus 4, Headnote), an application that might be seen as a fullscale remoralizing of the notorious ending of the *Roman de la Rose*. Finally, Kynde's (God's) last message to the dreamer in PP, that the one and only "craft" (*ars*) that he should seek to master is to "lerne to love" (22/B.20.207–8), focuses him only then on the goal that the *Rose* presents so confidently at the beginning, when it promises to present "the whole art of love." However direct or coincidental that last connection may be between the two poems, the parallel, like the other parallels, is also significant for emphasizing their differences. PP overtly presents that goal only at the end, defines it in a distinctive register of supreme religious and social charity rather than erotic self-fulfillment, and shows that the embrace of it even as simply a goal comes only through a difficult and life-long process of inquiry, experience, suffering, and gradual discovery of charity that are all hallmarks of PP.

Whether any of PP's contemporary readers would have noted its responses to a major secular poem like the *Roman de la Rose*, if such they are, is a tantalizing but unanswerable question. The two known owners of PP from the late fourteenth century were both clerical: one, Walter Brugge, died 1396, was a wealthy canon of York who served as the chief financial manager of the vast Mortimer estates in England, Wales, and eastern Ireland (Davies 1999; see also Burrow 1984); the other, William Palmere, died 1400, was a London rector described simply as "clericus," who had exchanged his benefices in Sussex and Lincolnshire to serve as rector at St. Alphage, Cripplegate, London, from 1397 until his death, and who bequeathed a copy of PP to an unknown woman,

Agnes Eggesfield (Wood 1984). Mid-fifteenth-century named owners include a member of Lincoln's Inn, a rector, a London citizen, and a Speaker of the House of Commons (Middleton 1982:103, 48nn6–7; McFarlane 1973:237–38), most of whom, in keeping with the growth of secular literacy, were lay, but who probably represent some of the kinds of readers from L's own period. The manuscript contexts of the poem present abundant evidence of circulation with didactic and historical materials, and with some English romances and travel narratives (Middleton 1982). There is no explicit indication that any of the known readers or the extant manuscripts associated PP with the *Rose*, or much indication that it circulated initially in the kinds of aristocratic English circles where that poem was more securely known (for the late fourteenth-century aristocratic English readers of the *Rose* and other French poetry, see Burnley 1998:122–47). As McFarlane laments, "so very few inventories of the goods of the law-abiding have been preserved" (McFarlane 1973:237). Yet there is also no direct connection, in so thinly preserved a body of evidence, between owners and readers of PP and those of Guillaume de Deguileville's *Pelerinage de vie humaine*, whose influence on PP is widely assumed (see below), and which is itself a direct remoralizing of the *Rose*. Knowledge of ownership of PP, including its geographic range, is still being worked out (see, e.g., Hanna 2002); its readers' literary or indeed theological range is far more difficult to surmise. While it is clear that the poem was written for and from a clerical realm with blunt aspects of pastoral guidance and intricate matters of theology at issue, it is also clear that these matters are continuously brought to bear on broad social and institutional concerns, in a posture of addressing a lay and clerical audience whose "range of practical and speculative activity is well captured by Will's first two questions of Holichurche: the ownership and use of all 'this tresour' of the earthly field, and the salvation of the soul" (Middleton 1982:104).

Whether or not L was knowingly writing in the shadow of the *Roman de la Rose*, PP certainly falls within the *Rose*'s general tradition. In this tradition, the dream frame, whether it emphasizes sleep and thus (like the *Rose*) invokes the theories of the importance of dreams formulated by Macrobius or other ancient and biblical authorities (see Kruger 1992), or whether it simply identifies a narrator who is more or less casually granted a vision in some daily setting, serves to connect sublime or altered experience to the world of a pining lover or other accidental visionary narrator, and it does so in the distinctly novel realm of an intellectually complex but in some important ways still everyday and accessible vernacular literary language, marked throughout by a sense of more massive Latin authorities, and by an awareness of a wide range of potential readers. The vernacular dream-vision often ends, in fact, by returning the narrator at the end to a commonplace world where he must ponder and apply his new understanding, or begin finally to carry out an action for which the vision has prepared him. Such a genre in the vernacular usually maintains more uncertainties in those and other ways than the Latin visions do, particularly concerning the authority of the work and the status of its experience. Dreams are not always visions, though they might be, as ancient and medieval writers often emphasized (see below, B 6 and note; 11n); but nor are such portrayals of them mere entertainment or adventure, as is much other vernacular literary writing. Possibly an insistence on this latter point contributes to PP's concerns with and severe criticisms of most minstrels (see below, B 33–37n, 35–38n). A vernacular dream-vision poem thus opens an uncertain realm between didacticism and literary pleasure; a vernacular poet of such a work is as likely to present love poetry as social satire, even while emphasizing that the work is a "true vision," one of those "qui ne son mie mençongier" ("that are not at all lies" [*Roman de la Rose*, ed. Poirion 1974, line 4]), a "veray avysyoun" (*Pearl*, ed. Andrew and Waldron 1996, line 1184), or even the most "wonderful a drem" that anyone has ever dreamt, even though its status as "revelacion" or "fantome" is all the more uncertain (Chaucer, *House of Fame*, lines 1–65). Part of the point of a dream-frame in such poetry is to establish the possibility for this authority while allowing a deft evasion of its full claims; another part is to convey the tantalizing range of the force and mystery of direct experience, beyond even what the great *auctores* might speak of.

The form structurally allows a kind of suspension of claims of authority, as A. C. Spearing notes. In love poems like the *Rose*, "the dream may, in itself, have the force of a religious vision; but the turning of the dream into a poem provides for the possibility of a separation between inside and outside—between the Dreamer, who is absorbed in his own experience . . . and the poet, who is repeating the story five years afterwards." As Spearing says, "The Dreamer and the poet are both 'I,' but 'I' as poet does not necessarily endorse his reactions as Dreamer to the dream-experience of five years back" (Spearing 1976:28). The uncertainty that such displacement can imply is overt in PP, with its continuous arguments and disruptions of visions with new visions; as Anne Middleton notes, "the revelation of one adventure is retrospectively converted to the delusion or misapprehension of the next" (1982b:116). Thus in spite of any comprehensive ambitions suggested by the scope of PP, transplanting such narrative "separation" between past and present, inside and outside, from love poetry to social, ethical, and religious poetry makes the didactic and socially comprehensive materials of PP far less settled than they otherwise might be: they become points of doubt, debate, and boldly risky scrutiny and challenges, to the narrator if not also to many of the poem's readers and the poet himself.

Indeed, PP's use of a dream-vision and of a first-person dreaming narrator, so vividly if briefly established at the outset, leads directly to many of the central debates in the poem's critical history. As Bloomfield suggests, "Will is the bridge . . . between the soul and the world. This use of the central character . . . is the means by which Langland made the religious allegorical narrative serve his purposes, serious, ironic, and comic, at the cost of even its strong impersonality and clarity of aim and form" (1962:19). Scholars have long debated to what extent its recurrent and emphatic dream-vision framing and other rhetorical and narrative strategies should be seen as subterfuges for allegorical Christian meanings that can be uncovered only after "extensive consideration of alternative possibilities" by the modern scholar—and perhaps by the diligent medieval reader as well (Robertson and Huppé 1951:16; Kaske 1960); or which seem, as Donaldson argued in opposing the use of patristic exegesis to interpret the opening dream frame of PP, an "unwarranted intrusion upon the poem" (Donaldson 1960:7). More recently, literarily sensitive and theologically contextualized extensions of an exegetical approach to PP have argued that the poem's point is to show a necessary but arduous testing of religious faith through the narrator-dreamer's uncertain progress (Harwood 1992; see also Wittig 1972, 1975; Aers 1975). In a further extension and contextualization, this theological approach to the basic question of the status of the dream and the dreamer has sought the intellectual and religious contexts of the fourteenth-century problems of the will, where the effort to find "one's way out of the labyrinth of the Fair Field" includes continual criticism of sloth (*acedia*) in terms of the period's most acute debates about the nature of volition, by which the poem makes "the individual mind . . . a place for boundless exploration, but also a place for inevitably getting lost," whose ultimate solution for both the narrator and poet, and for other religious thinkers in the period, lies only in "simple fideism" (Bowers 1986:216–17). Further focus on the reformist implications of the poem's concerns with false signs and a hypocritically materialist Christianity has located it among other kinds of religious movements of the period, including those in which Franciscan ideals and anti-Franciscan satire are less easily distinguished than earlier scholars had thought (see Clopper 1997; Aers 2004).

A broader cultural basis has also been sought to account for the difficulties of intellectual clarity that PP's dream-vision mode and idiosyncratic and despairing narrator entail, not to mention the poem's unresolved contradictions and unanswered questions. In Muscatine's view, all this is more or less symptomatic of the period's "crisis" of authority in all manner of social, spiritual, and intellectual domains (Muscatine [1972]1999:65–88, 111–38). But cultural "crisis" may be read as cultural revivification, in which the poem's

debates and aporiae play a major role. In Middleton's view, the range of strategies destabilizing the poem's authority presents not a mere symptom but the
poet's "insistent" and fully conscious "openness to misappropriation" by a
wide range of readers, in order to test and revive a more creative spirit behind
a range of traditional and institutionally hardened teachings. Thus even
though it presents a "tantalizing and continued resemblance to familiar
instructive, factual, authoritative kinds of social discourse, the peculiar power
of the [poem's] literary fiction depends on its evasion or deferral of instrumental claims." By inviting diverse and uncontrollable uses by a very widespread audience, the poem's reassessment of the common teachings it presents
assisted a "full subjective repossession and communal renewal" of the culture's "almost blunted purposes" (Middleton 1982b:121).

The contradictions and evasive strategies established from the outset are
thus seen as either symptoms or veils or tests; they may be read as private
pursuits of faith, or as acts of cultural reflection or mediation. They may
chiefly answer to the poet's divergent audiences' concerns (see Benson 2004),
or to the poet's own tactical evasion of theological responsibility even while he
emphasizes his unusual legitimacy in religious and ethical terms (see Middleton 1997). The purposes and import of the poem's contradictions and evasions
are tantalizing elements of most of its debates and scenes of instruction or
trial, which often end with new problems (see notes on passūs 1, 3, and 4, and
especially their Headnotes).

The strategy of rooting a vision in the everyday human world, as well as
using such a dream-vision to displace ethical, social, and psychological
instruction into something separate from their everyday and narrowly immediate "instrumental" uses, is paralleled in part by the fourteenth-century
visionary French love and secular poetry that followed the *Roman de la Rose*,
especially Guillaume de Machaut's influential works, including the *Dit dou
Vergier* (before 1342) and the *Livre de la fonteinne amoureuse* (c. 1360), as well
as later works like Jean Froissart's *Paradise d'Amour* (1384; see R. B. Palmer
1993, especially xxxiv–xxxvii; also Spearing 1976:41–47). Although such fourteenth-century love visions are far removed in their erotic concerns from the
religious and didactic terms of PP, and thus have rarely been exploited as a
literary context for it, they occupy at least some of its readers' contexts and
define analogies to some of its broad gestures, including the general trend
toward intellectually complex and sophisticated discourses in vernacular
poetry. To a certain extent they provide analogies to PP's chief ethical problem
of what actions or "doing" one should carry out. In the French fourteenth-
century dream-visions, a solitary, often listless narrator is wandering or alone
(often in an idyllic setting, and often in a distressed state of mind), and falls

asleep or slips into "une vision" (Machaut, *Dit dou Vergier*, ed. R. B. Palmer 1993, line 152); there, he is granted an amorously or socially or ethically meaningful vision and is presented with an illuminating or troubling instruction or outcome for how to proceed with his dilemma in love, whereupon he awakens, often (especially in Machaut) with a newly focused appeal to his beloved that reflects the lesson about love and its ethics he has gained.

A similar frame is also clear in the mid-fourteenth-century trilogy of long Christian allegorical dreams and spiritual journeys by Guillaume de Deguileville, themselves a vigorously penitential and didactic response to and revision of the *Roman de la Rose* (see Huot 1993:207–32, Badel 1980:362–75): the *Pelerinage de vie humaine* (1330–31, revised 1355; ed. Stürzinger 1893), *Pelerinage de l'ame* (c. 1355–58; ed. Stürzinger 1895), and *Pelerinage de Jhesucrist* (c. 1358; ed. Stürzinger 1897). This trilogy, and especially the the first *pelerinage*, have long been considered likely influences on PP (see especially Woolf 1969; Burrow 1993:113–18). For some parallels with these last works to aspects of the first vision, see 1.3n, 4n, 6–9n, 6n, 63–64n, 68–71n, 77–78n, 115–25n, B 151n; 2.1–4n, 31–37n; passus 3 Headnote. These last works present often arresting allegorical personae but lack the uncertainties of where authority might be found that pervade and vitalize or disorder PP. The first of Guillaume's works is a direct moral revision and rectification of the *Rose*, which the narrator claims he has just been reading (ed. Stürzinger 1893, lines 8–10), and the *Rose* is still more severely treated in the revised 1355 version (not included in Stürzinger's edition of the first version) when Venus appears as a masked old woman on a pig who says that the *Roman* is "Myn owne book, (whan al ys do,) / And I my sylff made yt also" (in Lydgate's translation of the second version of the *Pelerinage*, ed. Furnivall and Locock 1899–1904, lines 13219–20). It may be better to see PP, however informed by the *Pelerinage*, as not simply modeled on that work so much as, in part, a parallel effort to reinterpret the *Roman de la Rose* in ethical terms, from a social as well as religious ethical perspective (see above).

If a body of French dream poetry constitutes an important background to PP, Middle English dream-vision poetry seems to have grown up around and perhaps in part in response to PP, whose A text is dated as early as 1369, rather than preceding and offering a pattern for L's initial poem (for a claim for PP's fundamental influence on other didactic alliterative poetry, see Lawton 1983; for possible influence on Chaucer's *House of Fame*, see Grady 1996). For instance, the dream-frame of a solitary wanderer appears in English before PP only for short lyric "encounters"; in this sense the whole poem's form, Middleton argues, has "sublimated" the short lyric mode by repeating it (Middleton 1982a:115, 118). The short alliterative "lament" for the brevity of kings' glory as they are tossed on Fortune's wheel, *Somer Soneday*, resembles some of the phrasing of PP and offers a similar portrait of a wandering narrator who has a vision, but there is no certainty when this poem, copied in a late fourteenth or early fifteenth-century hand, should be dated, and thus no indication of whether it precedes or follows or is roughly contemporaneous with PP (the earlier view that it was written in response to the death of Edward II or indeed any particular king has no basis; see Turville-Petre 1989:140–41; cp. Robbins 1959:301–2; and below, 153–59n). PP has no English precedent comparable in size and scope. The only likely Middle English precedent for PP's use of a dream-vision for social and ethical exploration is the incomplete alliterative poem *Wynnere and Wastoure* (ed. Trigg 1990), from which the debaters' resolution (if any) and the narrator's awakening are missing (c. 1352 by internal allusions but possibly considerably later if those are taken as "commemorative" allusions; for the common assumption that PP responds to *Wynnere and Wastoure*, see, e.g., Schmidt 1987:5, and more emphatically Hanna 1996:232–33, but compare the claim for the reverse relationship in Lawton 1983:80–81). PP's literary afterlife remains a complex puzzle, which cannot be pursued in this commentary (see, however, below 1–13n).

As PP establishes the dream-vision's general form—most clearly in the A text's first vision, with successive departures in later revisions and later visions—the narrator's wandering and lapse into sleep yields to a sweeping vision of the social estates in the Prologue (reminiscent of the more static parade of "soldiers" lined up for the armies of Wynnere and Wastoure, and also of the consortium of followers of Fauvel in the mid-fourteenth-century French *Roman de Fauvel*, as well as many other estates satires); in the next passus this gives way to an exposition by Holy Church on the principles of fidelity to truth (that is, the principle of fidelity to fidelity), followed by his entranced witnessing of Lady Meed's marriage to False as the center of the social practices he has initially observed, concluded by her departure to the king's court where she debates Conscience (as Wastoure debates Wynnere) in increasingly complicated and unsettling terms, whose resolution or at least cessation closes the vision.

Scholars have perhaps not sufficiently emphasized how clearly conceived yet dramatically varied are the genres comprising the first vision, and how adroitly those genres are knit together, in a bravura display of combining literary resources into a single form. A uniquely vivid estates satire is followed by a novel elaboration of a verse sermon, followed by an energetically sinful satiric marriage or preparation for a marriage, followed by a brilliantly articulate and dramatic debate, followed by a trial scene that combines elements of comedy, prophecy, and political theory (see Headnotes to the following passūs). Yet in spite of this extraordinary generic, characterological, intellectual and formal variety, the first vision is knit thematically by numerous strands, most broadly, perhaps, the issue of just merits and the place of mercy in social and religious domains (see e.g., 1.196–200 [B.1.201–5, A.1.175–79]; 2.207–19 [B.2.193–207, A.2.154–68]; 3.437–82a [B.3.284–330, A.3.260–76]; and 4.140–45 [B.4.143–48, A.4.126–31]). The same general themes or set of controverted issues punctuate the second vision as well, ending with the Pardon, and in less obvious forms many of the subsequent visions too, especially C.20 (B.18) and C.21 (B.19).

The Prologue exploits its literary resources fully for its novel purposes of social and ethical inquiry, and with increasing boldness in each of the versions of the poem. In A, after the poem has induced a visionary world in a lyrical vein by showing the narrator wandering and falling asleep (on the generic indications of the "chanson d'aventure" there, see below, 1–13n), it leads to a vision that recalls the tradition of "complaint" or "estates satire" (see 22–94n). But here this is a means not just to contemplate the failings of a wide range of social professions and "estates," but also to assess the concepts defining or justifying or expressed through the estates scrutinized. An inquiry into ethical choices and their practical expressions in social roles is clear already in the A version, beginning (unusually) at the lowest social rank with the choices that lead to becoming honest plowmen or followers of pride; from this moral crux the narrative rapidly turns to sharp complaint about the abuses and deceits of more urban estates and, especially, the self-interested or secularly focused clergy (in pastoral or administrative roles), lawyers, and urban craftsmen and tradesmen, with an immersion into whose street-cries and ballads the Prologue in all the versions concludes.

B considerably expands this social survey and complaint without altering its original materials—only six lines in A (90–95) are not taken up more or less exactly in B—inserting into the estates satire a description of founding a commonwealth and a description of the powers and limitations of a king, issuing successively from the mouths of a "lunatik," an "Aungel of heuene," a "Goliardeis," and "al þe commune," a section that (as long noted) might well draw on the coronation ceremony of Richard II in 1377, although its claims about the nature of a political contract are not narrowly topical. This is followed in B by another and lengthier addition: a description of a rat parliament, allegorically addressing the problem of how beings of smaller social status might avoid or hamstring the aggression of more powerful beings. This section evokes (but not exclusively) the greatest challenge to an English king's court favorites since the attacks on Gaveston and Despenser in the reign of Edward II: the Good Parliament of 1376. Together with a possible allusion to the schismatic election of Pope Clement VII at Avignon in 1378 (lines 107–11), these stretches provide the latest datable materials anywhere in B or indeed C, unless the reissued Statute of Laborers of 1388 is invoked in C.5 (see Hanna 1993:13–14; on C.5, see Middleton 1997; Clopper 1992 argues that the Statute of 1352 is the context there; see also below 134–37n, and 3.363–73n).

Topicality here—and further with the passages dealing with Lady Meed, as the notes to passūs 2–4 indicate—may be compared to the ways that "occasion" functions for other late medieval English poetry. As Chaucer included his "personal" chance meeting of pilgrims at an inn as an "occasion" for tale-telling, and as Gower included in the *Confessio Amantis*, as an occasion for writing the work, a chance meeting of "the poet" with the king, so L appears initially, in A, to have used the gesture of topical social satire, how people are sinning "these days" (a perennial trope of satire), to start off his vision on matters of sweeping cosmological, historical, and psychological or spiritual import. B does appear to have sharpened the loose topicality of the A prologue with further materials evoking particular historical events of the later 1370s, but those are retained in C, showing their supratopical importance. The manipulation of the sense of time, narrow or broadly extended, is one of the distinctive elements of artistry in the poem (see Trower 1973).

C's Prologue comprehensively and in detail reworks rather than simply adding to B, preserving only 164 lines from B's 231 lines in a more or less untouched state—that is, only about 70 percent of C's approximately equal length of 235 lines is taken intact from B. C appears to retreat from some kinds of topicality, particularly those that might be most immediately pertinent to a London and Westminster readership of the later 1370s. Most conspicuously it recasts B's presentation of the foundation of the commonwealth by omitting the lunatic, the Angel, the Goliard, and the commune—whose parallels to Richard's coronation ceremony would by then be superannuated or too specific to a London readership—and attributing the speeches of the first two to Conscience and omitting the speeches of the second two along with the speakers. All these changes serve to increase the king's claims to absolute power (see Baldwin 1981, and below 139–47n, 139–40n, 152n, B 139–45n, and 167–219n), but no longer with any suggestion of a particular king. C further frames all this material by introducing it with Conscience's sermon, which elaborates an exemplum of Ophni and Phinees (95–117), the two corrupt priests from 1 Kings 1–4 who were destroyed because they allowed "þe children of Irael" to sin. Just as the B Prologue contains materials suggesting that the poet's latest work in producing that version was devoted to elaborating the Prologue, so the section on Ophni and Phinees may, because of its uneven alliteration and in places nearly prose rhythms, represent a very late portion of the C version (see Pearsall 1981; Scase 1987; but cp. Hanna 1996:204–14). Finally, C alters the

Mouse's speech in the Rat Parliament slightly to emphasize the rats' sinful nature and their need to be ruled.

From the earliest version the tradition of surveying social types and professions, in the venerable tradition of the estates satire or "complaint," is inverted in its typical order of high to low estates, and used progressively to frame other kinds of social forms of political ethics and theory, from coronation to parliament to street-vending. In the later versions the form is made even more a means to ponder anew the bases of society: by including a coronation, a foundation of a commonwealth, and a parliament of rats and mice debating the self-rule of such a "commons," the Prologue extends the tradition of social critique into a many-sided and full-scale effort to theorize society. The tradition of estates satire—the survey of social estates or professions through a critique of how they at present fail to fulfill their ideal roles, often organized broadly by the "three estates" of those who pray, those who fight, and those who labor, and usually arranged hierarchically from high to low— has a long tradition in Latin, French, and English writing. One of the English versions of the genre closest to PP is *The Simonie*, a loosely alliterative rhyming "complaint" against many of the same social categories as in the Prologue. First written in the 1330s, *The Simonie* may have directly influenced PP (as well as other moralizing social complaints), and it was then revised in longer versions, the last of which might in turn have been influenced by a version of PP (ed. Embree and Urquahart 1991; see Salter 1967, Finlayson 1989:50). See especially below, 22–94n, also 12n, 57–61n, 64n, 72n, 160–66n; passus 2 Headnote, 2.60–63n, 223–24n; and 3.79n. PP's differences from this work are as obvious and fundamental as its similarities.

In every version, the first vision displays the overtly historical and political concerns of much fourteenth-century English alliterative poetry, which emerge even in alliterative poems quite removed from "complaints on the times." As precedents in this may be noted *Wynnere and Wastoure* and also, more securely datable, the mid-fourteenth-century work *William of Palerne* (after 1335 and before 1361; ed. Bunt 1985), translated from the twelfth-century French *Guillaume de Palerne*, which climaxes in a coronation, a triple marriage, and the restoration of a royal lineage and peaceful kingdom, as well as the unveiling of the hero from the animal disguises he and his beloved have been wearing, and the transformation of another heroic warrior from wolf form back to human. The Middle English version's author, also William, names himself as he punningly mentions the completion of his own "werke" along with that of the poem's hero; and the work seems to offer throughout an especially large overlapping range of rhetoric and language with PP. Indeed, on the grounds of western locale, general style, and the poets' shared forename, Lawton wonders why *William of Palerne* has not been considered Langland's first poem (1988:245; see also Kane 1989:282n4, and Warner 2006). Apart from such intriguing speculation, *William of Palerne* offers a good instance of poetic resources available to another poet writing in a similar poetic tradition. Thus rhetorical and other parallels to that early example of fourteenth-century alliterative poetry can (and will) be noted more often than parallels from most other English alliterative poems.

But a comparison with any other alliterative poem of the period merely serves to show how uniquely large, complex and brilliant the literary achievement of PP is, in any one of its versions and, especially, in its overall development between them. In all of these ways it is a quantum leap beyond—or (Lawton 1983) a formative example later unmatched by—anything else in the alliterative tradition, if not in medieval poetry more broadly considered. Thus Turville-Petre notes that the poet "modified the alliterative line, writing in a less tightly controlled style and avoiding the vocabulary restricted to alliterative poetry" (1977:45; see also Bloomfield 1962:34–36), and Schmidt notes the poet's ability to shift abruptly into and out of "the knockabout arena of *rum, ram, ruf* of which Langland is in his own way as critical as Chaucer" (1987:54). In concerns and style, PP's three versions might be said to focus increasingly on more specific objects of inquiry and condemnation, while extending the limits of what alliterative English poetry may be called upon to do. Both abstract ethical issues and social issues, for example, receive increasing detail in B and C, even as the formulae of alliterative poetry seem to diminish.

Considering the changes from A to B to C in terms of an increasing specificity in both ethical and social matters lets us see the three versions as progressing through a continuum, rather than stopping at particular "problems" until they are "resolved." If resolving problems were necessary for the poem to go forward, it would never have been developed into any significant size. For the poem perpetually poses extremely difficult problems in theology, society, and poetics, and continually leaves them unsettled at its conclusions of scenes and visions: the place and value of eremiticism, minstrelsy, mendicancy, mercantilism, agrarian labor, urban professions, deceptive or luxurious clothing, social governance and order, self-governance, vocation, and many other matters glimpsed here are all left unsettled and all returned to throughout the poem. If anything, a deepening sense of the difficulty of a given problem seems to allow the poem to move forward, rather than any resolution.

The Prologue introduces themes whose problems are only glimpsed and await the poem's fullest scrutiny after the first vision: the abuses of learning and intellectual labor; the importance yet the inadequacy of the clergy who are mandated to use their religious training and teaching skills to lead the rest of society; the uncertainty of the value of intricate intellectual and poetic play for its own sake; the inability of human administrations to control ethical behavior; the utter uncertainty of what salvation requires, yet the continuous likelihood that human beings will evade doing even what they already know should be done. In its perpetual return to such problems, the poem stands as a continual rereading of itself (see Schmidt 2000). The B and C continuations, culminating in the coming of Antichrist, make, in retrospect or second reading, the estates satire of the beginning of the poem darker than at a first reading, and this pessimism is anticipated or enhanced in the B and C Prologues by more savagely satirized figures, and more earnest denunciations, such as Conscience's speech in C. A's Prologue has a lighter satiric tone and (as Manly was first to stress in wholly positive terms) easier narrative consistency, "distinguished by remarkable unity of structure, directness of movement, and freedom from digression of any sort," where "the author marshals his dream-figures with marvellous swiftness, but with unerring hand" (Manly 1908:5).

The virtues of B's and C's increasing ethical and social complexity and precision seem matched by the increasing challenges of their larger poetic forms. If the A Prologue surveys a marketplace or at least a continuous social arena at a single if vigorously seething moment, the B and C Prologues' perspectives and scenes move backward in time to the founding of the commonwealth and outward in space to Westminster law courts and the abuses at sacred shrines. C's claims to social, moral, and even bookish authority throughout are of a more rigorous and ambitious kind than either of the other versions, a development that makes the three versions of the poem together a distinctly important example of the problems and opportunities facing a vernacular author pursuing literary authority in late fourteenth-century England.

C's more authoritative and prosaic explications conflict to some extent with a fundamental aspect of the poem in all versions: its surprises. This conflict in temper might be seen as the chief basis for the earlier theory of an altogether different author for C, but all the versions balance complex strategies of poetic and intellectual exploration and control with a seeming fascination with surprise and interruption. More than most medieval works, PP jars the reader with interruptions, indications of one genre that are then betrayed or ironized, and elements of initial mystery in the abrupt appearances of many of the figures (for this tendency, see below 1–13n, also 1.3n, and 3.90–107n). In part this effect may be our own conditioning. The tradition of Chaucer's generally clear boundaries of speakers and stories, as emphasized in modern editions relying heavily on the Ellesmere manuscript's careful divisions and rubrics and speech-attributions for *The Canterbury Tales*, appeals to a modern sensibility defined by clear notions of form and of literary personality. PP follows the more casual medieval narrative principle of a continuous series of speakers and venues, and sometimes uncertainty about the limits of those speakers' views or speeches, as found in such works as the *Roman de la Rose* (especially Jean de Meun's long continuation) and Guillaume de Deguileville's *Pelerinage de vie humaine*, as well as less exalted works in the minstrel tradition, such as the late fourteenth-century *Lybeaus Desconus* and the redaction of *Octavius*, apparently by Thomas of Chestre, which use some alliteration in their rhymed lines and have been said to display typically "a rearrangement of source-motifs that produces an illogical sequence, and the sudden introduction of a fresh character into the tale" (Mills 1969:17). But the difficulty of consuming the poem in easy morsels is not simply the result of its intimacy with such medieval principles of sprawling form and endlessly continued plots. From its first dozen lines, whose strategy is to suggest both a narrator's and a reader's shared wonder, shock, or unexpected broadening of social, intellectual, and historical vision, through its last words, an unanswered cry for grace at a moment of impending loss of all that has been established, the poem presents a mode of journeying that continually threatens to disrupt and demolish familiar settings and structures for the reader and the narrator, as rapidly as it deftly invokes them (for some of the wide critical notice of the disruptive style of PP and a variety of approaches to it, see Bloomfield 1962:37 and passim; Middleton 1982a; Salter 1983:106–8; Aers 1986; Lawton 1987; Justice 1988).

Rubrics and Passus Headings

Athlone editions and (except for Kane's A edition) Athlone's descriptions of manuscripts omit all information about the rubrics of medieval copies of PP, and we accept that these are most likely scribal in their extant forms. Yet they present suggestive details, which may reflect very early scribal or even authorial shaping of the poem, and a full dismissal is too easy a solution to these possibilities. Since Skeat's first edition of 1867, on the basis of many of the rubrics, the Prologue has often been taken as opening the *Visio*, that is, commencing the first of two "distinctly divisible" parts of a poem otherwise "thr[own] into the form of several successive visions" (1867:xxxix, iii). Skeat's structure follows an idealized form of the rubrics: the first part of PP was the "Vision of Piers Plowman" or *Visio*, ending with the Pardon passus (C.9 [B.7, A.8]); the second was the *Vita* ("life") of the three grades of virtue: Dowel (C.10–16 [B.8–14, A.9–12]), Dobet (C.17–20 [B.15–18]), and Dobest (C.21–22 [B.19–20]), all entities that the narrator openly pursues only after his encounter with Thought, who in all versions, including A, first provides the goal of seeking them (10.76 [B.8.88, A.9.69]). The *Visio-Vita* distinction and to a lesser extent the tripartite segments of the *Vita* have been unquestionably formative elements in scholarship; in his Parallel Text edition of 1886 Skeat assumes the scheme and expands on it (see, e.g., 1:x, xxii–xxiii, xxiv, lxxxvi–xci), and many studies have relied on it for its convenience or thematic implications, as even in Pearsall's recent edition that does not otherwise present the rubrics (e.g., Prsl's notes at 1.79–80, 10.1–2).

John M. Manly emphasized nearly a century ago the unlikelihood of the rubrics being the author's—or as he saw it, the several authors'—work (Manly 1909–10:94–96); more significantly, Kane's 1960 A edition noted some obvious scribal misapplications of the divisions (K-A 40–42) and established his grounds for ignoring them in the Athlone editions. This view has been as influential in diminishing use of the rubrics for significant kinds of interpretation as Skeat's view almost a century earlier had been for increasing such use. (Adams [1994:54] notes a 1981 letter in which Kane described his long-held view that rubrics in vernacular texts were typically due to the medieval publication process.) More comprehensive work, especially by Robert Adams (1985; 1994), has established the likelihood that the rubrics in their extant forms developed at a relatively early point in the scribal reception of the poem, were most clearly codified for C copies, then variously applied back to copies in the other versions, including A where the scheme cannot be fulfilled by the poem. Yet even Adams agrees that the *Visio-Vita* division with the Pardon reflects some authorial conception of a major break in the poem, and he notes that we can at least securely say "that the common ancestor of surviving A copies showed some sort of major division at the juncture of passūs 8/9, and that the rubric designating this division indicated the beginning of a segment involving 'dowel, dobet, and dobest' . . . It is quite possible, though by no means necessary, to imagine that Langland himself may have been responsible for some such heading in the holograph theoretically behind all A copies" (Adams 1994:62). Reconstructing just what such an early authorial conception of rubrics might have been there or elsewhere is not possible at present, or likely to prove so later. Although Skeat's useful summary of the poem is tidily organized by these segments (1:lxxxvi–xci), even in Skeat's own text the rubrics are complex and inconsistent, with signs of scribal uncertainties that Skeat made no attempt to smooth out, although he also did not present any of the rubrics' further textual tradition in his critical apparatus. His B text, in addition to "primus, "secundus," etc. for each part of the Dowel, Dobet, and Dobest lives, presents cumulative passus numbers, and (like many B texts) identifies many of the passūs in the *Vita* as also "de visione"; Skeat's A and B texts, but not his C text, present the first Dowel passus (just after the Pardon) without numbering it, as a prologue to all three lives, whereas his C text, which presents the *Visio* and *Vita* comprehensively like most C texts, omits a rubric for an initial prologue so that its overall numbering is ahead by one, and also begins numbering the Dowel portion without a prologue so that that numbering is also ahead of the other versions. And while Skeat felt his copytext for B, Laud Misc. 581 (L), was very close to the author's original (he even considered it to be the author's working copy [1:lxviii]), that copy of B is unusual in presenting rubrics that somewhat match the more consistent pattern of A and C texts: most B copies have systems of rubrics that fall outside the scheme Skeat proposed, and present conflicting and sometimes elusive points of division, such as the rubrics in most B copies beginning passus 15 "passus xv[us] &c finit dowel et incipit dobet" and then starting passus 16 "passus xvj[us] &c et primus de dobet," leaving doubt about where Dobet or its prologue might begin (see Clopper 1988:246, although Clopper defends the A/C rubrics as authorial). Both copies representing the important "alpha" textual stem of B, Oxford, Bodleian Library, MS. Rawlinson Poet. 38 (R) and Oxford, Corpus Christi College, MS. 201 (F), which in other ways witness aspects of the lost common ancestor or ancestors of the B text, lack all traces of the rubric scheme, except for a stray explicit at the end of R: "passus ii[us] de dobest," which possibly reflects consultation of a C manuscript since that form appears in the XU family of C, and thus indicates the spread of the rubrics laterally between versions (Adams 1985:214n; 1994:58). Yet one curious indication of a title for the poem that must have been conferred very early in the poem's textual tradition appears in the explicit of six B manuscripts, "explicit hic dialogus petri plowman"; Hanna notes that four of those manuscripts have some evidence of London dialect and suggests that this title might even be a vestige from the author's earliest conception of the poem, as a kind of continuation of *Wynnere and Wastoure* (Hanna 2005, chap. 6). It certainly reflects the form of the poem in many of its passūs in the early visions, most clearly in the first vision, in passus 3 (see below, passus 3 Headnote).

Significant use of the rubric divisions, and even of the strongly marked *Visio-Vita* division, has faded from scholarship in recent years apart from isolated appearances (but cp. Clopper 1988, 1995), as the tenuousness of their authority has become more evident. The major modern editions of the poem have decreasingly emphasized or even not mentioned the rubrics: Kane's A text lists the rubrics of A manuscripts only in the descriptions of the manuscripts, omitting them from the critical apparatus (K-A, pp. 1–18), and the subsequent Athlone editions of B and C do not list them even in the descriptions of the manuscripts. Schmidt's editions (Schm) list them in the critical apparatus, without full details; Pearsall's C text (Prsl), like the later two Athlone editions, omits mention of them, although they reappear in occasional comments of his edition, as noted above.

In omitting nearly all evidence of the rubrics, the Athlone editions make one part of the poem's reception history inconveniently absent; yet they also effectively challenge readers to confront the problems of categorizing the work without any simple structural and thematic assurances, such as those that its reception history has frequently imposed. The only relic of the rubrics in the Athlone editions remains in the series title, which announces the full title of the poem in a form that harks back to Skeat: *Will's Visions of Piers Plowman and Do-Well* (for K-A), and *Will's Visions of Piers Plowman, Do-Well, Do-Better, and Do-Best* (for KD-B and RK-C). Information about the main rubrics may otherwise be found throughout Schmidt's apparatus; fuller details of those in A are most conveniently found in Kane's descriptions of the manuscripts in his A text (K-A 1–18); those of the B tradition in Benson and Blanchfield 1997:116–23 or, more conveniently as a set, Adams 1985:215–31; and those of C in Adams 1994:70–84.

Much likelier authorial guidance than the rubrics, and worth more scrutiny than they have received, are the poem's basic named divisions, "prologue" and "passus." These headings Athlone (like all editions) retains, although Athlone does not note variants in the reception history of these, e.g., the C tradition that begins with "passus primus" rather than "Prologus," used by Skeat for his rubrics (see Adams 1994, and Schm); or the eccentric B manuscript at Oxford, Corpus Christi College 201 (F) that divides the poem's passūs according to dream-visions (see Weldon 1993; Galloway 2004b). The common term for large narrative divisions in Middle English writing, including the alliterative and romance traditions, is *fitte* (e.g., *Sir Gawain and the Green Knight*, c. 1400; ed. Andrew and Waldron 1996; and *Wynnere and Wastoure*, ed. Trigg 1990), a carryover from Old English *fitt*, "poem, song" (as in Cynewulf's signature in the *Fates of the Apostles*; ed. Krapp 1932:51–54, line 98), and applied in Middle English also to music or verse.

The divisions into "prologue" and "passus," found in all versions and all copies of PP (even if sometimes, as in "F," uniquely arranged), are somewhat unusual as titles in parts of Middle English poems but are attested in the alliterative tradition. Middle English *pas* ("step, pace, road, unit of five feet") is used as early as the *King of Tars* (c. 1330) to mean 'story' (ed. Perryman 1980, line 703; see MED *pas* 4 (b)); and it became well established in alliterative poetry: *William of Palerne* (between 1335 and 1361; ed. Bunt 1985), *The Wars of Alexander* (c. 1400, ed. Duggan and Turville-Petre 1989), *Siege of Jerusalem* (c. 1390, ed. Hanna and Lawton 2003), all use *pas* to indicate a section of their own story (e.g., *William of Palerne*, line 161: "Þus passed is þe first pas of þis pris tale"; at later points *William of Palerne* seems to refer to sections of the poem as a "lesson": "Leve we now þis lesson, and here we anoþer," line 1923; see 3528; for the casual nature of "pas" there in *William of Palerne* by comparison to the rubrics in PP, see Middleton 1982a:113). Both *Wars* and one copy of *Siege* (Cambridge University Library, MS. Mm.v.14; see Hanna and Lawton, ed. 2003:xix-xx) use, like PP, the Latin cognate passus as the name for narrative units (the units in *Wars* average about 250 lines, in *Siege* about 125 lines, both considerably smaller and in more regular sizes than the units in PP). *Wars*, *Siege*, and the late *Destruction of Troy* (c. 1450; ed. Panton and Donaldson 1968) also use the English term, while PP does not: "here a passe endes" (*Wars*, lines 2971, 5200; *Siege*, line 504; *Destruction*, line 663); but *Wars* more often uses "fitte" in the verse to mark such units (740, 3331, 3601, 4147), including the narrator's key statement at that poem's major dividing point, at passus 15, where the story shifts from the accounts of Alexander's triumphs to his decline and death: "Þe lattir ende of his lyfe me list ȝow to tell, / For all þe first is in fittis & folowand þe lettir" (3600–3601; see also *Destruction*, line 8420). This suggests that, in *The Wars of Alexander* at least, the English terms pas and fitt are readily synonymous; thus the Latin rubrics steadily numbering the passūs of *Wars* exist at a different discursive level from the English text of that poem, although not necessarily one less authorial. The Latin headings there and elsewhere in the alliterative tradition may be an effort by an author or a scribe to add a veneer of textual authority to an English alliterative work primarily geared for recitation.

Middle English *pas* in this sense in turn derives from Old French, Anglo-Norman, and medieval Latin usage, but usually to refer to a "passage" in the Bible or in other authoritative texts, a sense following the usage of "passus" established in Latin texts from the thirteenth century (thus the sense of the term in the famous letter to Can Grande de la Scala attributed to Dante, sec. 16; ed. Chiappelli 1965:864). The early fourteenth-century Anglo-Norman poet and preacher Nicholas Bozon, whose works have some affinities to PP (see below especially 167–219n, Headnote to passus 1, 2.178–96n), uses pas to refer to a passage in the Bible (Bozon, *La vie Seint Martha* 237; ed. Amelia 1947, line 54). In Middle English, the term is more widely applied but still appears to carry some sense of emphatically textual authority, as still more with *passus* as a textual division. The term "passus" as a textual unit is found as late as 1575, but probably as a jocular antiquarian reference (see OED *passus*).

It seems doubtful that a fashion for using the term to apply to a Middle English literary work's own division began—as so many elements of the "alliterative revival" are claimed to begin—simply with *William of Palerne*'s sole usage (at a point where the Middle English work lacks correspondence with the French *Guillaume de Palerne*). Yet some relatively narrow path of transmission or more or less definable regional context for PP's use of "passus" to refer to its units might be hypothesized. As noted above, *William of Palerne* is of special relevance for PP on the grounds of western locale and general style, if not indeed common authorship; moreover, one of the two manuscripts of the *Wars of Alexander* includes an A text of PP (Dublin, Trinity College, MS. 213 olim MS. D.4.12; see also below 2n). Yet with its structure of an ongoing pilgrimage or wandering, announced emphatically at beginning and ending of the poem, PP's use of "passus" suggests not "textual demarcation" but the etymological sense, "step," a notion strengthened by the poem's similarities to the medieval tradition of poetry or prose treatises presenting "paths" to heaven or to hell (see Barney 1988:126–27). Here, perhaps more than anywhere in the literary tradition, the vernacular poem seems closely tied in sense to the Latin word for its textual division, even though the English text itself does not include *pas*. Given the nature of the poem throughout, some such deeper tie from the outset between English and Latin in PP's textual presentation is not to be wondered at.

Opening frame

1–13 (cp. B 1–10, A 1–10): In a somur sesoun . . . Al y say slepynge, as y shal telle: The opening dream-frame of PP is briefer in all its versions than those of most dream poems, such as the *Roman de la Rose* and its French followers, Chaucer's *Book of the Duchess*, *Parliament of Fowls*, and *House of Fame*, Gower's Latin *Vox Clamantis*, and other English alliterative dream poems such as *Pearl*, *The Parlement of Thre Ages*, and *Wynnere and Wastoure*. *Somer Soneday* presents a terse set of phrases that seem more than coincidentally parallel: that poem's narrator rises when "Opon a somer soneday se I þe sonne" and he heads out to hunt: "I warp on my wedes, to wode wolde I wende," before encountering a vision of kings proclaiming their rise and fall on the wheel that Fortune is spinning (ed. Turville-Petre 1989, lines 1, 4). But PP's dream frame is densely seminal yet less specific, invoking a wide potential range of literary associations, hence a potentially wide range of readers' or listeners' expectations for interpretive postures and frameworks.

The warm season evokes the *reverdie*, popular in much French and English lyric poetry, and in more learned dream-vision poetry such as the *Roman de la Rose* or Chaucer's *Book of the Duchess* and *House of Fame*. *Wynnere and Wastoure* opens with a narrator not falling asleep, but kept awake by the loud sounds of a stream and birds, "For dyn of the depe watir and dadillyng of fewllys" (ed. Trigg 1990, line 44). In PP these elements are soothing for the narrator as well as the reader: in A and B, the water's sound here lulls the narrator to drift into the first vision (A/B 9–10); later, in all three versions, birds' singing draws him to doze and thus begin the third vision (10.61–67 [B.8.63–66, A.9.54–58]). The promise to tell all, **as y shal telle**, offers another kind of soothing reassurance, of confessional intimacy and veracity with a reader. The brief opening in all versions hints at a larger poem than any lyric; it responds at least indirectly to the medieval academic tradition of initial guidance for readers, the *accessus auctori*, whose statements explicitly relate who, what, and why (*quis auctor? quis modus? quae intentio?*; see Minnis 1984:9–28). Yet the responses here serve to thwart that scheme and to trouble, already, the strategies of reassurance: who the author is, is made tantalizingly enigmatic by the gesture of disguise; what the work's "mode" is, is made deceptive by its invocation of lyric and of bucolic bliss; what intention guides it is left dubious by the narrator's own uncertain intentions and unproven or unstable moral status, **vnholy of werkes** (3n).

Perhaps the most important literary gesture here is the evocation of a *chanson d'aventure*, a usually brief lyric, widespread in French but "fully naturalized" by the fourteenth century into English lyric forms (Middleton 1982a:114; see Sandison 1913). In this form, which Middleton calls "perhaps the essential paradigm of literary fictive narration in this period," a first-person narrator, "walking or musing alone, often in some named actual place (Rybblesdale, Peterborough, 'Huntle bankkes') . . . hears a bird song that carries an admonition, meets a fair lady, or overhears a complaint or revelation or debate." The literary form of such happenstance important discovery "implicitly argues" that "truth presents itself first to peripheral vision," and in turn resists final judgment (Middleton 1982a:114). In Middleton's view, L uses this mode to to enable "an examination of the social and personal value of literary didacticism" (1982a:115): a means, that is, to produce self-consciousness both about the endeavor of literary vagrancy and about offering earnest social and ethical teachings. Such a mode thus both affirms the "truth" of what follows and suspends its own judgment in order to preserve the delicately oblique way by which such truth must be perceived.

Latin lyrics offer another kind of background to the opening here that has been less fully explored than the French and English tradition of *reverdie* lyrics. Latin materials often stress the narrator's penance, satirically or earnestly, and deciding between the two for the narrator of PP is an issue of immediate uncertainty in the opening lines (see below, 2n, 3n). Many "goliardic" Latin lyrics—satires and social and ethical complaints from the twelfth and thirteenth centuries in particular—begin with references to a spring setting, then proceed to survey the abuses of the ecclesiastical orders and professions (e.g., "Apocalypsis Goliae Episcopi" and "Metamorphosis Goliae Episcopi," both ed. Wright 1841). Such lyrics offer a bridge to an earlier penitential tradition, which shows through the opening of PP too. An early medieval Latin work with relevant themes and a bucolic opening resembling that of PP is Bede's *De die iudicii* (ed. Fraipont 1955) and its Old English verse translation (Dobbie 1942:58–67): as PP by the third line defines its terms as both satirical and penitential (see below, 2n, 3n), so Bede's work begins with a description of a luxuriant landscape where the narrator, lamenting his sins, contemplates the Day of Judgment; the Old English version adds a rushing brook using diction much like that in the A and B openings (see B 5–10n below).

More learned and longer Latin poems may be pertinent as well: Alan of Lille's twelfth-century allegory, the *Anticlaudianus*, widely known in late medieval learned circles, also includes in its opening book a description of Nature's garden, complete with beguiling sensory richness not unlike the opening of *Piers* (see B 10n below). The fertile landscape implied in PP's opening might even be compared to the tradition of Latin historical writing, particularly in suggesting the exemplary "English" significance of the landscape through which the narrator wanders. Bede's *Historia Ecclesiastica*, following Gildas, opens with the British landscape as a scene of plenty; Geoffrey of Monmouth's twelfth-century *Historia Regum Britanniae* more closely suggests PP's opening lines, by opening with a description of England where it is noted of this country that "at the foot of its windswept mountains it has meadows green with grass, beauty-spots where clear springs flow into shining streams which ripple gently and murmur an assurance of deep sleep to those lying on their banks" (trans. Thorpe 1966:53).

After PP, the model of a *reverdie* followed by social satire is common in English writers, as in Gower's first book of the Latin *Vox clamantis*, which moves from June lushness to the rebellion of 1381 (ed. Macaulay 1902; trans. Stockton 1962) or Chaucer's *reverdie* introducing the satire of the General Prologue. PP's influence and afterlife is generally beyond the scope of the present commentary, but for the most direct poetic followers see the works in "the PP tradition" edited by Barr (1993); for the prose works invoking it or based on it see Hudson 1988b, with further references; and Somerset 2003. In addition to the works noted in those studies, the prose instructional dialogue called *Dives and Pauper* by an unknown Franciscan friar (c. 1405–10; ed. Barnum 1976, 1980; for the date, see Hudson 1988a:417–21) includes a passage that invokes some of the phrases of the opening of the Prologue, and perhaps also the opening of the next vision in passus 5, to which it can be usefully compared:

Pauper. Swych maner folc [hypocrits] han to maner of dedis, on in pryue, anoþer in apert. Here dedis in apert, ȝif þey ben goode, arn nout here but it arn cloþingys of schep vndir whyche þey wryyn hem as woluys for deseyuyn Godis schep. And þerfor Crist byddith in þe gospel [Matt. 7:15] þat we schuldyn ben war of false prophetys þat comyn to us in cloþinge of schep, for þey ben inward woluys of raueyn. Ȝif here dedys arn wyckyd it ben here owyn cloþinge wherby þei mon ben knowyn. But here pryue warkys & here pryue techynge arn here owyn frut, whyche comounly arn wol wyckyd. And so be þat þey don and techyn pryuely men mon best knowyn hem what þey ben. *Diues.* Y may wel assentyn to þyn speche, for so many wondris han fallyn in þis lond withynne a fewe ȝeris in sonne, mone and sterris, in lond, in watyr, in þe eyr þat we redyn in no book þat euere felle so manye in so lytil tyme; &, as men seyn, wol wyckyd lyueris don manye miracilis & prophecyyn and þou we wantyn grace on euery side and þe harde venchance of God is upon us nyȝt & day, schewynge þat God is greuously offendyd with us. *Pauper.* As seyth þe glose super illus, II ad Tessalonicenses ii [9], in signis et prodigiis mendacibus: forasmychil as þe peple is out of charite & wil nout knowyn þe trewþe but trostyn al in lesyngys and in falshed, þerfor God suffrith false schrewys for to doun wondris and miraclys for to deseuyn þe peple and to heldyn hem stille in here errouris. Y haue seyd as me þynkith. Sey forth what þu wyl. (ed. Barnum 1976:213)

The more definitive moral terms of *Dives and Pauper* demonstrate by comparison how PP's judgments and interpretations remain suspended, under a scrutiny that yields continual new perspectives rather than flat judgments. The B text is most likely the basis for this passage, since it was most widely circulated and none of the echoes here are to passages found only in C; as well as the statement based on Matt. 7:14, "false prophetys þat comyn to us in cloþinge of schep," which might have recalled PP in general, compare B.3.231 ("two manere of Medes"), B.Prol.56 ("Cloþed hem in copies to ben knowen from oþere"), B.Prol.65 ("Manye ferlies han fallen in a fewe yeres"), B.15.356–71 (e.g., 367, "Now faileþ þe folk of þe flood and of þe long boþe"; 370–71, "Astronomyens also aren at hir wittes ende; / Of þat was calculed of þe element þe contrarie þei fynde"), B.5.22 ("Ac I shal seye as I sauȝ"), and generally Repentance's sermon in B.5.

1–4 (B 1–4, A 1–4): In a somur sesoun whan softe was þe sonne . . . wondres to here: The hyper-alliteration of the first line, *aaaa*, produces a more formal rhetoric than the typical *aaax* (or looser) alliteration of the poem, decorously evoking one of the features of late fourteenth-century alliterative poetics (Oakden 1930:179): e.g., "Perle plesaunte, to prynces paye . . ." (*Pearl*, ed. Andrew and Waldron 1996); "Clannesse whoso kyndly cowþe commende . . ." (*Cleanness*, ed. Andrew and Waldron 1996); "Siþen þe sege and þe assaut watz sesed at Troye . . ." (*Sir Gawain and the Green Knight*, ed. Andrew and Waldron 1996; see also Schmidt 1987:29–32); "Opon a somer soneday se I þe sonne"

(*Somer Soneday*, ed. Turville-Petre 1989:142–47). While the first four lines of PP have various distinctly "poetic" features, including a simile (**as y a shep were**) and an inversion of the infinitive's subject with the infinitive (**wondres to here**; see also notes below)—the initial line uses unusually high style for this poem, with the location of the predicate adjective before the subject (**softe was þe sonne**).

Such inversion of the predicate adjective appears very seldom in PP; the two clear instances are also keyed to the sun, at moments of high drama: "derke bicam þe sonne" (C.20/B.18.60, at the Crucifixion), and "moste shene is þe sonne" (C.20.452 [B.18.409]), in Peace's song at Jesus' release of souls from hell at the Harrowing. Peace's words there are described as "of poesie a note" (C.20.451 [B.18.408]). The first four lines in PP also are linked by alliteration that, with cross-connections, shifts through 's-sh-w-h-w-h', a whisper with increasing vocalization that alternates softer with slightly sharper sounds, in a subtle instance of "linking" (Oakden 1930:148) or "translinear" alliteration (Schmidt 1987:52–55).

As in the *Parlement of the Thre Ages* (ed. Offord 1959, lines 1–2) and Chaucer's Prologue to the *Legend of Good Women* (G lines 89–90), **somur** here includes May, earlier included in "lenten" (MED *somer* 1a, 3; see Moore 1949:82–83). The opening thus may implicitly evoke not just summer but the return of spring after winter, that is, the genre of *reverdie* discussed above. The summer season, with its abundance of new life, vitality, and animal joy, provides an immediate contrast to the narrator's role **as an heremite** (3), one who seems to be contrite or aware of his unsanctified status (**vnholy of werkes**; see note below), and exhausted by travels, just as a *reverdie* typically contrasts the burgeoning of spring with a narrator's lovesick state: "Nou sprinkes the sprai, / al for loue icche am so seeke / that slepen i ne mai" (ed. Brown 1932, no. 62, before 1302, the earliest Middle English example noted by Sandison 1913:47–48). Many French and Latin poems open with such rhetorical and atmospheric contrast; the opening of Bede's *De die iudicii* tersely presents all the important elements of this topos: "Inter florigeras fecundi cespitis herbas . . . / Arboris umbriferae maestus sub tegmine solus / Dum sedi, subito planctu turbatus amaro . . . ." ("Among the herbs flowering in their fertile turf, while I, sorrowing, alone sat under the shady cover of a tree, suddenly distraught in a bitter complaint"; ed. Fraipont 1955); the Old English version elaborates the lush landscape still more fully before introducing the narrator's penitent state: "Wop wæs gehrered, / and min earme mod . . . eal wæs gedrefed" (ed. Dobbie 1942, lines 8–9; "Sorrow was raised up, and my wretched soul was entirely overcome"). The phrasing is designed to commence a poem or at least a scene, as e.g., *Alexander A* (ed. Magoun 1929), line 999, "In a somer seasoun soone therafter," a chance parallel (and there the phrase appears as "metrical padding"; Turville-Petre 1977:97); see also the passage in the tail-rhyme romance *Ipomadon* (1390 X c. 1450), where it more usefully announces the appearance of a love theme, well after the first stages of the plot: "In somer seson it befell / When flovrys were sprong swete of smell / And fowlys songe bedene . . ."; that passage continues by describing the amorous queen's troop pitching camp "Vppon a lavnde fayre and wyde / Be a rennande reuer syde . . . When they were wery for-rwne," paralleling or possibly even drawing on PP's opening (ed. Purdie 2001, lines 563–65, 578–82). Chaucer's rondeau to Nature in *The Parliament of Fowls*, a fully realized small *reverdie*, resembles the opening to PP in its opening line and the first line of its subsequent refrain: "Now welcome, somer, with thy sone softe, / That has thes wintres wedres overshake . . ." (680–92). This rondeau is possibly spurious, since it was added belatedly to early copies of the *Parliament of Fowls* (see Benson 1987:1150 n. to 680–92); its closeness to L's line proves nothing about Chaucer's personal knowledge of PP. But it may show the circulation of some popular springtime song to which PP also is indebted. For other possible songs evoked in and by the Prologue, see below, 198n, 222n, 229n, and 230–34n.

2 (B 2, A 2): Y shope me into a shroude as y a shep were: The first descriptive statements about the narrator in all three versions imply self-concealment as well as self-presentation, emphasizing his action of covering himself and offering, in **shep**, a much-debated word in a subjunctive clause for his hypothetical or assumed identity. The narrator characteristically presents his identity by means of such hypothetical clauses of manner using "as" with subjunctive (MED *as*, conj., 2; see 20.1–5n, and for examples 10.20, B.8.20, A.9.15; 15.2–3, B.13.2–3; perhaps also B.15.13). Yet his use of the same syntax in the Prologue and elsewhere to present other hypocritical figures elsewhere in the poem (e.g., the pardoner who preaches "as he a prest were," below, 66; see also C.7.66, C.9.248, B.5.452) makes it difficult to ignore the possibility that the narrator is hypocritical about his own vocation (for the syntax, see Mustanoja 1960:465, Nummenmaa 1973:75–6). This use of "as" to indicate hypothetical social identity resembles identifications of actual and legitimate social identity using "as" found elsewhere in Middle English (e.g., *Seinte Juliene*, "he set in dome as reue of þe burhe," R 141; ed. d'Ardenne 1961), a usage occurring "mainly with nouns denoting rank or position, often in a religious context," and suggesting not hypocrisy but rather function, evidently based on "as" clauses of similarity (Nummenmaa 1973:103). But these instances do not use the subjunctive.

The narrator describes his clothing or the action of clothing himself on five other occasions in C, usually as the preliminary to a dream sequence (5.2

[C only], "yclothed as a lollare"; 5.41, "in this longe clothes"; 10.1, "yrobed in russet"; 20.1, "Wollewaerd and watschoed"; 21.2, "And dihte me derely"). The action may evoke opening gestures of other dream-visions; the narrator of the *Roman de la Rose* also clothes himself at the opening of the poem, but as the first action within his dream itself, which also includes within the dream the process of going out on a May morning (lines 91–3); in the fourteenth-century dream-vision by Guillaume de Deguileville, *La pelerinage de vie humaine*, the dreamer initially seeks to know how he might properly dress himself to travel to the City of God he glimpses, and much of that poem concerns his implicated efforts to acquire the scrip and staff he needs and to hold onto those until he arrives, when he learns that he must finally enter it naked, at the point of death. Finally, much of *William of Palerne* presents the travels of William and his lover disguised, successively, in animal skins as white bears, and as stag and deer, through a necessary artifice that is often vividly described: "Þe hote sunne hade so hard þe hides stived [stiffened], / þat here comli cloþing þat kevered hem þerunder / [was] out bi þe sides sene" (ed. Bunt 1985, lines 3033–35; see further Warner 2006). In PP the question of the narrator's proper clothing does not develop so elaborately or insistently as any of these, yet it appears from the outset as an act of self-definition in both worldly and potentially spiritually meaningful terms. It flags the narrator's open potential, either to live up to an innocence and sanctity whose badge he seems to bear, or to become an example of the worst kind of hypocrisy.

In a similar gesture of self-definition, the phrase **Y shope me**, which, as Skt notes, "generally means 'I got myself ready,'" here implies vocational self-fashioning (see also Hanna 1994:85–86). But what vocation? **A shroud** may be a general set of clothing or specifically priestly vestments (MED *shroud* 1.a., b.); in neither case would resemblance to a sheep be literal (although a shroud would likely be made of wool, possibly a very rustic wrapping like those worn by some of the many hermits in the period [see Hanna 1997:34–36]). **a shep** is almost certainly 'a sheep,' although the ten witnesses to the "p" group of C manuscripts read "shepherde" and Skeat took **shep** in all versions to mean the latter (Skt). Evidently on the C manuscripts' basis or Skeat's authority, MED *shep* 5 cites this occurrence only as meaning 'shepherd' (but MED inconsistently does not accordingly grant *shep* as 'shepherd' a separate lexical entry). In contrast, OED *shep* n. emphatically excludes this line from meaning 'shepherd' although it presents two early examples for "shep" as 'shepherd.' In fact neither of the other early examples in OED of this sense of "shep" is secure: the first is a surname from an account of the 1381 Rising, "Chep [var. Schep]," which may not be an occupational surname, and if it is, might easily be from the "cheap/chapman" group (Dr. Paul F. Schaffner, personal communication); the second is from a line only in the spurious stanzas to Lydgate's "Churl and the Bird" found in the seventeenth-century *Theatrum Chemicum Britannicum* but not attested in early copies of the poem (see MacCracken, ed. 1934[1961]:486). No examples of "shep" meaning 'shepherd' can be securely identified before this seventeenth-century example, followed only by later dia-lectical or faux-dialectical usage (northwest Lincolnshire; see OED). "Shep" elsewhere in PP consistently means 'sheep' (C.3.412, 5.18, 9.265, glossing *disper-gentur oues*), while "shepherdes" appears on numerous occasions (B.10.467, B.12.152, B.15.361 [C.17.99], B.15.368). Those C manuscripts reading "sheph-erde" at Prol.2 also all read "shrobbis" for "a shroud" (probably based on confusing a hastily written Anglicana lobed 'w' with 'bb')—"Y shope me into shrobbis as y a shepherde were"—suggesting that their paired reading "shep-herde" is a clarification impelled by the reading "shrobbis," which fits a sheep even less than a shepherd. OED thus seems justified in excluding **shep** here from meaning 'shepherd' (for further support of 'sheep,' see Kane 1989:95n25). The sense of 'shepherd' offered by the "p" family of C manuscripts, and by Skeat's emphatic advocacy, has, however, persistently influenced lexicogra-phers, editors, and critics (in addition to MED, see Salter and Pearsall 1967 and Prsl, "shepherd [a possible sense of *shep*]"; Mills suggests that the narrator sees himself "in terms of the rôles of 'active' shepherd and 'contemplative' her-mit, neither of which he fills"—although Mills goes on to reject the sense 'shepherd' for the line; 1969:340n13).

To dress as a **shep** evokes either the good sheep or the "wolf in sheep's clothing" of Matt. 7:14–15 (so Robertson and Huppé 1951:33–34). The latter phrase was routinely applied to "false religious," either heretics or bad priests, from early medieval culture on. The proof-text from Matthew is often found in sermons on the related notion in John 10:14, Jesus' statement, "I am the good shepherd" ("ego sum pastor bonus"). Thus sermons on John 10, the text for the second Sunday after Easter, ensured that the Matthew text was wide-spread, and invoked to describe the duties of priests and condemn the failings of bad ones (see, e.g., the thirteenth-century sermon cycle of Jacobus de Vora-gine, *Sermones*, very widely known in late medieval England, as in Lambeth MS. 43 cols. 200–17 [on this sermon collection's English circulation, see Gallo-way 1992a:9–10n16; see also Hanska 2002:302–4, for Hugo of Prato's sermon on John 10]). In the late fourteenth century, the passage in Matthew was also used equally both by the orthodox clergy criticizing the Lollards and by Lol-lards criticizing orthodox clergy: for the first, Archbishop William Courtenay calls Lollards "wolves in sheep's clothing" (quoted in Workman 1926, vol. 2.204); so too the chronicler Henry Knighton emphasizes the hypocrisy of the Lollards who wear russet "as if displaying an exterior simplicity of heart" but are wolves in habits of sheep (*Chronicon* ed. Martin 1995:298–303); in turn, Lollard sermons condemn the "false prophetys þat comen in cloþyng of schep" of Matthew 7:14, identified as "false frerus" (ed. Gradon and Hudson 1983–96, vol. 1.252–55; see also vol. 1.438–42, on John 10, where the Matthew text as usual in such sermons has a significant role). The text from Matthew 7 is also an insistent point in Fals Semblaunt's damning self-portrait in the *Roman de la Rose* (ed. Poirion 1974, lines 10993–11128), and it informs many representations of religious hypocrisy: "Trichery" in Deguileville's *Pelerinage de vie humaine* involves a similar posture (ed. Stürzinger 1893, lines 8349–8551).

3 (B 3, A 3): In abite as an heremite, vnholy of werkes: If the opening self-portrait uses a language of potential hypocrisy, it also uses a language of aspiration toward religious vocation. Clothing oneself in sheepskin was appropriate for ancient hermits; the writings of John Cassian, both *De institutis coenobiorum* and *De octo principalium vitiorum remediis libri xii*, enjoined hermits to wear sheepskins in imitation of Old Testament ascetics (see Bowers 1986:33n100; 102n18; Scase 1989:91), although as Richard Rolle's construction of his own habit from his sister's dress indicates, they need not literally wear rough sheepskins in the fourteenth century, certainly not in warm weather (on Rolle, see Watson 1991; Hanna 1994). As Bloomfield observes, "Will dresses as a hermit because he is seeking what a hermit seeks—perfection" (1962:70).

Thus (as Bloomfield implies) **In abite as an heremite** may mean that the narrator's vocation is *comparable to* that of a hermit, if **as an heremite** is taken as elliptically repeating the hypothetical "as"-clause of the preceding line: i.e., **In abite as [if y] an heremite [were]**. Mills aptly suggests the simultaneous possibilities of a sinister portrayal of the "wolf in sheep's clothing" and a portrayal of the narrator's wish "to be a 'sheep' as opposed to a 'goat,' one who is among God's chosen and will be saved," and adds that "both these senses become stronger as the poem progresses" (1969:186–87). A similarly ambiguous persona is evoked in 5.2–4 (C only), where the narrator says he is "yclothed as a lollare," and dismissed even by "lollares of londone and lewede Ermytes."

His identity is difficult to categorize at any point. He bears traces of a hermit (see Hanna 1997, and also next note), but also of a vagrant, and even of a friar in the sense of following the most extreme version of their abandonment of settled and secure lives (on the last, see Clopper 1997; e.g., Will's "life imitates that of many friars insofar as it aspires to the mendicant ideal but falls short of it whenever he falters in humility or patience or whenever he takes more alms than he needs or takes them instead of providing by physical labor. He is the image of the friar whom he attacks. He is the idle 'lollare' he rebukes"

[Clopper 1997:304]; see also Cole 2003 for scrutiny of how all these categories of vagrancy coalesced and were reformulated during the period of PP and in the poem's development of them). Other mentions of "lewede heremites" recur throughout the poem, including those who "clothed hem in copes, clerkes as hit were / Or oen of som ordre of elles a profete" (9.211–12; C only), suggesting another self-deprecating parallel for the narrator (see 9.139–40, 9.189–280, both C only; and for a hermit in a tavern, 6.368; this line C only). Below, hermits who do not follow rules rigorously are unambiguously condemned in the example of Hawkin, in similar cadence and phrasing, as "Yhabited as an heremyte, an ordre by hymselue, / Religion saunʒ rule and resonable obedience" (B.13.285–86, partly shifted to Pride's confession in C.6.35–38).

Also only in B, Anima condemns hypocritical vagrant religious with a similar use of the subjunctive to describe their professional status: "þer are beggeris and bidderis, bedemen as it were, / Loken as lambren and semen lifholy, / Ac it is moore to haue hir mete on swich an esy manere / Than for penaunce and parfitnesse, þe pouerte þat swiche takeþ" (B.15.205–8). Even humble clothing, if chosen in order to define one's spiritual authority, may be a sign of pride in one's own perfection, as the comment below on lewd hermits suggests (see below 51–55n, and see also the "fair maiden" "Pride of parfit lyuynge" that later chases the narrator: C.11.174, 192 [B.11.15, 33]). As Clopper says, the poet places his persona "on the knife edge between legitimate and illegitimate beggary" (Clopper 1997:321 finds this daring position itself "central to the mendicant mission as represented by Francis," although whether the poem sees that as so is less certain, given its pervasive attacks on friars). Will's "life," his "living" in every sense, may be considered one of the preeminent problems that the poem addresses; the sheer multiplicity of interpretive challenges at his first announcement of who he is and what he does is an appropriate prelude to this theme, although it begins to be directly engaged only in the following passus.

vnholy of werkes: The narrator's "withdrawal from the world may mean that he does no evil but also does no good works" (Mills 1969:186), or that he is "unsanctified of conduct," as Kane translates the phrase (1989:95), or, as Bloomfield proposes, means either "that as a new hermit, he is not yet holy or that he is, as a hermit, more sinful than is normal" (1962:24). Medieval religious writers in many contexts apply brief penitential epithets to themselves; an early sixteenth-century devotional treatise, *The fruyte of redempcyon*, claims in its explicit that it was written by "the Anker of London wall, wretched Symon" (the bishop providing an imprimatur for this work presents a similar epithet, as if in competition with the author's humility: this "deuoute treatyse I Rycharde unworthy bysshop of London haue studyously radde & ouerseen":

STC 22557; Winkyn de Worde, 1514 and many editions thereafter until 1532). But the phrase gains particular resonance throughout the poem. Shortly, Holy Church herself will conclude her speech to the dreamer by emphasizing good works, pinning this on James 2:26, "faith without works is dead" (see 1.181–83a and note). But Paul also says in Romans (using the revised Wycliffite translation) that justification by works is inevitably inadequate for salvation: "For if Abraham is iustified of werkes of the lawe [*ex operibus iustificatus est*], he hath glorie, but not anentis God . . . Sotheli to hym that worchith not, but bileueth in to hym that iustefieth a wickid man, his feith is arettid to riȝtwisnesse, aftir the purpos of Goddis grace" (Rom. 4:1–5). The difficulties that these views present to the value of **werkes** are central to many of the poem's theological dilemmas (see Adams 1988b); they come to a crisis in the central portion of the poem where the A text breaks off, when the narrator reflects on how, for example, the thief on the cross next to Jesus "was yraunsomed . . . Withoute penaunce oþer passioun oþer eny other peyne" (C.11.259–71a [B.10.427–36a, cp. A.11.285–92]). The poem opens in uncertainty about the worth of **werkes**, and the narrator is himself definable only by negation (for the use of negation to define identity, see also 4.140–45n).

4 (B 4, A 4): Wente forth in þe world wondres to here: The line motivates the narrator's initial actions and thus all that follows. Robertson's and Huppé's argument that the narrator is initially presented as "erring" is apt, since he is indeed literally given to wandering (*errans*) and to *curiositas* (on *curiositas* see Zacher 1976)—as to some extent is Robertson's and Huppé's claim that the narrator is presented from the outset and throughout the poem as an allegory of the will (*voluntas*) through "whose errors, the reader may learn the pitfalls which lie in the path of any Christian in a corrupt church" (1951:35; see the fuller and more nuanced version of this view in Bowers 1986). Thus too Schm (at B.8.1) contrasts the impulse here with the later desire to seek Dowel at the beginning of the third vision (C.10/B.8/A.9).

   Whitaker (1813:xix) began the modern academic attention to Will as simply "the will" (partly because Whitaker took the poet's first name to be Robert). The idea has been fruitful, if sometimes overemphasized. Other contexts show the importance and plausibility of the literal aspects of Will's identity and actions. His penchant for wandering, for example, does not in itself render him unlike many other late medieval hermits (see Bloomfield 1962:70 and nn4–5; Hanna 1997). Indeed, as cases of late medieval hermits who traveled, begged, engaged in necromancy, and even married show, stability and obedience in the monastic sense were not required for the fulfillment of that vocation, which allowed great variety of ways of life (Clay 1914:88–91; Hanna

1994:85–94). Hermits in the order of St. Paul were especially free from institutional connections and rules (Davis 1985). The suggestion that the narrator is motivated by *curiositas* certainly lays him open to comparison with those he describes below who choose an eremetical vocation for dissolute purposes (see 51–55n). As Scase observes, his travels also potentially align him with the type of the *gyrovagus*, the unaffiliated religious who were the target of St. Benedict's strictures in the Benedictine Rule (based on concerns as early as Augustine's about monks wandering in pursuit of various earthly and social goals [*De opere monachorum*, cap. 28, PL 40:575–76]); by the eighth century the name *gyrovagi* was given to wandering and unaffiliated monks, especially Irish religious who were subject to prosecution, and by the fourteenth century to a broad range of vagabond religious (see Bloomfield 1962:24–25, 70–71 and n38; and Scase 1989; for a valuable discussion of the general late medieval "shock" at the notion of itinerant religious figures, especially friars, see Clopper 2003, and Cole 2003).

Again, however, since the implicit syntax of his claim to be a hermit may elliptically be in a hypothetical "as"-clause of manner, he may not be a literal hermit after all, like those he goes on to describe, but instead somewhat and somehow *like* a hermit (3n). His posture as a traveller can invoke a writer's or poet's vocation: it resembles the prologue of Laȝamon's *Brut* (so Bnt), where the narrator says that he has fared "wide ȝond þas leode" in search of historical lore (ed. Brook and Leslie 1963, lines 14–15); or the "Goliardic," Latin satirical tradition portraying an author as a clerical poet who has dissolutely travelled all his life: "Feror ego veluti sine nauta navis, / ut per vias aeris vaga fertur avis" ("I am borne like a boat without a sailor, as a wandering bird is carried on the drafts of air"), as the narrator of the *Confessio Goliae* says (ed. Wright 1841, lines 9–10; see also Hugh Primas #23, lines 72 ff., "Domus mea totus mundus, / Quem pererro uagabundus . . ." ["My house is the whole world, which I wander through as a vagrant"; ed. McDonough 1984]). Will's travelling forth, as the reader embarks as well, is like the quests in Deguileville's *Pelerinages*, which that narrator begins after falling asleep reading the *Roman de la Rose*; such travels may further invoke a knight's "motiveless quest" (Weldon 1987:261), an association clearer in B with its features of romance (see also Shepherd 2001; and B/A 6n). Benson notes that the line connects PP to travel narratives like *Mandeville's Travels* and sets the terms for a similar emphasis on "movement" as "both a stimulant and an impediment to [a book's] shape, producing new things to write about, even as it prevents the development of a single, unified story" (2004:122; see also Shepherd 2001:80–81, Middleton 1982b:105). The poem, Benson proposes, might even be called *Will's Travels*.

The motif of journeying pervades the poem in a wide range of valences, and these offer one principle for its unity (as in the word *passus*; see above, Headnote on the rubrics). In the B and C versions, this aspect of the beginning touches the end: PP's opening description of journeying is echoed by the last speech in the poem, Conscience's vow to become a pilgrim and "wenden as wyde as þe world renneth / To seke Peres the Plouhman" (22/B.20.380–81), a poignant vow to travel because of spiritual and cognitive need rather than interest in wonders, providing a redefinition rather than a repetition of the movement and wandering with which the poem begins. There, however, as at the start of the third vision with the search for Dowel, a more clearly spiritual desire motivates the wandering. But can we reject the value of **wondres**, which by definition are not assessible? Even here at the outset, the poem lays the foundation for a journey in pursuit of understanding, and thus of teachers to offer that. Exotic travel is not always a display of *curiositas*; Jerome's epistle to Paulinus, often presented as Jerome's prologue to his Latin translation of the Bible, opens with a long list of pious or intellectually earnest travellers who journeyed to seek new disciples or teachers: "So Pictagoras þe filosofere ʒede to þe filosoferes of memphies / So Plato wente to Egipt . . ." (in the Wycliffite translation; ed. Lindberg 1978:63). Chaucer similarly exploits the ambiguity of impulses for pilgrimage at the beginning of the *Canterbury Tales* (General Prologue 1–18; see Galloway 2005:288–89), perhaps another sign of Chaucer's knowledge and exploitation of PP's Prologue (see Cooper 1987).

The line's syntactic inversion of the infintive and its object is so commonplace in poetry that it might be considered a minimal marker of high poetic diction; such effects have received little comment in discussions of Middle English alliterative style (but see Lawton 1988:234). But this simple kind of syntactic inversion, an infinitive and its subject at the end of a line, is in fact a rarity in PP and contributes to the other markers of elevated or poetic style at the opening. Only 54 instances of such end-line inversion appear in the entire C text (6489 English or mainly English lines in RK-C), or on average about 1 every 120 lines, used as often for satiric as elevated effect; their frequency rises slightly in the later passūs (using the C text: Prol.74, 87, 196; 1.51, 72, 74, 78; 2.21; 3.49, 203, 207; 5.180; 6.208, 215, 435; 7.74, 102, 108, 127; 8.11, 13, 78, 181, 343; 9.12, 81; 10.302; 11.38, 58, 74, 78; 12.150; 14.43, 55, 64, 94, 126; 17.286, 294; 19.67; 20.388, 399; 21.164, 223, 240, 241, 360, 374, 445, 466; and 22.128, 131, 230, 290). For comparison, 36 instances appear in the 1340 lines of *The Siege of Jerusalem* (on average about 1 every 38 lines). Statistics do not capture the stylistic difference between rather "mannered" poetry like *Siege of Jerusalem* (most recently edited in stanzas by Hanna and Lawton 2003) and the longer periodic use of such overtly "poetic" strategies in PP. The prosy syntax of other alliterative poetry such as the *Wars of Alexander*, however, or *Wynnere and Wastoure*, rarely uses this feature at the ends of lines; the very loosely alliterative *Simonie* lacks it entirely. PP navigates freely between several distinct kinds of alliterative style.

5: And say many selles and selkouthe thyngus: C adds a line to the opening that offers a series of synonyms for "marvels" to replace A/B 6 (see note); compare the opening claim in *Wynnere and Wastoure*: "There hathe selcouthes bene sene in seere kynges tymes, / Bot never so many as nowe by the nyne dele" (ed. Trigg 1990, lines 3–4); the line in PP is in turn imitated at the opening of *Richard the Redeless*: "Sodeynly ther sourdid selcouthe thingis" (ed. Barr 1993, also Dean 2000), line 5. Hall considered the new line "futile and pithless," proof, in his view, that C was another and inferior poet's work (1908:7). Yet the line offers a touch of retrospective vision in the self-portrait of the narrator: it transfers the experience of 'marvels' from the dream itself in A and B to marvels in waking life that the narrator has already experienced *before* experiencing his dream-visions and thus before beginning to recount his poem (at least in the C version). The portrait of the author implied by this new line with its temporal perspective is like that of the narrator of Laȝamon's *Brut* or the Old English *Widsith*, about a minstrel/historian who "monna mæst mægða ofer eorðan, folca geondferde; / oft he on flette geðah mynelicne maððum" ("travelled through peoples, the greatest groups of men across the earth; often on the hall-floor he received abundant treasure"; ed. Krapp and Dobbie 1961:149–53).

Some prior life experience is implicit in the previous line in all versions, "Wente forth in þe world wondres to here," but this is made definite and overt by the new line: the narrator has already seen many things; he has a past. The line deepens the narrator's poetic authority and suggests his greater age than the unseasoned narrator of A and B. Possibly this is some indication of writing for an audience that already knew the author's earlier work; at least it incorporates into the opening portrait the similar claim in the Land of Longing episode for a long stretch of unrecorded life experiences or adventures (C.11.167–12.40 [cp. B.11.1–106]).

B 5–10 (A 5–10): Ac on a May morwenynge . . . sweyed so murye: For a close parallel, although within the dream proper, see the *Roman de la Rose* (ed. Poirion 1974, trans. Dahlberg 1986), lines 45–128. The A and B openings thus assert more direct affiliation to the tradition of *reverdie* dream-visions like the first part of the *Rose* than does C, which omits B's and A's portrayal of a waterbank scene and the allusion to the wonders **of Fairye.** In C's series of small compressions, B 6–7 (A 6–7) become C 7; B 8–9 (A 8–9) become C 8; and B 10–11

(A 10–11) become C 9 (on C's "reluctance to linger over the detail of B's description," see Donaldson 1966:52); for the more authoritative persona of the C narrator that replaces these lines, see above 10–13n. C's compressions omit B's and A's languid description of the narrator's slide into unconsciousness, a descriptive detail that the poet is capable of elaborating for ironic, paradoxical, or psychologically revealing possibilities (see, e.g., 5.107 [B.5.8]): here in A and B, he is seduced by natural sounds, as the reader is by the language of romance and adventure, in distinction from the more elaborate prologues of many other Ricardian poets (see Middleton 1982b:112–13; Galloway 2005).

6 (B 5, A 5): on maluerne hulles: Dream-vision poems and *reverdies* rarely provide specific place names for their opening setting, although some English *chansons d'aventure* do (see above 1–13n). **maluerne hulles** recurs at the close of the second vision in all three versions as the narrator's setting for these two dream-visions (see 9.296 [B.7.147, A.8.129]). From at least the sixteenth century, the Malvern area, northwest from London in southwest Worcestershire on the Herefordshire border, has been considered the birthplace or early home of the poet (see Kane 1965:38), and the dialects of many of the C manuscripts can be placed in or near this area (Samuels 1985). This last point may confirm Skeat's durable suggestion that the poet returned in later life to the Malvern area (first in ed. Skeat 1873:lxxiv) or at least maintained special connections in the area (Samuels 1988:208). Such connections could derive from holdings by the Despenser family in the area, for the Eustace Rokayle who is identified in an early fifteenth-century note in Dublin, Trinity College, MS. 212 as the father of "Willielmus de Langlond" held land of a Despenser (see Hanna 1993:7, 18). "Malvern Hills" fills out a proverb in the narrator's later condemnation of lawyers (165–66n).

But the geographical designation should not be used simply as biographical evidence, just as details of the Malvern landscape should not be used to explain the opening of the dream (cp. Bright 1928). Skt commented on the poem's opening sleeping geography as a mere foil for its focus on London: "to remember the *London* origin of, at any rate, the larger portion of the poem, is the true key to the right understanding of it. Though William is supposed to be bodily present on the Malvern hills he is soon *fast asleep* there; and it is of the London world that he dreams" (n. to line 6). Malvern was not a distant edge of the cultural landscape; it is near the Berkeley center, patrons of John Trevisa's translations (see Hanna 1989), and close to Bristol and the trade passages of the Severn. Thematically, however, Malvern locates the narrator's viewpoint decisively outside the administrative and civic world of London, which he can thereby contemplate from a moral and intellectual distance, allowed by the dream-vision form as well (see also 21.480–81n, and Pearsall 1997).

The location of Malvern for dreaming the first two dream-visions in both A and B is ruptured or overlaid by the location of the new waking episode in C.5 of "Cornehull . . . Amonges lollares of londone" (5.1, 4), a kind of waking within a waking, just as passus 13 (B.11) presents a dream within a dream. The C narrator attaches that brief awakening in London, in C only, to the later, preexisting awakening at the end of the second vision in Malvern Hills by stating, "Thenne mette me muche more then y byfore tolde / Of þe matere þat me mette furste on Maluerne hulles" (5.109–10). Yet by that statement, the narrator invokes a subtle distinction between actually returning to dreaming on Malvern Hills for the second vision, and returning to "þe matere" he dreamt there. Moreover, in the phrase "þat me mette furste," he acknowledges that he has presented the first of several dreams, and possibly acknowledges that he is revisiting his previous version of the poem. This contributes to a narrative position in C further displaced distinguished from the participant in the dreams (for other indications of this in C, see also 10–13n and 14–18n; see also 20.350–58n, par. 3).

B 6 (A 6): a ferly, of Fairye me þoȝte: ferly is a "marvel," here in the positive or enticing sense of the initiation of romance adventure, or the miracles of a "Breton lai," equivalent to the phrases at the opening of such works. *Sir Launfal* (first half of fifteenth century) begins, "Ther fell a wondyr cas . . ."; the late fourteenth-century *Awntyrs off Arthure* begins with a hunt in the forest in a distant time and place "In the tyme of Arther" when "an antur betydde . . ." (ed. Shepherd 1995:219–43). Yet near the opening of the *Awntyrs,* a ghostly woman prophesies deaths and other horrors for Gawain and Arthur's court as "seche ferles" (298, 299), and the narrator summarizes the unnerving encounter in the center of that poem as "this ferli" (708). The sense of "ferly" in PP shortly becomes menacing (see below, 62–63n). **ferly** and **of Fairye** are part of the characteristic diction of magical, surreal, or whimsical literary adventure, or even romance, all elements that C consistently avoids or parodies and that explain C's omission of the line here (see below 11n). In *William of Palerne,* when the emperor sees the handsome foundling William living in a shepherd's cottage, he thinks "þat feiȝþely it were of feyrye for fairenes þat it welt [possessed]" (ed. Bunt 1985, line 230); so too at the poem's end, the transformation of the werwolf back to human being is a wonder described as "þat ferli þat was fallen þere" (line 4764).

Five early copies of PP are copied with works that might be classified as chivalric romances, and one, Lincoln's Inn Library, London, Hale MS. 150, includes an A version of PP with an anthology of such works, many of which predate PP (*Libeaus Desconus* [mid- later fourteenth century], *Of Arthour and of Merlin* [c. 1320], *Kyng Alisaunder* [c. 1320] and *The Seege of Troye* [c. 1350]; see Shepherd 2001:72]). To suggest PP's affinity with such works, Shepherd (2001) focuses on the theme of the "righteous heathen" with which PP A (the version most often found with such romances) ends, as the romances some-times present righteous Saracens; Shepherd also proposes that, more broadly, the romances found with the A text "feature *will*-ful lone male heroes involved repeatedly in life- (or soul-) threatening struggles" (2001:73; see also N. Clifton 1993, who focuses on the disguised duel in C.20/B.18 as another romance motif). As with other works of this kind, "ferly" appears several times in *Libeaus Desconus* and *Of Arthour and of Merlin*; in the latter, Merlin, the off-spring of "a feond of gret poustee [power]" who has secretly had intercourse with Merlin's human mother—that is, he is surely "of fairy"—describes him-self as "a ferly sond" ('a wondrous messenger'; ed. Macrae-Gibson 1973, Auchinleck line 1119). Something of the nocturnal visitation of Merlin's fiend-ish father, responsible for Merlin's own vatic powers, might be evoked by the A/B line describing the origins of PP's dream-vision, even hinting at the dream's prophetic powers like those of Merlin himself. The PP narrator's explanation here is analogous to the helpless appeal of Merlin's mother: "as y slepte on a nyȝt / By me lay a selcouþ wyȝt / Bote y ne wist what hit was, / Þerfore y do me in þy grace" (*Of Arthour and of Merlin*, ed. Macrae-Gibson 1973, Lincoln's Inn MS., lines 919–22). He is a passive recipient of his own poetic incubus.

On other grounds, Bowers suggests that crediting the dream to **Fairye** might here imply for a fourteenth-century reader a demonic source (1986:139). This seems too closely oriented to the dichotomies of exegetic interpretation to describe many literary readers' reactions, but the line might arouse some spiritual concerns about the vision's origins and nature. Theological debate about the divine or demonic status of visions, deriving from 1 John 4:1, "believe not every spirit; but try the spirits [*probate spiritus*] if they be of God," grew in the fifteenth and sixteenth centuries. In 1415 Jean Gerson wrote *De Probatione Spirituum* elaborating the difficulties of assessment: an image of a sacred entity must be carefully tested; and what is presented as revelation must be weighed not only for its immediate appearance of piety but for its long-term consequences, just as John Hus sounded pious but revealed himself as heretical (ed. Glorieux 1973, vol. 9:177–85). Such concerns were more common in a period of reawakened mysticism, with which indeed PP has been variously connected (see Jusserand 1894[1965]; Vasta 1965; Phillips, ed. 1990).

The casual suggestion in A and B that the vision in PP is **a ferly, of Fairye** does not, however, induce the narrator to any sense of "testing," *probatio*, the vision that begins to unfold. That begins only when Holy Church suggests that the narrator "test all things," when he asks her to explain the Prologue's vision (see, e.g., 1.81–204n). Her insistence on such probing sharply contrasts with the narrator's passive acceptance here of his initial vision. Emmerson emphasizes that mentions of the "dubious sources" of the narrator's dreams appropriately announce the uncertain forms those dreams and their messages take: "The poem's fragmented, directionless, and inconclusive dreams do not resemble the coherent, guided, and progressive dreams of the Macrobian tradition, but suggest the kind of naturalistic explanation developed by the scholastics that closely links the state of mind and passions of the dreamer when awake to the substance of his dream when asleep" (1993:104). But the initial dream and the state of mind of the dreamer cannot be linked together at the outset at least; instead, the line simply licenses any unpredictable forms and interruptions that may follow. The line, that is, emphatically refutes the narrator's control at the outset; it sharply contrasts the opening poetic gesture of the *Roman de la Rose*, which begins by citing an authority like that brought into PP only with Holy Church: "one may have dreams which are not deceitful, whose import becomes quite clear afterward. We may take as witness an author named Macrobius, who did not take dreams as trifles . . . [and] in this dream was nothing which did not happen almost as the dream told it" (trans. Dahlberg 1986, lines 3–30). And only after the end of the second vision does PP's narrator assert a textually sanctioned validity of his dream-visions, at last presenting the gesture found at the beginning of the *Roman de la Rose*; as the *Rose*'s narrator cites Macrobius initially to justify his prophetic authority, PP's narrator only then cites the book of Daniel to propose the truthfulness and divinity of some dreams, implicitly including his own; the citation is balanced by others that dispute the value of dreams (see C.9.303–17 [B.7.154–72, A.8.131–50]). This inverted approach to a strategy of self-authorizing, by which any possible support from textual authority is only gradually earned and then still tentatively claimed rather than announced at the outset, suggests another way in which the end of the second vision marks a major moment of structural completion for the poem, indicated in the rubrics by the division of the *Vita* and *Visio*.

7 (cp. B 7, A 7): for werynesse ofwalked [B, A: wery forwandred]: "Weary" appears from early Middle English on with a past participle, usually with the prefix "of-" or "for-" (and both are attested here in the variant readings of all three texts). Later in the Middle English period, these formations of prefix plus past participle are often treated as prepositions, and made to precede present participles: thus textual variants here in all versions show "of wandryng," "for wanderyng" (see Mustanoja 1960:560–63, and Nevanlinna 2000). The present participial forms are to be rejected as later scribal simplifications. The idiom is repeatedly found in *William of Palerne*, sometimes in the same kind of moment and in similar rhetoric; e.g., "And as he aweited to þe windowe, wiȝtly þerafter / he slod sliȝli adoun, aslepe ful harde, / as a wo-wery weiȝh for waked tofore" (ed. Bunt 1985, line 2236; see also 739, 790, 2236, 2868, 3686); "wery forfoȝten" appears in *Wars of Alexander* (ed. Duggan and Turville-Petre 1989, lines 1394, 4045).

The combined state of exile and weariness often impels PP's dreamer into his visions (e.g., 20/B.18.1–4; see Huppé 1950:186–88 for a tabulation of the elements in the various passages describing the dreamer). Yet while logical and plausible as a prelude to sleep, weariness from the wanderings of an exile is not a common state of dream-vision narrators, apart from those of Chaucer, whose over-insistence on his sleepiness is parodic (*Book of the Duchess*, lines 25–29, *House of Fame*, line 115, *Parliament of Fowls*, lines 92–93). The contrast with Chaucer's bedridden drowsiness emphasizes not just the PP narrator's more hardearned fatigue, but also his rootlessness and continual wandering as the basis for that fatigue, establishing a position somewhere between a pilgrim's, a vagrant's, and, especially by the end of the poem, an exile's seeking to found a new city, like Aeneas, *fato profugus* ("driven forth by fate": *Aeneid* 1.2). The framework of continued wandering and questing decisively distinguishes PP from the triumphant allegorical battle against sin and founding of a New Jerusalem in Prudentius' *Psychomachia*, which has otherwise at least indirectly contributed to PP's overall form (for comparison between those, see Barney 1979:82–104, and especially 109).

B 10 (A 10): sweyed [A: swiȝede]: The onomatopoetic verb describing the river in B and A is variously spelled by scribes and variously interpreted by lexicographers: as well as obviously scribal substitutions (e.g., "semede" and "sownede"), numerous plausibly authorial readings are found, including "sweyed," "swede," "swyed," "sweyued," "swyȝed," "swiȝede," and "sweuenyd," shifting the sense between *sweien* (1) 'to sound'; *sweien* (2) 'to move in a sweeping motion'; *sweiven* 'to move with a whirling motion'; and *sweven* 'to put to sleep or (of the sea) to become calm.' The homophones of *sweien* (1) and (2) show that no clear distinction of sense is possible or needed here between sound and motion; the differences between K-A and KD-B's readings are mere fidelity to the copytext's spellings. K-A p. 433 notes that the EJ reading "sweiued" ('move' or 'put to sleep') offers a strong alternative; but **sweyed** ('resound' or 'move in a sweeping motion') appropriately presents a descriptive word with the most suggestive ambiguities of lulling. Compare the

opening of the Old English version of Bede's *De die iudicii,* "Judgment Day
II," "þær þa wæterburnan *swegdon and urnon* / on middan gehæge, eal swa ic
secge" ("There the streams of water swirled and ran / Amidst a field, all as I
shall say": ed. Dobbie 1942, lines 3–4); the parallel may show some tenuous
continuity between Old and Middle English alliterative verse or rhythmical
alliterative prose traditions (although "Judgment Day II" is only unevenly
alliterative), sustained by ecclesiastical and especially monastic milieux (on the
context of this continuity see Blake 1969b; Salter 1978; Pearsall 1982). The sensory fullness of the line in PP helps evoke a scene like that of the opening
garden of Nature in Alan of Lille's *Anticlaudianus,* which "has and holds
everything that feasts the eye, intoxicates the ear, beguiles the taste, catches the
nose with its aroma and soothes the touch" (1.71–73, ed. Bossuat 1955; trans.
Sheridan 1973:47). The topos is richly developed by the later fourteenth century. The alliterative *Wars of Alexander* describing May mentions the "swoȝing
[whispering] of þe swift wynde & of þe swete wells" (ed. Duggan and Turville-
Petre 1989, line 4514).

B 12 (A 12): I was in a wildernesse, wiste I neuere where: In many dream
visions, an idyllic and mysterious garden is the initial setting of the dream, as
in Guillaume de Lorris' *Roman de la Rose* and its fourteenth-century French
followers; e.g., "Je ne say que ce pooit estre / Fors que le paradis terrestre": "I
didn't know what it might be / If not the earthly paradise" (Machaut, *Dit dou
Vergier,* ed. Palmer 1993, lines 65–66). But the dreamer's location in a **wildernesse** is a floating position in an undefinable place that contrasts and is soon
eclipsed by the busy scene he looks out on. It is a transitional landscape that
might open into a visionary Edenic garden like much dream vision love
poetry, but that already seems less pleasant than the Malvern riverbank, perhaps hinting not at a recovery of Eden but a state of exile from that other
Edenic scene (see also 15n below). In A and B especially, to dream is not to
enter Eden again but, usually, to exit Eden again, in a continous fall from
innocence. For the dreamer's clearer recapitulation of the Fall, in a dream
within a dream, see C.13.132–232 (B.11.324–422).

10: Al þe welthe . . . and þe wo bothe: The C opening reduces the descriptive-
ness of the scene in B, but continues to invoke alliterative literary formulae:
the phrase **Al þe welthe of the world** is found in *Wars of Alexander* (ed. Duggan and Turville-Petre 1989), line 3382; see also *William of Palerne* (ed. Bunt
1985), line 4758. Neither has the antithesis, although *Wars* uses the phrase to
declare how all such wealth "worthis at þe last / To cayrayne & corupcion."
The usual antithesis is between "wele" and "wo" (see Whiting and Whiting

1968, W132–40). C's line adds social and ethical terminology, both entailing major contrasts and vast range, and suggesting a sharper sense of ethical responsibility and authorial control from the outset on the part of the narrator. In C he is not simply a hapless and passive witness to good and evil scenes but an expositor of issues that he already knows he can comprehensively organize (into antitheses) and recount, establishing an increased degree of authoritative bookishness and omniscience to his poem and authority behind his position of presenting it. The opening narrator of B and A seduces the reader with the promise of a lyric interlude; that of C commits the reader to something of epic scale. With parallel ambition, the *Roman de la Rose* opens with a statement that "ce est li *Romanz de la Rose*, / ou l'art d'Amors est tote enclose" ("This is the Romance of the Rose, in which the whole art of love is enclosed"; ed. Poirion 1974, lines 37–38). On the possible relations of PP to this work, see above, Headnote.

11: Wynkyng as hit were, witterliche y sigh hit: The emphasis on truly having dreamed this differs between C and the other versions; this line compensates for, or explains, C's omission of the A/B claim that the dream was a marvel "of Fairye" (see above B 6n). There is a stronger hint in the new line that the dream is a fictional disguise for serious and true materials (compare Gower's Latin annotation to the opening of the first book of the *Confessio Amantis*, where after the narrator begins to recount his love-struck state, the annotation declares that "the author is here fashioning himself as if he were a lover, as if in the persona of those whom love binds" ["hic quasi in persona aliorum, quos amor alligat, fingens se auctor esse Amantem"; ed. Macaulay 1900, book 1, by lines 59–65]). Like the other uses of "as" in hypothetical clauses (see above 2n), the qualification that the narrator is only **as hit were** dozing (OED *winking* vbl. sb[1] 1) expresses a hypothetical comparison, no longer claiming that this was an otherworldly dream-vision (on C's tendency to use **as hit were** "as part of a plan to make the simplest reader recognize the presence of allegory," see Donaldson 1966:64–65).

12: treuthe and tricherye, tresounn and gyle: C's early notice of **treuthe** points toward a key term; see below 15n. This single notion is here balanced against three species of sin and evil, perhaps already evoking the multitude of personified versions of such sins around Meed (see e.g., 2.5–9 [B.2.5–8, A.2.5–8], 2.25–26 [B.2.25–26, A.2.19–20], 2.44–46 [B.2.41–43, A.2.22–25]). The alliterative linkage of **tricherye** and **treuthe** is a fundamental one for the poem and for late medieval culture; compare the early thirteenth-century Anglo-Norman poem *Le Bestiaire* of Guillaume le Clerc which opens by defining the essential,

dichotomous terms of human existence, established by God along with his creation of the world: "A home dona tel franchise, / Qu'il sout conistre la divise, /
Qui esteit entre ben e mal, / Entre tricheor e leal, / Entre paraïs e enfer" ('to
man [God] gave such freedom that he might know the distinction that exists
between good and evil, between treachery and truth, between paradise and
hell': ed. Reinsch 1890, lines 10–14). The "B" and "C" versions of *The Simonie*
at the opening contrast "Falsnesse and Trechery in londe" to Rome where
"Trewþe scholde begynne" (ed. Embree and Urquhart 1991, lines B 27–28 [C
14–15]).

13: as y shal ȝow telle: for an Old English poetic analogue to the opening frame
which also has the phrase, "eal swa ic secge," see B 10n. To this point the narrator has said that he knows marvels and that he has dreamt "merueylous-
liche" (9), but he has only hinted that he could present more ("as y may ȝow
telle," 9). Donaldson notes that the poet's habit in C of repeating a line or
half-line is "at least half deliberate," a case, as here, "where an aging Prospero
is nervously undertaking one final fling at the creation of magic and is filled
with a sense of responsibility toward his audience" (1969:61). The shift from
"may" to **shal** also marks a more direct promise than line 9 above, a sign of
C's more rapid shift from the seductive hints left from A and B to urgency and
directness.

Setting of first vision

**14–18: Estward y beheld . . . and wikkede spiritus / B 13–16 (A 13–16): Ac as
I biheeld into þe Eest . . . dredfulle of siȝte**: All versions of the poem have a
vast cosmological frame for the contents of the dream—contrasted in a few
rapid strokes with the highly local setting of the narrator's sleep on **maluerne
hulles**. Only C, however, balances **Estward** with **Westward**, and only C identifies the tower as the dwelling of "truth" and the dale as that of "death," leaving
between these sharp dichotomies a morally indeterminate space for human
action. Visually realized, the scene in all versions is comparable to the *platea*
in medieval drama, itself a realization of a widespread moral cosmology in
which the inner world and the outer world, the microcosm and the macrocosm, echo one another (see the survey of instances in Brinkmann 1980:52–70
and especially 49–51nn). The setting of a "feld" enhances this sense (see below
19–21n), although in a rural register while *platea* is a town setting. Analogues
for this scene have often been proposed from morality drama, such as the fifteenth-century *Castle of Perseverance*, which locates in its manuscript illustra-

tion the World, the Flesh, the Devil, and God at various points around the
traditional outdoor circular stage (Skt; Jusserand 1909:310; see Southern 1957);
hell mouths are clear in sacred drama from the twelfth-century on (e.g., the
Ordo Representacio Adae; ed. Bevington 1975:78–121).

Estward evokes Eden "in the East" (Gen. 2.8), usually at the top of
medieval maps; Holy Church (in C only) provides a more explicitly Christian
gloss for the line: "Estward til heuene . . . / There treuthe is, þe tour that trinite
ynne sitteth" (1.133–34 [cp. B.1.131–33]). A long discussion of this orientation is
found in the early fifteenth-century dialogue, *Dives and Pauper* (ed. Barnum
1976:113–16). In PP 1.111a–22a the cosmology of the cardinal directions is
extended further when Lucifer is located in the north and Jesus implicitly in
the south (see also 1.115–25n). A/B's axis of orientation of the tower and the
valley is vertical; it is not clear for several lines that the location of the folk is
"bytwene" these reference points as on a flat plain. C's landscape, while omitting the visually descriptive adjectives for the tower and the valley, immediately positions the folk "bytwene" two points on a horizontal, east-west axis.
The dreamer's point of view looks both east and west, and thus stands between
the two, where the human action is.

**15 (cp. B 14, A 14): And say a tour . . . treuthe was thereynne [B, A: I seiȝ a
tour on a toft trieliche ymaked]:** The image of the **tour** passes in just two
lines, but in all versions its initial presence is clearly significant, and evocative
in numerous dimensions. For some medieval readers, it might invoke the edifice in the *Roman de la Rose* from which Raison first descends ("de sa tour,"
"from her tower"; ed. Poirion 1974, line 2976); the connection is more clearly
suggested when Holy Church descends "doun fro þe castel" (see 1.4n; for the
problem of whether much of the readership of PP can be assumed to have
known the *Rose*, see above, Headnote). The connection is fleeting and general,
although since Raison, at that first encounter, berates Amant for having followed "Oiseuse" and "Deduit," Leisure and Pleasure, a connection might be
seen between those elements and the motives of PP's dreamer that have been
schematically glimpsed so far, although in a radically different social and physical setting from the courtly and erotic garden where Raison finds Amant (see
also above, B 12n), and opening at once into a vision where the hypocritical,
avaricious, and unlovely figures painted on the wall outside the garden in the
Rose are here the content of the central field, an inversion of the *Rose*'s social
tableaux.

More clearly, however, the **tour** invites religious associations and guidance for the vision and the poem, and these indications emphasize fundamental distinctions of purpose from French and any other visionary love poetry.

The **tour** where **treuthe** dwells has elements invoking numerous allegorical edifices in biblical and medieval Christian writing, such as God as the "tower of strength" (Psalm 60:4 and Prov. 18:4), and especially the adaptations of and commentaries on Isaiah 12:8, "I am upon the watchtower of the Lord, standing continually by day," which are legion in medieval culture, spanning periods and purposes. Since Zion, as Jerome declared, means "watchtower" in Hebrew (Vulgate *specula*), and since, as Psalm 75:4 says, God's "abode is in Zion," commentaries and other writings stress the connection of Isaiah's "watchtower" to the city of Zion, and both to God's dwelling there, understood in a range of allegorical senses. Jerome's gloss on *et habitatio eius in Sion* (Psalm 75:4) present the set of connections that became widespread through medieval Christian culture: "secundum litteram possumus dicere Jerusalem, et Sion: quoniam ibi fuit templum. Secundum tropologiam vero, et anagogen dicimus: quia in Sion habitatio Dei sit. Sion interpretatur, 'specula.' In quacumque ergo anima notitia Scripturarum est atque doctrina, ibi inhabitat Deus": "according to the literal sense we can speak of Jerusalem, and Zion, since the temple was there. We can speak according to the tropological and anagogic senses, however, that 'in Zion was God's dwelling': Zion means 'watchtower.' Therefore, in whatever soul is the knowledge and doctrine of the Scriptures, there God dwells" (Jerome, *Tractatus lix in psalmos*, PL 26:1035; see also his *Commentarii in Isaiam*, glossing the sense of Isaiah's "watchtower" in a further way: "we can say that this refers to the Church, or to a holy man's soul, since that can rightly be called a watchtower and vision of peace when the Father and the Son and the Holy Spirit dwell in it": "possumus haec referre ad Ecclesiam, vel ad sancti viri animam, quae recte appellari potest specula et visio pacis, quando Pater et Filius et Spiritus sanctus habitaverint in ea"; PL 24:625). Following these and other connections, other exegetical writers use the synonym "truth" (*veritas*) for God to describe the watchtower's omniscient inhabitant: a twelfth-century commentary on the Pater Noster, for instance, declares that "Veritas namque dei de excelsa providentiae suae specula universa considerans quid cuique conveniat perspicit et hoc quod convenire singulis cognoscit adcommodat" ("for the truth of God, considering from his lofty universal watchtower of his providence what for each he perceives to be appropriate, and what he thinks is appropriate to each, he applies to each"; Frowinus, ed. Beck et al.: 2004, bk. 2, cap. 1; noted by Thomas Hill). In this tradition, the Archpoet in his twelfth-century Latin satirical "Confession" can allude to the "tower of truth" ("turris Alethie"), as also can the twelfth-century Latin debate poem, the *Ecloga Theoduli*, a basic Latin schooltext used throughout the later Middle Ages (cp. Raby 1965; and 1.149–50n; see also 21.317–34n).

The images produced by this understanding of Zion as God's "watchtower" are very widespread in English religious writings: the "hehe tur of Ieru-salem" in *Hali Meiðhad* (ed. Millett and Wogan-Browne 1990:2), the "tur of heouene," in the *Lofsong of ure Lefdi* (80, ed. Thompson 1958); and God's "tor," as the maiden in *Pearl* describes the heavenly Jerusalem (line 966, ed. Andrew and Waldron 1996), all follow the traditions that Jerome established. The Wycliffite *Lanterne of Liзt* says that the church "in heuene . . . holdiþ þe toure," and adds that Christ came "fro þe toour of heuene" (ed. Swinburn 1917 for 1915:35, 54). The same phrase is the entire theme of a short lyric found at the bottom of a copy of Robert Grosseteste's *De Veritate Theologie*: those who can enter the "richз ture" of heaven will find "Mirthes ma þan ert [heart] may think" while the "Sinful man" will enter "neuer mare þar-Inne" (Brown 1957, no. 50). The fifteenth-century East Anglian *Mary Play* begins with a prayer that "God þat is hevyn kynge / Sende us al hese dere blyssyng, / and to his towre he mote vs brynge" (ed. Meredith 1997, lines 22–24).

The versions of PP differ in the license they provde for free-association through these possibilities. A and B offer only an allusive and punning descrip-tion of the tower: it is on a **toft**, that is, a small hill, or a plot of land for a dwelling, often enclosed. B/A's **trieliche ymaked** produces a pun on 'excel-lently' (French *trier*), 'truly,' and, in the context of other uses of "trie" and "trielich" that soon follow, the Trinity: 'in a triune or trinitarian way' (see 1.81n, 1.136n; Huppé 1950:180; Robertson and Huppé 1951:35). The adverb **trie-liche** is otherwise attested, though without such religious implications, only in *William of Palerne* (ed. Bunt 1985, lines 1228, 3198, 4819, 4861). **trieliche ymaked**, with its further hint of visual detail, also parallels the description in *Mandeville's Travels* of the Church of the Holy Sepulchre in Jerusalem as "craftyly wrought" (in the Latin version, "artificiose ornatur"; ed. Seymour 1963:50–51). Absent any explanation, A/B offer a tower amenable to any num-ber of courtly adventures: we may expect a maiden (and we shortly get one); we may await a knightly tournament (and that eventually follows too). A very noncourtly world and satiric perspective, however, rapidly dispel the reader's associations with courtly (and romance) conventions.

C's identifications of the **tour** as the home of **treuthe** and the "depe dale" as the dwelling of the "wikkede spiritus" dispels these associations more quickly, advancing information that the dreamer learns only later in his con-versation with Holy Church (see 1.12–40n, 55–67; Donaldson 1966:49). Such initial definitions, like other details mentioned above (6, 10–13 and notes), show C's narrator displaying greater authority, presenting a retrospective con-spectus rather than visions and teachings as they are thrust upon him: com-pare Chaucer's narrator opening *Troilus and Criseyde* (lines 1–7) with a similarly comprehensive summary of themes. C's interpretive authority at the outset suggests the posture of an *auctor*, commanding a wide point of view and interpretation of the poetic scene (see Minnis 1984:94–117, 160–210).

The tower's Christian significance, gradually rapidly revealed, is to distinguish sharply between those entering a dwelling of salvation and those excluded; thus it may also echo Psalm 14, used repeatedly in PP: "Lord, who shall dwell in your tabernacle? Or who shall rest in your holy hill [*in monte sancto tuo*]?," universally assumed in Christian culture to refer to the question of who shall enter heaven (see 2.39–42 [B.2.36–39], B.3.234a–41a, and notes; see Robertson and Huppé 1951:234). Psalm 14's answers to its own initial question likely contributed to the opening conceit of the tower of Truth: "who shall rest in your holy hill? He that walks without blemish, and works justice: He that speaks truth in his heart . . ." In all versions of PP, however, the kind of question with which Psalm 14 opens echoes more profoundly than the answers.

treuthe: Even here at its first, brief mention in C only, one may identify **treuthe** as a name both for God and for the essence of social and religious faith and loyalty. Based on John 14:6, "I am the way, and the truth, and the life," and other scriptural passages (Jn. 8:32, Ps. 30:6, Ps. 84:12, and 1 John 2:4, 2:8, etc.), Jesus was commonly called *Veritas* in medieval commentary; Wyclif and the Wycliffite English writings use this appellation with special consistency. Below at 9.59 (in C only) the narrator directly identifies God and Truth ("oure lord treuthe"), and at B.11.164 (B only) Truth is aligned with Jesus in the harrowing of hell. *Veritas* in medieval writings also refers to Scripture, a sense implicit in many of the citations of Truth in PP but not the narrow sense in any. Middle English **treuthe** is richer still; it can mean the principle of right or justice; virtuous living, integrity; a true account or testimony; and, especially, loyalty, faith: it is a virtue incorporating all of the above (Alford, *Gloss.*; Kane 1980:9–10; Green 1999). As a principle of loyalty and fidelity in all senses, it occupies the highest position in late medieval culture, counterposed by treason, duplicity, and faithlessness. In social dimensions, this remained a supreme value even in a period considered based on the contingent social contracts of "bastard feudalism" (see Hicks 1995:84–93; 116–17). Yet how to apply the principle among the uncertainties of any social world or individual mind and soul remains a central doubt in the poem. Holy Church's elaboration of the word emphasizes the need continually to explore by experience and learn the possibilities for finding Truth, rather than assuming that there are simple ways to grasp it; see passus 1, and especially 1.81–204nn.

As an agent, Truth is outside the "field of folk," the realm of the humanly knowable, except, perhaps, by knowing its opposite. Truth acts in the poem but always as an elusive and removed presence, known only through indirect evidence like the tower, or through messengers like Holy Church and messages like the Pardon, or, as a smaller instance, through the "tokene" that Truth would have sent Meed by way of the king (see 3.133n). A Wycliffite sermon on the Prodigal Son of Luke 15:11–32, exiled into a "fer cuntre" and made to eat husks, describes the desire for Truth in pertinent terms: "Þis hungir þat fel in þis cuntre is wanting of knouyng of treuþe wiþ kyndely desire to knowe treuþe. One of þe citeseyns is þe fend, as al þis world is Goddis cuntre; and dyuerse fendis of helle han wille to tempte to dyuerse synnes . . . . But al þis shewiþ greet nede of man" (ed. Gradon and Hudson 1983–96, vol. 3.103). Yet, as Embree and Urquhart point out, PP's "Truth has not been exiled; he is just keeping his distance. His *toure on a toft* may be difficult for the pilgrims to find, but there is no suggestion that Truth himself would have difficulty getting back to the *felde ful of folke*" (1991:61n52). In PP Truth at least remains present as a beacon focusing the desires and views of the dreamer and some other allegorical figures and "folk" in the poem, at first vaguely in the first two visions then with increasing intensity in the later portions, though throughout eliciting rather than fulfilling human beings' desire for it. For possible relations to Augustine's definition of "the true" as a self-sufficient and permanent force, opposed to the derivative and deliberately deceptive actions of "the false," see his treatise *De vera religione* (ed. Daur 1962), and below, 1.141–45n; and his *Soliloquia* (ed. and trans. de Labriolle 1939), and below, 2.1–4n.

17–18 (cp. B 15–16, A 15–16): a depe dale; deth . . . / Woned in tho wones [B, A: A deep dale byneþe, a dongeon þerInne . . . dredfulle of siȝte]: In keeping with the iconography of drama and other traditional depictions of sacred cosmology, B and A pair the tower of truth with a **dongeon** in the dale, a word that can mean a dark prison or pit, and in this sense the word is commonly used in Middle English to refer to hell (MED *dongoun* 2.(b), 3.(b)). In the "Legend of St. Michael" in the *South English Legendary*, Lucifer is described as falling "To þe deope put of helle as is wonynge is" (ed. D'Evelyn and Mill 1956:407, line 172). A/B's **dongeon** would then similarly invoke the *abyssus* in which Satan is bound (Rev. 20:1–2). But **dongoun** can also mean castle or keep (MED *dongoun* 1); and Holy Church later refers to the "Castel of Care" (1.57). A castle or keep could have a subterreanean prison, the feature that the narrator's eye falls on in A and B: **Wiþ depe diches and derke and dredfulle of siȝte.** Thus Alford declares that the scene presents two castles, and that it poses the question, "to which castle or lord do these folk owe their faith, their loyalty or (to use the feudal term) their *truth*?" (Alford 1988a:32).

The description chiefly emphasizes the opposed imagery of heights and depths, and C simplifies the details to stress that opposition and to make clear immediately its Christian implications, by omitting A/B's somewhat ambiguous reference to another fortress or simply a pit, the **dongoun**, and by directly identifying the inhabitants of the **depe dale** as **deth** and **wikkede spiritus**, i.e., hell, with a possible basis in "the valley of death" (*in valle mortis*), the Vulgate's second, Hebraic translation of Psalm 23:4. **spiritus** is not Latin plural, thus not the first Latin in the poem, but a southwest Worcestershire plural often used in the Athlone C copytext (Huntington Library, MS. HM 143, = X; see Samuels 1988:211). The word is not rubricated as Latin in X; the other important copy, the northwest Worcestershire copy British Library MS. Add. 35157 (= U), has "spirites." **woned in tho wones**: For the same formula with the cognate accusative see *Alexander and Dindimus*; ed. Skeat 1878, line 1103.

19–21 (B 17–19, A 17–19): A fair feld ful of folk . . . as þe world ascuth: A capacious social vision is announced, suggesting a survey of the various estates and occupations; see below, 22–94n. For the poet's tendency to generate occupational lists, see below 222n. The turn to social satire after a springtime opening is not generally found in previous *reverdie* or estates satires, although it appears in somewhat later works (e.g., *Parlement of Thre Ages*; ed. Offord 1959, *Somer Soneday*; ed. Turville-Petre 1989:140–47, and Chaucer's General Prologue; for the likelihood that Chaucer knew PP's A Prologue, see Cooper 1987). The phrase **feld ful of folk** offers common alliterative stave words: see, e.g., *William of Palerne*, "boþe partyes here place pertiliche hade chosen / in a ful fayre feld, feiþly to telle" (ed. Bunt 1985, lines 1150–51); and *Wars of Alexander*, "all þe fild full of folke fyue mile large" (ed. Duggan and Turville-Petre 1989, line 3175), describing a battlefield (also "When Phylyp with his faire folkie had þe fild won"; line 454; see also 1455, etc.). *Wars* also has "efter wele comys wa, for so þe werd askis" (line 4750), another commonplace formula in alliterative tradition; see below.

The opening of PP thus echoes the common rhetorical strategies of alliterative poetry emerging plentifully by this date, yet it splices the scenic capabilities of that poetry with its satire, developing both into allegory, in which phrases usually used for military adventure become means of scrutinizing moral and intellectual issues. A **feld** may, as in *William of Palerne* and *Wars*, be a battlefield, or simply open or rural land as opposed to woodland or a town, or indeed more generally the surface of the earth (MED *feld* 1, 3, 5); the term stands undefined and capaciously suggestive of human existence, with a suggestion of a stage for conflict. A spiritual battlefield is indeed a possible implication, supported further by the tower and dungeon; but the immediate reference to plowmen makes 'open land' another obvious sense here, whatever the threat and promise of the tower and dungeon might mean (MED *feld* 2; see also the "half aker to erye by þe heye way" where Piers Plowman in the second vision leads the "thousand of men" who have gathered for a pilgrimage [8.2 (B.6.4); 7.155 (B.5.510)]). Pearcy (1997) suggests that **fair** and **feld** could potentially read with equal stress, to signify "market fair," on the grounds that "Fairfield" and other names show that phrase; *Troilus and Criseyde* 1841 has "al nys but a faire, / This world" (for further analogues and references to that, see Barney's note in *The Riverside Chaucer*, 1057 ad loc.). But that possibility is unlikely; at the beginning of the second vision, in a line present from A on (although not found in one cluster of related A manuscripts, TChHN), the narrator uses the terser phrase "felde ful of folk" (as in *Wars*, line 3175) to recapitulate at the beginning of the second vision his opening return to a dream-vision, and (briefly) to familiar alliterative literary features (A.5.10, B.5.10, C.5.111).

The **feld** on which the poem is set is a general arena and productive agrarian image for a theater of human economic labor and spiritual struggle (compare B.6.140). Such agrarian images are the basis of the poem's central metaphors, from the fruit-filled tree of Liberum Arbitrium and the Barn of Unity to Piers Plowman himself. These metaphors define human existence in terms of labor, growth, and yield, sustained on many social, moral, and theological levels (see, e.g., 12.178–247, 13.23–25, neither in B); the vegetative and agrarian ideal sometimes appears in perverted forms (see, for example, Wit's speech on offspring, 10.242–77 [B.9.148–75], and especially the anti-plowing of Antichrist, 22.53–57n, although that is another kind of battlefield). Yet many of the professions and practices surveyed are mercantile and urban rather than agrarian and manorial; thus the agrarian space of the opening survey "serves to criticise the actual practices of many groups within that society," in which "the complexity of the mercantile and bourgeois world . . . cannot be constrained by the . . . simplicity of the space in which it is set" (Simpson 1990b:33). Thus, like the analogous sequence of expansions of the social scheme in the versions of the Pardon passus, and like the emphases on "craft" prominent at the end of the poem (22.213–57n, 21.229–51n, etc.), the insertions by B and C into the Prologue register the poem's increasingly specific and complicated portrayals of vocation and estate, leaving the agrarian plane of human action the successively overlayered foundation.

20 (B 18, A 18): þe mene and þe riche: From the A text on, the poem proposes a comprehensive social scope using two basic social categories, a pattern that C develops prolifically into its other dichotomous opening terms, "wele" and "wo," "treuthe" and "tricherye," with "tresoun" and "gyle" as further contrasts to "treuthe"; see also above, 12n, and below, 222n. The line is echoed at the end of the Prologue (see 222n). The mass of people here recalls the vast mixed crowd of followers of "Fauvel," the allegorical horse representing all manner of flattery and deceit, whom everyone wants to curry in the popular early fourteenth-century French *Roman de Fauvel*, likely a source for the estates satire here (see below 136–37n) and whose presentation of Fauvel's effort to marry Fortune is probably a source for the marriage of Lady Meed in passus 2 (see 2.25–26n). Near the beginning of that satiric work, Fauvel is surrounded by "gens de toutes nacions / Et de toutes condictions / Que c'est une trop grant merveille" ("people of all countries and conditions, which is a very great marvel": ed. Långfors 1914–19, lines 29–31); the brief description there of various estates, from kings to townspeople, the pope to parsons, ends by saying that all have come to curry Fauvel, "Riches, moëns, gros et menus" ("the rich, the commoners, the great, the small," lines 169–70).

Whether *Fauvel* was a particular model, **þe mene and þe riche** is a formulaic and widespread phrase, based (like the French *gros et menus*) on the common Latin phrase, *minores et majores* ("the lesser and the greater"). For a partial English parallel, compare *William of Palerne*, ed. Bunt 1985, line 1310, "forto riʒtleche [rule] þat reaume real, of riche and of pore"; note also *William of Palerne*, "þe grete after here degree . . . / and menere men as þei miʒt" (lines 1936–37). As this last example shows, **mene** includes a wide range of social meanings, loosely divisible into either "inferior in rank" (adj. 1 [2a], from Old English *gemæne* 'common'), and "of middling status" (MED *mene* adj. 2 [3], from Old French *moiien* 'middling').

Several C manuscripts here read "þe mene and þe pore" (as printed by Prsl from his copytext), evidently taking **mene** as "of middling status" (thus needing the contrast of "pore") rather than "(economically) inferior." The latter sense, however, is the likelier here, and the Athlone reading correct, since it allows a sharper dichtomy in the line in keeping with the other wide dichtomies here, and since the line reappears below at 222. The vague meaning of **þe mene**, which allows this textual variation, points to the wide social range that this word was obliged to cover (for the parallel wavering in the French phrase *menu peuple* in the later fourteenth century, see Dudash 2003). The reference to "þe pore" in the C-variant phase here probably shows scribal awareness of PP's general focus on the poorer social classes, and possibly reflects a Franciscan bias of that scribal tradition; for the focus on the poor, particularly in the first two visions, see Shepherd 1983, Pearsall 1988, Hewett-Smith 2001, Kim 2002, and Scott 2001 and 2004; and for the Franciscanism implied by such a view, Clopper 1997, especially 226–38.

21 (B 19, A 19): Worchyng and wondryng as þe world ascuth: This final doublet before the vision itself invokes the pattern of the previous clear dichotomies but thwarts any definitive clarification, in moral or interpretive terms. **Worchyng** may refer broadly to those who "win" or produce rather than consume or "waste" (see 22–26n), or to those fulfilling properly their social roles (MED *werken* 3.(a)), and in the Prologue the verb by itself remains positive, but already by the beginning of the next passus it is modified to refer to doing evil (1.26, but in A/B not until B.1.128 [A.1.117, C.1.130]). And as we immediately see in "summe putte hem to pruyde" (25 [B/A 23]), focused endeavor is not in itself necessarily laudable. **wondryng** (evidently let stand by RK-C as a by-form of B/A's **wandryinge**, but emended by Prsl to "wandryng") may be aligned with the "wasters" described in line 24 just below. Elsewhere in the poem the word "wandryng" is used to describe what "wasters" do: e.g., "And tho wolde wastor nat worche bote wandred aboute" (8.324; see also B.9.198 on "fals folk" who "Wandren as wolues and wasten if þei mowe"). The narrator, of course, is more literally a "wanderer" than any of those he surveys, an association that increases the possibilities for moral uncertainty in the term (see above, 4n). But *wandren* can be morally neutral, encompassing *la condition humaine*, especially as a consequence of the Fall (see Dyas 2002). Thus B.7.97: "of alle oþere manere men þat on þis moolde wandreþ"; yet C changes that phrase to "men þat on this molde walken" (9.173), so perhaps some slight pejorative view of *wandren* is indicated in this revision. For a review of further negative and neutral views of **wondryng** here see Dyas (2002).

    as þe world ascuth: A recognizable formula of alliterative verse but applied with powerful if elusive import. For the formula, see *Sir Gawain and the Green Knight* (ed. Andrew and Waldron 1996), line 530, *Alliterative Morte Arthur* (c. 1400, ed. Benson 1994), line 2187, *Death and Liffe* (c. 1425, ed. Donatelli 1989), line 5; variants are common (e.g., *Wars of Alexander*, line 4750). Waldron (1957:797) suggests dozens of examples of b-verse lines that follow the same structure of thought, phrasing or meter; PP often uses such b-verses with "saying" or "asking" or "displaying" verbs to specifically meaningful rather than formulaic effect (e.g., "as this lettre sheweth," 2.209; "as the world techeth," 9.88). Here, the phrase closes the differences between **Worchyng and wondryng**: both follow the world's demands. To do so does not necessarily imply sinful activity (thus Donaldson 1960:7, against Robertson and Huppé 1951:17), or even a case of an "empty tag[] . . . made satirically mordant" (Lawton 1988:236), for that would thus extend to **worchyng** too. Yet although Robertson and Huppé, and Lawton, go too far in their flatly pejorative reading of the phrase, to act according to the demands of the world is indeed elsewhere in the poem a potential ethical trap, as when the figure Need brings to focus the ethical problem of acting *simply* as physical need requires,

"Withouten consail of Consience or cardinale vertues" (22/B.20.21), or when Lady Meed offers arguments of expediency to justify her influence (3.221–83).

Thus the effect of the phrase is not simply blandly quotidian ("The people are behaving in accordance with their position in the world"; Griffiths 1985:6). Prominently placed in the context of the poem's opening broad vision, the formula releases a potential not commonly possible for it, allowing it to be moving and monitory, but not decisively judgmental: demands and circumstances as well as commitments and self-interest necessarily define human beings' actions and lives. The sweeping view implies a perspective outside yet conscious of the inevitability of such self-interested purpose and action for living beings. Compare Keats' comment, "the greater part of men make their way with the same instinctiveness, the same unwandering eye from their purposes, the same animal eagerness as the Hawk . . . . I go among the Fields and catch a glimpse of a stoat or a fieldmouse peeping out of the withered grass— the creature hath a purpose and its eyes are bright with it—I go amongst the buildings of a city and I see a Man hurrying along—to what? The Creature has a purpose and his eyes are bright with it" (letter to Mr. and Mrs. George Keats, 19 March 1819 [ed. de Man 1966:340]). Beyond even the distancing strategy of a dream-frame, the resigned and encompassing perspective in the line in PP fundamentally distinguishes the poem from other kinds of "complaints" and estates satires, even as the poem now turns to the more pointed criticisms of those modes.

Survey of estates

22–94 (cp. B 20–96, A 20–83): Somme potte hem to plogh . . . in stede of stewardus and sitten and demen: The phrase of line 20, "Of alle manere of men," announces the social survey that follows. This survey occupies the rest of the Prologue in the A version, and is varied after line 94 in C and 96 in B by deeper and more vigorous allegorical and topical explorations of the nature of the bonds and the fundamental principles of that society. The previous literary tradition of "estates satire" sprawls across Latin, French, and to a minor degree English (see Mohl 1933, Yunck 1963, and especially Mann 1973, including a list of estates satires at pp. 203–6); an atypically full precedent in English is a thirteenth-century poem in MS. Jesus College 29 surveying fancy-dressers, rich men, arrogant poor, and variously immoral types of monks, priests, knights, lawyers, merchants, plowmen, proud ladies, and nuns, called by Morris "Sinners Beware!" (ed. Morris 1872:72–83, lines 91–174). The apparently more popular English work written c. 1330 and adapted into several forms, *The*

Simonie, uses a very loosely alliterative six-line rhyming stanzaic form to survey abuses methodically and hierarchically through the three estates, from
cardinals down to physicians, barons down to squires, various lay professionals down to laborers (ed. Embree and Urquhart 1991). *The Simonie* includes
small scenes of corruption and laments the departure of Truth and the
approach of famine, and one of its versions may very well have directly influenced PP's Prologue as well as the arrival of Hunger at the end of the second
vision (Salter 1967, Finlayson 1989; Embree and Urquhart 1991:59–62). This
genre of a survey and a description in the third person is related to, but distinct
from, sermons *ad status*, designed for direct address to particular estates,
although that mode of speaking to "you" of a certain social order does appear
elsewhere in the poem, indeed more readily than in other literary "estates satires" that merely survey the estates (e.g., "Ʒe lordes and ladies and legatus of
holy churche" [C.7.81]). For a model for the focused addresses in *ad status*
sermons, see Honore d'Autun (PL 172:861ff); see further references to the
genre in Muessig 2002.

   Although PP's narrator almost disapppears from view, the survey follows
his gaze and its roving discovery of the practices displayed. This heuristic style
for surveying social order somewhat resembles twelfth- and thirteenth-century
Latin "Goliardic" works of estates satire such as the *Apocalypsis Goliae Episcopi*, where the narrator's flight to heaven in a vision leads to his chance to
read about the vices of the clergy, or the *Speculum stultorum*, where Burnel the
ass travels to each of the religious orders and dutifully notes (and later tries
to consolidate into one conglomerate order) their hypocrisies. The mode also
resembles the genre of "path of hell" or "path of paradise," a genre that
Barney suggests might be called *voie*, in which the narrator moves from station
to station in hell or heaven, surveying various ethical classes of people under
various rubrics of virtue and sin (e.g., *La Voie de Paradis*, which presents
such vignettes in the "lieus" one visits; ed. Diekstra 1991; c. 1280: Diekstra
1991:30–32; Barney 1988:126–27).

   This way of presenting a social survey differs from static descriptions of
the ideal qualities of social groups as in, for example, the French *Romans de
Carité* (c. 1185, ed. Van Hamel 1885) or the abuses of the social groups and
occupations in John Gower's *Mirour de l'Omme* (ed. Macaulay 1899; trans.
Wilson 1992) and *Vox clamantis* (ed. Macaulay 1902, books 2–8; trans. Stockton 1962), both roughly contemporary with PP B. In PP, each social group or
occupation is caught in its typical mode of action, and its abuses are thus presented as modes of doing. Yet abstraction, heuristically unfolded, governs these
social types in a different way: laborers and wasters are presented (at least initially) not as expressing the different talents that God has divided among

human beings, as in 1 Cor. 7:7, 12:4–11, a principle suggested later in the poem (see C.21/B.19.229–61, 21.229–51n), nor as creatures of mindless routine, but rather as those who have chosen and continue to choose among major ethical options: plowmen **potte hem** to supplying the needs of all and repairing the losses that "wastoures" inflict; others **putte hem** to exacerbating those losses through displays of "pruyde"; still others **potten hem** to prayer and penance. For all, their lives as various kinds of social "estates" or professions is merely a consequence of that initial ethical or even quasi-allegorical choice. The heuristic mode here is echoed later in the quasi-naïve point of view of Chaucer's General Prologue; but here this strategy is not self-parodying or coyly ironic in itself. Rather, it expresses a kind of philosophically heuristic inquiry of how social roles develop from fundamental choices of principle, and how those choices continue to be expressed in the modes of action exhibited by those sustaining those roles. The viewpoint of the Prologue is not that of a naïve narrator, but of a mind seeking to ponder the fundamental rationale for society in its present forms and modes of action.

Estates theory provided a basis for such conceptual inquiry; a typical division was that of king and knighthood (*bellatores*), clergy (*oratores*), and "laborers" or "commons" (*laboratores*)—the last a category that sustained continual elaborations and expansions in keeping with developments in professions and urban specializations (see Duby 1980; Rigby 1995; Galloway 2000). Originating in the eleventh century, tripartite social analysis was still common in fourteenth-century writings; in the 1380s, for instance (possibly in 1387), Thomas Wimbledon preached a widely copied sermon, extant in fifteen manuscripts, on the interdependent functions of the three estates and the necessity of preparing for the impending Apocalypse. Wimbledon's sermon (not a sermon *ad status* but a survey) argues for the distinction between human beings and animals on the principle (from Avicenna) that the former must have a tripartite division of labor, into those who fight, those who pray, and those who labor (ed. Knight 1967). The sequence in PP begins with the principles defining the last, agrarian labor, and proceeds to frame all human endeavors in sum as extensions of the principles of agrarian labor, in a way deeply connected to the biblical definition of all lapsarian human life: with labor and toil shall you eat from the earth for all the days of your life (see Gen. 3:17).

Indeed, PP does not entirely present an "apparently random mass of social types . . . offered initially as something merely observed, not ordered or explained" (Godden 1990:31). For at least at the outset, the promise of clear principles prevails over details, but then details of what those principles mean in practice swim into view, and then again, still other principles are uncovered that help account for society and its ethical as well as interfunctional structure.

A structuring principle of the "Three Estates," of laborers, knights or court-iers, and clergy, lies behind the beginning of the survey by the emphatic echo in the sequence of those who **potte hem to plogh**, those who **putte hem to pruyde** (with the implication that these are courtly affectations and fashions), and those who **potten hem** to prayers and penance. But the echo there of the traditional scheme is then thoroughly violated, as if to insist that the principles defining society need fundamental reassessment—an impulse to which the refounding of the whole commonwealth in the coronation scene answers, as does the less momentous debate between the mice and rats about their relative standing and function next to the cats of court (see below 139–59n, 167–219n).

Some satirical literature of the fourteenth century is likely to have con-tributed to L's mode of prompting such reconception of social order. The opening of the *Roman de Fauvel* presents a similar general division in the brief description of the social world following Fauvel, between secular figures (from nobility down to urban citizens) and ecclesiastics (from pope down to par-sons). *Fauvel*'s literary conceit redefines society as so many different ways to "curry favor." But PP's pervasive emphasis on proper action, *doing* well, and choosing one or another ethical or inethical option to pursue as a mode of doing, takes a more fundamental approach to the divisions of society. The closest contemporary analogues to PP's sequence are Lollard estates descrip-tions: in the *Lanterne of Liȝt*, the "true church" is described, in sequence, as composed of "symple labureris . . . þe lowest astaat þat we clepen comunes," then "þe ordir of knyȝthod to defende Goddis lawe, to maynten good lyuars & to iustifie or soore punysche mysdoars," then "þe hiȝe ordir of presthood" (ed. Swinburn 1917 for 1915:33–34; for the importance of the poor laity in the Lollard perspective, see Barr 2001:128–57).

The same sequence is followed by Bishop Reginald Pecock, a later antago-nist of the Lollards who often used (to his own eventual downfall) their own mode and arguments; in his mid-fifteenth-century *Donet* he lists the estates and to some extent the principles of human ability and need in terms like PP's:

as manye parties or degrees or statys as ben necessarye to þe nede and profite of þe comounte, be ordeyned and stabliid to be and abide, as ben þese vii: The first, erþeti-liers, wiþ beestys multipliyng; The ii[e], craftys men; The iii[e], merchauntys; The iiii[e], mynistris or seruauntis or laborers; The v[e], leerid men or scolers, boþe of natural kun-nyng and of moral kunnyng; The vi[e], prelates, or curatis, wiþ vndir hem helpers, as louȝer preestis and oþire ordrid men, and wiþ religiouse persoonys profityng forto be able, if god so graunte, to be takun into state of prelacye or curacye; The vii[e], þe prynce wiþ hise helpers vndir him, as dukis, and oþire officers. (ed. Hitchcock 1921:74–75)

But Pecock's list is still a steep and regular "hierarchy," if one inverting the traditional three estates. The scheme of PP's survey—from which it is difficult to exclude the entry of the king and founding of the commonwealth there, as well as the parliament defining the nature and division of the mice, rats, and cats of court—probes and reshuffles its principles within the progress of every version, and progressively across the three versions (sections that are inserted or deleted in any revision are bracketed and indented progressively for B and C, and the section on the sergeants of law which is repeatedly moved is bracketed and its various appearances linked by asterisks):

Those committed to plowing (C 22–24; B 20–22; A 20–22)
Those committed to pride (C 25–26; B 23–24; A 23–24)
Those committed to prayers and penance (C 27–32; B 25–30; A 25–30) . . .
  e.g., anchorites and hermits (C 30–32; B 28–30; A 28–30)
Merchants (C 33–34; B 31–32; A 31–32)
Minstrels (bad: C 35–40; [good, then] bad: B 33–39; A 33–39)
Beggars (C 41–46; B 40–45; A 40–45)
Pilgrims (C 47–55; B 46–57; A 46–54)
. . . e.g., hermits on pilgrimage (C 51–55; B 53–57; A 50–54)
Friars (C 56–65; B 58–67; A 55–64)
Pardoner, who relies on help from priest and bishop (C 66–80; B 68–82;
  A 65–79)
Parsons and priests (C 81–84; B 83–86; A 80–83)
[Sergeants at law (A 84–89)]*
Bishops and bachelors (C 85–94; B 87–99; A 90–95)
    [Conscience's denunciation of shrine-keepers and other clergy: C
      95–127]
    [The power entrusted to Peter (= papacy) (C 128–29; B 100–101)]
    [Cardinal virtues / cardinals at papal court (C 130–37; B 102–11)]
    [Royal coronation / refounding the commonwealth (C 139–59; B 112–
      45)]
      [Sergeants at law (C 160–66)]*
    [Mice and rat parliament (C 167–219; B 146–210]
    [Sergeants at law (B 211–16)]*
Miscellaneous laborers (C 223–35; B 217–31; A 96–104)

The survey invites but frustrates discovery of its unifying principles, and the additions of the later revisions as well as the shifting of the sergeants at law in all three versions suggest that the poet was himself inclined to rethink the overall sequence continually. The survey offers a general impression of moving toward figures holding increasing measures of power; but the narrative's progress in that direction is uneven and unpredictable, and the rat parliament and still more the laborers at the end finally dispell that impression of any such clear order and hierarchy. The focus on characteristic action and "doing" tends to break down the sense of how the sum of social parts contributes to what Pecock calls "þe nede and profite of þe comounte." But rather than ending in anomie and professionalized relativism (as Mann has implied for Chaucer's General Prologue: Mann 1973:187–202), PP's figures are viewed not in isolation as "portraits" but typically in moments of social interaction and social endeavor, as well as in social choices. The wide swath of exploration throughout raises questions about the nature of each social role, and the relation of any one or group of some to any other or group of others.

At the next major break in the poem, the Pardon passus will similarly offer a variety of ways to reconceive society; its opening sequence of estates likewise begins with plowmen followed by kings and courtiers and then ecclesiastics, before proceeding to other kinds of professionals who, as in the Prologue, distend the Pardon passus beyond any clear hierarchy (C.9/B.7/A.8). Other brief or implied estates surveys or satires appear at 3.265–81 (B.3.209–26, A.3.196–213), 21.230–51 (B.19.229–51); see 21.230–51n. The sequence in the Prologue particularly raises questions about which larger categories subsume which particular professions or roles (e.g., are the priests and bishops as they practice their professions conceptually subordinated to the pardoner, just as they are responsible for his appearance before the people?); so too, the poem throughout displays a tendency in apocalyptic visions to prophesy or imagine the "higher" estates reduced to the level of humble laborers, further showing the impulse not to rest content with any present structure of society, or with any settled scheme for justifying it: see especially 3.437–82a (B.3.284–330, A.3.260–76) (and notes), 4.108–45 (B.4.113–48, A.4.100–131) (and notes), and 8.7–18 (B.6.9–20, A.7.9–22).

22–26 (B 20–24, A 20–24): Somme potte hem to plogh . . . in many kyne gyse: The opening opposition of kinds of action in the Prologue presents only the barest descriptive detail, but it serves at once to evoke contrasting outlooks on life and contrasting degrees of self-indulgence or common utility. The repeated verb "putten to," 'set oneself to a pursuit or craft' (see MED *putten* 22.(a)), links the first two ways of life superficially, but the zeugma renders their contrasts more evident (see Huppé 1950:177, Raabe 1990:118, Simpson 1990b:22). **potte hem to plogh** evokes the idiom "putten in ploughes," 'to begin to plow' (MED *putten* 11c); **putte hem to pruyde** also exists as an idiom, 'turn to pride' (MED *putten* 22b), but the parallel with **potte hem to plogh** allows the satiric sense 'set themselves to the vocation of pride,' even 'applied themselves to the tool, "pride."' The verb suggests an inchoative sense, as if displaying the moment of choosing or reaffirming a profession—"they *began* to put themselves"—by which the dreamer sees the moment at which each group takes up and thus creates an occupation. The present tense verbs suggest a particularly portentious historical moment, perhaps even hinting at rebeginnings after the Black Death, at which each will choose how to apply effort or indulge in sins. A more explicit view in the Prologue of the origins or the making anew of the social division of labor appears when Kind Wit and the commune contrive "alle craftes" and make for the "peple" a "plogh," in a scene that presents the foundation of the commonwealth as a whole (142–44; see 141–47n).

The two initial "classes" or "professions" here are presented throughout the poem as fundamental social and moral antitheses. The lack of detail allows a rapid grasp of broad choices. The morally abstract category of those who **putte hem to pruyde** retrospectively allows those who **potte hem to plogh** to be understood equally abstractly, as anyone who takes up earnest labor for God and the common good.

Plowmen who perform their labors diligently are assumed throughout the poem to be supremely and self-evidently moral, unlike virtually any other occupation. On actual plowmen's activities the poem elsewhere supplies some details (contrast the vague idealism of Chaucer, General Prologue, lines 529–40); lore relevant to **settynge** (i.e., putting seedlings in the ground [MED *settinge* 2a]) and **sowynge** is presented elsewhere in the poem, although often by way of allegory or analogy (see 12.179–93, 219–34 [both C only]; 21/B.19.309–16). But except for Piers' first appearance when he describes his occupation (again in allegorical terms: 7.182–94 [B.5.537–49, A.6.25–36]), plowmen themselves are rarely seen carrying out such labors, and in spite—or because of—their ethical and ideological import, they are remarkably scarce in the poem; Piers himself disappears after 9.296 (B.7.148, A.8.130), except for a brief appearance in C only at 15.137, and then in the penultimate passus. Recklessness produces the examples of "ploughmen and pastours and pore comune peple" and "Lewed lele laboreres and land tulyng peple" strictly as a contrast to the abuses and corruption of the learned clergy (11.292–93 [B.10.465–66, A.11.309–10]), an idealizing and passage that, spoken by the narrator in A and B, brings the A version to a close.

The sources for the ideal of plowmen, and for the character "Piers Plowman" (the one part of the poem that enjoyed a substantial afterlife, at least in name; see Hudson 1988b), are diverse and obscure, and should not be attributed simply to a ready-made "folk tradition" before PP, although some outlines are dimly visible. One English saint, St. Walstan of Bawburgh, who lived in the tenth century, was said to have abandoned his prospects as a member of the royal family to live as a field laborer; his distinctive image, with crown and harvest scythe, was widespread in church windows, wall-paintings, and statues in Norfolk, many now defaced or destroyed or overlaid with reconstructions, and his shrine outside of Norwich was the focus of pilgrimage through the sixteenth century, "all mowers and sythe folowers sekynge hym ones in the yeare" on his feast day, 30 May, as the seventeenth-century recusant who transcribed his life noted (30 May; see Duffy 1992:200–2005, plates 79–81; Twinch 1995, especially plates on pp. 56 and 153). Because of the suggestiveness of the images and life of this saint, his tradition may be considered a general part of the cultural background to the poem, and perhaps by some path his combination of scythe and crown suggested some of the multiplicity of the identies of Piers Plowman himself. But St. Walstan appears to have had notoriety mainly in Norfolk, and there is no evidence of direct connection between the poem and this saint. Some medieval accounts spell the name of Wulfstan, the last Anglo-Saxon bishop of Worcester, in whose see Malvern is located, as "Wulstan" or "Wlstane," leading to some confusion between them (see Twinch 1995:30–33); the north choir clearstory of Great Malvern Priory contains a full-length portrait of Wulfstan dating from the rebuilding of the Norman priory in the fifteenth century, where his name is represented as "S(an)c(tu)s wolstanus" (see Hamand 1995:27, and plate I). But there is no evidence that the fourteenth-century religious community of Malvern would have conflated Wulfstan (or even "Wolstanus") with Walstan's story and way of life. More certainly, positive homiletic uses of the metaphors of "plowing" and gardening are very widespread in intellectual culture, dating from the Bible and including a continuous tradition of commentary on such passages as John 15, "I am the true vine; and my Father is the husbandman" (see Barney 1973). But these images, so signficant in the poem, did not create what might be called a precedent for the poem's emphasis on and development of them. Perhaps many of the elements of the poem's most positive group of workers and of Piers Plowman himself should be sought less in a particular tradition preceding the poem, than in the negative images of other figures and classes of workers against which the ideal is contrasted throughout the poem.

Wastors, prevalent figures in the poem, are apparently here distinct (because of the new start, **And summe**) from those who **putte hem to pruyde**; while not again mentioned until the beginning of the second vision, 5.126 (B.5.24, A.5.24), and not described extensively until the plowing of the half-acre (C.8/B.6/A.7), **wastors** are throughout contrasted to true laborers who produce, as opposed to consume (e.g., 8.139–40: "ʒe been wastours, y woet wel, and waste and deuouren / That lele land tilynge men leely byswynken"). With a strong bias towards making over consuming or displaying, PP's sense of **wastors** is morally pejorative throughout, unlike the figure Wastoure in the debate of *Wynnere and Wastoure*, where, since Wynnere is attacked as much for miserly hoarding as Wastoure for the opposite, it is not obvious whether winning or wasting is finally superior (see Roney 1994). PP's laborers are never liable to a charge of hoarding or miserliness, only to the charge of rebellion against their task. The type can be found as early as Walter Henley's early thirteenth-century *Hosebondrie*, which opens by condemning those "who have lands and tenements and know not how to live . . . because they live without rule and forethought and spend and waste more than their lands are worth yearly, and when they have wasted their goods can only live from hand to mouth and are in want, and can make no bargain that shall be for their good" ("ke vnt teres e tenemens e i ne seuent pas viure . . . pur coe ke eus viuent santz ordinance fere e purueyance auant mayn e despendent e gastent plus ke lur teres valent par an e kant il vnt degastes lur bens adonc ne vnt fors ke de mayn en gule e viuent en angoysse ne chiuisance ne puent fere ke bon lur seyt": ed. Lamond 1890:2–4). Wasters take many forms in the poem; the indictment of the rats and mice at the end offers them as just one example (see below, 167–219n).

What is entailed by the portrait of those here who "apparel themselves after pride" or **In continance of clothyng in many kyne gyse** is similarly vague, more a moral perspective than a material description, and as such part of a large tradition of such satire in sermons (see Owst 1933:390–414). The category of "the proud" is socially broad in the poem; see the arrival of Pride at 21.335/B.19.351, "With such colours and queyntise cometh pruyde yArmed" (see 21.335–36n), evocative of the Pride of Life in I John 2:16. In late medieval homiletic writings pride is usually linked to sartorial extravagance, and often courtly affectation: as the late thirteenth-century *Somme le Roi* says (in the 1375 translation known as *The Book of Vices and Virtues*), "On signe þat men and wommen wolen plese þe world is þat þe herte nys not al to God and to grete arraie and queynte atire about þe body, for non wolde neuere seche ne desire grete araie ne queynte atire of robes or of oþer aperail but þei wenden to be loked on and seyn of folke; but who-so moste purchaseþ suche fairenesse wiþ-out-forþ, þe more he leseþ þe fairenesse wiþ-ynne, wher-wiþ þei schulde plese God" (ed. Francis 1942:253); so too Robert Mannyng, *Handlyng Synne* (begun 1303), "Ne dysgyse nat þy cloþyng / Ouer mesure for þy preysyng. / Alas, hyt shulde so betyde, / Many one are lost for here pryde" (lines 3323–26, ed. Sullens 1983). **in many kyne gyse** (B/A: **comen disgised**) most simply means "in many forms," but, especially as a sharpening of B/A's reading, probably refers particularly to the burgeoning fashions of this century of which many homilists, poets, and chroniclers took notice (e.g., Mannyng, *Handlyng Synne*; ed.

Sullens 1983, lines 3355–406, the prose *Brut* s.a. 1345; ed. Brie 1908:296–97, John of Reading's *Chronica*; ed. Tait 1914:167, Higden's *Polychronicon*; ed. Babington and Lumby 1865–86, vol. 2.76), and which were accompanied by the first sumptuary laws in England in 1363 (SR 1.381). No one fashion is described by these sources—Mannyng's "a kote perced queyntly wyþ pryde" in a story of an accursed coat (3358) is an early reference to the typical detail of "dagged" clothing—but the perception of novel fashions and hence novel social identities and loyalties is often evoked in comments on the "newe gyse" or *nova gysa*, a term apparently first used in the 1340s and proliferating thereafter (Newton 1980). As the late fourteenth-century Augustinian canon, Henry Knighton, says under the year 1388, "For the lesser people were so puffed up in those days in their dress and their belongings, and they flourished and prospered so in various ways, that one might scarcely distinguish one from another for the splendor of their dress and adornments: not a humble man from a great man, not a needy from a rich man, not a servant from his master, not a priest from another man, but each imitating the other, and striving to shine in some new fashion and to outdo his superior in the splendor of his pomp and habit" ("Nam tanta elatio in inferiori populo illis diebus in habitu et apparatu in diversis guysis pullulabat et crevit, quod vix quis de populo dinosceretur ab alio per splendorem vestitus aut apparatus. Non pauper a potente, non egens a divite, non servus a domino suo, non sacerdos ab alio de populo, sed unusquisque imitabatur alium et nitebatur inducere noviorem gysam et transcendere in elatiori apparatu et habitu suum potentiorem" (ed. and trans. Martin 1995:508–9).

27–32 (B 25–30, A 25–30): In preiers and penaunce potten hem mony . . . here lycame to plese: Those who "set themselves to" carrying out the vocation of the eremitic and anchoritic life are defined by contrast to those who abuse this vocation (see 9.196–203, C only, for a further portrait of holy hermits, and 17.7–36 [cp. B.15.269–306] for the historical decline of hermits in their ethics of gaining sustenance). For the phrasing to describe the eremetic mode of life, compare *William of Palerne*: "Sone were þe ladies to an hermitage brouȝt, / and liveden þere in god lif, wil our Lord woled, / in penaunce and in prayeres priveli and loude" (ed. Bunt 1985, lines 4801–3). In PP the positive exemplars pursue their vocation with a singleness and purity of intent and practice that the poem imitates adverbially: **Al for loue of oure lord lyueden *ful* streyte** (the last word would in Latin be *recte*, which appears shortly concerning the proper rule of kings; see below B 139–45n). Anchorites are linked to hermits again in the scene of the plowing of the half-acre, where the ideal instances of these figures are praised in the A version as they are here at line 30 (B 28, A 28), "þat holde hem in here sellis" (A.7.133); that line is slightly adjusted in B and C to "þat eten but at nones" (8.146 [B.6.145]), perhaps because the poet noticed the exact repetition, or because in the later plowing scene, where food production and famine are the central issues, it was more logical to insist on their frugality than their stability. If the traditional sequence of revision is assumed, therefore, the phrase here (as at A.7.133) is the first one that comes to the writer's mind no matter what the context, to describe the ideal of hermits and anchorites.

Anchorites are traditionally defined by their enclosure, and the formula is most obviously apt for them. But hermits were not required to be confined; instead, they were often expected to maintain roads and bridges and attend to particular shrines. John of Gaunt, for example, supported one at the shrine of Thomas, Earl of Lancaster, who was murdered during the reign of Edward II (see Walker 1990:98; Hanna 1994). Thus the formula that brings hermits together with anchorites seems to invite special scrutiny and criticism of hermits, who are much less likely to be among those **þat holdeth hem in here selles**. Both kinds of religious are plentifully documented in England up to the Dissolution (see Warren 1985; Clay 1914). Some hermits, such as the Monk of Farne Island and Richard Rolle, contributed significantly to the mystical and contemplative literature of fourteenth-century England, in English and Latin (for the Farne Monk see Pantin 1944; for the Farne Monk's Latin writings see Farmer 1961; for Rolle, see Allen 1971, Ogilvie-Thomson 1988, and Watson 1991). The Farne Monk, after probably a period at Oxford, seems to have remained in his isolation; but the more famous Rolle moved among various patrons and areas.

29: In hope to haue a good ende and heuenriche blisse / B 27 (A 27): In hope for to haue heueneriche blisse: C inserts the phrase **a good ende** into B's line, allowing alliteration of 'h' and a vowel. The general (if not universal) ideal of having **a good ende** was clearly articulated in the Middle Ages; Augustine, for example, says in a letter quoted in Wimbledon's sermon, "Wel auȝte euery man drede þe day of his deeþ; for in what state so euere a mannes laste day fyndeþ hym whan he goþ out of þis world, in þe same state he bryngeþ hym to his dom" (Epistola 199, PL 33:905; *Wimbledon's Sermon*, ed. Knight 1967:108–9). By the fourteenth and fifteenth centuries the topic of "How a man comeþ to good ende" occupied numerous treatises of instruction for all Christians in the *Ars moriendi* tradition, including a large section in the *Somme le Roi* (see the Middle English translation in *The Book of Vices and Virtues*, ed. Francis 1942:68–71), a section frequently used separately in adaptations of that work (see also the *Disce mori*; Raymo no. 11, 1986:2263–64). John Ball used the phrase in one of his letters of the Revolt of 1381, charging political change with spiritual redemption: "Nowe is tyme, Lady helpe to Ihesu þi sone, and þi sone to his fadur, to *mak a gode ende*, in þe name of þe Trinite, *of þat is begunne*" (ed. Green 1992:194; emphasis added).

The idea is the correlative of the first half of the Pardon: "*qui bona egerunt ibunt in vitam eternam*" (9.287 [B.7.113, A.8.95]); on the pervasiveness of the Pardon's terms in the poem, see Lawler 2000. But the phrase **a good ende** appears only in C, where it is inserted into five passages, often as "Grace of good ende and gret ioye aftur" or some variation. (This might be evidence that John Ball's letter of 1381 drew on C, but scholarly consensus places C in the later 1380s.) In C, Holy Church tells Will that those who follow her shall have it (2.35); Conscience tells the king that those who make proper retribution will receive it (3.340); the Pardon from Truth promises it to lawyers who help the poor (9.50); Will hopes for it when talking to the friars (10.60). So too in C only the narrator expresses his hope to Conscience and Reason that he will set his "los at a leef at the laste ende" (5.97). We might speculate that C's special emphasis on making a good death is due to the advanced age of the poet himself. But the specter of the narrator's death had since the B text been inscribed in the poem: see 20.163–65n; and see the apocryphal passus A.12 for John But's summary of the poet's death, which uses the phrase itself, possibly evidence of John But's awareness of this emphasis in the C text (on the phrase, and on But's effort to give the poet a better end than the poet himself seems to allow, see also Middleton 1988).

The phrase sounds a note of optimism or desperate hope, and it presents one of the distinct tempermental and lexical features of C (for other distinctive terms in C, see below, 87–88n, and 3.242–57n). A "good ende" would most clearly feature "the grace of repentance, mediated through the Church's sacramental system, confession and penance, anointing and viaticum" (Duffy 1992:310). The final state of mind is critical, and would outweigh the need for others to offer post-mortem obsequies, or pay to have them offered, including the sort condemned below at 81–84 (see n), as well as, ironically, those in which the narrator in C.5 seems to be involved (see especially 5.48).

31 (B 29, A 29): Coueyten . . . in contrey to cayren aboute: A typical complaint against clerics is that they travel on pleasure when they should be in their churches or religious houses. John Audelay's poems include a verse against priests who "callun hit permetacion cuntreys about to kayre" (ed. Whiting 1931, line 730); for "caired over cuntres" as a formula see *William of Palerne* (ed. Bunt 1985, line 2714), *Wars* (ed. Duggan and Turville-Petre 1989, line 1180), and *Sir Gawain and the Green Knight* (ed. Andrew and Waldron

1996, line 1670), and below at B.4.24/A.4.22: usually, the formula here is used for knights or secular heroes on their travels, perhaps emphasizing the inappropriate actions of the hermits. PP's focus on hermits' wandering and living licentiously is entirely topical; in the fourteenth and early fifteenth centuries are recorded numerous cases condemning the wanderings and teachings as well as the illicit earnings of hermits. In the early fifteenth century, for instance, William Blakeney, kettlemaker, who was "able to work for his food and raiment," was indicted because he "went about . . . barefooted and with long hair, under the guise of sanctity, and pretended to be a hermit . . . and under color of falsehood he had received many good things from divers people" (quoted in Clay 1914:89); on the valence of "barefooted" here see 20.1n, 8–12n, 12n. His transgression appears to be his preference for an itinerant and mendicant life in spite of his ability to work as a craftsman. Such cases, like the false hermits condemned in the poem, also cast light on Will's persona as a "heremite, vnholy of werkes"; see generally Middleton 1997; for the narrator as a hermit, see Hanna 1994, 1997.

32 (B 30, A 30): For no likerous liflode here lycame to plese: Very often, satire against clerics (friars or monks) in the tradition of "estates satires" stresses gluttony and the eating of dainties, but that focus appears only faintly here, in abstract terms of principle. It is developed more fully in the banquet with the Doctor of Divinity (C.15/B.13).

    liflode: The word often means 'sustenance,' 'diet,' in PP but is also often used metaphorically, spiritual sustenance, in a slightly increasing number of cases in the A-B-C succession: see, e.g., 4.115 (not in A/B); 6.68 (B.5.87; not in A); 13.114 (B.11.300); 15.248 (B.14.47); 22.239 (B.20.239). See also Spearing 1960. Thus this is the first reference to a major theme: the material necessities of the moral life. Compare Piers' description of his "huyre" from Truth (7.194 [B.5.550]), and the narrator's final question to Kynde," How shal y come to catel so to clothe me and to fede?" (22.209 [B.20.209]). The issue is highly charged within debates about "perfect poverty" and mendicancy, ecclesiastical possessions generally, and efforts to control the disruptive possibilities of higher wages for the diminished number of workers after the Black Death, all topics that seized the period (see generally Middleton 1997, Clopper 1992 and 1997).

33–34 (B 31–32, A 31–32): And summe chesen chaffare . . . suche men ythryueth: merchants, that is, those engaging in wholesale trade on a large scale, are here seen rather more than others as outsiders, whose actual prosperity can only be guessed at (**as it semeþ to oure sighte**); the passage may form a basis

for Chaucer's emphasis on the secrecy of the merchant in the General Prologue, "Ther wiste no wight that he was in dette" (280; Cooper 1987:75); so
too, Chaucer's merchant in the Shipman's Tale tells his wife, "We [chapmen]
may wel make chiere and good visage, / . . . And kepen oure estaat in
pryvetee, / Til we be deed" (VII.230–33). Merchants are emphatically "other"
to these literary points of view, as **suche** men and **oure** sighte show. The isola-
tionism of those in what is sometimes called "the merchant class" is clear in
the guild societies that had fully developed by the late fourteenth century; their
strong advantage in urban political position kept them distinct from craftsmen
and retail tradesmen. The connections, from economic to marital, between
merchants even of different companies contributed to a cohesive social identity, as did high entrance fees and long apprenticeships into their guilds (see
Kermode 1998:66–69; Thrupp 1989:53–102; Thrupp 1966:284–88). This view,
however, must contend with the view (not necessarily one excluding the previous claim) that they lacked any distinctive social identity in this period (see
Patterson 1991:322–66; Smith 2004; see also Thrupp 1989:288–319). For the a-
verse alliterative formula, compare *William of Palerne*, "semes in mi siȝt . . ."
(ed. Bunt 1985, line 444, also 446, 2880).

   semeþ suggests some complexity, ethical or economic, beneath the surface of the merchants' prosperity. Soon the ethics of using and gaining money
will be opened to intense scrutiny and debate (see especially notes to 3.221 ff.),
and the uncertainty of what is beneath what **semeþ to oure sighte** hints at the
long tradition of medieval debate about the "hidden" morality of trade and
monetary profit. To didactic writers and preachers, merchants' moral status
was, by the fourteenth century, no less secure than any other estate's, although
in earlier centuries they possessed less certain legitimacy in those perspectives
(see Le Goff 1980:29–42, 58–70). Aquinas offers a diffident view of trade as a
way of life: "trading in itself is regarded as somewhat dishonorable, since it
does not logically involve an honorable or necessary end. Gain, however,
which is the end of trading, though it does not logically involve anything honorable or necessary, does not logically involve anything sinful or contrary to
virtue; hence there is no reason why gain may not be directed to some necessary or even honorable end" (*Summa Theologica* IIa IIae, ques. 77, art. 4; trans.
Monroe 1948:63). Elsewhere in the poem, gauging merchants' rectitude
involves investigating closely just how they gain and spend, and with what
motives. In the Pardon scene below, they do not have complete pardon *a pena
et a culpa* because of their "couetyse of wynnynge," but Truth nonetheless
sends them a special letter close "vnder his secrete seal"—again, with emphasis
on their professional privacy—allowing them to make profits off their resales
so long as they put such "wynnynge" to charitable uses (9.27–42 [B.7.18–39,

A.8.20–44]). The point of the proper use of profit from trade is traditional. "Thriving" in mercantile (or other) activity was never in itself sinful in the general tradition of Christian doctrine; 1 Cor. 9:7 was a proof-text for a reasonable and self-sustaining level of profit in all labors: "Who serves as a soldier, at any time, at his own charges? Who plants a vineyard and eats not of the fruit thereof? Who feeds the flock and eats not of the milk of the flock?" Thus Aquinas, in his *questio* "Whether a man may lawfully sell a thing for more than it is worth," elaborates the rationale for a merchant making some profit; in his view, "a man may," provided that there is no fraud, since the rule of doing unto others as you would have them do unto you (as in Matthew 7:12) applies to commerce (*Summa Theologica* IIa IIae, ques. 77, art. 1; trans. Monroe 1948:53). The "just price" should be determined by the value of "the thing sold" as well as "the loss incurred by the seller in parting with it"; yet Aquinas says that one who lives by trading may legitimately acquire "moderate gain" from trading provided that is used "for the support of his household, or even to help the needy; or even when a man devotes himself to trade for the public welfare" (art. 4, resp; trans. Monroe 1948:63).

Most of these Thomistic views appear directly in the early fifteenth-century English dialogue *Dives and Pauper*, itself cast in the Thomistic structure of dialectic. In one exchange, Dives reopens Aquinas' *questio*: "May a man sellyn a þing derere þan he boute it to?" Pauper replies (in similarly Thomistic terms): "Ellys myȝte no man lyuyn be hys merchaundye ne be his craft. He must takyn up his costis & susteynyn hym & hese & worchepyn God & holy chirche & helpyn þe pore, and for þis ende it is leful & nedful to þe chapman and to þe warcman to sellyn þing derere þan he bouȝte it to" (ed. Barnum 1980:155). The discussion in *Dives and Pauper*, while it affirms the legitimacy of "chapmen," shows that the question or doubt implied in PP's cautious phrase remained alive through the later Middle Ages.

Whereas "thriving" may be virtuous (or not), profiting from loaned money—usury—was categorically sinful throughout the Middle Ages, according to canon law (see Noonan 1957:180–90; Langholm 1992), although it was evidently common in London's mercantile world (see 3.108–14n). In PP, usury is linked to avarice (2.94 [B.2.87, A.2.63]) and to "winning" "with wrong" rather than "with riht," although that distinction becomes impossible to determine under the regime of Antichrist and Pride (see 21.350 [B.19.350]). The distinction is, in fact, already hard to make here in the Prologue: placed between holy anchorites and minstrels both holy and unholy, the merchants can only be said to "seem" to be thriving, and how moral or immoral their gains are is impossible for the narrator or the reader to assess.

B 33–37 (A 33–37): And summe murþes to make . . . to werken if hem liste: "Minstrel" can cover all manner of entertainers, from actors to jugglers, drummers, acrobats, harpers, trumpers, etc. (see Woolgar 1999:28–29); it can refer more broadly to any servant, retainer, or administrator, and thus is used in PP for Activa Vita/Hawkin, 15.190–217 (B.13.221–240). "Jangling" is associated throughout the poem with indiscreet and sinful speech and thought, a common association: the English exposition of *Qui Habitat* attributed to Walter Hilton urges the "louere of god" to be in peace in his tabernacle, the shadow of God, "whiles oþur men rennen out and fihten and striuen, sweren and be-gylen, Iapen and Ianglen, pleyen & syngen" (ed. Wallner 1954:39, quoted in L. Clifton 1993:33, along with other examples in contemplative writings of "jangling" as "vanity and foul speech"). Sweeping criticisms against both minstrels and "janglers" are more common than PP's distinction; in the Wycliffite *Lanterne of Liȝt*, giving alms "to mynstrals to iogullers & oþir veyn iapars" is a sign of being an almsgiver in "þe fendis chirche" (ed. Swinburn 1917 for 1915:54). One late medieval didactic tract, *The Fyve Wyttes*, similarly warns in sweeping terms against all poetic and narrative entertainments, though the writer suggests that listeners can find a way to ponder any manner of "merþes þat ben honeste" in spiritually profitable ways:

in as muche as þou myȝt þou schalt fle al manere of vayn merþes of tales and gestes and songes, bot yf it be of eny such matere þat may stire þy soule to sobournesse and loue of þy Lord God. Mynystralcye also, yf it drawe þyn herte into itself for to delyte þerynne, it is nouȝt profitable for þe to hure muche. Neþeles, yf þou conne reduce alle suche manere merþes þat ben honeste þy soule to mynde to a maner lyknesse of þe blysse of heuene, it may somtyme be hurde profitable for a recreacioun in refreschynge of þe spirites, bot nouȝt muche be occupied þerynne. (ed. Bremmer 1987:20)

PP's considerations of the kinds of poetry are more subtle than such views of prosaic religious expositors, heretic or orthodox. Like *Wynnere and Wastoure*, which opens with a wistful praise of a lost time when "lordes in londe . . . loued in thaire hertis / To here makers of myrthes þat matirs couthe fynde" (ed. Trigg 1990, lines 19–20), that is, knew how to write original materials, and a condemnation of upstart poets "Þat neuer wroghte thurgh witt thies [*read* thre] wordes togedire" (25), PP distinguishes not only legitimate from illegitimate poetry but also legitimate from illegitimate poets. But the terms of such "professions" are elusive. The A/B distinction between legitimate minstrels and illegitimate **Iangeleres** may be between entertainers attached to a great household and itinerant entertainers (so Bnt); but even minstrels attached to great households, at least before the later fourteenth century, had looser ties to households than other servants. From the later fourteenth century on they sometimes wore lords' livery, but they were often required to be in residence only at the main feasts. Their payments could be generous but seem more sporadic than those to other servants, and they seem not to have received many of the benefits other servants did (see Woolgar 1999:26–29, 94–95).

More likely than a distinction of steady or occasional employment, the A/B distinction between **giltlees** minstrels and **Iaperes and Iangeleres, Iudas children** (A/B 33, 35) traces the elusive line between those whose "proper" work is poetic entertainment (i.e., professional minstrels in any capacity, so defined because they **geten gold with hire glee**), and those whose "proper" work is something much more spiritual (their paying "work" is something else). Only the latter are criticized as having **wit at will to werken if hem liste** (A/B 37), implying that for them, poetic entertainment constitutes an abandonment of their proper vocation, like many of the other figures satirized in the Prologue. In this general sense, PP follows Boniface VIII in the Sext, c. 1300, where are set the terms of canon law against clerics who for lesser or greater lengths of time abandon their proper calling and take up artistic entertainments: "clerici, qui, clericalis ordinis dignitate non modicum detrahentes, se ioculatores seu goliardos faciunt aut bufones, si per annum artem illam ignominiosam exercuerint, ipso iure, si autem tempore breviori, et tertio miniti non resipuerint, careant omni privilegio clericali" (Sext 3.1.1, ed. Friedberg 1959, vol. 2.1019): "let clerics by law lose all clerical privileges who, detracting not a little from the dignity of the clerical order, make themselves jokesters and goliards and buffoons, if throughout the year they ply that wretched art, or do so for a shorter time but do not desist after three warnings." For the form of the alliterative line here, compare *William of Palerne* (ed. Bunt 1985), line 2746, "and hadde wind at wille to wende whan hem liked."

Minstrels are not commonly depicted in estates satires, but their role and ways of life achieved some measure of a literary tradition. Many of the stereotypical vices of minstrels, as well as an instance of the wisdom they can speak in their "folie," are collected in the description by an idiot-savant jongleur to a king of his way of life, in a fabliau titled "Le Roi d'Angleterre et le Jongleur d'Ely," the sole copy of which is found among the works in English, French and Latin collected in MS. Harley 2253 (fols. 107ᵛ-9ᵛ; ed. Montaiglon and Raynaud 1877, vol. 2.242–56):

Nous sumes compaignons plusours,
E de tiele manere sumes nous
Que nus mangerons plus volenters
Là où nous sumez priez,

E plus volenters e plus tost,
Qe là où nous payons nostre escot;
E bevoms plus volenters en seaunt
Qe nus ne fesons en esteaunt,
E, après manger que devant,
Pleyn hanap gros e grant;
E, si vodroms assez aver,
Mès nus ne avoms cure de travyler,
E purroms molt bien deporter
D'aler matyn à mostier;
E ce est le nostre us
De gysyr longement en nos lys
E à nonne sus lever
E puis aler à manger;
Si n'avoms cure de pleder,
Car il n'apent à nostre mester;
E nus vodroms estre tot dis,
Si nus pussoms, en gyws e rys;
E si vodroms aprompter e prendre,
E à nostre poer malement rendre;
Nus n'avoms cure de aver,
For que nus eyoms assez à manger;
Plus despondroms à ung digner
Qu'en un mois pourroms gayner;
E uncore volum plus,
Quar orgoil est nostre us,
E à bele dames acoynter,
Ce apent à noster mester.
Or savez une partie
Coment amenons nostre vie;
Plus ne puis par vileynye
Counter de nostre rybaudie. (ed. Montaiglon and Raynaud 1877, lines 165–200)

[We are a large company, and we live in such a manner that we eat more willingly where we are well supplied, both more readily and quickly than where we have to pay our pay; and we drink more willingly sitting than standing, and after eating rather than before, a full goblet huge and tall. And if we want to have wealth, we never have any wish to work, and we can very well do without going to church in the morning. And it is our custom to lie for a long time in bed, and to rise at noon, and then go to eat. We have no concern with legal debate, since that does not pertain to our craft, but rather we wish to spend all day if we can in games and laughter. We like to borrow and take, and make bad amends by our effort. We have no interest in wealth, except insofar as we have enough to eat; we spend more at a single meal than we can gain in an entire month. And we want still more, since pride is part of our custom; and to flirt with pretty ladies, that belongs to our craft. Now you know part of how we lead our life; because of its villainousness, I can tell no more about our ribaldry.]

For this work, see also below, 148n.

Although condemning minstrels here on similar if far terser grounds, PP appears below to approve clerical or quasi-clerical minstrels who tell edifying or scriptural tales. Thus Dame Study condemns "Harlotes" and "Iangleris of gestes" in contrast to one who speaks with "holy writ ay in his mouþe" (B.10.31–32; C lacks the line with "Iangleris of gestes": C.11.26–29; cp. A.11.35–38); given her own eloquence in describing him, the one with holy writ in his mouth seems to be as much a poet as a preacher or chaplain. Below, the B narrator near the encounter with Hawkin praises "kynges minstrels" as fit for clerics and knights—like the guiltless minstrels who receive gold—but adds that "Muche moore . . . riche men sholde / Haue beggeres bifore hem þe whiche ben goddes minstreles" (B.13.436–39, transposed in C to a commentary in Sloth's confession, 7.96–99). "Kynges minstrels" have a clear professional status, but "goddes minstreles," while unimpeachably legitimate, do not. Among a long list of minstrels recorded in York civic records as present at Corpus Christi celebrations in 1447 (where the lost "Crede Play" was performed) are many references to minstrels attached to various lords' households, as well as "one blind minstrel called God's minstrel": "j Ministrallo seco vocato ministrallo dei" (Johnston and Rogerson 1979, vol. 1.70); it is not stated how he earned this nickname. Such distinctions of minstrels' professional status add to the problem of clerical identity in the poem. It is never fully clear, for instance, if Will is a cleric, just as Hawkin's mode of being a minstrel is part of a confusion of professional elements in his identity. See also 35–38n; and compare also the tradition of Franciscan friars as "joculatores Dei" ("jongleurs of God"; see Fleming 1977:177–89).

B 35 (A 35): Iudas children: A common insult in polemical language of the late fourteenth and early fifteenth century; see also "Upland's Rejoinder," line 348 (ed. Heyworth 1968).

35–38: And summe murthes . . . yf þei wolde: C, avoiding ambiguities and elusive distinctions, folds the first line of the A/B passage dividing good and bad minstrels directly into the description of bad minstrels, producing a single massed group that is roundly condemned: "some [chose] to make entertainments as minstrels know how, [and] want neither to work nor sweat but to swear great oaths." This much parallels other critical views, and indeed by merging minstrels with slothful beggars more closely echoes the description of a minstrel's life in "Le Roi d'Angleterre et le Jongleur d'Ely" (see B 33–37n above). But C retains A/B's elaborate distinctions between legitimate and illegitimate minstrels in a later extrapolation on the "braunches þat bryngeth men to sleuthe," shifted from the encounter with Hawkin to Sloth's confession (7.69–118a [B.13.421–56]). As Prsl remarks (ad loc.), "the hostility to 'minstrels' is throughout C more clear-cut than in A/B, perhaps because C has clarified the problem by recognizing a new class of 'God's minstrels.'" Although this last "class" has been present since B.13.421–56 as noted above (a section found only in the two manuscripts R and F, thus representing either the alpha stem of the B archetype, or perhaps representing a transitional point of the poet's revision between B and C: see Hanna 1996:215–29), they are somewhat more fully limned in C, especially as beggars who are "not solicitous" for their life (Matt. 6:25; see 9.133–39, C only; see also 4.191–94n; Donaldson 1966:136–37, and Clopper 1997:143, 200–214, who finds these figures crucial examples of the apostolic life that the dreamer himself partly and unsteadily resembles).

Perhaps because no standard professional grounds define such pious story-tellers, or perhaps because the spiritual implications of their ways of life are elaborated so fully in C's pardon passus, C.9, and in the figure of C's Reckless-ness, C.12–13, they find no place in C's Prologue. For a more typical moralist's complaint that listeners forever flock more eagerly to things less edifying than to what he has to present, see *Pricke of Conscience*, lines 183–96 (ed. Morris 1863); see also following note.

37 (B 36, A 36): fantasies/ foule fantasyes: The term "fantasyes" is particularly common in fourteenth-century vernacular guides to pious meditation, refer-ring to the general sins of thought that such guidebooks typically offer advice for overcoming. The word is consistently pejorative in those contexts. Walter Hilton's *Scale of Perfection* (c. 1380) recommends that beginners in the path to meditation say out loud prayers such as the Pater Noster as a crutch or baby's milk, to avoid "errours ne fantasies bi his veyn meditacioun," while still learn-ing how to achieve more mature (and silent) meditations (1.27, ed. Bestul 2000). The "Remedies Against Temptations" of c. 1359 by William Flete, Cath-erine of Siena's English confessor, focuses throughout on the theme of over-coming "trauelous [burdensome] fantasyes" (sometimes called "wykkyd vilenous þoughtes"), but also atypically asserts that "fantasyes" do not neces-sarily constitute "gret synne," so long as one has a generally good will toward God: "For þer schulde non demen yuel of man ne woman for a thinge þat is oncerteyn or in weere or doute; and right so it is yuel and not skylfully don ony resonable creature to deme his owne soule in swich plyght, þat it were parted fro god for on wersum [wearisome] fantasie or douteful [fearful]" (chap. 22, ed. Colledge and Chadwick 1968:223).

Yet the focus here in PP is not on private temptations but on the sinful thoughts that these minstrels "invent" ("fyndeth out" 37), and dredge from their minds to offer to others. Although **fantasyes** as a term for immoral literary products is apparently unparalled, characterizations of the worst sins of storytellers or poets include prurient stories or fabliaux, the "tales / Of putrie and of paramours" that Lechery, as soon as physical ability to sin has waned, listens to (6.185–86; also 193–94: C only). Other evil words include scurrilous indictments of others, such as the "tales" that Wrath circulates and instigates (6.154 [B.5.172]), or the self-serving "Bostyng and braggynge with many bolde othes" that, in C only, Pride (developing a passage in B's Hawkin) relates to promote his own lineage and wealth (6.34 [cp. B.13.280]), and more generally dubious reports that beggars or boasters tell "in tauernes and in stretes" (6.49–58 [cp. B.13.302–10]; see generally Craun 1997).

The vague indictment here would apply either to "nonprofessional" story-tellers, to which the line refers in A/B (see B 33–37n above), or "professional" story tellers, to which the line refers in C (see 35–38n above). For the latter, compare the deft implications Chaucer's Pardoner is able to lace into his sermons defaming those he is afraid to attack openly (Pardoner's Tale, lines 412–22), or the insulting "fables" by minstrels that Nicholas Bozon, in his early fourteenth-century *Char d'Orgueil*, mentions: the nostrils of the horse "deleauté" (disloyalty) pulling the cart of Pride are minstrels, who "now know how to say well of you, but now put forth nothing but fable" ("Ore set bien dire de wus ore le tient tut fable"), depending on whether you have given them enough (181–84, ed. Vising 1919). The more common term, in fact, in French and Middle English for a disreputable literary work is "fable."

39 (cp. B 38, A 38): That Poul precheþ of hem preue hit y myhte: The reference to Paul's words has been identified on the basis of the preceding lines about having "wytt at wille to worche yf þei wolde" as 2 Thessalonians 3:10, "If someone does not wish to work, let him not eat" (Skt), or, on the basis of the following line, "*Qui turpiloquium loquitur* is luciferes knaue," as Ephesians 5:4, "But let not fornication or any uncleanness, or avarice be attributed to you . . . or impure talk, or foolishness, or scurrility [aut turpitudo, aut stultiloquium, aut scurrilitas]" (Bnt), or Colossians 3:8, "But now let you put away . . . foul speech from your mouth [turpem sermonem de ore vestro]" (Alford, *Quot.*). For the last, the Old Latin text reads "turpiloquium" for "turpem sermonem" (Alford, *Quot.*). Peter the Chanter's collection of ethical and social topics, the *Verbum Abbreviatum*, opens a long passage against minstrels and entertainers by citing 1 Thessalonians 5:14, "rebuke the unquiet" (PL 205:153). The reference to what **Poul precheþ** might be all of these possibilities, although the Latin following suggests the likelier indication. See next note.

40 (B 39, A 39): *Qui turpiloquium loquitur* is luciferes knaue [B, A: luciferes hyne]: "Who speaks filthy talk . . ."; for the possible sources in Ephesians 5:4 or Colossians 3:8, see preceding note. The scenic potential of this line is realized in 7.114–18a (B.13.455–56), where is mentioned the gathering of those who enjoy such minstrels at "luciferes feste, / With *turpiloquio*, a lay of sorwe and luciferes fythele," expanding the statement into a description of a satanic banquet. The association of Lucifer and sinful and seductive minstrelsy, however narrowly or broadly such minstrelsy is understood, is old in homiletic literature. In the tenth-century collection of Old English homilies in what is known as the Vercelli Book, homily 10 includes Lucifer's assertion to Jesus of his ability to sway morally weak people away from the pious reading that they were engaged in on Jesus' behalf, by drawing them with his own "harp":

Þonne hie gehyrdon þine bec rædan & þin godspel secgan & hira lif rihtan & him ecne weg cyðan, hy symle hiera earan dytton & hit gehyran noldon. Ac ðonne ic mine hearpan genam & mine strengas styrian ongan, hie ðæt lustlice gehyrdon, & fram þe cyrdon & to me urnon. & ic hie mine leahtras lærde, & hie me hyrdon georne. & ic hie to þeofðum tyhte & to geflite scyrpte & to inwitfullum geðancum, þæt ic wolde þæt hy þe afremdedon. Ac, hwæt, woldon hie in minon hordcofan, & þin cynerice eal forgeaton. Æt me hie leornodon scondword & lease brægdas, & þine soðfæstan lare hie forgeaton & þinne dom ne gemundon; ac minre neaweste a wilnodon & þine forgogodon. (ed. Scragg 1992:200–201)

[When they were listening to your books being read and your gospel being spoken and their lives being set straight and their eternal path being made known to them, they at once fastened up their ears and did not want to hear it. But when I took down my harp and began to strum my strings, they lustily listened to that and they turned away from you and ran to me. And I taught them my lessons and they eagerly obeyed them. And I seduced them to theft and incited them to strife and to evil thoughts, because I wanted them to be alienated from you. And lo, they wanted to be in my private chamber and to relinquish your kingdom entirely. From me they learned blasphemy and false oaths, and your eternally truthful lore they relinquished and your judgment they forgot; and they were ever seeking my companionship and spurning yours.]

The early thirteenth-century allegorical journey to Hell by Raoul de Houdenc, the *Songe d'Enfer*, concludes with the king of Hell's request that Raoul read aloud from a book presenting the "laws of kings," and he reads an entire quire devoted to "Les vies des fols menestrels" ("the lives of wicked minstrels"), which include all the sins (ed. Mihm 1984, lines 623–58).

    As these precedents suggest, the foul speech and "songs" of Lucifer's fiddle have far-reaching consequences beyond momentary bawdy entertainment. So too the Wycliffite *Lanterne of Liȝt* (c. 1400, ed. Swinburn 1917 for 1915) declares that Lucifer "regneþ in his malice ouer þe children of pride" (60/3), part of the "devil's church" in which are also included those "preiars in þe fendis chirche" whose minds are "cumbrid wiþ vnclene þouȝtis & wiþ veyn fantasies & þi tounge in minstralsie or on lewid iangling" (50/29, 51/1–2), as well as "syngars in þe fendis chirche" who "breken curiouse nootis . . . to plese þe peple wiþ likerouse voice & fylle her eeris wiþ veyn dyn" (58/13–15).

Further lore connecting Lucifer directly with minstrels may also be pertinent. Lucifer is a common alternate name for Venus, as the morning star, who in twelfth-century Latin translations of the Arabic texts relevant to the tradition of the "children of the planets" governs the qualities of "amor, irrisio, gaudium, solatium" ("love, laughter, joy, pleasure") and is called the "parent" of all lovers, actors, and dancers (see Avenare 1521:xx-xxi; and Albumazar [trans. in the twelfth century by Adelard of Bath] 1506:fol. d2a, d3a; Klibansky et al. 1979:205). The late thirteenth century encyclopedist, Bartholomeus Anglicus, summarizes this background (in the translation of John Trevisa c. 1395):

> Uenus, þat hatte Lucyfer also . . . is an goodliche planete, female, and a nyȝt planete . . . In mannes body he disposiþ to fairnesse, volupte, and lykynge in touche and groping, in smyl, in taast and in songe; and þerfore he makeþ singers, louyers of musik, and makers of confexiouns of spicerie and spicers. [gen. ed. Seymour 1974–1988, vol. 1.481–82.]

The figure Hawkin would be under the planet Lucifer, as at once a "mynstral" and a maker of confections (see 15.190–209 [cp. B.13.221–40]).

41–46 (A, B 40–45): Bidders and beggers . . . sueth hem euer: The urban beggars seen here vigorously swarming elicit the poem's harshest vocabulary for wasters and vagabonds, from "faytors," to "gluttons," down to a quasi-allegorical representation of their being followed by **Slep and slewth** (on the partial personification, see Griffiths 1985:10). The issue of urban labor, and urban unemployment, is broached directly with these figures who present analogues for the narrator, whose identity hovers in a range from "minstrel" to "beggar," especially in C with the addition of C.5.1–104 where he is criticized for pursuing a life "in Citees to begge" (C.5.90). From that retrospect in C, the point of view of the narrator of the Prologue, so deeply informed in all the practices he surveys, is potentially redefined as that of a participant in this urban scene; perhaps the more omniscient and "authoritative" posture of C's opening lines compensates for that potential relativism (see above 1–13 and nn). **Bidders** may refer to mendicant friars, or perhaps to a specific kind of illegitimate beggar; it does not necessarily denote an official status (see Scase 1989:68–69, and further below at 22.48n).

Fayteden: Derived from "faitour," 'deceiver'; a verb that L uses far more frequently than his poetic contemporaries though the term is common in anti-mendicant writings (see Scase 1989:69–71; see MED *faiten* 1). The word implies a calculated display of one's injuries to elicit alms illegitimately (see 8.128–29 [B.6.121–22, A.7.113–14]: "faytours . . . / leyde here legges alery as suche lorelles conneth"). As *The Book of Vices and Virtues* says, "faytours" "schewen al here pouerte and alle here maymes and hirtes, and euere-more þei leggen þe worst forþ to schewe, and al for þei wolde þat þe folke hadde rewþe of hem and ȝeue hem almesse" (ed. Francis 1942:176). The word is applied to the dreamer himself on two occasions: 5.30 (C only) and 22/B.19.5 (see notes on these lines, also Kerby-Fulton 1990:123, 146–47), again suggesting a retrospective complicity between his own mode of living and these beggars'. The notion is broadly paralleled in the acts against *faiterie* in the 1376 Good Parliament (see 22.5n), and also the 1388 reissue of the Statute of Laborers, all moments along what Middleton has defined as a "complex ideological invention, the pejorative figure of the alms-seeking able-bodied vagrant," whose particular pejorative names and images include "stafstrikers," "faitours," and later "lolleres" (Middleton 1997:229). See also 2.132–39n, 22.1–51n.

here bagge: In C especially, a bag indicates beggars who take thought for the morrow (cp. Matt. 6:25–34), accumulating their gain beyond immediate need (as is emphasized in their also having a **bely** that is **bretful ycrammed**); hence they violate "goddes lawe" (9.158), the ideal in Jesus' commissioning of the disciples in Luke 9:3 (where "bag" is *pera* in the Vulgate): "And he said to them 'Take nothing for your journey, neither staff, nor scrip [*peram*], nor bread, nor money; neither have two coats" (behind which too is Exodus 16:19–20). Thus too, "beggares with bagges þe whiche brewhouses ben here churches" are condemned in the C revision of the pardon passus (9.98), while in contrast those beggars who go "Withoute bagge and bred" are "Godes munstrals and his mesagers and his mury bordiours," "For they bereth none bagges ne boteles vnder clokes," like the apostles (9.120, 136, 139; see also the narrator's claim at 5.51–52).

To Franciscans, the fact that Judas took a *loculus* when Jesus sent him forth to collect food (John 13:29) was a symbol of material possessions with which Judas' own hypocrisy was associated; William of St. Amour in his *De periculis novissimorum temporum* (1255) opposed the friars' position that the original apostles had been mendicants by arguing that John 13:29 indicated that the apostles typically carried a bag for their common possession, and that they were not in fact beggars (see Szittya 1986:49–50). The Lucan ideal is emphasized in the "Earlier Rule" of St. Francis, "When the brothers go through the world, let them take nothing for the journey, neither knapsack, nor purse, nor bread, nor money, nor walking stick" ("Earlier Rule," trans.

Armstrong et al. 1999:73]), and in Thomas of Celano's *First Life of St. Francis* (1.9, trans. Armstrong et al. 1999:201).

Sermons on the topic of pilgrimage and pilgrims sometimes stressed that the scrip should at least be small and modestly filled (see Birch 1999:86), but PP does not represent this moderate position. Curiously, the same theme of faith in divine support for righteous vagrants appears in *William of Palerne*, when William's lover answers his fear that "we schul deie for hunger" by declaring that "We schul live bi oure love, lelli, atte best, / and þurȝth þe grace of God gete us sumwat elles" (ed. Bunt 1985, lines 1805–13). The theme is of course a common one in medieval Christian culture. In contrast to the apostolic ideal mentioned at 9.120 and implied here, the urban poor depicted here frequent ale houses, engage in fights, and depend on deception for their alms. For another literary scene of fighting among "riotours," in a deadly struggle feigned as "pleye," see Chaucer, Pardoner's Tale, lines 826–32; earlier, the urban poor are shown fighting over being chosen for jobs in the later thirteenth-century poem *Havelok* (ed. Smithers 1987, lines 858–909).

45 (B, A 44) robardus knaues: Clearly some sort of disreputable figures, probably thieves, as also suggested by the effort at penance by "Robert the ruyflare" at 6.315 and 6.321 ("Roberd þe Robbere" at the parallel passages B.5.461 [A.5.233] and B.5.467 [A.5.241]), including the remark that Robbert the Rifler "hadde layȝe by *latro*, luciferes aunte," that is, had intercourse with "theft" (6.329 [B.5.476, A.5.250]). In the early twentieth century, the location of Robert the Robber under "sloth" in A/B (B.5.461–76, A.5.233–50), shifted in C to "covetousness" (6.315–29), was the basis for much discussion about whether one or several authors wrote the poem's various versions (see Manly 1906; 1908; Jusserand 1909:16–25; Manly 1909–10:21–34; Jusserand 1910:306–7; Chambers 1910:3–6); the debate, which questioned the fitness of A/B's location of a thief under sloth, and thus the question of single authorship, led usefully to consideration of evidence pointing to the broader sense of dishonesty, including sloth, in Robert's nickname. At B.6.148 Piers declares that "Robert Renaboute shal riȝt noȝt haue of myne," in the context of condemning illegitimate religious beggars who take alms falsely. As often in PP, stock names are stirred into life, even when glimpsed elusively and in passing; a parallel stirring into life of stock names occurs with "Purnelle" (see 4.110n), and "Kit" and "Calote" (see C.5.2n; C.20.467–75n).

The name "Robert the Robber" denotes a characteristic identity or an everyday alliterative taunt, and both appear in the historical record: as early as a Latin gloss dated to the twelfth century, a scribe says of his brother Robert, "dicebatur Robertus quia a re nomen habuit, spoliator enim diu fuit et praedo" ("he is called Robert because he takes his name from his substance, for he has long been a pillager and thief": ed. Wright 1839, line 354; see Mustanoja 1970:61–63); a "Robertus Robbeioye" is listed in the Subsidy Roll of 1332 (MED *robben* v., 5.), and a statute also from 1332 notes "Diverses roberies, homicides, & felonies ont este faitz . . . par gentz qi sont appellez Roberdesmen, Wastours, & Draghlacche" ("divers manslaughters, felonies, and robberies, done by people that be called 'Roberdesmen,' 'wasters,' and 'drawlacches'") (5 Edward III c. 14, SR 1.268; first noted Skt; see also Chambers 1910:3–4, who, intent on arguing the fitness of A's inclusion of the line after Sloth in A/B, takes the nicknames as varying synonyms, any one of which would thus refer to those engaged in "vagabondage, leading to ribaldry, gluttony, and theft"; see also Roberts 2000). Possibly the term is linked to *ribald*, "scoundrel," "low entertainer," attested from the early fourteenth century in English, and earlier in Old French (*ribaud*) and Latin (*ribaldus*), whose origins are obscure. Manuscript variants for **robardus** include "Robberes" (C and B) and "rybaudys" (C and A), both clearly showing the direction of textual variation, but also indicating the loose range of malfeasance that **ryseþ with rybaudrye** could suggest, and the association with low social status. The social valence of the word here is far humbler than the cognate "robeur" used in Old French, as when fifteen "robeurs" who are also called "chevalers" seriously wound a sleeping knight and steal his horse, in the mid-thirteenth-century Anglo-Norman romance, *Gui de Warewic*; ed. Ewert 1932, lines 4717–58; when Gui tracks them and kills all fifteen it is an honorable slaughter.

So too elsewhere the category of "thief" in **robardus knaues** and "Roberdesmen" can include a range of illicit activity, again implicitly at a low social level: *Pierce the Ploughman's Crede* has the Franciscan declare that Carmelites "ryght as Robertes men raken aboute, / At feires and at ful ales and fyllen the cuppe, / And precheth all of pardon to plesen the puple" (ed. Barr 1993, lines 72–74). In two of the gnomic English Rebel Letters of 1381 is also mention of "Hobbe Robbyoure" who is to be "wele chastysed for lesyng of ȝoure grace, for ȝe haue gret nede to take God wiþ ȝowe in alle ȝoure dedes": here as at B.6.148 the name indicates loss "not only of material goods but of 'grace'" (Justice 1994:94), possibly as an admonition for the Rebels not to tolerate looters among them (see Green 1992:183–84), and probably showing direct or indirect contact with PP (Mustanoja 1970:57; the letters are in Green 1992:193–95, as Knighton [2] and Walsingham; see also Hudson 1988a:251–52). The connection is likely both because of the citation of "Peres Plouȝman" in the Rebel letters near that of "Hobbe Robbyoure," and because PP uses and develops the epithet for Robert more than any other Middle English literary work.

47–50 (B 46–49, A 46–49): Pilgrymes and palmers . . . al here lyf after: From here to line 135—that is, the balance of the estates survey and Conscience's sermon against false priests—the survey considers the sins of those in religious professions, official and unofficial. First treated are pilgrims and **palmers,** that is, those who wear the badge of a palm leaf or palm fronds as a sign of having travelled to the Holy Land, a word often used for those who devote their lives to pilgrimages, often as paid substitutes for deceased persons or those otherwise unable to do so, as distinct from those making a single pilgrimage for a specific purpose (Bnt; Rickert 1948:267–68; Sumption 1975:298–99; Webb 2000:201). As well as receiving an indulgence, before departing from a shrine a pilgrim would usually acquire a lead or pewter badge with an open-work design set off by a small background of colored paper or parchment, including pins to fix it to the traditional pilgrim's hat; more expensive badges in copper, bronze, or even gold were available (Nilson 1999:115; Koldeweij 1999). The necessary outfit is summarized in the *Alliterative Morte Arthure* (ed. Benson 1994), lines 3468–76, and below 7.162–69 (B.5.517–24, A.6.5–12).

As with the other portraits, the pilgrims' "profession" is portrayed by means of a significant moment of choosing or commencing it, here the vow by which a group **plighten hem togyderes / To seke seynt Iame and seyntes at Rome**, that is, to seek the two most popular continental goals of pilgrimage, St. James of Compostella and the Roman shrines. Numerous instances of sworn communities of pilgrims from the fourteenth century are known, before Chaucer made the gesture into a pact for storytelling while on pilgrimage. The notion here is also part of the homiletic repertoire: John Mirk's *Festial* (c. 1390) includes a story about "thrytty men" who "plyȝten troþis forto goo to Saynt Iamys and to abyde togedyr yn helth and yn sekenes" (ed. Erbe 1905:212–13). The sworn company is punished when they leave one of their members behind in spite of their vow. Lollards sometimes also picked out the social element of pilgrimages for special criticism: the Lollard William Thorpe, for instance, in the early fifteenth century attacked the existence of fellowships of pilgrims as a departure from communion with the fellowship of God and the saints: "manye men and wymmen now gon hidir and þidir on pilgrymage . . . more for to haue here worldli or fleischli frendschip þan to haue frendschip of God or of hise seintis in heuene" (ed. Hudson 1993:63).

leue to lye al here lyf after: Telling tall tales was commonly associated with pilgrims from at least the fourteenth century on (see Chaucer, General Prologue, lines 771–74; *House of Fame*, lines 2122–23; John Heywood's sixteenth-century play, *The Four Ps*, presents a pilgrim as a contestant in a lying contest; B. Brown 1937 presents an exemplum from Caesarius of Heister-bach in the thirteenth century describing a layman asked to tell a story to clerics travelling with him: he tells one wittily disparaging the gluttony of the cardinal who has asked him for a story). The claim that pilgrims milk minor pilgrimage experiences for talltales is paralleled (again) by William Thorpe: "And if þese men and wymmen ben a moneþe oute in her pilgrymage, manye of hem an half ȝeere aftir schulen be greete iangelers, tale tellers and lyeris" (ed. Hudson 1993:64). **leue** ironically echoes the indulgences customarily granted by ecclesiastical authority for taking a pilgrimage (for the technical sense of **leue** as "ecclesiastical permission" see below, Prol.83n, and MED *leve*² 1a; for the usage of "leve" + infinitive as here, see MED *leve*² 1b). As with the portrait of minstrels, the portrait focuses on the abuse of stories and narrative: false pilgrims are another species of false poets and storytellers. Rather than the lives and miracles of the saints that they are visiting, these pilgrims begin their journeys with **many wyse tales**, and they acquire from those journeys an indulgence to lie about their experiences forever after.

PP almost always presents praiseworthy pilgrimages as spiritual journeys traced in allegorical terms, often contrasted to the sins of physical pilgrimage, but PP never directly rejects real pilgrimage outright (see 7.160–291 [B.5.515–638]; compare Thorpe, ed. Hudson 1993:62; Burrow 1965[1969]). Instead, as Burrow notes, the poem presents a "'serpent-like' movement" in taking up such issues as pilgrimage and rendering them gradually into "more inward statements" (Burrow 1965[1969]:227). Thus Reason repeats and glosses the lines in the Prologue satirizing pilgrims: "ȝe þat seketh seynt Iames and seyntes at Rome, / Seketh seynt treuthe in sauacioun of ȝoure soules" (5.197–98 [B.5.56–57, A.5.40–41]). PP does not overtly resemble Lollard (and later, humanist and Protestant) attacks against literal pilgrimage as such (see Zacher 1976:47–9, 170n36): Will, Conscience, and Patience are all very like pilgrims at the end of the banquet scene (15.182–90), and the very construction of the poem in *passūs*, "steps," implies a traditional Christian idea that human life is a pilgrimage, a literary motif or even genre (Wenzel 1973) that often entails literal wandering and pilgrimage; see Chaucer's Parson's Prologue and Tale (lines 48–51, 75–80; see also Fleming 1985). PP ends with a return to the state of wandering and searching established at the beginning, when Conscience vows to "bicome a pilgrime / And wenden as wyde as þe world renneth" (22/B.20.380–81), echoing but immeasurably deepening the narrator's opening posture (see above 4–5n).

B 50–52: I seiȝ somme þat seiden þei hadde ysouȝt Seintes . . . Moore þan to seye sooþ, it semed bi hire speche: C's excision of these lines, again inveighing against pilgrims' tales, returns to the sequence in A, which also lacks the lines. The lines unique to B are probably authentic, although rather empty and redundant with the preceding lines: perhaps the lines show an attempt to rewrite or elaborate A 46–49, and were then cancelled by L but inadvertently left in by a copyist early in the B tradition. The lines echo the phrasing of C.16.146 (B.14.312): "He tempreþ þe tonge to truþeward þat no tresor coueiteþ." The use of *tempren* ("to govern") to refer to the tongue's mendacity or to its verity is exemplified in MED by only these two appearances in PP (MED *tempren* 6.c.).

51–55 (B 53–57, A 50–54): Eremites on an hep . . . here ese to haue: Clearly hermits would not ideally define their vocations by being pilgrims, any more than they would by travelling in crowds: the Benedictine Rule defines their vocation as dwelling alone in a set area (usually imagined as deserted), and even in late medieval England they were characteristically settled in cottages, often bridge entrances, where they depended on the charity of passersby and maintained the bridge (*Regula* 1; see Hanna 1997; Jusserand 1961:68n). The denunciation against vagrant hermits ("londleperis heremytes . . . alle swiche þei faiten") becomes explicit at B.15.213–14 (C omits this). When they did travel, hermits tended to restrict their destinations to English shrines whereas "palmers" went abroad; the fifteenth-century mystic and autobiographer, Margery Kempe, for example, persuaded a hermit to travel with her to the shrine of Walsingham as part of the first leg of her third pilgrimage overseas; the hermit leaves her at Ipswich and swiftly returns home, clearly conscious that he should not depart for too long or travel too far away (ed. Meech and Allen 1961:226–28). **Eremites** and **hep** alliterate here as at 8.183 (B.7.187, A.7.175), "An heep of Eremytes henten hem spades"; in the present passage, **on an hep** carries a more clearly pejorative sense because it is applied to hermits for whom travel in groups is distinctly noneremetical behavior. However, **on an hep** is not usually pejorative or colloquial when referring to groups or clumps of people, in battle and elsewhere (MED *hep* 4).

These lines thus further elaborate the Prologue's depiction of sinful pilgrims, now hermits heading **to Walsyngham**, i.e., the shrine of St. Mary of Walsingham, in Norfolk, a popular and lucrative shrine vividly described in the sixteenth century in Erasmus' sixth colloquy (trans. Thompson 1957:56–91). **hokede staues**, more commonly described as "pikstaves," are iconographic type-identifications of professional pilgrims of all kinds; the illustration of the professional palmer in the PP manuscript, Bodleian Library, MS. Douce 104, carries a "hooked" or forked cane at B.5.535 [C.7.180]; reproduced in the facsimile by Scott 1992. For the near-formulaic association of pilgrims with "pikstaves," see Robert Mannyng's *Chronicle* (c. 1338), "a schorte staffe . . . as palmers in handes take, / square gronden, scharp euenlike" (ed.

Sullens 1996, Part 1, lines 15127–29); Chaucer, Summoner's Tale III.1737, etc. The grave of a mid-fifteenth-century pilgrim from Worcester discovered in 1968 includes a long ash staff with a double-pronged iron spike at the bottom and traces of a horn tip at the top, which may have had a pierced cockleshell attached to it (Webb 2000:210–12).

Hermits' choice of special clothing in order **to be knowe fram othere** (54 [B 56, A 53]), in spite of the humbleness of the clothing in question, may align them with those who "putte hem to pruyde, aparayled hem þeraftir" (25 [B 23, A 23]). Justifications for why Franciscans sought distinctive habits sometimes use the same phrase (see 2.223–45n, Pecham's *quaestio*). Hermits also developed distinctive clothing: a brown habit over which a white scapular was worn, which the aspiring hermit brought before a bishop and which was ritually granted back by the bishop in the service of making the hermit (see Davis 1985:209). "Lewed hermits" are condemned in detail in C's additions to the Pardon passus (9.140–52, 189–280; see also 5.2–3), following the same general argument that they gain status and leisure by adopting such a role with little or no ecclesiastical authority; a positive countertype to hermits who beg **here ese to haue** is found in "Paul *primus heremita*" described by Liberum Arbitrium (Anima in B), who makes his own clothing from leaves and relies on birds to bring him food (17.13–16 [cp. B.15.286–89]).

52 (B 54, A 51): and here wenches aftir: Walsingham was noted as a shrine that women visited (see Morrison 2000:16–35), and literary satire is rife against single women on pilgrimage (like satires of other kinds of pilgrims) as sexually licentious (Morrison 2000:106–24). Probably the meaning of **aftir** is adverbial, "They went to Walsingham and then went to their wenches" rather than prepositional, "They went to Walsingham and their wenches followed after them." Both uses of **aftir** are attested in PP. Supporting the first sense is the description by William Thorpe: "peple wasten blamfulli Goddis goodis in her veyne pilgrymageyng, spendynge þese goodis vpon vicious hosteleris and vpon tapsters, whiche ben ofte vnclene wymmen of her bodies" (ed. Hudson 1993:64). Such criticism of pilgrims is found from the eighth century on (see Zacher 1976:170n36). For the syntax of the second sense, that is, here implying women pilgrims, compare 2.197–98 (B.2.184–85, A.2.145–46): "Thenne fals and fauel ryde forth togederes / And mede in þe myddes and al this meyne aftur."

53 (B 55, A 52): Grete lobies and longe: lobies can mean a kind of fish (pollack), but it is first attested in some metaphorical sense here in Middle English, and subsequently appears only in *Richard the Redeless* (ed. Barr 1993, also Dean 2000), 2.170, apparently on the basis of this line. The word is usually glossed 'lazy lout,' or 'lubber' (from thin attestations; see MED *lobre*, *lob* b.), from Middle Dutch *lobbe* and Old Norwegian *lubba*. But possibly it is derived from Old French and Anglo-Norman *lobeur*, 'flatterer,' 'deceiver,' 'toady.' Huon de Méri's *Torneiment Anticrist* includes the figure Loberie among a group of sins of speech such as Lying, Detraction and Betrayal (ed. Bender 1976, lines 796–800), sins that are here associated with the pilgrims. The reference to **longe** people who are unlikely to work carries a potential self-reference, realized at C.5.24 and B.15.152.

56–65 (cp. B 58–67, A 55–64): I fonde þer Freris . . . mounteth vp faste: The poem's criticism of friars begins here, possibly sparked by "Bidders and beggers" above at 41–46 (A/B 40–45). They are here considered together as **alle þe foure ordres** (i.e., Carmelite, Austin, Dominican or Jacobite, and Franciscan or Minorite, often referred to in antifraternal writing as a collective acronym, CAIM). B and A always have the standard number of four; C retains it only here, elsewhere speaking of "fyue ordres" (8.191, 9.344). Prsl (ad loc.) proposes that the fifth order was the "Crutched" or Cruciferous friars (see also "Jack Upland," line 83, ed. Heyworth 1968:57 and 119n), but the identification is not certain. The mention of five orders is unusual in medieval discussions, and their identities would likely be difficult for contemporaries to specify with complete confidence. Perhaps the change reflects a wish to distance the poem from the acronymic Wycliffite condemnation of the four. It may be relevant also that near the end both B and C condemn the number of friars as uncountable (see 22/B.20.267).

The topic brings the critical voice of the Prologue most clearly into open denunciation. The criticisms display the polymorphous capabilities and dangers that such religious orders themselves are said to embody. In a rapid shuttling of embodiments, they are presented here as preachers, "glosers," **maistres**, **mendenant freres**, personified **charite** become a merchant, and **shryuars** of lords, all summed up as **The moste meschief on molde**. Lawton (1988:241–44) notes the idiomatic wordorder of the passage, and observes that in many of the lines of the B version, the things the friars would keep hidden are presented in the understated nonalliterating lifts (the *x* in *aaax*) (e.g., **Siþ charite haþ ben chapman and chief *to shryue lordes*** (B 64; see also 21.221–24n). In general, C's slight adjustments provide more subtle specificity, retaining the basic points from antimendicant satire: C's **For coueytise of copis contraryed somme doctours** for B's and A's **For coueitise of copes construwed it as þei wolde** (B 61) suggests they promote themselves specifically by means of hairsplitting disputation and commentary, rather than simply by willful exegesis. C's replacement, with **contraryed**, hints at academic dialectic or public theological debate, such as those between possessioners and friars that were not uncommon in London (see, e.g., Galloway 1992a:23–25). C's **maistres of mendenant freres** (60) for B's and A's **maistres mowe cloþen hem at likyng** speaks with careful precision, avoiding the possibility that any other "maistres" might be intended and keeping the criticism pointed at the friars (and almost arriving at the oxymoron of "Maystres of þe menores" [10.9 (B.8.9, A.9.9)]). The specter of friars who are **maistres** implies an increased sense of the heavy involvement in university life of the friars, and of some inevitable pride in such a status (see Chaucer, Summoner's Tale, III.2184–86). The ties of the poet himself to the university realm are uncertain (see Galloway 1992b).

57–61 (B 59–63, A 56–60): profyt of þe wombe; coueytise of copis; Here moneye and here merchandise: Imputations that friars want profit and preferment are common in antimendicant satire. The claim that friars preached "for material gain rather than the spiritual good of the faithful" appears widely, perhaps earliest and most explicitly throughout William of St. Amour's *De periculis novissimorum temporum* (1255) (see Szittya 1986:52). Here, however, many of the references to profit are analogies, showing that the concepts of monetary profit govern every kind of gain the friars seek. **profyt of þe wombe** is presumably a reference to gluttonous indulgence, **coueytise of copis** a reference to sartorial greed and implicitly professional advancement (see also 22/B.20.58). Both invoke long satiric traditions, the first against gluttonous clerics (more often, in earlier literature, monks than friars), the second against friars offering service to gain status, signified by fine clothing (Mann 1973:18–20, 43–53). Payment for services at all social levels in the Middle Ages was often made in clothing, often bought in a single large bolt by a lord and used for all his followers, which displayed one's position in his good favor: even "charite," allegorically considered, will take the "robes" of "riche men" if they "lelelyche lyuen and louen and byleuen" (16.358–59; see many references in Green 1980; Hicks 1995:63–65).

here merchandise is evidently a reference to their "trade (in souls)" (Prsl)—that is, their facile granting of absolution after hearing confessions in return for a donation, a form of simony. The linked language of monetary profit shows how this mode of thought controls all the various sins that satirists commonly imputed to contemporary friars; see also 3.38–67n. The critique culminates in the last passus of the poem, from 22/B.20.230 on; see notes there. Compare the similar denunciation of clerical professionals driven by love of profit in *The Simonie*, "For Coveytise and Symonie han the world to wille" (ed. Embree and Urquhart 1991, line A 30, C 36; on this work, see above, Headnote).

62–63 (A 61–62, B 64–65): sith charite hath be Chapman . . . in a fewe ȝeres: I.e., "since the time when those who should embody charity [as Francis did, 16.355–57 (B.15.230–32)] have become merchants and are the foremost who provide absolution to members of the higher social estates, many novel and horrific things have rapidly occurred." The elliptical syntax, and the overtly paradoxical claim that charity could become its antithesis, allows the word **charite** to be hollowed out into a mere sign, capable of contradicting the ethical meaning to which it refers (see Simpson 1986:172). A more authentic and lexically stable sense of "charite" immediately follows in the next line, as if directly to contrast with the lexical instability of the word in this one. A similar quasi-allegory of venality appears in the contemporaneous apocalyptic treatise *The Last Age of the Church*: e.g., "Chaffare walkynge in derkenessis is þe pryui heresie of symonyans / bi resoun of whiche þe thridde tribulacioun schal entre into Cristis Chirche" (ed. Todd 1840:xxv; see Kerby-Fulton 1990:184). The selling of spiritual goods is in a general sense simony (Acts 8:18–20 is the proof-text), but friars are identified specifically as preachers about charity (as noted above, and at 16.289–94, in C only). In contrast, foundational Franciscan documents often stress the opposite movement: from Francis as materialist merchant to Francis as spiritual merchant, "a salesman of the gospel" (Julian of Speyer, trans. Armstrong 1999:372), who "Like an experienced merchant, concealed the pearl he had found from the eyes of the mockers and selling all he had, he tried to buy it secretly" (Thomas of Celano, *Life*, 1.3, par. 6, trans. Armstrong 1999:187; on the mercantile elements of Franciscanism, see Little 1978). Whether by specific reference or by manipulation of broader cultural associations, PP here reverses the metaphoric language of Franciscanism (or reinverts it, since that "language" is itself a reversal of the commercial world).

　　ferlyes: "novelties and horrors"; the sense has decisively shifted from the positive usage above in the A/B opening frame, A/B 6: Rogers observes that this tracks the different generic demands of the dream vision and the estates satire, and the shift in this word helps mark these genres' "obvious and abrupt juxtaposition . . . as if not the speaker, but the drift of the discourse, is determining [the narrator's] consciousness" (2002:57). It might be added, however, that "ferly" always has instability in its movement between alluring and sinister senses, as the usage in *Awntyrs off Arthure* shows (see above B 6n). For the phrasing of the line, compare *Wars of Alexander*; ed. Duggan and Turville-Petre 1989, line 501, "Anoþir ferly þare fell within a fewe days." As here, the

sense there is of a menacing or at least awesome omen, a broken egg representing Alexander's world conquest but also his death.

**64: But holi chirche and charite choppe adoun suche shryuars / B 66 (A 63):
But holy chirche and hij holde bettre togidres**: A and B closely resemble a
passage in *The Simonie*, whose critical survey of English society under Edward
II's reign offers one model for the estates satire of PP's Prologue: "For hadde
the clergie harde holden togidere, / And noht flecched aboute noþer hider ne
þidere, / But loked where the treuþe was, and there haue bileued, / Þanne were
the barnage hol, that nu is al todreued / So wide" (ed. Embree and Urquhart
1991, lines A 451–55). C's change introduces **charite** as the active, even destructive force that it is later in the poem, a force that must destroy false images of
charity such as hypocritical friars in order to reestablish authentic charity (see
especially 19.275 [B.17.294]: "Thus 'veniaunce, veniaunce!' verray charite
asketh"; for other appearances of charity in an active and sometimes nearly
personified role, see (in C) 2.37, 7.257, 11.63, 15.275, 16.35, 16.290, 16.350, 17.49,
17.148, 18.206, 19.276. Lawler (2002) notes that **charite** here "must mean the
secular clergy and specifically the bishops, whose responsibility it is to chop
down abuses"; thus he suggests that here the Prologue shifts from the friars to
the secular clergy (Lawler 2002:95–96). Lawler argues further that "charity" is
a word commonly used in the poem to represent the secular clergy (see further
Lawler 2003).

C adds to the B Prologue both this reference to **charite** and a reference
to "true" charity (see 87n below). Against Lawler's view, partly on the basis
of B.15.149–248 and 557–67, Scase notes that "charity" in fourteenth-century
anticlerical writing, particularly that of Wyclif, was used as a principle to argue
that the clergy should be divested of illicit, and hence in some arguments any,
civil dominion (1989:84–119). But as Lawler's claim indicates, the C version
differs from B in equating or aligning charity explicitly with the church on
several occasions, including the present one (see also 17.125, 19.276). C also
omits most of the anticlerical claims of B.15.196–215 in the discussion of charity
(see 16.339–49). The topic remained notable up to and beyond the Reformation: a late gloss on this line in the C manuscript U (BL MS. Add. 35157, fol.
7ᵛ) notes of this phrase, "þe light of þe truthe," and a later note adds, "Kinge
Henrye viij fulfiflled in his time."

Choppe can be one of two verbs, to mean either 'strike down' (MED,
choppen v. 1) or 'buy and sell' (*choppen* v. 2); MED shows the second only from
the late fifteenth century, but in *Dives and Pauper*, c. 1420, a patron of a church
who sells the patronage, or adds to the price of a manor because it has a
patronage attached to it, is condemned for simony on the grounds of "chop-

pyng of chirchis withoutyn autoryte of þe buschop" (ed. Barnum 1980:183). The main sense of the line here is 'strike down,' but the overtone with the other sense implies the practice for which they ought to be struck down. The noun "choppe-chirches," i.e., those who buy and sell benefices or patronages, is attested from 1391, in a letter from Archbishop William Courteney to all English bishops "*contra Choppe-Churches*" (cited in Wilkins 1964, vol. 3.215– 17). The second sense emerges probably by similarity less to 'strike a bargain' (so MED) than to 'chap-man' (Old English *ceap-man*), 'trader' (see Lawler 2002:96n12). Certain benefices were traded so rapidly in London that Mc-Hardy observes they functioned "almost as currency, once they had fallen into the hands of the benefice-brokers" (1995:66); a contemporary instance of someone involved in this market is the chronicler and civil lawyer Adam Usk, who owned or transferred at least twenty-five benefices (Emden 1959:3:1937–38; see Galloway 1997:306–7). Lawler notes of the PP line that "in a brilliant piece of wordplay, the priesthood is divided into chapmen and choppers" (2002:96). The double sense of **choppe** implies an intricately apt justice of a sort typical of PP (and of satire generally): those chopping the church will be chopped by the church.

66–80 (B 68–82, A 65–79): Ther prechede a Pardoner . . . yf þe ne were: Official complaints against pardoners (*quaestores*) selling indulgences on the grounds that these provide remission from sin without further contrition date from the mid-thirteenth century and persist to the end of the fifteenth century; literary satire of pardoners dates from about the same period (Delahaye 1926, 1927, 1928; Mann 1973:145–52). Wyclif's attacks on the sale of indulgences were vehement (Wyclif, *De ecclesia* cap. 23, ed. Loserth 1886:549–50), and a later Lollard sermon may even draw on this passage in PP, as the echoes of nearby language in the Prologue, and the general use of alliteration, suggest: "in þis blyndenesse beþ alle þoo þat bileuen / þat for a bulle purchasid of a fals parde-ner, þoru a fals suggestion and symonye of seluer, and þei paie him þanne a peny and leie hit on hire heuedes, þei beþ asoiled of alle hire synnes, as þei witterli wene" (sermon 10/285–89, ed. Cigman 1989:113). But in spite of the satire and polemical attacks on several sides, indulgences themselves were never designed in theory to offer facile *quid pro quo* release from the punish-ments of sin; pious action or thought remained a premise of indulgences, and indeed these elements seem more stressed by those offering (rather than critic-izing) indulgences in the late Middle Ages (see Minnis 2003).

Originally, indulgences provided remission simply from a specific num-ber of days of temporal, worldly punishment for sin, granted after confession and "after the guilt of sin has already been forgiven" (*Codex Iuris Canonici*

can. 911); by the late Middle Ages, they seem to have offered a kind of time
remitted from punishment in purgatory as well. Payment for such indulgence
was officially defined as a specific contribution to the work of the church, not
monetary payment for a pardon that absolved one without need of confession
or contrition (see Southern 1970:136–42; Delahaye 1926:342–45). How an
indulgence actually could measure time in purgatory was similarly unclear;
forty days of indulgence would not remit forty days of time in purgatory
directly. Rather, whatever the spiritual merit might be of forty days of penance
on earth, that amount was deemed potentially acquired by a forty-day indulgence, an addition to whatever more immediate penance and thus remission
of penalties of sin a sinner might undergo in life. Perhaps seeking to balance
this difficult calculus, the *Pricke of Conscience* (c. 1350) suggests that "a man
sal thynk þare a day . . . Þe space of alle ane hale yhere [year]" (ed. Morris
1863, lines 3931–33).

As the laity's dazed eagerness for indulgences here in PP suggests, the
uncertainty of just what was being gained did not lessen desire to heap up such
possible remissions of purgatory, which were less expensive than other means
such as having Masses sung, and thus more broadly and popularly disseminated. Their popularity was enormous; vast numbers were produced in late
medieval England and into the early decades of printing (Gutenberg's first
product was an indulgence, as probably was the first item to issue from Caxton's press, and the first known printed item in England [Blake 1969a:79]).
Individual indulgences were widely sold, often for as little as 4d—about the
amount a thatcher could earn in a day—although sometimes a sliding scale
was used depending on income (Swanson 1995:219–20; Dyer 1989:215). The
view that indulgences provided some direct remission of the punishments of
sin after death was probably inevitable, even though the notion that the pope
could grant indulgence to those in purgatory officially prevailed only by the
late fifteenth century, promulgated in 1476 by Pope Sixtus IV (see Oberman
1983:405–6). By 1343 Pope Clement VI had, however, defined the idea of the
Treasury of Merits, by which the saints and especially Jesus had built up a
"super-abundance of merit before God which the church could direct to other
causes," only a small step from claiming the pope's power to remit punishment in purgatory (Swanson 1995:27). Thus if indulgences were "sold, as many
were, by the unscrupulous; if inflated out of all proportion, as they were after
1350; and if acquired by the credulous; they might wrongly be seen as securing
total release from the effects of sin" (Swanson 1995:218).

The *Pricke of Conscience* (c. 1350) in defining the pardon of indulgences
strives to walk a fine line between clarity and blurriness on all these matters,
where blurriness might be useful to an individual cleric charged with explain-

ing such things to his parishioners: the "pape has swa large powere / To assoyle a man, and hym forgyfe, / Alle þe dette of payn þat may greve" (ed. Morris 1863, lines 3859–61), but only so long as the penitent fulfills "the law of the gospel"; bishops have less power to pardon than the pope, but may nonetheless delegate their power to pardon to their underlings ("Til þair hawen underloutes" [line 3877]). Those pardoned must be "out of dedly syn" (line 3881), but if they are, they can be pardoned from the "þe remenand of payns, þat es, dett / Þat parchaunce es lefte undon here" (lines 3897–98), a "remnant of the debt of pain" that might exist because penance was not well or fully done, including left "forgeten thurgh reklesnes" (line 3909) and thus might otherwise require time in purgatory. "For swa mykel pardoun may a man / Purches here, þat he may þan / In purgatory qwyte all þe dett, / Þat hym fra blis may tary or lett" (lines 3918–21). But the writer cautiously adds, "bot som clerkes counsailles / Þat we it spare and reserve halely, / Until we com til purgatory, / And do here penance whilles we lyf may" (lines 3927–30). The narrator of PP returns to ponder the validity of papal pardons at the end of the second vision; but, like the *Pricke of Conscience* author, he leaves their validity neither fully endorsed nor fully denied (see C.9.319–46 [B.7.174–200, A.8.152–78]).

The Prologue's pardoner, who **preched . . . as he a preest were** and claims **þat hymself myhte assoylen hem alle**, operates loosely within ecclesiastical law, since he has a bishop's "bulle" (67) with a "seel" (77); a letter of Archbishop Simon Sudbury in 1378 condemns pardoners who preach to the people and offer indulgences without displaying the proper letters from the bishop (Reg. Sudbury fol. 49a; quoted. in Wilkins 1964[1737], vol. 3.131). But the pardoner here seems to have come by this illicitly (see 78n). Moreover, his claim to **assoylen** his listeners is blatantly against religious law: only a priest may absolve, as only a priest may consecrate (see Swanson 1995:34). Here *as* he a preest were is unambiguously a sign of hypocrisy (see above, 2n). That he will absolve them **hymself** adds to the many indications of illegitimacy, even as a parish priest seems near at hand or behind the scenes (see below 79n). And whereas the doctrine of indulgences depended on a spiritual Treasury of Merits whose potential beneficent effects could, it was hoped, reach up to God's mysterious judgments, the laity giving money to PP's pardoner foster an economy of expanding cycles of sin, a kind of "treasury of sin": **Thus ȝe gyue ȝoure gold glotons to helpe / And leneth hit lorelels þat lecherye haunten.**

67, 71 (B 69, 73; A 66, 70): Brouth forth a bulle; to kyssen his bulle: The Pardoner's first gesture is to produce the document that establishes his authority to preach and defines the quasi-dramatic moment and place of his sermon (see also Chaucer, *Canterbury Tales* VI.335–40); the object of authority remains in view and is worshipped at the conclusion of his performance. The **bulle** marks the beginning of the poem's presentation of documents (see generally Steiner 2003:93–142); this document is not read aloud but functions as "stage property" (Hughes 1992). The two further documents of the first vision, Meed's marriage charter (see 2.80a-118n) and Peace's bill of complaint (4.45n, 46–48n), are both read aloud and their particular terms made part of events and debate. The later documents are occasions for diverse reactions, and elicit debate or conflict; however disruptive such reactions might be, the evil of the Pardoner's bull is that it does not produce any questioning or criticism apart from the narrator's.

The listeners' abject worship of the bull echoes a portrayal of Islamic idolatry that John Mandeville describes, when he comments on the power of the Sultan's signet and documents in Jerusalem: "the folk of the contree don gret worschipe & reuerence to his signett or his seel & knelen þereto as lowly as wee don to Corpus Domini. And ʒit men don full grettere reuerence to his lettres, For the Admyrall & alle oþere lordes þat þei ben schewed to, before or þei resceyue hem þei knelen doun & þan þei take hem & putten hem on here hedes & and after þei kissen hem & þan þei reden hem knelynge with gret reuerence & þan þei offren hem to do all þat the berere asketh" (ed. Hamelius 1919:54). In the kiss the pardoner elicits, an obscene pun or suggestive gesture is also possible. Indeed, the majority of PP manuscripts of B and C, and four of those of A, read "to kyssen his bulles." The Athlone editions correctly emend to follow the minority of witnesses with **bulle** since the author is unlikely to have broken consistency in the details of the scene. The obscene implication is made overt in Chaucer, *Canterbury Tales* VI.946–55.

69 (B 71; A 68): Of falsnesse of fastynge and of vowes ybrokene: The sin of simony, selling a sacrament (absolution), is serious. But a further irony is the relative smallness of the sins for which the **Lewed men** here eagerly seek absolution, which contrasts with the pardoner's own grosser sins of hypocrisy, gluttony, lechery, and avarice. Canon law distinguishes criminal from venial sins in terms closely similar to the sins of the pardoners and the laity shown here, defining "capital crimes" as sacrilege, homicide, adultery, fornication, false testimony, plunder, theft, pride, envy, avarice, wrath ("if it be sustained for a long time"), and intoxication ("if it is continuous"), and the "lesser sins" as excesses in food, drink, speech (and silence "more than is expeditious"), eating while others are fasting, and vows that are made "incautiously" and cannot be fulfilled (Dist. 25, c. 3 *post*; ed. Friedberg 1959). The distinction is maintained in literary sources: in the fourteenth and fifteenth centuries, various poems declare that simply looking upon the Host when elevated in a Mass absolved the viewer of many venial sins: Lydgate's *Virtues of the Mass* declares, when a man hears Mass "Hys veniall synnes, rekenyd manyfolde, / Of neglygence and othes that byn lyght, / They byn foryeuen, for grace passyth golde" (MacCracken 1911:112, lines 597–99; further examples are at Duffy 1992:100–102). The pardoner thus offers for pay a spiritual good that should be and often was obtained free (note Lydgate's glance at the same sin with "grace passyth golde"). At least one confessor's guide, in English from the fifteenth century, similarly divides venial and deadly sins (see Hodgson 1948:3). Of course some breaking of vows (e.g., adultery) might be serious, but PP's pardoner, unlike Chaucer's, is portrayed as relatively cautious, and perhaps somewhat realistic, in what he offers to absolve, for all of the simony and duplicity in his offer. Chaucer's Pardoner's simoniacal offerings include his promise to cure everything from livestock illness to gluttony, lechery, and avarice itself, a surreal self-advertisement that seems to hint at the young men's similarly hyperbolic effort to kill Death in his tale (*Canterbury Tales* VI.352–76; 895–912).

72 (B 74, A 71): blered here yes: The phrase also appears, in discussing deceptive doctors, in *The Simonie*, line A 223 (ed. Embree and Urquhart 1991); discussing the general similarity of that poem with the estates complaints in PP, Salter notes with particular aptness to this passage that "the mingling of abstract concepts and classes of people in a designedly realistic setting [in *The Simonie*] is highly suggestive of Langland's method" (1967:249). The present expression is a remarkable if minute case in both poems of proto-allegory: being struck in the head by the pardons hard enough to blur their vision suggests judgment blurred by deception.

76–78 (B 78–80; A 75–77): Were þe bischop yblessed . . . þe boy precheþ: Bishops were blessed at their consecration ceremonies (Bnt), so a technical meaning seems likely; but the clause is contrary-to-fact, thus it allows an ironic invocation of **yblessed** as simply "a truly holy man" (as Skt takes it). The bishops were consecrated by ritual but not truly blessed.

   worth bothe his eres: Bnt suggests a colloquial phrase, "worth his salt," "alert to what is going on" but speculates about another technical sense: "worthy to keep his ears" rather than lose them in the pillory as an accessory to a fraud. Phrases of "wagering" one's ears ("legge myn eres," "wedde myne eris") appear several times in PP (see B.4.146/A.4.129; C.8.289). The tone of such phrases is that of everyday asseveratives, but with a suggestion of continual rough reminder of public justice, and implying ears' special value and special vulnerability to being lost or amputated. Probably at least as important as any precise implications in the present line is its tone of speaking of bishops, figures of dauntingly high status, as if they were commoners.

But the next phrase backs away from this stance: **nouȝt be the bischop**, "not with the bishop's permission"; having denied that the bishop was truly consecrated, the thought then insists the bishop did not in fact offer permission either. In the lines here to this point, the verse delivers scandalous contempt for bishops; but in the nick of time, this shift exempts them from responsibility for what is taking place. The satire thus avoids dwelling too long on the powerful and turns to a lower order and a more immediate agent.

boy, a term most used in the southeast midlands although spreading in alliterative poetry generally by the end of the fourteenth century, usually has no sense of youth before the mid-fifteenth century; in PP as elsewhere, the term is one of contempt, either to refer to someone of lower social standing or a generally disreputable figure. Each version of PP uses the word more frequently, Dobson suggests as possibly a sign of an increasing general use of the word, or possibly an increasingly easternizing of language in the versions of the poem (see Dobson 1940). The last would oppose in a minor way the southwestern dialect of many of the C manuscripts (see Samuels 1988).

77 (B 79; A 76): His seel: The charge against bishops for somehow allowing their seal to be sent out for such purposes is anticipated in the physical description of the "bulle" or "breuet" that the pardoner produces, as dangling "with bischopis selys" (67); indeed this is the meaning of the further synonym for the document, "his Rageman" (73), a document tricked out with ragged strips on which hung the authenticating seals, often called a "ragemanrole," the origin of our "rigmarole" (see Alford, *Gloss*. s.v. *ragman*). Bnt notes that the term *ragemen* appeared in the late thirteenth century to refer to those royal inquisitors in eyre who collected sealed depositions from witnesses, and who were viewed also as collectors of money for the royal treasury; he speculates that by the later fourteenth century, by which time the eyres had fallen into disuse, long rolled documents with episcopal seals would still carry the same sense of predatory intrusion. Some collective indulgences carried multiple seals; each bishop's seal would be considered worth forty days of indulgence, with the total calculated cumulatively (see Zutshi 1995:282). But the document here is a stageprop, illicitly acquired and deployed. Seals, the signs of authoritative documents, are as notable in the poem as documents themselves (see 2.117–18n, 2.223–45n, 3.184n, 9.27–42 [B.7.18–39, A.8.20–44]).

79 (B 81; A 78): þe parsche prest and þe Pardoner: Shifting from blame of bishops for the pernicious endeavors of pardoners, the narrative focuses on local priests as the true means by which pardoners might find a footing. This alliance is perhaps the earliest example of what became a topos of simony, by which traveling preachers or pardoners would collude with local parish priests for alms (Fletcher 1990). Fletcher makes a pertinent comparison to a Wycliffite tract from after 1383, in which parish priests are condemned who

assenten to pardoners disceyuynge þe peple in feiþ and charite and worldly goodis for to haue part of here gederynge . . . for whanne þere comeþ a pardoner . . . grauntynge mo ȝeris of pardon þan comen bifore domes day for ȝeuynge of worldly catel to riche placis where is no nede, he schal be sped and resceyued of curatis for to haue part of þat he getiþ. (Matthew 1880:154)

Here, even in this satiric phrasing, the pardoner graunts not sheer absolution (see above 66–80n) but years of remission from purgatory (although the years are so many that the remission is tantamount to absolute). See also *Dives and Pauper*, ed. Barnum 1980:182.

81–84 (B 83–86, A 80–83): Persones . . . seluer is swete: Having opened the topic of the sins of priests, the satire expands on the possibilities for the corruptions of that group in other ways (on the poem's special attention to parish priests throughout, see Lawler 2003). Just shown colluding with pardoners to deceive the bishop, parish priests (here, by distinction from parsons, vicars who would collect only a small portion of a dependent church's tithes) are now condemned along with parsons (i.e., rectors of an independent parish church) for wheedling permission from their bishops to be absent from their parishes in order to gain additional income from singing prayers for the dead. That even vicars, themselves standing in for other rectors or another religious house, and in theory obliged to carry out the care of souls personally, could gain permission to be nonresident (and thus to hire for an even cheaper salary some further vicar for their parish duties) was an increasing feature of the fourteenth and fifteenth centuries, when all parish benefices generally shifted from rectories to vicarages, and thus to more fungible positions (see Swanson 1989:44). The general topic is deepened and expanded at B.11.283–317, where chantry singing is just one of the ways that priests may be simoniacally and unworthily advanced, and where appears further condemnation of those bishops who have consecrated (again, "blessed") priests who lack means to be supported steadily and legitimately, and who lack proper knowledge to serve their flocks. Below, the narrator says of his own livelihood that "y synge for here soules of suche as me helpeth" (5.48), on the basis of which Skt influentially proposed that L himself was a chantry singer, a priest who pursued temporary engagements to say Masses for the departed (note ad loc.; see also Jusserand

1965:88–94); Donaldson used the same passage to suggest that L was not a chantry priest but an acolyte, who had lost his ability to serve as parish clerk because he had married, but who still sang prayers for those living whom he visited (1966:203–16). See further C.5.1–105.

Perpetual chantries employed permanent chantry priests, "cantarists," who were like other beneficed clergy in England "usually presented by a patron, instituted by the bishop of the diocese, and inducted by an appropriate local ecclesiastical official" (Kreider 1979:5), and who remained in their position as a priest would, often effectively with tenure for life; unlike parish priests, they primarily carried out incessant prayers for the soul of the founder, rather than pastoral duties, and thus could be seen as having abandoned a curacy for this apparently easy life (see Chaucer, *Canterbury Tales* I.508–10, "leet his sheep encombred in the myre / And ran to Londoun unto Seinte Poules / To seken hym a chaunterie for soules"). Chantries could also employ stipendiary priests, "annueleres" (see Chaucer, *Canterbury Tales* VII.1012, the Canon's Yeoman's Tale) whose hiring and dismissal did not require such a tier of authority but simply rested with the trustees of the chantry; these often performed duties for a specific term, often one, three or seven years, and their status was quite distinct from those with permanent benefices (Kermode 1998:127–32; Kreider 1979:5–6; McHardy 1995:68). There were, further, free chapels, colleges (groups of chantry priests), and guilds that all offered opportunities for short- or long-term employment for those offering prayers, litanies, and other rituals for the dead on an annual or more frequent basis (in York and Bury, town criers are recorded as hired to ring a bell through the city to "excite the people to pray," and elsewhere some were hired to sprinkle holy water on graves, etc. [Kermode 1998:132]).

In London, parish fraternities proliferated after the Black Death. These functioned as communal chantries for those who could not afford private chantries, employing a fraternity chaplain "who would pray for all the members, living and dead" (Barron 1985:23–24). At least 2,200 intercessory institutions of some sort, capable of supporting at least one priest and as many as a dozen or more, existed in late medieval England, and of these London had at least 314, many with groups of cantarists or stipendiary priests (Kreider 1979:14–15). St. Paul's alone supported 74 by 1366 (Myers 1972:141–42). The average annual salary in the period for chantry priests was 7 marks (£4 13s 4d; Kermode 1998:128), over twice the maximum wage for a laborer (see Dyer 1989:29), but many chantry chaplains were poorly paid: Robert Braybrooke, bishop of London from 1382–1404, sought by combining chantries to make sure that London chantries provided adequate incomes (see McHardy 1995:69–70; Hill 1971), a period too late to account specifically for PP's criticism of episcopal approval of London chantries but indicating a general basis for its view. Most chantry foundations were small scale and limited in duration, but major merchants might found permanent chantries with enormous sums of £400 or more (Kermode 1998:128). Chantry priests might have so many souls to pray for that those funding prayers would take special efforts to be sure their own requests were honored, like one Richard Wartre of York who had his own name and those of his parents and two wives written on "bills" so that "the chaplains could have the names in front of them as they sang" (Kermode 1998:131). For a range of forms for the prayers, see the Sarum *Manuale* (ed. Collins 1960:144–52).

From a rigorous canonical perspective, the possibility of simony lurks in all such requests, however popular, if those seeking such employment are motivated by some manner of personal desire rather than need, if the prayers are too precisely purchased with an explicit *quid pro quo*, or if the desires of those requesting such a service are somehow worldly rather than spiritual. Thus *Dives and Pauper* says, summarizing canon law on this matter, "As anemyst [regarding] ȝifte of seruyce of þe tunge þat stant mychil in preyer & wardly fauour, þu must takyn hede wheþer a man is ordryd or chosyn by his owyn preyere or be oþir mennys; ȝif be his owyn preyeres it is symonye; ȝif it be don be oþir mennys preyerys, or it ben [either it is] charnel or spiritual; ȝif it ben charnel & for hym þat is nout worþi it is symonye, but ȝif it be don for hym þat is able & worþi it is no symonye, so þat þe ordynour & þe cheser takyn non gret heed to þe preyere but principaly to God & to abylte of þe persone. Netheles ȝif a man hadde nede & fele hymself able he may askyn a symple benefyce withoutyn cure, for þat is no symonye. But ȝif he haue no nede þerto, ȝif he aske it he synnyth" (ed. Barnum 1980:177; see also Raymund of Penafort, bk 1, title 1, cited there in the text). Courteney's letter against "Choppechurches," Gower, Chaucer, and other English satiric materials describing parish priests seeking to be absentee beneficiaries and enjoy more profitable opportunities in London, are all pertinent for the complaint in PP of mercantile treatment of spiritual goods (Wilkins 1969[1734], vol. 3.215–17; Gower, *Mirour de l'Omme* [ed. Macaulay 1899], lines 20209–832; Chaucer, *Canterbury Tales*, I.507–10). In works more thoroughly involved in moral theology and canon law, however, the issue is often a finer one of nuance and intent; thus *Dives and Pauper* at a later moment probes the precise nature of simony here as dependent on the degree of a bargaining mentality. Dives remarks, "It semyth bi þi wordys þat þei þat syngyn þe gyldene [golden, i.e., profitable] trental gon wol nyhȝ symonye, for þei makyn wondirful comenant [covenant, i.e., contract] of her syngynge," and Pauper replies, "It may ben don withoutyn symonye ȝif it be don frely withoutyn swiche comenant. But

comenant-makyng makyth oftyn symonye þat schulde ellys nout ben symonye, as ȝif þe ȝeuere aske, 'What is it worth to synge so many messys?' and þe
prest answere, 'Twenty schyllyngis' . . . & þus barganyyn & brockyn aboutyn
syngynge of þe messe, þat may nout ben sold ne bout, as men don aboutyn
byyng & sellyng of an hors or of a cow & of a calf, & so þei fallyn boþin in
cursyd symonye" (ed. Barnum 1980:186). PP's glimpse of a different, but
related scene, shows bargaining priests claiming "need" before the bishop,
whose acquiescence is again an oblique target of the satire.

After this section, A shifts to criticism of sergeants at law, lines displaced
in B and C to after the fable of the rats and mice (see below A 84–89n, after C
89n; and see 161–62n, 85–94n). A then continues with its survey of clerks as
royal servants (below, A 90–95n, after C 165–66n).

82 (B 84, A 81): sithe þe pestelence tyme, part of the priests' indirect speech
to the bishops, offers a topical dating for the first time in the poem, a construction of history "before and after the plague." The year 1349 is inscribed deeply
in later fourteenth-century culture, found widely in legislation, and responsible for dropping the London population substantially, from perhaps 100,000
in 1300, to less than half of that a century later, with a host of other related
social changes (see Palmer 1993, Herlihy 1997, and Barron 2000:396–97).
Although the plague recurred in 1368 and later, its first arrival seems invariably
defined as the most devastating and historically pivotal one. John Trevisa, e.g.,
in his 1385 translation of the *Polychronicon* notes that widespread efforts to
learn French disappeared "to fore firste deth" (BL Cotton MS. D VII, fol. 50v:
"tofore þe furste moreyn"), leaving the English knowing only English (*Polychronicon* 160–61; see Galloway 2004a:46–48). As Bnt notes, some valid
economic pressures may have contributed to the point here: the reduced population of parishioners after the Black Death made it impossible for some
clergy to live on their tithes and oblations; but of course the comment is indirect discourse, recording the arguments used by those applying for absentee
status, with the true motives displayed in the following lines.

The argument that need transcends law here marks the entry of a key
issue in the poem, of both legitimately necessary excuse (*necessitas non habet
legem*, C.13.44), and of illegitimate claims that simply rationalize immorality
on such grounds. That large topic is most fully addressed with the encounter
with Need at 22/B.20.1–51 (see nn on those lines); it appears obliquely in matters such as distinguishing the worthy from the unworthy poor, and even matters of which vocations and expenditures are legitimate, which not.

83 (B 85, A 82): licence and leue indicates the basic administrative step necessary for the priests' and parsons' requests for absenteeism, seeking an episcopal

licence or a papal dispensation (see, e.g., the blanket dispensation for Cambridge students, in Zutshi 1988). The same phrase appears in Wrath's confession below, C.6.121, now directed by wrathful prelates themselves against friars who confess parishioners without "licence and leue." The administrative detail is missing from Chaucer's and Gower's portrayals of the phenomenon; it suggests more intimacy with administrative pastoral culture than do those writers, while also condemning bishops if only for compliance with those of uncertain motives and real needs, in an exchange that we seem partly to overhear.

84 (B 86, A 83): synge þer for symonye: The phrase (possibly echoing "sing for one's supper," although that phrase is attested only from the eighteenth century) slides out of the parsons' and parish priests' plea to the bishop, disclosing to readers the sin that the bishop does not perceive, or to which he prefers to turn a deaf ear during the request for license that, implicitly, he grants.

85–94 (cp. B 87–96): Bischopes and bachelers . . . sitten and demen: C and B expand on the sins of bishops, now in their involvment with legal occupations. This section on the higher clergy and university graduates pursuing administrative professions evidently elaborates A 90–95, where A's survey of ecclesiastical abuses reaches its highest levels (A 90–95 is discussed after 165–66n below). B and C, the latter after an insertion of Conscience's monitory exemplum of Ophni and Phinees against false priests, go further in addressing ecclesiastical abuses to treat cardinals and, obliquely, the pope (C 134–37). B and C at this point move away from A's schematically clear consideration of ascending ecclesiastical rank by a series of insertions and displacements: B places after the description of the foundation of the commonwealth a section about sergeants at law (B 211–16) that in A precedes the materials at 90–95, which in turn are made into the present passage; C puts the sergeants at law passage at the close of the foundation of the commonwealth (see below, 160–66n), now as the climax of the description of the inside of Westminster ("Court" [160]).

The ecclesiastic authorities here may be those who happen to come to court on behalf of their institutions, or figures with regular employment in Westminster as canon or civil lawyers. Criticism of the "Caesarean" clergy, those dedicated to civil service, is found in Wyclif and Lollard writings; in the *Tractatus de Ecclesia* Wyclif argues that the clergy should never be judges since the issues in court are worldly wealth and must often be settled without considering the will of God; thus clerics who are judges must necessarily act against their true calling as the followers of Christ who do not carry a sack or a bag, nor wear shoes or salute anyone, as Luke 10:4 teaches (*De Ecclesia*, cap.

19, ed. Loserth 1886:449; see also Gradon 1980:189–90. For PP's invocation of the same gospel passage see above, 42n). The poem's legal concepts and language are precise and informed, helping situate its author and possibly some of its early readers as at least in contact with the Westminster royal courts, if not as participants in some roles (see Alford, *Gloss.* ix-xx; Hanna 1996:236–37; Kerby-Fulton and Justice 1997; see also above, Headnote). The busy transactions that stand behind any bishop's register or any religious account book are glimpsed here in the audible rumble of legal proceedings. For a range of such transactions between a distant religious house and Westminster, see, e.g., the collection of royal writs to the bishop of Lincoln, in McHardy 1997.

In Cheker and in Chancerye chalengen his dettes / Of wardus and of wardemotis, wayues and strayues offers a fluent list of legal means to claim goods, inheritances, and other monies, on the part of religious institutions who have sent their agents or heads to Westminster (where such business nationwide would be conducted), or on the part of the crown who employs its own. **chalengen** here is "to claim (something) as one's right, due, privilege, or property" (Alford, *Gloss.*), and the following phrases describe more specifically the kinds of **dettes** such royal administrators sought (see Alford, *Gloss.*). **dettes / Of wardus** refers to the substantial revenues that the king received from estates belonging to those over whom he could claim guardianship, especially minors left as heads of estates that were owned by the king's tenants-in-chief, whose income he could collect until the heirs came of age (Bnt). The king's government gave close attention to such income; the poet John Gower was briefly investigated by the king's justices in 1366 for having bought such an estate before its head had fully come of age, thus depriving the king of the estate's profit that he would have received until that point (see Fisher 1965:51–54).

dettes / . . . of wardemotis refers to the collections by exchequer clerks of monies due the king at the wardmotes, irregular meetings of the citizens of each of London's wards. These were the "basic unit of civic governance" and numbered twenty-four until 1394, twenty-five thereafter (Barron 2004:121–27). All assessments of royal taxation on Londoners were made in the wards (Barron 2004:122). But this point, and the phrase in PP, is from a royalist not a civic perspective. The chief functions of the wardmotes (first attested in English here) were to organize London's citizens for military purposes, to collect juries, and, in the fourteenth century, to hold elections of aldermen and of representatives to attend the great assemblies at the Guildhall (Cam 1963:86). The alderman of a ward, who usually summoned a wardmote once a year, would then bring the resulting legal business of indentures and inquest verdicts to the mayor's special court, the "Great Court of Wardmote," held on the Monday after the feast of the Epiphany (which falls on the earliest Sunday after January 6), that is, the first working day after Christmas. Barron notes (following the editor of the London Letter-Books) that this Monday was known as Plough Monday (2004:122; see Sharpe 1907:276n), and, suggestively enough for PP, throughout England playful rituals would be held then involving a young man with a plow, who would plow up in front of any house that did not pay him a token (see Duffy 1992:13; the feastday was suppressed in 1548; Duffy 1992:461 and index, s.v. "plough Monday").

wayues and strayues (modern "waifs and strays," still used in British law) refer to the animals, treasure, and other property found ownerless and therefore falling to the king or lord of a manor if unclaimed within a specific period after due notice is given. Such goods are being collected or assessed here. "Weyf et stray" are listed from the thirteenth century on among other legal rights in charters in Latin and French; PP is the first attested wholly English context (MED *weif* (b) and (c); another reference in Ratcliff 1946:45–46).

As the center of such pursuits in the kingdom, Westminster brings to focus the striving for gain and material advantage that perverts sacred callings and draws all to it; see also 3.1–146nn; 4.27–31n and passus 4 passim. The narrator's target here is less the legal machinery for royal income than the clergy who take on the duties of administering the financial rights of religious or manorial households, implicitly abandoning any pastoral vocation: **summe aren** *as* **seneschalles . . .** / And ben *in stede of* **stewardus.** Other alliterative poetry commonly refers to clerks in administrative terms without irony or criticism, e.g., the phrase "clerk with countours" (*Siege of Jerusalem*, ed. Hanna and Lawton 2003, line 132). As Hanna and Lawton point out (note ad loc.), PP "is revolutionary within the alliterative tradition in imagining that *clerkes* should be those learned and in orders. Most other poems consider *clerkes* those domestic servants most useful for keeping accounts." Here the judgment is not overt, although the indications of an assumed role are clear. Both seneschals and stewards are legal and domestic officials in the household of a lord (Alford, *Gloss.*); historical evidence suggests that bishoprics were conferred on effective civil servants as rewards (see Pantin 1955:14, 41), and conversely that bishops were promoted to chancellors. PP often regards such promotion in either direction as dubious (see 21.256n and 461n). Yet in 5.53 ff. (C only), complaints against the worldly involvements of clergy are used by the narrator in a less authoritative way, to argue that the narrator should himself not be asked to labor as others do. For the issue in PP and fourteenth-century culture, see also Galloway 1992b.

86 (B 88): That han cure vnder crist and crownyng in tokene: Their **cure vnder crist**—that is, the "care of souls" which is entrusted to priests—may implicitly condemn their "curial" (courtly) occupations; their **crownyng in tokene**—that is, the tonsure which reveals their vocation and office—may implicitly condemn their labors for the earthly crown (so Bnt). But both judgments remain unspoken, and the condemnation is made part of the mystery of the vision, depending on the reader's interpretation or recognition of other textual or lexical keys (see also above note). One key to the judgment here is the explication of the tonsure in Guillaume de Deguileville's early fourteenth-century *Pelerinage de vie humaine* (see Headnote). There Raison explicates what Lydgate's translation calls the "Tookne of your crowne": the tonsure, circled like a castle or garden but open in the middle, signifies a barrier against worldly preoccupations and an inner openness only to God (*Pelerinage de vie humaine*; ed. Stürzinger 1893, lines 889–932; see Lydgate, *Pilgrimage of the Life of Man*; ed. Furnivall and Locock 1899–1904, lines 2103–27). Deguileville's Raison compares those given religious tonsure to sheep being fleeced (lines 924–32).

87–88: Ben charged with holy chirche . . among lered and lewed / B 89–90: And signe þat þei sholden shryuen hire parisshens, / Prechen and praye for hem, and þe pouere fede: In sustaining the emphasis in the entire passage on the true vocation of prelates, C here generalizes B's definition of that vocation (apart from these lines C 85–94 is otherwise identical to the parallel section at B 87–96). By doing duty for the more specific list of functions in B, C's **charite** as elsewhere in C is directly aligned with **holy chirche**, further distancing C from the possible anticlerical implications of the discussion of charity at B.15.196–215 (see also above 64n). C's change subsumes into its general injunction B's specific assertion that bishops must feed the poor, a point of canon law that was the basis for the medieval equivalent of poor law and was realized in bishops' responsibility to provide the necessities to the poor in their diocese (see Tierney 1959:68; and *Corpus Iuris Canonici* sec. pars causa xii quest. II cap. 71, *Gloria episcopi*, vol. 1:710–11 [ed. Friedberg 1959]). A fuller description of bishops' duties appears at 17.283–92, where preaching, prayer, and support of the poor are listed; the C version there replaces the suggestion in B that it would be "charite" to "deschargen" prelates of their lands (B.15.565) with the assertion that a bishop should "enchaunten hem [his peple] to charite on holy churche to bileue" (C.17.286). The phrase and the plowing conceit, **charite to tylie**, are echoed in Grace's and Piers' efforts at the end of the poem "to tulye treuthe / And þe londe of bileue, the lawe of holi churche" (21/B.19.334); for a survey of the history of metaphorical ideas of plowing in medieval Christian culture, see Barney 1973.

   lele loue and lyf: Donaldson notes that C dramatically increases the uses

of *leel* and *leelich* (1966:65); indeed, there are no appearances of *leel* in B until
B.10.355, and 19 instances before that in C. He suggests translating it "just," as
in *William of Palerne*, "alle lele lawes" (ed. Bunt 1985, line 1312), in keeping
with "C's preoccupation with justice" (1966:66). *Leel* and *leelich* are common
in *William of Palerne*.

89 (B 91): in lenton and elles: I.e., year-round, although Lent is a particularly
egregious time to indulge in London's luxuries, since then the cure of souls
would be most active, with the heightened liturgy and the need to confess the
flock for the Easter communion. The like-sounding words **lenton / London**
stand for two opposed value systems. The narrator also grows drowsy during
Lent at 20/B.18.5, but there his obliviousness to the Easter liturgy is more than
compensated for by a vision of the events themselves.

A 84–89: Þere houide an hundrit . . . til mony be shewid: For details, see
below 160–66n and 161n. A's **Þere** does not distinguish the setting of these professionals from those of any others; they are on a continuous stage or field. B,
shifting these lines to after the Rat Parliament, implicitly locates the lawyers in
the Westminster buildings of that scene; C more explicitly moves them to the
scene of court that opens up when Conscience and the King arrive there.

Conscience's Accusation

**95–135 (cp. B 97–111): Consience cam and accused hem . . . "Contreplede hit
noght," quod Consience, "for holi kirke sake"**: Unlike the preceding parts of
the Prologue's vision, C's open denunciation of those priests and prelates who
allow the laity to make offerings idolatrously to images of saints in hope of
reward or cure is a call to action. In this sense C here offers the first direct and
sustained emphasis on *doing* as well as *saying* (or seeing), ironically provoked
by the topic of priests, biblical and modern, who merely stand by and do nothing to keep sins from occurring. In B, the first introduction of such a mood
for a direct call to action—albeit there one thwarted—might be said to be the
parliament of rats and mice (see below 167–219n); the A Prologue might be
said to have no such call overtly presented, apart from the hint that the initial
phrase "vnholy of werkes" presents (see above 3n). All these are signs that the
A-B-C trajectory need not be seen as one of increasing "social conservatism"
as is sometimes thought; here, the passion of the denunciation can barely be
contained within a semblance of literary features such as alliteration and char-

acter attribution, and the passage may be a very late and only partly finished one, or at least one preserving a looseness of form that matches the directness of its statements.

Although Conscience first appears here in C, he is of course a developed figure in later parts of earlier versions, starting with passus 3 and reappearing throughout the poem. Conscience's new speech in the C Prologue is constructed by splitting into two B's condemnation of the higher legal servants of the king and other nobility, B 87–96 and B 97–104; in C these passages— separated by the new section of Conscience's discourse up to 121—become C 85–94 and 122–29. Amidst those C also adds material from B.10.285–88, perhaps because the long stretch at B.10.257–336 on the sins of parsons and parish priests seemed out of place in Clergy's mouth (the portions from there that were not placed in the C Prologue went to C.5; see C.5.146 ff.). The Prologue's condemnation of bishops and others serving the laity's administrative needs, along with the following discussion of the pope and the cardinals, is thus now enclosed within Conscience's speech, as the new speech tag line 135 indicates. That line, alternately, may be Conscience's interruption into a discourse that, by design or inattention, has slid back into the narrator's voice where the text says, **I parsceyued of þe power that Peter hadde to kepe** (125), for in B that line explicitly refers to the narrator (for a parallel uncertainty about an inserted speech tag in C, see 12.58).

The 40-line insertion could be easily contained on a single folio; RK-C suggest that the placement of the whole section is the work of early scribes or a "literary executor" (pp. 87–88; compare the early speculation of Donaldson: "it almost seems possible that the autograph MS. of C, if it should ever come to light, would prove to contain a text of the *Visio* without the later additions. These were probably written on separate sheets and their position in the text indicated by one of those complicated systems of arrows and carets that every reviser finds himself adopting" [1966:28]). The section is (as RK-C note) more general in focus than its immediate context, but this criticism in milder form might be applied to other sections of the poem, revised or unrevised. Clearly, the reformulated section has a discrete unity and self-sufficiency. Deflected into the mouth of Conscience, the speech is no longer, like its small seed in B, the personal discourse of the narrator (see B.Prol.97–99), but the powerful accusation by a major figure in the poem, whose role here is in the tradition of the force of conscience in legal contexts (see 95n). The original passage from B.10.285–88, spoken by Clergy, may have seemed less suited to its speaker; arguably too, Conscience carries more authority than that figure. So re-situated, the discourse offers views with which the narrator here and elsewhere overtly aligns himself (see below 107–17nn).

To 'accusen' is "to charge (somebody) with an offence; to impugn; to indict" (Alford, *Gloss.*). As Alford points out (*Gloss.* s.v. *Conscience*), this is the special duty of Conscience in the "court of conscience" (*in foro conscientiae*) within the private mind, which itself is a harbinger of God's judgment. A long tradition of commentary, and of literary elaborations of that, based chiefly on Romans 2:15–16, presents *conscientia* as a legal accuser, defendant, or witness at the Last Judgment, where, Paul says, conscience will give witness even to the Gentiles at the Last Judgment, their "conscience bearing witness to them; and their thoughts between themselves accusing or also defending one another, in the day when God shall judge the secrets of men by Jesus Christ, according to my gospel." This text, combined with Daniel 7:10 and Rev. 20:12 (and others, e.g. 2 Cor. 5:10–11), was the basis for a quasi-personification of "Conscience the accuser" at any point in one's life (see, e.g., Gregory the Great, *Moralia in Job*, Book 22, chap. 13, par. 26 [PL 76:229]; Bernard of Clairvaux, in a sermon on the parable of the unjust steward (Luke 16:1–9), allegorically describes one of the overseers of the cultivators of the estate as "Conscience the accuser" [PL 184:1024]). But the role is most prominent at Judgment Day. See *The Pricke of Conscience* (c. 1350), "First sal þair awen conscience / Accuse þam þan in Cristes presence," followed by a long succession of other accusers of the damned and saved crowded in a vast group together, "bathe yhung and alde, / And gude and ille . . . / Swa mykel folk com never togyder, / Ne never was sene sythen þe werld bygan" (ed. Morris 1863, lines 5440–41, 6011–14; see also 21.5–14n). With C's insertion, an aura of apocalyptic judgment, which pervades the end of the first vision and still more the end of the poem, appears more openly in the Prologue than in the earlier versions.

The basic identity of Conscience in medieval understandings and in PP is clear here from his open opposition even to established institutions and powers. These qualities spring readily from what, according to Aquinas, we mean by *conscientia*, as both knowledge (stressing the root *scire*) and judgment, the latter involving the role of accusation:

We use the word "conscientia" in accordance with both types of application [i.e., "discovery" and "judgment"]. When knowledge is applied to an actualization in order to direct it, *conscientia* is said to goad or urge or bind us. But when knowledge is applied to an actualization by way of testing what has already been, *conscientia* is said to accuse or worry us if what has occurred is found to be out of accord with the knowledge by which it was tested, and to defend or excuse us if what has occurred is found to have turned out in accordance with the piece of knowledge. (*Quest. disp.*, trans. Potts 1980:131)

Since conscience depends on knowledge (indeed, much of the scholastic discussion of the complexities of conscience focuses on the problem of whether fallible human reasoning is able to inform conscience correctly [see Potts 1988]), the burden of Conscience's indictment is against those charged with proper instruction of the laity: the clergy. An adequate public conscience requires an adequate public moral understanding. As Lawler (2003:88) notes, the accusations here return to the abuses of parish priests, now those who have left their flocks to become custodians of popular shrines in terms that mislead lay worshippers to the priests' own profits; the abuses are also those of **prelates** in charge of such shrines. Both groups directly or indirectly **soffren** the laity worshipping at the shrine to commit **ydolatrie** and **vntrewe sacrefice, That lewed men in mysbileue lyuen and dyen** (96, 98, 101–2). The repeated emphasis on **soffren** and **soffraunce** (96, 101, 119, 124) implies a sin of omission, a dereliction of teaching and chastisement of just the sort that Conscience himself presents; the priestly sin of tolerating sin is a point particularly emphasized elsewhere in C (see below 124n). This is further amplified by the further repetition of the word in the exemplum of Ophni and Phinees, who **suffred** the children of Israel to sin without rebuke (107–10). The wealth of shrines provides another kind of sin, covetousness, **þe tol** (98) that **profiteþ ʒow into pursward** (101), a point that is implied as well in the sins of Ophni and Phineas (see below).

Conscience's role in demanding such proper guides to understanding is emphatically judicial, a glimpse of the role that Conscience will also occupy in debating Meed in passus 3. Thus C here as elsewhere stresses a legal force and posture, distinctly more prominently and technically than does B, and that version more than does A (thus Kirk 1933, considering this issue from the viewpoint of the multi-author question; on the question of legal style in B and C, see also Galloway 2001b). The legal structure and setting of Conscience's speech in the Prologue is also in accord with medieval emphases on conscience in institutional legal proceedings, a focus that by Richard II's reign was leading increasing numbers of law cases that could not be solved by common law precedence to be passed to Chancery, where the chancellor was able to offer a subjective ruling based "not on precedent, but on the circumstances of each case" (Beilby 1990:73), in a procedure that by the sixteenth century was formalized into equity justice, carried out in "a court of conscience." It is also likely that petitioners' shift to Chancery in this period was due to the more effective machinery that Chancery had for bringing offenders into court, for the subpoena "was not limited by restrictions of venue and privilege; it could be used to summon parties for offences committed at sea and could penetrate the great franchises" (Avery 1969:141).

Canonists from the late twelfth century on emphasized the priority of conscience over the judgment of any legal system; in one passage the influential commentator Hostiensis says that if "in the judgment of the soul" (*in iudicio animae*) a man knows he is acting rightly, he should tolerate excommunication passed against him "in the judicial forum" (*in foro . . . iudiciali*), since no one should act against conscience (*Summa aurea* iv, tit. *de cland. despon.*, no. 3, quoted by Helmholz 1974:63). By the later Middle Ages, judges frequently invoked the "law of conscience" to settle legal cases where other kinds of law, especially common law, were in conflict or deemed inadequate (for examples, see Baker and Milsom 1986:61–4, 66, 96, 104); by the sixteenth century there were complaints about the arbitrary and socially disruptive nature of so many judgments made "by conscience" (Baker and Milsom 1986:103–4). For the general indication of support for equity law in the poem, see 4.5–7n.

The poem's emphasis on the legal and morally authoritative function of this figure in the C Prologue is, then, at once traditional, topical, and timeless, part of an increasing emphasis on court procedures pursuing justice outside statute or common law, part of a strong concern in PP and elsewhere with the clergy's proper instruction of the laity, and also a presentation of a fundamental element of Christian ethics and the forces that, sooner or later, are expressed in Christian history. For other points in the Prologue where the C version emphasizes the role of Conscience, and perhaps points to the growth of equity procedures, see lines 140, 149, 157; and see 21.5–14n.

95: Consience cam . . . and þe comune herde hit: Wherever Conscience is located here, his words carry force with the popular world if not with the clergy committing such actions. Whether Conscience is already at the king's courts just surveyed seems less clear, since later he goes back with the king "into Court" (160). Probably Conscience is here best seen as unlocated, possibly to be more closely fitted in revision, but possibly a lone and unlocatable voice like that which Conscience has at the ending of the poem (22.380–86). The *Roman de Fauvel*, amidst its condemnation of monks and canons along with other ecclesiastic professions and figures who "curry Fauvel" and are possessed by avarice, declares that "Conscience ne les remort / Comment il sont au siecle mort / Sans avoir propre affection, / Mès tout au contraire redonde: / Mort sont a Dieu et vif au monde / Et mourir font religion" ("Conscience does not remind them how they are dead to the world without having any self-interested feelings, but quite the opposite happens: they are dead to God and alive to the world, and they cause religion to die": ed. Långfors 1914–19, lines 903–8). For other connections in the Prologue to this work, see below, 136–37n.

96–102: "ydolatrie ȝe soffren . . . lewed men in mysbileue lyuen and dyen": the poem's only use of the word **ydolatrie** appears here; the topic was a regular accusation by Wyclif and the Lollards, often linked to pilgrimage, which in the Lollard view led to worship of "þe gaye peyntyng of þe rotun stok and nouȝt þe seynt in whos name it is seett þere" ("Images and Pilgrimages," ed. in Hudson 1978:85; on the parallel between PP and Wyclif here, see Gradon 1980:193–94). Complaints against donations to and worship of images are also widespread in Wycliffite texts (e.g., *On the Twenty-Five Articles* [ed. Arnold 1869–71, vol. 3.454–96], at 463). The **boxes . . . yset forth ybounde with yren** are the strong boxes or pyxes (Latin *pyxides*) placed in shrines near the altar; in earlier times the money and wax given as offerings had been placed directly on the altar, but by the fifteenth century accounts from offering shrines commonly list offerings *de pyxide* (Nilson 1998:105–6). Most surviving pyxes are of oak bound with iron (Nilson 1998:106). Wax was given copiously as well, often of the same size as the ill person being prayed for or a simulacrum of the diseased or injured bodily member (Finucane 1977:95–96), and in value greatly exceeding money offerings (Nilson 1998:135): thus **In menynge of myracles much wex hangeth there**. But **menynge** is empty signification here, as the following line declares: **Al þe world wot wel hit myghte nouȝt be trewe** (100). As often in Middle English writings, especially homilies and chronicles, **lewed men** are discussed here as distinct from the literate community that the narrator or poet assumes as an audience. But the opinion might be indeed somewhat widely shared; after 1400, donations to shrines gradually dropped, after a sharp increase following the Black Death (Nilson 1998:171).

107–23: For Offines synne . . . and Fines or on her fader: Homilists addressing the laity usually took from the story of Ophni and Phinees the point that the two **fals prestis** of 1 Kings (1 Samuel) 1–4, who steal offerings from the church, refer to how fathers should correct their children. For Ely, their father, is usually seen, as here, bringing down God's wrath on all the Israelites because he **suffred hem [Ophni and Phinees] do ille / And chastisid hem noght þerof and nolde noght rebuken hem . . . And al was for vengeance he bet noght his children** (see, e.g., *Handlyng Synne* [ed. Sullens 1983], lines 4919–5044; *Dives et Pauper* (ed. Barnum 1976:324); Bromyard 1484, s.vv. *correptio*, and *ordo clericalis*). But sermons that are more pointed to the clergy, such as visitation sermons or those for audiences including clerical members, and usually preserved in Latin, often present the story as an exemplum of clerical abuse (see Wenzel 1999). Conscience's use follows this second tradition, a rare instance of that in English rather than Latin, and a sign (if one were needed) that PP clearly includes the clergy in its assumed audience (**ȝow prestes** are directly addressed at 118 ff.).

The need for the clergy to guide their flock is a general point of PP, but the question of the poem's speakers' right to utter such denunciation is occasionally raised and never fully settled. The issue of the narrator's right to deliver just rebuke *in propria persona* is debated in his exchange with Leute at 12.24–40a (B.11.84–106a); and Conscience himself later observes that criticism of the powerful is no easy task no matter what one's right: "For so is the world went with hem þat han power / That he þat sayth men sothes is sonnest yblamed" (3.435–36). See also 220–21n below. For an equally bold and direct address to priests see 13.104–7 (B.11.290–93), given further weight in C by a long new passage before it on true poverty (C.13.1–99); for the general theme of the crucial responsibilities of the clergy as spiritual "techares" and the dangers of a corrupt clergy, see 16.242–85 (B.15.89–148). The general point reappears throughout late medieval writing up to the Reformation: see *Everyman* (c. 1495), lines 750–68 (ed. Bevington 1975:959).

The exemplum of Ophni and Phinees appears in most C texts in the metrically and alliteratively loose state printed in the Athlone text; one manuscript, the "Ilchester" manuscript (Univ. of London, MS. S.L V.88), presents improved alliterative lines for the section and certain deeper differences and omissions (RK-C 186–94). The Ilchester text is related to that of MS. Huntington 114, and Scase argues that these witness an independent version of the section circulating before the C version was released in its full form (if indeed that form ever was "full"). Whether, as Scase claims, Ht and J show a prior circulation of this section of C before the whole was completed and released cannot be definitively settled. Hanna views the Ilchester version as a scribal "completion" of what was perceived to be an unfinished part of the poem (Hanna 1996:204–14, as also Pearsall 1981; Russell 1989:176–77, 188n6), but if so, how its revised sections match only those passages that end up as C additions to B remains to be explained (see Galloway 1999:72–74; and Warner 2002:11–13).

The passage in the main C tradition here, very deficient in alliteration, is loosely correct in its distribution of metrical stresses, though no more so than some alliterative prose (e.g., the poor meter of **And for þei were prestis and men of holy chirche** followed by **God was wel þe wrother and took þe raþer vengeance** [116–17]). In this it resembles the late fourteenth- or early fifteenth-century polemical and satirical chain of works known as *Jack Upland, Friar Daw's Reply,* and *Upland's Rejoinder,* which appear in the manuscripts in various combinations or choices of verse and prose: sections that Heyworth prints as prose include such phrases as "Go now forþ frere and fraiste ȝoure clerkis, and grounde ȝou in Goddis lawe, and ȝeue Iacke an answere" (*Jack Upland,* ed. Heyworth 1968:72, lines 407–8); and sections printed as verse include many metrically correct but alliteratively deficient lines, e.g., "Who shal graunten to myn eyen a strong streme of teres / To wailen and to wepyn þe sorwyng of synne . . ." (*Friar Daw's Reply*, ed. Heyworth 1968:73, lines 1–2). Various passages in the Lollard sermons collected by Cigman (1989) intermittently present similar features: e.g., "alle suche [idolators] ben maad blynde or blyndefeld for a tyme, as men pleyen abobbid, for þei beþ bobbid in hire bileue and in hire catel boþe bi suche lepers ouer londe þat libbeþ bi hire lesyngis" (sermon 10/ 302–5, ed. Cigman 1989:113–14; see also above 66–80n, and passus 1 Headnote). Possibly PP's section is not unfinished but an extreme form of C's loosening alliterative style (see Duggan 1990:159n8; and generally Barney 1995a). Perhaps its style was chosen here to suit an extemporaneous social complaint and exemplum, nearly a style of roadside preaching, albeit different from the crafted imagistically rich style of Holy Church in the next passus and indeed different from what is flagged most distinctly as homiletic discourse elsewhere in the poem (e.g., by Repentance [C.7.122ff. (B.5.478ff.)]; Hunger [C.8.205ff. (B.6.198ff., A.7.185ff.]; Scripture [C.12.42ff. (B.11.108ff.)]).

124: shrewed soffraunce: "Evil acceptance of others' sins" (as distinct from, but condemned equally with, **ʒoure oune synne**). The evils of tolerance are particularly pertinent to those holding power, whether of spiritual or secular kinds. This and two other passages in C suggest special attention to this sin: "vnsittyng soffraunce" appears as a fleeting figure at C.3.208 (see 3.203–10n) and C.4.189 (see 4.187–90n).

126–27 (B 98–99): drede is at þe laste / Lest crist in constorie acorse of ʒow manye: The first reference in the poem to the Apocalypse, **þe laste**, the end of history when all will be resurrected and be sent to eternal salvation or damnation; the framework might have suggested the apocalyptic touch of having Conscience "accuse" all (see above 95–135n). This and a later reference to the Apocalypse in part also prepare the poem for its own presentation of that time in the narrator's last dream-vision (22/B.19.51–386; see also 3.437–83). The absence of the line from A may indicate A's lack of visions after the third. Yet the reference point is commonplace in any case; *Wynnere and Wastoure* refers to "dredfull Domesdaye . . . at the laste when ledys bene knawen" (ed. Trigg 1990, lines 16, 29).

constorie: The image of Last Judgment is based on Matt. 25:31–46, when Jesus in glory will sit on his throne of glory and condemn (**acorse**) the "goats" for their dismissive and proud treatment of him in life. Consistory court usually referred to a bishop's court, over which the bishop's administrator the *officialis* presided, as distinct from the bishop's personal court, the Court of Audience; its verdict could be appealed only at the Court of Arches (MED 1;

Morris 1963:155; cp. Alford, *Gloss.* s.v. *constorie*, who says that no appeal from consistory could be made). The thirteenth-century *Mirror of Justices*, an imaginative treatise preserved in a London custumal and covering a variety of moral and legal views, describes Jesus' challenge to the pursuers of the woman caught in adultery (John 8) as a moment when "God made himself judge in his consistory" ("dieu [se] fist juge en consistoire"); but the *Mirror*'s author adds, "to give us a perpetual example that there can be no lawful judgment without three persons—judge, plaintiff, defendant—God told her to go without a day [i.e., to be acquitted], since it does not pertain to a judge to act as both judge and party" (ed. Whittaker 1895:43). See also 3.473n.

128–38 (cp. B 100–111): I parsceyued of þe power . . . for holi kirke sake": The first two sentences of this section are taken over intact from B, the first sentence presenting the ideal, the second the reality of the offices of cardinals and pope. With C's new sentence at 138, these statements are then either framed as part of Conscience's speech or—if the voice of the preceding passage is understood to have shifted back to the narrator's as in B—seconded by Conscience. RK-C's punctuation asserts the first interpretation, but no certainty is possible here since the matter of speech tags is related to the larger question of how distinctly realized "character" in the poem is at any given point, and how separate a character's direct discourse might be from the narrator's words. If the whole section is understood to be Conscience's, it retains a denouncing tone quite different from later speeches attributed more securely to that character in the poem; compare C.15.

In offering first an ideal for the social estate thereafter portrayed, this section marks a turning point: so far, the Prologue has defined estates by present observation of them first "as they are" (albeit in a perspective moving between sensory detail and moral perspective: see above 22–94n). At this point, the rhythm or direction of emphasis shifts to positing ideal bases for social roles, a presentation persisting from here through the section describing the founding of the commonwealth (line 159 in C).

128–33 (cp. B 100–106): I parsceyued of þe power . . . in kynedom to close with heuene: As the opening of the Prologue has defined social callings by large principles of moral commitments, so here the papacy and the papal court are defined by large moral concepts and traditions. The pope is not mentioned as such. Instead, the principle behind the office of pope is described: the transmitted **power . . . / To bynde and vnbynde**, invoking Matt. 16:19: "And I will give to you [Peter] the keys of the kingdom of heaven. And what you shall bind upon earth, it shall be bound also in heaven: and whosoever you shall

loose on earth, it shall be loosed also in heaven." This foundation for the papacy's claims of authority dates from Leo I's claims in the mid-fifth century and
is restated in, for example, Gratian, Dist. 21 *ante* c. 1, "Petrum vero quasi in
summum sacerdotem elegit, dum ei prae omnibus et pro omnibus claves regni
celorum tribuit et a se petra, Petri sibi nomen imposuit" ("he chose Peter as
the highest priest, whereby he before all and on behalf of all granted to him
the keys of the kingdom of heaven and he imposed the name of Peter for him
from the word for rock"; ed. Friedberg 1959; for Leo I, see Ullmann 1975:22–
28). Leo I defined the pope's "power" as a *plenitudo potestatis*—with both universal jurisdictional and more local ordinational features—but even from this
early date a distinction was made between the right of Peter to hold such
power, and the right of his successors to wield it (Ullmann 1975:25–26).

That distinction was made absolute by the Lollards, who denied the pope
any legitimate spiritual authority over the whole church on the basis of Ephesians 1:22, Colossians 1:18, and 1 Corinthians 3:11; e.g., "The Thirty-Seven Conclusions," article 21: "Cristen men ben not holden for to belieue þat þe bishop
of Rome þat nowe lyueþ in þis peynful lijf is heed of al holy chirche in erþe.
Þis sentence is open by þis, þat Crist alone is heed of holy chirche, as Poule
seiþ . . . if þe pope chalengiþ þis dignite to hym, he is a blasfemer and Lucifer
and antecrist" (ed. Hudson 1978:122). In turn, such attacks on the office of the
pope led to more extreme formulations of the pope's "infallible" status, a view
that earlier was far from universal (see Tierney 1972:83). See further at 21.182–
90n, 21.182–86n, and 21.413–23n.

This **power** (**it**) is left in the "keeping" of **loue** (130 [B 102]), which then
is called **Amonge foure vertues most vertuous of vertues** (131 [B 103]), introducing the question of what ethical principles justify the existence of cardinals.
The phrase likely depends on Augustine's assertion that the four cardinal virtues of prudence, justice, fortitude, and temperance are at bottom expressions
of God's love (or the love of God): "for that virtue that is called four-fold, is
said to be, as far as I understand, from a certain varying affection of God's
love. For those four virtues—and would that their strength were in our minds
as their names are in all our mouths!—I would not hesitate to define in that
way: namely, temperance is the whole love offering itself to that which is loved;
strength, a love easily bearing all things on account of what is loved; justice, a
love both serving its sole beloved and ruling rightly; prudence, a love wisely
distinguishing between those things by which it is helped and those by which
it is hindered" ("namque illud quod quadripartita dicitur uirtus, ex ipsius [i.e.,
dei] amoris uario quodam affectu, quantum intelligo, dicitur. itaque illas qua-
tuor uirtutes, quarum utinam ita sit in mentibus uis, ut nomina in ore sunt
omnium, sic etiam definire non dubitem, ut temperantia sit amor integrum se

praebens ei quod amatur; fortitudo, amor facile tolerans omnia propter quod amatur; iustitia, amor soli amato seruiens, et propterea recte dominans; prudentia, amor ea quibus adiuuatur ab eis quibus impeditur, sagaciter seligens": Augustinus, *De moribus ecclesiae catholicae et de moribus Manichaeorum*, chap. 15, PL 32:1322).

Augustine's point, and this passage declaring it, appear in every major discussion of the four cardinal virtues from at least the twelfth century on: those of Philip the Chancellor, Albert the Great, and Thomas Aquinas, and vernacular recastings of those (for the scholastic sources, see the texts assembled and translated in Houser 2004: Philip the Chancellor, *Summa de bono*; Albert the Great, *Summa Parisiensis*, Part 6, Tr. 1, art. 1; and his *In tres sententias*, d. 33, art. 1; Aquinas, *Quaestio disputata de virtutibus cardinalibus*, art. 1; for all these, see Houser 2004; see also *The Book of Vices and Virtues*, ed. Francis 1942:124). From this tradition **Loue** thus appears here for the first time in B and C as a distantly glimpsed personification, who later occasionally speaks and even sings (see 3.379n), but here is no more personified than the "lok of loue" (1.197): like that notion, which releases grace, **loue** here is entrusted with a sacred keeping, rather than a doing. For the elusive entity Love elsewhere in the poem, see 1.153–58n, 1.196–97n. As Schmidt notes, **vertues** conflates two senses of *vertue*: 'powers' and 'moral excellence' (OED 1, 2), an ambiguity played out when the actual cardinals are described who, Schmidt notes, mistake their power for the original power of moral excellence (Schmidt 1987: 120–21).

132–33 (cp. B 104–6): That Cardinales ben cald and closyng ȝates/ Thare Crist . . . to close with heuene [B: That Cardinals ben called and closynge yates / There crist is in kyngdom, to close . . and heuene blisse shewe]: A gated heaven is a venerable topos, based again on Matt. 16:19, as well as typical understanding of Psalm 99:4 ("go ye into his gates with praise [*in confessione*]"; see, e.g., *La Voie de paradis*, sec. 63, "*confiteor* . . . euvre la porte de Paradis qui est close au pecheeur . . . laquele porte touz les sainz et toutes les saintes de Paradis ne peüssent autrement ouvrir que par confession"; in the Middle English translation, "'I me schryue' . . . openyth the ȝates of Paradys that arn schet to synful man . . . the whiche ȝates alle the seyntes of men and wemmen of Paradys ne mow non otherwyse openen than be confession": ed. Diekstra 1991:136–37). The metaphor is elaborated by use of the etymology of *cardinalis* from *cardo*, 'hinge.' In their discussions of the cardinal virtues, Albert the Great and Aquinas both invoke this etymology (Albert the Great, *Summa Parisiensis*, part 6, Tr. 1, art. 2; Aquinas, *Quaestio disputata de virtutibus cardinalibus*, art. 1, resp.; see Houser 2004:123–24, 162–63): Albert comments that "these four [virtues] are called cardinal because they are like a hinge for the principal acts of the motive powers of the soul, to which the acts of the other virtues are connected, as to a hinge"; Aquinas elaborates the image in terms that suggest the source for the passage in PP: the term cardinal is taken from *cardo*, "the hinge on which a door turns, as in Proverbs [26:14], 'As a door turns on its hinges, so does a sluggard on his bed.' Therefore, we call those virtues cardinal on which a human way of life is founded, and through which as through a door one proceeds . . . [Res. to Obj. 4]: [But] wisdom, since it is not about human but divine matters, has no subject-matter in common with the moral virtues. Therefore, it cannot be counted along with the moral virtues so as to be denominated with them a cardinal virtue, because the very notion of 'doorhinge (*cardo*)' is inconsistent with contemplation. Contemplation is not like a door, by means of which one goes somewhere else. Rather, moral deeds are the door through which one enters into the contemplation of wisdom" (the last is a notion Aquinas equates with being in the presence of God).

The use of *cardo* to explain cardinal virtues is found in other works of moral theology; see also the thirteenth-century confessors' manual, the *Summa virtutum de remediis anime* (ed. Wenzel 1984:55). More often, the metaphor is used to describe the cardinals, key figures of church and papal governance, whose mention in the next line is anticipated here; in 1054 Pope Leo IX used the metaphor for the definition of cardinals, that the papal see is the head and "hinge" of the universal church: "Like the immovable hinge that sends the door forth and back, thus Peter and his successors have the sovereign judgment over the entire Church . . . Therefore his clerics are named cardinals, for they belong more closely to the hinge by which everything else is moved" (quoted in Kuttner 1945:176).

134–37 (B 107–10): Ac of þe Cardinales at Court . . . þe grete eleccoun: Ac introduces the narrator's shift to the dubious ethics of actual cardinals; these individuals have merely **caught . . . such a name**: that is, they do not possess the substance or *res* beneath the *nomen*, in medieval philosophical terminology. The slippage between the cardinal virtues and the cardinal deacons of the pope is registered again by the irony in the speech of the "lewd vicar" (see 21.409–64 [B.19.409–58]); a similar sense of revulsion at the blurring between cardinal virtues and human cardinals is evident in the Wycliffite "Thirty-Seven Conclusions," article 21, which asks rhetorically "wheþer þe vicious and vnkunnynge colegie of fleishly cardynals shal ȝeue more grace and holynesse to a worldly prest, chosen of hem by fleisly eiþer worldly affeccioun, þan Crist, God almyȝtti, ȝaf to Iudas, chosen of hym by souereyn wisdam and goodnesse and loue to al holy chirche, his spouse?" (in Hudson 1978:123). The most notable and controversial **eleccoun** of a pope in the later fourteenth century was that of Urban VI at Rome, which quickly led to the counter-election of Clement VII by French cardinals at Avignon in 1378, instigating the Great Schism which lasted until 1417. The reference here is often taken as dating the B text after 1378; as Hanna notes (1993:13–14), this is the latest potential date-marker for B.

Yet specific reference to the Great Schism of 1378 is not certain. The English attacked many an earlier pope (and hence attacked the election of those popes), especially the French ones, and some cardinals were notorious enemies to the English well before the Schism, such as Cardinal Talleyrand de Perigord, called in 1343 in Parliament "le plus fere Enemye que soit en la Courte, et plus contrair a les busoignes nostre Seigneur le Roi" ("the most fierce enemy that there might be in court, and the most opposed to the business of our lord the king" [Rot. Parl. 2.144; see also Pantin 1955:82]). While a post-1378 date for B seems likely, secure dates should not be sought from such evidence; L seems close enough to building sentiments at court and elsewhere to be able to predict events from trends before the fact, as well as allude to them later (see Galloway 2001a). Direct discussions of the Schism in English materials usually focus directly on the scandal of two popes, as commonly in Wycliffite writings (see Gradon and Hudson 1996, vol. 4.99–101 and references there), not the role of cardinals (rather than the cardinal virtues) which PP here focuses on, and which would obtain for any papal election. For clear contemporary comments on the Schism, see Gower, *Confessio Amantis* (ed. Macaulay 1901), Prol.360–77, and his *Mirour de l'Omme* (ed. Macaulay 1899), lines 18829–40, 19024–32; and see Harvey 1983.

The disapproval of cardinals in PP is due to their presumption of the **power . . . in hemself a pope to make / To haue þe power þat Peter hadde**, a power just identified as in the keeping of "love," conferred on Peter but with no indication that he had the power to transmit it further: that authority was love's. Cardinals were granted the right exclusively to elect popes by the Third Lateran Council of 1179 (Southern 1970:152–55). But Peter is not describing as "presuming" his power (i.e., 'seize without right,' MED *presumen* 3) but 'having' it "to kepe" (128, cp. 136). The critique may reflect the traditional, even formulaic distinction between Peter's right to his power and that of his "unworthy" heirs, a distinction first articulated by Leo I in the fifth century and sustained in the rhetoric of the pope as *indignus haeres* (Ullmann 1975:25–26). But the criticism seems more pointed than that general topos; perhaps it reflects a general English discontent with invasive Roman officials. Compare the portrayal of simoniacal cardinals in Gower's *Mirour de l'Omme* (ed.

Macaulay 1899), lines 18841–19056 (just after mentioning the Schism). Some twelfth-century homiletic poems such as the *Vers de la Mort* also criticize cardinals (the *Vers de la Mort* punningly compares the name "chardonal" to "charbon" [charcoal] and "chardon" [thistles], "wherefore they take their name" ["Et por ce ont chardonal non": stanza xiv, ed. Wulff and Walberg 1905, who note other instances of these puns in twelfth-century poetry, 1905:v]).

136–37 (B 109–10): inpugne y nelle: The lines are surely an ironic invitation to "impugnen" or "counterplead" the issue of the pope's power further (on evasions of responsibility in satiric writing, see Simpson 1990a); compare Holy Church's more direct satire of the pope, 2.23n. The *Roman de Fauvel* presents a similar grave protestation about satire against the pope at an analogous spot in its estates satire—just where it is about to attack the Roman pope most emphatically: "Mès je fais protestacion / Que ce n'est pas m'entencion / D'aleir contre l'ennour de Romme, / A qui doit obeïr tout homme" ("but I emphasize that it is not my intention to go against the honor of Rome, which every man must obey": ed. Långfors 1914–19, lines 99–102). The closeness of the parallel suggests the possibility that the expansion of A into B involved the poet's return to a source he had already used for his first version (see above, 20n); and, if the slighter indication of a parallel at C 95 is a further sign of use (see 95n), he again consulted that source for his final revision. Such an indication of his personal library is wholly speculative, but it usefully supplements the religious service books shown in the narrator's self-portrait of himself carrying out his everyday spiritual "labor" in C.5.45–47.

138: "Contreplede hit noght," quod Consience, "for holi kirke sake" / B 111: Forþi I kan . . . speke more: C's phrase, whether punctuated as an intrusive corroboration by Conscience—that is, set off with quotation marks at the beginning of 135—or as the final comment of what has been throughout Conscience's speech from 96 (see 95–135nn), consorts ill with Conscience's immediately preceding condemnation of those who "nolde noght rebuken" the sinful laity and with Conscience's own rebuke of such complacent clergy, and it shows how delicately balanced is the voice of rebuke against the voice of restraint throughout the Prologue especially, and the poem as a whole; see, e.g., above 76–78n. The line replaces B's evasive and teasing statement (see also above 136–37n). Conscience's advice in C that the listeners (and perhaps the poem's readers) should **Contreplede hit noght** does not deny problems with any one election, but more earnestly urges listeners not to press any public complaint. This may be a specific appeal **for holi kirke sake** not to exacerbate further the divisiveness within the Universal Church that the Schism had already generated, or it may be a general appeal not to condemn the clergy openly before the laity. For the poem's concerns about discussing particular or "privy" sins publicly, see the qualifications at 12.27–40a (B.11.86–106a).

The founding of the commonwealth

139–59 (cp. B 112–38): Thenne cam ther a kyng . . . "de pietate metas": From theory of ecclesiological power, springing from estates satire on religious orders, the narrator shifts to theory of kingship; together, these two topics occupied intellectuals and polemicists from early medieval centuries, often in the context of glosses on Romans 13:1–7 and the "two swords" of Luke 22:38 (see Robinson 1988:288–305). This bipartite concept of social order often coexists with a tripartite concept of estates. For obvious reasons, however, kings do not typically appear as instances of "estates satires," where they would be criticized against an ideal; B's folding in of the coronation and definition of kingship is an instance of the poet's bold effort to reconceive all society as well as the genre that the Prologue has taken up. Within other kinds of medieval writing, the topics of whether royal or papal power was dominant received intense development, especially from the late eleventh century and the "investiture controversy," and both kinds of power received much attention in the thirteenth and fourteenth centuries, notably those by Giles of Rome, Duns Scotus, and Wyclif. Indeed, the two topics are inextricably related; works on the scope of papal power imply a view of, and therefore must often explicitly treat, the scope of royal power and vice versa. Both focus on the issue of sovereignty.

L's topic here is broader than rule, however; it encompasses, with a recapitulation of ultimate origins, the founding of the *communitas regni* as well, and it does so with greater focus on this goal in C than in B (A lacks the entire section). C eliminates some of the notably controversial figures introduced in B: the Lunatic, the Angel, and the Goliard, who all speak portions of the principles or "lessons" to the king about kingship. The chronicler Thomas Walsingham describes a pageant for Richard II on the day before his coronation including an encounter with a mechanical "golden angel" that bowed and offered him a crown (see Walsingham, *Historia Anglicana*, ed. Riley 1863, vol. 1.331–32; *Chronicon Angliae* ed. Thomson 1874:153–56; the latter is conveniently translated, along with another account from the *Anonimalle Chronicle*, in Carlson and Rigg 2003, appendix 2; see also Barron 1999:150–51, Kipling 1998:6–47, 115–81).

The king's "reconciliation" with London in 1392 after the conflict between the king and the city, according to Richard Maidstone, included a "tower" in Cheap suspended in the air with ropes, on which stood a crowned woman and a young man dressed as an angel; the ceremony included the presentation of a tablet mentioning the king's virtue of *pietas* (that is, pity and forgiveness), in a plea for reconciliation since he had punished the City for refusing to lend him money (see Carlson and Rigg 2003; Galloway 2002:93–94). Such pageants constituted the most theatrical expression of an idealized social contract between king and people (and perhaps fed the king's expectations that this contract would always involve the latter's submission).

C distances itself from the spectacle of such a public celebration by shifting the speeches by the Lunatic, Angel, and Goliard to the more abstract and psychological entities Kind Wit and Conscience, and by other adjustments so that B 112–45 is compressed to C 139–59. C also advances the sergeants of law from after the Rat Parliament at B 211–16 (= C 160–66; see n) to follow the section here describing the role of kingship and the foundation of the commonwealth. Law is thereby made more visible as a founding element both in the speeches and in the social institutions that should be carrying it out.

139–47 (cp. B 112–21): Thenne cam ther a kyng . . . while lif on londe lasteth: Thenne cam is the poem's typical formula for introducing new characters and, usually, an entirely new situation and set of topics (see 3.27 [B.3.26, A.3.25], 4.42–45 [B.4.44–47, A.4.31–34]; 6.196 [B.5.188, A.5.107]; 7.1 [B.5.385, cp. A.5.213]; 15.25, 32, 42, 59 [B.13.22, 34, 37]; 20.35 [B.18.36]; 21.200–202, 360, 465 [B.19.199–202, 360, 465]; 22.121, 129 [B.20.121, 129]). The phrase suggests both a perpetual condition of surprising arrivals or unpredictable changes of topic, and a continuous processional movement to the whole, in keeping with the principle of a passus as a continuous "pace" or "step" (see Headnote, and below). The formula is a simple strategy to allow seemingly endless and unmotivated shifts and arrivals of characters, and is surely useful for inserting new sections in revision as here; but since the scenes that assemble by this means are inevitably meaning and dramatic, the phrase deftly forces the reader to grope for the meaning and full implications of each new arrival, situation, and topic. It is a form of dramatic parataxis, requiring the reader to supply the syntax of interpretation, association, and connection to other moments in the poem.

Up to the advisory speeches to the king—introducing the king, Kind Wit, and the commune, and (in C) deploying Conscience for the first time as the king's agent (or perhaps the abstract governing principle of the king's office, a personal faculty rather than any external constraint)—the section is nearly identical in C and B, with the significant exception of the change from B's **Might of þe communes made hym to regne** (B 113) to C's **Myght of tho men**

made hym to regne (C 140), and the replacement of the subject-agents in the first line of B's statement that **The kyng and knyȝthod and clergie boþe / Casten þat þe commune sholde hire communes fynde** (B 116–17) with C's **Conscience & kynde wit and knyghthed togedres** (C 143). Baldwin notes that placing **þe communes** in the contract with the king in B parallels Bracton's contractual claims about kingship, and Baldwin argues that C's change there parallels C's omissions of other moments of contractual kingship, B 122 and 141–42 (see below B 122n, B 139–40n). "In the C-text of the 'Coronation Scene,' the 'commune' is given no political power: it neither makes the king reign . . . nor helps make the law" (Baldwin 1981:15).

The absolutist implications here have a deep basis in late medieval legal theory by civil lawyers and commentators (post-commentators, as they are called in this period), who effected a shift generally in defining sovereignty, from doing so in terms of law and custom to doing so in terms of will. "By the middle of the fourteenth century, a new doctrine of authority had emerged in the writings of the jurists that penetrated every crack and crevice of the *ius commune*," Pennington claims; "for the old norms of custom, feudal obligations, honor, loyalty, reason, and tradition [the jurists] exchanged cause, necessity, and the public good" (1993:119). The relationship between these ideas of sovereignty as defined by law or custom, and as defined by will and the public good, remains as complex in both B and C as in any of the jurists of the period, but a general shift in accord with the emerging thought Pennington describes can be noted in the Prologue. The stanza that the Angel speaks in B, and Conscience in C, epitomizes the emerging focus on "cause, necessity, and the public good" (see below 152n). As Baldwin characterizes C's shift, "human laws [are not] given authority over the king; they are not even mentioned. The advice the king is left with puts no political restraints upon him, but only moral and religious ones. Indeed it encourages him to take full responsibility for the social justice of his kingdom, *whether or not* he acts through law" (1981:15; her emphasis). Absolutism, of a morally ideal ruler, is one solution to such demands, but, pursued far enough, the need for perfect morality in fulfiling such an ideal can lead to disenchantment about kingship as such (see Galloway, forthcoming), just as PP focuses on the evils of tyranny near the end of the poem (see below 20.417–41n). Richard II's most extreme claims of absolutism from the 1390s follow somewhat similar lines of argument, especially his claims from civil law concerning the king's power, including his notorious claim reported at his deposition that the law is in the king's mouth (see Saul 1999); the extent to which PP might have contributed to such later political arguments remains unexplored.

The presentation here follows something like a processional display of the traditional "three estates" of much medieval social theory—but the procession is the procession of historical creation of social order: first appear the king and knighthood (*bellatores*), then the clerks (*oratores*), then the commons and "peple" (*laboratores*) (see above, 19–21n). As noted above, a "functionalist" tripartite social analysis was common in the fourteenth century, showing the need for all three estates (see above 22–94n). Presenting the historical *emergence* of such estates is far less common; in the historicized view of the division of the estates and professions, it presents many of the features of the commonplace "decline from the Golden Age" but in terms that look progressively toward improvement, not degeneration (for some fourteenth-century English uses of the tradition of seeing a decline, see Galloway 1996).

The passage portrays social and political interdependency in terms of an intertwining of power and authority—the terms (*potestas* and *auctoritas*) traditionally distinguishing the lay from the ecclesiastical orders. The secular arm—the king and knighthood—is described first, and in terms of **Myght** (compare *potestas*); the clerical arm—Kind Wit and clerks—is described in terms of their ability to **conseillen** (*auctoritas*). An entrenched medieval combination of *fortitudo et sapientia*, "strength and wisdom," is evident, including its particular political form in *auxilium et concilium*, "help and counsel" (see Kaske 1963; Hill 2002). These two kinds of social estate, secular and clerical, are then yoked—as **Conscience & kynde wyt and knyghthed togedres** in C 143, as **The kyng and knyȝthod and clergie boþe** in B 116—to offer technical, craft knowhow to **þe commune** in gaining sustenance, **here communes** (for **kynde wyt** see below, 141–47n). The referent for the possessive seems to include their own food and the food of others (perhaps B's **casteth** 117 more clearly suggests that the commons are to produce food for the military and clerical orders, while C's set of mostly abstract entities leading the commons to learn to produce more clearly suggests they will then produce for themselves as well). Compare Wimbledon: "laboreris . . . geten out of the þe erþe bodily loflode for hem and for oþer parties" (ed. Knight 1967:63). Clopper, who observes that L generally (like Chaucer and Gower in the *Confessio Amantis*) "prefers to begin his images with kings and knights rather than clergy" (1997:153), sees the functions of the social estates here as exemplifying the Trinity's functions of "power" (i.e., the Father), "wisdom" (i.e., the Son), and "goodness" or "benignity" (the Holy Spirit; Clopper 1997:134, 153–54, 166). The political implications of this "exemplarism" and of the passage, Clopper argues, implicitly leave the king, "as a consequence of the Fall," in sole possession of "ownership of all goods and lands" which he "lends to his people," while the clergy are left as counselors only, "without ownership of goods so that they exhibit supremacy in spiritual matters"—a stance consistent with Franciscan ideals of "the absolute separation of civil *dominium* from the highest status of perfection," leaving the clergy only the use of worldly goods (Clopper 1997:153–55, 163, 166). The "commons," whose name already elevates them to a special claim on authority, are by this analogy granted the unusual authority of being repositories of the Holy Spirit and the receptacles of God's grace. For a recapitulation of the need for "crafts," and for its divine distribution, see C.21/B.19 and notes, especially 213–14n, 213–57n, 229–51n.

139–40 (cp. B 112–13): Thenne cam ther a kyng . . . made hym to regne: The general concept that kingship depends on the **Myght** of subordinates has a long lineage, although how this dependency is realized is highly variable. In a tenth-century Anglo-Saxon homily, Ælfric, prior of Evesham, declares in a simile that just as the people have the power to choose the king but then are bound to obey him, so one is free to choose sin but then is bound by it (see Godden 1987). In the "Addicio de cartis" in the thirteenth-century *De legibus et consuetudinibus angliae*, "Bracton" (or one of the other hands apparently responsible for the work known as Bracton's) declares that the king's counts and barons are his "partners" (*socii*) and ought, if the king is "without a bridle, that is, without law," to put a bridle on him (*Et ideo si rex fuerit sine fraeno, id est sine lege, debent ei fraenum apponere*; see Bracton, trans. and ed. Thorne and Woodbine 1968, vol. 2.109–10; for discussion see Nederman 1988:415–29; Baldwin 1981:13–14). The mid-thirteenth century saw the first convening of Parliament on a semi-regular basis (see also 4.45n), and in the fourteenth century two kings were deposed by the barons. The coronation *ordo* of the fourteenth century reflects, to be sure, a contract between ruler and ruled: from Edward II on, the *ordo* included the formal question to the king, "Sire, graunte vous à tenir et garder les Loys, et les Custumes droitureles, les quiels la Communauté de vostre Roiaume aura esleu . . . ?" ("sire, do you agree to uphold and protect the rightful laws and customs that the community of your realm will choose?", quoted by Donaldson 1966:106). As Donaldson notes, however, the king's essential contract in all versions of PP, as in medieval law and culture in general, is not with the people or the barons but with law (see Donaldson 1966:106–7).

The official account of Richard II's coronation in June 1377 in which the king arrived "una cum ingenti multitudine Procerum Magnatum Militum et Armigerorum in secta sua se circumdancium," "along with an enormous multitude of barons, magnates, knights, and esquires surrounding him in his following," offers "an almost exact equivalent" of the descriptive first line here (Donaldson 1966:116). The section in PP is political and social theory rather than topical reportage, but the possibilities of the latter have dominated discussion here. The identification of an allusion here to Richard II begins with Tyrwhitt, who thought it referred to the period after the Black Prince's death on June 8, 1376, and before Richard's accession a year later (so Skt, who thereby dates B to this narrow range). Bennett first aligned the line with Richard's coronation and thereby opened the date of the B text to the period sometime after June 1377 (1943b:57). The argument for such a dating and such a topical poetics for the B text is helped (but not proven) by the reference to a young king at B 193–95a—*Vae terre ubi puer est Rex* (see below, 206–9n). But when all these passages are carried over into the C text it is difficult to say how well they can sustain such topical interest. By the late 1380s, if that is C's date, the focus had shifted to the antagonism between the king and his nobles, especially the lords appellant (see Saul 1997:176–204).

That shift may account for C's small change for the basis for the king's regnal power from B's **Might of þe communes** to **Myght of tho men**; or that may respond to contemporary readings of the poem which saw it as extolling too broadly the powers of the "commons." Whatever the reasons for the change, the new demonstrative pronoun refers to **knyghthede**, producing a statement that is more politically specific and focused on the group of higher nobility around the king. These were increasingly important in Richard's reign, from their regency period when Richard was crowned at age 10, monitored by the council appointed by the Good Parliament, through their impeachment of his chancellor in 1386 and the toppling of his government in 1388, to the special supervisory council that the higher nobility imposed that year to monitor his household expenditures and other actions (see e.g., Tuck 1974; Saul 1997). C.4 ends with Reason's careful selection of such councillors, an addition to B (see 4.195–96n). The connotations of "commons" shift in the period between the narrow sense of the "commons" in Parliament—the minor gentry who were increasingly submitting parliamentary petitions to the king's council, the higher nobles who, with the king, dominated parliament— and the broader sense of the coronation *ordo* and elsewhere, of the "community" of the realm as a whole (see below, 169n). Donaldson argued that L's usage of **commune** is in the B passage a general one, referring "not to that group which we associate with the House of Commons but to the whole commonwealth" (1966:106). If so, C here suggests a more realist view of oligarchical parliament and central government. See also 21.213–14n.

141–47 (cp. B 114–22): kynde wytt: Following the king in procession, **kynde wytt** constitutes the first allegorical agent in B; in C he—or it—is preceded by Conscience, yet even in C, **kynde wytt** exhibits a more dramatic presence and more powerful agency than Conscience, who in this passus merely "accuses."

The A text does not introduce **kynde wytt** until A.1.53, where this principle occupies a role in good management; however, A introduces **kynde wytt** in the role of a creator of a kind of society at the end of passus 3, where its power is conceived as an apocalyptic renovation of the present world (see 1.51n; 3.452n). In B and C, **kynde wytt**'s action of "making" clerks is followed by the more ambitious action of contriving **alle craftes** (145; on which see passus 21), capped, in C only, by a speech to the king on his duties (149–52), a speech attributed to the "clergial" Lunatic in B (B 125–27). **kynde wytt** here thus constitutes in some measure an organizing, creative principle behind all the crafts discussed in the Prologue, a founding capability instanced in C as making **a plogh** as **for most profit to þe peple**—that is, as the economic basis of society broadly and most archaically considered. In B the commune is the agent, acting "by means of Kind Wit" (**contreued of kynde wit**), and ordaining plow-*men* rather than the tool of the plow. C's Kind Wit thus allows a more specifically technological force in society to be emphasized rather than a social estate. The interest is typical of the period; Herlihy (1997) argues that the Black Death was a widespread instigator of technology to replace manpower, and generally the period saw a rise of intellectual and technical specialization (see Galloway 1996).

"Kynde" can mean 'natural,' 'grateful,' 'that which pertains to one's kin,' 'generous,' 'authentic,' or 'proper'; L's use of the word and of its cognates exploits much of this range and, hence, has occasioned much scholarship. The meanings of the locution **kynde wytt** in particular seem to shift in the poem and between the versions. Although in this passage it appears aligned with or fundamental to "clergie," later it seems distinguished from Christian teaching by being strictly the attribute of natural or naturally acquired intellectual knowledge (14.17 [B.12.55]), the *sapientia huius mundi* displayed by pagan philosophers (14.70–88a [cp. B.12.127–38a]), and in a simpler form by animals (14.157 [implied in the rest of the parallel B passage, B.12.222–30]). **kynde wytt** is clearly crucial for human ingenuity, as in the basic ability to use tools or construct buildings or perform more complex "crafts." Yet **kynde wytt** can, although it need not always, possess a strongly moral valence: after Reason's speech against Meed, **kynde wytt** ratifies Reason's judgment (4.151–59n); in the case of Piers himself, **kynde wytt** is a teacher who is clearly distinct from the book-learning sense of "clergie"; along with Conscience he is Piers' guide to Truth (7.184 [B.5.539, A.6.27]). Ymaginatif explains the idea as knowledge derived from sense experience and then transmitted by teaching to subsequent generations (14.72–80 [B.12.129–32]); its appearance as a guide to the structure of society and of economics (1.48–53nn) might be understood as based ultimately and *historically* on simply sensory knowledge, but clearly exceeds this scope in the powers it displays in the poem. The closeness of such a function to an innate connection to God is clear in the next passus, especially via its close cognate, "kind knowing" (see 1.78n, 137–38n, 141–45n). (For important discussions, see White 1988:3–40; Quirk 1953; Carruthers 1973:54; Harwood 1976; Morgan 1987.) Ultimately, **kynde wytt**'s dispensation of society and its structures (and vulnerability to sin, as in the sins of the professions that it brings into being) will, Conscience implies later, be replaced by an order established by Kind Love (see 3.452n).

B 122: Shopen law and leaute, ech lif to knowe his owene: This line, omitted from C, introduces **leaute** as the creation of "The kyng and þe commune and kynde wit þe thridde" (B 121); on this as an entity see 149–51n below. Their other creation is **law**, paired with **leaute**, and, though created jointly by the king and the commons, thenceforth a binding force on both of them, as the speeches by the Goliard and the Commons below declare (B 139–45 and nn). A parallel passage in C only, 3.374–82 (see nn) was perhaps inserted in tandem with C's omission of this one; there, "Lawe, loue and lewete" are what the "commune" demand of a king (3.379n). Both the B and the later C passages show that **law and leaute** equally bind the king and his subjects; C's later passage adds "love" and elaborates the king's non-partisan role. Here, **law and leaute** are shown created in tandem, and jointly by the king and his subjects: a feature that, as Baldwin notes, characterizes B and is typically suppressed from C (Baldwin 1981:13–15; see also above, 139–40n, 139–47n). For **leaute**, see below 149–51n.

   ech lif to knowe his owene: The phrase echoes Ulpian's definition of justice, quoted at the opening of Justinian's *Institutes*: *justicia est constans et perpetua voluntas jus suum cuique tribuens* ("justice is the constant and continual will to render to each his own right"). The line is often elliptically invoked, as for example in the English king's coronation oath, as *uniquique tribuere quod suum* ("to render each his own") (Alford, *Gloss.* s.v. *his (own)*). As the seventeenth-century political and legal theorist Thomas Hobbes translates and elaborates it, "Justice is the constant will of giving to every Man his own; that is to say, of giving to every Man that which is his Right, in such manner as to Exclude the Right of all men else to the same thing" (*A Dialogue Between a Philosopher and a Student of the Common Laws of England*, ed. Cropsey 1971:72). But **ech lif to knowe** varies the phrase from the maxim's "to render to each," generating a range of interpretations of the sense here. The phrase has been claimed to be a provision for each man to know his place in society (so Donaldson 1966:85–87); to be an evil "lesson" in the self-serving principles of fourteenth-century society ironically antithetical to Christian ideals (so

Robertson and Huppé 1951:27–29, contrasting the phrase to 1 Cor. 10:24, "Nemo quod suum est quaerat," "Let no man seek what is his own," and comparing it to Augustine's condemnation of *amor sui*); and to be a provision for the justness of private property (so Kean 1969:134–35, aligning the phrase with discussions by Aquinas). Of these, Donaldson's general interpretation seems in the present context of a social survey the most plausible, yet Kean's view is supported by other passages in the poem that emphasize the importance of knowing one's rights to property: Kean takes **knowe** as 'acknowledges,' 'accepts' (Kean 1969:135); as possible confirmation of this, the parallel C addition in passus 3 compares the king to a visible boundary marker between properties (3.381–82; see 3.374–82n). Yet again, in a medieval Christian view, private property, albeit grounded in common law, was long held a sign in some measure of original sin, supported by Acts 4:32–35 and other New Testament texs (see Coleman 1988; Pennington 1993:122–32). Thus Robertson and Huppé's sense of the line as indicating a postlapsarian state of being may be valid as well.

148: Thenne kynde witt . . . saide / B 123–24: Thanne loked vp a lunatik . . . clergially he seide: Skt took B's **lunatik** as a persona of L himself (so too Rogers 2002:44), an identification possibly depending on the piety of the "lunatyk lollares" treated in C only (see paragraph below) as well as on Will's similarly marginal social status and similar boldness in addressing the powerful. The **lunatik** who offers a learned ("clergial") address to the king in B recalls many hermits, beggars, fools and minstrels who speak truth in or about court. The early fourteenth-century fabliau "Le Roi d'Angleterre et le Jongleur d'Ely" in MS. Harley 2253, which presents a minstrel answering all the king's questions with paradoxical and scandalous answers (see above, B 33–37n), concludes with the overtly sinful and foolish minstrel offering the king wisdom about reigning wisely: he should not be too cruel or too gullible towards his people, but instead "vus portez meenement" ("maintain the middle ground"); for "um puet oyr sovent / Un fol parler sagement. / Sage est qe parle sagement, / Fols come parle folement" ("one often hears a fool speaking wisely; he is wise who speaks wisely, and foolish who speaks foolishly"; ed. Montaiglon and Raynaud 1877, vol. 2, lines 411–13, 242–27; for the various views of kingship in Harley 2253, see Corrie 2003). In Hoccleve's *Regiment of Princes*, a "foole sage" stands before the king to chide him for having pardoned a murderer (ed. Blyth 1999, lines 3145–57). Late medieval images of a Roman "triumph," associated with medieval royal entries at least by the time of Lydgate, include the figure of a fool accompanying the king and reminding him "know thyself," taken in such contexts to mean recognizing his mortality rather than, as elsewhere, his immortality (Nolan forthcoming, chapter 4). Here, in B, the **lunatik** is paired dramatically with an angel, and C's omission of both acknowledges their somehow linked or contrasted identities as principles of advice to a king (see below, 152n).

C's substitution of **kynde witt**, while a less scandalous adviser to a king, confirms that the speaker is meant to provide advice from outside the courtly world, like those of most of the speakers to the king in the B Prologue. As C's replacement speaker, **kynde witt** is a counselor to the king but is also associated with the clergy's knowledge and with the people's crafts and technology, neither possessing courtly associations. Inserting **kynde witt** here offers some further development in C of this figure, who speaks nowhere else in the poem as an allegorical personification, although referred to by Holy Church and, in a less personified sense, by Imaginative (1.51–2; 14 passim). Further, omitting the Lunatic may be linked to C's concomitant expansion of "lunatyk lollares" (9.105–38), who are similarly prophetic but playful spokespersons of God's messages; their treatment reveals a more elaborate treatment of the characteristics merely hinted at here.

149–51 (B 125–27): "Crist kepe þe . . . in heuene": The first speech to the king—the Lunatic's in B, retained as Kind Wit's in C—is a benediction rather than criticism (although far from "flattery" [Robertson and Huppé 1951:29]). This speech emphasizes **lewte** as the essential element of royal governance, immediately declaring that one of the principles the king himself has helped establish must govern him as well; the following speakers, the Angel, and in B the Goliard and the Commons, all emphasize law. Although the speech is humble in its assumption that the king *will* live up to these standards and **be rewardid in heuene**, it is bold in using the singular/familiar pronoun "thou," a mode of address allowed to scholarly advisers to royalty in some medieval traditions, including early humanist ones (see Burnley 1990, and 1986; for a more general discussion of the development of a familiar vs. a formal second-person singular pronoun, see Brown and Gilman 1960; see also below, 1.4–5n). Moreover, the speech carries a reminder that the king is subject to God, as Bracton also asserts (e.g., 2.109; trans. and ed. Thorne and Woodbine 1968); more important, it carries the proviso that the king must **lede þy londe so lewte þe louye**.

Lewte (loyalty, fidelity, justice, 'faith' in the sense of 'keeping faith'), based on Latin *legalitas*, is a figure widely important in the poem, although more as a notion in the minds of the poem's speakers than as a personified presence, appearing and speaking only in B.11.85–91. For comment on the evolution of the figure in the poem, see 2.51–52n. The term, which passed from

Latin into the French form that is found in Middle English, retained the associations that it had in French chivalric romance, indicating "faithfulness" and "lawfulness" in a sense appropriate to amorous, social, and finally religious duty. In the mid-thirteenth-century Anglo-Norman romance *Gui de Warewic*, for instance, Gui is praised for this virtue, especially at the end when, with his pious death, the word has a religious as well as a knightly valence:

Fei e lalté tut dis ama,
Sur totes riens Deu honura;
E Deu le gueredun li rendi . . . (11635–37; ed. Ewert 1932)

[He loved faith and lawfulness every day, and honored God in everything; and God rendered to him his reward . . .]

Other important, and similar, instances of this word in Middle English literature include *Cursor Mundi* (ed. Morris 1966, lines 1655–58), where God tells Noah that because of his "leute" he and his children will be saved, and Barbour's *Bruce* (ed. Duncan 1999), 1.365–74, which stresses the preeminent value of the ethic, there defined as "to love wholeheartedly":

Leawté to luff is gretumly, [wholeheartedly]
Throuch leawté liffis men rychtwisly.
With a vertu and leawté
A man may yeit sufficyand be, [still be adequate]
And but leawté may nane haiff price [without "leawté" no one is worthy]
Qether he be wycht or he be wys . . . [Whether he be powerful or wise . . .]

The speech in PP reverses the grammar of the commonplace claim that a proper hero does or must "love 'leauté'" to invoke an active personification that puts the king on notice, "provided that you rule your country in such a way that 'leauté' loves you." As Kean (1969:148–49) points out, **Lewte** in PP means something broader than "keeping faith" to an individual; rather, it means living according to law, and, Kean argues, uniquely in PP means simply "justice" (see also 3.379n). The merging of "loyalty" with "justice" resembles Eccles. 33:3: "a man of understanding is faithful to the law of God: and the law is faithful to him" ("homo sensatus credit legi Dei et lex illi fidelis"). Indeed, Kane suggests that the personification in the phrase here means "your loyal subjects" or even, "more probably," "law-abiding people" (Kane 1989:96–97). But this dismisses the degree of abstraction allowed in PP's personification allegory, which in a more muted way the word possesses throughout its literary history. **Lewte** is the abstract notion, applying to kings and subjects as well as lovers and knights, of steadfast adherence to ethical ideals proper to a given relation or social position. Nicholas Bozon implies this with a presentation of its opposite, Deleauté, in *Le Char d'Orgueil*: the allegorical features of this, the third horse drawing Pride's cart, include, for example, as its head prelates who do not at all carry out the tasks of their office but seek their own comfort ("Qe rien ne font lor office mes querunt lor solaz" [173]); as its eyes, evil sergeants; as its nostrils, treacherous minstrels who concoct slanderous songs about those who do not pay them enough; as its teeth, evil, backbiting neighbors; as its tongue, troublemakers who destroy love between neighbors by evil stories; as its ears, aggressive beadles; as its feet, indolent youths who rarely go to church but continually eat (ed. Vising 1919). Political theory emphasizing the need of the king to keep "faith" in this sense is found in a section in the pseudo-Aristotelian thirteenth-century *Secretum secretorum*, entitled in an early sixteenth-century translation "How a kynge ought to kepe his fayth or othe": "Aboue all thynge . . . beware that thou breke not thy faythe and othe that thou has made. . . . Wyte thou than that by kepynge of faythe is made þe goodly assemblynge of men. Cytees ben inhabyted with comyns and soo is the good sygnouryes of kynges. By kepynge of fayth castelles ben holden and kepte in lordshyps" (ed. Manzalaoui 1977:327). Indeed, Kean notes the pertinence of the opening of the *Secretum* to the Lunatic's / Kind Wit's speech: "God almyghty saue our kynge & the glory of all his frendes, and conferme his realme in the faythe of god. And cause hym to reygne in thexaltacyon, prayse and honour of his people" (ed. Manzalaoui 1977:253; Kean 1969:138). Personified or not, the ideal of upholding a contract with society and God is pervasive in the poem, governing all estates' and professions' observance of ethical ideals (stoutly rejected by the brewer near the end; see C.21./B.19.396–490 and n). Thus, although B.Prol.121–22 is omitted from the C Prologue, an added passage at C.3.374–82 emphatically reasserts in these terms the contractual aspects of the king's duties to his people.

The entity **Lewte** in PP elsewhere develops into a principle of publicly speaking the truth, like Sothness; see 2.20–21n, 2.24n, and, again, 2.51–52n. Against that more active personification, the proviso to the king here may hint at **Lewte**'s public recrimination if the king does not guide himself appropriately.

152: Consience to Clergie and to þe kynge sayde / B 128–31: And siþen in þe Eyr an heiȝ an Aungel of heuene / Lowed to speke in latyn . . . forþi seide þe Aungel: Like the Lunatic, the Angel has been identified in topical terms. Owst (1925) suggests it is Bishop Brinton; the basis for the comparison lies in the similar fables of the Rat Parliament that PP and Brinton present (see below, 164–216n). More broadly, preachers generally were sometimes likened to angels (Owst 1933:579). Indeed, as well as its general Christian authority as a messenger or announcer, the Angel's authority likely evokes a variety of particular associations. An angel bearing a golden crown was part of the pageant held the day before Richard II's coronation and on other occasions (as recorded in the *Anonimalle Chronicle*; see Carlson and Rigg 2003:104–5, and see above 139–59n). The tradition of "guardian" angels might be involved too, since these figures involve guidance and teaching (see Wilmart 1932:537–58), although the Middle English contribution to this tradition is typically contemplative and privately penitential (e.g., Gray 1975, no. 70). There was also a widely spread tradition that an angel spoke "an heigh" at the granting of the Constantine Donation, the document (actually an eighth-century forgery) purporting to be the basis for the church's right to temporal endowments. The story was familiar from the twelfth century on (see 3.165n, 17.220–25 [B.15.557–67]). Dramatically, an angel counterbalances an address by a fool, to suggest a range of sources, high and low, from which a king may gain guidance.

C's replacement of the Angel with Conscience omits B's emphasis that this Latin speech—one of four extended Latin speeches in the poem (see the others in C.16 [B.15])—marks a vast chasm between those who know Latin and those who do not, the "lered and lewed" or *literatus* and *illiteratus* (see Clanchy 1993:226–33; on the kinds of literacies in the late Middle Ages, see Swanson 1994; on the status of a written vernacular and of unlicensed literacy in the late Middle Ages, see Hudson 1994, Hudson 1986; Aston 1987). B's Angel allows the king to be constrained by a power far beyond human abilities, as Baldwin notes (1981:16), while C's Conscience places the advice simply within the king's mind. The angel is condescending from a higher level; he literally "lowers himself" (Rogers 2002:45), and by speaking to human beings in Latin he keeps his celestial authority. Indeed, a further potential resonance for this figure is with the seventh angel's blowing of the trumpet in the Apocalypse to found the kingdom of God on earth, followed by verses of praise to this divine ruler (Apoc. 11:15), a model following Ezekiel 1:10 and in turn followed by the *Shepherd of Hermas* (see Kerby-Fulton 1990:94–95). The pattern of powerful teachers descending to a human level is found throughout allegorical poetry (see Headnote to passus 1, and Piehler 1971, e.g., 12–13, 38–39, 138–43); often they are feminine, but PP's angel is masculine (**hym** 139). The angel's celestial status is made clearer by the earthy **Iangle ne Iugge** used to describe what the commoners cannot do, and perhaps suggesting their idiom for all the authoritative speeches so far. Clifton suggests that **iangle** indeed accurately characterizes the speeches of the king's advisors, which are contradictory and ultimately "lost beneath the babble of the Rat Parliament" (1993:41).

The attribution of the verses to Conscience in C increase this figure's importance to royal rule (as at C.4.186; see also passus 4 Headnote, 4.6–12n, 4.105–6n, and 4.151–59n). In contrast to the Angel's complete and unbroken existence in a higher world of Latin, Conscience is able to navigate a wide range of languages and levels of style, perhaps (in C especially) the widest of any figure in the poem (compare his earlier diatribe to the commons at 96–138, and, at the other extreme, his arguments in C.3). His taking the speech here may specifically weaken the forces constraining the king's authority, but his role in C also generally collapses the cosmic and social divisions of the poem. In C.4.157, the commons themselves can address Conscience directly, allowing the king to overhear them (see 4.151–59n).

þat Iustifie hem sholde (B 130): Take þat as "those who," a caution against the commons judging their superiors. Interpretations that take Iustifie as 'justify' are unlikely (Skt; Owst 1925:273n4); here the primary sense is 'govern' (MED 1).

153–59 (B 132–38): "Sum Rex . . . metas": "[You say] 'I am King, I am Ruler'; neither perhaps [will you be] in the future. O you who administer the sublime laws of Christ the King, in order to do that better, as you are just, be pious! Naked law needs to be clothed by you with piety [*or* pity]. Sow the grain you wish to reap: if the law is nakedly administered [*lit.* stripped bare] by you, then let [judgment] be measured out [to you] according to the letter [*lit.* naked law]. If piety is sown [by you], may you reap according to piety." The verses are also found in Lambeth MS. 61, fol. 147v, as a scribal insertion into a sermon preached in 1315 by Henry Harclay, Chancellor of Oxford (Alford, *Quot.*). The line invokes the "wheel of fortune" often appearing in literature on the "falls of princes"; in some visual displays, a wheel is turned by Fortuna and a small royal figure at each compass point appears, declaring "ero rex" (I will be king), as he climbs up one side, "sum rex" (I am king) as he perches in glory at the top, and "eram rex" (I was king) as he falls down off the other side (see Nelson 1980). For a literary analogue to that general "fall of princes" background, see *Somer Soneday* (ed. Turville-Petre 1989:140–47), a short alliterative vision of three kings at different points on Fortune's wheel; so too, the *Alliterative Morte Arthure* presents Arthur's dream of Fortune and her wheel with its "climband" and falling kings (ed. Benson 1994, lines 3230–455). The topic seems especially pervasive in alliterative poetry; see also the *Wars of Alexander* (ed. Duggan and Turville-Petre 1989), "I þat was ȝustirday so ȝape & ȝemed all þe werld, / Today am dreuyn all to dust" (lines 3433–34, the death of Darius).

Within that broad evocation, the point here is a more particular admonition. As the Lunatic has stressed that the king is subject to the "lewte" that he has helped create, so these lines emphasize that he is subject to whatever kind of law he puts forth: promoting a mercilessly "naked" law will yield the same back to him. Assuming that he is just, he is asked to cover that with pity (*pietate*; for the importance of this notion in the period, see Galloway 2002); a similar demand that a king be governed by both *justicia* and *pietas* appears as early as Isidore, in a couplet resembling the Latin lines following in B (B 141–42; see following note). These two kingly virtues are constantly repeated in the final three passūs, especially 21/B.19. The present lines emphasize the contractual nature of the king's office vis-à-vis the law, in another anticipation of later contractual theories of kingship (see above 146–48nn). On justice and mercy as kingly virtues, see also 21.15–62n and 21.83–95n.

B 139–45: Thanne greued hym a Goliardeis . . . *"legis"*: "Since *rex* [king] is said to have its name from 'rectification' [*regere*], it has the name without the substance unless he is zealous to uphold the laws." The basis of the etymology is play on the word *regere*, 'set right,' 'make a straight line,' and 'govern.' Introduced in B but omitted from C, the lines add a third quasi-allegorical advisor to the king, who reminds him of a contractual relation between the king and the law by which he governs. As Baldwin notes, the claim limits royal power, and its omission from C allows a more absolutist principle of kingship (1981:12–13). A "goliard" was a stock figure of a wandering cleric and often a satirical critic of the powerful (see Mann 1980); Robert Mannyng describes in *Handlyng Synne* a disruptive and sinful minstrel as a "gulardous" (ed. Sullens 1983, line 4705). In PP, however, the figure of the **Goliardeis** is, like an Angel and a Lunatic, a voice of truth outside the courtly world, like the Sothsegger in *Mum and the Sothsegger* (ed. Dean 2000). His brief speech in PP is a commonplace sometimes found directly associated with English kings: it appears in the eleventh-century laws of Edward the Confessor: "Rex eris dum bene regis; quod nisi feceris nomen regis non in te constabit, et nomen regis perdes" ("you will be king so long as you rule well; since if you will not, the name of king will not remain unmoving in you, and you will lose the name of king": Liebermann 1903, vol. 1.637); in Matthew Paris' thirteenth-century chronicle a prior alludes to this proverb when arguing with Henry III (see Clanchy 1968:211; Alford, *Quot.*). Ultimately the notion reaches back at least to Horace, who quotes children who commonly say in their games, "rex eris . . . si recte facies" (*Epistularum Lib.* 1.1, lines 59–60); with a similar pun, Augustine mentions in his *enarratio* on Psalm 44 that the rod of God that corrects one ("qui te regit") is the rod of direction ("virga directionis"), and since "rex a regendo," therefore the God that corrects is the God that is king of all our rectors (or guides): "non autem regit qui non corrigit; ad hoc est rex noster rectorum rex" (PL 36:504). The most influential use is Isidore of Seville's, who doubtless takes it from Horace since he elaborates the form of it found in the *Epistles*. He calls it a "proverb" found "among ancient writers" (presumably based on Horace's context of children's chants): "Rex eris, si recte facias: si non facias, non eris" ("you will be king if you act rightly; if you do not, you will not be": *Etymologiae* 9.3.4; ed. Lindsay 1911). He goes on to declare that royal virtues are especially "justice and mercy." Isidorean semiotics, where the linguistic bases of a (Latin) word define or should define the properties of the possessor of the name, are epitomized in the second line of the Goliard's speech, *nomen habet sine re* ("he has the name without the substance"), and this common medieval view, cited widely in learned vernacular poetry as well as legal commentary or Latin writing (compare, e.g., Dante, "nomina sunt consequentia rerum" ["names are the results of realities": *Vita Nuova* pr. 13; ed. Chiapelli 1965:377], Chaucer, "The wordes moote be cosyn to the dede" [*Canterbury Tales*, I, General Prologue 742]), governs much of the satirical view of the estates and callings in the Prologue. The later fourteenth-century English preacher John Bromyard in his influential *Summa Praedicantium* cites the Isidorean couplet under the topic *Regimen* ("rule"), and comments, "hoc ergo faciendo nomen regis tenet scilicet seipsum et alios quantum potest a peccatis custodiendo. Et hoc non faciendo nomen regis amittit et veraciter servus est" ("that is, by doing this [governing himself] he keeps the name 'king,' namely by protecting himself and others as much as he can from sins. And by not doing this he loses the name 'king' and truly is a slave"; Bromyard 1484, R.iiii.v). Bromyard's use shows more fully than the others that the verses were common in homiletic discourse.

Precepta Regis sunt nobis vincula legis: "The precepts of the king are for us the chains of law!" The people do not support the Goliard in his subtle warning to the king, since they are willing to take the king's word as law regardless of the lawfulness of those words. Bnt (followed by Alford, *Quot.*) notes that the statement is "a metrical variant of a maxim of Roman law: *quod principi placuit legis habet vigorem*," "what pleases the king has the force of law," the *Lex regia*, found in numerous legal commentaries (Gierke 1900[1958]: 39, 147n142). Gierke notes that this maxim constitutes "an act of alienation performed by the People" of their own power, and thus ultimately shows the people's will as the source of rulership (39). The shout of public acclamation is traditional in England, from William the Conqueror's coronation on (although on that occasion, when knights who were guarding the church where William was being crowned heard the popular acclamation, "a tremendous shouting in a language they could not understand, they thought that something had gone wrong, and under this misapprehension they set fire to the environs of the city"; William of Poitiers, *Gesta Guillelmi*, 220; J. Nelson

1982:122–23). The late fourteenth-century *Anonimalle Chronicle* notes that at Richard II's coronation, the archbishop of Canterbury "asked the commons if they would like to agree and hold prince Richard as their king. And they with a great shout and cry answered, 'Yes, we wish it!'" (ed. Galbraith 1927:110; see Bennett 1943b:57). The popular acclamation in PP appears more submissive and binding on the people than usual; it marks a shift, perhaps, toward a status of kingship and sovereignty not bound by the law, a view dominant in C (Baldwin 1981:12–13).

160–66 (B 211–16, A 84–89): Consience and þe kynge . . . til moneye be shewed: The first line in C is added; the other lines are carried over from the section's different locations elsewhere in the other versions' Prologues. In A, the section falls just before the condemnation of bishops (A 90–95, expanded into B 87–96/C 85–94), which in turn concludes the overt estates satire of the A Prologue before the more sweeping and nonjudging view of laborers (for which see below 222–35n). In B the section appears after the Rat Parliament and so climatically closes B's overt estates satire of the Prologue. C's relocation before the Rat Parliament, along with a new transitional line, allows Conscience's and the king's entry into court to provide a more literal framework for that scene, and to provide continuity with the coronation scene, thus emphasizing the proper ideals of law and maintenance of its institutions as crucially important to the commonwealth (see above, 139–59n).

The passage thus begins as "complaint" against lawyers and judges, a common issue in PP and other medieval satire. In PP such satire features both lawyers' simonical sale of a divine gift, knowledge (see Post et al. 1955; Yunck 1988:146). The poem, like other medieval satires, also focuses on their pursuit of profit instead of a resolution of their clients' conflicts, thus ignoring the spiritual health of those they represent. For further discussion of various aspects of these criticisms, see 2.20–21n, 39–42n, 65–66n; 3.14–25n, 387–93n; 4.66–68n, 148–50n, and throughout the notes on passus 4. See also B.7.57–60a (A.8.59–62); and see 20.350–58n, where other addresses to lawyers are noted.

Here, the particular estate of sergeants at law is presented. As the most prestigious rank—virtually a knightly "order" with special clothing and distinctive silk cap (the coif), and high prestige (see Baker 1984:3–27)—these draw notice and satire from many late medieval writers: see Chaucer, General Prologue, *Canterbury Tales* I.309–30; Gower, *Miroir de l'omme*; ed. Macaulay 1899, vol. 1, lines 21772–74 . The job of sergeants, known as *narratores*, "counters," and "plaideurs," was, at first, to represent a client, then settle with the judges the amount of the fine to the king, and finally, after the judge ordered "Criez la peas," the serjeants would recite in French the terms of the concord (see Baker 1984:12–13). After 1315, some appear as "servants of the king" by which they alone could plead at the Bench of Common Pleas, but others remained for hire by any party. Their "order" gradually came further under royal control; from 1382, the king took an active role in overseeing the nominations of all new sergeants (see Baker 1984:24–27, 28). PP's satire against them seems focused on those for hire by any party; king's sergeants would be paid by royal salary and would therefore be in principle less subject to the particular standing of a client they were arguing against. Compare *The Simonie* (ed. Embree and Urquhart 1991), A 343–48, "countours in benche þat stondeþ at þe barre, / Þeih wolen bigile þei in þin hond, but if þu be þe warre. / He wole take xl pans for to do doun his hod / And speke for þe a word or to and don þe litel god, / I trowe. / And haue he turned þe bak, he makeþ þe a mouwe." Thus too, Chaucer more suavely notes of his sergeant "of fees and robes hadde he many oon" (General Prologue 317): that is, he collects fees from his many clients. On lawyers' uncertain relation to wages rather than retainers' fees, see Ramsey 1985. For a contrasting ideal, see L's understanding of the line *super innocentum* from Psalm 14 (2.39–42n).

161–62 (B 211–12, A 84–85): houed an hundrid in houes of selke / Seriantȝ it semede: For the three versions' locations of this passage see above, 160–66n, and A 84–89n. Sergeants' distinctive silk caps (**houes**) identified them as members of the Order of the Coif, from which judges were chosen (see Baker 1984; see also 3.448–49n [B 295–96]). The coyness or slyness of the narrator's identification of his subject here—**Seriantȝ it semede**—resembles his hesitation in B and C to interpret his dream of the Rat Parliament (Prol.220–21 [B 209–10]), and his more postured coyness in a line dropped from C (B 111; see above 138n). But the hesitation may be a way of denying lawyers the honorable name **Seriantȝ** (i.e., "servants"), once more a case of *nomen sine re*. The caution reflects the social prestige and power of those in such a rank. A similarly oblique identification of the powerful group of sergeants at law appears in the quasi-allegorical battle of estates described in *Wynnere and Wastoure* (ed. Trigg 1990, lines 149–52), where their authority and dignity is more explicit and more respectfully treated: "Anoþer banere es vpbrayde with a bende of grene / With thre hedis white-herede with howes one lofte, / Croked full craftyly and kembid [combed] in the nekke. / Thies are ledis of this londe þat schold oure lawes ȝeme [guide]." **houed** recalls the term for 'hovering' at a joust, i.e., awaiting the order to begin (MED *hoven* v.(1), 2. (a), as 20.80–94n), hence possibly specifically recalling the jousting in *Wynnere and Wastoure*, but in any case generally connecting court action with jousting, a connection literalized in passus 20 (B.18). On PP's **an hundrid**, Baker remarks that this "must have been a considerable exaggeration, though there may well have been a hundred lawyers if all the clerks and attorneys were included" (1984:27n1).

163 (B 213, A 87): Plededen for penyes and pounded þe lawe: For **pounded** most manuscripts (all versions) read "poundes," construing "penyes and poundes" as a phrase (adopted by Schm in all texts). The Athlone emendation of all three texts, a felicitous one, is offered as the hard reading that explains both the A reading "poundyt" and the "alpha" B readings "pownded" and "poudres" (K-A 434). Kane (K-A 434) takes the sense of the amended word as 'shut up, confined' but Wittig 2001 lists as MED *pounden* v., where it is identified as an acephalic form of *expounen*, 'expound,' the only example listed. Possibly there is also a bilingual pun on Anglo-Norman *pouner*, *pondre*, used in Law French of the fourteenth century, 'to lay, be based,' of law, sometimes used reflexively of a lawyer's legal basis (as in, e.g., "vous vous ponet tut sour ceo q'il ne put," "you base your legal position entirely on what cannot be based on"; *Year Books of Edward II* ix.104, quoted in A-ND). A further pun on "pulverizing" the law seems possible (see MED *pounen* v.). The gavel does not seem recorded yet as in use in the period, although if it were used that would suggest a yet further pun.

165–66 (B 215–16, A 88–89): Thow myghtest betre . . . til moneye be shewed: Unattested earlier but with the witty specificity and assonance characteristic of proverbial comparison; the use in the early fifteenth-century poem, *London Lickpenny*, likely derives from PP's use here (ed. Robbins 1959, line 31, "He would not geve me a momme of his mouthe"). Other attested proverbs refer to the age of Malvern Hills (cp. "old as the hills"): "yf I lyff the age of malvornn hyllys" appears in a fifteenth-century schoolbook (Nelson 1956:37); "All about Malvern Hill a man may live as long as he will" is recorded elsewhere (Apperson 1929). **meten:** measure or, perhaps, mark out or survey (as land); see MED *meten* v. (1), 1a, 3a. **Mum** (i.e., an inarticulate sound, a mumble, hence any noise at all) became an allegorical figure in the later alliterative *Mum and the Sothsegger* (ed. Dean 2000) where he embodies those who "withseye neuere" sovereigns (line 245), presumably because any disagreements he might have are mere mumblings.

A 90–95: I sauȝ bisshopis bolde & bacheleris of deuyn . . . þe cuntre to shende: A concludes its view of "caesarian clergy" by focusing on the highest clerical ranks doing service for the king's civil service and, especially, his higher law courts (B and C take the issues of this passage into consideration of still higher ecclesiastics: see 85–94n). A's form **I sauȝ** emphatically continues the regular, and organized, device of the A Prologue's first-person rhetoric (see A 14, 55, 97); compare the repeated use of this in Chaucer's *House of Fame* to present the visionary exploration of the *Aeneid* there (lines 150, 174, 209, etc.). In PP A, the narrator directly criticizes the powerful and sympathizes with the larger social community (**To preche þe peple & pore men to fede**), tapping into a tradition of political verse and political commentary, as does Robert Mannyng's *Chronicle* (see Turville-Petre 1988). **cuntre** is generally a shire or other judicial district, with a possibly narrower sense "the jurymen of a shire" (if the king's lawyers are seen as specifically deceiving the jurors of provincial courts). But the word allows a broad social complaint about the national destruction that the king's officers allow, as in English poems dating back to Edward I's reign (see also Robert Mannyng, *Chronicle*, ed. Sullens 1996, part 2, lines 7617 ff.). For the cognate notion in B/C, "common profit," see below, 169n. Complaints against legal corruption of royally commissioned judges operating in the shires were common before and during the Rising of 1381 (see Harding 1984). For corrupt assizers in the shires see C.2.65, "sysores of contrees" (changed from B.2.63 "Sisours of courtes").

The Rat Parliament, C and B texts

167–219 (cp. B 146–208): Than ran þer a route of ratones . . . "ʒe couthe nat reule ʒowsuluen": The moralized fable used in this passage is found earliest in Latin in the mid-thirteenth-century collection by Odo of Cheriton (# 54a, in Hervieux 1896, vol. 4:15–16; trans. Jacobs 1985:129–30); it appears in Anglo-Norman in the collection of fables by the early fourteenth-century Franciscan, Nicholas Bozon (ed. Smith and Meyer 1889:144–45), but Bozon's version shows signs of an earlier English version, since it names the cat "Sire Badde" and includes a final proverb in English, "Clym! clam! cat lep over dam!" It then appears in the popular late fourteenth-century sermon manual the *Summa praedicantium* by the Dominican, Johannes Bromyard, chancellor of the University of Cambridge in the 1380s (Bromyard 1484, s.v. *ordo clericalis*, art. 7). Resembling Bromyard's version (and possibly dependent on it), it appears in Bishop Thomas Brinton's sermon preached to a convocation of clerics during the Good Parliament on 18 May 1376 (Devlin 1954, vol. 2.315–21). In all these uses, the fable's point is that plans to control the strong are easy but execution of those difficult: having unanimously decided to bell the cat that harasses them, the mice find that none of them is willing to carry this out. The specific or implied social applications reflect the authors' settings and audiences: in Odo's collection, the fable is applied to insurgent lower ranks of

religious against their religious superiors (*episcopum, priorem, vel abbatem*);
Bozon applies it both to pusillanimous members of lower orders generally, and
to prelates, both of whom cower in the face of rulers (and perhaps his application to two kinds of "mice" points the way to the use in PP of rats and mice);
Bromyard uses it to illustrate the point that laws against clerical abuses are
rarely satisfactorily carried out (he grants that this use requires some looseness
in the application of the fable's details); Brinton applies it to the fear that
preachers now have criticizing lords of the kingdom "since many of them in
the past, when preaching at St. Paul's Cross touched on lords' sins, are immediately arrested like criminals and hauled before the king's council, where they
are examined, condemned, and banished or have their rights to preach permanently suspended" ("tacent predicatores quia multi eorum si ante hec tempora
in sermonibus apud crucem vicia dominorum generaliter tetigerunt, statim
isiti tamquam malefactores arestati coram regis consilio erant ducti, vbi exa-
minati, reprobati, banniti vel a predicandi officio perpetuo sunt suspensi": ed.
Devlin 1954, vol. 2.317).

The fable is, then, a parable describing the gap between merely judging
and carrying out or publicly expressing judgments, thus the gap between
words and deeds in a large political sphere. It is thus consummately suited to
the poem's broader theme of "doing well"—and to the problems this entails—
rather than just perceiving or condemning abuses in oneself or others; and
indeed it introduces this issue before its explicit appearance in Holy Church's
sermon in the next passus (see 1.49n). In C that issue can be said to have
already been emphasized with Conscience's accusation (see above 95–135n);
but it pervades the poem in all versions from the third line. This focus is especially clear in Brinton's presentation, for his whole sermon is structured
around the text *Factor operis hic beatus* (James 1:25), "this doer of the work
[shall be] blessed," and Brinton focuses throughout on *opus*, on works as well
as faith, using this key scriptural text as well as others. While the question of
dating versions of PP that were circulating in 1376 becomes more pressing with
the suggestion, it seems possible that Brinton preaching on 18 May 1376 was
using and alluding to this passage of PP in some form: Brinton's sermon
includes a version of the Pardon as translated in 9.290 (B.7.116, A.8.98), "quia
prouerbialiter solet dici *Benefac et bene habe*" ("because this is proverbially
called 'do well and have well'"; Devlin 1954, vol. 2.318). Traditionally, PP has
been seen to be responding to Brinton, but the other echoes are intriguing.

PP nowhere else uses a beast fable, in the sense of an anthropomorphizing
and moralizing narrative of animals. Like the applications by Bozon and Brinton, PP's use of the fable is applied to secular powers, more specifically the
higher nobility (as the phrases **Cat of a Court** and **grete syres in Cytees and**

in townes make clear [170; 218; 179]; the phrase **comune profyt** indicates the general secular application [169; 186; 204]). With its two species of rodents, PP has more clarity than the other extant versions of the fable; apart from PP only Brinton mentions a parliament of both rats and mice, although Bozon implies two orders of "mice" (*soricez*) with his initial explanatory rubric, "contra pusillamines subditos et prelatos." Yet the fable in PP serves a very different purpose from that of either Bozon or Brinton: PP's fable argues against political action by inferiors who are incapable of governing their own willfulness. In PP's version, it seems a good thing that nothing can be done to fulfill the rats' judgments, **For hadde ȝe ratones ȝoure reik ȝe couthe nat reule ȝowsuluen** (219). The point draws on a tradition of political poetry; for a poetic version of an earlier political argument between the king's barons and the king himself, who "smartly" answers them in terms like those of PP's Rat, see Pierre Langtoft's and Robert Mannyng's description of the Parliament of 1300, and the arguments between Edward I and his barons, where, for instance, King Edward declares, "Sall no man put þorgh skille his lord lowere þan he, / ne I ne salle no wille to while I kyng salle be" (ed. Sullens 1996, part 2, lines 7639–40).

   Huppé argued that the fatalistic moral put on the fable by the final **mous þat moche good couthe** (199) is an "ironic" statement about the failure of the decrees of the Good Parliament of 1376 in the "Bad" Parliament of 1377, governed by John of Gaunt. However, C's later reuse of nearly all of B's section with only minor rhetorical repointing shows that the fable's points are readily susceptible to broad application in the general political context in which L wrote. The oppressive power of lords like John of Gaunt over somewhat lesser lords and knights, yet the arguable usefulness of such brutality for preserving "oure comune profit" by restraining the middling lords and knights, did not cease or begin in 1376 or 1377. As Armitage-Smith notes, "this allegory [of the rats and mice], which the poet probably meant for the events of 1376 . . . fits the circumstances of 1386 equally well. The Lancastrian power, which Richard regarded with suspicion and Robert de Vere with hatred, had at least imposed a check on the forces of disorder and of rival ambitions" (1904:337). As commons and knights, the rats and mice can themselves be aligned with elements of oppression and "waste"; Simon Walker observes that "contemporary complaints about the quality of law and order singled out the great lords and their followers as the chief culprits, and were never more vehement in doing so than during Richard II's reign. In 1381, the speaker of the Commons identified the oppression of the common people by magnate dependants as one of the principal causes of the Peasants' Revolt; in 1384 the Commons demanded a statute against certain local potentates, who were protected from justice by their magnate patrons; in the Merciless Parliament [of 1388] they returned to the attack on the 'second kings' of the shires, identified this time as royal officials and magnate stewards" (Walker 1990:4). The further question of whether the lesser provincial lords and officials were capable of maintaining order became if anything more pressing in the later decades of the century, with the Peasants' Revolt of 1381 and perhaps also with the disruptive rise and subsequent quashing of John Northampton, a populist London mayor, in 1384.

In casting doubt on the self-rule of the somewhat lesser lords and officials even while indicating their oppression under the higher gentry, the narrator affirms the logic of autocratic royalist ideology in the preceding part of the Prologue, and the utility of keeping the lesser lords in a state of fear. This royalist position (sharpened further by C: see Baldwin 1981:12–15]) is consistent with the apparent sympathy in all versions with "pore peple of þe parsche" (80 [B 82, A 79]), for those are as much harmed by the rats and mice eating up "many mannys malt" (214 [B 198]) as they are by any other "wastoures." The Prologue that has begun with plowmen who "wonne þat þis wastors with glotony destrueth" (24 [B 22, A 22]; see above, 22–26n); it closes by approaching that issue in a more specific if not topical example.

167–68 (B 146–47): a route of ratones . . . And small muys mid hem: The two species are often distinguished as the higher and lower Commons in Parliament (Bennett 1943a). Each shire would send two knights and two burgesses. Such a group was not, however, essential for Parliament to conduct its most important business, in which the nobility and the king were the chief participants (see Sayles 1988:32–35). The central role of the Commons in the Good Parliament was exceptional.

169 (B 148): þe comune profyt: The phrase, and various cognates, refers in the late fourteenth century to a broadly disseminated ideal of the importance of collective and communal benefits over any one group or individual's benefits, opposed to "singuler profit" by Gower, *Confessio Amantis* 8.3039; another poetic use (purportedly based on Macrobius' *res publica* [Benson 1995:180– 84]) appears in Chaucer, *Parliament of Fowls*, line 47, where it is contrasted to "brekers of the lawe" and "likerous folk" (78–79). As Thomas Usk's figure of Love defines it, "commen profyte in comynaltie is not but peace and tranquylite with just governaunce proceden from thylke profyte" (*Testament of Love* bk. 1, lines 553–56, ed. Shoaf 1998:95); see also the quotation from Reginald Pecock above at 22–94n, and 139–40n. For Usk, this idea is opposed to "covyns of wicked men" (bk. 1, line 629, ed. Shoaf 1998:100); likewise, the point in PP seems to be the importance of the good of a larger community over any one faction's interests: not individualism as such, but party politics seems at issue.

A significant origin for the idea was in Magna Carta sec. 61, the "security clause" mentioning the power over the king by the twenty-five barons and "the commune of all the land" (trans. Holt 1972:182; see also Turner 2003:197]). For comments on the term in political theory from the thirteenth century on, stressing the subsuming of individual rather than partisan rights to a larger community's benefit, see Black 1988:595–96; Bennett 1957:33–34 and n.; and Olson 1980. The phrase "common profit" often appears in official letters and in chronicles as a call to a purpose on a national or more vaguely capacious scale (e.g., the Anglo-Norman *Anonimalle Chronicle* 1307–1334, "le commun profist"; ed. Childs and Taylor 1991:82, 124, 126, etc.); yet it frequently also appears as a legal principle to justify a prince's power (see Pennington 1993:235–36). See also Quillet (1988) for a useful survey of medieval social ideas of "common/commune/community."

170 (B 149): For a Cat of a Court cam wham hym likede: The **Cat of a Court** is readily exemplified by John of Gaunt, Duke of Lancaster (see Huppé 1941), but more generally opposes courtly power to the subjects of such power: compare Bozon's "Sire Badde." Gaunt, Richard's uncle, was the most powerful baron in England well beyond Edward III's senescence and Richard II's youth in 1376–77, and widely hated: his London residence was destroyed by the rebels in 1381. Gaunt himself stated to the assembled Commons in 1384 that he was greater than any other lord in temporal matters and worldly power (see Walker 1990:5). With this line and 209 (see below), the fable seems to make clear that the king himself is not the figure of the cat intended here.

171–72 (B 150–51): And ouerlep hem lightliche . . . and potte hem þer hym lykede: One of the descriptive touches that renders PP's fable different from and his cat more realistically feline than in the other versions extant is the facile aggression of his "Cat of a Court," whose activities are ironically described as "play" and "game." John of Gaunt's famous temper (as when he stopped the Parliament convened after the Peasants' Revolt for three days demanding an apology from his third cousin Henry Percy for not having given him hospitality [see Armitage-Smith 1904:254–59; Galloway 1994]) indicates a similarly aggressive temperament. But PP's cat displays calculating feline cruelty rather than uninhibited rage.

B 152: "For doute of diuerse dedes we dar noȝt wel loke" / F MS.: "And for drede of deeþ we dar noȝt wel loke": The line was deleted in C after the preceding lines, perhaps because some criticism against Gaunt is implied (and made much harsher in F). Note also F's reading for B 206 (below, 196–216n).

177 (B 157): "We myhte be lordes alofte and lyue as vs luste": Evidence of the rats' wistful longings and repressed willfulness, whose fulfillment is hopelessly unlikely. Compare the fantasy of the three rioters in Chaucer's Pardoner's Tale, who imagine that with the gold "Thanne were we in heigh felicitee" (VI.787), and then, when two conspire against the third, that "Thanne may we bothe oure lustes al fulfille" (VI.833). The phrase **lordes alofte** recalls statements about divine (or quasi-divine) exaltation: B.1.90–91 (A.1.88–89) "He is a god by þe gospel, a grounde and o lofte, / and ek ylik to oure lord" (referring to the true Christian); C.1.112–13, "Lord! why wolde he tho, þat wykkede lucifer, / Luppen alofte . . . ?" (referring to Lucifer's presumption); C.6.424, "Thow lord þat aloft art and alle lyues shope . . ." (Glottony's prayer to God). If the rats were indeed exalted in the utopian terms they imagine, they would not be any more moral than the lords currently in power, since both seek to **lyue as vs luste** (C's stronger self-indictment than B's "lyuen at oure ese").

178–88 (cp. B 158–71): A ratoun of renown, moste resonable of tounge . . . ". . . or rometh to pleye": In presenting the idea to bell the cat as the proposal of a single **ratoun**, L's version of the fable most closely parallels Odo of Cheriton's: where L's rat, **moste resonable of tounge** (178) says, **Wer ther a belle on here beygh . . . men Myghte ywete where þei weente and here way roume** (182–83), Odo's "quidam Mus sapiens" ("certain wise mouse") proposes to the assembled parliament, "Ligetur campanella in collo Cati, et tunc poterimus ipsum quocumque perrexerit audire et insidias eius precauere" ("let a bell be tied to the throat of the cat, and then we will be able to hear wherever he is headed and avoid his treacheries"; Hervieux 1896:4:225). In the context of late fourteenth-century England, the **ratoun of renown**, who offers smooth-sounding arguments for how the rats might remain continually aware of the cat's movements and moods, is usually assumed to recall Peter de la Mare (see Huppé 1941). Sir Peter was a mere knight, but became the first Speaker appointed for the Commons when he delivered the Commons' complaints to the higher lords in the Good Parliament of 1376; a year later, when the resulting impeachments were overturned, he was imprisoned in Nottingham Castle. Peter's speech set forth the Commons' reasons for not supplying the king the special war taxes he had requested until the king's more corrupt counselors, servants, and followers, including his mistress Alice Perrers and the merchant Richard Lyons, were discharged and punished (see *Anonimalle Chronicle*, ed. Galbraith 1927:86–90). The *Anonimalle Chronicle*, which presents the most detailed and consistent account of the Good Parliament, describes him as singularly eloquent on this occasion, "si bien parlaunt et si sagement rehersaunt les maters et purpose de ses compaignouns et les enfourmaunt pluis avaunt qils mesmes ne savoient" ("speaking so well and so wisely rehearsing the matters and purpose of his companions and informing all of them what they did not know": ed. Galbraith 1927:83).

180–81 (cp. B 161–62): beyus of bryghte gold aboute here nekkes / And colers of crafty werk, bothe knyghtes and squieres: Possibly such necklaces and collars are symbols of high office, or, more likely, symbols of livery worn by men who were "maintained," that is, identifiably in a lord's retinue, sometimes as extensions of his household or his military undertakings, often but not always for life, and usually paid annually (rather than, as earlier, receiving grants of land [see generally Hicks 1995]). Abuses of power by such "affinities" were a focus of petitions from the Commons in the period, who complained of the legal pressures and political factionalism that such entities might impose (see Walker 1990:94–96; and see 1.94–101n). John of Gaunt's followers were particularly famous for wearing necklaces of linked Ss, whose precise signification is not clear but whose social power was unmistakeable (see Walker 1990:94–96; Fisher 1965:68; Strohm 1992); a fifteenth-century image of the Lancastrian collar (worn by a diplomat and servant of Henry VI) appears in Woolgar 1999:10, pl. 2. PP's Rat of Renown wittily suggests that bells could be conveniently hung from all such insignia, an image merging the animal fable with the social satire.

184 (B 167): reson me sheweth: A common phrase, of course, but particularly suited to parliamentary and legal proceedings, where versions of it are used often (see 1.50n); for a form of the phrase as a springboard to the emergence of Reason as a personification, see 4.5–7n.

185–91 (B 168–74): "A belle to byggen . . . and yf hym wratheth ben war and his way shonye": The argument is tactful: that the rats would still serve the Cat of the court so long as they knew when it was safe to do so, but would have ampler opportunity to escape when it was not. The Rat of Renown is not proposing to make the rats into lords, their hyperbolic desires notwithstanding; his views are somewhat more practical, even intrinsically servile, although still too ambitious for the rats to accomplish.

198 (B 181): And leten here labour ylost and al here longe study: Brinton's brief summary of the fable includes a close parallel to this lilting line, "Hoc non fuisse in parliamento diffinitum, et per consequens inualidum erat et inane" ("this was not concluded in the parliament, and thus it was void and null": Devlin 1954, vol. 2.317). L's line itself echoes the "newe Frenshe song" to which Chaucer alludes in *Fortune* and the Parson's Tale: "wel may that man that no good werk ne dooth synge thilke newe Frenshe song, '*Jay tout perdu mon temps et mon labour*'" ("I have lost all my time and my labor": Parson's Tale, line 248; *Fortune* 7). For other possible popular songs evoked in the Prologue, see above 1–4n, and, with more frequency as the Prologue comes to a close, below 229n, 230–34n. See also the phrase at C.16.40 (B.14.199).

199–219 (cp. B 182–208): A mous þat moche good couthe . . . "ȝe couthe nat reule ȝowsuluen": An explicit denunciation of the rats' true abilities to be rulers, already hinted at in 177 and 185–91. This speech, arguing for restraint and patience in the face of social oppression (214: **soffre and sey nouȝt**) is not paralleled in the other extant versions of the Rat Parliament. The **mous**, implicitly a member of humbler ranks than the **ratoun of renown**, openly announces the servile role implied in the Rat of Renown's speech. Huppé plausibly argued that such a resigned conclusion proved that the preceding description of the Rat Parliament was "ironic," and that this tone had force in reference not to the Good Parliament but to the undoing of that parliament's decrees a year later, in the "Bad" Parliament of 1377 which John of Gaunt packed with his own associates and followers (Huppé 1941). **"Thow we hadde ykuld þe Cat ȝut shulde ther come another"** may even be a reference to a popular attempt to assassinate John of Gaunt in 1377 (Huppé 1941:37–38). But the Prologue continually swings between calls for change and deference to existing powers. Here, the line recalls Boethius' *Consolation of Philosophy*, 2.pr6, "If you saw one mouse among many claiming to have rightful power over the rest, how you would laugh!" ("Nunc si inter mures videres unum aliquem ius sibi ac potestatem prae ceteris vindicantem, quanto movereris cachinno!": ed. and trans. Stewart, Rand, and Tester 1978).

C moves B's 198–201, where the mouse condemns the typical activities of rats and mice—"And many mannes malt we mees wolde destruye, / And also ye route of Ratons rende mennes cloþes"—to the end of the speech, where the concluding statement emphasizes this point: **For hadde ȝe ratones ȝoure reik ȝe couthe nat reule ȝowsuluen** (219 [B 201]). In the F MS.'s readings, the mouse's speech itself expresses more open resentment of lords; C's **soffre and sey noȝt** is, in F only (whose reading KD-B accept here), "suffren as hymself wolde to slen þat hym likeþ" (B 206; Schm more plausibly adopts the reading of the main B tradition with a smaller emendation for the sake of meter: "But suffren as hymself wolde so [for manuscripts' "to"] doon as hym liketh"). Bitterness at the Cat's lethal violence is thus here thrust forward along with the advice to acknowledge their servile status.

206–9 (B 193–96): For y herde my syre sayn . . . *Ve terre vbi puer est Rex*:
"Wo to the land where a child is a king" (cp. Eccl. 10:16). Critics usually
assume that the tag here refers to Richard II in his minority (who was 11 years
old when he assumed the throne in 1377). This possibly overemphasizes the
topical and underemphasizes the proverbial traditions of political thought
here: the line is a popular saying (see Walther 1982–86, no. 32852c), framed as
such by mentioning the parental source (for the framing of popular and biblical proverbs as parental advice, see Manciple's Tale, e.g., line 317; *The Good
Wife Taught her Daughter*; ed. Mustanoja 1948, etc.). The statement appears in
general political commentary and theory such as Brunetto Latini's *Li livres dou
Tresor*, ed. Carmody 1948:352; it also appears in the London *Custumal* begun
by Andrew Horn in the early fourteenth century (see Benson 2004:26n56; on
Horn, see Cannon 2003). A fifteenth-century collection of proverbs, riddles,
and translation excercises includes several lines on the same pattern: "Þere
childe is kynge / & clerke bysshop, / And chorle reue / all is greue" (Pantin
1930:102, no. 15–16). But topical implications are inevitable in Richard's minority. Adam Usk, responsible for helping confect the legal arguments for depos-
ing Richard, quotes the biblical passage in his chronicle in describing the
inevitability of Richard's fall (ed. and trans. Given-Wilson 1997:6–7); Gower
more blatantly says, "The king, an ignorant boy, neglects the moral acts / By
which he can grow from boy to man" ["Rex, puer indoctus, morales negligit
actus / In quibus a puero crescere possit homo"; *Vox clamantis*, VI.7, lines
555–56; ed. Macaulay 1902:246).

The topical understanding here must allow the one cat to bifurcate into
an adult cat (John of Gaunt) and a kitten (Richard), and this is indeed suggested by B 203: "Shal neuere þe cat ne þe kiton by my counseil be greued." C
complicates, or simply generalizes, the possible referents even further by
changing B 200, "Nere þe cat of þe court þat kan yow ouerlepe" into "Ne were
þe Cat of þe Court and ȝonge kitones toward" (218). The youthful lords and
heirs were as dangerous as the older lords in Richard II's court; possible candidates for "ȝonge kitones" could always be imagined, whether other royal children or simply young members of the nobility.

220–21 (B 209–10): What þis meteles bymeneth . . . by dere god almyhten:
Another sign of the narrator's timidity in interpreting his dreams appears in B
111 (see above 138n). The caution here does nothing to obscure the topical
meanings, but shows that restraint and introspection are as native to the Prologue (and the poem) as denunciation (see Simpson 1990a). Even Conscience
is sometimes similarly restrained; see 3.363–73n, 3.436n.

Conclusion of estates survey

222–35 (cp. B 217–32; A 96–109): ʒut mette me more of mene and of riche . . . and seuene sythes more: The remnants of his **meteles** that occupy the rest of the Prologue stand even further from easy explication. What was in A and to a lesser extent B the more or less orderly completion of the estates satire becomes in C—with the shifting of the sergeants of law (B 211–16; A 84–89) to before the Rat Parliament (C 160–66)—a brief and elliptically recounted return to the mass of people amidst their "working and wandering," especially London's lower trades and mercantile activities but also including various agrarian laborers. The close offers not ordered conclusion to an estates survey but a final interpretive puzzle of social order and its moral interpretation. The promise to recount **Al y say slepynge** thus is no clear promise for clarification.

The reference to doing **dedes ylle** enigmatically alludes to abuses; indeed, many of the trades mentioned are those elsewhere directly criticized for profiting at the expense of the **mene** people (222), especially bakers, brewers, butchers, and cooks (see 3.80–88n, 21.396–42). The criticism against such independent workers is presumably an economic individualism that violates an ideal of regimented and direct production and consumption. But the point is not developed here as it will be in the debate with Meed (see passus 3). None of the abuses that such trades are indicted for later in the poem are presented here, but the portraits of such tradesmen might well be calculated to make the medieval reader think of trade deceits that were "widely practiced, widely condemned, and widely punished in fourteenth-century London" (Barron 1992:97). For instances, see 3.80–88 (B.3.78–86, A.3.67–73), 6.208–85a (B.5.198–269a, A.5.114–45), 16.130–32 (B.14.295–96), and 21.396–442 (B.19.396–442).

222: ʒut mette me more of mene and of riche: C inserts a tagline echoing 20 and beginning to close the Prologue with a series of balladic lines that echo the Prologue's opening; see also 235n. Clattering lists of occupations appear in short and longer form throughout the Prologue and first vision especially, as well as elsewhere in the poem (esp. 2.57–64 [B.2.54–63, A.2.33–47], 2.112–16 [B.2.104–12, A.2.68–76], 2.223–47 [B.2.213–35, A.2.171–94]; see also 21/B.19.258–60n). The enumerative tendency is basic to the paratactic form of a single alliterative line; the list extending from here to the end seems to release the potential of the brief pair of terms mentioned at line 20. Barney (1982) surveys the trope in rhetorical manuals (where it is variously called *congeries, congregatio, accumulatio, frequentatio, enumeratio*, etc.) and Chaucer. In those other sources, lists of traits, synonyms, or scenic details such as plants or trees, but not occupations, are the norm.

223 (B 217, A 96): As Barones and Burgeys and Bondemen of thorpus: The mixture of widely diverse groups glimpsed from here to the end is especially clear in this line, which links an extraordinary span of social ranks through alliteration. **Barones** are the highest nobility in the land; **Bondemen**, the "unfree" or "servile," are those who owe a fixed, lifelong rent and sometimes labor service to their lords, who had first claims on what the bondmen owed and often had a monopoly over the further stages of whatever the bondmen produced, as in milling, brewing, and baking. Bondmen's lords had other rights over their lives, such as "merchet," the fine leviable when a bondwoman married, and "leyrwite," the fine leviable when a bondwoman fornicated (see Keen 1990:39–40). Keen notes that the fixed rent due from bondmen was an advantage to them during the rising rents before the Black Death, but that after that it was a heavy burden on them, leading lords to pursue claims of servile status more aggressively; he suggests a growth of class-consciousness as a result, one of the backgrounds to the Revolt of 1381 (Keen 1990:40–41). Bondmen are not often featured in surveys of estates; their identification here speaks to a clear sense of their collective identity. But see Turville-Petre 1988 for the view that Robert Mannyng's *Chronicle* in the early fourteenth century offers particular attention to bondmen in the Lincolnshire area (Turville-Petre also includes a good survey of the conditions of bondmen there), thus constituting a literary predecessor for PP's focus here and again at 8.42 (B.6.45, A.7.44). The narrator invokes bondmen contemptuously, however, in his defense of his own vagrancy before Conscience and Reason (C only, 5.68, 5.70).

229 (B 225, A 103): *dieu saue dame Emme*: "God save Lady Emma!" Apparently the refrain of a popular London song, perhaps about Dame Emma of Shoreditch, mentioned at B.13.339 along with "þe Soutere of Southwerk" as a magical healer or "wicche" (B.13.337) (so Prsl). See also above, 1–4n.

230–34 (B 226–30, A 104–8): Cokes and here knaues . . . "the roost to defye!": Cooks are overtly but briefly criticized at 3.80 but not elsewhere; an idealized cook is Contrition who (in C only) prepares a "pytaunce" for the banquet with the Doctor of Divinity: a small prayer (15.59–60). **Tauerners** are glimpsed at 6.226 (B.5.218, A.5.134) (an alewife) and the brewer at C.21./B.19.396 ff.; complaints against their sale of "corupt wyn" are legion in civic records (see Chambers and Daunt 1931:99–101, 125). In an essay on Chaucer's Cook's Tale, David Wallace surveys materials on such vendors in fourteenth-century London to suggest the issues and materials that Chaucer could have developed in his unfinished tale; Wallace (1992) argues that the London concerns of that tale could not be developed by Chaucer because no coherent, single ethos of urban culture existed in late fourteenth-century London. In PP, the absence of any explication in this final section of the Prologue, flecked only by enigmatic details, supports Wallace's view that the conflicting issues and claims of the London world challenge any effort to define this world as an "estate" (and even as exclusively "urban," as the inclusion of ditch-diggers and other laborers shows).

Wynnere and Wastoure (perhaps 1352) similarly ends with a scene of a street vendor selling his wares to Wastoure, which may include a snippet of the vendor's street cry (as Trigg's quotation marks propose):

Brynge hym to Bred Strete, bikken þi fynger,
Schew hym of fatt chepe scholdirs ynewe,
"Hotte for þe hungry" a hen oþer twayne. (ed. Trigg 1990, lines 480–82)

Vendors' cries in literary works are usually more or less overtly moralized or satirized; as in *Wynnere and Wastoure* the songs are enticements to "waste," so other appearances of such cries are pointedly meaningful. In the satirically utopian early fourteenth-century Anglo-Irish *Land of Cockaygne*, the geese themselves fly already spitted and roasted to the abbey, advertising themselves: "Gees al hote, al hote!" (ed. Bennett and Smithers 1974:138–44, line 104); in Gower's *Vox clamantis* (ed. Macaulay 1901), young Fraud stands outside a shop shouting "Hic . . . est quos vos queritis, ecce veni" ("Here're the ones you're looking for, come here": 5.13.750). John Bromyard's late fourteenth-century preacher's compendium, the *Summa praedicantium*, says that those preachers who do not correct their own sins are like those vendors who call out to sell ornaments and clothing "in towns as is often done" in order to correct the clothing and accoutrements of others, but whose own clothing and ornaments are mere scraps that they do not repair and correct ("tales assimilantur istis qui per villas clamant sicut mos est quod ornent utensilia etc., quo clamore videntur se velle defectus in alienis utensilibus corrigere, et tamen vestes proprias et utensilia habent satis exilia nec ea corrigunt" [Bromyard 1484 s.v., *correctio*, art. vii]). The early fifteenth-century *London Lickpenny* mentions the popular songs sung by street venders as examples of the supreme power of money: "Then come there one, and cried "Hot shepes fete!" / "Risshes faire and grene," an othar began to grete; / Both melwell and makarell I gan mete, / But for lacke of money I myght not spede" (85–88, ed. Dean 1996). For French examples see Abrahams 1934. The morality is hidden but obvious in a satiric first-person presentation of a peddlar's song to accompany his wares (chiefly sexual ones, it seems) which form the substance of a mid-fifteenth-century lyric, beginning "We ben chapmen lyȝt of fote" (Robbins #7, 1952:6). The "weep, weep" of William Blake's Chimney Sweeper presents a continuation of this implied moralized tradition of street-vendor cries.

In PP, the concatenated songs by street vendors are left unjudged and uninterpreted, in something closer to their own idioms, and perhaps even with some evocation, for contemporary audiences, of their rhythms and melodies. The cries may imply satiric judgments: e.g., like Bromyard's use, they show no signs of self-reflection; and the ethic (if it can be called that) expressed by such cries is essentially "seize the day"—"get it while it's hot"—standing as one possible relation to life. But the Prologue concludes by leaving the reader to judge, in perhaps a sign that the political questions of the preceding satire have reached an impasse (so too, Chaucer's parliamentary poem *The Parliament of Fowls* can turn only to song once it has reached its final impasse).

The cries quoted have partial rhymes—**pyes / grys / defye**—that may capture or imitate aspects of the originals. Indeed, the more appropriate tradition for the final songs in the Prologue of PP may be musical rather than literary or homiletic. The earliest musical and literary representations of street vendors' cries are in thirteenth-century motets, such as those preserved in the Montpellier Codex, where poems in praise of Paris are knit together by an ostinato tenor uttering a vendor's cry, "Frese nouvele! Muere france!" ("Fresh strawberries! Wild blackberries!"; see Maniates and Freedman 2001). By the sixteenth century, whole musical compositions appeared as pastiches of street cries (see Maniates and Freedman 2001). The English musical tradition reaches a climax in the *Cries of London*, c. 1600, by Thomas Weelkes and others, where hundreds of street cries appear. This musical tradition is woven into Thomas Heywood's *Rape of Lucrece*, c. 1607, in the "cries of Rome" section (ed. Holaday 1950:139–141; see also 173); but the vendors' own musical tradition preceded and superseded its place in literature and music. Christopher Marsh describes an effort to reconstruct the melody of a ballad of c. 1620, entitled "A Merry New Catch of all Trades," said to be sung "to the tune of the cleane Contrary way"; in print, it contains "a somewhat perplexing list of mainly urban occupations" (e.g., "The Taylor sowes, the Smith he blowes, / The Tinker beates his pan . . ."), but when Marsh enlisted "a group of Queen's University music studens, most of whom had backgrounds in Irish traditional music," to sing it, the song was "steadily transformed into a rhythmic, fast, relentless, accelerating and pulsating thing . . . highly charged and infectiously repetitive" (Marsh 2004:178–79). In his mid-twentieth-century autobiography, the poet John Holloway records, with musical notation, from London in the 1920s the chants of milkmen, bells of muffin men, and songs of old-iron men and other hawkers: a length of memory that suggests the "infectiously repetitive" quality of such songs (1966:43–45). Clearly a chief impression of London and other cities even before the Industrial Revolution is of much song and human (rather than automotive) cacophony: thus the sixteenth-century poet William Dunbar notes of Aberdeen, "Your burgh of beggeris is ane nest, / To schout thai swentyouris [rascals] will not rest; / All honest folk they do molest, / Sa piteuslie thai cry and rame [scream]" ("Quhy will ye marchantis of renoun," in *Poems*, ed. Kinsley 1989, no. 31, lines 43–46). The first scene of the poem's dream thus shifts from overwhelming sight to overwhelming sound, a sensory shift also accomplished at the end of the poem with Conscience's crying after grace.

235 (B 231, A 109): Al þis I seiȝ slepynge . . . more: The line resembles the first-person asseverative just above at 224, "Al I say slepynge," also present from the A version on (B 218, A 97). C's 224 (perhaps due to scribal tradition) parallels this final line much more closely, just as C's 222 closely echoes C 20. The two proximate lines 224 and 235 are ballad-like or chanting asseveratives, both building the Prologue euphoniously to a close. Such a chanting style may draw inspiration from the vendors' songs just mimed: the ending of the Prologue is the poet's own vendor song. Some manuscripts in all three versions, especially in B, omit this final tag line, with a loss only of literary framing and euphony but not sense. But the significant witness to B's alpha stem, R, has the line, and few A and C manuscripts omit it (only X for C). The echo between C 224/B 218/A 97 and this line argues that the chanting or balladic or street-song effect achieved was deliberate, perhaps an aspect of the lyrical principles of didactic writing that Holy Church, in the following passus, identifies as "preaching in your harp" (see 1.146–58n, A.1.137n).

C Passus 1; B Passus 1; A Passus 1

Headnote

With the second passus, the vision shifts scope, perspective, and mode dramatically, while retaining, obliquely, a connection to the scene just viewed. Whereas much of the Prologue is a social survey or "estates satire" embedded in a dream and, in B and C, extended into political theory, much of passus 1 is an instructional dialogue, which begins the narrator's expansion of his own quest and voice. Given its parallels with a range of prose and poetic didactic writing in Middle English, the genre of passus 1 might chiefly be classified as a "sermon," or a "religious dialogue" or "catechism," since it combines religious teaching with dramatic interaction (for general connections of PP to sermons and homiletic writing, see Owst 1933:548–93; Bloomfield 1962:32–34; Wenzel 1988; and Fletcher 2001). But apart simply from being in verse, its rhetorical flights and imagery suggest a distinctly poetic didactic style. The genre that has been called the "verse sermon," that is, homiletic poetry and lyric presenting material often found in sermons but often in a structure and development closer to song or narrative, is recognizable from the twelfth century on in French and Anglo-Norman, from Helinandus of Froidmont's *Vers de la Mort* (ed. Wulff and Walberg 1905), the *Grant mal fist Adan* (ed. Suchier 1949), and the *Sermon* of Guischard de Beaulieu (ed. Gabrielson 1909) (all from the twelfth century), to Jean de Journi's *Dime de Penitance* (ed. Breymann 1874) (later thirteenth century) and the early fourteenth-century verse sermons of Nicholas Bozon (see Levy 1981; Jeffrey and Levy 1990), the last of which have direct parallels with other stretches of PP, at some of which they are likely influences (see Prol.167–219n, 2.178–96n, also in the Crucifixion passus: see 20/B.18.8–34n, 20/B.18.21n, 20/B.18.298–311n, 20/B.18.330–31n).

In English, the same category is usually exemplified by brief devotional lyrics and by lyric collections, sometimes as found among Latin sermon materials, as in the lyrics punctuating John of Grimestone's preaching book, the lyrics of the Vernon manuscript in which a copy of PP also appears, or, less densely, those found in the *Fasciculus Morum* (see Brown 1957; Wilson 1973; Wenzel 1978; Wenzel 1988). Other English parallels may be found in some Middle English sermons laid out as "prose" which are also sometimes nearly scannable as alliterative poetry (see Prol.66–80n, 107–23n). By the early thirteenth century, the French "verse sermons" had shifted emphases from punishment and fear to contrition and redemption (see Payen 1967:489–515; Levy 1981:13–15), and most devotional English lyrics are similarly pitched. Holy Church's rhapsodic affirmation of her views captures some of these elements but remains capable of wit and irony, never adopting the sentimental tones of many pious lyrics. For hints that the poet was conscious of using or developing here a genre that presents preaching in musical or lyrical terms, see below 135n, 146–58n, and A 137n.

The abrupt turn to such a genre establishes early in PP the capacity of the poem to shift genres with a new narrative unit, and in terms no less dramatically apt than the shifts of Chaucer's collection of genres in the *Canterbury Tales*. Whereas Chaucer's premise for connecting his diverse display of genres in that work is a social drama, L's connections between the diverse literary modes of each passus are forged by rhetorical and thematic means, here a query about the "meaning" of the previous passus. The explanation of the Prologue's castle, dale, and "feld ful of folk" is offered via a guide commanding almost supreme authority to speak in moral, theological, ecclesiological, and cosmological terms. Implying for the first time real uncertainty about the "meaning" of the Prologue—first the reader's perplexity, then his own—the dreamer seeks to interrogate a beautiful woman whose degree of scriptural understanding is awesome and mysterious to him but who turns out to have a lifelong intimate knowledge of him dating from the baptismal font, putting herself in the role of a supreme mother. This invokes the common phrase for the medieval church, "the mother of us all," originally from Gal. 4:26 describing Jerusalem, hence the New Jerusalem of the community of saints, a term also applied to the church on earth by, e.g., Augustine, *Confessiones*, 1.1, as where he describes his own baptism (ed. and trans. Watts 1999, vol. 1.32–37). After she identifies herself as Holy Church, the narrator inquires about his own salvation and receives a densely allusive and rich discourse on "treuthe" and "love," notions that have, as she shows, deep connections.

As a concept, if this entity can be so reduced, "Holy Church" here is especially Christian doctrine as stored, expounded, and conveyed through apostolic tradition with complete authority, and put into sacramental action. But it is significant that the figure does not return to the poem after her departure at the beginning of the next passus, except perhaps in the abstract notion of Unite as the place to which the righteous flee: "unite, holy chirche an englische" (21/B.19.328; see the final passus). Apart from that spectral return, the entity of Holy Church is elsewhere dissolved into the figures and texts and issues who make up that entity, including the multitudinous members of the church. Clergy, in B only, declares that Holy Church "is a commune lyf . . . on holy chirche to bileue / Wiþ alle þe articles of þe feiþ þat falleþ to be knowe" (B 10.238–39); in C only, Will is told by Liberum Arbitrium that Holy Church is simply "Charite," but again more particularly is defined as "Lief in loue and leutee in o byleue and lawe . . . Alle kyne cristene cleuynge on o will" (17.125–28). Abraham declares her the "moder" of all the "childrene of charite," invoking Romans 9:8's definition of the "true" Israelites as the "children of the promise" (18.206–8 [cp. B.16.197–99]).

Those later definitions follow standard definitions of Holy Church: the sixth of the seven articles of faith promulgated by the Lambeth Council in 1281 as basic teaching for the laity (chapter 9 of the canons of the Lambeth Council) says that the church is sanctified "through the Holy Ghost, the sacraments of grace, and all other things in which the Christian church communes" (Powicke and Cheney 1964:901). In re-presenting the point in 1357, Archbishop Thoresby turned it into a definition, stating that the "holy Catholic church" (*sancta ecclesia Catholica*) consists "in the congregation and the communion of the faithful, and in the sacraments of the church and other things by which the Christian church communes" (Simmons and Nolloth 1901:25); as John Gaytryge's "sermon" presents this, translating Thoresby's catechism into English in the archbishop's register for wider distribution (at least eight manuscripts are extant), "Haly Kirke, our modir, es hallyly ane thorowowte the werlde, that es comonynge and felawrede of all cristen folke that comouns togedir in the sacramentes and in other haly thynges that falles till Haly Kyrke, withowtten the whilke ne es na saule hele" (Simmons and Nolloth 1901; Blake 1972:76; on the work's influence and context see Pantin 1955:189–218; Shaw 1985; Boyle 1985; Powell 1994; Raymo 1986). The Lollard treatise *Lantern of Lyȝte* (dated 1409–15: see Hudson 1988a:318) is a sustained treatise on what the church is. Drawing on Nicholas of Lyra and other authorities, it distinguishes the church into three entities: first, the small flock of the saved, including the larger "congregacioun, or gedering-togidir" of those "feiþful soulis þat lastingli kepen feiþ and trouþ, in word and in dede, to God and to man"; second, "þe material chirche wiþ hir honourmentis," made by "mannes crafte, of lyme, of tymbre and of stoon," and providing no guarantee of holiness but merely gathering "good and yuel in a place þat is halowid, fer from worldi occupacioun, for þere sacramentis schullen be tretid and Goddis lawe boþe radde and prechid"; and third, the church triumphant at the end of time, when the "fendis chirche" that has coexisted with it will be separated from it and annihilated on the Day of Judgment (partly ed. in Hudson 1978:115–16; see also Swinburn 1917 for 1915:22–23, 36–40; for discussion, see Hudson 1988a:314–27).

Yet none of these definitions stressing the collective and unified membership of Holy Church reach the critical mass necessary for an allegory, especially one so authoritatively and distinctively loquacious. Of other figures in the poem, perhaps only Liberum Arbitrium (B's Anima) instructs the dreamer in so extensive, confident, yet metaphorically rich a manner. Holy Church's luminous, iconic power here derives not from prosaic definitions of the concept, but from a deep and widespread range of imagistic and literary traditions, biblical and medieval, with a rhetorical complexity and ambition at least comparable to the earlier fourteenth-century Anglo-Norman "verse sermons" by Nicholas Bozon (see Levy 1981).

Such a figure's descent from a holy place to inform a narrator evokes the vision of the "holy city, the new Jerusalem, coming down out of heaven from God, prepared as a bride adorned for her husband. And I heard a great voice from the throne, saying, Behold the tabernacle of God with men" (Apoc. 21:2–3), a scene understood by exegetes as, among other things, referring to the true church (see Robertson and Huppé 1951:36–37). Her relation to the narrator draws from many other traditions and contexts as well. Debate between a transcendentally authoritative feminine figure—the kind of entity that Piehler calls a *potentia animae* ("power of the soul"; 1971:12–13)—and a human being (who is almost always, apart from Christine de Pizan's works, a male) seeking or needing assistance has many sources and parallels. The most influential medieval basis of the tradition is the dialogue with Lady Philosophy in Boethius' *De consolatione Philosophiae* (c. 520), a work known, and a model followed, throughout medieval literary and intellectual culture; its direct impress is particularly clear in such works as Alan of Lille's *De planctu naturae* (c. 1170), Jean de Meun's portion of the *Roman de la Rose* (c. 1170–85), and Guillaume de Deguileville's three "pelerinages" from the early to mid-fourteenth century (ed. Stürzinger 1893, 1895, 1897), as well as other, less influential works in Latin, French, and English (see Piehler 1971, and Prologue Headnote). A widely disseminated and repeatedly translated early twelfth-century Latin debate on the elements of Christian faith, the *Elucidarium*, contributed to the tradition behind Holy Church's teachings if not to L's creation of the passus itself.

Probably exerting the most direct influence on the main framework of the scene here are the *Pelerinage de vie humaine* and perhaps the *Roman de la Rose* itself (see Prologue, Headnote). Deguileville's didactic trilogy, with its *pelerin* who seeks or is subjected to a series of interlocutors, from sins on earth to the passage to heaven, provides a very broad display of the same kind of scene of instruction that PP portrays in denser and smaller canvas. PP's passus 1 roughly resembles the pilgrim's first and second encounter in the *Pelerinage de vie humaine*, with Grace-Dieu then Raison, both scenes of which respond to the debate between Raison and Amant in the *Roman de la Rose* (see below 3n, 4n, 6–9n, 77–78n). Yet just as Holy Church is a different kind of entity—an institution as well as a spiritual community—so the substance of her presentation differs substantially in style and detail from Deguileville's work. Boethius' *De consolatione* is directly visible only in a single, adapted line that was circulated separately in that form in preaching manuals and elsewhere (13.224a [B.11.416a]; see Alford, *Quot.* 78), yet its influence is discernible throughout the dialogue with Holy Church; "certainly Langland must have known it" Bloomfield concludes (1962:21). Direct influence from the *Shepherd of Hermas*, known in northern Europe but not necessarily widely in England, where Ecclesia instructs the narrator in the commandments interspersed by enigmatic "similes," is possible as well (see Kerby-Fulton 1990:79–96). A further possible basis, though not identifiable as a direct source, is Augustine's *Soliloquia*, which provided an important model for Boethius, the *Roman de la Rose*, and many medieval dialogues (ed. and trans. de Labriolle 1939; for an assertion of its importance to the *Rose*, see Fleming 1984:3–63): here, Reason (Ratio) instructs Augustine in the elusive yet transcendent nature of truth, and in the pervasive yet ultimately illusory existence of "the false," issues (if not precisely similarly treated) that are as significant to Holy Church as to Augustine in that dialogue and in other works (see below, 141–45n, and 2.1–4n).

For more contemporary analogues in literary style, one may also look to the pedagogical tone and strict biblical and sapiential posture of the instructors in many didactic poems of the later Middle Ages, in Latin, French, and English, especially those framed as instructions or dialogues and based on the distichs of pseudo-Cato from the third century, itself quoted at various points in the poem (see Galloway 1987). The late medieval tradition includes the collections of proverbs known as *Facetus*, the works of Albertano of Brescia (c. 1260; used by Chaucer), *Le livre du chevalier de La Tour Landry* (c. 1380), and various fifteenth-century works such as *Stans puer ad mensam*, "How the Wise Man Taught his Son," and "How the Good Wife Taught her Daughter" (ed. Mustanoja 1948; for surveys see Louis 1993, Utley 1972; for the genre, see Davenport 1988; for pedagogical contexts and uses, see Orme 1973:102–6; Miner 1990). These works establish the kind of pedagogical dialogue found in passus 1. Few of these frame social ethics in terms of Christian love, but the development of schoolbooks in the fourteenth and fifteenth centuries moved away from the focus on pagan authors in the twelfth and thirteenth centuries, and casting Holy Church as a teacher is consistent with this trend (see Orme

1989:23–31). Holy Church's power draws from the poet's sense of the enormous power of the Bible's language and images in total: she not only speaks "holy writ," she *is* that writ, as it extends into sermons permeating and guiding every aspect of life. She is the poet's effort to capture the sacred page as the living entity it was in late medieval culture (surveyed by Evans 1992).

The broader cultural occasion for such a dialogue is the fourteenth-century English emphasis on basic religious teaching to the laity, demonstrated in the large numbers of pastoral manuals produced by midcentury and in widely disseminated summaries of the basic teachings legislated by Archbishop Pecham at the Council of Lambeth in 1281 as mentioned above, such as John de Thoresby's catechism of 1357 and Gaytryge's widely disseminated translation and expansion (ed. Blake 1972:73–87). Will's ability, however, to answer back, sometimes expressing doubts more comprehensible than Holy Church's teachings, points to a late medieval temper of lay questioning of clerical authority and teaching, in what Middleton (1978) has noted is the fiction of a "common voice" widespread in Ricardian poetry, which interrogates traditional teachings in contemporary tones and with immediate concerns. Such lay self-determination is not wholly without ironic undercutting here, yet it raises issues, such as the topics of the rights of dominion over worldly goods, that pervaded and persisted both in heretically anticlerical, rebelliously anti-institutional, and orthodox and socially conservative lay culture (see Hanna 1990b; Galloway 1990). Will's questions here have the authority for representing a common, contemporary range of concerns; like the voice of the Prologue, the queries of the narrator here are not continuously or fundamentally parodic, although more wit pervades the instructional dialogue here than is common in the genre.

Important topics treated later in the poem do not appear here, such as the question of the friars, the status of learning, the nature of penance, of kingship, or of labor; thus it is claiming too much to see this passus as defining explicitly the concerns of the poem as a whole. But clearly the passus adumbrates important topics in the rest of the poem, from natural goods and worldly wealth to "the great Christian 'goods' of truth and love" (see Kaske 1974:326; see also Dunning 1980:19–47). Others have noted that the notion of "kind knowing," later a motto in Will's request for answers, is first advanced here (see 141–45nn). Moreover, the poem's main literary pattern of allegorical instruction and debate is first established here as a central mode, through which the poem not only includes the voices of supremely authoritative speakers but also submits them to interrogations that put them on their mettle. The primary connection between the passus's themes and exposition is that of the range of ways in which "treuthe," denoting 'fidelity' as well as 'accuracy' and 'righteousness' and God, is linked at its root with "love," denoting all of these things as well. Hence her reliance on 1 John, where a "new commandment" of light and truth for the "sons of God" combats the lies and sins of the Antichrist (for particular reliance on 1 John, see below 12–40n, 22n, 59–60n, 62n, 69n, 82n, 84–87n, 141–45n, 175–79n, 185n).

Most of the changes between A, B, and C occur in the second half of the passus, at the point where the focus shifts to teachings on more explicitly Christian matters: up to C 103—that is, through Holy Church's lessons on material and social ethics—relatively few lines are altered. Both B's and C's most significant locus of alteration is the fall of the angels, which undergoes first greater cosmographic specificity in B, then greater contemporary English specificity in C.

The meeting with Holy Church

1–11 (B 1–11; A 1–11): What the montaigne bymeneth . . . ". . . what may this bemene?": In an instant, and within the new sphere of a one-on-one discussion, the dreamer achieves a quasi-awakening from the social vision of the Prologue, entering a more abstract level of investigation and understanding, but also a more tangible approach to ideas, since instructional personifications now fully enter the poem to begin their guidance of the narrator. The pattern of weaving ideas into the appearance of their personifications is clear from twelfth-century Latin allegory on (on this feature see Piehler 1971:21–30). Bernardus Silvestris' *Cosmographia* (trans. Wetherbee 1973), e.g., opens with Nature's request that Silva (inchoate mass) "be drawn forth to assume the image of a nobler form," a gambit that there simultaneously demands instruction in the universal creative process of making form from formlessness (which Silva itself is), and allows that poem to start generating personifications who can speak and interact; the sequence of gestating personification here in PP also recalls Ovid's opening to the *Fasti*, where Ovid poetically apostrophizes Janus, only to have the god Janus actually appear, offering answers to the questions Ovid has posed about him (*Fasti* 1.89–98; for a suggestion of a possible echo of Ovid elsewhere in PP, along with a valuable comment on how the poem "teases us to know" by its extraordinary range of possible allusions, see Barney 1995b:8).

In PP, the narrator announces this shift from idea to personification by implying there *is* a further "meaning" in what we have read and he has seen. Thus at a stroke interpretative depth is created for the poem and greater textual authority for the preceding vision, making way for Holy Church's explanatory "preaching in her harp" (for this notion, see below 146–58n, A 137n). The opening lines of the passus pick up the thread of Prol.217–18 (B 209–10), "What þis meteles bymeneth, ȝe men þat ben merye, / Deuyne ȝe, for y ne dar." But there the question of meaning is coyly taunting, and the "meaning" hinted at there seemingly no deeper than deciding to which groups or persons the fable of the Rats and Mice refers. Here not just some one deeper meaning, but a hunt for meaning, potentially endless, opens up. For the underlying medieval academic tradition of interpreting philosophical significance beneath the *integumenta* of the literary forms of authoritative visions, such as those in Virgil, Boethius, and Martianus Capella, see Wetherbee 1972.

Here, since the answer to the question of what the mountain means (truth) leads to the other questions (what is truth, how may it be sought in spiritual and worldly endeavors, how can an individual know the truth), the invitation for endlessly inductive thinking is offered from the outset, in a style that characterizes the dreamer's quest throughout the poem and the elaborate answers he receives, whose pregnant implications immediately cancel the narrator's initial promises of certainty.

3 (B 3, A 3): A louely lady of lere in lynnene yclothed: The hints of the mysterious woman's identity are suggestive but enigmatic (see Middleton 1982b:115). The Pilgrim in Deguileville's *Pelerinage de vie humaine* initially does not know who Grace-Dieu is when he encounters her, but he feels "gret gladnesse" (in Lydgate's translation, ed. Furnivall and Locock 1899–1904, line 671), and immediately reasons his way toward her identity: she seems to be the "douhter of som Emperour, / Somme myghty king, or gouernour; / Or off that lord that guyeth al, / Wych ys of power most royal" (line 678; "Vi une dame en ma voie, / Qui de sa biaute me fist joie, / Fille sembloit d'empereur, / De roi ou d'autre grant seigneur"; ed. Stürzinger 1893, lines 231–34). The opening description uses an alliterative and romance formulaic phrase: **louely lady of lere** (PP's only use of **lere**, a rarity that suggests how far the poem is from such usage) invokes the romance tradition although in terms long appropriated for sacred settings in the alliterative tradition: see *Juliana* (ed. d'Ardenne 1961) 17/ 196, *Katherine* (ed. d'Ardenne and Dobson 1981), (1) 313; *Pearl* (ed. Andrew and Waldron 1996), line 398. So too, **in lynnene yclothed** is appropriate for a beautiful woman, for this is a delicate white material, suitable for summer as opposed to wool for winter; the material was also used as an altar cloth. But the phrase is also pointedly evocative of biblical descriptions of visionary figures, often apocalyptically judging ones: Daniel's ninth vision is of "a man clothed in linen [*vestitus lineis*], and his loins were girded with the finest gold.

And his body was like the chrysolite, and his face as the appearance of light-ning, and his eyes as a burning lamp . . ." (Dan. 10:5–6); Ezekiel similarly has an apocalyptic vision of a terrifying group of armed figures with "one man in the midst of them clothed with linen [*vestitus lineis*], with a writer's inkhorn at his reins" prepared to go through Jerusalem to mark the Thau on the fore-heads of all those who will be saved, leaving the rest to be butchered (Ezek. 9:1–8). Robertson and Huppé note that in the Apocalypse, "the holy city, the new Jerusalem, coming down out of heaven from God," has "the glory of God, and the light thereof was like to a precious stone" (Apoc. 22:2, 11), and they add that in one patristic author, Bruno Astensis, linen clothing signifies the *justificatio sanctorum* (Robertson and Huppé 1951:37 and n41). Such traditions are likely mediated through Deguileville's portrayal of Grace-Dieu, who like a noble lady as well as a heavenly figure is also in "fine array" ("de si grant atour": 255).

The mode of introducing new figures as mysterious appears prominently in later passūs (especially presenting Meed, as noted, and Jesus, passus 20/ B.18); it follows PP's general style of abrupt shifts of expectations, and may owe something to the practice of Middle English romance (see Prol., Headnote; Prol.1–13n, 3.90–107n), as well as the *Pelerinage de vie humaine*. Typically the dreamer soon asks who they are (within four lines, for instance, he asks about Liberum Arbitrium, "Thenne hadde y wonder what he was" [16.162; C only]). Here, however, the dreamer does not express curiosity about her identity until line 68 (B 71, A 69). The long delay is more a mark of the greater intrinsic fascination of her words, which immediately and completely engage his thoughts and questions and seem to crowd out any other thoughts, in spite of her remarkable presence and features mentioned immediately following here. When he does finally ask who she is, he does so, he says, not because of her astonishing features but because he marvels what woman "suche wyse wordes of holy writ shewede" (69 [B 72, A 70]). Meed will ravish the dreamer with her appearance (see passus 2 Headnote; 2.5n; 2.10–15n; 2.16n); Holy Church enraptures him with her words. The biblical echoes in **lynnene yclothed** noted above show, like much else of her discourse, that she not only speaks, she *is*—in some measure—"holy writ" (see Headnote).

4 (B 4; cp. A 4): Cam doun fro þe castel [A: fro þat clyf]: In the *Roman de la Rose*, Raison has been watching the lover from on high in her tower ("de la haute . . . de sa tour"), and she descends to help him when she sees him des-perate: "de sa tour avalee" (ed. Poirion 1973, lines 2971–77). Compare the arrival of Raison in Deguileville's *Pelerinage de vie humaine*, "Tantost vers eus une pucelle / Descendit d'une tournelle" ("then towards them a young maiden came down from a turret"; ed. Stürzinger 1893, lines 573–74), where there is no tower described before this moment, presumably because the topos was so securely established by the passage in the *Roman de la Rose*.

4–5: calde me by name . . . "Wille, slepestou?" / B 4–5 (A 4–5): called me faire . . . "Sone, slepestow?": In PP, the dreamer's reverential and subordinate relationship to the woman is immediately defined by both parties: she at once uses and persists with the "thou" form of address, he uses the careful title "madame" (11), then later the "you" form of address (41, etc.; see the same distinction in the Prol.149–51n). Still later he settles more often into the familiar "thou" form (see 55–67n, 79n).

Wille: Holy Church's explicit naming of the narrator in C, the first in the poem, emphasizes that he is known to Holy Church personally, as indeed she "met" him at baptism and gave him his name (below 73–75n). C's naming dramatically identifies Will as a visionary, less magisterially, or parentally, than B/A's **Sone**. For C's slight diminishment of the human figuration and intimacy of the church with the dreamer, see also 2.31–37n. Apart from this striking initial naming, C reduces the number of times that the narrator is named. In other versions his proper name first appears at the brief glimpse of his confession (6.2 [B.5.61, A.5.44]); that instance is followed in A by his being named as scribe of the Pardon (A.8.43, dropped from C/B), and that is followed by his introduction to Wit (B.8.129, A.9.118, dropped from C). The doubtful A.12 has four mentions not in the others; B has two others (B.11.45, 15.152), the last climactic as a signature of William Langland, but only the first of which, describing the Land of Longing when Will "hath al his wille," is preserved in C (12.2). Simpson (2001) argues that the naming of Will performs a function opposite to those in the naming of many of his poetic contemporaries, where their self-inscriptions of their names reestablishes their place in an orderly political realm in which they are subjects of the institutions around them; in PP, such naming serves to open opposition to authoritative institutions, embracing the possibility of a common or public "will" that resists these. See also Middleton (1990) for a wide exploration of the advantages of self-fictionalizing in the late fourteenth century. C's gesture here appears to resist, however, both common or shared identity, and self-fictionalizing: it announces the author's direct responsibility for his "sleep." C's reduction in mentions of his name elsewhere, while an opposite symptom, may in fact be a further sign of this shift toward a more directly authorial posture.

slepestou: The genre of the dream-vision is ironically acknowledged and granted a thematic, spiritual meaning by this "inner" rousing, implying that the narrator is being called from sleep to a state of higher awareness, perhaps evocative of the sleep of the apostles in Gethsamane, similarly awakened (Mark 14:37), or of those asleep in Luke's account of Jesus' transfiguration on the mountain, similarly into "white and glittering" clothing (Lk. 9:28–35). The phrase also echoes the first words by an angel (soon identified as the archangel Michael) in the popular mid-thirteenth-century Anglo-Norman *Gui de Warewic*, sent by night to tell Gui, who at this point has become a hermit, of his coming passage to heaven: "Une nuit, cum il s'endormi, / Deus un angle li enveia, / Qui apertement a li parla: 'Gui,' fait il, 'dormez vus? . . .'" ("One night while he was sleeping, God sent to him an angel, who spoke to him aloud: 'Gui,' he said, 'are you sleeping?'"; ed. Ewert 1932, lines 11450–53). This popular romance is not likely to have offered much as a whole to the author of PP, but it does present a hero who, here, has become a hermit, and since Gui proceeds to die in a saintly manner, this passage might well have seemed notable. For other small parallels to the Anglo-Norman romance, see Prol.149–51n, and below, 14–19n.

6–9 (B 6–9, A 6–9): seestow þis peple . . . halde thei no tale: The lady's first brief statement is her only reference to the folk on the field; almost immediately, she shifts to a more general referent: **The moste party of this peple þat passeth on þis erthe**, and her subsequent discourse, except for brief references to "ȝow riche" (171) and greedily ambitious "men of holy chirche" (187–88; only in C), mostly lacks social specificity. Her tone is sympathetic though lofty, taking note of the difficulties, temptations, and conflicting promptings of most of those who pass through this world. The Raison of the *Roman de la Rose* similarly begins immediate instruction about the allegorical figures the lover has already encountered (2998 ff.); Grace-Dieu of the *Pelerinage de vie humaine* immediately begins indicating to the dreamer how he might reach the city of God he has seen (ed. Stürzinger 1893, lines 292 ff.).

6 (B 6, A 6): mase: "Miscellaneous and undirected human activity . . . the restlessness of people caught in the labyrinth of the search for worldly gain" (Bnt). So too at B.Prol.192, and C.3.198 (B.3.160, A.3.149). The noun is from the verb "masen" (frequently used by Chaucer), in turn probably from an aphetic form of Anglo-Norman "esmaier," "amaier," "enmaier," 'to upset, dismay' (see Rothwell 1994: 63–64). This look back at the confusion of the worldly city directly contrasts the consideration of the City of God that forms the subject of Grace-Dieu's first speech in the *Pelerinage de vie humaine* (ed. Stürzinger 1893, lines 340 ff).

8 (B 8, A 8): Haue thei worschip in this world thei wilneth no bettere: Holy Church begins her sermon with a traditional topos. In Boethius' *Consolation*

of Philosophy, honor (*gloria* or *fama*) is one of the partial goods (ed. and trans. Stewart, Rand, and Tester 1973, 2.pr7, 2.m7), and the point is widespread in medieval Christian culture. Didactic poetry or "verse sermons" frequently open with a condemnation of excessive interest or faith in worldly pursuits; the early thirteenth-century *Poème Moral* (ed. Bayot 1929) opens each of its three parts by stating variations on "Ki cest secle trop siut, ne vait pas droite voie / Quar joie d'icest secle, c'est uns venz, n'est pas joie" (1–2; "who follows this world too much does not proceed on the straight path, for the joy of this world is a mere puff of air, it is no joy"); Guischard de Beaulieu's late twelfth-century verse *Sermon* takes its theme as "Ki se fie en cest secle por fol tenc mult celui" ("who trusts in the world is held a fool"; ed. Gabrielson 1909).
worschip had the special sense by the late fourteenth and early fifteenth century of the ideal authority and proper decorum pertaining to membership in a given social caste or institution. In these terms by this period, "Englishmen constantly alluded to their *worship*" (Hicks 2002:17–19; see also Kermode 1998:40), often in terms that defined the authority and ideal status of a particular estate or caste, such as "the king's worship" or "the worshipful," who "should be sat with their peers, but sometimes, unavoidably, they 'may be coupled with any worship'" (Hicks 2002:18, quoting from Edward IV's Black Book). In the early fifteenth century, Margery Kempe defined her early, sinful pride as several kinds of versions of this social ideal: "sche wold sauyn þe worschyp of hir kynred what-so-euyr ony man seyd. Sche had ful greet envye at hir neybowrs þat þei schuld ben arayd so wel as sche. Alle hir desyr was for to be worshepd of þe pepul" (cap. 2, ed. Meech and Allen 1961:9/23–7). The term seems a key one for both particular kinds of caste-consciousness and general social prestige. Thus like many of the poem's direct condemnations, this statement is a particular reprimand of the socially successful laity. Similarly, the example of Lucifer below figures prominently, where his pride in his status is the main concern (see 107–29 and nn). The posture of "verse sermons" (like other sermons) often is to condemn the successful members of the audience (see especially *Les Vers de la Mort*, ed. Wulff and Walberg 1905), but Holy Church's approach to such criticism is gently oblique, assuming her listener is not necessarily one of such people (**thei**). Will indeed seems hardly a candidate for such a criticism. **in this world** further allows sympathy for misdirected or misunderstood desires: people are too easily satisfied. Holy Church herself seems to display her own version of concern with "worship," when she disdainfully compares Meed's debased lineage to her own "bettere" one (see 2.30n), but her prestige and authority are not limited to the terms of **this world**.

10 (B 10, A 10): I was afered of hire face: Boethius' Lady Philosophy's beauty of face and clothing is similarly featured at the opening of her portrait in the *Consolation of Philosophy*; the narrators of both works feel reverential terror at the sight of their unknown interlocutor's face ("visa est mulier reverendi admodum vultus" [1.pr1]: "a woman appeared of exceedingly awesome face" [ed. and trans. Stewart, Rand, and Tester 1973]).

The lesson of truth as faith and moderation

12–40 (B 12–42, A 12–40): treuthe is þerynne . . . ben ywar what wolde þe desseyue: This is the first of three issues that she explicates, framed as responses to Will's questions: what Truth is; what worldly goods are for; and how Truth is the best good or "treasure." Will treats the three topics as unrelated (note "Ac" [42 (B 44, A 42)], and his protest at 79–80 [B 83–84, A 81–82]). But the three topics unfold from each other in turn: Truth is shown to be a form of faithful mediation of and moderation between opposing forces, and a means to avoid fully falling into the seductions of the body and the world; then worldly treasure is shown to be a good that may be used but governed by principles of reason and moderation; finally, Truth is redefined as the principle of humility, fidelity, and charity (see below 42–53n, 81–204n).

treuthe: As in C.Prol.15 (see n), the term here encompasses the pure principle of fidelity as well as of veracity, and is identical or continuous with God. A pattern of key ethical and theological terms beginning with *tr-* starts here, linking much of Holy Church's speech below and, perhaps, many of the poem's key terms (see Huppé 1950:180–86). Here the word picks up the many senses of *veritas* in 1 John, including its alignment with *fiducia*, which provides the basis for many of Holy Church's associations. Here, e.g., compare 1 John 2:4: "He who says that he knows him, and keeps not his commandments, is a liar; and the truth is not in him"; 1 John 2:8: "Again, a new commandment I write unto you; which thing is true both in him and in you, because the darkness is passed and the true light now shines"; 4:6: "We are of God. He that knows God hears us. He that is not of God hears us not. By this we know the spirit of truth and the spirit of error [*ex hoc cognoscimus Spiritum veritatis et spiritum erroris*]." See also below at 81–204nn.

12–13 (B 12–13, A 12–13): treuthe is þerynne . . . as his word techeth: In A/B, the start of Holy Church's first discourse offers a revelation, but in C that has already appeared in Prol.15 (see n). Even in C, this is a moment of bold assertion: Holy Church's statement is less tentative than the narrator's "as y trowe"

(Prol.15), and she adds the crucial idea that Truth is a being who **wolde** that people follow his word. As she describes Truth as a quasi-allegorical agent, so her own allegorical existence embodies, to a considerable extent, the words and teachings of the Bible, whose authority establishes her own (cp. below line 69 [B 72, A 70]; and see 44n for further cross-references).

14–19 (cp. B 14–19, A 14–19): For he is fader of fayth . . . to make ȝow attese: Holy Church's discourse begins with beginnings, implying a promise of foundational completeness in her information and the control of her exposition and, in turn, God's perfect and rational control of existence (on "beginnings" as a central issue and problem in the poem and late fourteenth-century England, see Smith 2001). The discourse begins with scriptural echoes: **fader of fayth** is a calque on the Latin *pater fidei*, usually referring to Abraham (after Rom. 4:9–16), but as an epithet for God perhaps formulated in contrast to "Fader of falshede" (below, 59–60n; see John 8:44); A/B's **formed yow alle / Boþe with fel and with face** invokes Gen. 2:7, even in the sound of the key terms **formed** and **face**: "*formavit* igitur Dominus Deus hominem de limo terrae et inspiravit in *faciem* eius spiraculum vitae et factus est homo in animam viventem" ("And the Lord God formed man of the slime of the earth, and breathed into his face the breath of life; and man became a living soul"). C 15's **To be fayful to hym** (**fayful** is a regular alternate spelling of "faithful") is somewhat redundant against the following **For to worschipe hym þerwith** (16), and it replaces an attractive locution in A/B: **Boþe with fel and with face**. Yet the C changes stress the divine intention **to worschipe hym**. Moreover, C's recasting of the sentence includes a small but precise change in the preceding line, from God has **formed yow alle** to God as **formor of alle**, the latter an epithet whose Latin parallel *formator omnium* is particularly found in works by Augustine, such as the *De libero arbitrio* (cap. 31; PL 32:1300; see also Augustine's *Sermones*, PL 38:662; *De natura boni*, PL 42:569; *Contra Julianum*, PL 44:813, etc.). The revision allows the echo between **fayth** and **fayful**, stressing how the father of faith intends to engender faith, and emphasizing that this is *why* God creates the five senses (**wittes** 15), as do the string of logical connectives (**For, To be, Wherfore**).

Holy Church's initial passage unfolds a small prayer of praise into a stretch of basic advice. It appears as a humanly focused version of Boethius' influential lyric of praise, "O qui perpetua" (ed. and trans. Stewart, Rand, and Tester 1973, 3.m9). Just as that lyric praises God's rationally governed universe, so does Holy Church; just as Boethius' hymn praises God for having "bound the elements into order," so does Holy Church. But her eloquence is likely not inspired directly by Boethius; instead, the ingredients of her capacity for magnificent arias are simply the common elements of sacred address in late medieval poetry and prose; note the form of prayer in *Gui de Warewic*, "Deu . . . omnipotenz, / Qui fesis les quatre elementz . . ." (ed. Ewert 1932, lines 8491–92). In a lengthy description of the universe inserted in the story of St. Michael, the late thirteenth-century *South English Legendary* mentions that "Oure Louerd in eche of þis foure [elements] sseweþ alday is miȝte" (ed. D'Evelyn and Mills 1956:419, line 515); the mid-fourteenth-century *Pricke of Conscience* elaborates in detail how the "lower" world, "Whare þe sternes and planets er, / God ordaynd anly for our byhufe," with the sun-warmed air nourishing and illuminating the world and its inhabitants, and made subject to human beings, "to serve man, and man noght it," although the world has become a den of human sin populated by "worldishmen" who are "over bysy" with it (ed. Morris 1863, lines 1014–95). Holy Church's vision is one of attainable harmony: through God's ordering, the elements' powerful forces can be balanced and thus made temperate for human beings, **in mesure thow muche were** (a passage statement that begins a theme taken up fully below; see 33n). Later, Anima (Liberum Arbitrium in C) notes (like many other versions of the microcosm/macrocosm) that human beings can no longer effectively predict the elements because of a decline in learning and religious rigor (C.17.95–124 [B.15.367–96]), suggesting a sense of contemporary crisis that Holy Church's paean utterly lacks, but that was common in didactic passages of late fourteenth-century literature (e.g., Gower, *Confessio Amantis*, ed. Macaulay 1900, Prol.880 ff.).

fyue wittes: Basic didactic teaching in the fourteenth century typically began by mentioning the **wittes**, even though this has no basis in the influential instructions of the Fourth Lateran Council or the Lambeth Council, or perhaps "any official church document" (for a survey of the history of this emphasis, see Bremmer 1987:xxxiv-xlviii). The late fourteenth-century Wycliffite elaboration of Gaytryge's Sermon is typical of orthodox teaching when it interpolates a lengthy section on the five 'inner' and five 'outer' wits, including a statement that closely resembles the phrasing of L's poem: "These be þe wittys þe whiche god has geuyn vs to know hym with and to rewle vs thorwȝ wysdam" (ed. Simmons and Nolloth 1901:21; see also the treatise *The Fyve Wyttes*, ed. Bremmer 1987).

bothe lynnen and wollene: lighter and heavier garments, often treated as a pair to define all seasons of clothing (see B.11.267, C.13.102); the sumptuary legislation of 1363 allows clerics to use fur in winter, linen in summer (SR 1.381.xiii). Possibly the description of these as two kinds of **bilyue** or ways of life suggests that two estates are implied, either lay and clerical, or aristocratic and laborer, or a suggestive indication of any sort of social plurality. On the merging of clerical and secular estates in the passus, see below 88–136n, 135n, 146–58n, A 137n, and 175–79n.

17–19 (cp. B 17–19, A 17–19): Wherfore he hette þe elementis [B, A: þe erþe] to helpe ȝow alle tymes . . . to make ȝow attese: elementis here refers to the four simple substances (earth, air, water, fire), thus more broadly to the idea of a surrounding nature created to serve human beings (see Gen. 1:26); on God's power over the elements see also the analogues in the above note. B's and A's **þe erþe**, with **to make ȝow attese**, may more precisely track Gen. 2:9, "produxitque Dominus Deus de humo omne lignum pulchrum visu et ad vescendum suave" ("And the Lord God brought forth of the ground all manner of trees, fair to behold, and pleasant to eat of"), as well as the general emphasis on "earth" as the base material made into life in the second creation scene of Gen. 2 (e.g. 2:5, 2:6, 2:7, 2:9, 2:19). See also 20.246n. Before declaring what human beings should do for God, Holy Church defines what God has done for them, "of his cortesye" (20).

13–20 (B 13–20, A 13–20): ȝe, ȝow: The section marks one of the three points where Holy Church shifts to plural pronouns; when first describing God's creation of **alle** (or B, **yow alle**), her words take in and speak to all human beings. Soon she reverts to addressing simply the dreamer ("reherse hem wher þe liketh" [22]). See also 50–53n, 171–80n.

21–24 (B 21–25, A 21–25): Aren non nidefole but tho . . . fode . . . vesture . . . And drynke: See Eccles. 29:28, "initium vitae hominum aqua et panis et vestimentum" ("the chief thing for man's life is water, and bread, and clothing"), possibly influenced, as **nidefole** suggests, by Eccles. 39:31–32, "initium necessariae rei vitae hominum aqua ignis et ferrum lac et panis similagineus et mel et botrus uvae et oleum et vestimentum" ("The principal things necessary for the life of men are: Water, fire, and iron, milk, and bread of flour, and honey, and the cluster of the grape, and oil, and clothing"). Eccles. 29:28 and more emphatically Eccles. 31 (e.g., 31:19) go on to stress the virtues of temperance, as does Holy Church. In B/A her balanced explanatory phrases for these **nidefole** things—**vesture from chele þee to saue; mete at meel for mysese of þiselue; drynke whan þee drieþ**—resembles a passage in Gregory the Great's *Moralia in Job*, discussing Job 14:1 ("Man, born of a woman, living for a short time, is filled with many miseries"), where Gregory comments, "Ipsi etenim corruptioni carnis seruire ad necessaria atque concessa miseria est ut contra frigus uestimenta, contra famem alimenta, contra aestum frigora requirantur" (11.49; PL 75:982–83: "for serving this weakness of the flesh in the necessities and misery granted it, clothing is required against cold, food against hunger, coolness against heat"). The point is paralleled at the end of the poem; see 22/B.20.11–19n.

22 (B 22, A 22): rekene hem by rewe: reherse hem wher þe liketh: Holy Church casts her speech as a lesson to the dreamer to be memorized and kept as a constant reference point in his mind, evoking in this baptismal context the Church's responsibility for instruction of catechumens through the catechism. Fuller reference to the dreamer's early education appears at 5.35–41 (C only; see also Galloway 1992b). Holy Church's advice links her speech to late medieval pastoral teaching; Gaytryge elaborates Thoresby's advice about the promulgation of his catechism in similar terms: "our fadir the byschope . . . byddes and commandes in all that he may that all that hase cure or kepynge undir hym enjoyne thair parischennes and thair sugettes that thay here and lere thise ilke sex thynges and oftesythes reherse tham till that thay cun tham, and sythen teche tham thair childir, if thay any have, whate tym so thay are of elde to lere tham" (ed. Blake 1972, 75/33, 45–50; see also Woods and Copeland 2002). Yet Holy Church enjoins Will to do this for himself wherever (**wher**) he wishes. Later, she exhorts Will to teach as if he were the sort of parish priest that Thoresby and Gaytryge were addressing: "Lere hit thus lewed men, for lettred hit knoweth" (below 135). At this point, however, she is addressing his formation of himself, not his instruction of others.

25–31 (cp. B 27–33, A 27–31): Loot in his lyue thorw likerous drynke . . . Thorw wyn and thorw women there was loot acombred: Lot's incest with his daughters was a common example of the dangers of drunkenness; other Middle English literary uses of the topos include Chaucer's Pardoner's Tale (IV.485–87) and Hoccleve's *Regiment of Princes* (ed. Blyth 1999, lines 3844–64). Lot is mentioned in this connection as early as Jerome's letter 59, but his fullest condemnation appears in the twelfth century with Peter Comestor (on Comestor's criticism see Taitt 1971). Late medieval pastoral manuals locate Lot's drunkenness under **glotonye**, for gluttony often focused centrally on inebriation, and didactic poetry follows this (thus Rutebeuf's Gloutonie in the *Voie de Paradis*, for example, "fu en la taverne ier / Autant comme ele a hui esté" ["was in a tavern yesterday just as she has been today"; ed. Faral and Bastin 1959–60, vol. 1.336–70, lines 411–412]; Raoul de Houdenc's *Songe d'Enfer* describes a river called "Gloutonie" next to the Vile Taverne that the narrator visits [ed. Mihm 1984, lines 142–46]; the main action of L's Gluttony is his visit to a tavern [6.350–418]). Ranulph Higden's (unedited) *Speculum curatorum* of 1340 mentions Lot's drunkenness in a discussion of gluttony, quoting from

Jerome's fifty-ninth letter: "Looth per temulentiam nesciens libidini miscet incestum, et quem Sodoma non vicerat, vina vicerunt" ("Lot, unaware through his drunkenness, mixed incest with lust, and him whom Sodom had not conquered, draughts of wine did": Illinois MS. 251 H53s, pag. 210; for Jerome see PL 22:663). Probably Jerome's statement, by way of such pastoralia, "quem Sodoma non vicerat, vina vicerunt" ("him whom Sodom had not conquered, draughts of wine did"), informs L's **Thorw wyn and thorw women there was loot acombred** (for *acombren* as 'conquer,' see MED 1(b); see also note to 30a below). The phrase "wine and women" derives from Ecclesiasticus 19:2 ("wine and women make wise men fall off"), thus certainly available in English citations well before the first attestation by Thomas Burton in the seventeenth century (*Anatomy of Melancholy*, I. ii. III. xiii, "Those two maine plagues . . . of humane kind, Wine and Women, . . . haue infatuated and besotted Myriades of people"). Lot is cited again in these terms at 10.177–78 (C only).

A and B show Lot subject to allegorical agencies of evil, which are at least as prominent in their effects on him as his **drynke**; C's Lot inhabits a world not of demonic agency but of human responsibility, desire, and denials. Elisa Narin van Court observes that here and in the C transformation of Saul at 3.407–32 (B.3.259–77, A.3.238–57) and of Mary at 12.134–35 (B.11.246–47), "allegory is suppressed to locate a heightened personal responsibility in the scriptural figures" (1996:72 and n20), a shift she suggests is part of C's project to demote the Jewish figures of the Old Testament: their personal failings make them patently fallible historical antecedents to a superior Christian truth. The A/B-C shift in the present passage is stylistic as well as theological. In A/B, while Lot is the lustful sinner who **Delited hym in drynke**, he does so **as þe deuel wolde**, a line C drops (A/B 29). A/B also has **And Leccherie hym lauȝte** (A/B 30), locating the agency of sin in a personification of evil, a feature of Holy Church's presentation elsewhere in all versions (see, e.g., below 61–67 [B 65–70, A 62–68] and notes); C's Lot does not perform the devil's wishes nor is he taken possession of by **Leccherie**, but, more simply and crudely, **In his dronkenesse aday his doughteres he dighte**. In A and B, **And al he witte it wyn þat wikked dede**, located before the narrative of his downfall, suggest that the narrator supports the view that other entities guided Lot's will here; in C, where the line is shifted to the more logical position after the event, it seems to echo Lot's own bitter denial of responsibility. Many C manuscripts (including the Athlone copytext, adopted by Schm) go further in suggesting Lot's indirect speech here, reading here "*his* wikked dede."

30a (B 31a): *Inebriemus eum . . . semen*: "Let us make him drunk with wine and let us lie with him, that we may preserve seed of our father" (Gen. 19:32).

The Latin is the first directly presented in the poem, introduced in B (but cp. the echoes to lines 14–19 as above); its syntactic independence from the surrounding English is evidence on a small scale that B was a revision of A, suggesting "a kind of teacherly citation of authority, as if in the margin" (see Lawler 1996:171; cp. Mann 1994:28). Taitt (1971) notes that the Vulgate passage, presenting Lot's two daughters' plans, undermines medieval condemnations of Lot's responsibility for his own sinfulness. Holy Church, however, takes note of the literal sense of the Vulgate by immediately adding that Lot was conquered "Thorw wyn and thorw women" (31, B 32). So too, when Chaucer presents the story he emphasizes, "So dronke he was, he nyste what he wroghte" (Pardoner's Tale, line 487). These responses closely follow Jerome's emphasis on Lot's obliviousness (see above 25–31n).

33 (B 35, A 33): Mesure is medecyne thogh þow muche ȝerne: The topic has now decisively shifted to moderation, temperance, "mesure," frequent issues in discussions of gluttony. The transition from cosmology to diet may seem abrupt or bathetic. "The Lady answers [the dreamer] in substance: The tower on this toft is the place of abode of Truth, or God the father; but do not get drunk," as J. J. Jusserand wryly summarizes the passus to this point (1909:310). Jusserand's observation was made during the heat of early twentieth-century debate about single or multiple authorship, at a moment when defense of single authorship required that A's narrative be shown to be not uniquely tight and elegant, but as clumsy and unpredictable as anything in B or C. Manly's rebuttal (in the same context of debate about authorship) defending the turn of thought in Holy Church's speech is now the standard view: the focus on moderation is appropriate in a religious context because "excess is sinful and dangerous to the soul . . . The question was not irrelevant, nor, to one familiar with mediaeval discussion, ought it to be unexpected" (1909–10:127; see further Dunning 1980).

Measure is featured as a physical and moral virtue; the seventh and last virtue in Gaytryge's translation and elaboration of Thoresby's catechism says that "methe [moderation] or methefulnes . . . kepes us fra owterage and haldes us in even hede, lettes fulle lykynge and luste of the flesche and yemes [restrains] us fra yernynges of werldly gudes and kepes in clennes of body and of saule. For methe es mesure and mett of all that we do if we lyffe skillwysly als the lawe teches" (ed. Blake 1972:84). "Mesure / ys tresur" appears in a late medieval collection of proverbs and riddles in Latin and English for teaching grammar and elementary translation, next to Latin lines on the great wind of 1361–62 that are also supposed to help date PP A (Pantin 1930:101, no. 9; for the wind, see A.5.13–14; Hanna 1993:11); the phrase is proverbial and widespread (see Whiting and Whiting 1968, M461). The topic often emphasizes physical benefits; Robert Mannyng in *Handlyng Synne* (c. 1303) commands, "Ete ne drynk but þat nede ys. / Who so doþ hyt out of mesure, / Hele of body may nat dure" (ed. Sullens 1983, lines 7188–90). The point is often bolstered (as by Mannyng) by reference to the medicinal value of temperance in Cato's distich: "Hoc bibe quo possis si tu vis vivere sanus: / morbi causa mali minima est quaecumque voluptas" (4.24: "If you'd live healthy, drink in temperate measure: Oft ill diseases spring from trivial pleasure"; ed. and trans. Duff and Duff 1982:618). Understandably, it is linked to the sin of gluttony too; see Chaucer's Parson's Tale, X.828. Against such moralists, satirists, and medicinal advisers, Holy Church is the gentler teacher, since in spite of her condemnation she acknowledges the desire that prompts overindulgence: **thogh þow muche ȝerne** (although this can be used rather formulaically: see *Havelok*, ed. Smithers 1987, line 299).

The tradition that "virtue stands in the mean" has a moral range that explains the centrality of the point here and its place in the larger topic of "truth." The history of the claim is vast, because it reaches back to Aristotle (*Nichomachean Ethics* 2.8) and Horace (e.g., *Satire* 1.1.106–7), and is found in Boethius' *De consolatione Philosophia* 4.pr7, "Firmis medium viribus occupate!" ("hold to the mean with firm strength!" [ed. and trans. Stewart, Rand, and Tester 1973]), whence it reaches many writers in the homiletic tradition (e.g., Alan of Lille, *De arte praedicatoria* cap. 25; PL 210:161 ff.). Peter the Chanter's twelfth-century *Verbum Abbreviatum* fills two long chapters with examples of the virtues of *mediocritas*, the term that, like *mensura*, informs L's **mesure** (chap. 18, 67: PL 205:70–72, 202–4). The twelfth-century *Poème Morale* includes a section on the virtue, as a way to conquer every one of the sins (ed. Bayot 1929, lines 2997–3020); it is the "wise message" that the foolish *jongleur* from Ely finally delivers to the king of England, in a fabliau (ed. Montaiglon and Raynaud 1977, vol. 2, lines 412–27). So too, in Jean Bruyant's 1342 *Chemin de Povreté et de Richesse*, an allegorical dream-vision, Raison's sister is "Mesure," whom Raison says is "well ruled" ("bien ruilée"; see *Le Ménagier de Paris*, ed. Brereton and Ferrier 1981, vol. 2.16, 27). *Mandeville's Travels*, included in some copies of PP, opens with a geographically literal application of this ethic: Jesus chose Jerusalem for the Incarnation because it is the "herte and the myuddes of all the world, Wytnessynge the philosophere þat seyth thus: Virtus rerum in medio consistit that is to say: the vertue of thinges is in the myddes" (ed. Hamelius 1919:1).

Holy Church's immediately following emphasis on the heart as the center of religious faith and understanding may show some similar web of association to the idea of moderation as "central" (see below 36–40n, 141). Holy Church's use here broadens the application to all physical desires and points beyond those to principles of law, reason, and social and moral harmony and order: proper mediation and moderation of conflicting forces are the practical ethics of "truth." Possibly this range explains why the present line is reused in *Richard the Redeless* 2.139 (ed. Barr 1993, also Dean 2000) for a political point far from dietary concerns: there it implies the need for King Richard to restrain his corrupt followers and hear the complaints of those oppressed by them.

The transition from diet to politics and Christian cosmology in Holy Church's own speech shows how well chosen this part of her theme is. Yet the emphasis on balance and moderation is severely tested by the stark terms of Christian judgment in Reason's speech at the end of the present vision in passus 4, and in the Pardon at the end of the second vision (C.9 [B.7, A.8]). The balanced view she espouses is repeatedly abandoned in favor of radical oppositions.

36–40 (cp. B 38–42, A 36–40): Leef nat thy lycame for a lyare hym techeth . . . þi soule . . . wysseth þe to ben ywar what wolde þe desseyue [B, A: And for þow sholdest ben ywar I wisse þee þe beste]: The focus on intention and desire persists in her survey of bad *exempla*, humanizing the stories and the advice. The conclusion of Holy Church's first lesson alerts the dreamer to the distinctions between spiritual and physical desires and goods perceived by his own soul, rather than insisting he rely on her authority alone: **þat seeth þi soule and syth hit the in herte**. So too she will later tell him that her lessons are easily supported by the "kynde knowynge that kenet in thyn herte" (141).

That both **thy lycame** and **þi soule** are implicitly speaking or arguing here faintly evokes the tradition of body-soul debates. As Holy Church says that **a lyare . . . techeth** the body, so in a common and widely translated body-soul debate from the thirteenth century, the soul asks the body, "From whom have you learned such very sharp words as you just spewed forth?" ("a quo didicisti / verba tam acerrima quae jam protulisti?"; ed. Wright 1841:93–106, lines 143–44; on the adaptations, see Utley 1972:691–95). The ironic implication in the body-soul poem is that the soul itself has taught the body such sophistries; in Holy Church's passage, however, the **lyare** that has instructed the body is **þe wrecchede world**, constituting at least two of the three traditional enemies of the soul: the world, the flesh, and the devil, often defined as the father of lies (John 8:44; see below 59–60n). The implicit "debate" in L's passage takes place during life, not after death. Holy Church is already telling the dreamer how he may save his soul, not how it will be judged. To this end, C's changed final line places the authority not on Holy Church but on the dreamer's own soul, which in C (instead of Holy Church as in A and B) is what **wysseth þe to ben ywar.**

For all of the importance of Holy Church's advice in C for the dreamer to listen to his soul, the lines are textually vexed, and Athlone's editorial decisions have been inconsistent (see Galloway 1999). B's text, as edited by Athlone, makes a quite different point: KD-B's reading for B 41 (also Schmidt's in his first 1978 edition of his B text), **And that [shendeþ] þi soule; [set] it in þin herte**, removes the common B reading **seeþ** in favor of the A manuscripts (plus, uniquely among C manuscripts, RK-C's C copytext, but written as a correction) that read "shendeþ" or the like. Only A manuscripts consistently read "shendeþ"; the majority of B and C copies read **seeþ**. Thus for K-A and for KD-B, the A manuscripts, and the correction in one C manuscript, preserve the correct reading corrupted in the archetype of B. The line then would assert in A/B not idea of the soul speaking **the in herte**, but the more common medieval idea of the destructive power of the world, the flesh and the devil. But RK-C alter their copytext, the sole C copy with the reading "shendeþ," back to the majority B/C reading, "And your soul sees that and speaks in your heart." If definitive views rather than simply a change of opinion, this sequence of the Athlone editors' decisions implies that C's final line, emphasizing the authority and perspicacity of the dreamer's individual soul but based on a reading in the B archetype that KD amend as corrupt, involves C's acceptance or sanctioning of archetypal scribal error in the copy of the previous version that the C reviser used. A simpler theory, used by Schm (and Rigg and Brewer; ed. 1983:44, note to Z.Prol.129]) is to see the A reading as archetypally corrupt, and change it to cohere with B and C, assuming that the poet always preserved the line as it stands in the C text. Yet A manuscripts do not show descent from a single scribal archetype, but five archetypes; thus claiming a shared error in all of them violates the understanding of A's complex textual tradition (see Kane 104–5, Hanna 1996:234–38). Either the poet made a small but quite important change, one suspiciously like the common visual errors of scribes, or archetypal emendation of some kind, however problematic, is necessary. Assessing at just what stage the poet (or some scribe) advanced the idea that Will need only listen to what his soul is saying in his heart remains unusually difficult, a small glimpse of the complex interactions everywhere between the poet and the scribes.

The lesson of worldly treasure

42–53 (B 43–57, A 41–55): "Ac þe moneye of þis molde . . ." ". . . For hosbondrye and he holdeth togederes": Will introduces the second of the major

themes that Holy Church explores, the status and uses of money, as a departure (**Ac**), but the theme of the money **of þis molde** develops directly from
Holy Church's capacious view of the "wrecchede world" that "wolde þe
bigyle" (37). The phrase **þe moneye of þis molde** makes a clever play on a
common, rather wordy, romance and alliterative poetic phrase, "man on
molde" or "man on this molde," but the transition ingeniously exploits the
formula. Will's question shifts the topic from "natural riches and their place
in the general scheme of things" to "artificial riches" (Dunning 1980:22). The
transition may also involve the association between money and "measure" or
"medium," terms that were commonly used to define money's function in the
fourteenth century (see Kaye 1998:137–46). Considered as further inquiry into
what the vision of the Field of Folk may "bemene" (11), Will's question moreover returns matters to the many activites there in which money figures, especially the clerical abuses of money, to which Holy Church returns at the end
of her speech (see 186–94nn). The narrator's question is a shrewd challenge to
the vision Holy Church has supplied of God's complete satisfaction of human
needs through the "elementis." As Rogers observes, "It is not obvious at all,
on the premise of an orderly ecology where everything we need is provided,
why there could be or should be a money economy" (2002:87). Will's further
simple but vast question, **To wham þat tresour bylongeth** (43), has both a
particular relevance to elucidating the preceding vision of the profiteering friars, pardoners, parsons, priests, lawyers, royal administrators, and higher
ecclesiasts (see Prol.55–94, 156–63 and notes), and a broad ethical, historical,
and ecclesiological import concerning the disposition of wealth, which defines
various pressing issues in the later fourteenth century, especially that of the
status of monetary profit, and that of ecclesiastical wealth or "dominion."

   The first major issue was the status of profit that an economy based on
money generates. The resistance to considering monetary surplus or profit
legitimate was pervasive in medieval culture; the concern often focused not
simply on usury but on the role of the market in determining the "just price,"
the price that preserved a "just equality between buyer and seller" in Aquinas'
phrase (see Kaye 1998:87–137). Profit is figured as the error of believing that
one actually can "own" money; the true owners are Reason, Kind Wit, and
Husbandry (see below 48–53n); Judas is the ultimate example of action driven
by desire to own "iewene suluer" (63 [B 67, A 65]). For the status of profit in
canon law and moral theology, see Prol.33–34n.

   The second major question was whether the church justly owned its
"treasure" and whether the lay state could legitimately mulct the church when
need demanded, a question that Will does not ask directly but that cannot be
ignored when Will's interlocutor is Holy Church herself. The Spiritual Francis-

cans, and Franciscanism in sum, with its rigorous views on religious poverty, brought the ecclesiological aspect of the issue to the fore in the early fourteenth century, although the extreme Spiritual position was condemned by the pope (Moorman 1968:188–204). In this context, the issue of the church's right to temporal possessions was elaborately addressed in Giles of Rome's treatise *De ecclesiastica potestate* (1302) to argue for the church's right to lordship by its manifest claims to grace. By the 1370s, Giles' conjunction of lordship and grace came to dominate Wyclif's and, later, his followers' thought and writings but in service of an opposite conclusion closer to that of the Spirituals: the church and especially its corrupt, "caesarian" clergy had no right to temporal possessions (see Gwynn 1940; McKisack 1959[1991]:289–95; Kenny 1985:42–55; Scase 1989:84–89).

In the 1350s the clashes between Richard FitzRalph and the friars, in which FitzRalph argued that they should have no civil dominion, laid the groundwork for widespread claims against clerical property as such. In 1371, two Austin friars argued in a Parliament, where Wyclif was present, that, in order to raise war funds, the state should not only tax but confiscate church properties, an argument that resembles the fundamental level at which Will approaches the question of all ownership of money. Since, according to the Donation of Constantine, all ecclesiastical property was ultimately a gift from the secular ruler, it could lawfully be demanded back when national needs demanded (Gwynn 1940:215–16). Wyclif's most extensive and influential treatment of the question, the first book of *De civili dominio*, which mentions this Parliament, was probably written too late (in the early 1370s) to have affected PP's first presentation of Will's question in the A text; but the topic was widespread in the period's intellectual climate (see Gwynn 1940:212–24, who suggests connections to other passages in PP). For the Constantine Donation, see below, 3.165n. More direct comments on the need to disendow the church of the "poison" of material treasures appear at 17.220–35 (B.15.557–69); see also 5.168–79, B.10.328–31, and 21.1–51n.

The two questions point to how a human economic order can replace and compete with a divine order; the challenge persists in the next two passūs with the presentation of and issues surrounding Meed, and the question of proper profit or "reward" governs the later passūs of the poem as well (see 21.389–93n).

44 (B 46, A 44): Go . . . and se what god sayde [B, A: Go to þe gospel . . . þat god seide]: Much of Holy Church's speech is based, overtly or not, on scriptural texts; apart from the gospels, Genesis and, especially, 1 John lie behind her statements (see Headnote). See especially notes to 12–40, 22, 62, 69, and

82. **Go to** can pregnantly mean "consult [a text] for confirmation," as at B.6.232/A.7.216 and B.15.82 (a sense not precisely distinguished by MED or OED, but cp. MED *gan* 11b, and closer OED *go* 33, where More's *Confutation of Tyndale* is quoted, "Go me to the newe lawe and to those sacramentes which Tyndall agreeth for sacrements"). C's Holy Church advises Will not simply to **Go to þe gospel** as A and B, but also to **se** for himself **what god sayde**. The exhortation may be simply equivalent to "Go we now," but the emphasis on private reading may also be reflected in other changes in C, such as Conscience's comment on Lady Meed's failure fully to read a gospel passage she cites: in C, Conscience says that she should herself have "loked in þe luft half and þe lef turned" (3.493). In B, she "failed a konnynge clerk þat kouþe þe leef han torned" (3.347). For the growth of private reading in the fourteenth century see Hudson 1994, and Saenger 1997:256–76.

48–53 (B 52–57, A 50–55): "*Reddite cesari . . .*" . . . For hosbondrye and he holdeth togederes: "Render unto Caesar [the things that are Caesar's], and unto God the things that are God's" (Mt. 22:21, Lk. 20:25, Mk. 12:17). Holy Church's answer to Will's query evokes Jesus' qualified approval of taxation, perhaps with some topical relevance to the parliamentary debates in the mid-fourteenth century about the king taxing the clergy; complaints against English kings' household operations and taxations were legion; for Edward III, see Ormrod 1990:157–58, and below 21.258–60n. However, just when Holy Church appears to be literally suggesting centralized secular control of wealth, by Caesar, her following statements offer an allegorical sense of what Jesus intended by "Caesar," and what this ruler's royal household should be like, avoiding any claim that an actual central secular authority should control the money of this earth. The medieval homiletic capability for generating allegorical "households" is displayed in rapid strokes here; an elaborate further Middle English example of the species is the *Abbey of the Holy Ghost* (ed. Blake 1972:88–102), an earlier one *Sawles Ward* (ed. Bennett and Smithers 1974:246–61). The tradition is well developed in French allegories (e.g., the household duties of the sins in Huon de Méri's *Torneiment Anticrist*, where Bras-de-fer, "Iron-arm," in this respect an antitype to L's Reason here, is chamberlain of Antichrist "and guards his silver and gold" ["Et gart son or et son argent": ed. Bender 1976, line 295]; see also Gower's *Mirror de l'Omme* [ed. Macaulay 1899], passim), and it remains central to English allegorical narrative through the Renaissance. Wit's Castle (10.129–50 [B.9.1–24, A.10.1–24]) and the Barn of Unity (passus 22/B.20) are two of PP's more developed instances.

As Holy Church unfolds Jesus' words, the "ruler" of money ought properly to be **resoun**; and the owner of money ought to be the **wardeyn** and **tutor** (guardian and funds dispenser or overseer) of King Reason's wealth, **kynde witte** (see below 51n), who is closely allied with **hosbondrye**. By allegorizing the parable in terms of these ethical abstractions, her answer unites the "spiritual" and the "earthly" economies far more closely than does the original gospel passage; she allows human use of money but not final human ownership, which belongs instead to principles of common benefit. The scope of the question and answer remains broad and in that sense theoretical not practical: Will has asked about "þe moneye *of þis molde*" (42), not just of England, and the king she describes is a universal rather than a national entity, one meant to govern the goods of this world considered in the context of the ethics and spiritual scope more abstractly involved.

ʒe don ylle; ʒow alle; ʒoure welthe; ʒoure tresor: Holy Church allows the plural pronouns of the scriptural quotation to govern her further comments on the allegorical royal administration. As she addressed a collective humanity in describing God's creation of the world at 13–20, so she now addresses a large collectivity of contemporary readers.

49 (B 53, A 51): or elles ʒe don ylle: Added to the scriptural quotation are words introducing the poem's large theme of "doing well" and "doing ill," a theme that Holy Church further develops briefly at 130 and 132. The continuous use of the second-person plural/formal pronoun from this closing tag into the following lines effects a seamless transition between Jesus' original audience and Holy Church's (and the poem's) present one, and between the historical moment and its present meanings (see above note). Modern editors' use of quotation marks—used by RK to separate the last phrase as within Jesus' speech and to exclude it from what follows—inevitably blurs the artistry that the medieval manuscript, lacking quotation marks, allows, by which the speaker presents the meaning of the passage as springing smoothly from the scriptural basis for it, and her voice as merging with Jesus'.

50 (B 54, A 52): resoun: The first reference to this entity as an entity (see Prol.184n, 4.5–7n), too fleeting to suggest any features of the full personification introduced in passus 4. He is not 'rationality,' for which PP reserves the term "wit" and its variants (Alford 1988b:205; see next note). Several senses of the word are appropriate for the present context: Middle English "resoun" (like Latin *ratio*) may mean 'an account, a reckoning' (MED 6a), and PP frequently and punningly collates these words with Reason (12.66, etc.). PP's **resoun** also means 'mesure' (e.g., 13.142, 179, etc.; see Alford, *Gloss.* s.v. *resoun*). But above all it is directly linked to the idea of law. A common Anglo-Norman collocation found in chronicles and parliamentary records and meaning

"divine and human justice and order" is "Dieu et resone et les leys del roi-
alme" ("God, reason, and the laws of the realm"; e.g., *Anonimalle Chronicle*
ed. Galbraith 1927:96). By the mid-fourteenth century it was commonplace to
equate law and reason: "ley est resoun," as one judge remarked in 1346 (Putnam 1950:104–6, where other instances are collected). As the principle for the
specific applications of judgment that Conscience carries out, Reason's importance shifts in the different versions, most notably in B's replacement of Conscience with Reason as a preacher at B.5.11. The two are increasingly conjoined
in the versions; the solitary appearance here is a relic of the first level of L's
development of the figure.

51 (B 55, A 53): kynde witte: In the sequence of A-B-C composition, this is L's
first reference to and treatment of the mysterious entity **kynde witte** (A 53).
Here **kynde witte** is subsumed under Reason; hence it is a principle of rational
social and economic order, an aspect of "husbandry" reemphasizing the economic sense of *ratio* (see note above). For **kynde witte** as a vital part of the
ideal state, and for some of its other properties, see Prol.141–47n; yet chrono-
logically prior to that development, and in tandem with the appearance here,
A develops the entity as a social renovator at the apocalypse (see A.3.275, and
3.452n [B.3.299]). In the assumed order of composition, the role of **kynde
witte** in founding society on earth and before the apocalypse is a secondary
stage in conceiving the entity's social functions. **wardeyn . . . And tutor:**
"Reflects the formula *custos et tutor*" (Alford, *Gloss.* s.v. *warden*), "guardian
and overseer," that is, a highly trusted counselor and dispenser of funds. The
office of treasurer of the Exchequer (which in the fifteenth century became
"lord high treasurer") first appears in the later fourteenth century; Holy
Church may allude to it with **tutor of ȝoure tresor.** Pertinent holders of the
office include Richard, lord Scrope of Bolton (1371–75), Richard Fitz Alan, earl
of Arundel and Surrey (until 1380), and William le Scrope, earl of Wiltshire
(until 1399; see Cokayne 1912, vol. 2:618).

**55–67 (B 59–70, A 57–68): "the dep dale . . ." . . . "þat is his kynde and his
lore":** Holy Church maintains the allegorical mode she has taken up in
describing King Reason's household; see also the place where evildoers live
after death "ther wrong is" (131). Hell with its "gates" (20.272 [B.18.262]) is
presented later as both a dark pit and a walled fortress. **y þe byseche:** B manuscripts at line 60 universally read "y yow byseche"; most C copies (at 56) omit
the pronoun. The A majority reading **þe** (at 58) has been adopted for the other
versions by both KD-B and RK-C, with unnecessary fidelity to K-A (Schm
accepts "yow"). The pronoun probably should be the second-person plural/

formal "yow," distinguished throughout the poem from the second-person singular/familiar pronoun, since the dreamer changes to the familiar pronoun only when he knows who she is (see 79–80n).

59–60 (B 63–64, A 61–62): wrong . . . Fader of falshede fond hit firste of alle: As is clear from lines 107–31 (B 111–29, A 110–118) below, Wrong should here be aligned with Lucifer, who is not in this passus (as in passus C.20) distinguished from Satan. That Wrong is not directly named Lucifer but merely made coextensive with him, may, however, imply for the word a fundamental principle of evil that the historical figure Lucifer simply expresses; note below how the poem proliferates the identities of devils such as Lucifer and Satan in C.20 (B.18). PP offers a broad and complex elaboration of the word **wrong**, which in other Middle English contexts typically means a narrower or more singular principle such as sin, injustice, and physical damage or other injury (MED; see also Alford, *Gloss.*, where primarily the legal sense is treated). The French synonym, *tort*, appears as an allegorical figure in Huon de Méri's thirteenth-century *Torneiment Anticrist*, but he is there a secondary figure who appears as the combatant against Droit (legal right) and Justice (ed. Bender 1976, lines 723–60). In PP, allegorical appearances under Wrong's name are amorphous and changeable between versions, their variety perhaps an indication of the essential elusiveness of this force or principle in this poem and its making. Wrong appears as Meed's father in A passus 2 (see below 2.25–26n). In passus 4, Wrong appears in the more common sense as a personification of civil and criminal wrongs, the opponent of Peace and implicitly of the king's justice (see below 4.45–63n). The proliferation of such allegorical expressions of Wrong ceases with passus 4.

In the present passage, aligning the name with the devil places it more clearly in antithesis to "treuth" (12), God. In a similar way, **fader of falshede** completes a contrast with "fader of fayth" (14). See John 8:44, where Jesus tells the unbelieving Jews that their father, the devil, "was a murderer from the beginning . . . he is a liar, and the father therof"; also 1 John 3:8: "he that commits sin is of the devil; for the devil sins from the beginning." See 20.352n. For the general dependence of Holy Church's discourse on 1 John, see Headnote and references to other notes there.

61 (B 65, A 63): Adam and Eue he eggede: Gen. 3:1–5, possibly influenced by the reference at 2 Cor. 11:3 where the serpent's power of "corruption" is generalized to a present danger. The same verb is used for this scene at B.18.289. Sometimes multiple demons are pictured urging or helping Adam and Eve to eat the forbidden fruit in medieval and later art; see, e.g., *Queen Mary's Psalter* (ed. Warner 1912), plate 5.

62 (B 66, A 64): Conseylede Caym: See Gen. 4. But the point is from 1 John 3:8–12: "this is the declaration which you have heard from the beginning: that you should love one another. Not as Cain, who was of the wicked one and killed his brother." The verb in PP, like "of the wicked one" in 1 John, emphasizes the source of evil, with Cain as a mere vehicle for it.

63–64 (B 67–68, A 65–66): Iudas he byiapede . . . anhengede hym hey vppon an hellerne: See John 13:27 where Satan "entered" Judas. The verb **byiapede / iapede** always describes a despicable, never a simply humorous action in PP; cp. Chaucer, e.g., *Canterbury Tales* VII.693. At B/A.Prol.35 above the verb is similarly linked to "Judas children." The series of parallel clauses in which Wrong (Satan) is the active agent mitigates Judas' own blame: he is another victim of Wrong, an implicitly tragic view of Judas common in medieval culture. Similarly, in the late twelfth-century *Benediktbeuern Passion Play* the devil comes forth to lead Judas to his hanging (Bevington 1975:219, lines 215 ff.); in Guillaume de Deguileville's *Pelerinage de vie humaine*, Peresce (Sloth) carries a rope, Desperation, with which she says she hanged Judas (ed. Stürzinger 1893, line 7231). When the narrator of that last poem meets Avarice, who claims to be a hangman too, he asks which of them hanged Judas; Avarice replies that both she and Peresce did, but mainly "ma main en fist le pendement" ("my hand did the hanging"; 9562).

    hey vppon an hellerne: Avarice in Deguileville, in the exchange just quoted, similarly emphasizes "haut le pendismes" ("high we hanged him"; 9556); the tree is not specified. Early elaborations of the gospel account of Judas' suicide in Matt. 27:5 (e.g., Juvencus, Bede, Peter the Deacon, Rupert of Deutz) considered Judas to have hanged himself from a fig tree (perhaps because of the blighted one at Matt. 21:19; see Bede, *De locis sanctis*; ed. Fraipont 1965, cap. 3; Petrus Diaconus, *De locis sanctis*, PL 173:1121; Rupertus Tuitiensis, *Commentaria in Johannem*, PL 169:498). The change to an eldertree, or sometimes to a sycamore (perhaps because of its height mentioned at Luke 19:4), is perplexing, but the elder is consistently named in Middle English and later English sources. The Anglo-Norman *Holkham Bible Picture Book* calls the tree Judas used an elder ("se pendiit desure un seur": ed. Pickering 1971:50), but Bnt notes that this manuscript illustrates the line with a sycamore. *Mandeville's Travels* says that the very elder tree that Judas used was still there, adapting claims by Bede and others that the fig tree he used still existed (*Mandeville's Travels* 1.61; Bede, *De locis sanctis* loc. cit.; see also the *Speculum*

Sacerdotale, ed. Weatherly 1936:120/31). Note the confused exchange between a Pedant and a Boy in Shakespeare, *Love's Labor's Lost*, 5.2.595–606, suggesting that Judas' hanging was part of schoolboy information through the sixteenth century (ed. Evans et al.:1974). Elsewhere in PP, an eldertree is presented as the consummate bad tree, an example of bad origins: Wit declares that grafting an apple to an eldertree results in bitter apples, as sons of bad fathers will "haue a Sauour after þe sire" (B.9.152–55). But Wit's point may depend on arboreal lore rather than Judas: the late thirteenth-century encyclopedist Bartholomeus Anglicus says (in John Trevisa's translation of c. 1395) that the eldertree's fruit "is blak with horrible smylle and sauour and þis vnprofitable to ete," though it has various medicinal uses, especially as a purgative (*De proprietabus rerum*, bk. 17, chap. 144; gen. ed. Seymour 1974–1988, vol. 2.1044–45).

67: To combre men with coueytise, þat is his kynde and his lore: C's only major change to the description of the Castle of Care, the added line emphatically links the present discussion to the preceding comments on worldly wealth, more explicitly contrasting the prudent and moderate management of worldly treasure by Reason and his household (although the point is made in the preceding line also present in A/B, B 70: "That tristeth in tresor of erthe he bytrayeth sonest" which more resonantly completes Holy Church's theme). For **combre** as "conquer," "overwhelm" by sin's power (MED 2, 3, 4), see 31 (25–31n); the assertion of the burden of sin versus the lightness of grace is also pertinent (see Lawler 1979). Again the origin of sin in its full power is attributed to the devil, not human beings, whose error is reduced to reliance on "tresor of erthe" (66), a motive that Meed is later blamed for inciting (see 3.158–215n).

    þat is his kynde: Wrong, or Lucifer, has been made the source of evil by all of the preceding statements, and questions about his own motivations are deferred to a consideration of his "nature"—albeit that this nature is paradoxically both angelic and evil, a mixture that is all the more sinister. For roughly contemporaneous presentation of Lucifer's rage and bitterness at losing his angelic "kind," see the York "Fall of Man" (ed. Beadle 1982), lines 1–22. The argument of "kind" appears elsewhere, as in the narrator's explanation for the king's courteous tones to Meed in spite of his outrage (3.130), and Jesus' explanation for being merciful to human beings because of his shared nature with them (20.417). A brewer uses the same justification of his innate nature for his persistent chicanery (21.396–401). Below, 112–14, the dreamer addresses the mystery of Lucifer's motivation directly, but Holy Church is again evasive—or gives an answer appropriate to his pedestrian understanding (see 115–25n): in either case this is one of the points that leads the dreamer to his first outburst of frustrated incomprehension.

68–71 (B 71–74, A 69–72): Thenne hadde y wonder in my wit . . . þat wissede me so faire: Compare the *Pelerinage de vie humaine*: "A donc ne me pue plus tenir, / Comment qu'il m'en deust avenir, / Que tout ne vousisse savoir / Et son nom et qui elle estoit" ("Then I could no longer hold back, no matter what might happen to me. I wanted to know everything—her name and who she was": ed. Stürzinger 1893, lines 283–86); these lines inform the following exchange as well (see 77–78n). Delayed identification is common in the Boethian tradition (as in *De consolatione*, 1.pr3; ed. and trans. Stewart, Rand, and Tester 1978); see above 3–11n. Here, since Holy Church presents an entire mini-sermon before the dreamer has an opportunity to intervene, this allows Holy Church's authority to be demonstrated through a bravura performance before she is named: as the dreamer admires her elegant and learned discourse, so the reader is offered a substantial opportunity to appreciate it as well (see also 41).

on the hey name: For the formulation see Phil. 2:9, and the same asseverative at *Castle of Perseverance*, line 1122, where in Envy's mouth it is reduced ironically to mere expletive (c. 1450, ed. Eccles 1969:36). Will has already used the highly reverential style of invoking God's name for making an inquiry of Holy Church (54); since she is God's daughter this is more literally apt than the dreamer yet knows (see 2.31–33), a "positive" dramatic irony, quite unlike the *Castle of Perseverance*. For the rhetorical form of such imploring to know a speaker's identity, compare *William of Palerne*, "I conjure ȝou be Crist, þat on croyce was peyned, / þat ȝe seie me swiþe soþ ho-so ȝe bene" (ed. Bunt 1985, lines 4518–19; see also 1327–30, 4058–60, 4243–46).

73–75 (B 76–78, A 74–76): Y vndirfenge þe formeste and fre man the made [B, A: and þi feiþ þee tauȝt] . . . al thy lyf tyme: See Boethius' recognition of Philosophia as his first teacher: "when I looked on her clearly and steadily, I saw the nurse who brought me up, whose house I had from my youth frequented, the lady Philosophy" ("ubi in eam deduxi oculos intuitumque defixi, respicio nutricem meam cuius ab adulescentia laribus obversatus fueram Philosophiam": *De consolatione Philosophiae*, ed. and trans. Stewart, Rand, and Tester 1973, 1.pr3). A/B's **and þi feiþ þee tauȝt** distinctly refers to the catechetical rite of baptism: before the blessing of the child over the font, the priest would admonish the godparents to see that the parents kept the child from "fyer and water and other perels" and that they would "lerne or se yt be lerned the Pater noster, Aue maria, and Credo, after the lawe of all holy churche" (a late gloss in the Sarum *Manuale*, ed. Collins 1960:32; see also Duffy 1992:53–

87). The A/B phrase thus implies a kind of parental or god-parental intimacy with the dreamer; for this overtone, see also Headnote, and 4–5n above.

C's **fre man** is a Pauline phrase; see Romans 6:18, "Being then freed from sin, we have been made servants of justice" (see also Donaldson 1966:57–58); on the replacement of A/B's reference to his already being taught his faith, see also 77–78n. When Holy Church first "received" the dreamer she made him **fre** from original sin by baptism; at a desperate moment later Will thinks back on this basic privilege (12.50–74a [B.11.115–39a]). The standard brief formula for the efficacy of baptism is "remission of sins" (as in the Sarum *Manuale*: after the child is dipped in the font the priest declares, "Deus . . . dedit tibi remissionem omnium peccatorum tuorum" ["God . . . has given to you remission of all your sins; ed. Collins 1960:37; see also Peter Lombard, *Sententiae Liber IV. Dist.* 3 cap. 5; ed. 1981, vol. 2.247–48]); the fourteenth-century *Speculum sacerdotale* says that in baptism one receives "innocense and clennes" (ed. Weatherly 1936:4). The phrase **fre man** also invokes the language of high civic status, denoting enrollment as a full citizen in late medieval London and other major cities, where only a select group of merchants could attain a status prohibited to women, craftsmen, laborers, apprentices, servants, and "foreigners," i.e., English-born noncitizens, and "aliens," i.e., those born overseas (see Waugh 1991:50; Thrupp 1989:2–3; Barron 2004:93, 204–6). In passus 3, C also inserts a passage specifically addressing the high standards that must be maintained when "mayres . . . maketh fre men" (3.108–14n).

74 (B 77, A 75): Thow broughtest me borewes my biddyng to fulfille: The **borewes** are the human "pledges" who must be present at baptism, godparents who function as guarantors that the baptisand will be given basic Christian instruction. Such **borewes** may not be the parents or clergy, but must be confirmed and must themselves have a minimum of Christian knowledge. On the requirements of the godparents' learning and teaching, the *Speculum Sacerdotale* comments that "none oweþ to be chosyn in-to borowe for the childe but that can the Pater Noster and the Crede, the which two yche borowe oweþ for to techen here godchildren, for they be therefore here borowes and bonden for to kepe in alle that they mowe þat they go noȝt oute of the way of feiþ and bileue, as they woll answer þerfore in the day of dome" (ed. Weatherly 1936:116). Holy Church represents herself here as a living presence at the baptism; her **biddyng** is the words of the liturgy and the instructions to the godparents (as immediately above 73–75n).

75 (B 78, A 76): To leue on me and loue me al thy lyf tyme: For the diction and phrasing, compare *William of Palerne*, at a similar moment of solemn promises of mutual loyalty, there secular and military: "þer nis god under God þat I may gete ever, / þat it schal redeli be þin at þin owne wille, / ne no dede þat I may do þat ne schal be do sone; / and love lelli what þou lovest al mi lif-dawes" (ed. Bunt 1985, lines 4716–19). The agreement at baptism to **leue on** the church is in the question and answer of the Creed recited by the priest and those who have brought the infant, who answer on its behalf: " 'Credis et in . . . sanctam ecclesiam catholicam . . . ?' 'Credo' " (" 'Do you also . . . believe in the holy Catholic church . . . ?' 'I believe' ": Sarum *Manuale*, ed. Collins 1960:36). Possibly there is a particular attention to believing **on** Holy Church as reflecting the use in the Creed's Latin of *credere in ecclesiam*; see 3.356–60n. Thoresby's *Instructions* mentions that baptism establishes a commitment of loyalty to Holy Church (in Gaytryge's translation): "the firste synn that we ere borne with and alkyn other synnes ere waschen awaye . . . and the trouthe [*fides*] of Haly Kyrke es taken tharein" (ed. Blake 1972:80/199–203; ed. Simmons and Nolloth 1901:62). With **loue me** the lines also evoke a romance or marriage between Holy Church and her followers, as below B only (B.2.31–35; see C.2.31–37n), but love is throughout an emphasis of her discourse.

76 (B 79, A 77): y knelede on my knees: As Burrow notes, the narrator here, in the "common form of submission to the lordship of God and the mysteries of religion," kneels as soon as his interlocutor identifies herself, and, as Burrow observes that A/B.2.1 shows ("*Yet* kneled I on my knees"), he remains kneeling as long as he is speaking to her (Burrow 2002:22; emphasis added). Kneeling on both **knees** is reserved for religious worship, while only on one knee is appropriate for honoring "a lord temporall," according to John Mirk in his late fourteenth-century *Festial* (ed. Erbe 1905:50). C.2.1's "*Thenne* y kneled," indicating that in C, he is not continually on his knees before Holy Church, is probably a slip, unless Will is imagined to have risen when "leue at me she lauhte" (C.1.204), a line also only in C. C may elsewhere moderate or refine the dreamer's gestures of supplication somewhat: in A/B the narrator kneels to Study (B.10.147, A.11.100); in C there he slightly less self-abasingly bows (11.85)—perhaps thus restricting the greater reverence implied by kneeling. Conscience later says (like Mirk) that kneeling is an appropriate response to knighthood (21.28 [B.19.28]), but this is by pale analogy to honor of Jesus: no one in the poem kneels to a contemporary human knight (cp. 8.23 ff. [B.6.24 ff., A.7.38 ff.]). The narrator's kneeling to Scripture "on my knes" at A.12.47 is within a probably spurious section but follows the pattern here. For the view that kneeling to Jesus himself in the final two passūs of the poem specifically reflects Philippians 2:10, invoked at C.21/B.19.15–22 ("that in the name of Jesus every knee should bow, of those that are in heaven, on earth, and under the earth"), see Weldon 1989; that text presents an outlook and range of gesture so fully absorbed into medieval Christian culture that it need not be in view in other places in the poem.

77–78 (B 80–81, A 78–79): preyede here pitously . . . kenne me kyndly on crist to bileue: The narrator's request begins by continuing with supplicant gestures, then by that means introduces the notion of knowledge conveyed or achieved somehow **kyndly**, the first oblique mention of a theme that develops more openly below (137–38n, 141–45n). As Davlin notes, the position of **kyndly** in Will's question allows two senses to his question: "**kyndly** instruct me . . ." (thus as part of the gesture of supplication established by **pitously**) or "instruct me to believe **kyndly**" (1981:11), a more suggestive and mysterious notion. The latter possibility seems more prominent not only because the topic with the adjectival phrase "kynde knowyng" is developed below, but also because the narrator has, as the exchange about his baptism and godparents so far shows, already been given basic instruction in the Christian faith: thus he must now be asking for some different and deeper form of instruction, and doing so with an eagerness that emphasizes the difference from what his early teaching has allowed. In Guillaume de Deguileville's *Pelerinage de vie humaine*, the narrator cannot keep back his desire to know the lady Grace-Dieu's name and identity (see above 68–71n), but in PP the urgency is not to discover her identity but to learn answers to his questions.

To understand **kyndly** may suggest a manner of belief that is personally transforming, or perhaps deeply comprehending, or both (see Harwood 1976, 1992:2–32 and further below here). The adverb can mean 'graciously' or 'naturally,' 'with gratitude" or 'fitly' or 'according to familial relationships'; along with the adjective "kynde" it frequently receives punning treatments in fourteenth-century writings (see Galloway 1994:373–74). The word is imbedded in the language of religious lyrics. One that retells the life of Jesus in a voice that shifts between that of the Virgin, child, lover, and penitent and found in at least fifteen manuscripts, elaborates the word in several of these senses, also framed as a request for learning:

I pray þe, lord, þat *lare lere me [*teaching teach me]
After þi luf to haue langyng,
And sadly sett my hert on þe
And of þi luf to haue lykyng . . .
If I for *kyndnes suld luf my kyn, [*natural affinity *or* graciousness]
Þan me think in my thoght
Be *kyndely skyll I suld be-gyn [*natural reason]
At him þat has me made of noght.

His sembland he sett my saule within
And þis world for me he wroght,
Als fader of *fude my luf to wyn [*child]
Herytage in heuen he has me boght.

As moder of him I may mak mynde
Þat be-for my byrth to me toke hyed,
And sithen with baptym wesched þe *strynd [*race]
Þat *fyled was wyth Adam dede. [*defiled]
With noble mete he norysched my kynde,
For with his flessch he dyd me fede . . .
My kynd all swa he toke þare tyll . . .
When I was went fra him with *wrang, [*wrong]
Fro heuen to erth here he me soght;
My wrecched *kynde for me he *fang, [*nature; *took]
And all his noblelay he sett at noght . . .
For my luf his ded was *dyght, [*prepared]
What kyndenes myght he do me mare? . . .
His lufly lare with hert full fyll
Wele aght me wirk if I war *kynde [*grateful *and* aware of a shared nature],
Night & day to do his will
And euermare haue him in mynde . . . (Brown 1957, no. 48; see also the Vernon lyrics,
ed. Brown 1956, e.g., no. 95)

PP invokes such devotional language but allows more ironic edge, since its narrator's question seems provoked partly by a characteristic dissatisfaction with whatever he learns: he has just been told that he has received proper instruction in childhood from this entity, but immediately he demands a deeper and fuller form of it. C's omission above of B's reference to his having already learned the principles of Christianity (above 73–75n) might be motivated by a wish to remove the odd effect of this repetition. In all versions, however, his hunger for learning is already a defining feature of his character (see, e.g., A.11.103, and C.16.212–13 [B.15.50–51]).

Ultimately such insistence on immediate understanding and believing is shown to be wrongheaded, since the true way of knowing goodness and holiness in the poem is shown to be from gradual and unending experience. Thus Peace in the C text notes the need to experience opposites in order to understand anything: "Ho couthe kyndeliche whit colour descreue / Yf all þe world were whit or swanwhit all thynges? / Yf no nyht ne were no man, as y leue, / Sholde ywyte witterly what day is to mene" (20.213–16). The Incarnation itself is premised on God's desire to know in a "kyndly" manner what Adam suffered and what all sorrow is, in order for God fully to understand goodness (20.227–34a [B.18.218–25]). To know and to believe **kyndly**, then, is to know by the framework of experience, especially by trial of opposites and contrasts. This principle defines and finds expression in much of the poem. A concise and widespread earlier formulation of it appears near the end of the *Roman de la Rose*, although in a very different context, in the author's musings when he is about to use his "harness" finally to enter into the *Rose*: "il fait bon de tout essaier / Por soi miex es biens esgaier . . . . Qui mal essaié n'avra / Ja du bien guieres ne savra; / Ne qui ne set d'onor que monte / Ja ne savra connoistre honte . . . . Aussi va des contraires choses, Les unes sont des autres gloses; / E qui l'une en vuet defenir, / De l'autre li doit sovenir" ("it is good to try everything in order to take greater pleasure in one's good fortune . . . . he who has not tried evil will hardly ever know anything of the good, any more than will he who does not know the value of honor know how to recognize shame. . . . Thus things go by contraries; one is the gloss of the other. If one wants to define one of the pair, he must remember the other"; ed. Poirion 1974, lines 21550–52, 21562–74; trans. Dahlberg 1986). The point is reapplied by other readers of the *Rose*; compare Chaucer's *Book of the Duchess*, "I sey nat that she ne had knowynge / What harm was, or elles she / Had koud no good, so thinketh me" (996–98).

Will's journey will soon begin to unfold in these terms, when Holy Church ceases to answer him about "truth" and turns him toward its opposite, "the false" (see 2.1–4n). His urgent question in the present passage appears well intentioned, but only later does he realize the principle of gradual understanding by experience, that "yf y may lyue and loke y shal go lerne bettere" (10.56–57 [B.8.57–58, A.9.48–50]). Note too her insistence, C's insertion, at 2.47, "Soffre and thow shalt see." See also below, 81–204n.

79–80 (B 83–84, A 81–82): "Teche me . . . How y may saue my soule, þat saynt art yholde": The question assumes a technique that may instantly be conveyed to him, a **How** that he may apply, which in turn assumes that he, in his present state, is a fit responsible agent for this act. This set of assumptions comes to focus on the terms of the Pardon, and finally collapses for Will after his efforts to ask such questions about technique end in a curt dismissal by Scripture and his own or (in C) Recklessness' diatribe, culminating in the doubt of whether he has been "chose or nat chose" (12.52 [B.11.117]). Thus while the Pardon offers an abrupt answer to the present question: "just do well," it also opens up another "how" that continues the poem in its unsettled balance between immediately applied individual efforts or techniques and larger forces and more gradual processes of learning. The answer to the impatient "how?" here is patience, suffering, and long experience of constrasting values.

þat saynt art yholde: "you who are considered holy" (with common Middle English use of a relative pronoun without antecedent noun or pronoun). In C and B, Will has not used second-person singular/familiar verb forms to Holy Church until now (**art**), if manuscript evidence is correct (see 55–67n). Below, at 137 (B 138, A 127), he returns in most manuscripts of all versions to the second person plural/formal pronoun "ʒe," but some copies in A and C continue the second-person singular/familiar pronoun there as well. On the poet's care in this distinction, see also Prol.149–51n.

The lesson on "treuthe" as humility, fidelity, and charity

81–204 (B 85–209, A 83–183): "When alle tresores ben tried treuthe is þe beste . . ." . . . leue at me she lauhte: Holy Church's last answer, encompassing the rest of the passus, is structured as a homiletic elaboration of this opening claim. **treuthe**'s meanings of 'fidelity,' 'integrity,' and 'veracity' define goodness in domains from the religious to what we would call the psychological and social, reinforced by the identity of "truth" with Jesus, based on John 14:6 and behind that Psalm 30:6 as well as other scriptural texts (see Prol.15n). Holy Church's elaboration of multiple aspects of her theme's term offers what in preaching contexts is called *divisio* or the making of *distinctiones*, which often proceeds by taking each word of a scriptural quotation and expounding a series of senses, uses in other scriptural passages ("concording" it), and uses or elaborations by other approved or appropriate authorities, and the use of narratives, with fearful or inspiring explications, for amplifying the theme's meanings (see Higden, *Ars componendi sermones*, chaps. 9–19, ed. Jennings 1991:21–60, and further references there to other preaching manuals). Since the key phrase here links **tresores** with **treuthe**, a process of using *divisio* is already at work on the term **tresores**. This term invokes and changes the sense of the earthly treasure mentioned earlier (above 52 [B 56, A 54]), now reinterpreted in terms of Matthew 6:19–20, "Lay not up to yourselves treasures on earth . . . but lay up to yourselves treasures in heaven."

Yet as Simpson notes, the dreamer's earlier question seeks to separate earthly from spiritual economies, whereas Holy Church uses "the very term which potentially threatens Truth [i.e., **tresor**], to describe Truth," in a way that does not reject all **tresor** but argues that Treuthe is the *best* **tresor** (1987:89–95). Holy Church's theme does not declare, like Matthew 6:19, that worldly treasures should not be laid up, but rather that after "trying" or testing all treasures, Truth will emerge as best. The emphasis on proof and gradual experience as a means to understanding is crucial to her lesson, and a contrast to the narrator's expectations of instant understanding. The principle is clearest in the motto *omnia probate, quod bonum est tenete* ("prove [i.e., test] all things, hold fast that which is good": 1 Thess. 5:21), quoted by Conscience at 3.491, 495, and repeated in C as part of Peace's discussion in both B and C of even God's need to learn by experience (20.227–34a [B.18.218–25]). As at that climactic moment, understanding truth here also is said to involve knowledge by contrasts and accumulated experience; in this sense, Holy Church prepares for Will to "try" worldly treasure by being drawn to ponder Lady Meed in the next passus. Her own theme asserts that he cannot fully know the True until he has proceeded to experience the treasures offered by False. The point is logically fulfilled by the literal "trial" of Lady Meed in passus 4 (see passus 4 Headnote). For a parallel in the *Roman de la Rose* to the idea of knowledge by contrasts and experience, see above, see above 77–78n.

This section is the poem's first significant elaboration of a single Middle English word, using the methods and materials of preachers and preaching manuals but bringing these to bear on a nonscriptural, vernacular, and possibly original statement (for later instances of elaboration of a single Middle English word, see Wit's speech on "kynde" [10.151–307 (B.9.25–210, A.10.26–218)], Conscience's elaboration of "Meed" [B.3.231–51 and C.3.286–412], and the late elaboration of "Nede" [22.1–51n]). For an example of a preaching manual's description of this technique in the context of elaborating a scriptural passage, see Jennings 1991:xl, and 16–32; for discussion of the relation of Holy Church's speech to sermon methods and actual materials see Wenzel 1988:165–67. It is Holy Church's bravura performance, marshalling in a thick series of quotations a wide range of materials to support her carefully crafted finale, the climax to her verse sermon, and her return to what the vision of the the Field of Folk with its two towers means.

81 (B 85, A 83): When alle tresores ben tried treuthe is þe beste: Given the importance of testing knowledge in the poem, the further claim for a trinitarian pun on "tried," "triȝed," and "three" already at this instance seems unlikely, but that possibility is stronger below at 136 (see Huppé 1950; and Prol.15n). Holy Church takes this line as her theme and, in good sermon fashion, at the conclusion repeats this theme as proven "by siht of this textes" (201–2). Instead of a biblical phrase elaborated into points supported by other kinds of examples and materials, as is the common procedure of sermons, Holy Church takes the same care with an original, vernacular, alliterative statement supported by a series of scriptural authorities. The choice of a nonscriptural theme shows that her discourse, for all of its evocation of actual late medieval sermons, is not after all a sermon in a fully official sense. Basevorn and Higden, for example, in their preaching manuals insist that a sermon's initial *thema* must be from the Bible, with strict rules about which words may be altered when quoting it (Basevorn, in Charland 1936:250–53; Jennings 1991:17–20).

82 (B 86, A 84): I do it on *deus caritas* to deme þe sothe: "I adduce the text 'God is love' [1 Jn 4:8 and 4:16] to prove the truth of this." The phrase **do it on** (or "upon") functions in PP as a technical idiom for invoking as support for an argument an example or text, corresponding to *adducere* in Latin sermons (and perhaps influenced phonetically by that word). See 2.39, B.3.188, and B.10.38. To "undo" something is to explicate it or provide an answer to it (see 2.39, 41n). The general relevance of 1 John to Holy Church's themes has been widely noted (see Davlin 1996 for consideration of PP's use of both the Gospel and the Epistle of John). Wenzel argues that Holy Church's exposition of the theme falls in two halves, the first developing the notion of **treuthe**, the second that of love in relation to this concept of **treuthe**. The reference to 1 John anticipates the second section by invoking love at the opening where it is "implicitly set in relation" to **treuthe**, and later this connection receives fuller development (Wenzel 1988:165–66; Davlin 1996:90, 116–18). Taking the reference as 1 John 4:4–8 and connecting the section to the continued emphasis on proper use of worldly goods (which reappears at the end of Holy Church's speech), Dunning sees in the passage an implied opposition between the false teachings of the avaricious worldly and the truth of the spirit of love and charity (Dunning 1980:29–30). Prsl notes that other passages in 1 John support Holy Church's overall focus on keeping God's word.

The second use of *Deus caritas* in 1 John is particularly pertinent. The Latin in the Vulgate passage just following that use of *Deus caritas* reveals a specific connection to Middle English "treuthe" in a discussion of *fiducia*:

[4:16] et nos cognovimus et credidimus caritati quam habet Deus in nobis; Deus caritas est et qui manet in caritate in Deo manet et Deus in eo; [4:17] in hoc perfecta est caritas nobiscum ut *fiduciam* habeamus in die iudicii quia sicut ille est et nos sumus in hoc mundo.

[And we have known and have believed the charity which God has to us; God is charity; and he that abides in charity abides in God, and God in him. In this is the charity of God perfected with us, that we may have confidence (Wycliffite Bible: "trist") in the Day of Judgment; because as he is, we also are in this world.]

Holy Church's theme on **treuthe** thus appears supported by the reference to the *fiducia* we hold with God and God with us concerning the Day of Judgment, a trust constituting both a sign and means of our "contract" with God for salvation. Holy Church thus answers Will's question, How may I save my soul? by alluding to a text describing the *fiducia*, the trust or "troth" we have concerning our final judgment. In Gatrynge's sermon, "trouthe" similarly translates *fides*, and it is the first virtue that "Haly Writte teches." By "trouthe," "we trow anely in Godd that made all thynges, with all the other artycles I touchede before. And this es nedfull till all that cristenly lyffes, for trouthe es begynnynge of all gude dedis; for nother es troughe worthe withowtten gud werk, ne na werke withowtten trouthe may pay Godd Almyghtty" (ed. Blake 1972:83).

In B, Wit also cites 1 John 4:16 to support his statement that "ale þay lyuen good lif are lik to god almyȝty" (9.65; see also C.3.403a, B.5.486b).

83 (B 87, A 85): Hit is as derworthe a druerie as dere god hymseluen: With **druerie** in the sense of 'treasure'—a sense often applied figurally in religious contexts (MED 3b)—the statement repeats the theme; with **druerie** in the sense of 'love-token' (MED 3a), the statement sustains the point of 1 John 4:17 that God's *fiducia* for human salvation is the mutual love between God and human beings. With a mildly scandalous echo of love-talking, **druerie . . . dere god** practically translates *deus charitas*.

84–87 (B 88–91, A 86–89): For who is trewe of his tonge . . . by saynt Lukes wordes: Holy Church's most exalted view of human potential, amounting to deification of the human being who speaks, acts, and intends according to the love that is God (as described in 1 John 4:16). This seems to speak of the mystical and contemplative tradition of union with God (so Vasta 1965); but in PP it does so within the terms of a fully active and secularly involved life, invoking the activities of urban professionals and laborers as well as clerics, and looking forward to the half acre (C.8, B.6, A.7); see also Tommy Trewe-tonge (4.18 [B.4.18]), whose antitype is Tommy Two-tonge (22.162 [B.20.162]). Indeed, when Thought presents similar exhortations later they define merely the first level of "doing well"; the C reading of line 84 is identical to the B and C line in Thought's lesson to Will concerning Dowel (see 10.78).

by saynt Lukes wordes may refer to Luke 6:35 ("love your neighbors, do well, lend money without expecting repayment . . . and you will be sons of the Most High"). But **a god by þe gospel** more closely resembles John 10:34, where Jesus quotes Psalm 81:6: "you are gods" (so Prsl); see also 1 John 3:1–2, "Behold what manner of charity the Father has bestowed upon us, that we should be called and should be the sons of God . . . we are now the sons of God." The phrase also parallels the similar claim that those who "restrain the tongue" can become divine, in the Distichs of Cato, assumed to be pagan: "Virtutem primam esse puto, compescere linguam: / proximus ille deo est qui scit ratione tacere" ("To restrain the tongue I judge the first virtue; he is nearest to a god who knows how to be wisely silent" [1.3; ed. Duff and Duff 1982]). This range of Christian and pagan sources for her statement may be why Holy Church adds that "cristene and vncristene claymeth it echone" (89 [B 93, A 91]; see Galloway 1987). Her purposes of course are Christian. To be able to grant **hele**, "health" evidently in the spiritual as well as physical senses of this word, invokes the healing powers of the apostles (as in Acts) and the sacramental powers transmitted down from them to priests, and looks more generally toward Holy Church's later comment on love as a "most souerayne salue for soule and for body" (147).

88–136 (B 92–137, A 90–126): Clerkes þat knowen hit . . . treuthe and trewe loue is no tresor bettre: Holy Church's discourse shifts to specifying the ideal of **treuthe** for two social estates: the clergy and knighthood. The clergy are only briefly treated at the beginning and end of this section: their task is teaching, making **hit**, "treuthe," widely known in its *true*, that is Christian, form. Her discussion of the ideal of **treuthe** in the estate of knighthood emphasizes the loyalty to principles of justice and impartiality that military actions must sustain: they must maintain **treuthe** (here loyalty) according to **resoun**, and their punishment of transgressors is not summary execution but an imprisonment defined by the sentence **treuthe** passes (93). Will is addressed at the end of this section as if he were himself one of those responsible for instructing those who do not know this **treuthe** and its value: **Lere hit thus lewed men, for lettred hit knoweth** (135), although he quickly distances himself from possessing any such authority (137). There and elsewhere Holy Church appears to limn his role as a poet who is didactic yet somehow removed both from clerical and from secular cultures, or somehow positioned at the point of those two estates' overlapping dependence on Holy Church. Will's posture as too humble socially to be of significant lay status and too unlearned to be of significant clerical authority merges the two in a complex social address, allowing his manifestly inadequate persona to function as the necessary communicator to both (see also below 135n, 146–58n, and A 137n).

92 (B 96, cp. A 94): *transgressores* [cp. A: *trespassours*]: The terms are general names for law-breakers; the French calque used in A, **trepassours**, is often found in legal documents as "offender" (see A-ND; Alford, *Gloss.*). **transgressores** says the same thing, but its Latin form may evoke James 2:9: "But if you have respect to persons, you commit sin, being reproved by the law as transgressors [*transgressores*]." The passage in James was frequently invoked in medieval discussions of impartial justice (Alford, *Quot.* 35). Here there may be a particular insistence on how knights should be firm with those who try to curry favor with the rich like themselves (so Rogers 2002:95–96); C's further addition at 95 supports the connection to the passage in James with its concern for avoiding corrupt favoritism, but there cautions the knights from being *transgressores* themselves by favoring the powerful: "And for no lordene loue leue þe trewe partie." Holy Church near the end of her discourse quotes another passage from the same chapter of James (see below 181–83a), and another of her statements may reflect that chapter too (see 96–98n). All the overt or likely Latin quotations from James are added in the B and C texts.

94–101 (cp. B 100–104, A 98–102): And halden with hym . . . in hope to lac-che syluer: C has shifted and expanded a discussion where the B and A texts, after the comments on David (which C locates after these lines), define knighthood as a sacred **ordre** (for the sacralizing of this estate, see below 96–98n). C's shifting of this passage may be due to the corrupt B text the poet used to make his second revision, since the B archetype here also has the lines disordered; KD-B argue that in making C, L "smoothed the incorrect sequence in the scribal manuscript before him" (104). The expansion, however, goes beyond minor smoothing; it also features greater specificity in knights' and kings' relation to legal endeavors: at 94, C adds the admonition that knights must **halden with hym and with here þat han trewe action**, that is, join with others only in legitimate legal procedings (see MED *accioun* 2.(b), OED *action* II.7.a; Alford, *Gloss.* s.v. *accioun,* apparently based on MED *accioun* 2(a), "cause or grounds for lawsuit" rather than the legal process itself, is misleading here). The following line (95), also added in C, further specifies that knights, once entered into such legitimate legal proceedings, should not be swayed in their testimony or jury decisions by loyalties or obligations to other lords: **And for no lordene loue leue þe trewe partie. lordene** is genitive plural, a survival of Old English *–ena* found throughout the West Midlands and South, most commonly in a subjective genitive (compare C.5.31, "lollarne lyf") rather than an objective genitive as here (see Mustanoja 1960:73). But **lordene** appears in alliterative diction elsewhere (e.g., *Somer Soneday*, "Last litel lordene lif, / fikel is fortune"; ed. Turville-Petre 1989, lines 125–26). Two C manuscripts of PP use "lordene sones" at C.5.74 (the rest present "lordes sones" there, chosen by RK-C).

Complaints of legal corruption are common in late medieval England, but historians have long disputed the period's degree of and fundamental reliance on legal corruption. Some have seen such corruption as regular practice of the period's "bastard feudalism," by which lords exerted their power through what were in effect private armies, those employed (for an annual wage rather than a grant of land, as earlier in medieval culture) by them for all manner of services and usually garbed in their livery or other emblems of affiliation (Bellamy 1989); others see the monetary ties of lordship characterizing "bastard feudalism" as not producing legal corruption as the norm but as a by-product, and not a novel one, of a functional social world increasingly using monetary rewards but nonetheless based on the value of "service" and loyalty, however subject to the self-interest of all cultures (McFarlane 1973:1–18, 102–21, 228–47; Hicks 1995:84–93). Juries could be "challenged" on the bases of the biases that Holy Church mentions—on the grounds that in relation to the defendants they were "dyvers ways syb or alyed, old howshad [household] servandes, free tenandes reteyned be fee or lyverey"; and gift-giving in the context of bribery was a condemned if common practice in all legal endeavors, from jury to advocates to judges to the royal court (see Bellamy 1989:63–67, 81–97, 102–22; 1498 case at 65). Thus C 101 (slightly revising B 103) declares: **neuer leue for loue in hope to lacche syluer**; i.e., "do not neglect [pursuing justice or supporting a just cause] because of political loyalty, with the expectation of gaining some reward." As Owst shows, *munera, amor, favor, odium* ("money, love, partisanship, grudges") are the key terms of many homiletic complaints about abuses of the law by lawyers, judges, and lords in charge of rendering justice: "all the satires and complaints of English medieval preaching against the law do little else than ring the changes on these unhappy themes" (Owst 1933:341). Yet Palmer declares that "no one who has spent even a couple months reading the court records or who has examined the rigor with which legal argument in the courts was pursued can believe that only violence and wealth, not law, determined relations in that society" (Palmer 1984:13). McFarlane, however, finds a discernible shift toward manipulation rather than outright breaking of the law by those so inclined: "feuds that in an earlier century would have ended, if not begun, in bloodshed, were now pursued within the framework of justice—with no loss of zeal. Hence from the end of the thirteenth century the growth of a demand for legislation on such topics as maintenance, champerty, conspiracy, and embracery. But it is as well to remember that the offences were not necessarily as new as the remedies provided to deal with them" (McFarlane 1973:115). See also 2.60–63n.

96–98 (cp. B 100–104, A 98–102): Trewelich to take . . . appostata of knyghthed: The early fifteenth-century Lollard treatise *The Lanterne of Liȝt* succinctly parallels the statement: "it parteyneþ to þe ordir of knyȝthod to defende Goddis lawe, to maynten good lyuars [those living justly] & to iustifie or soore punysche mysdoars" (ed. Swinburn 1917 for 1915:34); but the connection simply shows that this much of the idea was widespread, not a sign of "Lollard" influence (Wycliffite writings often go on to say that knights and secular lords should also teach the law of God in English, in the absence of sufficiently learned priests; Aston and Richmond 1997:10). From the twelfth century, clerical writers defined knighthood as a religious "order" (see Morris 1978), and the Knights Hospitaller and Knights Templar date from that period. The Templars especially sought to follow as much a monastic rule as a military code, and their strong establishment in Britain—until they were arrested and dispersed in 1308 on various charges of heresy, apostasy, homosexuality, and misuse of wealth—remains visible in their distinctive round church at London, the New Temple (built 1166; see Lord 2002:22–40). Their foundation was encouraged by Bernard of Clairvaux, whose tract "In Praise of the New Knighthood" (c. 1130) defines the ascetic clothing and regular hours of an "order" that "indefatigably wages a twofold combat, against flesh and blood and against spiritual hosts of evils in the heavens" (cap. 1; see Greenia 2000:33). Several poems and treatises on the "order" of knighthood as such also appear in the thirteenth and fourteenth centuries, and in the fourteenth and fifteenth centuries, kings in England and elsewhere in western Europe created various elite "orders" or societies of knighthood on the model of lay confraternities and thus with quasi-religious outlooks and trappings of ordination and membership, but none with the ascetic ideals of the Templars (see Keen 1984:5–15, 179–99). Some occasion for the general trend lies in the fourth-century Latin guide to military arts by Vegetius, *De re militari*, well known throughout the later Middle Ages in scholarly, courtly, and practical military realms (see Green 1980:144; Lester 1988:12–17); this work opens by declaring that those who are "piscatores, aucupes dulciarios linteones omnesque, qui aliquid tractasse uidebuntur ad gynaecea pertinens, longe arbitror pellendos a castris" ("fishermen, fowlers, confectioners, linen-weavers, and all who will seem to have done things that pertain to womanly affairs, I think, ought to be kept far from the camp": ed. Önnerfors 1995:17). All these terms are transformed into medieval moral and social forms by Jean de Meun in his popular late thirteenth-century translation of Vegetius: "on ne doit pas eslire pour estre chevaliers hommes pereceus, oiselleurs, rabardiaus, jougleurs, tresgetteurs, bordeliers, ne gent qui s'entremetten d'office appartenans as delices" ("one must not choose to be knights men who are lazy, idle, ribalds, cheap entertainers, lowly tricksters, pimps, or anyone involved with any role in serving pleasures": ed. Robert 1897:11–12), and further (probably via consultation of Jean's translation) by the late fourteenth or early fifteenth-century Middle English translation possibly by John Trevisa: "ffissheres, fouleres, rymoures and gestours, lechoures and holoures [fornicators or adulterers] ne schulde noʒt ben chosen to kniʒthod" (Lester 1988:54). Beyond the tradition of Vegetius, the early thirteenth-century verse *Ordene de chevalerie* (ed. House 1919) describes the investiture into the "sainte ordene de chevalerie" (line 85) in the words of a knight, Sir Hugues of Tiberias, who has been captured by Saladin and compelled to explain and demonstrate the investiture of the order of knighthood to the Islamic sultan. This widely copied work is in turn a source for the late four-teenth-century prose *Livre de chevalerie* by Geoffroi de Charny, which lengthily contrasts the "orders" of the priesthood and of knighthood (sec. 42, ed. Kaeuper and Kennedy 1996:181–91).

appostata (a masculine Latin noun directly incorporated into Middle English and Anglo-Norman) refers to a Christian who renounces Christianity, more narrowly a clerk in holy orders who returns to a secular life (Niermeyer 1997). The reference to "apostasy" from the "order" of knighthood parallels a phrase in the mid-fifteenth-century verse translation of Vegetius, *Knyghthode and Bataile*: ". . . chiualers, the worthiest of fame, / That wil with wisdom & with wepon smyte, / Noo knyght apostata, noon ypocrite, / Feers, feithful, ofte approved, olde & wise / Knyghtys be thei . . ." (ed. Dyboski and Arend 1936, lines 1785–89). But this, which is not in the Latin original (3.14, ed. Önnerfors 1995), likelier refers to a knight who is an apostate from Christianity than from the quasi-religious "order" of knighthood, the latter a notion that Holy Church develops with unusual boldness, as if it could fully compete with the spiritual authority of religious orders. But in milder terms late medieval writ-ers discussing knighthood were often drawn toward comparisons with reli-gious principles and orders. The fifteenth-century verse translator of Vegetius recounts that when he presented his work to Henry VI, the king declared, "For my seruyse / Heer wil I rede (he seith) as o psaultier" (ed. Dyboski and Arend 1936, lines 57–58).

For **þat poynt**, compare James 2:10, "whoever keeps the whole law but fails in one [*in uno*] has become guilty of all of it" (so Prsl; for other passages from this chapter of James, see above, 92n, and below 181–83a and note). Yet Holy Church's language is also closely keyed to the nomenclature of a knight's military profession: the **poynt** of fighting and winning **Trewelich** is not only the essential "point" or goal (MED *pointe* 6(b)) of knighthood but also its chief weapon (MED *pointe* 11 (a, b)), which, like a spear or arrow, must not miss or "pass" its target (MED *passen* 1(e)).

99 (cp. B 101, A 99): For thei sholde nother faste ne forbere the serk: This departs from many guides to the "order" of knighthood, which often suggest that the knights follow some measure of observance suited to Christian reli-gious orders (see note above). The *Ordene de chevalerie* declares that a knight should fast rigorously on Fridays if he is at all able to (ed. House 1919, lines

275–89). Bernard of Clairvaux specifically emphasizes that the Templars utterly forsake the "feminine tresses" of "worldly knights," and instead "both in raiment and in rations they shun every excess" (cap. 2, 4, tr. Greenia 2000:37, 45); the Templars' calling themselves the "poor knights" in spite of their eventually massive wealth sustains this image of austerity (Lord 2002:5). Holy Church's view that knights are not to follow the rules of professional religious is a further bold claim that their "profession and pure order" has a spiritual legitimacy of its own, just as it is. Her comment is perhaps also in response to the increasing austerity in clothing and burial of some knights in terms that resembled (but was not necessarily identical with) Lollardy, to which late fourteenth- and early fifteenth-century knights were often said to be attracted, making them "appostata" in the broader religious sense that was receiving much attention in the period (see Catto 1982; Hudson 1988:110–17).

forbere the serk: C's addition probably means not that knights should avoid going without a "shirt" altogether as a form of penance (so Skt), but that they should not put aside their soft knightly clothing in favor of the rough gown of a religious, as at 6.6 (B.5.65, A.5.48). Compare the advice for abstemiousness in *Cursor Mundi* (ed. Morris 1876), line 17243, "Forsak þi serc o silk and line." The forms of assuming knighthood often involved the donning of robes and a coif and elaborate ceremonial: see the *Ordene* (ed. House 1919, lines 137–66), and the *Livre de chevalerie* (sec. 36, ed. Kaeuper and Kennedy 1996:166–71).

102–3 (B 98–99, A 96–97): Dauid in his daies dobbed knyghtes . . . to serue treuthe euere

102–3 (B 98–99, A 96–97): Dauid in his daies dobbed knyghtes . . . to serue treuthe euere: Donaldson (1990, ad loc.) notes 1 Chron. 12:18, where David receives a group of Benjaminites and Judahites and makes them the leaders (*principes*) of his troop; more broadly the list of David's heroes in 2 Kings (Vulg.) 23 is pertinent. The chivalric view of this "dubbing" may derive from the tradition of the nine Worthies, in which pagan, Jewish, and Christian heroic figures are presented in various works, including the *Parlement of the Three Ages*, in similarly chivalric terms. Uriah, for example, is there called David's "ownn knyghte" (ed. Offord 1959, line 451). It may be pertinent that Bernard of Clairvaux's treatise on the "new order" of the Templars opens by declaring that with this order, a "horn of salvation" has again been raised up "in the house of [God's] servant David" (cap. 1, tr. Greenia 2000:33; cp. Luke 1:69). The chivalric presentation of all previous heroic history, including scriptural history, is of course prevalent in medieval writing, emphatically so below in the Crucifixion and Harrowing (passus 20 [B.18]). Holy Church's comment, however, is no general "medievalizing" of the scriptural past but a calculated use of biblical materials to argue for the connection between knighthood and "treuthe."

104–8 (cp. B 105–6, A 103–4): And god whan he bigan . . . on of goddes knyghtes: For the phrase and some basis for the chivalric vision of heaven, see 2 Timothy 2:3–4: "Labor as a good soldier of Christ Jesus. No man, being a soldier to God, entangles himself with secular businesses." The *Pricke of Conscience* calls martyrs "Godes awen knyghtes" (5524, ed. Morris 1863); the New Testament term *miles* (for a Roman soldier) is regularly construed in Middle English as "knyght." For the image of heaven as a royal court, an ancient Hebrew idea, compare the more elaborate courtly structure presented in the *Legenda Aurea*, where after describing the hierarchies of the angels, Jacob of Voragine says,

This ordering and ranking of the angels can be understood by its similarity to the organization of a royal court. Among the king's ministers, some, such as chamberlains, counselors, and assessors, work in immediate contact with him: the orders in the first hierarchy are similar to these. Other officials have duties pertaining to the overall government of the kingdom, not to one particular province: of this class are the commanders of the militia and the judges in the courts of law, and they are similar to the orders in the second hierarchy. There are also minor officials, for instance, prefects, bailiffs, and the like, who are put in charge of a particular part of the kingdom: these are similar to the orders of the lowest hierarchy. (trans. Ryan 1993:203)

   creatures tene . . . suche seuene and anoþer: Heaven is often said to have been originally populated by ten "orders" but PP presents these as individuals, as if not understanding that "seraphim" and "cherubim" are plural; the confusion is still greater in B when these are more clearly treated as individual knights (105–7). Taking "seraphim" and "cherubim" as singular is, however, a common medieval error (even Isidore of Seville takes words with such endings as both singular and plural). Seven of the remaining eight cannot, however, be mistaken as singular in the usual sources: thrones, dominions, virtues, powers, principalities, archangels, and angels; the final one, **anoþer**, is dramatically left unnamed at the line break until the next line identifies this as Lucifer (for a narrative description of the "orders" see the Legend of St. Michael, Archangel, in the *Legenda Aurea*, trans. Ryan 1993:203; see also Dionysius the Areopagite, *On the Heavenly Hierarchy*, chaps. 6–9, tr. and ed. Parker 1976). The solution appears to be that the ten "knights" are each the leaders of large companies of their own, as when Lucifer fell so fell "mo þousandes myd hym þan man kouþe nombre" (B 116). But the other "creatures" do not have their own "menyee" since in heaven there is only "God's "meynee" (B 108). Later, Liberum Arbitrium (Anima in B) tells Will that his incessant thirst for knowledge shows that he is "oen of pruydes knyhtes," a parallel to "luciferes knaue" (see

Prol.40n), thus followers or "children" of Lucifer who "ful fram heuene" (16.212–13 [B.15.50–51]).

B 107–10 (A 105–8): Yaf hem myȝt . . . nouȝt ellis: A/B's remark emphasizes that they gained their understanding by being taught, just as the dreamer seeks to be taught. Having the heavenly beings receive instruction þoruȝ þe **Trinitee** literalizes in a witty way early catechetic teaching about the Trinity. C's omission may endeavor to restrain such energetic wit in sacred matters, or to avoid the implication that beings who are pure intelligences needed instruction in the human terms that are whimsically suggested here.

111a (B 119): *Ponam pedem . . . altissimo*: "I will set my foot in the north, and I will be like the most high." Having suggested how the human being who follows "treuthe" and abides in love can become "lyk to oure lord" (87), Holy Church now shows how the archangel who had "*lust* to be lyk his lord" but who with his followers "helden nat with treuthe" (109) fell to the deepest hell. For the different kind of "fall" of the Incarnation, see below 149-50n. *Desire* to be "lyk to oure lord" is the antithesis of the love and obedience that may produce a truer similitude to God, as Liberum Arbitrium (B's Anima) implies when scolding Will and evoking Lucifer with the same Latin passage (16.213a [B.15.51a]; see above 104–8n). The quotation was originally derived from Isaiah 14:13–14 and then, with alterations, applied typologically to Lucifer, especially in Augustine's commentaries on Psalms 1:4 and 47:2, where it appears in nearly the form that L uses it except that it reads "seat" (*sedem*) not "foot" (*pedem*). L need not have taken Augustine's version of the phrase directly from the commentary on the psalms, since the quotation is found elsewhere and in more pertinent contexts. It appears, for example, in commentaries on two fables by Avianus, where proud entities are allegorically interpreted as representing Lucifer (Risse 1966). Another likely intermediary source is the *Vita Adae et Evae*, preserved in over a hundred manuscripts and translated widely in medieval vernacular languages, including several Middle English poetic and prose versions (see Murdoch and Tasioulas 2002:1–34), among them the late fourteenth-century Vernon manuscript that includes a copy of PP. This work also includes a summary of the sacred history that Holy Church is presenting. There, Lucifer rejects St. Michael's warning that God will be angry if Lucifer does not honor Adam, and asserts, "If he is angry with me, I will place my seat above the stars of the sky and I will be most like God." A fifteenth-century manuscript of the Latin version has the "Augustinian" reading "in the north" for "above the stars of the sky" ("ponam sedem ad aquilonem et ero similis altissimo"), and this version appears to have been circulated in England, for the Vernon translation follows it: "Ye yif he beo wroth with me I wot where to abyden: I schal sette my seete in the north syde and I wol be lyk the hexte that is aboven us" (ed. Blake 1972:106; the Latin text is ed. Meyer 1878:214, 226). One sermon by Augustine presents both this passage and one like that on the "warmth" of the south added to C just following it; see below, 115–25n.

In all of these cases the quotation reads, "*Ponam* sedem . . .," "I will place my *seat*"; since we have no other example of the change, the shift from "seat" to "foot" seems L's own (see Kellogg 1972:413–14; 1972:32–59, confirmed by Hill 2001b). That this change is authorial, not scribal, is supported by line 119 below, present only in C: "For theder as þe fende fly his *fote* for to sette . . .". It is just possible that the change in the Latin was originally an archetypal error in B, and that the C reviser using a corrupt copy condoned and exploited it further, but the attention in the whole section to Lucifer's fall and location seems too consistently energetic to make this likely. The insertion of the motif of Lucifer misstepping and plummeting, coming to rest finally in the lowest place, confers a sense of vigor, drama, and physicality on Lucifer's attempt to occupy the seat of God. The alteration of the Latin text may draw on the references elsewhere in Augustine's commentaries on the psalms to the "foot of pride," *pes superbiae* (see Kellogg 1958:386–90; see also Freccero 1986:29–54; Hill 2001b); or it may be L's own conflation of the passage in Isaiah with such biblical passages as Psalm 35:12: "Let not the foot of pride come to me: and let not the hand of the sinner move me," or Psalm 59:10, "Into Edom will I stretch out my shoe: to me the foreigners are made subject." To "put one's foot" also invokes Middle English idioms for entering a place (see MED *fot* 14q, OED *foot* 28b), and for combating or striving against another (OED (28a)). The sense of the devil putting his foot in unsavory places has some echo in Chaucer, when the Manciple tells the Cook, "Hoold cloos thy mouth, man, by thy fader kyn! / The devel of helle sette his foot therin!" (*Canterbury Tales* IX.38).

112–14: "Lord! why wolde he tho . . . roweth?": Added in C, the dreamer's intrusion addresses the mystery of Lucifer's disobedience, which none of Holy Church's comments have plumbed. The most general form of the dreamer's question would be, If human beings' sins derive from Lucifer, what are the origins of his? But the dreamer does not in fact ask that more general question. Instead, his question, based on the scene Holy Church has unfolded, is too literal to allow an answer: why should he be *in the cold north* rather than (**thenne** relies on the implied comparative in **wolde**) in the sunny warmth? **þe sonne syde þere þe day roweth** opposes the north to the sun, possibly because of the double meaning of Latin *meridie* as 'midday' and 'south'; see following note.

115–25: "Nere hit for northerne men . . . knaues, when þei worche": Continuing the new materials in C, this passage both elaborates and allegorizes the remoteness and ruggedness of the north as a fitting place for Lucifer's overweening character. The elaboration of north and south in terms of sacred history follows the clearer cosmology of C (see Prol.14–18n, and below 122a n). In art and architecture, the north of a church was usually associated with night and cold, and often carried the symbolism of the Old Testament; it was the place for the Virgin, and for women parishioners to sit. The south was often associated with warmth and light, and bore the symbolism of the New Testament, and provided the seats for the male parishioners (see Ferguson 1966:43–44; Aston 1990). For the north in England as a notoriously barbaric region see *The Owl and the Nightingale* (ed. Cartlidge 2001), lines 905–22, 995–1030, and for another location of the devil there, Chaucer's Friar's Tale line 1413. See also Guillaume de Deguileville, *Pelerinage de vie humaine* (ed. Stürzinger 1893), line 7242, referencing the north wind as the influence of Despair, and implicitly of Satan.

In one of his treatments of the verse *pone pedem* (from a recently discovered sermon collection preserved in a single fifteenth-century French copy), Augustine moves from the Isaiah verse to Song of Songs 1:6, "show me, o you whom my soul loves, where you feed, where you lie in the midday" (*ubi cubes in meridie*), the final word of which means either 'midday' or 'south'; he suggests that north and south are symbols of darkness and light, respectively, and thus of bad angels and good, pride and humility. He then notes, as Holy Church in C implies, that the northern region "stands for spirits that are cold and darkened, while the South stands for those that are enlightened and fervent; so those who are good, as in the South, are fervent and shining brightly, while those who are bad, as in the North, are cold and covered with dark, dense fog" (Sermon 26 [= 198 Maurist], ed. Dolbeau 1996:377). His general movement of thought and perhaps of underlying scriptural texts parallels that of the C insertion in PP; at any rate, the double meaning of Latin *meridie* accounts for PP's new association in C between 'south' and 'midday.' **southe þer þe sonne regneth** answers and neatly echoes the dreamer's phrase "why wolde he . . . sitten in þe sonne syde þere þe day roweth?" Its answer presents a pun on the Son of God (viz., *sol justiciae*, Malachi 4:2), who reigns over "fervent souls." Yet in spite of these further allusions and puns, Holy Church's answer remains dutifully close to the dreamer's precise question. Such a narrow method of answering derives from medieval scholastic sparring, and is in this context itself a form of instruction on the importance of asking the right questions, a lesson in inductive reasoning.

The half-playful comments in PP here taking account of how **northerne**

men might feel about the cosmology suggested may express the poet's awareness of the increasingly national readership of his poem by the time of the C version. A sense of large audience evidently informs Holy Church's return to a second-person plural pronoun: **Nere hit for northerne men anon y wolde ʒow telle** (115). See also 124–25n.

121: helle is þer he is: In C, Holy Church moves away from south or north to identify hell as simply where Lucifer is. But this is not the same as the "ubiquism" of some radical sixteenth-century theologians, who deny any location for hell other than wherever the damned are; nor is it like the early thirteenth-century heresy of Amaury de Bene, who was burned for postulating that only states of mind, not real places, define hell (Allen 1956). In PP Lucifer is bound in hell, a fixed cosmological location (see 21.57 [B.19.57]); Holy Church's comment merely emphasizes the impossibility of Lucifer being anywhere other than hell, and thus assures readers that this is not in fact where northern men dwell. Her view is therefore fundamentally unlike both Mephistophilis' in Marlowe's *Dr. Faustus*, "where we are is hell, / And where hell is there must we ever be'" (ed. Wine 1969, lines 513–15), and the ubiquism of Satan in Milton's *Paradise Lost*, "Which way I fly is hell; my self am hell" (ed. Fowler 1980, IV.75).

122a: *Dixit dominus . . . meis*: "The Lord said to my lord, Sit at my right hand" (Ps. 109:1). The passage is quoted by Jesus and later Peter to prove that David considered Christ his Lord (Mt 22:44, Mk 12:36, Lk 20:42; Acts 2:34). C continues to show that heaven and hell are not simply regions where people live; the poet's growing sense of a national landscape conflicts with the cosmology that he has laid down from the A text on. As Prsl notes, from a point of view facing east (confirmed by 133 below), that is, the direction of the Tower of Treuthe and also the direction of an altar in a church, Lucifer in the north is on the left, Jesus on the right in the south. Medieval world maps position east at the top, thus the poem's orientation fits global geography (see Woodward 1987:297). For further associations of the left side with evil, see 2.5, 8n. The psalm's following verse also quoted by Jesus and Peter, "Until I make your enemies your footstool," is also relevant but with a different orientation to Lucifer's position in hell "lowest . . . of hem alle" (128).

124–25: Hewes in þe haliday . . . when þei worche: "Laborers look for warmth in holidays, but care not if it is cold while they are working." A **haliday** was both a holy day and a day of rest from "servile labors," leading to penalties for those who carried on their crafts during those times of rest (see Pfaff 1970:2;

Cheney 1961). The lines are abrupt, and enigmatically gnomic. Prsl's suggestion that they refer to the suffering that people are willing to undergo in this life in the hope of greater pleasure in the afterlife is persuasive but general; this point, with a metaphor of winter and summer, appears explicitly in Patience's speech at 15.287–97 (but not in the parallel B.14.125–30), and at 16.18–20 (B.14.157–73). Possibly the more specific point is that Lucifer went north because he was setting himself to work, of an illicit sort. The lines may also offer a final concession to "northerne men" after Holy Church declares that she will argue no further for a cosmology that places them near hell (123). For northerners' distant, colder world may be anagogically like hell, but the cold literally does not affect them while they are at work, and the nature of that work will determine where they go to rest. Thus as often, a tantalizing metaphoric sense emerges while Holy Church adheres to the precise terms of the dreamer's question, at once frustrating and inspiring him.

126–28 (cp. B 116–26, cp. A 112–15): Wonderwyse, holy wryt telleth . . . lowest lith of hem alle: A and B progressively elaborate the description of Lucifer's fall but C omits much of the detail. In A, it is in the act of falling that Lucifer and his **felawis . . . fendis bicome** (112); B adds details of the kinds of fallen angels (see following note) and says that the fall lasts **ful nyne dayes togideres** until God establishes quiet in heaven (121; see also *Paradise Lost* 1.50–53, 6.870–74: Hesiod says that the fall of the Titans takes nine days; *Theogony* 664–735, but this, while it influenced Milton, would not have directly influenced L). C omits details on the fall and the kinds of fallen angels (except for a trace in line 127 of B's discussion; see B 118–25n below) possibly because the central lines in B's description (122–23), which are corrupt in all B copies, were already incomprehensible in the copy of B that the poet used when creating C (see KD-B 98–127).

B 116–25: And mo þousandes myd hym þan man kouþe nombre . . . somme in helle depe: B elaborates A to generate a glimpse of the ranks of angels who were firmly committed to Lucifer (**þei leueden vpon Lucifer**) as well as those more tentatively looking for Lucifer's success (**And alle þat hoped it myȝte be so**), as Hill (1974) notes. C reduces B's passage to its final survey: **summe in erthe, summe in ayr, summe in helle depe**. According to some medieval sources, the varied disposition of the fallen angels depended on their degree of rebellion against God and loyalty to Lucifer. In the legend of St. Michael in the *South English Legendary* (ed. D'Evelyn and Mill 1956, lines 197–98), the variously suspended angels' degrees of loyalty against God or Lucifer will be finally settled only at Domesday, when it will be determined whether they ascend again or descend forever. The Vernon translation of the *Vita Adae et Evae* similarly adds to its Latin source the information that the angels' degree of assent to Lucifer was established at the moment of the fall, locating them at varying suspended points of exile in phrasing closely resembling L's: "And after that while heo beon pynet, summe more and summe lasse . . . . And he and alle his feeren fullen out of hevene . . . summe astunte in the eyr and summe in the eorthe" (ed. Blake 1972:106/77–79). But according to Jacob of Voragine in the Legend of St. Michael, all the fallen angels are suspended in our "dark air" until the Day of Judgment in order to experience multiple torment: "they are not allowed to live in heaven, or in the upper part of the air, because that is a bright and pleasant place, nor on the earth with us, lest they do us too much harm. They are in the air between heaven and earth, so that when they look up and see the glory they have lost, they grieve for it, and when they look down and see men ascending to the place from which they fell, they are often tormented with envy" (trans. Ryan 1993:205). Instead of this, PP appears to follow the view expressed in the *Vita Adae* and elsewhere, but C's compression may indicate the poet's awareness by then that other views were possible, or simply a retreat from engaging cosmological theories.

129 (cp. B 127, A 116): pruyde that hym pokede [BA: pride þat he putte out]: C's refinement turns to Lucifer's psychic experience rather than his behavior, using the idiom found also at 7.263 (B.5.611, A.6.97).

130–34 (B 128–33, A 117–22): And alle þat worchen þat wikked is . . . that trinite ynne sitteth: The major theme of "doing well" and "doing evil" and their rewards is first announced, although anticipated at 49; for the next significant statement of this theme, see 4.140–45n; the theme climaxes with the Pardon (9.287–92 [B.7.113–18, A.8.95–100]); for the seeming absence of the power of repentance in this severe dichotomy, see Lawler 2000:119 and passim. Holy Church returns to the theme near the end of her discourse, 2.31–37n. C's addition of the references to **Estward** and **þe tour that trinite ynne sitteth** plots Lucifer's actions and consequences directly onto the cosmology of the poem's opening (see Prol.14–18n, and above, note to 122a); as there, so here human choices are literally given a moral compass. Such a "compass" may be aligned with the medieval concept of *synderesis*, the orienting instinct of right and wrong (see Prol.95–135n).

135 (B 136, A 125): Lere it thus lewed men, for lettred hit knoweth: Considered in terms of the poem's fourteenth-century audience, her address to knights by way of those like the clergy who can "translate" her discourse manages to include both as readers of or listeners to the poem; the known contemporary audience was chiefly clerical (see Prologue, Headnote). Lay authorities are addressed by indirection at this point, as if overhearing what Will should pass on to them; yet clerics are similarly placed in a secondary role: at this point Holy Church does not yet address them directly, and they at any rate can at best only emulate or represent vicariously her authority and teachings (see also below 171–80n). The phrase resembles a definition of the role of a parish priest (see above 22n), but Will himself is not clearly clerical here, as he quickly makes obvious (see also above 88–136n). Yet he is also not secular, as the charge Holy Church gives him here makes clear. Her urging of what Will should do is a specific warrant for the poem, not pastoral teaching in the usual sense (see above 88–136n). Here the warrant is overtly to be a translator or amanuensis, as (in A only) Will is a scribe of the Pardon (A.8.43); below, the encouragement to write a kind of didactic song or "harped preaching" suggests fuller license to elaborate (see below 146–58n, and A 137n). More fundamentally, her words and the passus as a whole help create a role for the poet that merges or transcends simple clerical or lay identity and authority by means of a poetry that engages both.

136 (cp. B 137, A 126): Than treuthe and trewe loue is no tresor bettre / A/ B: That Treuþe is tresor þe trieste on erþe: C explicitly draws together two major themes of the passus, or rather unpacks A/B's **Treuþe** into its components. **trewe loue** brings out the linking notion between the terms of fidelity (*fiducia*), as applicable to the feudal relations defined in the chivalric vision of David's knights (and their antitype Lucifer, formerly God's chief knight), and of true treasure—the spiritual treasure that has been tested and found best of all treasures, the definition of the treasure that is explicit here only in A/B. The dreamer's following question refers in all versions to the themes Holy Church has summarized as "it" (138 [B 139, A 128]), indicating the unity of the terms into which C has amplified A/B's **Treuþe**. A/B's adj. **trieste** ("choicest") recalls the initial A/B description of the "tour on a toft" as "trieliche ymaked" (A/ B.Prol.14; see Prol.15n), and appears again at B.16.4 to describe the Tree of Charity. In that last instance, "a ful trie tree" likely puns on "trinity," supporting a sense of that pun here as well.

137–38 (B 138–39, A 127–28): I haue no kynde knowyng . . . my menynges [B, A: By what craft in my cors it comseþ, and where]: As soon as he is told by Holy Church that he should teach her lesson of "treuthe" to "lewed men," Will professes his unworthiness and ignorance, wanting in B more specific physical, and in C more specific psychological information about the origins and workings of "treuthe." The vocation of teacher appears to be a role he is routinely uncomfortable with (but see B.11.101–2; C.20.468–75 [B.18.427–31]; see Galloway 1998a). His restlessness in seeking understanding is already cast as somewhat challenging to his authoritative interlocutors; in a more condescending way, Walter Hilton remarks that those who have fully opened their spiritual vision ("goostli iye") to divinity achieve "a siker feelynge and a soothfast. Yif thou may come therto and holden it, thee thar not neden to renne aboute heer and there and aske questions of ech goostli man what thou schalt doon, hou thou schalt love Jhesu, and how thou schalt serve Hym, and speke of goostli materes that passen thi knowynge, as perchaunce some doon" (*Scale of Perfection* 2.42, ed. Bestul 2000:248). Here Will seems to anticipate such criticism against him; he is later subjected to it by Imaginatif (B.12.16–19); and in general his posture suggests that of one whose thinking and speaking stand outside authoritative institutions of learning but who is continually absorbed by the questions asked in such contexts.

The phrase **kynde knowyng**, denoting some specially intimate or accurate knowledge, cannot be translated in an unchanging form, since its point seems to shift across the poem and across all versions, and indeed its tantalizing elusiveness may reveal its relation to gradual and inevitably inconclusive pursuit of understanding "the true" (see above, 77–78n, and Prol.141–47n). In Holy Church's answer here (line 141), it appears to mean "divine wisdom" and be aligned with desire for mystical knowledge (see Davlin 1971, 1981; Vasta 1965); but in the dreamer's question, it seems more an indication of his limited understanding of the right questions as well as the right answers. In his usage here it appears to mean "intuitive cognition" (Harwood 1992:2–32), but not in a sense that implies that he has yet worked hard at such understanding, and his interest in it here seems precisely that it does not seem to depend on long labor or experience. When the dreamer makes specific queries in B and C about where "treuthe" is located in his body or mind he appears to seek impossibly specific, literal, and immediate information. The overly materialist nature of his own understanding of **kynde knowyng** as implied in his questions about it may reflect the root of his problem in attaining it. Holy Church's response again tracks his level of understanding very closely, pushing it beyond itself by seizing on the phrase he has inaugurated.

138 (cp. B 139, A 128): By what wey it wexeth and wheder out of my menynges [B, A: By what craft in my cors it comseþ, and where]: The A/B form of the question may be tied to the "powers" (*crafts*) of "facultative psychology," which in the Latin Avicenna tradition linked human with divine intellectual powers, and in other medieval traditions located specific mental operations in specific regions of the cranium (so Kaulbach 1993:18–19, 65, 83). But recondite sources need not be sought here; the question of bodily powers also bespeaks the more common language of treatises of vices and virtues. The popular, anonymous thirteenth-century *Summa virtutum de remediis anime*, for example, opens by differentiating the categories of virtues as the natural virtues, political virtues, and virtues of grace; natural virtues include the powers of the soul and the body (*vires anime et corporis*), and the writer adds, "the sensitive powers of the body are also called 'bodily powers' [*virtutes corporee*] by many philosophers, because they are located in the instruments of the body" (ed. Wenzel 1984:52–53). A/B's dreamer's effort to ascertain the bodily origins of "treuthe" rings impertinently, but it appears to fall within the range of legitimate definitions of the faculties in this treatise: "natural" and "spiritual" powers are grouped together, distinguished as the "rational spirit" with intelligence, memory, and will, the "animal spirit" with imagination, memory (*sic*), and appetite or desire, and the "vegetable spirit" with growth, nutrition, and generativity. C's question less technically asks how love or truth develops, and humbly suggests that the topic might exceed his understanding (MED *menynge*, ger. (1), 2). The climax of the topic is at 22.207–8 (B.20.207–8), that the best "craft" is to "Lerne to loue," a view already implied by the answer here and below at 141–42, "to louye thy lord leuest of alle."

140–40a (B 141–41a): To lyte Latyn . . . *duxi vitam iuuenilem*: "Ah me, what a useless life I led as a youth!" The Latin, as often, is spoken *in propria persona* of the speaker. B wittily introduces the Latin tag to comment on a lack of Latin learning, using a proverbial line in leonine verse (Walther 1982–86, no. 6232, 10736b). The line is also found (as Prsl notes) in a manuscript, John Rylands Library MS. 394, along with other Latin quotations used or invoked by L; in keeping with the schoolroom atmosphere of Holy Church's lesson, the manuscript possesses other contents suggesting an educational context and function (see Pantin 1930; see B.10.266a; and see also Galloway 1995). The line also appears later in Sloth's confession in B and C (7.54a [B.5.440]), a portrait that Bowers notes "brings into high profile certain moral features shared by the Dreamer" (1986:88; see generally chaps. 6–8). Criticism of unlearned clergy is pervasive in the poem, but the dreamer is often treated with particular exasperation (see e.g., Dame Study in passus 11 [B.10, A.11]).

141–45 (B 142–46, A 130–34): Hit is a kynde knowynge . . . and so thow myht lerne: Hit has typically been taken as an impersonal construction referring proleptically to **kynde knowynge**, an assumption often used to define the latter phrase. But as White points out, **this y trowe be treuth** allows **Hit** to refer to "truth," the topic of Holy Church's lesson (White 1988:52). If "treuth" is linked to the *fiducia* of salvation that, according to 1 John 4:16–17, human and divine love establishes (see 82n), then this "treuthe" or *fiducia* is easily described as **a kynde knowynge that kenet in thyn herte / For to louye thy lord leuest of alle**.

By echoing but redefining the dreamer's phrase **kynde knowynge** (see above 137–38n), Holy Church is only superficially assuring him that he does indeed have such detailed and intimate information as he has asked for. More profoundly, she is showing him the limits of his curiosity about material and analytic details of her topic. She does partly address his physiological question posed in B about "By what craft in my cors it comseþ" in her comments on **thyn herte**; and she does answer his facultative question posed in C about his "menynges" with her comment on how he is naturally taught (**kenet**) by his heart. But in both versions, her answer turns his request for external authority into a reminder of his internal "teacher" (see also 36–40n). Given that she is pointing to his inner sources of such knowledge, there is ironic duplicity in her comment **ho kan tecche þe bettre / Lok þow soffre hym to seye**: he should indeed **soffre** the guide in his heart **to seye**. While her comment is preparing the poem for further scenes of instruction, it is also suggesting his own inability to "know himself," summarized in the final comment of his last dialogic teacher, Scripture, in the longer versions (see 11.163 [B.11.3]).

The complexity of Holy Church's advice here therefore somewhat follows Augustine's twisting definitions of truth (*veritas*) in his treatise on "true religion," a logical background to Holy Church's teaching: "noli foras ire, in te ipsum redi. In interiore homine habitat veritas. Et si tuam naturam mutabilem inveneris, transcende et te ipsum" ("do not seek without; return to within yourself. Within human beings resides truth. And if you find your own nature mutable, transcend even yourself"). For Augustine, however, such transcendence does not require any other teacher apart from logic (or Reason, like the "Ratio" in his *Soliloquia* who presents a similar argument when defining "the false" [see 2.1–4n]): for even doubt about truth results in a logical "proof" of truth in that the doubter believes his doubt to be true: "omnis ergo, qui utrum sit veritas dubitat, in se ipso habet verum, unde non dubitet, nec ullum verum nisi veritate verum est. Non itaque oportet eum de veritate dubitare, qui potuit undecumque dubitare" ("for anyone who doubts whether truth exists, holds that true in himself [namely, that he doubts]: wherefore he should not doubt, for nothing is true unless it is true in truth. Thus it is not necessary for him to doubt in truth, who was able to doubt in every manner"; ed. Daur 1962:234–35). These passages, and the description of "treuthe" "in thy sulue herte" at

C.7.255 (B.5.606), support White's view that truth and its bases remain the focus of the statement.

Melius est mori quam male viuere: "It is better to die than to live evilly." Introduced in B, the motto restates the preceding English line; versions of it are proverbial (Walther 1982–86, nos. 14594, 38182d, and 38183), appearing in Innocent III's *De Contemptu Mundi* (1.24, ed. Lewis 1978), Thomas Usk's *Testament of Love* (1.7; ed. Shoaf 1998:105), and in a sermon cited by Alford (see *Quot*). This is the fruit of the sense of self-knowledge, a point similar to a passage in the *Pricke of Conscience*: here, self-reflection similarly leads to knowledge of God through "kyndely" knowing oneself, defined as a way of grasping one's mortality and the fragility of the world's "pomp": "a man suld first lere / To knaw him-self propely here; / For if he hym-self knew kyndely, / He suld haf knawyng of God almyghty, / And of his endyng thynk suld he / And of þe day þat last sal be . . . / Þe bygynnyng of alle þis proces/ Ryght knawyng of a man self es" (ed. Morris 1863, lines 219–36).

146–58 (B 148–62; cp A 135–38): For treuthe telleth þat loue ys triacle . . . the mercement he taxeth [A: For þus wytnessiþ his woord . . . ʒif men bidde þe ʒedde]: C's and B's mercurial succession of images describing **loue** replaces A's brief suggestion by Holy Church that love is **þe plante of pes**, followed by her assertion that the dreamer should **preche it in þin harpe / Þer þou art mery at mete** (A 137–38). The A text, that is, by supplying the dreamer "a theme for a song, not the gift of song itself" (Donaldson 1966:148), opens toward the dreamer's future elaboration (see below); B and C enact that elaboration but disallow the dreamer the authority to be the one carrying out that performance. C/B have more fully realized the key genre of the passus and of Holy Church's discourse, whereas A presents a flourish of self-consciousness about that genre; see above 135n, and next note.

A 137: preche it in þin harpe: For the phrase and the sense of genre, compare the (second) Wycliffite translation of Jerome's epistolary introduction to the Vulgate, which declares that "Dauiþ þe sownere of symphonye, Pandarie & Alcheus, Flaccus & Catullus & Serenus, prechiþ Christ wiþ an harpe; & in a sautre of ten cordis he reisiþ him up fro hellis, þat roos fro deþ to liyf" (ed. Lindberg 1978:131). The Latin presents the idea of David's musical preaching with less clear resemblance to the phrase here: "David, Simphonides noster, Pindarus et Alcaeus, Flaccus quoque, Catullus atque Serenus, Christum lyra personat et in decachordo psalterio ab inferis suscitat resurgentem" ("David, our Simphonides, our Alcaeus Pindar, our Flaccus, and our Catullus Serenus, sings about Christ with his lyre, and raises him up from the nether regions in his ten-string harp"). The association with David emphasizes an ideal of sacred but highly musical poetry that the poem frequently adduces; see B 33–37n, also "goddes minstrels" at B.13.436–39, transposed in C to an excursus within Sloth's confession, 7.96–99). Here, the idea may epitomize a sense of the genre that Holy Church herself here offers, the "verse sermon," or what might in her idiom be called harped preaching. For a range of other rhetorical theories and views potentially behind the poet's theories about "versifying fair," especially Isidore and Alan of Lille, and a series of examples of his adept merging of point with form, see Schmidt 1987. Perhaps the phrase was cut to avoid identifying the novice Will here too closely with the poet.

146 (cp. B 148): triacle for synne [B: triacle of heuene]: The image of love as a medicine resembles traditional exegeses of Num. 21:8–9, where, following John 3:14, the brazen serpent which Moses made (hence perhaps the reference to Moses in B 151) and which could heal those stung by serpents is often interpreted as Jesus; as Hugh of St. Cher says (commenting on John 3:14), "just as from a serpent is made venom, and from a serpent is made a medicine [*tyriaca*, lit. 'snake skin'] to cure venom, so once the Serpent was made from venom, that is, from the devil, the Lord wanted to be made a serpent, that from him might be made the tonic against the venoms of the devil" (see Smith 1966:22). A Middle English sermon (in MS. Royal 18 B 23) quotes John Chrysostom, "Like as triacle distroyse all maner of veneme and is nedefull to mans bodye in euery sekenes, ryght so þe loue of God all myghtye, þe wiche is goostely tryacle, fordoþe all maner synnes and kepeþ a mons sowle euermore in clennes" (ed. Ross 1940:199; noted by Wenzel 1988:167); so too, the French *Voie de Paradis*, and the English translation, note that "ainssi conme le triacle chace le venim chace la confession le pechié et le deable" ("as tryacle chaseth venym, confession chaseth synne and the deuel": ed. Diekstra 1991:179–80). Possibly there is a continuation of punning allusions to the Trinity in words starting in *tri-* (see above 136n, and Prol.15n).

A further context for the metaphor is the evidence of wide use of church sacraments for medical disorders, literally applying consecrated water or a service book to diseased body parts (see Gurevich 1994). The Sarum *Manuale* includes in the service of baptism an extra blessing of the infant baptisand, "quia secundum doctores maxime valet pro morbo caduco" ("because according to teachers this is very effective against the falling sickness," i.e., epilepsy; ed. Collins 1960:38). Yet in C, Conscience condemns the "idolatrie" of those who seek miracles at shrines, which would include similar pursuits of healing (see Prol.95–135n). See also 20.154–60n and 20.400–412n.

B 149: þat spice: Possibly "that species" of remedy for sin (Skt, see MED *spice* n. (2)) but much more likely "that spice," that aromatic substance from plants, as in glosses on *nardus* as charity (Smith 1966:22; so Bnt). The second possibility is supported and refined by the sense 'medicinal spice' at MED *spice* n. 1 (2b), with texts cited there such as MS. Welcome 584, fol. 86a-b, "Þe triacle þat Galien makiþ . . . is maad of iiij spicis . . . And ech of þese iiij spicis is triacle by him silf." The medicinal sense is confirmed by C's "souerayne salue for soule and for body" (147); see also above 146n.

B 151: And lered it Moyses for þe leueste þyng: The B line briefly offers a glimpse of salvation history, presumably alluding to Moses' postscript to the commandments that the Israelites should "love the Lord your God" (Deut. 6:5), an exhortation made central to Jesus' teachings (e.g., Matt. 22:37). In Guillaume de Deguileville's *Pelerinage de vie humaine*, at Moses' arrival, with horns on his head (a common image), Reason lengthily teaches Moses the meaning of his horns: as means only for gentle and merciful corrections of sinners (ed. Stürzinger 1893, lines 635–796). C's omission of the line may be aligned with other C revisions where Judaism is effaced, thus presenting Christianity as supplanting rather than fulfilling its precepts (see C.12.95–96 [B.11.166–69]; and Narin van Court 1996:50–51).

148–50 (B 152–54, A 137): þe plonte of pees: As Adams shows, the notion of the Plant of Peace, the next image here, ultimately derives from the Septuagint version of Ezekiel 34:29, "phyton eirenes," where it appears in a series of promises of Israel's restoration: "and I will raise up for them a plant of peace" (becoming in the Vulgate "bud of renown"). The notion entered Latin Christendom probably via Augustine's citation of it (*plantam pacis*) in his sermon 47, where it is an image of the unity of the church that even heretics can rejoin, as part of the "plant of charity" (see Adams 1991:7–13). Of fundamental importance too is Isaiah 45:8, commonly used in sermons on Advent to describe the Incarnation in the terms of a natural force: "drop down dew, you heavens, from above: and let the clouds rain the just. Let the earth be opened and bud forth a Savior; and let justice spring up together"; see, e.g., Alan of Lille, *Sermo VII in Adventu Domini* (PL 210:214–18); see also below 149–50n. In Holy Church's development, the image charts a vigorous vegetative movement, fecund and invasive, and managing to evoke as a single, growing entity the Incarnation and the spreading of the message and love of Jesus. In a roughly analogous fashion, the tree of Good and Evil and the wood of the Cross were often cited as identical in medieval exegeses (see Daniélou 1953); that arboreal connection, however, completes history. Holy Church's image suggests open, future possibilities for the plant of divine love. The close of her discourse returns to this image of divine and human love as natural forces (see 159–64n).

148 (B 152): vertues: Healing-powers as well as spiritual goods, like "spice" and "souerayne salue" (see above B 149n). L typically uses the double sense.

149–50 (B 153–4): For heuene holde hit ne myghte . . . Til hit hadde of erthe yʒoten hitsilue: The initial heaviness of the plant of peace expresses God's simultaneous desire and decision to become incarnate as the bursting of a natural and progressive force, assimilated to a seedpod becoming heavy and falling. Compare the Pauline image of God "emptying" himself, "taking the form of a servant, being made in the likeness of men . . . he humbled himself, becoming obedient unto death, even to the death of the cross. For which cause, God also has exalted him" (Philippians 2:7–9). Holy Church's image is full of a similar paradox—that which was so heavy that it fell, became lighter than a leaf once it had fallen (see Lawler 1979:152). The lineage of such a moment of rhetorical and metaphorical power reaches deep into Christian tradition. Augustine's *Confessions* discusses the movement of the Spirit on the waters (Gen. 1:2) in terms that resemble Holy Church's physics of heaviness and lightness, but to a different end, stressing the weight of the human body and the lightness of love, although these terms are reversed near the end of Augustine's passage:

cur ergo tantum de spiritu tuo dictum est hoc? cur de illo tantum dictus est quasi locus, ubi esset, qui non est locus, de quo solo dictum est, quod sit donum tuum? in dono tuo requiescimus: ibi te fruimur. requies nostra locus noster. amor illuc attolit nos et spiritus tuus bonus exaltat humilitatem nostram de portis mortis. in bona voluntate tua pax nobis est. corpus pondere suo nititur ad locum suum. pondus non ad ima tantum est, sed ad locum suum. ignis sursum tendit, deorsum lapis. ponderibus suis aguntur, loca sua petunt. oleam infra aquam fusum super aquam attolitur, aqua supra oleum fusa infra oleum demergitur: ponderibus suis aguntur, loca sua petunt. minus ordinata inquieta sunt: ordinantu et quiescunt. pondus meum amor meus: eo feror, quocumque feror.

[Why therefore is this said of thy Spirit only? Why in this case only is a sort of place, where he should be mentioned (which, however, is not a place), why in his case, of whom alone it is said that he is thy gift? In thy gift we rest; then we enjoy thee. Our rest is thy gift, our life's place. Love lifts us up thither, and thy good spirit advances our lowliness from the gates of death. In thy good pleasure lies our peace. Our body with its lumpishness strives towards its own place. Weight makes not downward only, but to his own place also. The fire mounts upward, a stone sinks downward. All things pressed by their own weight go towards their proper places. Oil poured in the bottom of the water, is raised above it: water poured upon oil, sinks to the bottom of the oil. They are driven by their own weights, to seek their own places. Things a little out of their places become unquiet: put them in their order again, and they are quieted. My weight is my love: by that I am carried, whithersoever I be carried.] (*Confessions* 13.9, ed. and trans. Watts 1999, vol. 2.390–93)

As perhaps another source or influence here, Alan of Lille's twelfth-century Advent sermon on Isaiah 45:8 (see above 148–50n) includes an elaboration of the earth as the Virgin who germinates the seed of the Savior, suggestively paralleling and explicating other aspects of the imagery that Holy Church uses here:

Terra est virgo Maria, terra inarabilis, terra promissionis, terra melle manans et lacte: haec est terra, quae non ut nostra infirmitas, rastris et ligonibus concupiscentiarum vexata, fructum fecit, non fluctibus luxuriae perfusa germinavit, sed solo Spiritus sancti rore Filium edidit. Semen vero fuit Virginis caro, opere Spiritus sancti a reliqua carne separata, et in corpus Christi formata. Si tamen semen censeri debeat quod non per luxuriae pruritum, sed per Spiritus sancti refrigerium est separatum. Germen fuit corpus Christi quod ex praedicta carne processit; et ita germinavit Salvatorem, id est Christum. (PL 210:217)

[The earth is the Virgin Mary, the unplowable land, the land of promise, the land offering milk and honey: this is the earth, which not as our weakness, vexed by the draghoes and mattocks of lusts, makes fruit, does not germinate suffused with waves of lechery, but solely by the dew of the Holy Spirit gave forth the Son. For the seed was the flesh of the Virgin, separated from the rest of flesh by the work of the Holy Spirit, and formed into the body of Christ. If only that seed could be valued that is separated out not through prurience of lechery but through the coolness of the Holy Spirit. The sprout was the body of Christ which proceeded from the aforesaid flesh, and thus she sprouted the Savior, that is Christ.]

Compare Psalm 84:12: "Truth is born from the earth" (*veritas de terra orta est*), commonly glossed as referring to the Resurrection (see Greenhill 1954).

Whatever its sources, PP makes the sequence of images wholly its own. The fall of the Incarnation, with its immediate return to soaring, echoes and reverses Lucifer's downward movement into bondage, both with a sense of inevitable momentum of these movements. As often, L appears more able to convey depths and heights in his spatial perspectives and in his sense of movement than he does horizontal expanses, which rarely open up without encountering some new absorbing figure or another interruption of movement.

yȝoten hitsilue: "begotten itself." Many B manuscripts read "eten his fille" (so Schm 365, who notes that the line thus "avoids anticipating the explicitly incarnational statement" of the second following line). The B reading has support from arboreal lore: the late thirteenth-century encyclopedist Bartholomaeus Anglicus notes that a tree consumes the earth, so that (in John Trevisa's translation, c. 1395), "þe roote [is] in þe stede of þe mouþe. By þe roote humour is ydrawe to feede al þe tree" (*De proprietatibus rerum*, bk. xvii, chap. 1; gen. ed. Seymour 1975–1988, vol. 2.882–83). The C change, however, which is well supported by C manuscripts and which KD-B prefer for B as well, clarifies that the Incarnation is the subject.

153–58 (B 157–62): And portatif and persaunt . . . the mercement he taxeth: The succession of images Holy Church now pursues begins with the invasive, sharp qualities of a vigorous plant or vine at its growth buds, then blends into qualities of military conquest and leadership, then into civic leadership, and then closes on legal authority. In spite of their threatening implications, all the images following that of the plant manage to sustain connotations of life, love, peace, and, especially, forgiveness. The comment on piercing **Armure** and **heye walles** is apt for either a plant's gradual invasion or a weapon's sudden penetration; it probably draws on Heb. 4:12, "For the word of God is living and effectual and more piercing than any two-edged sword and reaching unto the division of the soul and the spirit, of the joints also and the marrow, and is a discerner of the thoughts and intents of the heart." The military connotation is fulfilled in **loue** being a **ledare of þe lordes folk of heuene** (on the development of this as another entity see also C.3.452n [B.3.299]), but this shifts the thought into another form of leadership, the mayor's, which involves not battle but mediation between greater and lesser powers (note the common epithet of Jesus as "mediator"); finally, springing from the metaphors of civic and royal authority appears the technical reference to legal monetary punishment, **the mercement he taxeth** (called an "amercement" because its amount was assessed "at the mercy of the king" rather than established by statute), where the sense of "mercy" emerges as a possible double meaning, made explicit in Jesus' plea for "mercy" for his executioners at 166–69 below. As Benson comments, "the only fine that Christ imposes is no fine at all but mercy" (1980:199). A similar elaboration of this pun appears in Robert Mannyng's *Handlyng Synne* (ed. Sullens 1983, lines 5489–98):

Beþ mercyable for ȝoure prow
Þat god ne take veniaunce on ȝow.
Ȝyf þou haue be so coueytous
To mercye men ouer outraious,
And pore men specyaly,
Þat ferde þe wers for þat mercy,
Syker mote þou be, syr styward,
Þy mercyment shal be ful hard.
Þy wrecched soule þarfore shal dwelle,
Þy mercyment shal be þe pyne of helle.

The career of Love as a personification, often distantly glimpsed, begins here. In the rest of the poem Love takes a series of forms, almost as mutable as those it passes through here. Love is a mocking audience member at Meed's trial (4.156 [B.4.161]; see 4.151–59n); Love is mentioned as Patience's "lemman" who taught Patience to love (B.13.139); Love is an initially distant figure in the debate of the Four Daughters of God, who has sent Peace "som lettre what this liht bymeneth" (20/B.18.185); Love then mysteriously appears as the final singer in the carol at the end of the Debate of the Four Daughters (20.466 [B.18.423]). In these cases, **loue** is not precisely identical to God or Jesus but seems to occupy or come from a place in heaven; perhaps sometimes to be understood as the Holy Spirit (often described in trinitarian theology as the principle of loving relation binding the Father and the Son; see Galloway 1998a), but elsewhere, as at Meed's trial, a rather obscure figure. For other aspects of this entity, see also Prol.128–33n, 3.379n.

155 (B 159): Forthi is loue ledare of þe lordes folk of heuene: For the elements of stock phrasing given new vitality here, compare *William of Palerne*, "for swiche a lorld of lederes ne lived nouȝt" (ed. Bunt 1985, line 3405).

156 (B 160): a mene, as þe Mayre is, bitwene þe kyng and þe comune: The basic point of a mayor's power as mediators between a city's needs and the king's law recurs at B.3.76–100, and in a different form at C.3.77–127. Conflicts between the City of London and the king increased in the fourteenth century as the city and the mayor's office grew in authority. The most pronounced conflict began in 1376, before B, as a struggle between the "populist" mayor John of Northampton and Nicholas Brembre, executed (along with the writer, Thomas Usk) in 1387 by the Lords Appellant as a supporter of Richard II (see Galloway 1997, 2002 for further references). The office of mayor was indeed at times a very dangerous position of mediation between the powerful entities of the barons, the city, and the crown, as anyone who had been in London and taken note of the Good Parliament would have known.

159–64 (B 163–68, cp. A 139–42): And for to knowe hit kyndly, hit comeseth by myhte . . . to amende vs alle: The C/B reading elaborates A's brief sugges- tion of a parallel between the regular physiology of "kynde knowyng" in human beings and God's loving feeling, then historical action of becoming incarnate. Both elements of the analogy define the emergence of a transform- ing love as a **myhte** that begins in the heart then is expressed in the world: implicitly, that can happen daily for human beings, but it happened once for God with particularly momentous consequences. The pairing suggests a paral- lel between the microcosmos of an individual's love and the macrocosmos of God's love and Incarnation, in general terms a common trope, but here linked by showing that God was moved by love in ways somehow comparable to how human beings are moved. The image is of a natural force like the descent and sprouting of the "plonte of pees" (see above 148–50n). As there, so here the imagery of Isaiah 45:8 may be pertinent; the notion of Advent, to which Alan of Lille and others link the passage in Isaiah "Rorate, celi desuper," etc., is often described as including the advent of love in individuals' hearts as well as the three "advents" of God (in grace, in the flesh, and finally at Judgment Day). **he was myhtfull and meke**: the paradox that is central to the **myhte** of love.

171–80 (B 175–84, A 149–58): Forthy y rede ȝe riche . . . þat no man desireth: The "riche" are condemned here openly in the poem for the first time, and the topic of avarice persists to the end of the passus (see above 135n). The notions here rely on Luke 6:37, "Forgive; and you shall be forgiven"; the verse following this in Luke is explicitly and repeatedly turned to below (174a [B 178a], 196–97 (B 201–2, A 175–76). Having explicated the paradox of "myhte" becoming meekness, Holy Church turns its application to a specific audience: the rich, responsible for legal judgments, hence **myhty to mote** (172), "of powerful legal authority," a continuation of the consideration of Jesus' "mercy" to those who unjustly executed him. A powerful clerical audience is the chief focus here, as the reference to divine service shows (179; see Lawler 2002; on addresses to the powerful in PP see 20.350–58n; for the known contemporary owners of the poem, see Prologue, Headnote). The point about lawful judgments and the voice here resemble Robert Mannyng's *Handlyng Synne* (ed. Sullens 1983), lines 5435–42:

> For ȝyf god shal deme wyþ lawe ryght,
> Shal no man come to heuene lyght.
> But þurgh grace & hys mercy
> Þan are we saued certeynly.
> Þarfore ȝe stywardes on benche,
> Þer on shulde ȝe alle þenche.
> Ȝyf þou of þe pore haue pyte,
> Þan wyle god haue mercy on þe.

174a (B 178a): *Eadem mensura . . . vobis*: "with the same measure that you shall mete withal it shall be measured to you again" (Lk 6:38). Implied in lines 171–80 (see note above), Luke 6:37–38, with its call for forgiveness in order to receive forgiveness, emerges directly again below, 196–97 (B 201–2, A 175–76). The point here also looks back to the Latin counsel delivered to the king in the Prologue (Prol.153–59n), now focusing the point on a broader audience of the wealthy and powerful.

175–79 (B 179–83, A 153–57): For thow ȝe ben trewe of ȝoure tonge and trew-eliche wynne . / . . But yf ȝe louye leeliche and lene þe pore . . . / ȝe ne haueth na . . . meryte in masse ne in oures: Prsl notes that the syntax and theme, "the nothingness of 'virtue' without love," echo 1 Cor. 13:1–3. The language and moral theology here and in the following further examples also echo 1 John 3:18–19: "let us not love in word nor in tongue, but in deed and in truth. In this we know that we are of the truth and in his sight shall persuade." The focus on Masses and prayers are directed to clergy (see Lawler 2002), but has obvious importance to those laity seeking to gain merit from chantry prayers they have paid for (for the topic, see Prol.81–84n, and see above 88–136n, 135n, 146–58n, and A 137n).

180 (B 184, A 158): malkyn of here maydenheed þat no man desireth: A saying in Middle English found in numerous late fourteenth-century writers, including John Trevisa, here criticizing claims to a fugitive and cloistered virtue by the rich as like pride in virginity by the homely. For the various instances of the phrase and its different applications, see Fletcher 1986, Cassidy 1948. Here, the sense of virginity as a spiritual treasure that is not truly valuable because it is not defended for any virtuous reason carries forward the motif of "true treasures," tested and not tested. The evident misogyny in most examples of the motto is somewhat mitigated by this focus on Malkyn's presumed lack of being tested.

181–83a (B 185–87a; cp. A 159–61): For Iames þe gentele . . . *mortua est*: "Faith without works is dead" (Jas. 2:26). All the versions present a punning translation of the text in James: **fayth withouten feet** [i.e., without *faits*, Fr. 'works'] **is feblore then nautht**. The odd image is suggestive of the need to "ground" faith so that it can stand and walk. The A text, lacking the Latin text of James, does not present the key to the pun (for the B and C texts' additions of explicit mentions of James, see above, 92n). The same pun may be worked into the odd scene in the late fifteenth-century play *Everyman*, where Good Deedes (i.e., *bons faits*) "cannot stande" because Everyman's books of works "lie under the fete" (ed. Bevington 1975, lines 498, 504). The line is perhaps related to a proverb attested in Latin, Italian, and Spanish versions, "lies have short legs" (*Verum proverbium est, mendacia curta semper habere crura*: see Singer 1995–2002, s.v. *lügen* 4.3). The pun on *feet / faits* is followed in PP by a further proverb on the concept of "act," with perhaps another punning echo on (but here, radical distinction between) **dede** and **ded: as ded as a dore nayl but yf þe dede folowe** (see Whiting and Whiting 1968, D352). At this pitch of rhetorical invention, Holy Church's voice resembles more densely allusive riddling moments in the poem (e.g., 15.159–61 [B.13.145–55]), far beyond everyday homiletic style, toward a distinctive kind of "harped preaching" (see Galloway 1995; and Wenzel 1988:169–70).

185 (B 189, A 163): as lewed as a laumpe þat no liht is ynne: Compare Mt 25:1–13 (the virgins who have no oil for their lamps); the application of the Matthew text to "Chastite withouten charite" derives from Chrysostom's widely known commentary on Matthew, where it is emphasized that the parable applies only to those with virginity, who must in addition to this also have charity (see Wailes 1987:177–84; for the Chrysostom see PG 56:713; for the wide dissemination of this work in Latin medieval culture see Galloway 1992a:18–19n27). This application of the parable appears in Middle English as early as the early thirteenth-century treatise *Hali Meiðhad*: "for al meiðhad, meokelec is muche wurð, ant meiðhad wiðuten hit is eðelich & unwurð, for alswa is meiden i meiðhad bute meokeschipe as is wid-ute liht eolie in a lampe" ("for all virginity, humility is precious; and virginity without it is a poor and worthless thing, for a maiden in virginity without humility is like oil in a lamp that has not been lit": ed. and trans. Millett and Wogan-Browne 1990:40–41). Another traditional interpretation of the parable, applying it to all good works (not just chastity) in relation to charitable intentions, is less relevant to Holy Church's usage (e.g., *Fasciculus morum*, 3.8: "Just as the clearest lamp without oil and fire does not shine . . . , so all works before God are vile and profitless without charity" ["sicut lampas clarissima sine oleo et igne non lucet . . . , sic omnia opera coram Deo sine caritate vilia sunt et nichil prosunt"; noted by Wenzel 1988:166n]; so too the *Book of Vices and Virtues* uses other metaphors to express the same Pauline point about the preeminent importance of charitable intentions behind other kinds of virtue: "For as moche as þer is bitwexe a cole of fier and a ded coole, oþere a ded man and a quek man, riȝt so moche is þer bitwexe vertue wiþoute charite and vertue wiþe charite"; ed. Francis 1942:124). Possibly the text with "light" in it appeared in association (i.e., by concordance) with the emphasis on God as light in 1 John, e.g. 2:8–10: "the darkness is passed and the true light now shines. He that says he is in the light and hates his brother is in darkness even until now. He that loves his brother abides in the light; and there is no scandal in him."

    lewed: as "foolish" (MED 2.(a)), this odd adjective for lamps applies better to the virgins who are the unstated tenor of the biblical simile. Probably it is simply a transferred epithet ("as foolish as a lamp with no oil," i.e., as fool-

ish as not remembering to fill your lamp with oil). It is remotely possible that
lewed here means "unhallowed" (MED 3. (b), as at 1 Kings 21:4, "non habeo
panes laicos," "I haue not lewid loouys" (Wycliffite Bible); even if its colloquial sense of "foolish" is primary, the sense "illiterate, lay," and thus
"unsanctioned," may also apply to the uncharitable chaplains (185 [B 190, A
164]).

B 199 (A 173): And lernynge to lewed men þe latter to deele: B/A's line is
ironic: "a lesson for the laity to give the more slowly." C 195 clarifies emphatically and forthrightly, taking no chances of misunderstanding: "a luther
ensumple, leef me, to þe lewed peple." The assumed audience is more clearly
clerical here, with the laity presented as above as overhearing (at best) how
they should be instructed (see above 88–136n, 171–80n). A sense of the risk in
presenting the teachings of Holy Church in terms that might be taken as heresy or blasphemy, i.e., that Holy Church is teaching the laity to be uncharitable, may guide the revision, as too when her speech in C is carefully separated
from Jesus' words; see next note.

196–97 (B 201–2, A 175–76): *Date & dabitur vobis . . . þat vnloseth grace:*
"Give and it will be given to you" (Lk 6:38), with a return as in a sermon to
the *thema* at 174a, the focus on "true treasure" that also recalls Matthew 6:21,
"where your treasure is, there is your heart also" (see 81–204n). *Date* defines
the paradoxical **lok of loue**: charitable giving, and implicitly the key to heaven.
From here to the end the discourse is climactically rich in metaphor and paradox, as if a treasury of language were opening up with the treasury of charity.
Thus the flat sense "key" MED offers for this one case of **lok** may be narrow-
ing the word too quickly to its function in the passage (MED *lok* n. (2), 1c (b));
it may also in the simplest sense be 'lock,' then secondarily the opening of that
lock. The paradox of love as binding yet freeing is commonplace. In PP, charity is also figured as a "cheyne" at B.5.607, and love may release **grace** to the
extent that love locks or binds: thus the common "love-knotte" that Chaucer's
Friar wears (GP 197), thus Thomas Usk's "knot in the hert" (*Testament of Love*,
ed. Shoaf 1998:158 ff.).

The image of love's **lok** which **vnloseth grace** inverts the pernicious
effects of the preceding image of avarice as something that has "yhapsed"
together covetous clergymen (192), as well as the chains that such avaricious
people deserve to be held by in hell (184). Images of heavenly cities in the
poem involve locks of love in the sense of gates, as here: love is a gate-keeper
of heaven in Prol.128–33 (see n); and Grace, then the Virgin, are identified in
this role at 7.248–53 (C's "þe hye gate of heuene" there clarifies this referent in

the equivalent B passage, B.5.595–604). The **lok of loue** here, as a metaphorical gloss on Jesus' saying about giving, may easily be associated with his mother who released him as a kind of gift to the world, as well as the "church . . . In thyne hole herte" where "all manere folk" may find food, a powerful vision of a citadel holding and thus making available universal social charity: 7.259–60 (C only). **vnloseth grace [A, B: my grace]**: in A/B Holy Church's gloss speaks as a continuation of Jesus' voice; C with a minor but careful change avoids this effect, perhaps with some concern for claims of heresy or blasphemy (see preceding note).

199–200 (cp. B 204–5, cp. A 178–79): So loue is lecche of lyf and lysse of alle payne / And þe graffe of grace and graythest way to heuene [B: Loue is leche of lif and next oure lord selue / And also þe graiþe gate þat goþ into heuene; A: Loue is the leuest þing þat oure lord askiþ]: Many of the preceding images are here collected and, somewhat confusingly, piled into one another. The compaction seems calculated; each version further enriches the density of imagistic allusions to the preceding speech. A's relatively thin summation is enriched by B's allusion to the healing power of love (**leche of lif**), harking back to the discussion of love as a "triacle" (145), and faintly echoing the "lok of love"; C folds in a further allusion to the plant of peace in its reference to a "graft of grace," which neatly suggests a fusion in the Incarnation of earthly rootstock with a heavenly graft; the image is Pauline: see Romans 11:17–24 describing an eclectic new definition of the chosen people. Both C and B close by including a reference to the gate into heaven, hinting at the allegorical journey that Piers will later sketch out (see 7.206–82 [B.5.560–629, A.6.48–114]). On the career of the entity Love, see above 153–58n (B 157–62), and 3.379n.

203–4: "Loue hit . . ." . . . and leue at me she lauhte: C adds Holy Church's leave-taking, providing a formal end to the meeting and to the passus, and causing the narrator's request for more teaching at the opening of the next passus seem like a desperate tugging at her, by which his desire to learn is made all the more visible. Possibly he ceases kneeling here and rises to follow her, since in C he will shortly kneel again (see above, 76n, and 2.1n). His wish to understand what the world that he has seen "bymeneth" appears less satisfied after hearing Holy Church than before; this leaves the narrator's earlier promise to explain all to the reader in a similarly unfulfilled state. Her answers have stoked rather than quieted his desire; she offers not dogma but enticement to further understanding. The question of **what loue is**, which she here admits that she has simply no more time to try answering (**lette may y no lengore / To lere the what loue is**), remains pregnant in all the following scenes and lessons, even if the other themes in Holy Church's speech do not tightly control the poem. His last teacher in the poem, Kynde, or God, urges him even at the end that he must somehow "Lerne to loue" (22/B.18.208), late words effectively revealing that the dreamer has not even then accepted that his defining need remains simply that.

C Passus 2; B Passus 2; A Passus 2

Headnote

As the estates satire of the Prologue is linked to the verse sermon of passus 1 by means of a promise to explicate the "meaning" of the former, so in turn that verse sermon yields to satire in passus 2, by means of an inquiry into the one thing that Holy Church's presentation of "truth" has not explained. The shift of topic leads deftly to fundamental changes of style and drama, when Holy Church responds to the dreamer's request to show him "þe false" by indicating nothing less than False, who happens to be about to marry Lady Meed.

Literalized abstraction is a basic principle of PP's allegory, although so too are the ways in which the results combine surreal, fluid, and confusing elements. The satire of the present passus constitutes the poem's most volatile combination of social types and allegorical entities, presenting a challenge for the reader as well as the narrator-dreamer to "test" the nature of Truth (see 1.77–78n, 81–204n). In an inversion of the sacramental world that Holy Church has represented and described, passus 2 presents a parodic marriage, a parodic charter, and a parodic representation of reward, with a detail so energetically pursued that the style alone challenges the moral lessons just offered. The passus unleashes satire of the sort found in "devil's charters" and biblical parodies in what might loosely be called the goliardic mode, the tradition of Latin parody offering "carnivalesque texts . . . lampooning religious forms and ideas, . . . written by and for members of what has been considered the bastion of medieval seriousness, the Church" (Bayless 1996:2). The satire of Lady Meed's wedding presents a daring juxtaposition of genre to the lyrical homily of Holy Church's discourse, establishing a literary precedent (whether serving as such or not) for Chaucer's initial juxtaposition in the *Canterbury Tales* of the Knight's Tale with the Miller's Tale. For general comments on the use of satire in PP, see Bloomfield 1962:23–30, and Yunck 1988.

The passus is filled with action but this proceeds in a series of interruptions and unexpected side trips. After hearing about Meed's lineage, and its inferiority to Holy Church's, the dreamer witnesses Lady Meed's marriage to

False, or its preparation; at the last moment Theology challenges this, demanding that she be taken to Westminster, the nation's administrative and legal center, to test its validity. Meanwhile, alerted in advance by Sothness of the gathering of False and his companions, the king orders them to be arrested and executed and Meed to be brought before him, providing a second reason for her to come to Westminster. False and his companions manage to flee into such corners of London as may welcome them, a succession of urban crannies that the passus's final view pursues as vividly as it did the venders' cries at the ending of the Prologue, but it closes on a dramatic vignette of Meed being arrested.

Although the narrator is once again not an actor or interlocutor, the drama in the passus contrasts sharply with the stasis of the preceding passus. Whereas fixed views of Lucifer, Lot, and David, and the only slightly more mobile figures of Will and Holy Church, briefly appear in the previous passus, the numerous secondary characters presented here swarm around Lady Meed in a density and activity recalling the frenetic satire of the Prologue, a boisterous confusion reminiscent of the French satiric allegories such as the *Roman de Fauvel* and parts of the *Roman de la Rose*, and, though far more dynamically, like some of the sins encountered in Guillaume de Deguileville's first "pilgrimage" (see Yunck 1988). Meed is contrasted with Holy Church by more than lineage: they are competitors for human love (1.75, 2.34–38), and for political and social influence (2.22–23). They are both adept users of Scripture, but for opposite purposes (e.g., 1.81–83, 3.485–88). They present opposite degrees of agency: whereas Holy Church directly guided the contents of the previous passus, Meed is the pliable object, although no less the absolute center, of this one.

They are also shaped by and in turn evoke contrasting literary and cultural traditions: not simply those of the pure exegetical types of evil and good entities, with Meed as the Whore of Babylon and Holy Church as Jerusalem of Apocalypse (Robertson and Huppé 1951:52), but also a shift from the homiletic and scholastic traditions behind Holy Church, to a range of Latin satire and didactic French romance behind Meed. Meed, who is of good as well as bad lineage, is persistently of ambiguous moral value (see Yunck 1963:10; Dunning 1980:50; Benson 1980). She resembles the morally ambiguous figure Richesse (Wealth) in Jean de Meun's *Roman de la Rose*, and the portrait of Avarice in at least one other French allegory (see below, 10–15n and 12–13n). But whereas the relation of Meed to the broader tradition of venality satire, to satiric images and denunciations of "money" (Munus, Nummus, Sir Penny), and perhaps specifically the Latin satire "De Cruce Denarii," is clear from the topics with which she is associated (see below, 5–9n, 20–21n, 24n, A 38–47n,

151n, 223–45n), in one way this connection is surprisingly distant: few of the antecedents in that tradition were female.

Some reasons why Money is a woman here may be elicited from the answers to another question: why a marriage, or at least the festive preparations for one, to present her? As an antitype to the sacramental figure of Holy Church, Meed's marriage may, in the goliardic tradition, be an antitype to the very traditional and widespread topos of Holy Church as married to Jesus, which developed from commentary on the Song of Songs. Meed's drama may imply some parodic contrast to the parable of the wedding feast that Jesus presents to show that "many are called, but few are chosen" to enter the kingdom of heaven (Matt. 22:1–14), a parable that was commonly interpreted to refer allegorically to the marriage of Jesus with the Church (Wailes 1987:155–61); that feast is directly invoked and explicated at 12.47–49 (B.11.111–14), and more fully B.15.462–485. Another possibly pertinent scriptural basis is the wedding at Cana (John 2:1–11), where Jesus performed his first miracle. That biblical scene had a parodic afterlife as early as the sixth century, with the influential *Cena Cypriani* (with numerous later adaptations and copies). This work manages ludicrously to fold most of the figures of sacred history with their characteristic actions, postures, and clothing into the particular details of the wedding feast: Job, for instance, mourns that he must take his seat at the feast on a dungheap (see Modesto 1992:14–34, line 10; see Bayless 1996:19–56). Some of that work's terse, surreal assertions suggest the allegorical compression of sinful social types and social principles in Meed's festivities; as Noah in the *Cena Cypriani* takes his seat at the feast by sitting on the ark, so Liar somehow becomes "a lang cart" (178–96n). Another reason for an allegorical marriage is the fertile opportunity it offers to present an ideal or parodic meeting of different principles, and thus to explore their differences and the lore associated with them, as in Martianus Capella's fifth-century allegory, *De nuptiis Philologiae et Mercurii* (*The Marriage of Philology and Mercury*; trans. Stahl, Johnson, and Burge 1977). Yet no specific echoes of this work or the *Cena Cypriani* appear in PP. A likelier direct influence is the early fourteenth-century French *Roman de Fauvel*, which describes the failed efforts of the blithly pleasure-loving horse Fauvel (who embodies a variety of sins and forms of folly, especially "flattery") to marry Fortune; once he discovers that Fortune is unpleasant as well as pleasurable, he ends up settling, just as happily, for Vain Glory (ed. Långfors 1914–19; see Cornelius 1932:367; Yunck 1963:221–26; see also Prol.136–37n, and below, 25–26n). The plot and personages of that poem of over 3,200 lines are less complex, however, than those of the single passus in PP.

Yunck observes that, as "one of the rewards of fortune," Meed is "as amoral and unstable in her affections as *Fortuna* herself" (Yunck 1963:295), and this suggests another sense in which preparations for a marriage are pertinent. As Philosophia is in competition with Fortuna for Boethius' narrator's affections and commitments in the *De consolatione Philosophiae*, so Meed tests the loyalties of all those around her, beginning with the narrator's ravished attention and ending in passus 4 with the king's, Conscience's, and Reason's ability to judge and manage her and what she represents. The issue of making a match with her literalizes the question of how each figure encountering her must commit either to worldly rewards or to some higher principles and communities. But Meed is not cupidity or avarice as such, although she may bring those out in her suitors. She promises the peace of reconciliation. Fortune was considered most deceptive when she is blandishing and soothing, and most educational when she is severe (*De consolatione Philosophiae* 4.pr7 [ed. and trans. Stewart, Rand, and Tester 1973]; Chaucer, "Fortune"); but Meed's perennially assuaging demeanor, in spite of its invitation to corruption, may help achieve social harmony, another traditional element of marriages. Certainly, medieval culture depended on marriage as well as money as means to reconciliation; yet here these are inverted to the uses of corruption, trickery, and distrust. In a similar way, monetary reward has a tradition as a positive means for social harmony. "He was ful wis þat first yaf mede!" as the narrator of *Havelok the Dane* robustly says (ed. Smithers 1987, line 1636); see further passus 3 Headnote, 3.221–83n, and 3.265–81n. Yet Meed sows chaos, conflict, and deception around her. The glimpses of the victims of her followers confirm that the passus's antic energy is not an affirmation of her values.

Mixing social detail with allegory, the passus invites topical understanding. At least some early readers would probably have aligned Meed with Edward III's powerful and extravagant mistress, Alice Perrers, a prominent figure in London in the 1370s, who was publicly humiliated in the Good Parliament that proceeded from late April to late July 1376. Whether the poet initially designed Meed, even in part, to invoke Perrers is a matter of interpretation. Some allusion may always have been intended; it may have been added in B; or it may never have been a significant part of the poet's construction of the figure. The positions that scholars have taken on this are often involved with their conjectures of dates for the A version. Skeat, who favored a date for A of shortly after 1362 on the basis of the great wind mentioned at A.5.13–14, thought that the possibilities for allusion to Perrers, who was impeached in the Good Parliament of 1376, were "perceived" by the poet after writing A and then imbedded in B (Skt. 2:31). Cargill (1932), noting some plausible and some less likely allusions to Perrers and to her trial in the Good Parliament, followed this to date A after 1376 (see also Selzer 1980). Huppé (1939) did not accept the

Good Parliament as the basis for Meed's trial at Westminster argued by Cargill (and later Stevens), but thought that the range of allusions to Perrers, along with what he claimed were other allusions to military actions, dated A to the first half of the 1370s, when, he suggested, knowledge of Edward's personal relationship to Perrers was already public. Bennett (1943a), partly building on Huppé's views and partly rejecting them, accepted an initial allusion to Perrers in Lady Meed from A on, noted that Perrers' "connection to the court" could be dated back to 1364, then proceeded to demolish Huppé's other evidence for a date in the first half of the 1370s, arguing furthermore that A's reference to "rome renneris" in passus 4 (the earliest reference to the phrase) was meaningful only while the papacy was in Rome (rather than in Avignon, where it had been since 1308): that is, either in the narrow stretch from 1367 to 1370, when Urban V briefly established his court there, or after 1377, when the Holy See returned to Rome (see 4.125n). Bennett chose 1367–70 for A on the grounds of other allusions to the second half of the 1360s, although it implied a very fleeting topicality to the phrase "rome renneris." Yet this principle of dating cannot be supported, since references are made to the papacy as at the *curia romana*, or (in parliamentary petitions) "la Court de Rome, devant le seint piere le pape," even during the decades where it was in Avignon: where the pope was, there Rome was (see Rot. Parl. 2.82 [1334], 2.136 [1343], 2.172 [1347], etc.).

In his edition, Bennett continues to find details in the presentation of Meed "effective . . . topical allusions" (Bnt 120), but, like Huppé, emphasizes that the poet's primary intention is "illustrating in Meed (and in Alice Perrers in so far as she is identifiable with her) the vice of cupidity which has beset so many of the folk of the field" (120; see also Huppé 1939:61n46, and Robertson and Huppé's remark that Meed was meant to suggest Perrers but that all such "historical" suggestions in the poem are "illustrative rather than structurally fundamental" [1951:51n6]). As often, C's date is less determinate by these or other considerations (see, however, 3.367–70n).

In arguing for the early notoriety of Perrers, Bennett drew attention to an entry in the London Plea and Memoranda Rolls for 9 December 1364, in which five Londoners, including Geoffrey Chaucer's father John, stood surety that Richard Lyons, a merchant and royal financier (later also impeached in the Good Parliament) would keep peace with Alice Perrers, not harming her or preventing her from going where she pleased, or from doing the king's business as well as her own (quoted in Crow and Olson 1966:5; see the *Calendar of Select Pleas*, ed. Thomas 1932:11; Holmes 1975:79; Braddy 1946 and 1977). The isolated document suggests that Perrers was clearly a prominent and possibly already a controversial figure among Edward's court circle by this date, five years before the death of his wife Queen Philippa. Certainly, the association of Perrers, at that time *domicella* of the Queen's chamber, with both the king and various other serious matters (*negotia domini regis et negocia sua propria*) is intriguing as a basis for Meed; and certainly too Perrers gained most of her great wealth from the king's gifts; by the mid-1370s she was notorious as a powerful member of the king's *covyne*, styling herself, according to the sixteenth-century writer John Stow who calls her "the king's concubine," as the Lady of the Sun in the procession to the Smithfield tournaments in 1374 (ed. Morley 1908:351). When she was impeached in the Good Parliament of 1376 because of her interference in the bestowal of the king's favor (Rot. Parl. 2.329; Holmes 1975:68–69) she lost much of her considerable wealth, although she was pardoned later, and again pardoned for remaining in England after banishment. Tout shows that in 1398 she was still pursuing legal claims to regain her property (Tout 1920–33, vol. 4.29; see Given-Wilson 1986:142–47; Holmes 1975:160). The chronicles and legal documents suggest the career of a remarkably powerful and independent woman, whose properties confiscated in 1377 included a new hostelry on the bank of the Thames and a series of new houses that she had built in London; John of Gaunt, William of Wyckham, and the pope at various times all asked her for assistance (Braddy 1946).

However suggestive, arguments for allusions to Perrers in the two Meed passūs rest on impressionistic claims—not that such a basis in itself would be insufficient for a late fourteenth-century readership. The critical fascination with this pursuit and the poetic modality it implies for PP deserve scrutiny (on the former, see Trigg 1998). Yet it bears emphasizing that no one piece of evidence definitively shows that L at any point intended to allude to Alice Perrers; even the ingenious claim for word-play on "perreiȝe" at A 12 can also be explained by a likely literary analogue. Moreover, if the allusion is accepted, some of the transformations of its willful and powerful historical referent are profound. Nonetheless, in some form the claim remains one of the most durable proposals of topical allusion for any of the poem's allegorical figures (but compare Prol.167–219n). For specific aspects of Meed that may show allusions to Perrers, in some cases allusions possibly amplified by the poem's scribes, see below 5–9n, 10–15n, 10n, 12–13n, and 17n; also 3.5–8n, 128–46n, B 195–200n.

Although she evokes a range of probable other topical resonances that, like those inhering in the figure of Holy Church, are probably impossible for modern readers fully to appreciate—including debate about the conduct of the war with France, the power of the magnates, and the degree of real authority the king wields, all found throughout the Meed dramatic sequence in the following passūs—the figure of Meed primarily emerges from a complex knot of medieval definitions of women, reward, and self-interest, some antecedents to which are clearly found in the tradition of venality satire (see Yunck 1963). At least one twelfth-century clerical satire picks out and combines women, wealth, and honor as the "three enemies" assailing "holy habits":

Plurima cum soleant sacros avertere mores
Altius avertit femina, census, honos.
Femina, census, honos, fomenta facesque malorum,
In scelus, in gladios, corda manusque trahunt.

[Although many things impede holy habits, woman, wealth, and honor impede these most profoundly. Woman, wealth, honor are the tinder and torch of evils; they draw hearts to sin and hands to the sword.] (Hildebert of Lavardin, *De tribus inimicis* PL 171:1353–1430, at 1353; for further references see Yunck 1963:174n70; for a suggestion that L might have known some of Hildebert's works, see Schmidt 1987:74. An abridged version of this work is also found attributed to Marbod of Rennes, PL 171:1491–94)

Hildebert's "wealth" and "honor" are two of the "false appearing goods" or "partial goods" that Boethius treats (*De consolatione Philosophiae*, 2.pr5-pr6; ed. and trans. Stewart, Rand, and Tester 1973); and in the same clerical culture and the same period in which money satire most developed appeared a vast expansion of misogynist writings, though apparently never so directly merged as in PP (see, e.g., *Gawain on Marriage*, ed. Rigg 1986; Mann 1991; Blamires 1997, 1992). Yet even considered simply in terms of these elements, the figure of Meed does not so much combine them as articulate their range of implications with subtle and ethically provocative scope. It is as difficult to judge her definitively as it is to extricate her entirely from the corrupt aspects of society and judicial operations, as this and the following two passūs make clear. Perhaps as a consequence no final penalty is shown imposed on her; instead, as the end of the first vision shows, those who use her must be reformed (see 4.184–96 [B.4.190–95, A.4.153–58], and notes on those lines).

Medieval culture was the heyday of pecuniary satire because of a combination of cultural factors: official moral condemnations of many monetary practices were at their most pervasive and complex, while the dependence on money was rapidly increasing, prominently among the very group generating moral literature, the clergy. Circulation and use of money increased dramatically in all spheres of medieval Europe from the twelfth century on, primarily fueled by increases in trade, in civic manufacturing, and in use of wages, and further enhanced by the papacy's and the king's vast taxation system, by pilgrimages, by crusades with their ransoms and troop expenses, and in L's period by the Hundred Years' War (see Britnell 1996; Spufford 1988:157–62, 204–5, 234–35; Epstein 1991). A fifteenth-century carol says "Where indede, so

God me spede, / Sey all men whate they cane, / Yt ys allwayes sene nowadayes / That money makythe the man" (ed. Greene 1977:232, no. 393, stanza 20).

The literary tradition concerned with money and its abuses begins far earlier, in ancient Rome; its flowering, however, was in twelfth- and thirteenth-century Latin and French works, where the ambiguity of money's value, "to enable bribery or corrupt worldliness on the one hand, honorable rewards on the other" (Yunck 1963:289–90), is first developed. *Wynnere and Wastoure* marks the first full philosophical engagement of English writings with this theme, although money personified does not appear there but rather different modes of its use; the earlier fourteenth-century complaint against the abuses of all social types, *The Simonie*, focuses much of its criticism on the abuses of wealth (hence the closing colophon in Bodleian Library MS. Bodley 48, *Explicit Symonye and Couetise*; ed. Embree and Urquhart 1991). PP's intensely dialectical treatment of earthly reward was not followed by many other Middle English writers: some brief fifteenth- and sixteenth-century lyrics appear on "Sir Penny" (ed. Robbins 1952, nos. 50, 51, 57), and the fifteenth-century ballad-like "London Lick-Penny" condemns urban culture and its love of money (ed. Robbins 1959, no. 50). John Audelay fleetingly mentions "Mede þe maydyn" as "maintaining" corrupt rectors, "Because of ser Couetys is next of here kyn," but this is a passing and undeveloped allusion (ed. Whiting 1931:35, poem 2, line 705–6). The fullest successor to PP's elaboration of money personified is Spenser's ill-fated Lady Munera, directly based on Lady Meed but far less complexly developed (*Faerie Queene* 5.2.9, 20–28). Better known literary women, such as Chaucer's Wife of Bath with her similarly selective style of scriptural exegesis, may also owe something to L's character. But PP's sequence of passūs on Lady Meed stands as perhaps the most complex, probing, and thorough, and certainly among the most vivid and dramatic, literary scrutinies of material reward in any language. (For further discussion, see Yunck 1963, Benson 1980; Baldwin 1981:55–80; Stokes 1984:99–156; Simpson 1990b:17–60; Alford 1988; and Tavormina 1995:1–47.)

Introduction to the marriage of Lady Meed

1–4 (B 1–4, A 1–4): And thenne [A/B: ȝet] y kneled on my knees . . . ". . . to knowe þe false": The moment continues the drama of the dreamer's questions to Holy Church; here he holds her attention by remaining kneeling (or, in C, again kneeling: see 1.76n) as a supplicant, and makes a logical response to her claim to have fully explained to him "treuthe" and "love," by posing a question about their opposite. Yet in the context of his confessed failure to reach a "kynde knowyng" about Truth (see 1.77–78n), his further request sounds a note of exasperation, as if Holy Church had been proceeding by explaining the unknown by the less known, a recognized fallacy in arguments (see, e.g., Putnam 1950:112; Chaucer's Canon's Yeoman's Tale, line 1457). For the poem's continued emphasis on learning by opposites and through long experience, see 1.77–78n.

by sum craft: **sum craft** implies some skill or even supernatural power in Holy Church, a presumption that she has power over the vision that can be immediately fulfilled; see B.1.139 for the introduction (dropped from C) of the notion of **craft** (see 1.137–38n). In Deguileville's *Pelerinage de vie humaine*, Grace-Dieu obeys the narrator's request to have her "special servant," Raison, appear and take the dreamer by the hand and anoint him with protective ointments (ed. Stürzinger 1893, lines 473–78). This is the only moment in PP where the dreamer has direct control over which personification appears in his dream, although his request is for Holy Church to carry out a kind of conjuration or trick. For the form of the imprecation, compare *William of Palerne* (ed. Bunt 1985), when the eloping lovers "preyed hire [their go-between] par charite and for profites love / to kenne hem sum coyntice, ȝif sche any couþe, / to wisse hem forto wend awey unparceyved"; to which their confidante answers, "Bi þat blisful barn þat bouȝt us on þe rode, / I kan bi no coyntyse knowe nouȝ þe best, / how ȝe mowe unhent [unharmed] or harmles aschape" (lines 1664–66, 1669–71). There, the *coyntyse* ends up being a disguise; here, it ends up being a sudden creation of literary personification allegory.

þe false: As the idea of "the true" is extensively treated in Augustine's *De vera religione* (ed. Daur 1962; see 1.141–45n, and passus 1 Headnote), so the idea of "the false" is treated from several angles in the second book of Augustine's *Soliloquia*, a debate between Ratio (Reason) and Augustine, which may be a more or less distant source for the preceding dialogue of Holy Church and Will. In the *Soliloquia*, *falsum* is defined as that which is different from what it appears to be (2.3.3, ed. and trans. de Labriolle 1939), thus as wholly dependent on the senses (2.3.4); yet it is also defined only by contrast to the true, as "similar" to the true yet "dissimilar" enough to be false (2.7.13–14). Unlike poets and artists who produce fictions or lies (*mendaces*) in order to please, and thus are somewhat exempt from full moral condemnation, the false is something made in order to deceive and to lie (2.9.16). It is a product of the will. Yet unlike truth, which has permanent and self-sufficient force (it is "true" even if it disappears, since it "truly" disappears [2.15.27]), and which therefore proves the eternity of the soul because the soul has the attributes of the true (2.13.24), the false is simply the absence of the thing it represents, and thus it is ultimately founded on an absence: even to be able to declare that something "is not" shows the triumph of truth (because of *est*, "is"; 2.15.29). Augustine's general views, widespread in medieval theology although not often in so acute a form as in his own work, may have further literary consequences in the elusiveness of the identities, relations, and number of the personifications of False "and his felawes" (see below, 25–26n).

Augustine's Reason ends her discourse, therefore, with the unknowability because the non-existence of the false; L's Holy Church similarly ends her discourse abruptly at the dreamer's question of what the false is. She does not generate any definitions of it but instead allows the dreamer to experience the personfications and the rest of the dream. While touched with satire, therefore, the moment here is the beginning of the dreamer's realization of his need to **knowe** love and truth from direct, life-consuming experience of their opposites, learning to "suffer *stricto sensu*" (see Schmidt 1986:36; Galloway 1998a). The principle, notably elaborated in the *Roman de la Rose*, appears at several crucial points in the poem (see 1.77–78n).

5, 8 (B 5, 7, A 5, 7): thy left half: Since Holy Church has come "down fro þe castel" (1.4) in the east and Will is presumably facing her, the **left half** would place the marriage of False and Meed to the north, where Satan is (1.120; so Bnt). This incidentally takes up the sinister connotations of turning or looking **left**: note, e.g., Pope Gregory VII's comment in 1073 on a bishop's temptation: "he must know his right hand from his left. If he shall turn to the right we shall rejoice greatly; but if—which God forbid!—he shall turn to the left, it will certainly be a grief to us" (trans. Emerton 1932:9). The fourteenth-century *Book of Vices and Virtues*, a translation of the late thirteenth-century *Somme le Roi*, notes the importance of "looking on the left half to observe fools and folly":

it is grete nede þat a man loke wel forþ on þe lifte half, and þat is wiþ whiche eiʒe and and wiþ what degree, for men loken oþerwhile after schrewen þat ben on þe lifte side. Wel scholde euery wiʒte take ensaumple, first to haue of hem pitee and rewþ, after þat euery wiʒte fle here folies and here loos . . . wel behoueþ on þat half kepe wel discrecion and euenhed. (ed. Francis 1942:155)

Putting something to one's "lefte syde" is elsewhere an idiom for dismissing it (e.g., Usk, *Testament*, bk. 2, line 618, ed. Shoaf 1998:173). A sense of the moral and even supernatural consequences of such orientations was deeply imbedded in late medieval English culture. The early fifteenth-century dialogue *Dives and Pauper* includes (and ridicules) an apparently common belief that those passing "a man of holy chyrche" should keep to the right, with "hym on here lyft hond, for be þat þey wenyn to spedyn þe betere, and þe warse ʒif þey leuyn

hym on here riȝth hond" (ed. Barnum 1976:186). This suggests evil consequences if Will, facing Holy Church, not only looks to his left but also passes
her to his left, to approach the scene.

**5–9 (B 5–8, A 5–8): "loo where he standeth . . ." . . . a womman wonderly
yclothed**: The dreamer has asked to know "þe false" and Holy Church readily
complies, pointing out False and his companions. As often in the poem, an
intellectual abstraction or a single word becomes a tactile and dramatic personification (see 1.1–11n, 1.3n). The dreamer at once gazes not at this company
but the woman False is marrying; thus it seems as if he has made a mistake,
his attention drawn away by an attractive figure. But she embodies the antithesis of "truth" even more clearly than False himself because of her multiply
seductive appeal. Whether indeed she is more false than False remains in
debate for the rest of the vision. She is a figure who resists categorization, being
neither fully "true" nor fully "false," and in either case generally the center of
attention in any scene where she appears. Certainly the dreamer's own motivations in gazing upon her suggests that he is in moral danger (see especially
below, 16n).

Boþe fals and fauel and fikel tonge lyare: The figures surrounding Meed
are indefinite and changeable in all versions, perhaps indicating sin's nature as
swarming or indistinct; see below 25–26n. The Latin "goliardic" satire titled
"De Cruce Denarii" ("The Cross of Money") personifies similar figures when
it declares that "when money talks, truth falls silent; Fraud, Favor, Depravity,
and False reign" ("Cum nummus loquitur, tacebit veritas; / fraus, favor, pravi-
tas regnant, et falsitas"; ed. Wright 1841:223–26). PP's scene works from hints
of personification in this and a long tradition of similar works.

wonderly yclothed: Critics have long considered the extravagant and
mesmerizing clothing of Meed a signal that Alice Perrers is meant (see Headnote); Huppé remarks that "anyone contemplating the English court in 1374
would be arrested by the glittering figure of Alice Perrers" (1939:49). More
generally, male desire for the female as a force disorienting rational inquiry is
shown merged with the desire for worldly treasures, which, once possessed,
present the equally fascinating specter of a blurring of hierarchical social distinctions, that is, with *ambitio* and *honos* as Hildebert of Lavardin would call
this (see Headnote). In every version, however short or long the description of
the clothing, Meed and her dazzling clothing are irresistable distractions to the
dreamer, although the narrator's own fascination varies (see below, 10–15 and
notes). Holy Church's teachings about cupidity have described cupidity and
avarice eloquently in abstract terms, but the dreamer can only truly know such
sin by experience (see above note). Although he has assured Holy Church that

he needs to hear no more about worldly treasure (1.79–80 and n), almost as soon as he is at the end of her direct guidance, the wandering of his attention from the figure to which she is directly referring proves that "kynde knowynge" is more complex than objective moral teaching, and that on his own he will continue to go astray. See also below 16n.

10–15 (cp. B 9–16, cp. A 9–14): She was purfiled with pelure . . For to telle of here atyer no tyme haue y nouthe: Whereas scenic continuity is increased in each version of the poem, descriptive detail about Meed herself increases from A to B but contracts again in C, replaced by an abrupt comment. Meed's fluid iconography suggests various backgrounds and valences. The extravagant details in A/B, especially in the context of a holy guide indicating a figure of evil, recall the presentation in Apocalypse of the Whore of Babylon (Apoc. 17:4; see Robertson and Huppé 1951:50); C's compression somewhat reduces that association (see below). Latin and romance allegory offers more or less distant antecedents. Prudentius' female *Avaritia* (early fifth century) has large robes into which she stuffs the corroded baubles she finds, until she disguises herself as *Frugi*, "Thrifty," when she hides snaky hair under a white mantle (*Psychomachia*, ed. and trans. Thomson 1949, lines 454–563). The male Avarice in Huon de Méri's *Torneiment Anticrist* (mid-thirteenth century) has a large and tumultuous entourage, especially of Romans, and he carries a golden shield with jewels and a bend silver (ed. Bender 1976, lines 761–77). While Prudentius' detail of the flowing robes with ample pockets has a long afterlife in the iconography of Avarice, generally Avarice's iconography emphasizes more rapaciousness and violence than appears in the presentation of Meed (for the early tradition in moral theology of Avarice, see Newhauser 2000:73–85).

A much closer parallel and possibly a direct model for Meed is Richesse, from Guillaume de Lorris' early thirteenth-century portion of the *Roman de la Rose* (ed. Poirion 1974, lines 1053–1126; trans. Dahlberg 1986): she wears the most beautiful, costly, and splendid robe in the world, with a collar edged "mout richement" with gold and enamel, including plenty of glittering stones, one in her belt that would protect anyone against poison and another in its clasp that cures toothache and hunger pangs. She also wears a golden crown with further gems; and she also stands next to her lover, in Richesse's case a young man who "always thought to live a life of lavish spending." Further parallels to the *Roman de la Rose* are noted below. The motif of women wearing medicinal or protective jewels passes to English poetry by 1300, as in "The Fair Maid of Ribblesdale," a lyric from the early fourteenth-century portions of Harley MS. 2253 ("rubies on a rowe . . . ant emeraudes mo . . . a ston þat warneþ men from wo . . ."; ed. Brook 1964, lines 61–69).

Whether or not Meed's sumptuous clothing also alludes to Alice Perrers particularly, and already in the A text or only in B (see Headnote), Meed's outfit presents a general sense of high social station or pretension to one in fourteenth-century terms—as is suitable for the daughter of Amends who is kissing-cousin of the king (see below 148–49n), and as is generally the case for the tradition of Avarice (who in Huon de Méri is accompanied by Cruelty, armed to take the skin off of "la povre gent"; ed. Bender 1976, line 773), and of course Richesse. According to a (later suspended) statute of 1363, purfling of robes with pelure—lining and fringing them with fine fur—was prohibited to those below knightly rank or an income of 200 marks (SR 1.381, art. xiii). Women of the higher nobility or the royal family commonly wore very sumptuous clothing (Paley Baildon 1915–16; for Perrers' own clothing see Huppé 1939:43n21, which in general terms seems appropriate to those claiming royal connections). A longstanding association between luxury and feminity tended to increase the moral threat of both (note "Honor" in the poem by Hildebert of Lavardin: see Headnote).

These associations persist in C, but the narrative reductions there diminish some of the combined seduction of, and thus the apparent anxiety about, high social rank and femininity, just as the presentation there steps further away from the figure Richesse in the *Roman de la Rose* or indeed allusion to Alice Perrers. What is left of Meed in the initial portrait of C is a more abstract principle of intellectual and sensual distraction due to feminine sumptuousness and its various kinds of power, including the threat of losing all the moral distinctions that Holy Church has labored to impose (on Holy Church's discourse as devoted to establishing such distinctions see Robertson and Huppé 1951:43–44; and the poststructural restatement of this in Rogers 2002:98–100). The impulse to reestablish such distinctions in response to Meed defines Conscience's arguments in passus 3 (see B.3.231–51nn, and C.3.286–412nn).

10 (B 10): crouned in a croune, þe kyng haþ non bettre: Compare *Roman de la Rose* (ed. Poirion 1974), lines 1087–89: "Richece ot sus ses treces sores / Un cercle d'or; onques encores / Ne fu veüs si biaus, ce cuit" ("On her blond tresses Wealth had a golden circlet. No such beautiful one was ever yet seen": trans. Dahlberg 1986). In the *Roman de Fauvel*, Fortune holds two crowns, one packed with gems, the other cheap and dirty (ed. Lángfors 1914–19, lines 1871–96). Huppé collects this reference to **þe kyng** as further evidence pointing to Alice Perrers (1939:50).

12–13 (cp. B 11–14, cp. A 11–12): On alle here fyue fyngeres . . . and othere riche stones [B: Fetisliche hire fyngres . . . enuenymes to destroye; A: Alle

here fyue fyngris . . . þat prince werde euere]: In A, the parts of the description move from clothing to crown, to rings, back to robe; all these elements are vigorously expanded in B, then reduced to a skeleton in C. The treatment of the rings registers these shifts most fully; however unstable, these details have also persistently led scholars to see allusions to Alice Perrers. Bnt notes various notorious associations of Perrers with jewels: "in 1373 she was given the late Queen Philippa's jewels; at the Good Parliament of 1376 she was charged with using magic rings; and she is said to have stripped the rings off Edward's fingers when he died" (Bnt 119–20; for the last, see Walsingham, *Chronicon Angliae*, s. a. 1377: "since she sensed the royal foot to be placed at death's door, she decided to flee; but before departing, that she might make clear to all that she loved the king not on account of himself but on account of self-love, she furtively drew from his hands the rings that he wore for royal dignity on his fingers, lest anyone should have any doubt about the truth of the old proverb, 'no prostitute lacks the care of a thief' " ["ut praesensit regem pedem in mortis januis posuisse, fugam meditata est; sed ante recessum suum, ut cunctis manifeste monstraret se regem, non propter se, sed propter sua dilexisse, anulos, quos pro dignitate regia gestabat in digitis, de regiis manibus furtive subtraxit, ne cuiquam veniret in dubium verum fore vetus proverbium, quia nulla meretrix scrupulo caret furti"; ed. Thompson 1874:142–43]). The associations to Perrers may be reflected in at least some early copies of the poem: at A 96, the Vernon manuscript printed by Skt (his line 101) declares that "Meede is a Iuweler" (most other A manuscripts read "muliere"), possibly a scribal pun on Alice Perrers' name (Huppé 1939:51; see also next note).

A 12: Of þe pureste perreiȝe þat prince werde euere: Cargill, basing the suggestion on Skt's printing of the Vernon manuscript's reading "perre" (shared by many A manuscripts), argued that A's description of the rings contains a pun on Alice Perrers' name (Cargill 1932:360), the first of several claims about such punning in the poem (see above). Play on Perrers' name clearly appears in Gower's *Miroir de l'Omme* (ed. Macaulay 1900, lines 25573–96), as noted by Huppé (1939:51), but is much less certain in PP, for **perreiȝe** is a common alliterative term, and here also parallels the description of Richesse in Guillaume de Lorris' *Roman de la Rose*: "De riches pierres grant plenté" (1065). Possibly the poet cut the line to remove the potential allusion to Perrers.

B 13–14: double manere Saphires, / Orientals and Ewages enuenymes to destroye: B's vivid elaboration of the rings generally parallels the description of Richesse's medicinal and lavish jewels in the *Roman de la Rose*. Bnt identifies **Orientals** as pearls (based on Chaucer's specification of a "perle fyn" as "oriental"; *Legend of Good Women*, F line 221), and notes that Lydgate describes "ewage" (i.e., water) sapphires as "blew"; thus Bnt takes these as additional stones. But **Orientals and Ewages** are better taken as specifying the two kinds of sapphires mentioned in the preceding line: an Anglo-Norman lapidary specifically says that a kind of sapphire found in Turkey is "apelé oriental" (Struder and Evans 1924:140); **Ewages**, while used of sapphires by Lydgate, may similarly be used of any precious stone that has a watery appearance (e.g., Struder and Evans 1924:83, line 365, on hyacinths). Lapidaries define the healing and safe-guarding powers of gems in terms that suggest that Meed herself is well protected, regardless of what ills she inflicts on others (for the lapidary tradition see Brinkmann 1980:93–101). The powers of jewels to destroy **enuenymes** were proclaimed during eruptions of plague from the mid-fourteenth century on, at least in Italy (see Nohl 1971:68, 71).

In addition to various physical medicinal properties that a sapphire soaked in milk might bring (e.g., for headache and disorders of the testicles), sapphires are also said to be efficacious against treachery and fear ("contre tricherie et contre peur"), and to release one from prison (Struder and Evans 1924:140). The last might be particularly useful for Meed in her present circumstances, and indeed it is not clear whether she ever is jailed (see 4.162–65n).

15: no tyme haue y nouthe: In other alliterative writings the line would be a modesty topos, an emphasis on a lack of wit, rather than time: compare *William of Palerne*, "of here atir for to telle to badde is my witte" (ed. Bunt 1985, line 5024; see also 1425, 1941–44). C's narrator is not unable but rather unwilling to take the time to describe Meed's "atyer" beyond repeatedly stating that it was "rich" ("richeliche"; "riche"; "rychere"; "rychesse"), a repetition that Donaldson notes as part of C's impatience with physical details (1966:52). This emphasis might further serve to insist that the portrait of Meed was alluding to "wealth" (like the allegorical figure Richesse in the *Roman de la Rose*) and therefore not primarily to Alice Perrers. The sense of **tyme** as pressing and passing is pervasive in C, which has an increased emphasis on "a good ende" (see below, 31–35, and Prol.29n). The C text also emphasizes the evil of wasting time in idle speech (see Burrow 2003); see also below, 64n.

16 (B 17): Here aray with here rychesse raueschede my herte: The trope of a narrator's awe-filled attention at a spiritual or allegorical presence, reaching back to Boethius' *De consolatione Philosophiae* (1.pr1) and the Apocalypse (e.g., 1:17), and displayed at the words (but not the appearance) of Holy Church (see 1.3n), is here invoked with special intensity, although with a morally menacing tone and mood. Compare Marlowe's *Doctor Faustus*, on Faustus' equally ravished vision of Helen of Troy, "Her lips suck forth my soul—see where it flies!" (ed. Wine 1969, sc. xviii, line 101). The dreamer's reaction here explicitly combines male sexual desire for women with that for worldly riches, since the subject of the sexually charged verb, **raueschede**, derives not from Meed's body but **here rychesse**, although in her case that is ultimately perhaps indistinguishable from her being in every sense. Possibly the power of money's appearance was greater in a culture where it was scarce and dramatically displayed in every transaction; for a similarly enamored gaze at money, compare Chaucer, Pardoner's Tale, VI.774. The ancient and medieval sense of the visual seduction of money is clear in Cato's *Distichs* 4.4: "Dilige denarium sed parce dilige formam," "Love money, but love [its] beauty sparingly," quoted below at B.10.343a (modern editors emend the texts of the *Distichs* from "Dilige denarium" to "Dilige te ornari," "Love neatness," and indeed the focus on money's beauty seems more a product of medieval transmission of Cato than of any earlier original; ed. Duff and Duff 1982:614).

Colette Murphy's point about Conscience's denunciation of Meed is applicable even to Meed's first appearance: "the common ground between antivenal and antifeminist satire becomes clear: in both, the circulation of the female body as a currency between men of all social ranks can be used to figure debased values and social order" (Murphy 1994; see also Lees 1994). The convergence of these desires is satirically celebrated in the first clause of the marriage charter in B and C (below, 82–84 [B 75–77]). For the promise of wealth as inciting men to marry even old women with humble lineages, see 10.262–69 (cp. B.9.159–68, A.10.182–89), including the surreal statement, in C only, that a man who marries an old woman "for here welthe" will "weschen on þe morwe / That his wyf were wexe or a walet ful of nobles" (10.269), a stark display, in the wish to change his wife into the commodity of wax or money, of the dehumanizing effects of Meed and the longing that she inspires.

17 (B 18): Whose wyf a were: The dreamer does not yet know that a marriage is in progress, and his immediate curiosity about Meed's marital circumstances is an obvious preparation for the drama of the scene (so Tavormina 1995:1). A has only "What is þis womman . . . þus worþily atirid?" (15). Skeat considered the line added in B significant in relation to the discovery at the Good Parliament that Alice Perrers was already married even though she was evidently known to be Edward's mistress (Skt 2:31). The view that the poet was capitalizing on this added significance of his literary creation is an attractively dynamic approach to the poetic process. An allusion here to Perrers would presumably have less impact by the date (and the generally southwestern readership) of C;

yet the question not only remains in C but is now more explicitly spoken aloud, part of the dreamer's question to Holy Church rather than merely a matter that gave him **wonder** (B 18). Beyond topicality, therefore, the line can be understood as offering insight into the dreamer's and others' reactions to Meed, pointing to the desire to shape and possess Meed that she elicits in everyone around her, even in the intellectual terms of wishing to categorize and define her firmly, which becomes a central pursuit in the next passus. The dreamer's first point of curiosity thus displays his own desire to grasp Meed in categorical social terms, as a "free" or "unavailable" identity, a question linked both to women's status as possessions or objects of exchange between men and to a male viewer's immediate desire to possess her (see Lees 1994; Trigg 1998). If Perrers is alluded to, the question loses none of its power to reveal the dreamer's vicarious desires beneath his curiosity. See also Headnote to passus 3.

20–21 (B 21–22, cp. A 17): And lakked my lemman þat leute is hoten . . . lawes han to kepe [A: lakkid my lore to lordis aboute]: B introduces the personage Leaute into this passage as it has also at B.Prol.122 and 125–27, generating a figure out of A's **my lore.** C keeps all B's references to Leaute except the one at B.Prol.122. See C.Prol.149–51n for some of Leaute's properties, and below 51–52n. Here, Leaute is further defined as 'fidelity to justice,' and more, as 'a lord's counselor for justice,' since Meed has managed to spread lies among judges or other lords against Leaute (B's **bilowen** means 'spread lies,' as does RK-C's **ylow on** at C 21, which RK-C boldly inserts against all direct manuscript evidence to allow B and C both to read **lakked** in the first line here and a word for 'defame' on the second). In the Latin satiric tradition, money was often seen to foster disloyalty: "De Cruce Denarii" says that when money talks, "pietas fugiet; corruet aequitas; / locum non optinent lex, fides, charitas": "piety will flee, equity will be destroyed; law, faith, and charity will find no place" (ed. Wright 1841, lines 19–20). One of PP's persistent complaints concerning monetary abuses in legal settings where lords were often dominant is focused on "lovedays," special days for settling disputes by private or informal arbitration, and perhaps specifically indicated here among the arrangements controlled by **lordes þat lawes han to kepe.** For the direct conflict between Leaute and lovedays, and for more on the latter, see 3.196–97n. For references to other passages concerning legal corruption, see Prol.160–66n.

23 (B 23, A 18): In þe popes palays he is pryue as mysulue: Comments on the power of money (**he** is the southwestern *heo,* 'she') at the pope's court are a staple of venality satire; indeed, this is one of the concerns driving the earliest growth of such satire (see Yunck 1963:85–117). Compare the command by the king in *Wynnere and Wastoure* that Wynnere go "to þe pope of Rome," where the cardinals in the papal palace will "make þi sydes in silken schetys to lygge" (ed. Trigg 1990, lines 461–63); or the scene in the *Roman de Fauvel* of the pope stroking and complimenting Fauvel as a "beautiful animal" when Fauvel arrives in the pope's palace, upon which the cardinals applaud his good judgment (and display their own innate affinities to Fauvel): "Vous dites voir, sire saint Pere" ("you speak truly, lord holy father": ed. Långfors 1914–19, lines 105–16). In her terse rehearsal of the commonplaces of venality satire, Holy Church is more direct in her passing antipapal satire here than the narrator was in the Prologue (see Prol.136–37n).

24 (B 24): Ac sothnesse wolde nat so: "De Cruce Denarii" mentions that when money talks, Truth will be silent ("Cum nummus loquitur, tacebit veritas": see above 20–21n, 5–9n). In PP the figure **sothnesse** is a truthful informant and witness, reporting the truth to high places, especially to the king (thus the basis for the figure Sothsegger in *Mum and the Sothsegger*; ed. Dean 2000). Yet Sothness does not pronounce such truths publicly but rather as an informant, a spy, for the higher ranks, as, e.g., to Conscience at the king's court (A.2.150–53, B.2.189–92, C.2.203–6) and, in A and, as emended by KD-B, B, a witness to Love's whisper against Meed after Reason's public condemnation of her (A.4.137–38, B.4.162 [the latter emended against all manuscripts but to allow the meter at least some alliteration]; see 4.151–59n). In PP, Truth is not silent when money is talking, but it does speak quietly and privately, as perhaps a way of reimagining the statement from "De Cruce Denarii" in personified terms. Sothness' role as quiet informant to the powerful is thus partly contrasted with but otherwise closely tied to that of Leaute, just mentioned (see also below, 51–52n, and, again, 4.151–59n).

for she is a bastard: B and C add Holy Church's report on Sothness' view of Meed's lineage. Being cited by Holy Church constitutes high esteem for Sothness' authority; yet Sothness' opinion that Meed **is a bastard** contradicts Theology's later assertion that Meed is "moilere," that is, legitimate (see 123n). The topic of Meed's birth-status introduces a new problem about her status, compounding the initial question of her marital status. The legal status and thus property rights of bastards were complex, involving competition between the jurisdictions of canon law and common law which is possibly reflected here in the discrepancy. Common law (from the Statute of Merton of 1235) was usually rigorous in denying legal and inheritance rights to those born before wedlock, whereas canon law generally favored legitimation by subsequent marriage; yet common law usually did not bastardize children born from adulterous relations, whereas church courts usually did, to enforce the sacrament of marriage. Yet again, church rulings were rarely accepted by secular judges: "which procedure was most used is impossible to say" (Swanson 1989:147; see also Brundage 1987:408–9). Sothness, who as 2.203–6 shows is a strict supporter of the king's law, may generally be upholding the position of common law against the episcopal or papal courts, where Meed might be presumed to have some influence over a ruling about bastardy, as she would over every other legal decision. Elsewhere PP is particularly hard on bastards: see, e.g., 10.209–12a (B.9.121–25a). The one medieval notice of the poet's father presents a different name from the poet's, and this has long been taken, not fully convincingly, however, as evidence that he was himself illegitimate (see Prol.6n; the fluidity of surnames and the strong possibility of a pen name makes the question probably unresolvable). But the question about Meed, raised below (123n), is not how she should be treated as a bastard, but whether in fact she is one.

Smith suggests that an allegorical point explains Meed's two lineages: these define two distinct "circumstances under which the giving and receiving of meed begins. When meed is preceded by guile [figured by Holy Church's lineage of Meed at 25–26], it does become an avaricious force that disrupts social order. And unless meed is preceded by a willingness to honor bonds that have already been established [figured by Truth's previous plighting of troth here], it rapidly gives rise to guile" (Smith 1994:132). This explicates, and compresses, the details of her lineages allegorically as chains of actions and motivations involving reward; such a view is in keeping with how Conscience takes up the sequences of labor, merit, and reward in the next passus, and the issues here begin to move toward those concerns (see, e.g., 3.291–332n). Here, however, the more immediate emphasis and drama is on her marital, social, and legal status, from "whose wyf a were" (17n above) to the contradiction between Sothness' and Theology's claims about her status as bastard or legitimate. Like virtually all of the questions about her value, these issues are pursued with a detail that shows their importance but an irresolution that shows their futility.

25–26 (cp. B 25–26, cp. A 19–20): Oon fauel [B: Fals] was here fader þat hath a fykel tonge [A: wrong was hire sire] . . . bote yf he souche gyle: The idea of moral or intellectual relationships expressed as the kinship of personifications appears in the *Roman de la Rose* and elsewhere (e.g., in Nicholas Bozon's *Char d'Orgueil*, Pride is the daughter of Lucifer; ed.Vising 1914, line 2). But each version of PP changes the name of Meed's father, rendering the question of her legitimacy all the more difficult to settle, and perhaps also sustaining a general sense of the indistinct and swarming nature of sin (see above 5–9n; and 4.27–31n). The focus on Meed's father in any of his identities extends the attention in the previous passus to the "fader of falshede" (see 1.59–60n). The candidates for her father appear to be closely related, all members like her bridegroom "of þe fendes kynne" (44), and their identities shift elusively through each revision.

In A, Wrong, her father, is aligned with the devil (see A.1.61–68 [note at C.1.59–60]), and False, her husband, is "a bastard yborn of belsabbubis kynde" (A 95), suggesting at least a general kinship. According to the marriage charter in A, False has determined that Meed and her husband will go to dwell forever with her (or their?) father, Wrong (71); the charter, however, names not Wrong but Favel as enfeoffing Falseness to Meed (58), and perhaps Favel is already here an alternate candidate for her father, for Favel gives away the bride to False (49).

In B, her father, now named by Holy Church as **Fals . . . þat haþ a fikel tonge** (B 25), has nearly the same name (or is the same?) as her bridegroom, False Fickle-tongue (41). Favel, who as in A gives Meed away, is blamed for having "þoruȝ his faire speche . . . þis folk enchaunted" (42), and he yields her to False as a professional marriage-broker rather than a father (66). False, as either her father or husband or both, is also still the maker of the charter, which, however, records not his own but, as in A, Favel's enfeoffment of Meed and False to various territories and castles of sin (74–114); as before, Meed and False will dwell forever with the devil (103).

In C, her father, whom Holy Church now names as Favel but Theology as False (124), is thus either the same figure who has "foule enchaunted" Meed to undergo the marriage (45), who gives her to False "as a brokor" (68), and who enfeoffs False and Meed to various territories and holdings of sin (81–111), or, if he is False himself, as Theology says, then he is the incestuous beneficiary of Favel's machinations. Favel's new epithet in C as "fauel þat hath a fals speche" (86) confuses these distinctions while retaining the suggestion of his kinship with her bridegroom, False. When Theology in C like Holy Church in B names False as her father, and Fickle-tongue as, perhaps, her grandfather ("belsyre"; but see 124n), Theology makes the claim of incest directly, since in C as in B, he names False as her bridegroom as well (140 = B 124).

The different identities of Meed's father, and even their full names, not only suggest persistent uncertainty and multiplicity in her patrimony, they also hint at or directly declare her incestuous kinship with her proposed bridegroom. If Meed's father is not in fact her husband, those two appear in every version likely to be closely related, and whatever his relationship to her bridegroom, her father's pernicious control of the marriage arrangements is increasingly clear in the successive versions. The uncertainty of Meed's lineage presents an implicit contrast to the importance of the context, lineage, and grammar of transactions that Conscience elaborates in C especially (see notes to 3.333–406a, 336–39, and 340–40a). Perhaps related to the issue here is how the reproduction of money from money was considered "unnatural" by scholastics following Aristotle, especially Aquinas (*Summa Theologica* II IIae quaes. 78, art. 1, resp.; see Aristotle's *Politics* 1.3, 1258b; A). Yet Holy Church's marriage is presented as in some mysterious sense incestuous as well (see 31–35n). Her lineage, however, lacks the multiplicity of fathers and husbands that confers a strong sense of illicit promiscuity and back-room dealings on the marriage arrangements for Meed, and indeed on Meed's genesis, status, and identity.

Meed's fathers in A and B, Wrong and False, have names suggesting the devil himself. In C, Holy Church's identification of her father as Favel makes that connection somewhat more distant. Favel, whose role clarifies and expands in each successive version, had a generalized sense of "flatterer" (from its derivation from Latin *fabula*); thus Hoccleve contrasts his own true advice to Henry IV to that of Favel who "besieth hym . . . in sly portraituris" (*Regiment of Princes*, ed. Blyth 1999, lines 4439–52). According to the French *Roman de Fauvel* (see Headnote), Favel's name indicates his pedigree from many sins (see Prol.20n; for the lineage of sins, see passus 1, Headnote; see also next note):

De Fauvel descent Flaterie,
Qui du monde a la seignorie,
Et puis en descent Avarice,
Qui de torchier Fauvel n'est nice,
Vilanie et Varieté,
Et puis Envie et Lascheté. (ed. Långfors 1919, lines 247–52)

[From Fauvel is descended Flattery,
Who has the governance of the world,
And moreover from him is descended Avarice,
Who is not too squeamish to groom Fauvel,
Villainy and Changeability,
And then Envy and Sloth.]

The figure of Fauvel, as the horse of "favor" that sycophants curried, was well known in late medieval England. Thus a knight listening to a public sermon delivered by the London preacher Richard Alkerton before Henry IV and Archbishop Arundel in 1406 mocked the preacher for flattering the higher clergy by the mere gesture of having his servant present Alkerton with a horse's curry-comb (see Galloway 1992b:23–25; Spencer 1993:87, 395–96n35). The point was understood by everyone, including the archbishop, who forced the knight's servant to perform penance.

27–29a (cp. B 27–27a): And mede is manered aftur hym . . . *bonum fructum facit*: Although Holy Church is speaking, and the passages have religious origins, both quotations lose their religious associations. The first Latin passage in C and B, "as the father, so the son[, so the Holy Ghost is God]," may well be taken from the Athanasian Creed, where it appears (Alford, *Quot.*), but it is stripped of its religious point by the truncation, to mean simply "like father, like son," a proverbial phrase. The second passage, "A sound tree bears good fruit" (Mt. 7:17), is similarly made into proverbial wisdom without any overt Christian reference. Both quotations are used to support the view, a general one in the poem, of a continuity of moral as well as physical features between generations; see especially Wit's speech, 10.243–69 (B.9.150–68; Tavormina 1995:83–92), although a counter-trend insisting on the importance of teaching from an early age is clear throughout the poem: see Orme 1989:243–58. A substantial group of C manuscripts have "like father, like *daughter*" ("*Qualis pater talis filia*"), a more immediately pertinent reading (and one removing the connection to the Athenasian Creed). Yet although L could change a Latin quotation (see, e.g., 1.111a [B.1.119]), that variant is not supported by the use of the Latin to make a general claim about natural processes, **as men of kynde carpeth**. C's division of the two quotations and insertion of English exposition of the second between them allow the parallel English comments to precede each Latin quotation and thus stand as the primary exposition of each point, with the Latin tags as merely secondary support.

In this passus Holy Church's means of spurning Meed reduce her own language and her posture of authority from a sublimely religious to an earthly and social level, perhaps a function of the prevailing mode of satire of the present passus; see also below, 30n.

A 20: Out of wrong heo wex to wroþerhele manye: The A-text line, which the above lines replace, maintains a strict view of Meed's destructive power. In A, Meed simply ramifies and manifests **wrong**, in the sort of propagation of sins that the *Roman de Fauvel* and other late medieval penitential and homiletic works suggest. **to wroþerhele manye:** "as injury to many" (the dative **manye** is part of this archaic phrase).

30 (B 28, A 21): y com of a bettere: A's line, the only A line paralleling the development of this theme in the later versions here, shows Holy Church tersely and dismissively comparing herself to Meed; see also next lines and note. The implication of pride in her own lineage produces an ironic echo to her comment about others' pursuit of their "worship": see 1.8n. The expansions of this theme in the later versions may partly be efforts to explain that her pride in her own "worship" is a calculated paradox, rather than an uncalculated show of vainglory. Whether controlled by a didactic purpose or not, however, her self-presentation is daringly literal in social terms.

31–37 (cp. B 29–35): The fader þat me forth brouhte . . . a lippe of trewe charite: Holy Church establishes a series of contrasts between herself and Meed: her lineage; her dowry; her choice(s) of marriage partners; and the consequences of the marriage to that partner. Holy Church's mention of her lineage closely resembles the claims made by Raison in the *Roman de la Rose*, if Amant takes her as his lover: "Si avras en cest avantage / Amie de si haut parage / Qui'il n'est nulle qui s'I compere. / Fille sui Dieu le sovrain pere, / Qui tele me fist et forma. / Regarde ci quele forme a / Et te mire en mon cler visage. / Onques pucele de parage / N'ot d'amer tel bandon cum gié, / De ce ai, sans prendre, congié / De faire ami et d'estre amee" ("You will have a lover of such noble family that there is none to compare with her; I am the daughter of God, the sovereign father who made and shaped me so. Look at my form and at yourself in my clear face. No girl of such descent ever had such a power of loving as have I, for I have leave of my father to take a friend and be loved"; ed. Poirion 1974, lines 5813–23; trans. Dahlberg 1986). The statement is echoed by Grace-Dieu in Deguileville's *Pelerinage de vie humaine*: "Fille sui de l'empereeur / Qui sur tous autres est seigneur" ("I am the daughter of the emperor who is lord over all others"; ed. Stürzinger 1893, lines 297–98).

In the versions of PP, the point of the lines is consistent but the tone changes between B and C. B's Holy Church is, for a moment, an attractive and available, if somewhat prim, fourteenth-century maiden of good family, her father a benevolent though powerful lord. In C, however, both Holy Church and her father are more impersonally and more solemnly drawn. As Holy Church's father, God in B is fully humanized, with Holy Church as **his goode douȝter** to whom he has given **mercy to marie wiþ myselue** (i.e., the dowry of "mercy" to attract a husband to herself; so Bnt; possibly there is some further play on **mercy** as *mercien*, 'to reward' [MED v.1 (1b)], and 'to fine' someone [MED v.2]: i.e., God has given Holy Church the capacity to reward or fine her followers). God in C as Holy Church's father is *filius dei . . . / That neuere lyede ne lauhede in al his lyf tyme* (31–32), the last detail a point of Jesus' asceticism that patristic writers emphasized in commentary on his weeping at Lazarus' death (John 11:35; so Prsl); it appears in these terms in some vernacular lives of Christ (e.g., *Cursor Mundi*, ed. Morris 1966, lines 18855–56). In B, Holy

Church invites human commitment in the form of marriage and romantic passion, a mildly if confusingly erotic metaphor as her last bid for human beings to cleave to her rather than Meed before she exits the poem for good. Mystical marriage between humanity and God is, to be sure, a Pauline (and earlier) symbol for the state of salvation; see 2 Cor. 11:2, "For I have espoused you to one husband, that I may present you as a chaste virgin to Christ." But Holy Church's promise in B that any man who is loyal to her **Shal be my lord and I his leef in þe heiȝe heuene** expands the metaphor of marriage in an unexpected place—not in human beings' relations to God but their relations to the church—and does so with a confusion of positive but evidently inadequate metaphors for her relationships. Holy Church has, throughout B (and A), revealed that she is a parental figure to the dreamer and all of her flock, whose baptism she has attended and whose faith she has taught (see passus 1 Headnote, 1.4–5n, and 1.73–75n). Now she is suggesting she is also a spouse. For C's development of her quasi-incestuous relations to God, see below 31n.

In C the promise that human beings can marry her is abandoned; human beings are more coolly enticed to a commitment to the church, on the promise only of **grace to good ynow and a good ende** (on that last phrase, see Prol.29n). The passage includes the dichotomy of the Pardon (34–37), first appearing earlier in Holy Church's discourse (see 1.130–34n). The restatement here is parting guidance for the dreamer as he confronts choices for his loyalties.

31 (cp. B.29): *filius dei* [B: þe grete god]: In C, Holy Church is more remote both from human beings and from the enigmatic deity who created her, just as Meed is less directly the daughter of the devil; see above, 25–26n. And just as the candidates for Meed's father suggest the possibility of incest in her marriage, in making Holy Church specifically the daughter of *filius dei* C allows an implication of incest of a sacred and mysterious sort, since Holy Church is traditionally espoused to the Son of God (based on the typical understanding of 2 Cor. 11:2 and the traditional intereprepetation of the Song of Songs; compare Meed's incestuous marriage, above 25–26n). The idea of this marriage is pervasive in late medieval doctrine (see Headnote); but the emphasis on Holy Church as also the daughter of the God whom she marries is rare.

36 (cp. B 34): my lyf dar y wedde [B: myn heed dar I legge]: C's phrase, which overtly associates Meed with the pledging in which she is frequently involved, is reused by Meed herself (see 3.255), and structures her and her followers' actions (see 4.84–85n, 4.107n).

37 (B 35): a lippe of trewe charite [B: a lippe of *Caritatis*]: I.e., a taste of heaven, of full love of God. The line is already informed by Psalm 14, quoted below at 40 ff., which was routinely understood to refer to the question of attaining the "true charity" of heaven: e.g., the twelfth-century commentator Peter Lombard, glossing the line from Psalm 14 that appears below at 40, "*in tabernaculo tuo* . . . id est in aeterna beatitudine . . . ubi est visio pacis et super-eminentia charitatis, ubi nullus in agone contendet, sed in aeterna pace quies-cet" ("*in your tabernacle*, that is, in eternal sanctity . . . where there is the vision of peace and a very high eminence of charity, where no one will struggle in conflict but will rest in eternal peace"; PL 191:167). The phrase "supereminentia charitatis," possibly directly behind the last part of Holy Church's phrase here, is used by Augustine to define Jesus' ultimate charity in the eternal life (*In Joannis Evangelium Tractatus CXXIV*; PL 35:1507), and the phrase is adopted by other theological writers, especially in the mystical tradition (e.g., Richard of St. Victor, *De quattor gradibus violentiae charitatis* (PL 196:1207). In contrast to such writers, L restricts his few statements of enjoying heaven's or God's full love to mere tastes and small mouthfuls (**lippe**); see also C.11.224, "a lyppe of goddes grace"; and C.5.100, "a gobet [morsel] of his grace"; compare the self-serving "devouring" of charity below, 142–43n. Images of eating and drinking are pervasive in the poem (see Mann 1979); in "sipping" or "nibbling" charity or grace, this carries an obvious connection to the Eucharist. See also 20.403–8 (B.18.365–67), and note.

38: That helpeth man moste to heuene mede most letteth: The syntax is ambiguous, but the sense must be "Meed most hinders what most helps men to heaven" (not "What helps men most to heaven most hinders Meed"). For the sense of money as an obstacle or affliction, see B.4.154–56n. The carry-over from the immediately preceding line suggests that **That** ("that which") is "trewe charite"; but since the line is describing what **helpeth** man to heaven rather than what man will experience in heaven, the antecedent is more likely to be the love of and obedience to Holy Church (34), or even an unstated ideal of perfect poverty (see Clopper 1997:89–93). Compare Matt. 19:23–24, "it is easier for a camel to pass through the eye of a needle than for a rich man to enter into the kingdom of heaven"; the problems of defining perfect poverty are taken up especially in the C Pardon passus (e.g., C.9.61–166). The sense of **mede** here is thus "earthly reward" in its most immorally gained forms, the sense in which Holy Church invariably presents Meed, and as Conscience too will define her (see 3.286–500nn).

39–42 (cp. B 36–39): Y do hit vppon dauyd . . . *Domine quis habitabit . . . munera non accepit*: The Latin quotation in C and B of the first line from

Psalm 14, "Lord, who will dwell in your tabernacle?" and in C only the later line from the same psalm, "And [one who] has not taken a bribe against the innocent" (Ps 14:5), evokes a key psalm in the poem, often invoked by these two lines. The same two lines are used to define the nature of divine reward in Conscience's speech against Meed (B.3.234a, 237a, 241a), and again in relation to legal ethics in the Pardon passus in B (7.42a, 52a). These later instances are omitted in C, but in both B and C Conscience presents the psalm as one of Piers Plowman's two central texts for proving that "loue and leute and lowenesse of herte" are superior to "alle kyne connynges and alle kyne craftes" (see C.15.134 [B.13.127]). Psalm 14 was typically taken as defining the ideal of the true community and "unity" of the church, as obscured on earth but clarified in heaven: as Peter Lombard's commentary on it says, "agitur de unitate Ecclesiae praesentis, et de futura quiete. In praesenti namque Ecclesia, quia propter corporalem cohabitationem malorum cum bonis, non permittimur scire qui vere sint de unitate Ecclesiae, ideo quidam, licet indigni, jactant se esse de Ecclesia, cum tamen vere non sint" ("it concerns the unity of the present church, and its peaceful future. For since in the present church, where the good and the evil physically dwell together, we are not permitted to know who is truly part of the unity of the church, some unworthy ones boast that they are part of the church, though in truth they are not"; PL 191:167). The idea, although widely exploited by the Lollards, is a thoroughly traditional element of Augustinian theology of the "two cities" (on the Lollard views, see Hudson 1988a:314–58). The psalm may thus inform the poem's final portrayal of those fleeing into Unite, just as its images of a sacred mountain may be invoked at the opening of the poem (see Prol.15n). Its ethics of charity feature proper behavior to one's neighbor, prominently denouncing usury but also pointing to other aspects of economic ethics. L's citation of the psalm in terms of its absolute principles of heavenly reward for doing good and punishment for doing evil put it within the ethical reach of the Pardon (see Lawler 2000).

super Innocentem munera non accepit: This line is prominent in the poet's citation of Psalm 14: see also B.3.241a and B.7.42a, both dropped from C. At B.7.42a, the line appears next to the phrase, "þe Sauter saueþ hem noȝt, swiche as take ȝiftes . . . of Innocentȝ," and is interpreted there further as "Pledours sholde peynen hem to plede for swiche and helpe; / Princes and prelates sholde paie for hire trauaille": thus at least at that B line, L presents the line as meaning "take no gifts *from* the innocent" (rather than "do not accept gifts [bribes] *against* the innocent")—and for their fees in those cases, "pledours" should look to "princes and prelates." At B.2.243, the same line from the psalm is glossed to endorse those who "Wiþouten Mede doþ hem [þe Innocent] good" (see B.2.242–44n). But the sense of *super* in Jerome's translation from the Septuagint here, although unusual Latin, was widely and correctly understood as "against" not "from" (e.g., Peter Lombard, compiling comments by Augustine and Cassiodorus on the psalms, glosses it "id est, causam innocentis non deprimit pro munere alicujus" ["that is, he does not suppress the suit of an innocent man because of a bribe from someone else"; PL 191:169], and specifically glosses *super innocentem* "contra innocentes" ["against innocents"; PL 191:170]; Richard Rolle in his Latin commentary on the psalms ingeniously explicates *super innocentem* with a stem-word echo, "ad superandum innocentem in causa" ["for overpowering the innocent in legal suits"; Cologne ed. 1536; Porter 1929:61]). However, the early Middle English guide to confessors in dialogue form found uniquely in Stowe MS. 34 (olim 240), given the modern title *Vices and Virtues*, takes the phrase like PP as "from": "se ðe ne nimð none mede of ða innocentes, ðat bien uneilinde menn ðe none manne euel ne willeð" ("he who takes no reward from innocents who are harmless men who wish no evil to any man"; ed. Holthausen 1888:79/6–7).

The poet almost certainly understood the points of a psalm he knew and pondered perhaps more than any other, even in its rhetorical structure (see following note, and B.3.236–37n). The small but significant misconstruing of *super innocentem* at B.7.42 ff. and, implicitly, at B.2.242–44 may be a calculated endorsement of service by "pledours" to take no money to defend "the innocent" (perhaps exploiting some lost homiletic uses of the alternative sense, as captured also in the single twelfth-century copy of the vernacular *Vices and Virtues*, although that work does not apply the point to lawyers). The expansion at B.7.42 ff. shows that he takes *munus* not simply as "bribe" (a common particular meaning), but also as "payment" (its broad sense). Most broadly, this is part of L's sustained response to the tradition that all intellectual skill is a gift of God and therefore should be free; payment should especially not be involved in the legal process (see, e.g., Prol.160–66n; C.9.55–60 [B.7.53–59]; on the topic broadly, see Post et al. 1955). More narrowly, the interpretation of the psalm in these terms likely derives from oaths for various legal authorities: concerning ecclesiastical judges, Hubert Walter's twelfth-century *Legatine Canons*, quoting this psalm, notes, "since the Scripture testifies that he is blessed who withdraws his hand from accepting bribes, it is most carefully to be provided that justice be done gratis, and that no pay be taken for doing it, or laying it aside, or hastening, or delaying it in ecclesiastical cases" (Johnson 1851, vol. 2.78; noted by Alford, *Gloss.* s.v. *"Qui Pecuniam Suam Non Dedit ad Vsuram, etc."*). This concern prepares the ground for Magna Carta, cl. 40: "to no one will we sell, to no one will we deny or delay right or justice" (trans. Holt 1972:179), and thence for the oath that a royal justice from the mid-thirteenth century on swore: "to do justice to the best of his ability to all as well poor as rich . . . nor for hatred nor for favor nor for the estate of anyone nor for a benefit, gift, or promise given to him nor in any other way" (quoted by Brand 1992:150). Indeed, L's use of *super innocentem* at B.7.42 ff. mentioning "pledours" appears to refer specifically to sergeants at law. But his use here and elsewhere of *super innocentem* probably applies to judges and lawyers in general taking gifts or any payments from plaintiffs (on injunctions against these taking bribes, see Noonan 1984:178–79).

Just how closely L's ideal views reflected free legal representation of the innocent by any sort of "pleader" is unclear. From the twelfth century on, records show reprieve of fines "quia pauper est" ("because he is poor"; Hyams 1980:76), and Richard III and Henry VII appointed a master and Court of Requests to insure "equal remedies to those who could not afford existing tribunals" (Hicks 2002:25; on this court see also below 151n). There might be some parallel in the establishing of a house in 1423 in London where surgeons and physicians, in addition to giving lectures, treated the poor free of charge (Barron 2000:436). How London sergeants in L's period treated poor clients is, however, obscure; so too are the reasons for C's omissions of most examples of this unusual construing of *super innocentem*; see B.3.242–44n, B.7.41–42a.

39, 41: Y do hit vppon dauyd . . . And dauid vndoth hymself: On **do it** as 'cite in evidence,' 'appeal to,' and **vndoth** as 'explicate' or 'answer,' see 1.82n; see also B.13.157. PP's usage of these phrases is technically precise; for "undo it" in the simpler sense of 'present' or 'describe,' see Chaucer's *Book of the Duchess*, line 899. The balanced phrasing here shows C's emphasis on the psalm as a whole, indicating the question-and-answer structure that governs the entire psalm. Peter Lombard notes of this psalm, "Modus: Bipartitus est. Primo, interrogat Propheta . . . Secundo, subditur Domini responsio" ("mode: it is bipartite. First, the Prophet inquires . . . second, the Lord's response is given"; PL 191:167). L notes the bipartite structure but takes the speaker to be the same. So too, at B.3.236–37 (cut from C perhaps in order to advance the same point to the present location), Conscience notes about this psalm that David asks the question then answers it himself: "þis askeþ Dauid. / And Dauid assoileþ it hymself as þe Sauter telleþ." The same notice of Scripture's use of rhetorical questions appears in Walter Hilton's *Scale of Perfection*, where Hilton is translating and commenting upon Isaiah 66:2: "For oure Lord asketh bi His prophete thus . . . Upon whom schal My spirit reste? And He answereth Himsilf and seith: upon noon but upon the meke . . ." (ed. Bestul 2000:53).

39, 41: the doumbe wil noȝt lyen . . . as þe doumbe sheweth: Objects are mute in many proverbs ("dumb as a stone"); books are sometimes so called when they are difficult to use, as when they lack an index (MED *domb* 6d). The point here is not that, being mute, books cannot lie (so Prsl), for books can lie (as medieval Christian writers commonly said about ancient descriptions of pagan gods, for example). Rather, L here invokes a proverb hitherto recorded only as early as sixteenth-century Scotland, about mute objects whose import is so self-evident that they tell the truth better than any speaker: "Dummie will not lie" (Beveridge 1924:no. 244). An anonymous eighteenth-century expounder of Scottish proverbs relates the proverb "dummie will not lie" to the legal maxim *res ipsa loquitur* (the thing speaks for itself): "Spoken to convince our Servants, and others, of their ill Usage of what has been among their Hands: . . . my Horse is lean, my Utensils are broken, my Grain is eaten. *Nempe res ipsa loquitur*" (ed. Wilson 1970, no. 87). For an example of the legal demonstration of such an idea see 4.74–75n. L's usage of the proverb here, however, is a complex pun: he does not simply mean that the text cited is a *res ipsa* that transparently reveals his present point, the way a broken utensil bespeaks careless handling; rather, as line 41 makes clear, he is likely punning on how this psalm in particular both asks and answers itself (see note above): thus it "speaks for itself," and thus (paradoxically) it is **þe doumbe**, as in the later gloss on *res ipsa loquitur*. Instigating this pattern in the passage is perhaps the tradition, defined by Hill 2001a, that David the psalmist was "dumb" (based on Psalm 38:5, "I was dumb and was humbled, and kept silence from good things"), an idea that then is poured into the form of the proverb that L's line follows.

44–46 (B 41–43, cp. A 22–25): fals faythlesse / Fauel / [A: Gile]/ lyares led-yng: On False and Favel, see above, 25–26n. C and B present the actions of the sinful figures here so that each performs a somewhat separate function: False marries Meed, Favel enchants the populace to allow it, and Liar convinces Meed herself (although Favel also does this in these versions). The A text is less clear in its discrimination of activities: all four sinful figures perform the same function, convincing Meed to marry. Once the process of allocating discrete functions among the "persons" of the sinful figures developed in the B revision, there was no specific role for Guile to play, so he was dropped; in B and C he first appears in order to give False the charter of Meed's marriage (72). A relic of the A text's use of Guile in convincing Meed to marry remains at 129: "thow hast gyue here as gyle tauhte."

47: Soffre and thow shalt see: In C, Holy Church speaks of Will's learning as something he must await and gain over time. The language, and the use of an imperative, attribute graver and more solemn importance to the statement than B's "There myȝtow witen if þow wilt" (45). B's Holy Church hints that the dreamer (and the reader) may continue learning; C's Holy Church more sternly commands Will's and the reader's attention, and emphasizes the theme of learning by experience, in the face of which he must learn to cultivate patience and "suffering" in the fundamental sense. See 1.77–78n.

51–52 (B 48–49): Lacke hem nat but lat hem worthe . . . thenne pot forth thy resoun: Holy Church here licenses the dreamer, at some utopian future moment, to denounce Meed's followers, **that loueth here lordschipe**, once Leaute becomes a justice. This hints at, and surely bolsters, the narrator's authority for poetic satire that he is already displaying by writing his poem (see further 1.135n, 146–58n, and A 137n). **thy resoun** is both his formal legal accusation, and is also used later, in C only, to describe the narrator's guiding principle for his poetic denunciation of evildoers: in C, 5.1–104, the narrator, looking back to a time in London, claims that he had denounced "lollares of londone and lewede Ermytes" in his poetry ("made of"), and paid the price with their contempt: "For y made of tho men as resoun me tauhte" (5.4–5). This may be part of the false postures of authority and righteousness in the narrator's self-portrait, or an indication that the satire of the earlier versions of the poem was not in fact perceived to be evasive but pointed, direct, and unsettling, at least to wastrels (C.5.4). It may, however, take a more apocalyptic moment, when Leaute rules all justice, to **pot forth thy resoun** against the more powerful figures who follow Meed. The poet's constrained satire (see Simpson 1990a), in the present dispensation of history, and before the point where Leaute **haue power to punyschen hem**, cannot attain that discursive freedom. The deferment of his full authority to denounce evil anticipates the series of "until" clauses that Reason presents at the end of the Meed sequence, when he declares how long Meed must be resisted (3.108–45).

B originally introduced Leaute, "steadfast fidelity to principles of justice"; see above 20–21n, Prol.46–48n. In the present age, Leaute has been the recipient of Meed's abuse at a lord's court (above 20–21), but elsewhere Leaute urges the narrator and all laymen to denounce "Falsnesse" and "fayterye," provided that one is not the first to do so, provided (in the B version of this) that one is not a member of the clergy, and provided that one does not reveal "Thyng þat wolde be pryue," presumably individuals' names (12.23–40a [cp. B.11.84–106a]). The instigation to offer righteous "fraternal" correction has evangelical and Pauline bases (Mt. 18:15, Gal. 2:11–14; see Craun 2001); but the repeated mentions of **resoun** guiding, or being, the narrator's public denunciation points to a medieval tradition of that notion as "law" (see 1.50n). The postures of truth telling that Sothness and Leaute respectively embody are indeed both found as capabilities of Jean de Meun's Raison, in the *Roman de la Rose*:

Car se tu meffez ou mesdiz,
Ou par mes fez ou par mes diz
Secreement t'en puis reprendre
Par toi chastier et aprendre,
Sanz blame et sanz diffamement;
Ou vengier neïs autrement,
Se tu ne me voloies croire
De ma parole bonne et voire,
Par plaindre quant temps en seroit
Au juge qui droit m'en feroit. (ed. Poirion 1974, lines 7011–20)

[If, through what I do or say, you mispeak or misbehave, I can, without blaming or slandering you, correct you privately in order to chastise you and teach you. Or I can avenge myself in yet another way, if you do not want to believe my good and true utterance, by pleading, when the time comes to appear before the judge, who would give me a just decision.] (trans. Dahlberg 1986)

55–56 (B 52–53; cp. A 32–33): Thus lefte me that lady . . . metyng as it were: Holy Church has promised that Will will see the marriage "tomorwe" (43, 48), and B and C insert this brief transition accounting for the elapsed time. The time and scene change rapidly in setting the stage for Lady Meed's marriage, and these lines demonstrate further how L progressively smoothed the transitions (see above, 1–4n). A lacks any transition; B's insertion of **in Metels me þouȝte** allows a pause, and a hint of literary artifice or uncertainty about the nature of a vision; C's **metyng as it were** achieves the same with perhaps a more visible self-consciousness about the artistry or magic of dream-vision. There is still a sense of Holy Church conjuring all this up, as at the opening of the passus; her authority and power linger more after her departure than with most allegorical figures in the poem. Unlike Meed, Peace, or even Conscience, she does not seem to fade before her disappearance, but instead leaves an impression of continued control over the action that she began by presenting "the false" for the dreamer—possibly a reason why commentators have sometimes suggested that the entire poem springs from her teaching (Bloomfield 1962:153; Kaske 1974). The lingering sense of a numinous figure's power, as well as the compressed passage of "vision-time," may be compared to Margery Kempe's vision of Mary between the Annunciation and the Nativity: "The blysful chyld [i.e., the Virgin Mary] passyd awey for a certeyn tyme, þe creatur [i.e., Margery Kempe] being stylle in contemplacyon, and sythen cam a-geyn and seyd, 'Dowtyr, now am I be-kome þe Modyr of God' " (1.6; ed. Meech and

Allen 1961:18). Both L and the *Book of Margery Kempe* use the sleeping or trance-like state of the narrator to accommodate such rapid passages of time. On the potential compressions of temporality in PP, especially by way of its topological allusions to sacred history or points where the characters actually are "undergoing a movement within salvation history" (a wider movement than that occurring here), see Trower 1973 (quotation at 408).

Meed's marriage

A 38–47: Þer nas halle ne hous . . . in mariage was feffid: The Latin satire "De Cruce Denarii" neatly expresses the proverbial notion that "money is known by everyone," and L elaborates this point throughout the drama of Meed ("Nummus cognoscitur a cunctis gentibus," ed. Wright 1841, line 41). For the tendency to produce occupational lists in the poem, see Prol.222n. The A text here presents a much less precise and focused list of followers of Meed than B and C (see following note), including ropemakers and the redundantly inclusive **For lerid, for lewid.** In the A text Meed's marriage is a festive event, with **a pauyloun proud for þe nones / And ten þousand of tentis teldit beside,** and the assembled crowd is more a fascinated audience, energetically festive, than a parade of sinful figures.

From here A here proceeds directly into the parodic marriage vows; see below, A 49–53n. The other versions elaborate the preliminaries of the gathering, without ever quite making it as festive. Great marriages are often grandiose and crowded in medieval literature; although less common in alliterative poetry than in French romance, a spectacular triple marriage and one abortive but also splendid preparation for marriage occupy substantial and emphatic portions of the alliterative *William of Palerne* (ed. Bunt 1985, see lines 1463–1631, 4990–5105); see also following note.

A 40–42: In myddis a mounteyne . . . Was piȝt vp a pauyloun proud for þe nones, / And ten þousand of tentis teldit beside: The broader setting in A, cut from the later versions, parallels the first, paternally arranged marriage in *William of Palerne* (ed. Bunt 1985): "alle þe genge of Grece was gayli resseyved / and herbarwed hastely, ich hete þe for soþe, / in a place þer were piȝt pavilons / and of þe price tentes / semede as moche to siȝt as þe cite of Rome" (lines 1625–31). That marriage, imposed on the bride, ends with her escape with her true love William.

60–63 (B 58–61): Of knyghtes, of clerkes . . . and voketes of the Arches: To fulfill Holy Church's promise to reveal "suche as ben apayed / That mede is thus ymaried" (47–48), B and C identify "medes kynne" (59) as primarily from the lower-level administrative world. C/B extend the occupational list, and further fulfill the claim that money is well known to all people (see above A 38–47n). The broad pattern follows the presentation of all the participants at grand marriages, e.g., in *William of Palerne* (as above, A 38–47n and A 40–42n). Details in those presentations are often less clear than here, swallowed up in exclamations of extraordinary plenty, rather than, as here, specified in satiric identifications and sordid actions (see also below, 64n).

sysores: assizers, those who constituted the assize or inquest; sworn recognitors (OED; Alford, *Gloss.*). "Sysours" appear to name not substantial citizens called to a jury, but a class of individuals whose chief livelihood was serving in jury duty, where the costs of travel and, evidently often, something more, would be paid by the parties of the suit; hence their other name, "quest-mongers." They are often criticized for abusing the law. "Cisours" and "quest-mongers" were hunted down by the London rebels in 1381, as if these were known types or quasi-professionals (see Bellamy 1989:68, 63–67; Dobson 1970:158). In 1464, John Paston III described to his father a series of conversations with men who had been empanelled to sit as a jury at the inquest of his father's lawsuit, whose names John III had collected as a basis for determining their likely views; several led him to think that "they wold haue had a brybe of yow . . . for they haue non othyr leuyng but brybys" (Davis 2004, no. 322, part 1.526–27). In PP **sysores** are later directly condemned for perjury, and often grouped with summoners (see 21/B.19.369, 22/B.20.161).

sompnores: officials who summoned defendants to an ecclesiastical court, frequently the object of intense literary satire (e.g., Chaucer's General Prologue, 623–68; Friar's Tale), and also the object of real resentment and violence as they carried out their roles. In PP summoners receive relatively minor criticism; see also 4.162–65 (cp. B.4.166–72).

shyryues and here clerkes: **sh** commonly alliteratives with **s** in PP (see KD-B p. 132n10), as in *Richard the Redeless* and *William of Palerne* and infrequently in other poets (Oakden 1930:165). Generally substantial knights or esquires or simply well-off free tenant farmers, sheriffs had a wide range of authority and duties in their counties, including collecting money and fines from the populace for the king, detaining suspected criminals to turn over to the king's justices and sometimes trying minor crimes personally, and helping supply the king with provisions for war or his household, all opportunities for extortion or at least occasional misconduct, and sometimes for notorious and systematic abuse (see Gorski 2003:71, 102–25; Harding 1973:72–74; Palmer 1982:28–55). Sheriffs were particularly influential in the fourteenth and fifteenth centuries in their role of empanelling juries, where the sharpest suspicion (or hope) of their corruption often came to focus; "all knew that a single jury verdict could lead to a person losing his whole inheritance once and for all," and plaintiffs and defendants in land cases often tried to "labor"— bribe—the sheriffs of counties where the land in dispute was located (Bellamy 1989:11). As Conscience later declares, by means of sheriffs Meed "doth men lesen here lond and here lyf bothe" (3.174). In PP, sheriffs are mentioned persistently along with "sysours" and "sompnores," in large part perhaps for alliterative reasons; sheriffs and their clerks are persistently subjected to fuller criticism for corruption than the others (3.172–79 [B.3.134–41, A.3.123–30], 4.162–65 [B.4.167–70]; see further, Baldwin 1981:28–29). Historians debate the degree of systemic legal corruption in the period (see 1.94–101n), but the letter collections of the fifteenth century support the view that sheriffs were at least subject to multiple pressures in such legal matters, often by powerful entities. In one letter of 1451, John Paston I's legal advisor in a lawsuit against Lord Moleyns describes a circuitous conversation with a sheriff who has already decided to empanel jurors who will acquit Lord Moleyns, "in so meche as the Kyng hath wrete to hym for to shewe favour to the Lord Molyns and hese men. And as he seyth, the indytement longyth to the Kyng and not to yow, and the Lord Molyns a gret lord. Also . . . the Lord Molyns hath sent hym a letter, and my lord of Norffolk anoder, for to shew favour in these indytementes." Paston's adviser hints at a "surety" for his risk in not showing favor in that way, but he withdraws that when the sheriff says it would take £100 to cover his risks from Lord Moleyns and the king; "but be hese feyth, as he swore, if the Kyng wryte a-yen to hym he wol no lenger abyde the joporté of the Kyngges wrytynges." Paston's adviser concludes that Paston should purchase a letter from the king neutralizing the other letters to the sheriff: "it wold do goode and ye wold get a comaundment of the Kyng to the shereff for to shew yow favour and to inpanell jantelmen, and not for to favour non seche ryottes, &c.; for he seyde that he sent yow the letter þat the Kyng sent hym, and ye seyde a man shuld get seche on for a noble [moderately substantial coin]" (ed. Davis 2004, no. 479, Part II.72–73). The debasement of the king's writ, which here seems a fundamental source of the corruption of law, is significantly not a topic that PP satirizes (or other writings, outside of private remarks); sheriffs presented safer and more familiar targets. However, the legal principle by which an indictment is not the participant's but the king's, as suggested in the sheriff's remark to Paston's agent, "the indytement longyth to the Kyng and not to yow," and by the sheriff's evident wish to have the king's authority direct the preceedings rather than the plaintiff, receives extensive exploration in Peace's case with Wrong in passus 4 (see, e.g., 4.45n).

Bydels and bailifs: As in *The Simonie*, these are two sheriffs' **clerkes**:

compare *The Simonie* (ed. Embree and Urquhart 1991), line A 337–41, where these officials harrass the poor on behalf of the rich, whose shoes gradually carry more silver (unless those are the shoes of the bailiffs themselves): "And baillifs and bedeles vnder þe shirreve / Euerich fondeþ hu he may pore men most greue. / Þe pore men beþ oueral somouned on assise, / And þe riche sholen sitte at hom, and þer wole siluer rise / To shon." A sheriff might have as many as a dozen or more **bailifs**, who executed writs, made arrests, collected dues, and sometimes empanelled jurors and held inquests. The sheriff's beadle could be synonymous with a bailiff but often was an under-bailiff, a messenger of justice or a warrant officer (Alford, *Gloss.* s.v. *bedel*; OED *beadle* 2; Levett 1963:114–16; Palmer 1982:28–55). A beadle—in A/B another beadle of a sheriff, in C a beadle for another jurisdiction—is glimpsed below among small-time ruffians; see below 114n. The same alliterative phrase appears when naming the officers who lead Meed before the king in the next passus; there, they are doing their job, but they might also be seen as somewhat tainted (see 3.2n).

brokeres of chaffare: A general phrase for any middlemen buying and selling goods or currency or bills of exchange for profit. Profiteering, influence, and bribery are often associated with "brocage" in legal records and in PP. Meed's marriage charter, for example, enfeoffs her and her spouse to the County of Covetousness including "bargaynes and Brocages with the borw of thefte" (95).

Vorgoers and vitalers: "'Foregoers' or purveyors were men who travelled in advance of a great lord to commandeer provisions and accommodation . . . for a lord or king. The practice was much abused" (Prsl). Below, Gyle is literally made a "forgoere" to "guide" all the people, a sly literalization of this tainted word (see below, 201–2n). Wrong's assault against Peace includes more explicit elements of this role (see 4.45–63n). The practice of purveying was criticized from the mid-fourteenth century on, when Edward III's agents used the expenses of the war with France as justification for not paying for such provisions; William of Pagula's *Speculum de Edwardo Tertio*, "The Mirror of Edward III" (c. 1330; tr. Nederman 2002:63–139), possibly two treatises rather than one and its revision, focuses its prolonged criticism of Edward III primarily on this practice. In 1362 a statute was passed seeking to regulate it, and even change the name by which such royal agents were called: "est ordeigne et establi qe sur tieux purveances desore affaire pur les Hosteulx le roi et la roigne soit prest paiement fait en poigne, cestassavoir, le pris pur quel autiels vittailles sont venduz communement en marchees environ; et qe le heignous noun de purveour soit chaunge et nome achatour . . . et qe les prises soient faites en covenable et ease manere, sanz duresce, reddour, manaces, ou autre vilenie; et qe les prises et achatz soient faitz es lieux et places ou greindre plentee yad, et ce en temps covenable" ("it is ordered and established that payment will be made in hand henceforth for such purveyances to provide for the king's or queen's lodging, that is, at the price by which such provisions are commonly sold in the nearby markets; and that the heinous name of 'purveyor' be changed and named 'buyer' . . . and that the appropriations should be done in a convenient and easy manner, without duress, fear, menace, or other villainy; and that the appropriations and purchases should be done in areas and places where there is a great abundance, and at an appropriate time": 36 Edward III, st. 1; SR 1.365, 371–73, also printed in Crimes and Brown 1961:83–84). See further at 21.258–60n.

voketes of the Arches: Advocates of the supreme court of the ecclesiastical province of Canterbury, known as the Court of Arches, which sat in London at the church of St. Mary le Bow (Arcubus). For the position, doctors in civil or canon law were preferred, but bachelors were acceptable. This would be one home of Civil (see 22/B.20.136–37; and see below 65–66n).

64 (B 62): Y kan nou3t rykene þe route þat ran aboute mede: A topos in descriptions of spectacularly magnificent marriages; see *William of Palerne* (ed. Bunt 1985), "It were toor forto telle treuli al þe soþe, and to reherce þe aray ari3t of þat riche feste" (lines 5066–67); and "No clerk under Crist ne kowþe nou3t descrive / þe murthe for þat mariage þat was maked þanne, / þe richesse ne þe riaulte, to rekene þe soþe" (lines 5055–57). The topos of not being able to describe how splendid and well-attended a marriage is is familiar enough for Chaucer to toy with it ironically, to describe a shameful marriage conducted "prively" (see Wife of Bath's Tale III.1073–82). Here, PP's application of a topos for what is beyond "reckoning" has other ironic meanings, since the problem of measuring Meed's value will occupy so much of Conscience's assessment of money in passus 3 (see B.3.231–51 and notes; C.3.286–412 and notes).

65–66 (B 63–64): Ac simonye and syuile and sysores . . . of eny men me thoghte: B and C pick out Simony and Civil (i.e., civil law) early for criticism (on assizers see above, 60–63n). Both Simony and Civil have broad meanings, but here are both principles of ecclesiastical corruption, especially as involving ecclesiastical law. Simony appears as a quasi-official presence in this setting, specifically evoking the manipulation of legal judgments by bribery, a common complaint (see Noonan 1984:178); for the general sin of simony of buying and selling sacraments or ecclesiastical office, see Prol.62–63n. Civil here evidently represents the corrupt practices of those using civil law, that is, Roman law, which along with canon law applied to the dispensation of clerical property; it was much resented by those who felt that it violated English custom, in spite of various efforts to use and develop it as part of common law, notably by Richard II in the later 1380s, too late to influence this passage (see Saul 1999). Tenants of ecclesiastical lands, such as the peasants at St. Albans, sometimes complained about the use of *jura civilia* against them; the civil and canon lawyers retained by the abbot of St. Albans had to flee at the onset of the rising at St. Albans in 1381 (see Levett 1963:32). Wyclif and other Lollards persistently condemned civil law as a tool for clerical greed (see Gilbert 1981, and, with more detailed documentation, Barratt 1982), but orthodox religious also remark on the taint of career advancement in such law. Compare Thomas Wimbledon's sermon, c. 1388: "Why y praye ȝow putte men here sones raþer to lawe syuyl and to þe kyngis court to writen lettres or writis þan to philosophie oþer deuinite but for þey hopen þat þyse ocupacions shuld be euere menis to make hem grete in the world" (ed. Knight 1967:73; see also Scase 1989: 108–9).

As related entitites—the first is the sin, the second the technical training that helped make the sin possible—Simony and Civil function throughout the passus as nearly inseparable though not indistinguishable twins; in B and A, both read in unison the marriage charter (B 72–74, A 54–56); in all versions both notarize its sealing (see 117–18n). In 22.137 (B.18.137) in the coming of Antichrist, Simony goes to the Court of Arches and, in a fulfillment of this potential, explicitly turns Civil into Simony as well. Here, their institutional pairing also suggests canon lawyers employed "In þe Consistorie bifore þe Commissarie," whose life is tedious unless they receive silver, "And matrimoyne for moneie maken and vnmaken," as Anima in B declares (B.15.239–41; cp. C.16.364–65).

68 (B 66): as a brokor brouhte here to be with fals enoiyned: Since it usually designates a commercial intermediary, **brokor** is a satiric term for the father of the bride (but perhaps appropriate for the father of "reward"). The use of **brokor** to describe a "hired match-maker; a marriage agent or procurer" (Alford, *Gloss.*), appears in the late fourteenth century, but it is uncommon enough to be still an imported metaphor here. Wit mentions the issue of parents arranging their childrens' marriages for monetary reward, 10.256–58 (B.9.158–60, A.10.181–83).

69–70 (B 67–68): When simonye . . . at sylueres prayere [B: Thei assented for siluer to seye as boþe wolde]: Canon law required the couple's mutual consent for marriage (see Noonan 1973). In their continued expansion of A, B and C make it plain that only bribery will induce Simony and Civil to affirm Meed's and False's **wille**; C adds a quasi-allegorical elaboration of another of Meed's entourage, Silver. B and C only imply but do not express Meed's will; they do not record her actual marriage vow as does A (see below A 49–53 and note), an omission that coheres with the presentation of Meed as lacking any continuous, personal will (see below 127n).

Thus far, Meed has been coerced and deceived by Liar in B and C, and by False, Favel, Guile, and Liar in A (see 44–46n). Her father, Favel (or False, or Wrong), has in all versions kept a heavy hand on her choice. Her assent is never recorded directly and seems fleeting at best; only Silver's prayer compels Simony and Civil to affirm the marriage. Indeed, in spite of the principle of women's choice in canon law, women were not always provided real opportunity to choose in marriages, if doing so went against family wishes, although some, backed by canon law, were willing to risk such displeasure (Clark 1987; Goldberg 1992:245–49). But Meed never opposes any proposed marriage. Her utter lack of personal will—her complete submission to any and anyone's uses—constitutes a fundamental aspect of her nature, of which a corrupt friar absolves her (3.40–42) and which Conscience condemns (see 3.169–71). This lack renders the quest for defining her status, identity, and morality both tantalizing and futile. See also below, 83–84n.

A 49–53: Þanne fauel fettiþ hire forþ . . . to sewen his wille: A parody of marriage vows, presented with clear conditions: False agrees to supply all of her wants (**fynde hire for euere**), on condition that (**In foreward þat**) Meed will be obedient to him **At bedde & at boord**. False is presenting a conditional marriage, which would become effective as soon as the conditions were fulfilled. Such conditional vows were common; compare the "marriage" vows that Jesus takes in the *Book of Margery Kempe*: "I take þe, Margery, for my weddyd wyfe, for fayrar, for fowelar, for richar, for powerar, so þat þu be buxom & bonyr [obedient and willing] to do what I byd þe do . . . And þerto I make þe suyrte" (1.35, ed. Meech and Allen 1961:87; for other conditional vows in the period, see Helmholz 1974:50–57). False, however, is rehearsing both his part of the contract and Meed's as well; the instructions follow the official formulae in the Sarum *Manuale* and elsewhere, in which the groom, "with the priest instructing him," says "I N [name] take the N to my wedded wyf to haue and to holde fro this day forwarde for bettere for wers for richere for pouerer: in sykenesse and in hele tyl dethe vs departe if holy chyrche it woll ordeyne and therto y plight the my trouthe"; the bride is to answer "with the priest instructing her," "I N take the N to my wedded housbonde to haue and to holde from this day forwarde for better: for wors: for richer: for pouerer: in sykenesse and in hele: to be noere [*recte* bonere] and buxum in bedde and atte borde tyll dethe vs departhe if holy chyrche it wol ordeyne and thorto I plight the my trouthe" (ed. Collins 1960:47–48).

In this case, there is hardly any doubt that Meed would be obedient, since she agrees to all; False's conditional marriage vows seem designed to make the marriage valid immediately: by expressing her part of the normal marriage vow as his condition, he comes close to making her silent acquiescence sufficient to complete the vow. In A, Meed has no reply and never completes her part of this exchange—but False has not requested that she reply. B and C drop False's parody of a conditional marriage, making more persistently clear Meed's lack of choice or free will in any of her marriages (see 69–70n above, and 127n below). Her negotiations become more active in the next passus, but she remains chiefly the object of others' commitments and definitions. See *William of Palerne* (ed. Bunt 1985), lines 5115–38, for a more general and idealized presentation of the vows of marriage, folded into those of proper rule, and imposed on the bride who with joyous tears accepts them.

71–73 (B 69–71; cp. A 54–55): Thenne lup lyare forth . . . to rede hit [A: Symonye & cyuyle stondiþ forþ . . . þat fals haþ ymakid]: In keeping with Holy Church's claim about Liar's importance at 46 (B 43, A 25), C and B grant him the role of producing the document and introducing Simony and Civil as its formal readers and authenticators. Liar's bursting energy in C, an element of physical drama characterizing satire at its best in any period, also shows that the evil surrounding Meed has vigor and initiative, for which her passivity is a fertile occasion. Liar's role here as a sort of keeper of the charter leads him, paradoxically, to present truthfully and baldfacedly the damning marriage document, its duplicitous makers, and its deceitful public presenters.

loo! here a Chartre: for the phrasing when introducing and publically reading a document, compare *William of Palerne* (ed. Bunt 1985), 4824–43: "'Loo, here hire owne lettres . . . / Þe king komaunded a clerk keneli and swiþe / to loke on þo letteres and lelli hem rede." The rhetorical structure is elsewhere used for introducing other objects (see, e.g., *Wars of Alexander*, ed. Duggan and Turville-Petre 1989, line 2149).

75 (B 73, A 55): vnfoldeth the feffament þat fals hath ymaked: Steiner places Meed's charter in the developing presentation of salvation that, in her view, the poem's fictional documents trace out: as Meed's charter stands for the devil's record of how souls are damned, so Truth's Pardon stands for Christ's charter, thus (as Lawler elaborates [2000:124]), Meed's charter is directly "amended" by the Pardon, since this charter as it stands has only the sentence of punishment, the second line of the Pardon (Steiner 2003:110). Yet even here, the charter is challenged as soon as it is read. No document rests static in the poem, a feature perhaps related to the poem's own tendency to mutate in revision. See further below, 86–111n.

The **feffament** is a parody of a *maritagium*, a name used to describe a marriage settlement conferred by the bride's father. But the precise status of the object parodied (if it has one) is elusive both because of the shifting names of those surrounding Meed in the marriage, and because of the vicissitudes of legal history. Traditionally, a *maritagium*, designed to support the new family and its children, was presented by the bride's father and would offer lands with various stipulations that protected the woman and her children, including exclusions of collateral heirs (e.g., relatives of the groom if the couple died childless), and reversions to the donor or his heirs if no heirs issued from the marriage (see Biancalana 2001:37–69). By the early fourteenth century, with the seigneurial class often in need of money, the traditional *maritagium* of property only had often given way to the bride's father's grant of land and money to the bride, then increasingly frequently just of money to the groom's father, with the condition that the latter would grant his son and his new bride a dower of land in jointure. Originally, money in the form of the dower typically went from the groom and his family to the bride, and property went from the bride's family to the groom; but by the fourteenth century money went from the bride and her family to the groom, and property went from the groom and his family to the bride and hers. Thus the bride's father would purchase land from the groom or his father, and grant it back as *maritagium* (Biancalana 2001:150–51). Or the groom's father (who had been paid the dowry) would enfeoff the new husband and wife jointly with land granted them as a dower, presented in a writ granted at the wedding (Biancalana 2001:153–61). In the "new form" of marriage settlements, therefore, the bride and her family would be the source of cash, in order to fund the groom and his family as the source of property.

Meed's arrangment readily fits this "new form" all the more since the groom and her father seem either closely related or identical (see above 25–26n): since they are supplying the devilish properties, she can be understood implicitly to have supplied the money. The *maritagium* was an innovative instrument of property transfer, and left its mark on other kinds of property transfers (see Biancalana 2001 passim). But since the bride's and her family's wealth would ultimately determine the scale of the *maritagium*, it was sometimes the object of criticisms for its connection with mercenary marriages, e.g., on the part of a young man seeking a dowager's estate. A mid-fifteenth-century chronicler tersely summarizes the marriage of John Woodville, aged

20, with the aged and wealthy Katherine Nevill, widow of John Mowbray, Duke of Norfolk, as simply "maritagium diabolicum" (Stevenson 1864:783). Later in the C text, Conscience presents another kind of marriage settlement, with even greater detail, that is not a *maritagium*: see 3.367–70n.

vnfoldeth: The Pardoner in the Prologue simply "brouth forth" his bull (Prol.67, 71n); the act of unfolding this document, the second in the poem, makes its contents more visibly performative, dictating the poem's actions and entities and debates; compare the Pardon that Piers "vnfoldeth" (9.283 [B.7.109, A.8.91]). The opening of such documents also indicates their status as things made public; they are shown being made part of what Steiner calls the "poetics of publicness" that the various unsealed documents in the poem epitomize (2003:161–65).

76–80: Thenne saide symonye . . . "þat aftur mede wayten": A generalizing passage, almost but not fully announcing the moral point of the satire, at least enough to unwind its irony. See also 7 above and 105 below for two other generalizing C additions.

80a–118 (cp. B 74a–114, cp. A 57–71): *Sciant presentes & futuri &c.* **. . . By syhte of sire Simonye and syuyles leue:** "Let men, present and future, know . . .": an opening for any legal document, especially pertinent to a feoffment "invest-ing . . . a person or persons with an estate in land, tenements, rents, etc" (MED *feffement* 1). See, e.g., Bracton's form for feoffments, Thorne and Woodbine 1968, vol. 3.111: "Sciant praesentes et futuri quod ego talis dedi, concessi, et hac praesenti carta mea confirmavi tali, pro homagio et servitio suo, tantam ter-ram cum pertinentiis in tali villa": "Let men, present and future, know that I, so and so, have given, conceded, and by this my charter confirmed to so and so, for his homage and service, a plot of land of such and such a size with its pertinences in such and such a town" (noted by Baldwin 1981:97n26; see also Tavormina 1995:20). As Steiner observes, the clauses of Meed's charter trace implicitly the steps in the career of a sinner like Theophilus "who has despaired of salvation and must yield his soul to the devil" (2003:108–9): the story of Theophilus who signed a charter with the devil and then repented, an account widely available from the eleventh century in Latin and, from the twelfth and thirteenth centuries, in Old French, lies directly or indirectly behind the scene (for the tradition see the introduction to Garnier 1998).

The tradition of often detailed metaphoric or parodic charters of feoff-ment, of a lover and his "lady-lord," or a sinner and the devil, appear from the early twelfth century on in histories, sermons, and poetry; see, e.g., the lyric "Farai chansoneta nueva" by the first troubadour, Guillaume IX (ed. and trans. Goldin 1973:40–42, no. 7). An Anglo-Norman "Devil's Contract with the Covetous" of c. 1267 by Peter de Pecham offers a rough parallel to the satiric "lands" of sinful behavior granted to Meed and False: opening with the typical phrase, "Be it known by all my servants present and future" ("Sachent trestuz ke ove mey sunt / E ces ke a mey a venir sunt"), the Devil hereby grants the covetous "full support against any good deed they have committed" ("De teu feiz lur serrai garaunt, / Encuntre lur bienfeiz pleynement"), in return for the grantees' "service and homage, namely that each one who cheats another shall without exception quarterly for the rest of his life render to me alone, in the spite of God and good folk, the tribute of Greed, Pride, and Envy" ("Pur lur service e lur homage—/ Rendaunt a mey tut sulement / Encuntre Deu e bone gent / A trestuz les jurs de lur vie / Coveytise, Orgoil e Envie, / Pur tute manere de service . . . Quatre fiez par an genereument / Chescun ke de autri a tort prent") (ed. and trans. in Jeffrey and Levy 1990:137–41). In a similar mode, Nicholas Bozon wrote a letter from the Emperor Pride to his dependents (ed. Vising 1919:63–82).

Most of these parodies, like real land conveyances, demand services and homage in return, but the terms of False's charter are particularly unstable in such demands. What are described as part of the gift readily seem to become services demanded in return (**al þe lordschip of leccherye . . . in werkes and in wordes and waytyng of yes . . . Glotonye a gyueth hem and grete othes togederes / Al day to drynke at diuerse tauernes . . . And sue forth suche felawschipe til they ben falle in Slewthe . . .** [96–97, 100–101, 106 (B 89–90, 93–94, 99, cp. A 61, 64)]). The *maritagium* itself was unusual in that its grants were free of homage and services, at least until the third generation of descent from the donee (Biancalana 2001:43–51, 119).

83–84 (B 76–77): Mede is maried more for here richesse . . . for hey kynde: The charter's initial clause (added in B) proudly annouces the purity of the mercenary principles involved in this marriage. The emphasis starkly inverts the typical question about marriage contracts raised in legal depositions, where women were asked if they were bound in marriage by being "bribed or suborned" (Goldberg 1995:104, #24).

86–111 (B 79–104, cp. A 58–68): And fauel þat hath a fals speche Feffeth hem . . . With alle þe purtinaunce of purgatorye and þe peyne of helle: The charter, whose clauses and thus the descriptive features of the allegorical lands expand considerably from A to B then contract slightly from B to C (see B 105–7n), is structured rhetorically to follow the traditional marriage clause, "to have and to hold," in a series of echoes of that in other infinitives (which proceed in the "testamentary" form [Wittig 1986]): **To ben princes in pruyde . . . To bacbite and to boste . . . To skorne and to skolde . . ..** A/B retain the base phrase **to haue and to holde, and hire heires after** (B 102 [A 67]); C drops this so that only the echoes remain. The sins in Meed's *maritagium* are a basic string of deadly sins in A, then in B/C expand at once into energetic tableaux. Apart from **The counte of coueytise** and **þe lordschip of leccherye**, the B/C expansion prominently features sins of the tongue—the very sins that have arranged the marriage: backbiting, boasting, bearing false witness, slandering, "chaterynge out of resoun" (92), jangling and japing and judging "Emcristene" (102), and "ydelnesse in vayne speche" (104). On this topic, see generally Craun 1997. The extensive tracts of sin in Meed's satiric feoffment may be compared with the vast lands given the Black Prince at his investiture in 1362, and Skt suggests this inspired some of the general aspects of L's parodic *maritagium* (see also Tavormina 1995:21). But wide terrain is found in the allegorical landscapes appearing elsewhere in the poem: at the poem's opening (Prol.14–18 [B.Prol.13–16, A.Prol.13–16]); at Piers' path to "truth" (7.206–82 [B.5.560–629, A.6.48–114]); at the "lond of longyng" (11.167 [B.11.8]); and at "vnkyndenesse and coueytise . . hungry contreys bothe" (15.188 [B.13.219]). The poem often includes promises of wide vistas, although its movement through them is rarely swift or unimpeded.

The literary tradition of allegorical territories prominently includes Guillaume de Deguileville's trilogy (see Headnotes to this and the previous passūs). But here the motif of surveying an allegorical landscape more closely depends on a literary tradition of the "voie" to Hell, as in Raoul de Houdenc's twelfthcentury *Songe d'Enfer* (ed. Mihm 1984); see below 91–96n. Transforming a charter into such a voyage or "voie" is apparently original to PP A. The strategy may explain why the documentary metaphor becomes an unfolding set of vignettes. The B/C expansions here particularly militate against the static metaphor of a charter of lands being read. Dramatic actions and implied scenes immediately burst from each of the sinful domains mentioned: **To ben princes in pruyde and pouert to dispice** . . . (87). L's documents are thus less "stage properties" (Hughes 1992) than stages in themselves: they typically function like Chaucer's ecphrases, where visual description becomes present narrative action (see, e.g., *House of Fame*, bk. 1, Knight's Tale, lines 1893–2088). The scenes of Lechery and Gluttony that unfold here in the reading of the charter merely raise this tendency to a tumultuous and vivid degree: the worlds they suggest Meed and her mate would inherit are exuberant and dramatic, if sinful, a miniature version of the vivid drama of passus 2 as a whole.

91–96 (B 84–89, cp. A 60–66): The Erldom of enyue . . . al þe lordschip of leccherye in lenghe and in Brede: A's sinful properties (earldom of envy, lordship of lechery, kingdom of covetousness, isle of usury and avarice, gluttony, and seignury of sloth) imply all the seven deadly sins with the exception of wrath, also omitted from the Confession of the Sins in A. The omission from the latter generated considerable debate about the poem's unity of authorship (Manly 1906; see Middleton 1988:7–8), but the omission of wrath here as well did not feature in that debate. Compare the "path to Hell" in Raoul de Houdenc's *Songe d'Enfer*: it begins with the narrator departing his own lands ("ma terre": possibly "the earth"), and finds himself by that night "A Covoitise la cité" ("at the town of Covetousness") which is "En terre de Desleauté" ("in the land of Faithlessness"), and he travels from there to stay at a pleasant inn "chiés Envie," near the vile river of Gluttony (ed. Mihm 1984, lines 16–146). From there he wends his way to hell, where False's charter similarly leads. By coincidence or direct connection to the *Songe d'Enfer*, the latter work also does not include wrath in its landscape.

Poetic resources for condemning sloth, however, seem particularly strong among English writers; see Robert Mannyng's *Chronicle* (c. 1338) for a similarly reified list, there of the habits that the French king tries to persuade Edward I to adopt, in order to cease attacking the Scots, and in contrast to what Mannyng in his *Chronicle* sees as the tough character of the ancient Britons: "ffeyntise, liȝt duellyng, on mornes long to lie, / surfeyte in euenyng & luf of licchorie, / affiance of feloun, of enmys haf pite, wille without resoun, conseile of wise men fle, wynnyng forto hold, & gyue not largely, þe Bretons, men of told, forsoke suilk party" (ed. Sullens 1996 part 2, lines 7587–92).

B, followed by C, shifts gluttony below the sinful properties to a more vivid and dramatic exposition (see below 100–108n), and adds a line to encompass wrath among the properties (B 85/C 92): **Wiþ þe Chastilet of cheste and chaterynge out of reson** (just as B adds Wrath to the sins that confess, B.5.135–81).

95 (B 88): In bargaynes and Brocages with the borw of thefte: B, followed by C, also adds the gift not just of the borough of Theft but of illicit negotiations with that borough (unless the entire line is an abstract noun describing a section of devilish property). Technically, by the thirteenth century a "borough" was an independent entity owned by its "free" inhabitants whose "fee-farm" or collective tax went to the king alone and could not be purchased or sold by others; but the term **borw** (B: **Burgh**) was sometimes loosely used to apply to communities and markets owned by lords or religious institutions (and debate about the degree of legal independence of such communites figures in conflicts throughout the fourteenth century, climaxing in the rebellion of 1381; see Tait

1936:339–58; Campbell 2000; Kermode 2000; Galloway 2001a). The social level of the charter begins to shift here to less aristocratic domains, and soon will drop into taverns; ownership of the borough is clearly in a league of the powerful and wealthy, but negotiations and transactions with it are less so. For other associations of Meed with brokerage, see above 60–63n, 68n.

97 (B 90): in werkes and in wordes and waytynge of yes: Searching gazes are commonplace in descriptions of lust; B/C's expansion of the Land of Lechery closely follows the details of Hawkin's lechery in B (B.13.343–49), and almost precisely follows a line from C's confession of Lechery (C.6.177), indicating some cross-checking of spots like this one in the C revision of the Sins.

100–108 (B 93–101, cp. A 64–66): Glotonye a gyueth hem . . . he his lyf leteth: As Prsl notes, "the allegory of land-conveyancing dissolves here . . . into a tavern scene, anticipating that of" the later scene of Gluttony in the confession of the sins, where eating before noon (a violation of rules of fast-days), awakening to despair, and swearing **grete othes** (often an alliterative companion to Gluttony) all appear (see 6.350–417), just as the Land of Lechery recalls the C confession of Lechery (see above 97n). But the scenic potential of the charter has been evident from its first clauses with their depictions of actions, in the tradition of genre of "voie" (see above 86–111n, 91–96n). By this point, the social level implied by the charter's clauses has fallen precipitously, although it soon rises up again to offering large tracts of lands, a range that indicates the universality of Meed's following.

104–5: With spiserye, speke ydelnesse in vayne speche and spene / This lyf to folowe falsnesse and folk þat on hym leueth: RK-C transposes line 105 from where it falls in all C manuscripts after 108 (as in Schm and Prsl), a reordering that allows the preceding infinitive **spene** (104) to take as object **This lyf to folowe falsness**. Several C copies for the noun **speche** read the infinitive "speke"; thus Prsl and Schm, following that reading and retaining 105 in its manuscript location after 108 ("For a leueth be lost when he his lyf leteth") punctuate, with a period at the end, "speke ydelnesse, in vayne speke and spene" (i.e., to speak idly, to speak and to spend in vain). Thus punctuating and reading "speke" allows 105 to remain in its position in the manuscripts, since **spene** therefore does not need a further object and 104 is complete. But that does not explain the reading in most C manuscripts of **speche**, which cannot be an infinitive and which thus leaves **spene** dangling, a circumstance solved by manuscripts in various obviously scribal ways (e.g., for **speke ydelnesse in vayne speche and spene**, P²'s "Idelnes and vain speche speke þan afftur").

This suggests that the sequence of errors was, first, the transposition of 105 to after 108, perhaps assisted by eyeskip in the archetype between "his lyf leteth" at the end of 108 with **This lyf** of 105, followed by various accommodations in 104 including the alteration of **speche** to "speke." Transposing **This lyf to folowe falsnesse and folk þat on hym leueth** to follow 104 further allows the following phrase "suche felawschipe" (106) to refer back to **folk þat on hym leueth**, and groups the later "when he his lyf leteth" (108) with the rest of the clause pertaining to the penalty after death (109–11). So reordered, the passage also clusters 105's syntax, of object + *to* + infinitive + infinitive's subject, with a similar series from 101–3 in which *to* is expressed or clearly implied by parallelism, "to drynke . . . to iangle and iape and iuge . . . to frete," a series of infinitives dependent on "a [Favel] gyueth hem" (100), in the form that Wittig calls the "testamentary" infinitive (1986). The *to*, which as Wittig observes is normally used with such an infinitive, disappears with the infinitive "sue" at 106 and remains absent, in the new ordering, until the end of the paraphrase of the charter (111). Yet although RK-C's reordering fashions logical groupings of syntax and sense, 105 as it stands is not an easy fit in its new location either: there, it must mean "spend / this life in following Falseness and the people that believe in him," in which the infinitive **to folowe falsnesse** is no longer a "testamentary" infinitive but an infinitive of description, accompanied by an object not a subject, dependent by enjambment with **spene**. Perhaps a deeper archetypal error occurred in 105 before it was transposed; other errors by some copies in this section suggest a general uncertainty at some stage on matters of line breaks; and several copies significantly adjust the syntax of **This lyf to folowe falsnesse** in an effort to solve the puzzle of its infinitive: e.g., M's "this lijf is to folowe falsnesse . . ."; F's "This is to folowe falsnesse . . . ." Likely the documentary nature of the passage led to prosaic reordering and other liberties by scribes familiar with documentary conventions.

   With spiserye: Gluttony in his confession later similarly seeks "hote spyces" (6.358 [B.5.303, A.5.153]), which may there carry an ironic exegetical suggestion of failed penance (cp. Hanna 1990a). The tavern scene shows how Gluttony fosters additional sins of hypocrisy, judging others while violating a fast, and speaking idly.

111 (B 104, A 68): With alle þe purtinaunce of purgatorye and [B, A: into] þe peyne of helle: The **purtinaunce of purgatorye** ought to allow eventual passage to heaven, but this is only the outlying land of purgatory, used by ("leased to") hell for its purposes, with no sense that purgatory can still function as purgatory in those regions. The satire does not seem in A and B to have been designed to solve the theological puzzle this opens up concerning the different regions of purgatory (are only those eventually saved who are in the demesne of purgatory, rather than in its **purtinaunce**?). The A/B reading **into** mimics the style of boundary clauses in land-law charters accurately, but suggests that the claims of hell reach into purgatory. C's **and** more circumspectly distinguishes these realms. For L's tendency to allow cosmological boundaries to raise or address theological problems, compare Imaginatif's explanation that the crucified felon that Jesus saved must sit on the floor in heaven, and the righteous heathen Trajan "is in þe loweste of heuene . . . And wel losliche he lolleth þere" (14.135–52 [B.12.196–209]). The entire "field full of folk" is in an uncertain boundary region (see Prol.19–21n).

B 105–7 (A 69–71): Yeldynge for þis þyng . . . while god is in heuene: In A/B Meed's charter resembles at its close a devil's contract, as in the story of Theophilus, where worldly glory is granted for a particular span (see above, 80a–118n). C's omission of the clause achieves a closer resemblance to a land-conveyance charter, which the metaphor began as (on C's generally closer mimicry of legal matters, see Galloway 2001b, and below, 117–18n).

113–17 (cp. B 109–12, A 73–76): And Peres þe Pardoner . . . and monye mo othere: Those adding their names as witnesses to the contract are all of low and generally disreputable social standing, not the *probi homines* who would normally be sought as witnesses to a charter. Many of the precise professional roles of the figures are obscure.

113 (cp. B 109, cp. A 73): of paulines queste [B: of Paulynes doctrine; A: poulynes doctor]: MED under *Pouline* quotes *Gregory's Chronicle*, c. 1475 (ed. Gairdner 1876:74), declaring that the "ordyr of Powlys" were founded 1310 and called "Crowche Frers" i.e., the "crutched" friars (MED *Pouline*; also *Poule* n. 2b). In fact the Pauline order was composed of solitaries who had no formal connections with any religious order (Davis 1985:205). The fifteenth-century chronicler's confusion seems to have led lexicographers astray (see also OED *Pauline* 1). **paulines** may be local, satiric nomenclature referring to the pardoners who linger in the area of St. Paul's waiting for an opportunity to sell a pardon. "Every occurrence of the word *paulines* [in the poem] is in a legal context," Alford notes (*Gloss.* s.v. *paulines*); here the word appears amidst a list of witnesses just before official notarization, and below it appears at B 178–79 in a reference to the allegorical 'horse' that Civil will ride to Westminster: "Paulynes pryuees [i.e., participants in legal actions such as common suitors and approvers] for pleintes in Consistorie / Shul seruen myself þat Cyuyle is nempned." Alford thus concludes that **paulines** means "having to do with the consistory court held at St. Paul's Cathedral in London." Trevisa, writing in Berkeley in 1387, translates his Latin source's description of the Irish as *otio dediti* ("given over to leisure") as "alwey idel as Poules knyʒtes," suggesting some contact with this idiom (ed. Babington and Lumby 1865, vol. 1.349).

C's **queste** here likely means "body of questors," the official name for pardoners (Latin *questor*). This sense is not attested for **queste** in MED, although "body of inquisitors" and "body of persons serving at an inquest or a trial" are both attested (MED 2(a), 3(a)). Thus the C line likely means "a pardoner from the gang of pardoners lurking around the consistory court of St. Paul's." If so, B/A's **of Paulynes doctrine / poulynes doctor** is more archly ironic, invoking the religious authority of St. Paul the apostle to refer, in a mixture of local slang and learning, to this unofficial troop of ambulance chasers (and, as Trevisa's phrase suggests, customary loiterers) near the consistory court at St. Paul's. The poem's language here displays the colloquial wryness of close familiarity, using terms that were not widely known elsewhere (a regional limitation that might explain the somewhat clearer phrase in C).

114 (cp. B 110, A 74): Butte þe Bedel of Bannebury sokene [A, B: of Bokyngh-amshire]: B/A present the beadle of the sheriff of Buckinghamshire; see above, 60–63n. C's change to a beadle operating in **Bannebury sokene** is less clear. Banbury was not a county but a sizable town in Oxfordshire, substantial enough to serve twice in 1330 as the setting for the itinerant King's Bench (Musson and Ormrod 1999:194). A "soke" is a unit of land or of legal rights; if in a city it referred to an area under the control of a particular lord to whom the king had ceded rights, or to the king's own properties and legal jurisdiction: the king's soke in London included "the public streets and those private properties where he retained a socage rent" (Keene 2000:209). The phrase predominately implies criticism against the lower officials of lords who maintain their private and separate authority within the free public space of a city, and is probably not directed against ward beadles, who served under an alderman. Often the names of those holding such disreputable occupations are, in literature at least, paronomasic or alliterative type-names and nonce names (like Robert the Robber [see Prol.45n] or Sir Simony [see below, 117–18n]; see Mustanoja 1970). C's change to add mention of a western area may support the claim that the poet returned to that region late in life (see Prol.6n). The C manuscripts have clear indications of western dialects, in a tightly clustered area around Herefordshire (and Malvern).

115 (cp. B 111, A 75): Raynald þe reue and redyngkynges manye [B, A: Reynald þe reue of Rutland Sokene]: A/B specify that Reynald is the sheriff of

Rutland, in the east midlands, the smallest county in England, a mere 18 miles across its longest point. The county was governed by a succession of lords: the de Bohuns, whose Earl Humphrey IX commissioned the alliterative *William of Palerne*, held it in the mid- and later fourteenth century (although there is no indication that Humphrey maintained a manor in Rutland; Gorski 2003:34, 62; *William of Palerne*, ed. Bunt 1985:14–19; lines 5529–30).

C's addition of **redyngkynges manye is** of uncertain meaning but evidently refers to another disreputable craft, as below at 6.372 (B.5.315, A.5.165), where a "redyngkynge" consorts with a gang of pub companions including various figures from the lower reaches of urban culture, from a ropemaker to a stray hermit to a hangman. **redyng** perhaps refers to reed-thatching or red-dyeing, with the suffix "-king" applied to designate preeminence in a trade or manufacture (as in today's "copperking," etc.). The occupation is not recorded by this name in the printed calendar of late fourteenth-century London pleas and memoranda, but a John Redyngge was a brewer serving on the London Common Council in 1384–85 (Thomas 1932:92). Not far from St. Paul's, Dicereslane ("dicers' lane"), Newgate, was also called "le Redye" (Barron 2004:434, map 11 A1). For occupational lists generally, see Prol.222n.

117–18 (B 113–14; cp. A 77–78): "In þe date of the deuel the dede is aseled / By syhte of sire Simonye and syuyles leue [A: Be siȝte of sire symonye & signes of notories]": A private lay charter would normally not need the ecclesiastical authentication of a notary, or indeed of civil and canon law, nor would a binding marriage vow require any clerical witnesses. Yet participants in marriage vows sometimes arranged for clerics, including notaries public, to witness marriage vows, especially if there was reason to think that they might be challenged (see Pedersen 2000:202–3; for a late fourteenth-century case in York with a notary, see Pedersen 2000:107–8). A's concluding line, with notaries adding their **signes** (elaborate signs manual), directly satirizes such professionals for using their services to authenticate dubious cases; C and B, although removing the literal notaries and distributing their actions, and their identities, into those of Sir Simony and Civil, retain the official concluding clause from notary practice: an *inspexi* clause of Simony's notarization ('I have seen . . . '), plus a brief eschatocol or final phrase indicating Simony's authority from Civil thus to notarize it (Cheney 1972:107–8). For the poem's focus on documentary seals of various kinds, see Prol.77n.

The procedure focuses the satire on **notories** in all versions, all the more when their functions are subsumed by Simony and Civil, whose official authority explains why Liar presented the document to them to read (see above, 71–73n). Intrinsically evil here and more overtly so below at 142–43 (B

126–27, A 90–91), **notories** were a thirteenth-century clerical profession introduced from the Italian ecclesiastical system, called upon generally for ecclesiastical charters; in the later fourteenth and through the fifteenth century,
however, they were increasingly involved with the lawsuits and other legal
activities of the laity, and indeed were often lay themselves, as the evidence of
married notaries public shows (Cheney 1972; Ramsey 1991). In 1292 Edward I
used notaries to prepare documents adjudicating his claims to the Scottish
crown, because of the issues of royal succession that drew on canon and civil
law (Harding 1993:176). Possibly the broad public implications of just how
Meed, as "earthly reward," will be used suggests the relevance of ecclesiastical
law, even satirically figured in Simony and Civil. Notories are mentioned also
in the crowd gathered around Fauvel in the early fourteenth-century *Roman
de Fauvel* (ed. Långfors 1914–19, line 55).

   sire Simonye: sire here is a priest's title (MED 1(b)), and perhaps therefore the epithet is well established. Robert Mannyng in *Handlyng Synne*
(c. 1303) also briefly designates simony "syre symonye" (ed. Sullens 1983, line
5540).

**119–27 (cp. B 115–20, A 79–84): Thenne tened hym teologie . . . treuthe
plyhte here treuthe to wedde on of here douhteres**: Theology, suddenly present, challenges the marriage in four ways: on the basis of Meed's legitimacy;
on the basis of her maternally higher lineage than False's; on the basis of
Truth's prior "plighting of troth" (in C) or God's prior "grant" (in A and B);
and on the basis of her close kinship to the king.

123 (B 119, A 83): For mede is moilere, amendes was here dame: moilere is
'of legitimate birth'—probably here the adjective; like the Old French *moillier*
it can also be a noun (as at B.16.219). The word comes directly from "law
French" (see AN-D, s.v. *muilleré* for examples), and not all scribes were familiar with it, especially in the A and C textual tradition (C: "medeler"; A: "med-
lere," "a maydyn"; "a Iuweler"). The statement, which Theology emphatically
repeats at 148 (B 132, A 83), is the first dramatic interruption to the proceedings; it contradicts Sothness' claim about Meed's illegitimate lineage (see 24n)
and places pressure not only on the value of money but also on the value of
human systems of law. Theology offers no basis for his claim beyond the high
lineage of Meed's mother; in C only, he even goes on to grant that False is her
father (124). But this in itself would not prove that the marriage between
Amends and False or her birth from that marriage was legitimate, in any sense.
The assertion is as stark and unsupported as is Sothness'.

   Using the claim of the bride's higher lineage than the bridegroom's to
stop an allegorical marriage appears also in the *Roman de Fauvel*, when For-

tune tells Fauvel she will not marry him because she is the "fille du roy des rois" ("the daughter of the king of kings"), and because he does not know who she is: the very principle of history's many triumphs but also downfalls. Thus, Fortune reasons, Favel cannot actually want her as she is, since he seeks nothing except great success. He finds a better match with Vain Glory (ed. Långfors 1914–19, lines 2165–3222). Here, however, the objection of Meed's higher lineage may carry a more precise legal constraint on the marriage to False: she is a close cousin of the king, as Theology mentions when he repeats the term **moilere** (below, 148–49n). In English law from the mid-thirteenth century on, a member of the royal family holding an inheritance of the king in chief would need the king's license to marry, as the king soon reminds Meed when they meet (see 3.131–32n). If she were not legitimate, these limitations and promises of wealth and power would be nullified: she could not inherit by descent from the king, and she would not need his license to marry. Whatever its grounds, Theology's mere declaration of her legitimacy pulls her into the ambit of the king's claims on her, and the king proceeds as if that declaration were fact. Theology's ability to make this declaration may be a marker of the ability of the courts Christian to determine bastardy and legitimacy in their own terms, rather than those of common law, just as Sothness may speak from the perspective of common law (see above, 24n). The problem of fixing her status, however, like Fauvel's rather simpler problem of really knowing who Fortune is, remains, and dominates the debate in the following passus. At the same time, Meed's ability to generate fundamental uncertainties serves to reveal the limitations or debatable authority of the schemes of status and law used to define her, and even serves to weaken the claims of authority by the morally guiding entities who apply those. Her elusive lineage and identity leads Sothness and Theology to oppose one another's judgments fundamentally, just as Theology's challenge to her marriage to False does not impose an incontrovertible judgment but opens up further debate. Religious authority in this passus, and to a considerable degree from this point on in the poem, presents debatable claims rather than revelations of unquestionable truth.

amendes: Amends' powers of reconciliation are part of Meed's nature. Thus Peace later tries to drop his own suit against Wrong because "mede hath made my mendes" (4.97; see 4.94–98n). As the king's reaction there suggests, however, Amends herself is not always "objectively" moral and does not always lead to strictly just outcomes. Yet if morality is not an intrinsic part of Amends, Amends is an essential part of morality, as shown in the poem's recurrent theme *redde quod debes* ("render what you owe"): see especially 21.186–87n, and 21.135n. For the continued uncertain status of reconciliation in the poem, see further passus 4 Headnote.

124: Althow fals were here fader and fikel tonge her belsyre: Contradicting Holy Church's claim that her father was Favel (and perhaps suggesting that Favel was her grandfather instead, since Holy Church calls him Favel "þat hath a fykel tonge"; 25), Theology concedes the bad lineage on her father's side, and indeed perhaps implies that her current marriage is incestuous, itself an obvious impediment to a valid marriage. Theology does not appear to care much about her bad lineage or its details; he mentions this only to insist the more strongly on her mother's worth, and thus on the good kinds of authority that should govern Meed's marriage. **belsyre** may mean any ancestor (as at 10.234 [B.9.146]) but is usually 'grandfather.'

125: amendes was here moder by trewe menne lokynge: In C Theology emphasizes his claim, declaring more strongly that the "witness of trustworthy informants" attests to Meed's maternal lineage (OED *looking* 3; see also Alford, *Gloss.* s.v. *loken*).

126: withouten here moder amendes mede may nat be wedded: Theology bolsters his challenge to Meed's marriage by a legal argument, that her present agreement (if any) was preempted by her mother's choice. Parental consent is a common conditional stipulation to a marriage contract, but to be binding it would need to be part of the vow using words of the future (see Helmholz 1974:47–50). Just how directly part of that vow might be debated in court; Theology's suggestion that the matter could be argued legally is borne out by numerous cases concerning conditional marriage vows. But the king's courts or parliament at Westminster, where they go to settle the case, are hardly venues for upholding a mother's interest in marital matters: while common law granted that "marriage should be free," it focused on the rights of the lord of whoever sought to marry (see Pollock and Maitland 1952, vol. 1.318–29). Since Meed at this point lacks any known lord other than Wrong, her case under common law is most likely to favor False's and his companions' rather than Theology's claims on her. Usually the father's consent was sought primarily rather than the mother's, since "the children of [a woman's] marriage(s) were, in most vital matters before the law and in the eyes of her peers, [her husband's] children" (Rosenthal 1991:78). Examples exist, however, of endeavors to make sure that the mother in particular was "weel-willyng" toward a daughter's marriage (e.g., *Paston Letters*, part 2, no. 446; ed. Davis et al. 2004).

The missing element in this argument is Meed's own choice, which was required above all by canon law for any valid marriage (see Noonan 1973), but which Theology himself must find ways to render secondary. Meed's nature, as often, forces an established authority into an awkward position.

**127 (cp. B 120, A 84): treuthe plyhte here treuthe to wedde on of here douht-
eres [B, A: God graunted to gyue Mede to truþe]:** Tavormina suggests that,
"by the time of Meed's marriage, Meed's father and various 'friends' have
obviously ignored the grant to Truth, and made their own plans for bringing
Meed's *richesse* into the power of a husband much nearer their own kind.
Since Meed submits willingly to the latter arrangement, it might be difficult to
prove her earlier assent to her mother's plans" (1995:27). But an earlier assent
would not be enough in itself to enforce her mother's earlier plan to marry
her to Truth, since such assent would use *verba de futuro*, and thus would be
overridden by any later marriage using "words of the present" ("I, Meed,
do . . ."), unless she consummated the earlier vow sexually, a canonical safety
net that seems out of the question, or indeed redundant, next to a vow from
Truth (see Helmholz 1974:47–48). Theology's language in C somewhat
strengthens Truth's commitment in legal terms, since Truth's plighting of
treuthe cannot be surpassed in authority. C's line also suggests more strongly
than B Truth's personal desire to marry Amends' daughter—in B and A the
two "parents" arrange the whole thing by a "grant." But neither the grant nor
the troth-plighting surpass the force of Meed's personal and present choice;
Theology has no valid canonical claim unless Meed should seek to express her
present will to marry Truth, but will is what she characteristically lacks. The
drama of a marriage to her serves continually to bring forth the point that
reward is given its meaning exclusively by those who use it, by the motives,
desires, and systems of thought of its "lords," "husbands," or indeed intepret-
ers. As Colette Murphy points out, she epitomizes an eligible medieval woman's position as the object of constant male desires for control (1994:153–54);
but she also quickens this interest by being perpetually available, and perpetually challenging. Theology's appeal to a previous **treuthe**, and even Truth's
own plighting of his troth, are fundamentally incommensurate with Meed's
pliable nature, and the number of strategies Theology endeavors to use suggests the difficulty of his position and even the limitation of his authority in
the relativistic, wholly social world that Meed fully inhabits.

**132–39 (cp. B 122–23, A 86–86a): Y, Theologie, þe tixt knowe . . . no man bot
treuthe [B, A: The text telleþ þee . . . *Dignus est operarius* his hire to haue]:**
In B and A, Theology cites a text that reasserts a principle of **treuthe** in the
proceedings: "the workman is worthy of his hire" (Lk 10:7). This opposes
Meed's marriage to False because False's joining with and "having" of Meed
can involve no such just reward: by his nature, False cannot be "worthy" of
meed. Theology's use of a **tixt** against the marriage charter establishes the pattern of one document answering or clarifying another (see above, 75n). This

text, as a statement of just reward, also anticipates the Pardon, as do many other assertions of justice in the poem (see Lawler 2000). Since the literal terms of his text fit the dramatic situation, it presents both a literal objection (not False but the *operarius* should have Meed) and an explication of the moral allegory in what is occurring.

The text from Luke, however, directly invokes a question from the social world that Meed inhabits, and a particular topical domain of that where principles of authority were especially controverted. The question of the just wage was a charged issue throughout later medieval culture, notably by the later fourteenth century. As early as the twelfth century, the prooftext "the workman is worthy of his hire" was used to justify wages for teachers, doctors, and lawyers, that is, the first "professionals," who sold the intangible gift of God, knowledge (see Post et al. 1955). By the mid-fourteenth century, the issue of the just wage became widespread and incendiary because of demands for suddenly higher wages by the laboring forces whose numbers were severely reduced by the Black Death, and reprisals by landlords and the government, culminating in to a series of legislative efforts to keep wages and the prices of manufactured goods to the levels before the Black Death (see Waugh 1991:109–13; Ormrod 1986:178–80; Putnam 1908:10–15). As the monastic chronicler Henry Knighton says, under 1349, "operarii tamen adeo elati et contrariosi, non aduertebant regis mandaum. Se si quis eos habere uellet, oportuit eum eis dare secundum suum uelle, et aut fructus suos et segetes perdere, aut operariorum elatam et cupidam uoluntatem ad uota implere" ("nevertheless, the workmen were so puffed up and contrary-minded that they did not heed the king's decree, and if anyone wanted to hire them he had to pay what they asked: either his fruit and crops rotted, or he had to given in to the workmen's arrogant and greedy demands"; ed. and trans. Martin 1995:102–3). The Statute of Laborers seems directly alluded to in the narrator's debate with Conscience and Reason in C.5.1–104, either in terms of the 1352 Statute (Clopper 1992) or of its reenactment and expansion to include vagrants in 1388 (Middleton 1997); it is directly invoked in the aftermath of Hunger's blight on the plowing of the half-acre, where Waster "corseth þe kyng and alle þe kynges Iustices / Suche lawes to lerne laboreres to greue" (8.337–38 [B.6.317–18, A.7.298–99]). The broad issue of the just wage informs the struggles against Meed in this and the next passus, and indeed it appears at many of the points where the poem seeks a convergence between religious doctrine and present social conditions.

In C, perhaps to avoid that social controversy, Theology supports the need for marrying Meed to Truth with a different example of just reward, the dying words of St. Laurence, now declaring more directly that **no man bot treuthe** should have Meed. The change may be because the tag from Luke addressed too narrowly the right to receive just wages and not clearly enough the importance of heavenly rather than worldly reward. Laurence's dying words as recorded in the *Golden Legend* echo *dignus* in the Lucan passage: "I thank you, O Lord, because I have been worthy to pass through your portals" (trans. Ryan 1993:67). The paraphrase in PP adds the key word **mede**, now applied in the sense of heavenly reward; this pertinent addition was possibly suggested by the liturgy for the feast of St. Laurence, where for the octave, the York and Salisbury uses include Matt. 10:37–42 which speaks of the spiritual "reward" (*merces*) of the righteous (Tavormina 1987:251). The *Golden Legend*'s life of St. Laurence includes a comment by Augustine that has further pertinence: as Augustine is quoted there, "The man who is greedy for money and an enemy of truth is armed with two torches—avarice, which seizes gold, and impiety, which takes away Christ. Cruel man, you [Emperor Decius, Laurence's killer] gain nothing, you make no profit! The mortal material you looked for is taken from you, Laurence is gone away to heaven, and you perish in your flames" (trans. Ryan 1993:73). C adds yet another reference to St. Laurence, in Liberum Arbitrium's speech (17.65–70).

142–43 (cp. B 126–27, A 90–91): That ȝe nymeth . . . ȝe cheweth and deuoureth [B, A: Symonye and þiself . . . noyen þe peple]: C's somewhat convoluted syntax yields "What you [Simony and Civil] and notaries take brings to destruction holy church, and you chew and devour charity." For other uses of enjambement in C additions, see, e.g., above, 104–5n, and 18.226–28. On "chewing charity," a quasi-Eucharistic image perverted to avarice, see 1.190; such gusty and appetitive consumption, which 'devours' charity, contrasts the modest "sip" of 'true charity' (see above 37n). **notaries** are here starkly evil; see A 77–78, and above 117–18n.

148–49 (B 132–33, A 96–97): mede is moylore . . . A myhte kusse the kyng as for his kynnes womman: On **moylore**, see above, 123–26n. For the claim that her kinship to him is the reason for his direct interest in her marriage and her need to secure permission from him, see next note, and 3.131–33n.

151, 177 (cp. B 135, 161, A 99, 125): ledeth here to londone; To wende with hem to westminstre the weddyng to honoure: Theology's proposal to settle the legality of Meed's marriage in London has perplexed scholars because Meed's entourage understands this to mean Westminster. Yet marriage disputes were normally a matter for the ecclesiastical courts. Possibly Theology has in mind the courts Christian in London (e.g., the Arches; see above, 60–63n), and the playful and sinful followers of Meed are instantly twisting his suggestion. Or alliteration may explain **londone**. In any case, in C Meed's followers twist his demand for a legal ruling into an opportunity to celebrate rather than contest the marriage, turning toward Westminster **the weddyng to honoure** (cp. B/A's **to witnesse þis dede**).

The king's council at Westminster, which used equity procedures for determining civil suits, would consider some matrimonial cases if of great enough significance; in the later fifteenth century, the Court of Requests established at Westminster, also a secular court of equity, handled a variety of matrimonial disputes (see Harding 1973:107; Leadam 1898). So too, marriages involving the royal family, which Theology has declared her to belong to, might go before Parliament itself (see above, 123n; 3.131–32n; Giancarlo 2003). The nature of her allegorical identity is pertinent to her journey to Westminster as well. As Tavormina notes, Meed embodies the legal and other issues of temporal goods, "the treasures of this world, the things that are Caesar's," and matters concerning these things should be pursued before the king (1995:29).

153: And thow Iustices enioynen hem thorw Iuroures othes: Although Theology has pressed all the harder in C for the journey to Westminster, he also adds in C a comment on the likely corruption there, as well as (as in A and B) the presence of Truth and Conscience. He thus seems to concede all the more clearly that, for all his moral authority, he can at best invite more controversy, not impose simple clarification.

155 (B 139, A 103): Consience is of his consayl: Personified Conscience appears here for the first time in A/B. His role as a member of the king's council, a chancellor figure, is already evident, confirming the implication of an appeal to equity (see 95–135n).

156 (cp B 140, A 104): yf he fynde ȝow in defaute and with the fals [B, A: with fals]: C's reading, *the* fals, is also the reading of a heavy majority of A and B manuscripts, where it should also perhaps be adopted: the article adds an ironic and punning doubling of the abstract, non-allegorical point onto the vivid allegory of False—they will of course be convicted of being **with the fals**, since they are with False. The change is from singular to plural, and thus to the dangers of bad company. "The fals" appear again below at 167 (B 151, A 115), perhaps a more vivid instance of this demonstration of personification allegory confronting the bland abstraction. The opening of the passus performs the same operation, where the dreamer is shown the personification False after he has asked for the abstract moral concept of "the false."

160–66 (B 145–50, A 109–14): And bade gyle "go gyue gold . . ." grete was the thonkynge: The bribery is made festive by the joyous response, but since

gold is offered before these officials have done anything, it remains bribery. For the importance of paying after work rather than before, see 3.291–332n.

170–71 (B 154–55, A 118–19): For we haue mede amaystred with oure mery speche / That he graunteþ to go with a goode wille: False's and Favel's followers congratulate themselves for having so skillfully **amaystred** Meed; but their pride is misplaced: it is her nature to be so **amaystred** by each successive user or "wooer" (see above, 69–70n).

178–96 (cp. B 162–83, cp. A 126–44): Ac hakeneys hadde thei none bote hakeneys to huyre . . . "fobbes and faytours þat on here feet rennen": The satiric grotesqueness of a marriage to Meed, proudly displaying all the financial motives and corruption that moralists said should not be used for marriage, gives way to a nightmarish caravan of the allegories of sins clambering onto the social and professional figures that most "uphold" such sins.

Some of the social types carrying the sins have already been satirized as among the crowd attending the marriage; each is particularly suitable for carrying its allegorical rider. A sheriff, procured by Guile who has borrowed horses **at many gret maystres**, carries Meed herself, in keeping with sheriff's authority yet pecuniary corruption (see above, 60–63n); False and Favel gather assizers, in keeping with the lies and bought biases of such legal-beagles (see 60–63n); False and Favel also add reeves, on which they ride and outdistance Meed on her sheriff, perhaps suggesting the speedy effects of their lies and flattery. Simony and Civil, in C, make arrangements for priests and provisors to carry prelates: provisors are those clerics who possess a provision or grant from the pope to obtain the next available benefice (Alford, *Gloss.*)—itself a point of general resentment against such distant power over national ecclesiastical appointments, and often viewed as simony because of the payments made for such provisions (see below, 185n)—thus this suggests that Simony and Civil are upheld by the various arrangments in which prelates appoint to benefices. Simony and Civil ride on rectors and the sinful rich: if they are indirectly responsible for the appointments to benefices that prelates and the pope make, they are directly supported by established holders of benefices (Alford, *Gloss.* s.v. rector) and the wealthy laity who can make sure that those they want appointed are in fact given benefices. Notaries mount upon parsons who change their benefices frequently (and who thus need to buy off notaries to prove their right to make such changes), and on less wealthy provisors and appellants (treated as the abstract noun, **appels**) in patronage cases who have lost in local ecclesiastical courts and taken their cases to the Court of Arches. These are those who have been or are challenging a provision to a benefice, and who employ notaries as part of their deceitful legal efforts to win their case. Summoners and **sodenes**, subdeans, ride on lechers, because the first kind of official summoned fornicators to the archdeacon's court (and were, in satiric writing, often trumping up such charges to extort money from their victims; see Chaucer, Friar's Tale, Canterbury Tales III. 1369–74), while the second kind of official served in the role of judge at the archdeacon's court (where, presumably, a bribe would help produce a false judgment). The commisary, a bishop's representative in distant regions of the diocese, draws the cart of provisions, gathering it up from fornicators: he too takes bribes from these, perhaps to prevent him from indicting such sinners and putting them to the processes and punishments of the bishop's consistory court.

Kellogg (1958:390–98) notes that allegorical vehicles of sins go back to patristic allegorical exegeses of Exodus 15:1–4, Moses' song on the destruction of Pharaoh's chariot while crossing the Red Sea, and to Bernard of Clairvaux's exegesis of Cant. 1:8: in these exegeses, Pharaoh was Satan, his riders and chariots the sins. A closer analogue, and probably source, for L's passage is Nicholas Bozon's early fourteenth-century *Char d'Orgueil*, which presents a mixture of social satire and detailed allegorical iconography, including not just the cart of Pride but also its trappings and ornaments and four horses and their trappings and features, down to the nostrils, tongue, and teeth of each horse (the third horse, Deleauté, for example, has for teeth back-biters, evil neighbors who spread bad report; *Le Char d'Orgueil*, ed. Vising 1919). But what in Bozon are static equivalencies between various features of the cart and various sinful figures are here turned into instructions pregnant with drama and action. Closer to the bustle here at the end is the conclusion to Raoul de Houdenc's *Songe d'Enfer*, in which the devils in hell where the narrator has arrived, and read to them sinful minstrelsy, suddenly arm themselves and depart on horseback to invade the earth (ed. Mihm 1984, lines 659–64).

178 (cp. B 162, A 124): hakeneys hadde thei none bote hakeneys to huyre [B, A: caples to carien hem þider]: C's minor addition, that the group seeking to carry Meed do not own their own saddle horses and must pay to rent them, explicitly establishes the terms of the following allegory, in which the various corrupt officials are "hired" by bribes to "carry out" the various illicit or deceitful deeds that the allegorical riders personify. The social implications of this comment are more elusive. Horses were of course by far the most common way to travel, and large mobile households might keep as many as fifty horses, spending on average about a tenth of their income on keeping them. Dyer notes that smaller clerical households that did not need to travel much might have none, and hire them as needed (Dyer 1989:71; see also Willard

1926). The allegorical riders featured here, however, seem suited to considerable travel; thus their use of hired horses seems more a sign of a commercial and urban mode of life, an image of the power of commercial transaction itself, than of an infrequent need for transport. Perhaps urban dwellers typically (as often now) hired rather than owning transport.

180–81 (cp. B 164, A 128): a shereue sholde bere mede / Softlich in sambure fram syse to syse [B, A: Mede vpon a Sherreue shoed al newe]: In C's addition, Meed rides on a sheriff saddled in a sumptuous saddlecloth (**sambure** simply means "saddlecloth" in French, but the association with the language of the aristocracy insures its elevated status) in order to journey widely to assizes. The narrow plot of her journey to Westminster is opened to a larger satire against well-paid sheriffs who preside over assizes, by which bribery and obstruction of justice are carried out in all corners of the kingdom. B/A's **shoed al newe** make the basic point that the sheriff is "well heeled" because of the emoluments he receives in his corruption of justice, but A/B does not further derail the local plot with additional meaning as does C.

185 (cp. B 173–76, cp. A 137–38): prestis and prouisores sholden prelates serue [B: Denes and Southdenes . . . To bere Bisshopes aboute abrood in visitynge; A: denis & southdenis . . . shuln bere þise bisshopis & bringe hem at reste]: The A version begins a relatively simple line of allegory, that ecclesiastic officials are vehicles for simony, which B complicates with allegorical and literal details, whose visual realization C then clarifies by drastic pruning. To carry bishops, A introduces deans and subdeans—that is, church officials responsible for a subdivision of an archdeaconry and those in turn subordinate to them: the A Prologue alone has specified deans and archdeacons as among those who have reneged on their parochial responsibilities "To preche þe peple & pore men to fede" by having "ylope to lundoun" to serve as "clerkis of þe kinges bench" (A.Prol.92–95; see Prol.85–94n). B adds a full complement of similar ecclesiastical administrators, summoned for action: **Erchedekenes and Officials and alle youre Registrers**—that is, all the archdeacon's administrators responsible for prosecuting offenses against sexual morality and church discipline, always points where corrupt accusation was suspected (as in Chaucer's Friar's Tale). The image is further specified in B as the **deuoutrye and diuorses and derne vsurie** which the silver saddles will help these horses bear (B 175–76). **deuoutrye** is evidently "adultery" because of its resemblance to "avoutrye," but found in only two, notoriously sophisticated B manuscripts; nearly all others read "avoutrye," which KD-B rejects evidently for the sake of meter, and to choose the more difficult reading.

Alford suggests that **deuoutrye** may "have something to do with the corrupt practice of trading in benefices," perhaps L's "own coinage to signify one who misuses or interferes with the 'advowson' to an office (possibly influenced by Lat. *devotare*)," defined by Balbus' fifteenth-century *Catholicon Anglicum* as 'to breke Vowe; *deuotare, deuouere*' (Alford, *Gloss.* s.v. *devoutour*). See Prol.69n for those of a presumably humbler social standing who have "vowes ybrokene" and simoniacally seek to buy absolution from pardoners.

C sacrifices much of the allegory's complexity by merely having **prestis and prouisores** carry **prelates**. Provisors, as the holder of the pope's grant or provision to a benefice, were often the target of satire; the pope's ability to make this grant in English churches was assailed by Edward III and Richard II (allowing the king to make such grants himself, and to judge violators in the royal courts rather than in the church courts). The royal position was a relatively popular one, and became part of the satire against Rome's financial corruption. Parliament first passed a Statute of Provisors in 1351, along with the Statue of Praemunire in 1353: the first allowed the king to make an appointment to a benefice if bishops or a cathedral chapter were unwilling to appoint someone that the pope had already provided to a benefice; the second forbad any legal cases cognizable in the king's courts to be taken abroad (i.e., cases of disputed ecclesiastical patronage must be settled in royal court; for the legal principles see Pantin 1955:82–87). The Statute of Provisors was renewed in 1365, and provisions were further denounced in the Good Parliament of 1376 as the work of "brokers of benefices in the sinful city of Avignon"; provisors were legislated against again in 1390 (see Crimes and Brown 1961:74–76, 155–57; Pantin 1955:82–98). Wyclif's rise in authority under John of Gaunt's protection (but not necessarily his patronage) in the mid-1370s also contributed to this issue: calling himself "one of the king's own clerks" in his *Determinationes* of c. 1373, Wyclif defended the king's right to resist "tribute to the Roman pontiff," and after Richard II's accession in June 1377 he wrote a denunciation of papal taxation which appears to have been presented to a "great council," that is, the king's council supplemented by bishops and other lords (see Holmes 1975:166–69, and Rex 2002:28–32, who, however, questions Holmes' account of theological or financial support of Wyclif by John of Gaunt and other magnates in the 1370s and 1380s).

B's vigorous development of anticlerical allegory and the attendant issues may derive from, or seek to respond to, the vehemence surrounding this issue in the period of the Good Parliament and Wyclif's early prominence as a polemical writer, before the increasing condemnation of his sweeping anticlericalism capped by the "Earthquake" council of 1382 in which his views were declared heretical. In such a climate, C's trimming and focusing of the satire may be an effort for a more precise criticism.

186–87 (cp. B 171–72, 178–79, A 135–36, 139–40): y mysulue, syuyle . . . and ryche men deuoutours [B, A: late apparaille þise prouisours . . . myself þat Cyuyle is nempned]: In B and A, Simony rides on **prouisours** (B 171), and Civil on **Paulynes pryuees** (A: **Paulynes peple**), that is, suitors at the consistory court of St. Paul's (B 178–79; for the meaning of "Pauline," see above, 113n). In C, with provisors having already been used for prelates and notaries, Simony and Civil ride on two further groups, *Rectores* **and ryche men deuoutours** (187), that is, on those who held parish benefices (and were commonly satirized as absentee holders who paid vicars less than the parish's income to carry out parish duties), and on what appears to be wealthy adulterers (of whom John of Gaunt presented a preeminent example, as chroniclers frequently noted). Like **deuoutrye** in B 176 (see above, 185n), **deuoutours** appears only in PP and may refer to adulterers, a uniquely "altered form of 'avouter'" (MED). But Alford notes in connection to the C passage that "neither Syuyle nor Simony has any obvious connection with the prosecution of adultery," and he suggests that like **deuoutrye** the word may refer to those who break their oaths concerning a particular clerical "living," engaging in the corrupt practice of exchanges in benefices (see note above). But adultery would likely be tried in an archdeacon's ecclesiastical court, where civil law as well as canon law was used (see Harding 1993:88), and thus might easily be associated by this means with L's Civil and Simony.

190–92: Sommnours and sodenes þat supersedias taketh . . . On secatours and such men cometh softly aftur: In an addition, C repositions summoners and subdeans (also called rural deans), who were, respectively, the steeds of notaries and bishops in B and A; now they are called up to ride on lechers and **secatours**.

    lyppeth, rydeth, cometh: Civil's rousing commands (plural imperatives). In A and B, his commands to organize the cavalcade (with Simony in B) are responses to the notaries' grumbling about having no horses to ride; in C, he spontaneously displays his authority to organize the cavalcade.

    sodenes, subdeans or rural deans, were the lowest territorial church officials, who could hold their own court for relatively petty sins, for which they could impose fines (see Harding 1993:86–87; Alford, *Gloss.*); those carrying them here are those most likely to pay them such fines. **secatours** are executors, those entrusted with fulfilling the will of the dead regarding the disposition of their money and property, and of course liable to temptations to serve their own interests (as in 6.254 [C only], 16.279 [B.15.248], and 22.291 [B.20.291]). **þat supersedias taketh**: The summoners and subdeans who, for the right price, hand out writs that put an end to legal proceedings against such lechers and corrupt executors (for *taken* as "hand out," see MED 31a; on the corruption associated with these writs, see 4.187–90n). **þat supersedias taketh** allows a pun in context: *supersedeas* can mean either "let you desist" or "let you sit on top."

193–96 (B 180–82, A 141–44): And lat cople þe commissarie . . . fobbes and faytours þat on here feet rennen: The only section remaining intact through all the versions, and presenting the germ of the conceit of a cart of sins, just as Bozon presents the cart of Pride (the Prudentian tradition presents the cart of Luxuria; see Kellogg 1958). Cart allegories easily allow for allegorical multiplicity, since the details of the image are separately labelled. **commissarie**s are bishops' representatives who represented episcopal authority in various parts of the diocese, whose scope and authority in the early fourteenth century were roughly that of the archdeacon of such an area, but by the early fifteenth century had taken precedence over the archdeacon (and after 1500 merged with the archdeacon's office; see Morris 1959); for the potential for corruption of legal cases in the commissary's hands, see 16.364–65 (B.15.239–43).

   fornicatores: Those accused of sexual relations outside of marriage, liable to indictment and being fined by archdeacons, rural deans, or cathedral clergy (Helmholz 1974:145), or if they were of villein status, liable to "legerwite," a fee that lords could impose on unmarried villein women who were pregnant (Harding 1993:70; see Prol.223n). Because of these fines, and perhaps also bribes to ecclesiastical court officials, the group here supplies **vitailes** to the company of sins.

   a lang cart: The *longa caretta*, a four-wheeled military cart, a traditional conveyance for the army of sins, like the sort on which Luxuria is placed in the Prudentian and exegetical tradition, where the representation of sinners and sins as carts also appears (see Kellogg 1958[1972]:40–41). Compare the Cart of Christendom, 21/B.19.330–32 (and n); and see above, Headnote. The longer Liar becomes, the more entities are carried forward by lies. Possibly relevant to the image here is 1 Kings (Vulg.) 8:11, where Samuel announces the supreme power of a king over all subjects: "This will be the right of the king, that shall reign over you. He will take your sons, and put them in his chariots, and will make them his horsemen, and his running footmen to run before his chariots" ("hoc erit ius regis qui imperaturus est vobis: filios vestros tollet et ponet in curribus suis, facietque sibi equites et praecursores quadrigarum suarum"). The passage was used by commentators (including the *Glossa Ordinaria* and numerous legal commentators) to epitomize illegitimate, tyrannical power (see Pennington 1993:70). The tyrannical authority of Meed and her retinue is perhaps supported by their making Liar a **lang cart** (cp. Samuel's *quadriges*, but see also below 193–96n) and making **all this othere** run along **on here feet** (cp. Samuel's *praecursores*).

On **faytours**, see Prol.41–46n, and 22.1–51n.

199 (B 186): Y haue no tome to telle the tayl þat hem foleweth: The bookish metaphor for hyperbole is traditional in medieval poetry; see *Roman de la Rose* (trans. Dahlberg 1986), lines 6738–40: "I don't want to say more of him now; I would have to make a large book of it"; Chaucer, *House of Fame*, lines 1334–35: "Men myghte make of hem a bible/ Twenty foot thykke."

201–2 (cp. B 188, A 149): Ac gyle was forgoere to gyen al the peple: Gyle, who has helped supply the marriage charter and bribe the notaries to authorize it, now assumes his more general role of (mis)guiding **al the peple**: the word **forgoere** indicates that his own activities (and those of his followers) are a continual series of monetary depredations and fraud, like the hated purveyors and "vitaillers" who canvass the countryside in the name of a lord or the king (see above, 60–63n). C's additional line explaining Gyle's actions here, **For to wisse hem þe way and with mede abyde**, clarifies the point while still seeking to sustain the allegorical action.

203–4 (B 189–90, A 150–51): Sothnesse . . . prykede forth on pacience [B, A: on his palfrey] and passed hem alle: On Sothness, see above, 24n. Naming Sothness' horse **patience**, C adds an allusion to a proverb, *patientes vincunt*, "the patient vanquish" (see Whiting and Whiting 1968, P61, found among many of PP's contemporaries; it appears in Latin at 15.253 [B.14.54]). The importance of Patience grows throughout C (see passus 15 [B.14]).

205 (B 191, A 152): And kam to þe kynges Court and Consience tolde: The line, present from A, already indicates that Conscience is a member of the king's court, although his role there is not fleshed out to become a clear official. See Headnote to passus 3, and 4.184–86n.

207–19 (B 193–207, A 154–68): "Now, by crist!" quod þe kyng . . . "for eny preyere ich hote": Bnt notes "a case of a similar kind (a girl being imposed on by men acting as her guardians) which was brought to the King on private information": see Baldwin 1913:269–70, from 1376.

maynpryse: Release by surety or bail, to secure release for someone arrested (Alford, *Gloss.*). While bail was regular procedure at local courts, the crown often refused it for prisoners brought before it. A petition in 1449 concerning a gang's efforts to attack a member on the way to parliament says that the gang should be held "in þe kinges prison . . . withoute þat þei or any of þeym be hade in baille or put to mainprise afore þende of suche determynacion hade" (printed in Fisher et al. 1984, Doc. 216, line 28; noted by Alford, *Gloss.* s.v. *mainprise*). In Peace's trial below, Wrong's party tries to argue to the king for such bail (see 4.84–85n).

220–22 (cp. B 208–12, cp. A 169–71): Drede stod at þe dore and þe dome herde . . . bad falsnesse to fle and his feres alle: Drede stod at þe dore is proverbial, found in elementary Latin educational materials (Pantin 1930:114); it is also implied in an exercise from a fifteenth-century grammatical textbook from Bristol that Orme (1989:100, no. 6) prints: "Blodles an boneles stondyth by-hynd þe dore: *Exangue et exarsatum stant pone ostium*" (presumably a euphemism for 'blood-curdling fear'); see also Gower, *Confessio Amantis* (ed. Macaulay 1901), Prol.1082–83: "the comun drede, / Which stant at every mannes Dore." The fearful curiosity of the figure is L's development. But compare *The Abbey of the Holy Ghost*, a late fourteenth-century English translation of a French allegory:

The Levedy [Lady] Drede is porter that kepeth bysyly the yate and the cloyster of the herte and of the concyence, that chaseth out all unthewes [vices] and cleput in alle goode vertuus and so spereth [closes] the yates of the cloyster and the wyndowes that noon evel have entre into the herte thorow the yates of the mought, non thorow the wyndows of the eyen no of the eres. (ed. Blake 1972:95)

PP's sinful Dread does not disperse the sins in order to protect the soul but in order to protect the sins, keeping them from being brought to justice. Dread's moral valence is thus reversed from the usage in all the school-text and other contexts of the proverb.

   doom: The word has an elaborate history in the period of the authorship controversy, and serves to suggest some of the unresolvable editorial uncertainties that any small point in PP may elicit. Most C and some A manuscripts read "dene" or "dyne" ('din'), a point that Day (1928:4) used to argue for multiple authors, since C would not (Day felt) be based on such a wrong reading unless it were a different author's misunderstanding of the original. Chambers and Grattan (1931:29–37) energetically defended "dyne" as a harder reading, and argued it could not appear in three independent A manuscripts except as the correct reading. It also seemed to them "very much in the manner of A, whose power of visualisation is so remarkable, as has often been emphasised.

The more we think about 'din' the more attractive it is. It adds much to the picture, whilst the commonplace 'doom' adds nothing at all" (1931:32). Kane adopted **doom** for A, on the grounds that "dyne" could have appeared in A by memorial contamination from C; but Kane presented the choice as uncertain (K-A 155). RK-C more confidently emends the majority C reading to follow the common B reading and the earlier emendation of A. But certainty on such points remains elusive, as it was in the scribal and perhaps even the authorial tradition of the poem (see Galloway 1999).

223–45 (B 213–35, A 172–94): Falsnesse for fere tho fleyh to þe freres . . . And is welcome when he cometh and woneth with hem ofte: As Holy Church in the previous passus tends to abstract allegorical figures from visible human or even diabolical actions (see e.g., 1.25–31n and 59–60n), the present passus ends by showing the dispersal of the sins into visible and socially particular entities, as if extending the plot beyond the ending of Raoul de Houdenc's *Songe d'Enfer* with the departure of the sins into the world (see above 178–96n). Here, False's and Liar's flustered flights are followed by reassurances that they can find niches throughout London's religious and mercantile world, in the clothing in which they will not simply ride on literal social occupations, but practice within them. The section resembles the extant conclusion of *Wynnere and Wastoure* (ed. Trigg 1990, lines 456–503), where instead of a scene of sin fleeing the king is a scene in which the king himself decrees what social worlds Wynnere and Wastoure will, respectively, inhabit—Wynnere the court of Rome and the king's wars, Wastoure the taverns and bakeries in Cheapside. The satire in PP is more socially detailed, with bursts of unexpected satire in its rapid narrative. In the tradition of the fabliau, professional trickery is the focus of the satire (see Lawler 1980:33–53).

Falseness and Liar encompass fourteenth-century concerns with the crimes of artisans and others with urban occupations, and with the hypocrisy of doctors, friars, and pardoners, all long-standing topoi, but here aligned explicitly with other urban lower crafts. L's two figures of deceit both generate miniature curricula vitae. Falseness, urged frantically by Guile to flee for fear of death, decides to head to the friars, but having been kidnapped by merchants on the way, he is sent to sew in a shop and dress as an apprentice **the peple to serue**, no doubt a "service" of a sort to which his nature is suited (for "service" as a key social ideal of the later Middle Ages see Hicks 1995:146–50). Such workers are a characteristic target in the poem; for the deceptions of cloth makers, see the apprenticeship among them of Covetousness, 6.215–20 (B.5.207–12, A.5.123–28).

Liar has a more varied career, because it takes longer for various social and professional civic groups to warm to him, and presumably because his allegorical principle is shown to reach yet further in urban culture. His career rise is slower but ultimately loftier, and it allows more pervasive influence than Falseness'. Pardoners, a perennial focus of satire (see Prol.66–80n), are the first to show tenderness to Liar; their pity for him and washing and redressing him (232) suggest a brief parody on the Good Samaritan. Once they, Fabian-like, have set him up to sell sealed pardons on Sundays at church, doctors take notice of him and engage him for their more lucrative and easily deceptive services of urine analysis, **watres to loke**, an old commonplace for bogus technical advice found in "De Cruce Denarii" which offers numerous parallels to the passus (see above 5–9n, 20–21n, 24n, A 38–47n, 151n):

Quicunque medicus urinas viderit,
quivis causidicus causas inspexerit,
nisi pecunias ibi speraverit,
diffidit graviter et causam deserit.
[Whatever physician has looked at urine samples, or whatever lawyer has examined a case, and sees no hope for money, he gives up, gravely, and abandons the case.] (ed. Wright 1841, lines 61–64)

Treacherous imposter-physicians are legion in satire; one appears in Laȝamon's *Brut* (c. 1220 ed. Brook and Leslie 1978), lines 8845–47; one also appears (a likely influence on PP's instance) in *The Simonie*: "þer is anoþer craft þat toucheþ þe clergie: / Þat ben þise false fisiciens þat helpen men to die. / He wole wagge his vrine in a vessel of glaȝ / And swereþ þat he is sekere þan euere ȝit he was" (ed. Embree and Urquhart 1991, lines A 211–14). The illustrated copy of PP, Oxford, Bodleian Library, MS. Douce 104, presents the friar at the end of the poem, who is visiting Contrition, as holding a urinal flask (C.22/B.20.315; see Friedman 1994). So too, William Dunbar's late fifteenth-century poem, "As yung awrora with cristall haile" (ed. Kinsley 1989, no. 15), unfolds the long career of a corrupt medical practitioner. London records show concern with such professional claims and guises; in 1382, one Roger Clerk was punished on the pillory for pretending to be a physician (Riley 1868:464–65). More broadly, the ideas of "falseness" and "lying" may have particular relevance to an urban setting, as suggested in many historical records, lawsuits, and criminal proceedings against false weights, deficient or poisonous or rotten products, improper services, etc. Urban legislation and legal action against artisans often concern deceitful claims, breach of contract, false defamation, or false news; the ward beadle William Asshewell of the ward of Cornhill, for instance, was severely punished in 1388 for saying to "several men" that "he had heard a person say" that two aldermen had been arrested by the king's council (Riley 1868:507–8), a defamation deemed particularly heinous because as a beadle of the city, Asshewell's own duty was "to arrest such liars, and the inventors of such lies and rumours" (Riley 1868:508). Liar's career continues when spicers use both his knowledge of their craft and his increasing connections to high places (he **knoweth manye gommes**).

After sojourning with **mynstrals and mesagers** for six months, eleven days—precisely the duration of Edward III's French campaign in 1359–60, so perhaps a period when "rumour was rampant" (so Bnt; see also Bennett 1943a)—Liar reaches the culmination of his career dressed as a friar in which guise he can engage in the wandering and salacious activities for which friars were often satirized: **he hath leue to lep out as ofte as hym liketh**. His successful acquisition of status and complete freedom is gained by appearing as the religious profession most vilified in the poem.

for knowyng of comeres: "To prevent recognition by visitors" (Prsl). The sense of friars as hypocritical beings under their cloaks and hoods is pervasive in antifraternal satire, in which they often embody disguised sinful intentions. One side target here may be the apparent proliferation of "apostate" friars, those who, after the pope issued new restrictions in the early fourteenth century on more radical preaching about povery and criticisms of the institutional church, continued to preach in ways not licensed by the local bishop or even their own order, using disguises (especially secular clerks' habit) in order to avoid interference from the authorities. Such disguised (or simply unlicensed) Franciscan and even Dominican friars were frequent objects of complaint in the fourteenth century, and, in 1354, were legislated against, including orders against their using the clothing of secular clerks (see Clopper 2003:178–83). The concerns reach back to the founding of the Franciscan order, as when, in the late thirteenth century, John Pecham worried that hypocrites and heretics might use the clothing of the order (ed. 1898:363–64). The larger topic has complex resonance with the narrator's own use of a (seemingly unauthorized) "abite as an heremite" (see Prol.2–3n), and his ambigious claim to continue wearing "this longe clothes" as a beggar in spite of the suspicion by the king's officers, Reason and Conscience (C.5.41); see also Prol.51–55n. The tradition continues strong into the fifteenth century and even more the post-Reformation period. In Dunbar's "This nycht befoir the dawing cleir" (ed. Kinsley 1989, no. 14), the figure of St. Francis in a vision is revealed as a thoroughly unethical friar when he summarizes his career, then turns out finally to be the devil in disguise; in Marlowe's *Dr. Faustus*, the devil appears in a friar's cloak. Like Meed, friars present identities that seem doubtful, and they bring to focus uncertainties about status and identity that reach the late medieval and early modern period.

228–29 (B 218–19, A 177–78): Lyhtliche lyare lep awey thenne, / Lorkyng thorw lanes, tologged of moneye: The lines depend on common alliterative units of phrasing, but are notably spry and urgent, especially in the detail of evading clutching hands: compare *William of Palerne* (ed. Bunt 1985), "Whan þe clerk saw him come, for care and for drede / þe flagetes he let falle and gan to fle ȝerne, / þe liȝtliere to lepe his liif for to save" (lines 1892–94); or "Lorkinde þurth londes bi niȝt, so Lumbardie þei passed" (line 2213). **tologged**, from *luggen*, "pull," hence "pulled at forcibly," is attested only here. Barney (2001:106–7) notes the line's originality in many aspects, and suggests that Chaucer had it in mind in the Canon's Yeoman's Prologue's description of traversing the back alleys of a city, "Lurkynge in hernes and in lanes blynde" (658). "Are there any earlier representations of blighted urban spaces in English poetry?" (Barney 2001:107).

246–51: Symonye and syuile senten to Rome . . . "holy churche thorw hem worth harmed for euere": C's addition accounts for Simony and Civil after their dispersal: they go to Rome to supplicate the pope, persumably for mercy and protection from the king (see Alford, *Gloss.* s.v. *appel* II.), and perhaps more generally seeking provisions (see above 185n). The tradition of Latin venality satire often emphasizes how Rome or other central cities or courts are centers of sins and corruption associated with money; thus "De Cruce Denarii" says, "when money has come to consistory court, the lawyers know fraud's counsel by agreement and they litigate in collusion; they take turns winning, in a wicked alternation" ("Cum nummi venerint ad consistoria, / sciunt causidici fraudis consilia / ex pacto litigant et cum concordia; / triumphant mutuo, vice nefaria"; ed. Wright 1841, lines 45–48).

  thy kynedom thorw Coueytise wol out of kynde wende: An etymological pun, developing the relation between **kynedom** and **kynde**, as if to imply that a kingdom were a thing possessing a natural order (**of kynde**), a notion with Thomistic resonance (see Black 1992:38–40). See also 20.417–41n.

255 (B 239, A 198): wepte and wrang whan she was attached: To be **attached** is to be secured for legal jurisdiction; it means "arrested" if used for a person, but it may also be applied to a thing (see Alford, *Gloss.*). The late fourteenth-century alliterative poem telling the story of Susan and the Elders, *A Pistel of Susan*, in which Susan is falsely indicted for having an adulterous encounter with a young man, describes Susan's arrest in somewhat similar phrasing: "Homliche [impudently] on hir heued heor hondes þei leyed, / And heo wepte for wo, no wonder I wene" (ed. Turville-Petre 1989, lines 200–202). Susan's innocence and Daniel's argument in her defense suggest an apt contrast with the kind of trial for which the present moment is preparing.

C Passus 3; B Passus 3; A Passus 3

Headnote

With the journey to Westminster, the "goliardic" marriage of passus 2 leads directly, if not smoothly, into a debate before the king between Conscience and Lady Meed, nominally on the question of whether Conscience himself should marry her. With their debate, the poem turns again from action to discussion, an alternating pattern that generally characterizes the passūs of the first two visions. Direct debate between figures who represent opposing principles appears only here and after the Crucifixion near the poem's end, when Mercy, Peace, Righteousness, and Truth debate the principles behind the Harrowing of Hell and the Atonement (C.20.113–270n [B.18.110–262]). Yet six B manuscripts present the poem as a whole as a "dialogus," ending "explicit hic dialogus petri plowman" (Cambridge University Library MS. Dd.i.17 [C]; Cambridge University Library MS. Gg.iv.31 [G]; Cambridge, Newnham College MS. 4 [Yates-Thompson MS.] [Y]; Cambridge, Trinity College MS. B.15.17 [W]; British Library MS. Additional 35287 [M], Oxford, Oriel College MS. 79, part 1 [O]: details in Benson and Blanchfield 1997:118, 129, 150, 159, 169). This looser term presumably represents at least some early book-producers' or even the author's understanding of its general form (see Hanna 2005, chap. 6; for the general connection of PP to the genre of "debate," see Bloomfield 1962:21–23).

The term "debate" may be used to evoke the pointed and heated arguments of such works, which often present "two (and occasionally more than two) rather equally matched disputants who engage each other in an emotionally charged contest of words" (Conlee 1991:xii; for the Latin tradition, see Walther 1920). The genre usually (as here) pits antagonists who somehow embody what they argue for, whether in loose characterological terms as in the *Owl and the Nightingale*, the first Middle English debate extant (c. 1200), or in terms of personification allegory, as in the Carolingian debate known as the *Eclogus Theodoli* (ed. Huygens 1977:9–18), where Alitheia (Truth) and Pseustis (Falsity) argue the merits of pagan and Christian ethics and cosmologies by way of paired examples from classical and Christian literature. This last work was commented on from at least the eleventh century, included in the school-book collection known as the *Sex Auctores* of mostly pagan authors that was used in the twelfth and thirteenth century, then again still more widely circulated throughout the fourteenth and fifteenth centuries in the more Christian collection of writings used in grammar schools and known as the *Octo Auctores* (see Orme 1973:103–6; Theodolus had also been included in the earlier collection). Such literary traditions were surrounded by the staged debates of schoolrooms, of legal training and actual legal practice, and of less formal traditions of "flyting" or verbal abuse (elevated to a fine art by Scottish court poets in the fifteenth century), allowing the public debate format to pervade medieval culture.

Conscience is a logical opponent to or prosecutor of Meed. As he assumes that role, the issue of his marrying her, announced at the start of the debate, recedes from view. As passus 2 has already indicated, he is a member of the king's council (2.205–6n), a group of high lords usually with specific high royal positions or other close connections to the king (see Baldwin 1913); as the Prologue in the C revision has already made clear, it is his task, indeed his nature, publicly to "accusen" all evil, a role that in A and B is first displayed here (for the properties of this role, see Prol.95–135n). His is not the principle of private non-conformism or meditative soul-searching of the seventeenth century and later; rather, throughout the first vision he warns of public dangers to morality; he presses legal issues towards ethical and theological concerns; and he assumes energetically the role of royal counsellor. On the other side, Meed is a logical antagonist to any inflexible and impractical morality imposed on the community: she can point to how there "Is no lede þat leueth þat he ne loueth mede" (282), a point well founded in Aristotle's *Ethics* and its commentaries and influence, and thus she can argue for a morally as well as economically decentralized world, where individual efforts for reward are a force that cannot be controlled by any single moral principle or political or legal structure (see below 221–83n, 265–81n). Meed uses Conscience's official status as public spokesman for the kingdom against him, indicting him for the crown's and higher nobility's failed military and diplomatic ventures in the wars with France during the middle of Edward III's reign, and relying on the need for money that public policy on such a scale requires. In turn, Conscience can use her universal utility against her, as a principle that allows no distinctions of ethics or social hierarchy, and indeed makes possible a large host of sins. Both claim that the other damages the kingdom.

Although the positions here are sometimes forbiddingly complex or allusive to modern readers (and sometimes perhaps medieval ones), the basic terms of this debate seem broadly similar to those posing materialist or worldly or non-Christian views against more spiritual or transcendental ethics, thus standing in the large tradition of medieval debates between body and soul, Pseustis and Alitheia, and Jew and Christian. A series of debates originating or translated in the mid-fourteenth century are possibly relevant. *Wynnere and Wastoure* offers an antecedent for debate incorporating attacks on the abuses of money; there, both debaters describe their opponents' abuses of money, and both debaters present their cases to the king, who unlike L's king apparently does render a judgment himself, although its conclusions are lost with the ending of that poem. From about the same time, the French *Roman de Fauvel* offers a debate between Fauvel and Fortune with intriguing similarities between Fauvel's position and Meed's: Fauvel, having traveled to Fortune's dwelling at Macrocosm just as Meed has been taken to Westminster, seeks eagerly to marry Fortune just as Meed agrees to marry Conscience; Fortune rebuffs Fauvel in outrage (ed. Långfors 1914–19, lines 2135–38) just as Conscience rebuffs Meed. But Fortune expends her efforts not in criticizing Fauvel but in revealing her own many sided nature, which is far less appealing than Fauvel had thought. L's Conscience exclusively attacks Meed. Also pertinent from the same period, and possibly also directly influential, is the debate between Aristotle and Dame Sapience in Guillaume de Deguileville's *Pelerinage de vie humaine* (ed. Stürzinger 1893, lines 2921–3300; see in Lydgate's translation, lines 5545–6153), where Aristotle is undone by Sapience's Christian Eucharistic theology based on the analogy of other kinds of transmutations of large things into small ones (an object into a memory inside the head, for example). Conscience's and Meed's arguments proceed by similar dueling of forensic logic. An intriguing near-contemporary analogue is Nicholas Oresme's *Tractatus de commensurabilitate vel incommensurabilitate motuum celi* of c. 1360 (ed. Grant 1971), in book three of which is a debate between Arithmetic and Geometry concerning rational and irrational or "measurable" and "incommensurate" ratios in celestial motions, whose fundamental issue parallels one of the key matters in Conscience's grammatical analogy, commensurate and incommensurate reward (see below B 255–58n, and C 313–14n). Finally, misogamist works offer other parallels, since Conscience's position pivots in part on reasons not to marry. Many such works stem from the twelfth century, such as the long *Lamentationes* of Matheolus, a Latin satire translated into French in the mid-fourteenth century by Jehan le Fèvre (ed. van Hamel 1892–1905). In that work, the narrator recreates direct debate with various women to show their "lies and sophistry" (e.g., Latin text, lines 378–95, French text lines 843–902), and laments his loss of clerical honor by marrying which has made him in effect a bigamist and, as he briefly says, "Mon actif en passif mua" ("changed me from 'active' to 'passive'": Latin, lines 99–101,

French, lines 289–91), using the grammatical conceit that governs Conscience's extended analogy.

In the misogamist and misogynist tradition, the focus is often on women's duplicity: fair exteriors and evil interiors. Yet Conscience does not attack Meed on those traditional grounds, for she is not a female but *nummus, munus,* or *merces,* the usually unspeaking center of the tradition of venality satire, now brought to speech and life (fulfilling the claim by some works in that tradition that "nummus loquitur," "money talks"; see 2.5–9n). He attacks her as too amorphous, too susceptible to any use, and thus as presenting a problem of reward disconnected from merit. Within the terms of the poem and its world, such an issue is both urgent and densely complex, and indeed it receives rigorous elaboration and, perhaps, clarification (continuing in the successive versions of Conscience's response). Meed's argument is that Conscience is the example of duplicity: his authority and power are veneers for his and everyone's need for her. Indeed, although *Wynnere and Wastoure* is an important analogue and perhaps direct basis for the debate, Meed and Conscience never pursue the debate in terms of the merits of "wasting" or "winning," or indeed of "reward" or "conscience" flatly considered; rather, both endeavor shrewdly to exploit and define aspects of the other's identity in terms that help their cases. For Meed, Conscience is "royal policy" in the domain of worldy enterprise and power, who therefore needs money (see below, 147n, 231–32n, B 189–200n); for Conscience, Meed is "illicit reward," and indeed his process of diminishing her identity from "reward" broadly considered is a central part of his arguments (see below B 231–51n). Theirs is a war of mutual redefinition; and the very basis of their allegorical personification is an issue throughout.

Conscience and later his associate, Reason, have responses to each of the moments where Meed seems to be gaining the upper hand; Conscience's responses at those points increase in size and complexity with each revision, culminating in C's notorious "grammatical analogy," where the complexity and length of his exposition hardly allows the possibility of any counter response (see 333–406a and n). Here more learned distinctions are necessary than fourteenth-century English is typically asked to sustain, as the king notes (343n); in the C text especially the complexity of the analogies for true and false reward, within a theological context of salvation where direct "reward" and "merit" themselves are difficult ideas, has persistently challenged understanding. Indeed, Conscience's elaborate condemnations of Meed ultimately produce little effect on the king, who, as the opening of the next passus shows, loses his patience with them both. Other readers, modern and presumably medieval, have been attracted by the difficulties of this stretch of argumentation, as presumably the poet was when he continued so ambitiously to expand it.

The section is one of the poem's most daring and stylistically risky efforts to import inkhorn materials into sharply satiric and topical allegory, and a sympathetic pursuit of the points and meanings of Conscience's argument seems an appropriate response to a section that the poet at least thought worth intensely crafting and revising, even if some modern readers might agree with Skeat that the section is "barely intelligible, and very dull" (Skt 2.50). One may legitimately feel, as the king seems to, that Conscience has generally failed to rebut the claims Meed makes or resolve all of the problems she poses, including her own skillful redefinition of Conscience himself, yet still appreciate in his extravagantly learned final discourse a distinctive mode of high intellectual style with few parallels in any poetry, apart, that is, from passages in PP itself (consider, e.g., C.1.146–58 [B.1.148–62; cp. A.1.135–38], the "plante of pes"; C.15.157–69 [cp. B.13.148–63], Patience's riddles; C.18.226–38 [cp. B.16.220–24], Faith's matrimonial simile for the Trinity).

Meed's bower at Westminster

1–146 (B 1–109, A 1–98): Now is mede þe mayde and na mo of hem alle . . . "And teche the to louye treuthe and take consail of resoun": Before the trial, Meed rapidly collects at court an impressive entourage of followers from a series of professional groups. What she will be attacked for—her facilitation of bribery in all forms, her facile promoting of reconciliations between aggrieved parties that circumvent the king's justice and indeed any abstract notion of justice, and her rewarding of ungovernable and illicit services—is instanced in her interactions with a number of figures at court while she waits for the king to appear. Meed's reception is conveyed in tones of both courtly gentility and bitter critique, unstably mixing the generic conventions of romance and satire.

The invocation of romance conventions is clear in a stretch of courtly adverbs unparalleled elsewhere in the poem, describing the fashion in which she is treated and behaves: **Cortesliche** (9, 130), **Genteliche** (14), **Myldeliche** (21, 39, 77), **hendeliche** (30), **Solempneliche and softlyche** (54), **Loueliche** (55); as Zumthor notes, such "modal indexes" are crucial to the poetic tradition of *fin'amour* (1992:157). For a parallel in alliterative verse, see *William of Palerne* (ed. Bunt 1985): "William and his meskful [gracious] moder mekli and faire / ful loveli þe quen of Spayne led hem bitwene, / and hendeli into halle þanne hire þei brouȝt, / and derli on þe heiȝe des þei adoun seten" (lines 4309–12; also 3207–12).

The phrase **mede þe mayde** establishes this idealized, courtly tone here at the opening; as Wesling observes, as the phrase recurs throughout the passus it "receives incremental ironic force as the passus develops—especially after Conscience's 'she is tikil of hire taile' speech" (Wesling 1968:279). The court clerk's careful placement of her in a **Boure with blisse** (11), an elegant chamber apart from the king's court, sets the stage for a courtly romance; perhaps there is an allusion to the Painted Chamber at Westminster, a separate council room which from the time of Henry III held a large portrait of Largesse, an elegant gowned woman crushing Covetousness under her feet (Binski 1995:49–50). "Leuedyes in boure, knictes in halle," as the narrator of *Havelok* formulaically describes the two sexes' castle regions (239; ed. Smithers 1987); the *Pearl* narrator's request to the Maiden, "let me se þy blysful bor" (964), evokes the same conventions. Spenser's "Bowre of blis," Acrasia's paradisical retreat that Guyon destroys (*Faerie Queene* 2.12), fully literalizes the formula's language, and also literalizes PP's satiric and more direct discursive attacks on the romance conventions here invoked. No Latin quotations intrude to break this courtly texture for the first seventy-three lines, as successive suitors simultaneously try to comfort Meed and bid for her favor, outdoing one another in displays of their own corruption. As these conversations proceed, they are increasingly punctuated by the narrator's interjections that make plain the abuses involved, until the tone of romance entirely dissolves when the king summons her. Some parallels to the trial of Susan in the late fourteenth-century alliterative *Pistel of Susan* carry over from the end of the previous passus to the romance description of Meed here (see 2.255n): just as Susan takes her place at her trial in beautiful feminine array ("in sale sengeliche [hall elegantly] arayed / In a selken schert, with scholdres wel schene"; ed. Turville-Petre 1989, lines 196–97), so Meed brings the features of elegant femininity into the legal setting. Daniel's forensic defense of Susan in that work suggests, however, a different kind of literary brilliance in legalistic alliterative debate.

1–13 (B 1–12, A 1–10): Now is mede þe mayde . . . worschipeth here monye: The fleeting evocation of the style of romance in other alliterative poetry is lethally exact. The pattern of courtly etiquette for receiving a guest here resembles that in *Sir Gawain and the Green Knight*: when Gawain arrives at Bertilak's castle he is similarly greeted by a large crowd ("mony proud mon þer presed þat prynce to honour" [ed. Andrew and Waldron 1996, line 830]); the lord similarly directs a servant to see to his needs ("Þe lorde . . . chesly [solicitously] cumaundez / To delyuer hym a leude hym loʒly to serue" [850–51]); the guest is brought "to a bryʒt boure" (856) and led to take a seat (882), then presented with food and entertainment ("dere carolez" [1026]). Such initial generic markers suggest that a courtly dialogue or love-debate should follow, or an *aventure* like that between Gawain and the lady (1178–318, etc.).

1 (B 1, A 1): and na mo of hem alle: Meed's solitude is appropriate for a legal defendant, but the placing of her alone also emphasizes that she is not subsumable to the bad company she has been pulled from, that she is in fact an unknown entity. So far we have heard about her from Holy Church and from her powerful evil father and would-be suitor, but by placing her alone L stresses that we have not yet heard from her. Her solitude also seems to attract the king's sympathy, and to foster his vain belief that he is capable of assessing her if he can simply deal with her one on one (see 5–8n below).

2 (B 2, A 2): With Bedeles and Baylifs: See 2.60–63n, 2.114n. Their function here is routine, but since such figures have just been glimpsed among the marriage party, their reappearance immediately allows suspicion about the character of minor figures thronging the court world, soon confirmed.

3 (B 3, A 3): a clerke—y can nat his name: The remark seems to confer topicality and the patches of uncertainty of historical knowledge; compare Chaucer, *Troilus* I.132–33 and V.825, where the narrator pauses over unknown details in Criseyde's life; and General Prologue I.278 (the merchant's unknown name). The phrase is based on a formula; *William of Palerne*'s narrator similarly fills a b-verse by describing first the main heroes, then a vast host of knights, and then the narrator adds, "I knowe nouȝt þe names" (ed. Bunt 1985, line 5300). There, the formula is a gesture of plentitude; here, in PP's satire of Westminster, the phrase sharpens the general topicality already established, with a hint that even individual clerks are under scrutiny for their dealings with Meed. For Meed's own "calling of clerks' names," see below, 34n. Possibly the phrase here reveals the poet's intimacy with one of his likely audiences, of clerks and other administrators at Westminster (see Prol.85–94n); the same gesture appears below at C 129, and only in these two moments from the scene at Westminster. But although these moments seem to confirm topicality and realism, it is unlikely that the half-line here hints at some specific court officer, Clerk of the Council or other, serving at the time of the A version. Clerks of the Council appear to have been replaced or been rotated regularly, with the exception of John Prophet from the 1390s through the turn of the century (see Baldwin 1913:362–68); and as Baldwin notes, "Any clerk . . . might be employed on the errands of the council" (1913:363).

5–8 (B 5–8, A 5–8): "Y shal asaye here mysulue . . . Y wol forgyue here alle gultes, so me god helpe": The king's hope to find out what unmarried, beloved Meed would most love is doomed to failure, by the futile assumption that she is the romance lady she appears to be, while in fact she is by money's nature pliant to every man's desire (see 2.9–70n, 2.170–71n, and below 168–71). The king's involvement in her case may follow from her status as a kinswoman (see 2.151–52n) as well as from her allegorical status as the "weal" of the commonweal. But he seeks to settle the marriage case personally also because, like everyone else in this opening section to the passus, he is instantly charmed by her and wants to protect her from any punishment; compare 2.16n. If he can just clear up this matter of her complete inability to stay committed to one lover or husband, he will **forgyue here alle gultes**, with sentimental idealism. L's king does forgive her, with no rancor in B and A but with considerable intimidation in C (below, 139). The king's indulgence has occasionally been seen as a further indication that Alice Perrers is represented in Meed (Bnt 119–20, 139; Huppé 1939:52–53; Selzer 1980:259; see also passus 2 Headnote); but this indulgence also parallels the generic touches of romance. In any case, his plan to **asaye here mysulue** is rendered ineffectual as soon as Conscience arrives and refuses to follow the king's request to marry her, then undertakes a much more rigorous "assaying" of Meed. The king's immediate efforts to find some way to reprieve Meed palpably show that he is not the person to manage her singlehanded.

14–25 (B 13–24, A 13–23): Genteliche with ioye the Iustices somme . . . The leste man of here mayne a motoun of gold: Justices are the first of Meed's suitors; as usual, the poem's venality satire focuses first and foremost on law, with its dependence on "selling wit" (see Prol.160–66n, and below, 387–93n). The terms persistently suggest the allegorical meaning of the interaction, but the heavy romance diction for their offers keeps the irony for the time merely implicit. **Iustices** here are presumably king's justices, that is, judges in the Exchequer, the King's Bench, and the Court of Common Pleas; thus below, Conscience (in B only) declares to the king, "By Iesus! wiþ hire Ieweles youre Iustices she shendeþ" (B 155), and in C only the king later appoints Conscience himself to be "as kynges Iustice" (C 186). Such justices would in any case be part of the king's courts, and on his council (see Harding 1973:182–83). The scene here does not simply present Meed at her usual business, unrelated to the case at hand; rather, she is bribing those who will try her. The tactful style of bribery presented is notable. Meed makes no offer of such bribery; instead, the justices spontaneously seek to comfort her and assure her that they will **shape** her **way** in the coming suit. The narrator declares that they are already **of here mayne**, members of her following (25), before any abuse here takes place. She thanks them as delicately as any courtly lady in romance, but the language twists into a satirical punning: **Myldeliche mede thenne mercyede hem alle** (21), where **mercyede** means 'bribed' or 'repaid' as well as 'thanked' (MED *mercien* v. (1) b; see also the different pun on Jesus' "mercement" of human actions in 1.153–58n, and see below, 291–312n). The courtly tones are then punctured by a hint of vulgar clarification of just what **mercyede** here means, when she begins distributing her **riche ʒeftes** to them. For references to some other passages condemning judges and lawyers, see Prol.160–66n.

15 (B 14, A 14): Boskede hem to þe bour: The line is a formula in alliterative verse; see *Patience* (ed. Andrew and Waldron 1996, line 437), and *Cleanness* (ed. Andrew and Waldron 1996, line 834), and often in *William of Palerne* (ed. Bunt 1985, e.g., lines 1530, 1968, 2046, 2055, 2973). The conventions of such courtly formulae seem, again, deliberately and only briefly invoked.

27–37 (B 26–34, A 25–33): Thenne come clerkes to conforte here the same . . . "There connynge clerkes shal clokke byhynde": On the phrase **Thenne come**, see Prol.139–47n. The arrivals here, unlearned clerks who buy their way to promotion, are recurrent targets in the poem; see especially 13.112–28 (cp. B.11.298–319). Below, Conscience criticizes the abuses that Meed here encourages, nearly restating her words (187–88). Here, however, the satire is still half-cloaked in romance conventions, although persistently breached by bland assertions of venality.

Meed promises to the clerks in courtly terms **To louye hem leeliche** but then adds the vulgar promises to **lordes hem make** (31), **purchace ʒow prouendres** (32), and **bygge ʒow benefices** (33), the first an incentive to pride and worldly values, the second two clear forms of simony. **prouendres** are stipends from membership in cathedral or collegiate churches, whose purchase was commonly complained of as simony (see Alford, *Gloss.*); the purchase of **benefices**—from the twelfth century on the generic term for any ecclesiastical office or living to which was attached an endowment—was a basic definition of simony. The reference to **bonchef** (33)—'prosperity'—adds a gallicized courtly note (she is the ticket to their entry into the cosmopolitan set), but also suggests avarice. Her speech shifts midsentence from indirect to direct discourse, a frequent feature in the poem (see, e.g., 2.16–18 [cp. B.2.18–19, A.2.15]). The feature is a staple of early Middle English poetry (e.g., very commonly in Laʒamon's *Brut*); here it suggests how readily the narrator may move close toward or away from a character's point of view. The poem's satiric undertones are no less obvious when Meed speaks on her own behalf, a technique for which Chaucer is more famous (see, e.g., Donaldson 1954).

34 (B 31, A 30): in constorie at court do calle ȝoure names: Possibly this means for the clerics to be admitted as officials or judges in consistory court, the highest church courts in each diocese (on **constorie**, see Prol.126–27n). **do calle:** "cause to be summoned to a role" (see MED *callen* 3a); "call" is also used for appointing someone to a legal role in Chaucer, *Parliament of Fowls*, lines 524–25. By 1626, the noun "call" is recorded as meaning admission to the status of barrister (OED f).

35–37 (B 32–34, A 31–33): Shal no lewedenesse lette . . . clokke byhynde: That is, these ignorant, simoniacal clergy will be professionaly advanced ahead of the **connynge clerkes** who stumble behind (**clokken**, which otherwise means 'cluck' [like a hen], is recorded with this sense in Middle English only here; but cp. Anglo-Norman *clocer*, 'limp, hobble'). Meed is **byknowe** whenever this happens, a statement that may be taken both literally and allegorically: literally, she is proudly aware that, like any important patron, mentioning her name promotes her followers; allegorically, the spectacle of ignorant clerks promoted above more learned clerks makes known the presence of money.

38–67 (B 35–63, A 34–52): Thenne come þer a confessour . . . "euery seg shal se y am sustre of ȝoure ordre": The friar-confessor, a persistent object of the poem's criticisms (see Prol.56–65n, 4.140–45n, 10.6–60 [B.8.6–61, A.9.6–52], 22.315–72 [B.20.315–72]), requests bribes from Meed more overtly and extravagantly than the preceding groups, and this sets the stage for the narrator's abrupt direct comments. First, for absolving her for continuous polyandry and fornication, he will take a horseload (**seem**) of wheat (42); then, after absolving her—even after getting a further bribe from her, a **noble** (the gold coin worth a third of a pound first minted by Edward III), in exchange for spreading to others her request to **brynge adoun Consience** (43–44)—he adds yet another proposal: his order will pray for her if she will buy it a new window (a similar request, more elaborately describing the window in question, is implied by the Franciscan friar in *Pierce the Ploughman's Crede*, ed. Barr 1993, lines 118–29; see also Chaucer's Summoner's Tale, III.1974–80). His series of offers leap forward, carried further and higher by Meed's almost simultaneous positive reactions and signs. In Meed's reply the rapid bargaining of this section continues to escalate, as, in a section added in B, she also quickly tucks a final *quid pro quo* into the interaction: the friar's lenience to aristocratic lechers in exchange for her complete rebuilding of his order's house, roof, windows, and walls. The interaction between the two advances vigorously, and its pace suggests an approaching climax in the language and arguments awakened by bartering for spiritual services: a poetic energy is unleashed that the narrator seems so caught up in that he must aggressively wrest control by directly attacking the abuses so displayed, as he at once does.

The friar's negotiations with Meed are a stylish display of bribery. In most of the deals struck here, payment is offered *before* the favor is asked or along with the moment of it being asked, giving the negotiations the hypocritical semblance of gratitude and generosity; Conscience's "grammatical" analogy directly condemns such prepayment below: see 291–332n, 300n, and other passages cited there. A further and more direct renunciation of everything the friar is doing here to gather money for his religious order—so direct that it suggests simultaneous reworking with this passage—is presented by Repentance when told of Covetousness' sins (6.287–93).

B 41–42 (A 40–41): And ek be þe baudekyn . . . Conscience to felle: B/A's friar hyperbolically displays his corruption, offering to be a sexual go-between for Meed; the role is out of fabliaux, using a diminutive of "baude" attested only here (MED *baudekin* (2)), as if to display a kind of linguistic as well as sexual licentiousness (cp. Chaucer's friar's tendency "To make his Englissh sweete upon his tonge"; General Prologue, lines 264–65). Compare "fendekynes" in 20.415 [B.18.373]), and various proper nouns formed similarly in the poem: Malkyn, Haukyn, and most frequently Perkyn.

47–49 (cp. B 45–46, A 44–45): Tolde hym a tale and toke hym a noble / For to ben here bedman and bere wel here ernde / Among knyhtes and clerkes consience to turne [B, A: For to ben hire Bedeman and hire baude after]: In B and A her request that the friar be **hire Bedeman and hire baude after**, a plot from fabliau (see above B 41–42n), is only indirectly and rather awkwardly allegorizable: the allegorical point presumably is that friars condone monetary solutions to spiritual problems, and then serve as the means (**baude**) by which others are led to simony and other venal sins. But the literal plot in A/B is too vivid to make this point seem fully adequate. C's phrase, by which she exacts a promise to turn others against Conscience, is more immediately clear in the allegorical point, and, if less entertaining, unifies better the dramatic and the allegorical meaning of the court drama.

54–56: a suster of oure ordre . . . "Y shal be ȝoure frende, frere": The offer added in C to make Meed a member of a lay confraternity attached to the friar's order, in exchange for her patronage and financial assistance, is a typical arrangement; scores of such confraternities existed in late medieval London, and many letters of lay membership in them survive (see Barron 1985:17–18; Maxwell 1926 and 1929; Swanson 2000 and 2002). The arrangement was a regular target of Wycliffite writers; see also Chaucer, Summoner's Tale, 2124–28, and below, 22.363–67n. For **frende** as 'benefactor, patron,' see MED 1b.

57–62 (B 52–58): "The whiles ȝe louyen lordes that lecherye haunteth . . . þe skathe myhte sone be mended": In canonical and pastoral writings lechery is not so lightly treated, but there is enough tolerance to allow Meed an opening for her point. The *Book of Vices and Virtues*, a mid-fourteenth-century English translation of the late thirteenth-century French pastoral guide, *Somme le Roi*, says of lechery that "þer beþ somme braunches þat beþ not dedly synnes, as beþ many meuynges of þe flesche þat a man may not al wiþstonde; but þilke schal a man forbere and aȝenstonde al þat he may and noresche not hem and drawe hem not to hym" (ed. Francis 1942:4). Robert Mannyng (c. 1303) reports the view of "some of þys lewyd men" that if one believes strongly enough that lechery will be forgiven, then God on Judgment Day will in fact forgive it, because this sin is "but lyght synne": "Þus seye þey þat kan no gode," Mannyng emphasizes. The truth is, Mannyng says, any divine forgiveness for such sins must happen while you are alive, for in the next world "Þere ys but ryghtfulnes of dome" (*Handlyng Synne*, ed. Sullens 1983, lines 587–600). Mannyng elsewhere adds that of those that "haunte þe synne of lecherye" (line 7348), fornication between two unmarried people is the "lightest" sin of lechery; but even this "forbarreþ þe blys of heuene" (line 7358). Dives, in *Dives and Pauper*, presents a similar mention of the "comoun opynyon" that simple fornication is "non dedly synne": but Pauper sharply disagrees (ed. Barnum 1980:76). Meed's exculpation of lechery, even aristocratic lechery, of course has no place in any moral teaching that the friar ought to observe or teach. But friars were stereotypically prone to forgive lechery because they practiced it themselves (see 22/B.20.341–47).

B's and C's addition here thus adds to the antifraternal satire. For fines paid by fornicators to other kinds of church officials, see 2.193–96n. **lordes that lecherye haunteth** are also condemned near the end of the poem (see 21.352n); but before that, the Samaritan, like Dives and Robert Mannyng, is perhaps less damning of lechery itself, although editors usually insert quotation marks around the Samaritan's phrases defending it at 19.316–18 (B.17.336–38), as if he were merely ironically reciting common defenses for it by way of condemning it.

Discourse against church engraving and corrupt retailers

64–76 (B 60–75, A 50–64a): "y shal cuuere ȝoure kyrke . . ." . . . what thow delest with thi ryhte syde: With the friar's exchange, the narrator of the B text, and even more that of the C text, interrupts the wooing of Lady Meed to make plain the corruption and abuse involved in the requests. The aggressive interruption is a stylistic precedent for Spenser's narrative of the destruction of the Bower of Bliss. The elaboration of churches by donors for the wrong motives and God's knowledge of true motives are similarly described in *Dives et Pauper*:

As Sent Gregorie seyth in hise omelye, God takyth mor hede to a manys herte þan to his ȝifte and more to his deuocioun þan to his dede. He takyth, seyth he, no gret hede how mychil man or woman ȝeuyth or offerith in holy chirche, but he takith hed of how mychil deuocioun and of what herte he ȝeuyth or offeryth. . . . Ȝif þe makyng of chirchis and þe ornamentys and þe seruyse in þis lond were don principaly for deuocion and for þe worchepe of God, Y trowe þis lond pasyd alle londis in worchepynge of God and of holy chirche. But Y drede me þat men don it more for pompe and pride of þis world, to han a name and a worchepe þerby in the contre or for enuye þat o town hat to an oþre. (ed. Barnum 1980:188–89)

See also Chaucer, Summoner's Tale, lines 1974–77.

The basic concern with excessive church ornamentation was venerable: Gratian's Decretals includes a chapter, "A bishop's glory is not to ornament walls of the temple, but to provide for the poor" (*Corpus Iuris Canonici* secunda pars, causa XII, quest. II, c. 71; ed. Friedberg 1959, vol. 1:710–11). **god knoweth . . . Thi cost and here couetyse and ho þe catel ouhte** suggests, with its variation in pronouns, a very careful accounting of the misused funds and of the sinful desires. The distinctive self-representations that patronized engravings allow is overmatched by God's more accurate knowledge of particulars.

52, 66 (B 49, 62, A 48): graue ther ȝoure name / peynten and purtrayen ho payede for þe makyng: Patrons increasingly had themselves portrayed in the stained glass of churches they had funded, and mendicant priories in England, destroyed at the Reformation, likely showed the same sorts of displays. Hugh the Despenser's large full-length portrayal in the glass at Tewkesbury Abbey (c. 1340–44) is a lavish but not exceptional instance of donors displayed in churches (see Vale and Vale 1992:31 for a photograph). Other instances are the clerestory of Long Melford Church in Suffolk, "where the names of the benefactors are carved in the stonework, or . . . the stained glass windows of Merton College Chapel, Oxford, where the kneeling figure of Master Henry de Mamesfield appears with monotonous regularity in each of the dozen windows that he paid for" (Saul 1992:47). Such portraits were intended to evoke prayers for the donors and thus might be considered a form of simony. In England and

France, guilds and confraternities commonly financed cathedral and church windows; at Chartres Cathedral, forty-three windows are from guilds, with the names of those who gave them represented at the bottom of the window (Evans 1952:236). The narrator of PP declares that Meed's name—as the go-between for lords and friars, the means of facilitating the sins of both—is the "real" name that such portrayals show.

72 (B 68): Thi cost / here couetyse [B: þi coueitise] / ho þe catel ouhte: C presents an elegant variation of pronouns, succinctly evoking the motives and circumstances of the donor, the donee, and behind both those who used to own the wealth—who, as the past tense **ouhte** shows, were deprived of the **catel** even before the donor used it to pay the friars for an engraving. As Lawler points out, the past tense (ignored by Prsl's paraphrase, "to whom the money that is spent properly belongs"), offers a satiric punchline that recasts the point of the entire passage: "God is not fooled by the writing: he knows what's on your conscience, and just how unkind your will is, how the cost to you is simply the price the greedy friars have put on absolving you of the fraud by which you got the money" (Lawler 2005).

74a (B 72a, A 54): *Nesciat sinistra quid faciat dextera*: "Let not your left hand know what your right hand does" (Mt. 6:3–4), a reference to the proper attitude to supporting the clergy: without a simoniacal assumption of a quantifiable number of absolutions or prayers in return (see also Prol.81–84n). Donations to church structures were very common, no doubt often with an expectation of prayers in return (see above, 64–76n); some two-fifths of the wills from late medieval London examined by J. A. F. Thomson make bequests to religious orders, and, in spite of the narrator's condemnations here, increasing numbers of these—one-third, Thomson estimates—were for the friars (Thomson 1965).

A 63–64a: An aunter ȝe haue ȝoure hire . . . *Amen Amen dico vobis receperunt mercedem suam*: "Amen amen, I say to you, they have received their reward" (Mt. 6:2), with an ironic link between *merces* and Lady Meed: they indeed have their Lady Meed, but this worldly gain will be their only reward. The A text continues with the reference to Matthew 6 to emphasize the (merely) earthly reward of the hypocrites; the same quotation appears at different points in all three texts (see B 252–54a and C 311–12 and nn).

77–127 (B 76–100, A 65–89): ȝut mede the Mayr myldeliche he bysouhte . . . þe homes of hem þat taketh ȝeftes: Meed's meeting with the mayor presents a different kind of discussion from the preceding blandishments. The mayor is not a focus of venal satire as the justices, clerks, and confessor were, but he is clearly vulnerable to Meed. Meed is shown striving to convince him and his officers to be lenient in punishing civic abuses of money, and we do not know his response. The narrative intrusions increase dramatically beyond the preceding sections—indeed, it is as if the narrator were vying with Meed for the mayor's attention, an effect increasing in each version until with the C text the narrator nearly drowns Meed out with his excoriations of the abuses she is supporting. Bennett's view that the intrusions are the work of "an officious scribe's intrusion or a fragment of a larger episodic discourse that was missing from, or never completed in the *Ur*-text" (Bnt 136, at line 76–86) registers the stylistic shock of this moment, but the shift of focus and voice looks as much like an authorial error as a scribal one, and perhaps it is not an error in a sense that the C reviser would recognize as such.

Because of the first of these narrative intrusions, the present section appears abruptly in B and A: before allowing Meed to speak, the narrator emphasizes the duty of mayors to punish craftsmen prone to civic malfeasance, then shows her trying to subvert that duty. In C, an effort is made to smooth the initial abruptness, although difficulties and ambiguities remain in tying the narrator's long diatribe into the scene and even the syntax of the verse: Meed, **he**, entreated the mayor (77)—not, as Huntington Library MS. HM 137 (P) has it, the mayor "hure bysouhte," 'entreated her': although not all scribes with London dialects realized it, the pronoun **he** here, like the pronoun **a** in 115 and **he** elsewhere in the passus (161, 165, etc.), is a correct option for the female pronoun in the southwest Worcester dialect of the C copytext, which is close to L's own dialect (see Samuels 1988:210, 212). Thus the entire section is now thinly framed by Meed's incomplete entreaty to the mayor and his officers of law (MED *bisechen* 1), causing a prolonged suspension of syntax before we discover, with a restatement that she **bisowte** the mayor (115), what she requested. The narrator's intrusion that follows line 77 reminds those whom Meed addresses of their full duties; the passage becomes what the *narrator* entreats of the mayor, seizing her verb to preface her solicitous address with his own strident advice. The comma after **lawes** (78) should probably be omitted (as in Prsl) to show that the **lawes** are **To punischen** malfeasors, and to avoid taking **To punischen** as what Meed **bysouhte**; the narrator interrupts Meed to entreat the mayor **To punischen** various malfeasors and offers at still greater length, and with further complications of sense, the rationale for punishing them (81–114), before finally returning to allow Meed to say what she requested of the mayor and the other civic officials (115–16). Urban ethical advice in the poem is at its clearest here. For the poet's tendency to turn away from urban images and issues, however, see Pearsall 1997.

79 (B 78, A 67): pilories / pynyng stoles: Being held in the pillory (Latin *collistrigium*), a highly uncomfortable locking device to hold the hands and head as targets for abuse and in a standing but stooped posture, was the usual punishment for traders in foodstuffs who overcharged, underfilled a legally sealed winecask (see 88–89n) or sold rotten food ("vntidy thyng" [87]); often the offender of the last abuse would have the putrid meat or fish burned under his nose while he was held in the pillory, and sellers of bad wine might be forced to drink a draught, or have his crime named on a placard tied around his neck (see further Myers 1972:195–201; Robertson 1968:104–6; Chambers and Daunt 1931:94–96, 98, 100–105). Pillories were commonly located in central marketplaces (Palliser, Slater, and Dennison 2000:168, 177); PP itself "is most like a pillory in its fundamental concern with truth" (Benson 2004:238). The pining stool, usually called the cucking stool, a chair in which the offender was carried about for public humilation or abuse, was a less common punishment for such abuses; the two are mentioned together also in *The Simonie* (ed. Embree and Urquhart 1991, lines A 475–76, C 427–28), there too with hope for their more vigorous employment.

80–88 (B 79–86, A 68–75): As Bakeres and Breweres, Bocheres and cokes . . . that þe pore peple sholde potte in here wombe: The economic and social standing of the craftsmen and foodsellers was usually below the mercantile class, but might rise up to overlap with that class (Dyer 1989:195–99); hence such retailers of food and drink are distinguished from **þe mene peple** (on the word, see also Prol.20n), from whom they are here said to exact steep profits as retailers, to the degree that the retailers can build townhouses and live in burgages, which the narrator views as clear evidence of their fraudulent profits (see below, 84n). The narrator's basic view, insisted on elsewhere as well, is that the profit collected by such independent urban middlemen—especially brewers—violates the ideal of a direct movement of food supplies from producer to consumer (Dyer 1989:198); his condemnation speaks in the style of the urban authorities, who continually tried to monitor the practices of such vendors and retailers (Barron 2004:58–59). See also Prol.219–32n and other passages noted there.

82 (B 83, A 72): regraterye: Profitable retailing by victuallers (to whom the term **regraterye** was usually applied) was perfectly legal, but it was repeatedly subject to civic regulation in the fourteenth and fifteenth centuries (see Alford,

Gloss. s.v. *regrater*; Dyer 1989:198–99). The narrator's voice throughout this section coincides with the voice of London civic regulations; e.g., under "þe defautes and noisaunces founden with-inne þe warde of Chepe" in 1422 are condemned "all Pulters þat Regraton þe Market ayenst þe Maires crye" (Chambers and Daunt 1931:125). As the narrator declares below, the profits by middlemen were at the expense of "the peple þat parselmele mot begge" (86; cp. B 81, A 70).

84 (B 85, A 74): For tok thei on trewely they tymbred nat so heye / Ne bouhte none burgages: "If they took in [payments for goods] honestly, they would not [have the money to] build so high." Town houses, originally large plots with room for outlying buildings, were by the fourteenth century tightly packed along streets and often three or four stories high; a great hall might be set behind the frontage side of shops and chambers that reached outward over the street (see Grenville 1997:165–71). Town houses were often the homes of wealthy merchants but could also be divided for multiple occupancy and rented out: in such rentals in London's Cheapside, people were "sometimes housed in single rooms, with living accommodation adjacent to their neighbours' privies, and in some cases, to a churchyard" (Dyer 1989:189). But the more frequently leased or rather subleased properties were **burgages**, which required only an annual fixed rent to a lord that "represented exemption from the tolls paid by non-burgesses for the privilege of trading within the walls and from feudal dues owed to the lord" (Grenville 1997:161; see also Alford, *Gloss.*; Waugh 1991:50). The retail vendors have become so prosperous that they can buy **burgages**, usually the dwellings of the higher mercantile classes, and lease them out at a much higher rate than the burgage rents. A substantial amount of merchant income appears to have come from rentals, and seeing such mercantile control of urban housing as a sign of their sinful gain registers the importance of such rent in the growth of the medieval merchant class (see Hilton 1990:92–101). By the fourteenth century burgages were usually long, narrow plots with a row of dwellings, densely packed in town centers to allow the maximum number with street frontage, and more widely spaced farther from town centers where frontage was less at a premium (Grenville 1997:161–63).

88: thei fillen nat ful þat for lawe is seled: C adds this complaint; Patience later notes that the poor have at least not sinfully gathered wealth "with vnselede mesures" (16.130 / B.14.295). London ordinances in the late Middle Ages insisted that casks and barrels used by brewers had to be sealed with coopers' marks showing their capacity; such ordinances were not, however, regularly enforced until the mayoralty of William Crowmer in 1423 (for a list of brewers in that year caught with "Barrelles and kilderkyns [half-barrel casks] þe wheche wer nought seled with þe coupers marke," see Chambers and Daunt 1931:182–83).

90–107: Many sondry sorwes in Citees . . . forbrent forth alle þe rewe: This longer C addition appears to spring from the quotation from Job already in A and B, below, 124, but presented before that quotation and subordinating the Latin into the role of support for the English passage here. The focus on **fuyr** in both the English excursus and the scriptural quotation is relevant to the London issues taken up here: hundreds of hearths were used in London for cooking, heating, and industry, and fire among the close-set houses was a common occurrence, leading to civic ordinances ordering thatch on roofs to be replaced with less flammable materials (Dyer 1989:191). The concern appears as early as FitzStephen's description of London c. 1180 (copied into the London volume of memoranda in the early fourteenth century): "The only problems that plague London are the fools who drink to excess and the frequency of fires" (ed. Riley 1860:4). C's elaboration focuses on the fire hazards in a single block of connected buildings, possibly a single burgage—**alle þe rewe** (107)—an issue ignored by what in B was merely a brief discussion of fire falling on "The hous and þe hom of hem þat desireþ / Yiftes or yeresyeues bycause of hire Offices" (B 99–100 [C 125–27]). Thus in C, the merchants' sins in gaining so much that they can build and rent so many dwellings lead to a collective urban catastrophe.

But the role of the prayer **þat crist hem auenge** (93) suggests something more complex than measured and fitting retribution for sin. The whole insertion is based on Mt. 5:44–45: "pray for those who persecute and slander you, that you might be sons of your Father who is in heaven, who makes his sun to rise over the good and the evil, and rains upon the righteous and the unrighteous"; the Matthew passage is partly quoted at 21/B.18.431. Possibly relevant too is Romans 8:26–27, on inspired prayer: "For we know not what we should pray for as we ought; but the Spirit himself asks for us with unspeakable groanings. And he that searches the hearts knows what the Spirit desires; because he asks for the saints according to God." Augustine's *City of God* uses the Matthew passage and says that "blessings and disasters are often shared by good and bad" (1.8); C's brief allegory presents some of Augustine's terms to explore the ethics of another earthly city at a point where it meets the heavenly one. L's point is not simply that urban fires can spread catastrophically; instead, the brief allegory includes the spread of the "fires" of prayers for vengeance, tracing the passage of a prayer from innocent origins to unforeseen consequences: from good men in cities praying for divine justice against **fals men**, to Innocence praying in heaven to the saints, who then in turn pray to God and Mary to give **gylours on erthe** an earthly purgatory to amend themselves (100), leading God to send fire that burns both the evil and the just. The brief allegory also suggests elements of the destruction of Sodom, where Abraham besought God to agree to save the city if ten righteous men were found (Gen. 18:20–33); here, good men's entreaty to punish **fals men** leads God to destroy whole blocks of the city, including good and bad men.

The result does not seem Augustinian in spirit, although it may have Augustine's use of Matt. 5:44–45 behind it. Augustine stresses that ill fortune will produce a prayer from a good man and blasphemy from a bad; "stir a cesspit, and a foul stench arises; stir a perfume, and a delightful fragrance ascends" (1.8); PP reverses the sequence: an innocent prayer begins the general vengeance. The warning seems to be that "vengeance is mine" (i.e., God's; see Rom. 12:19), not human beings'. Elsewhere the poem displays particularly bad or uncontrollable outcomes to good but half-considered intentions; see, e.g., Piers' invocation of Hunger (8.169–352 [B.6.171–331, A.7.156–307]). The passage is a remarkable if negative articulation of the principle of unintended consequences, one that might be seen to govern, in more positive terms, the experience of much of the poem itself.

Like Augustine, however, PP here and elsewhere shows that earthly punishment, however it arrives, is potentially a path to moral remediation (indeed perhaps the only sure path), **grace to amende** (100). So too, in the Pardon passus the narrator argues that for the righteous humbly to submit to catastrophes of fire or flood or poverty gains them pardon at death from all sins (9.176–87 [C only]). As here, such catastrophes are described as **penaunce on puyre erthe** (101, 9.186), a use of "penance" that, as typically in PP, refers to punishment but not necessarily contrition. At the end of the poem, God sends plague upon a world overtaken by Antichrist, and after killing many God "sesede sone [in order] to se þe peple amende" (22/B.20.109). It is not clear that many do.

108–14: Forthy mayres þat maketh fre men . . . haue a fals name: C's insertion on urban ethics closes with a bold address to mayors—a socially didactic voice preemptively competing with the simpler arguments that Meed will offer the mayor—to investigate the mercantile practices of prospective **fre men**, that is, men granted citizenship in a city, especially the right to buy and sell without surcharge, and the right to elect or serve as civic officials: see 1.73–75n. City customs usually allowed for purchase of enfranchisement—hence **for eny speche of suluer**, "in spite of any persuasive language of money"—but increasingly in the fourteenth century the approved path was apprenticeship in that town. Complaints of admission of "unfit" men (especially merchants from other cities or other countries) as free citizens led some towns, including London from the fourteenth century, to constrict purchases of citizenship and insist on election by other citizens (see Waugh 1991:50; Sharpe 1907:309; Thomas 1932:xxiv-xxvi). The narrator's statements do not rule out the purchase of citizenship but urge high standards in granting it.

Hit is nat seemely . . . / That vsurers . . . / Be yfranchised: Usury—the lending of money or other means of exchange at interest (Alford, *Gloss.*)—is a recurrent concern in PP and in many late medieval moral theologians and canon lawyers; for some of the methods of usury, see 6.240–47 (B.5.238–49). Yet according to Thomas Usk in 1386, usury was common practice in London among "many of the worthiest of the town" ("Appeal of Thomas Usk," printed in Chambers and Daunt 1931:26, and Shoaf 1998:423–29). For **borw toun** (112) and **yfranchised** (114), see above, 85n.

115–20 (B 87–92, A 76–81): Ac Mede þe mayde þe mayre a bisowte . . . "to selle aȝeyene þe lawe": Restates and completes the syntax of 77 to allow Meed to entreat the mayor without interruption; see above, 77–127n. For the southwest Worcestershire feminine pronoun **a**, see also above, 77–127n; for **regraters**, see 82n.

118–18a: "Haue reuthe on this regraters þat han riche handes, / *In quorum manibus iniquitates sunt*": C inserts a quotation from Psalm 25:10: "in whose hands are iniquities." The rest of the line in the psalm is "their right hand is full of gifts," the basis for Meed's reference to **riche handes**: as at the end of the passus, she quotes only the pleasing half of a scriptural passage about money (see below, 485–500). The quotation is transferred from a later point in the debate in B/A, where Conscience uses it to rebut Meed: see below B 249n (A 228). Here, the remaining Latin that the narrator so quickly supplies provides further evidence of his persistent, intrusive condemnation of Meed's arguments while she is addressing the mayor. When Meed has no antagonistic interlocutor in the drama, the narrator typically takes on this role.

120 (cp. B 92, A 81): aȝeyne þe lawe [B, A: ayeins reson]: The change clarifies the sense of **reson** here, as nothing less than law (cp. the maxim *lex est ratio*); see 1.50n and other references there.

124 (B 96, A 85): *Ignis deuorabit tabernacula eorum qui libenter accipiunt munera*: "Fire shall consume the tabernacles of those who freely take bribes"

(Job 15:34). The passage here is B's and A's seed for the topic; for C's anticipation and expansion see 90–107n. Solomon was frequently named as the author of wisdom literature and sayings. By this point, Meed is implicitly defined as "bribes," although the other sense of *munus* as any "payment" is also latent and will be expressed in the debate.

The king's summons and Conscience's opening attack on Lady Meed

128–146 (cp. B 101–9, A 90–98): The kyng fram conseyl come . . . "louye treuthe and take consail of resoun" [B, A: "do þow so na moore"]: In B and A the king evidently convenes a private conference with Meed to chide her, but the courtly tones persist if not increase, with the king at least as amorously indulgent as the others: his sargeants **brouȝte her to boure wiþ blisse and wiþ ioye** (B 103), and the king himself **Curteisly . . . comseþ to telle** (B 104). In this intimate setting he barely scolds her before granting her his forgiveness and his **grace** (B 108). For the suggestion that these signs of special indulgence mark her as Alice Perrers and him as Edward III, see above 5–8n, though such treatment by an older male of any attractive woman under indictment is a general theme. In A and B the court's blandishing treatment of Meed fades only after Conscience rejects the marriage.

In C, the tone of romance and indulgence is fully dispelled upon the king's arrival. As in A and B he emerges from council but now has Meed brought before him in a public setting, where he is the first to rebuke her directly before an audience so packed that the narrator **myhte nat se þat ladde here** (129). The remnants from A/B lines only serve to emphasize how entirely the tone and setting have been reimagined. The king now speaks **Corteisliche** only because such courtly manners—as the rest of that line says—are **as his kynde wolde** (130), C's brief emphasis on his instinctively noble treatment of her in spite of his true feelings. In B and A the king seems to be restraining his affection for Meed; in C he, like the narrator, seems to be barely restraining harsh criticism. He lets her off with a sharp warning, which carries the poem's harshest tones from the antifeminist tradition, a development of the poem's persistent focus on Meed as uncontrollably promiscuous.

131–32: Lacked here a litel wiht . . . wilned to be wedded withouten his leue: C's explanation for the king's wrath emphasizes he is criticizing Meed for marrying without his **leue**, as well as perhaps for promiscuity—a new note for the king to strike (**for þat she louede gyle**, possibly referring to the constant companion to her father Favel [2.25–26n], but perhaps simply the general idea;

below, it is a figure, or simply a principle, of whom she is "eueremore a mayntenour" [287]). As in passus 2, the need for the king's **leue** implies that Meed, as a kinswoman (see 2.148–49n; Baldwin 1981:33), held an inheritance of the king in chief, that is, with the king as the direct lord of the holding in question, to whom all service would be directly due. As mid-thirteenth-century statute law declares, "women that hold of the king in chief any inheritance . . . shall not marry without the king's license" (SR 1.226; quoted by Baldwin 1981:33). Proper governance of Meed is thereby implied to be the king's direct responsibility, a position thematically intimated by 1.44–53 (see 1.48–53n), although the "king" defined in that allegory of the proper governance of wealth is Reason himself. The whole scene might, indeed, be imagined at a full Parliament, where such issues as royal weddings and major breaches of the peace were taken up (Giancarlo 2003). For the king's authority over Meed in C, see also next note. At this point, the purpose of the discussion about Meed adheres to the issue that caused her to be brought to Westminster, summoned by Theology (see 2.151n).

133, 140, 147: Til treuthe hadde ytolde here a tokene fram hymsulue; Thow tene me and treuthe; And teche the to louye treuthe: The C king begins to rouse his fury; here, the king is made a mediator or agent for Truth. Truth will send Meed notice by way of the king (**fram hymsulue**) when Truth decides to fulfill the marriage arranged with Meed's mother, Amends. The king will act on behalf of Truth when Meed enrages **me and treuthe**; and he will if necessary imprison her to **teche the to louye treuthe**, the last comment a moment where the drama of Truth as an allegorical personage takes second place to the abstract, moral meaning. Truth as always in the poem remains elusive and distant; when an agent, Truth is perceptible only by hearsay and messages like the **tokene** here, or the Pardon in passus 9 (B.7, A.8; see also Prol.15n). The king's authority in C is an authority delegated by and in service to Truth; with this new presentation no basis of Meed being a ward of the court is necessary for his claims of control over her.

141–42: In the Castel of Corf y shal do close the . . . woen ther as an ancre: The C king presents a naked threat of severe punishment, a complete shift from the solicitude of the B and A king, and a point where the indictment against her is clearly more than a kinswoman's marriage without the king's leave. The debate about her marriage is already assumed here in C to be a more sweeping trial of Meed's full range of actions and effects on the kingdom. The dungeons of Corfe Castle in Dorset were notorious (see Pugh 1968:128); Skt notes that Edward II was confined there before being moved to Berkeley, but apart from a letter by Jean Walewyn, declaring that a group had seized Edward II while he was being escorted to Berkeley Castle ("d'avoir ravi le pere nostre seignor le roi hors de nostre garde") the evidence is very tenuous (see Tanquerey 1916:127; Tout 1932–34, vol. 3.145–90). There was widespread belief, however, that Edward II was not only incarcerated in Corfe but brutally murdered there. The popular Anglo-Norman and English *Brut* (in its fifteenth-century English translation), expanding the information in the letter by Walewayn, says that Edward was removed from Berkeley Castle by two knights who "tok and lad him to þe castel of Corf, þe whiche castel þe Kyng hatede as eny deþ; and þai kepte him þere safly til þat it come to Seint Matheus day in Septembre, in þe ȝere of Grace M CCC xxvij, þat þe forsaide Sir Roger Mortymer sent þe maner of þe deþ, how and in what maner he shulde be done to deþ" (ed. Brie 1906, vol. 1.253). This popular account both mentions the preexisting horror of the castle "þe whiche . . . þe Kyng hatede as eny deþ," and suggests its further fearful association with that king's murder. The C king's threats for Meed's imprisonment there or in any prison, however, are not in fact fully carried out; see 4.162–65n.

144–45: That alle women . . . banne the and alle þat bereth thy name: The C king declares that Meed will specifically be a warning to **alle women**, emphasizing condemnation of her "feminine" qualities, or the proneness of women to fall similarly. For the fear of repute and the historical sentence of a permanent stigma on her **name**, see Chaucer's Criseyde, *Troilus and Criseyde* 5.1058–68, 1093–95. The sense of posterity's condemnation of women is paralleled by and perhaps ultimately based on medieval representations of Eve's guilt; for an early instance of her penitential self-consciousness of just such notoriety, see the twelfth-century *Ordo Representacio Adae* (ed. Bevington 1975), lines 459–60, 534, 555–64. Meed of course lacks all conscience, hence her antithesis to the figure she is about to meet.

147 (B 110, A 99): Y haue a knyght, Consience, cam late fro beȝende: C rejoins A/B's presentation of a more benign king, seeking to find a place for Meed in his court if under the governance of a more trustworthy husband. But since Conscience's role is as "accuser" (see Prol.95–135n), his arrival sets the terms in all versions for the genre to become that of a trial of Meed in general terms, not just her marriage. Once Conscience begins to speak, this shift is solidified. **fro beȝende** for "from biyond-se," the usual phrase for "abroad" (MED *biyond* 1b). Scholars have sometimes argued that John of Gaunt, often abroad at wars in the 1350s and 1360s, is meant to be identified with Conscience in this passus, and, while this is far too specific an identification to be sustained, elements of Gaunt's, the Black Prince's, and Edward III's own military endeavors should be set beside the references to Conscience's (see below, B 189–200nn). But Conscience is often a composite portrait of the actions and powers of the royal court (below, 226–28n), and his allegorical status can accommodate something like "royal policy," an identification that Meed shrewdly emphasizes in her arguments about his need for her (see below, 231–32n, B 189–200n).

152 (B 115, A 104): Byfore þe kyng and his consayl, clerkes and oþere: An unmarked change of scene may occur here, from a private meeting to full council (so Bnt), but it is simpler to assume that the king's interview with Meed has taken place all along in full council, which is here realistically described as including both clerks of various kinds, especially those trained in law, and secular lords, of middling to high rank. "The king's councilors, with great differences of rank and employment, . . . were retained largely for their individual services, some for law cases, some for diplomatic work, some to serve on commissions, and others for political counsel" (Baldwin 1913:112–13). There seems nothing to prevent the scene from being full Parliament, although that view has rarely been advanced (but see Giancarlo 2003). On the venue, see also 2.151n and 4.45n.

158–215 (B 121–69, A 110–56): "Ar y wedde suche a wyf wo me bytyde! . . . Such a maistre is mede among men of gode": The king's plan for this marriage is immediately shown to be impossible, and the point—and genre—of the passus is reconfigured as a full-scale trial and debate. Meed is necessarily ungovernable by Conscience, because she cannot cease representing payments of all kinds, not simply rule-bound kinds. Like the Latin word *munus,* which means 'gift' or 'payment' or 'bribe' depending on context, she is a creature of particular use and particular context, unable to divide herself permanently into specific kinds of payment, as Conscience will seek to do in his series of distinctions accumulating through additions in all versions. In all versions, Conscience's first attack on Meed surveys her social damage, group by group, in a dizzying pursuit of her transformations through society; his second attack, at least vestigially present in all versions (below, 285–500), scrutinizes in increasingly abstract terms the spiritual and philosophical nature of her pernicious influence. Even the first attack suggests the spiritual and metaphysical threat she offers: like Lucifer (1.66–67), she misleads by the **trist of here tresor** (161), which overshadows and destroys any other kind of social trust or faith, hence stripping authority and efficacy from any other procedures or institutions that allow people to maintain such trust and faith.

Thus women betray marriage vows and sexual restraint because they **lou-yeth here ʒeftes** (163); thus the documentary and other legal instruments and procedures of sheriffs, the king, justices, the pope, and other clerks are rendered hollow and ineffectual because of the greater power and attractiveness of monetary gain; thus intellectual endeavor in sum is transformed into schemes that pursue gain: **al þe witt of the world is woxe into Gyle** (212)—the last a recurrent complaint in the poem (e.g., 11.14–20 [B.10.17–22, A.11.17–22]). Conscience implies in the vignettes he offers of those who follow Meed a general attitude of insouciance towards institutions, catching echoes of their tones of cheerful self-determination. Governed by Meed's power they act when and as they wish: **when hem lust** (170); **wher hym liketh** (177); **a counteth nat a rusche** (180); **as sone as heresulue lyketh** (182); **as here luste** (196). To the energetic whirl of corrupt activity that Meed engenders, however, are contrasted desolate images of her victims, isolated amidst the pleasures in power that her followers and lovers enjoy.

Throughout his speech in the copytext manuscript, Conscience (or the scribe) uses the alternative feminine pronouns for southwest Worcester, **he** and **a**. The particularly heavy concentration of these, very likely the forms of L's original (Samuels 1988; above, 77–127n), confused some scribes of other dialects, who at points retained "he" while otherwise translating the text into their dialects.

158 (B 121, A 110): suche a wyf: Normally the demonstrative pronoun assumes an intensive, pregnant character only when followed by a result clause ("so evil" or "so great . . . that"; see Mustanoja 1960:177–78). Here **suche** has this intensive sense even though it is not followed by an explicit clause of result, since the consequences are implied, to be filled out in a series of later following statements. Compare *William of Palerne* (ed. Bunt 1985), "þi sone schal wedde swiche a wif to weld wiþ al Rome / as kinde keper and king" (2959).

164 (B 127, A 116): ʒoure fader she felde: An accusation of regicide that Meed takes as one of Conscience's most serious and unfair defamations: below, 233. The **fader** in question would be Edward II for the A text, a relic retained in B and C texts. A king coming to a bad end might easily be seen as having fallen into the corruptions or dangers of money. Edward III more notoriously enjoyed large amounts from hostage-taking, and often pressured his lords, the church, and the commons to come up with more to pursue his military enterprises. A topical criticism here of him might be made tactfully oblique by indicating his father, whom Edward helped destroy (see also below, 191n and 208–13n).

165 (B 128, A 117): He hath apoisend popes, he appeyreth holy churche: Benedict XI was thought to have been poisoned in 1305; but, as Bnt notes, the assertion that Meed has **apoisend popes** and **appeyreth holy churche** reveals the true reference: the Constantine Donation, a document (actually an eighth-century forgery) purporting to be the basis for the church's right to temporal endowments (see 17.220–25 [B.15.557–69], and other passages cited at 1.42–53n). An account common from the twelfth century on tells that an angel—or a devil, depending on the tradition of the story—cried out at the moment of Constantine's grant that the church was poisoned by the infusion of temporal wealth: "this day hath ydronke venym" (see 17.223 [B.15.560]).

The usual form of the story also includes another comment from Jerome on the decrease of the virtues of the church, and the two quotations may be tersely summarized in Conscience's two clauses and two verbs, **apoisend** and **appeyreth** ('impairs'). In John Trevisa's 1387 translation of Ranulph Higden's mid-fourteenth-century universal chronicle, which in turn uses Gerald of Wales' twelfth-century *De Principis Instructione*, the typical collocation is found: "it is writen that whan Constantyn had made that yifte to chirches, thanne the olde enemy criede openlich in the eyr, 'This day venym is yhelde and schad in holy chirche,' therfore Jerom in Vitas patrum seith, 'Siththe holy chirche encresed in possessiouns it hath decresed in vertues'" (ed. Babington and Lumby 1865–86, vol. 5.131; see Gerald of Wales, *De Principis Instructione*, ed. Warner 1891:87–88, where the voice is an angel's; see also Gower, *Vox clamantis*; ed. Macaulay 1900), 3.283; and further Laehr 1926:162–64, 172–73. The phrase attributed to Jerome is apparently adapted from a statement in his *Vita Malchi* par. 1; PL 23:53. When Lollards took up the story they invariably credited an angel with this announcement, seeing the Donation as the turning point in the church's decline from apostolic purity to modern materialistic decadence (see e.g., the "Lollard Chronicle" ed. Embree 1999:117; *Lanterne of Liȝt*, ed. Swinburn 1917 for 1915:96, where Augustine and Bernard are quoted as well: further 'angels' spreading this message; also in Arnold 1869–71, vol. 1.314, 3.340; and Matthew 1902:378, 475). Conscience is yet another "angel," showing one of L's parallels with Lollard thought although also with that of other clearly orthodox contemporary writers (see generally Gradon 1980; Bowers 1992; Pearsall 2003).

168 (B 131, A 120): tikel of here tayl, talewys of tonge: Sexually both lascivious and changeable (MED *tikel* 1b, c); and in talk, a gossip. Huppé notes that the consonance of **tayl** and **talewys** "suggests in the manner of a pun her close affiliation with lechery" (1950:165). Such features linking promiscuity of sexuality and of language tersely epitomize the medieval misogynist tradition (see

Patterson 1991:290–96); a similar play on "tail" and "tally" appears in Chaucer's Shipman's Tale, lines 414–34. On the synthesis of misogyny and venality satire in the portrait of Meed, see also passus 2, Headnote.

169 (B 132, A 121): As comyn as þe cartway: Whiting and Whiting (1968) C 64 lists this as the first English instance of a common proverb; to be added to Whiting's examples is Walter Hilton's *Scale of Perfection* (c. 1390) which says that a soul blinded by "wordli [*sic* for "worldli"] love" is "as comone as the highwai" (2.40; ed. Bestul 2000:239). More pertinent perhaps is the tradition surrounding the riddle in the Latin collection known as the *Joca Monachorum*, "Quid est mulier meretrix? –Sicut via lutosa" ("what is a prostitute like? –a muddy path"; ed. Suchier 1955, text C, no. 73; also text P, no. 27). Meed's "comyn cartway" threatens to blur social differences with her universal availability and usability; the pun depends on **comyn** as "given to prostitution" as at B.5.641 (see also MED *commune* adj. 9. (b)). Such social blurring is paralleled by Chaucer's Wife of Bath: "I ne loved nevere by no discrecioun, / but evere folwede myn appetit . . . . / I took no kep, so that he liked me, / How poore he was, ne eek of what degree" (622–26). However, Chaucer's Wife is speaking of her own desires; Conscience is describing Meed's complete lack of resistance to others'. On such pliancy see 2.127n. The principle of money's ability to make necessary "equivalencies" and form common social interactions is taken up by Meed below; see 221–83n. Her downfall uses **comyn** again (see 4.151–59n).

172–79 (B 134–41, A 123–30): Sysores and somnours . . . Shyreues of shyres . . . hangeth hym for hatrede þat harmede nere: For the collocation of assizers, summoners, and sheriffs, see 2.60–63n. The portrait of the trussed and hanged innocent victim of a corrupt sheriff is one of the more chilling depictions of Meed's victims.

184 (B 146, A 135): ȝoure secrete seel: Meed's power may specifically refer to bribed provisions from the pope having the power to outdo the king's requests in provisions (so Bnt); but the line also sums up the preceding activities that Conscience says Meed regularly does, which to this point evoke corrupt secular or royal power, to be followed by corrupt papal power. Fourteenth-century kings sought successively more private seals to exert their personal will against an increasingly large administration: the Privy Seal was created in the thirteenth century to identify the king's personal wishes in distinction to the Great Seal of the Chancery, then it became itself a great office, leading Edward III to create the signet or secret seal. By Richard II's reign, this seal too had become a distinct office, controlled by the king's secretary (Galbraith 1963:25–26; Waugh 1991:172). Meed's power outruns the speediest administrative means the king can create to impose his will. For the poem's focus on seals of various kinds, see Prol.77n.

185 (B 147, A 136): He is priue with þe pope, prouysours it knoweth: For provisors, and their relation to the pope, see 2.178–96n, and 2.185n.

190a: *Sunt infelices quia matres sunt meretrices*: "They are unfortunates, because their mothers are prostitutes"; source unknown. The quotation, a regular Leonine hexameter, inserted in C, turns attention briefly to the plight of the offspring of the illegitimate unions described. Canon law of course forbade priestly marriage in L's time. On priests and concubinage, see 6.135–36 (B.5.160), "dame purnele a prestis fyle"; see also Heath 1969:104–8.

191 (B 153, A 142): Ther she is wel with eny kyng wo is þe rewme: The point generalizes the outcome of the topically framed comment at 164 (B 127, A 116). The form of political proverb recalls *"ve terrae ubi puer est Rex"* (see Prol.209n).

193–95 (B 155–57, A 145–47): By iesu! with here ieweles the Iustices . . . here floreynes goth so thykke: Restates the general point of the satire above, 14–25, tersely generating a new allegorical tableau. A law court is in session in a manor or royal court, but **þe lawe** is kept locked outside, with the result that **fayth** is also kept from the proceedings by a throng of Meed's **floreynes**, suggesting a crowd of bought, hostile minions, "retainers of a powerful woman so crowding the streets as to obstruct the free movement of personified integrity" (Kane 1989:97). On the image of a snow, or perhaps a disease, of **floreynes**, see also B.4.154–56n.

196–97 (B 158–59, cp. A 148): louedayes maketh, / Thorw which loueday is loste þat leute myhte wynne: A "loveday" was a loose term for a number of different sorts of semi-official arbitration settlements, especially private settlements out of court, but also including arbitration in which the court was somewhat involved, on days set aside at court sessions or informally in manorial courts, and even including any kind of settlement of private or public quarrel (Josephine Bennett 1958; see also passus 4 Headnote). The semi-official kinds were presided over by a designated figure of some authority, such as a friar or other cleric who has been delegated the role of arbiter (like Chaucer's friar, who outfits himself to preside over these "lyk a maister or a pope": General Prologue 258–61); for L's condemnation of clerks assuming this role, apparently because it involves them in a quasi-secular office or because it gave them opportunities for illicit profits, see B.5.420, C.5.158 (B.10.312). The word could simply mean "reconciliation" (from the late thirteenth-century *South English Legendary*); L's contemporary, Thomas Usk, also uses the word to mean reconciliation, although he uses the metaphor of a semi-formal event with an arbiter, when Love rhetorically asks, "maked I not a lovedaye bytwene God and mankynde, and chese a mayde to be nompere to put the quarel at end?" (*Testament of Love* 1.2, ed. Shoaf 1998:67).

The A version's brief remark here, **She let law as hire list & louedaies makiþ**, seems elliptically to mean the illicit reconciliations that Lady Meed would make, not all manner of reconciliations. **loueday** is far from a term of opprobrium generally, and PP's categorical insistence on the evils of such arrangements is notable. B and C here seem to specify and defend A's original condemnation, while implying that lovedays are not evil as such but are particularly vulnerable to Meed's corruption. The usual concern, however, is the potential for violence among the large numbers of followers gathered by the parties of suits; for instance, for a brief period while the young Edward III was overseas doing homage (later renounced) to the king of France, he prohibited Londoners from (among many other illicit acts) maintaining groups of followers to hold lovedays in his absence "in disturbance of the peace of our Lord the king, or in affray of the people, and to the scandal of the city" (1329, Letter Book E, fol. cxciv; trans. Riley 1868, vol. 1:173; on retainers at such events, see Powell 1989:100, 105). But no general effort was made to repress lovedays as such on the grounds that they did not deliver adequate settlements, and indeed they were occasionally stipulated by legal authorities to settle conflicts in more locally suitable terms (see Rawcliffe 1984). Among PP's contemporaries, only Wycliffite writers approach the criticism of this point in PP, and usually the Wycliffites condemned lovedays not for bribery (if that is indeed the chief matter here in PP), but again for the violence they led to, associated with the private armies of retainers that were often assembled at lovedays: "grete men of þis world debaten [brawl], & meyntenen debatis at louedaies; & who so may be strengere wil haue his wille don, be it wrong be it riȝt, & ellis make debate among many hundrid & þousand men & sumtyme many countres, & by sich debatynge many men holden grete houses & grete araies & grete costis" ("Of Servants and Lords," ed. Matthew 1902:234–35). In the Wycliffite tract, the legal corruption, legal maneuvering, and outright reliance on power in such settlements as lovedays are seen to underlie lordly prosperity generally, which in a broader sense is like the hypocrisy that Conscience presents Meed as embodying (see above 158–215n, 172–79n). Elsewhere Wycliffite writers condemn lovedays for purporting to absolve sins as well as settle crimes (see pas-sus 4 Headnote), and this also may be implied in the present context.

It is difficult to find full parallels to the views in PP and the Wycliffites on lovedays as such. A 200-line poem of moral guidelines in English for "ʒe lordingis þat louedays wile holde" is found at the end of a fifteenth-century "holster" manuscript (i.e., a very narrow book, made for easy carrying by a friar or other itinerant cleric), possibly from the Hertfordshire area, Cam-bridge University Library, MS. Dd.1.1, fols. 300ᵛ-302ᵛ (noted and partly tran-scribed by Bowers 1952, and by Josephine Bennett 1958:365). The poem, while it nowhere condemns lovedays as such, warns those presiding over them against many of the evils that Conscience ascribes to Meed's corruption there, and indeed it includes some of the ethical terms that appear as allegorical per-sonages in her wedding. After using Pontius Pilate as an example of a corrupt-ible judge, for instance, the treatise says,

But wheþer domes men now on days
Don eny mor amys
Þan did sire Pontiuce Pilatus
Sum men supposen ʒis;
Þan wold I wete of wisemen
What schal ben hir mede
Þat mayntene falshed witingli
For loue or mede or drede? (fol. 302ᵛ)

The writer offers guidance for lovedays rather than not categorical condemna-tion of them; he assumes that "to confound al falsnes" is certainly possible in such a setting. PP presents less hope for this. The evils of unsupervised arbitra-tion and reconciliation become a central focus of the next passus.

198 (B 160, 149): The mase for a mene man thow he mote euere!: "[Such are] confusion for a poor man, even though he plead [his case] perpetually!" The line sums up the preceding vignettes of frustratingly corrupt legal proceedings. For a similar sense of **mase** see B.Prol.192, 1.6n.

203–10: Religioun he al toreueth . . . that no lond ne loueth the and ʒut leeste thyn owene: C's insertion is sweepingly concerned with all the spheres of late medieval life that Meed damages: religion, civic life, and the realm. **cus-tumes of coueytise** suggest a kind of "law" (with perhaps a pun on "custom-ary law") that Meed has insinuated into all these spheres of life. **Vnsittyng soffraunce**: "Unseemly Tolerance (of evil men)" (so Skt 2.xxxiv). The idea is first mentioned in Conscience's accusation against the negligent clergy, in C only (see Prol.124n); as an entity, it reappears at 4.189 below, also in C only.

208–13: the; thyn; thi: Conscience shifts to an informal pronoun in the heat of his warning to the king, and at the climax of his first speech against Meed, much of it added in C. With Edward II's fate as a general background, the warning that **thyne owene** land (213) will not love the king indeed evokes a serious threat to the king's authority if he permits such activities; if C is from the mid-1380s, such a threat might be suggested by Richard II's brutal conflict with the higher nobility, his uncles, in 1385–88 (see Goodman 1971). For the political point and the familiar pronoun, compare Chaucer's "Lak of Stedfast-nesse," especially the envoy requesting Richard II to "wed thy folk agein to stedfastnesse" (28). The issue exceeds topicality; it refutes the claim Meed will make later that rewards tie together a kingdom (see below 265–81n). The importance of the king sustaining justice throughout his kingdom is clear in the next passus (see especially notes on 4.166–96), already glimpsed in the coronation oaths inserted in the B Prologue (see Prol.136–56n).

Meed's defense

221–83 (B 175–227, A 162–214): "Nay, lord . . . gret lord oþer pore": Meed's defense relies on the basic theme that everyone needs and wants Meed, including Conscience. The idea has some foundation in Aristotle's *Ethics* 5:10–11, which was a touchstone for all later medieval commentary on the need for goods and services to be equated by the process of exchange, which implies the fundamental need for a principle of exchange that can equalize value and hence justice, and allow community itself to exist. As Nicholas Oresme, c. 1370, translates and glosses some of the pertinent passages:

convient il donques que le charpentier preingne de l'euvre au cordouennier et que il li retribue de la sienne. Et donques, se ce que a fait premierement le charpentier est equal selon proporcionalité a ce que il a receü de l'autre, ce sera ce que nous avon dit. [*C'est a savoir, juste commutacion tant pour tant, non pas selon l'equalité des choses, mail selon la proporcion de leur valeur; car une maison vault plus que un chaucement et une livere de saffren plus que une livre de chandele.*] Et se il n'est fait ainsi comme dit est, ce ne sera pas equalité et se il n'estoit ainsi, communicacion civile ne pourroit durer. Et n'i a force ou difference se l'euvre de l'un est meilleur que l'euvre de l'autre; car l'en peut bien faire et le convient selon justice tan que ily y ait equalité. [*Et que celui de qui l'oeuvre est moins bonne en face plus, jusques a la value de l'autre.*] Et en la maniere dessus dite est il es autres artz; car autrement periroient les artz, se celui qui a fait aucun ouvrage ne recevoit tant et tel selon valeur comme il a fait et se celui qui l'a receü ne fasoit tant et tel. Car communicacion qui est faite en commutacions ne est pas communelment entre personnes d'un artifice ou d'un mestier, comme sont .ii. medicins; mais est entre personnes de divers artifices, come sont .i. medicin et .i.

laboureur de terres qui son divers mestiers et ne sont pas equalz; mais il les convient reduire a equalité. [*Comme se le medicin a visité ou gueri un laboureur; donques le laboureur le servira de son mestier ou li baillera de son blé ou de son vin tant que il souffira selon raison et justice.*] . . . Et pour ce fu premierement trouvee monnoie et de ce vint elle. Et est monnoie aucunement le moien en commutacions, car par elle mesure l'en toutes teles choses et la superhabundance et la deffaute. [*C'est a savoir combien une chose vault plus ou moins que l'autre.*]

[Thus it is necessary that the carpenter should take the cobbler's work and that he grant him in return his own. And therefore, if what the carpenter has done first is equal in proportion to what he has received from the other, that will be as we have said. (*That is, a just price of so much for so much, not according to the equality of the goods, but according to the proportion of their value; for a house is worth more than a shoe, and a pound of saffron is worth more than a pound of candle-wax.*) And if it is not done as said, there will not be equality, and if there were not, civil communication would not be able to survive. And there is no matter or difference if one's work is better than the other's work; for one can do well and it would be matched according to justice as much as would be equitable. (*And that the other whose work is less good would do more of it, up to the value of the first.*) And it is so in the manner said above for the other arts; for otherwise the arts would perish, if one who had done some work did not receive such and such an amount according to the value of what he had done, or if the one who received that did not do such and such a work. For communication which is carried out in commutation is not commonly done between persons of a single art or occupation, such as two doctors, but between persons of various arts, such as a doctor and a worker of the soil who have different occupations which are not equal; but it is necessary to reduce them to equality. (*As if the doctor had visited and healed a laborer, and then the laborer would help him by his occupation or grant him some of his wheat or wine, as much as he should according to reason and justice.*) . . . And for this purpose was money first discovered and from this it arose. Money is entirely the medium in commutations, for through it [*literally,* her] one moderates all manner of such things, both superabundance and dearth. (*That is to say, how much one thing is worth more or less than another.*)] (ed. Menut 1940:294–95; see also Kaye 1998:51; Langholm 1992:189)

Conscience has already approached the Aristotelian principle of money's equalization as Meed's complete promiscuity (see above 168n); Meed seizes his terms of desire and approaches the Aristotelian principle from another direction, as universal desire for her, rather than for some higher principle of justice (as Aristotle does). In dialectical style, Meed's thesis is stated only at the conclusion: **Is no lede þat leueth þat he ne loueth mede / And glad for to grype here, gret lord oþer pore.** She makes sure to refute immediately the charge of regicide, a most dangerous one, and then diverts the argument to foreign policy and war policy, by which she stays with matters of special interest to the king; then she makes only brief reference to the brunt of Conscience's charges at the end. She proceeds by seeking first to weaken Conscience's personal credibility, then to prove to the king her own particular and universal value.

Thus her argument is organized mainly around two claims. First, she claims that Conscience himself depends on Meed but uses her ineffectually (226–64); thus Conscience depends on Meed to carry out his military endeavors, especially—and with a topicality that is weakened in favor of more general concerns with military conquest in the C text—his operations in the French war leading up to a complete relinquishing of English claims (implicitly at the treaty of Brétigny, 8 May 1360). The corollary to this is that Meed could have achieved a far greater national triumph without Conscience's pusillanimity and blinkered outlook. Second, Meed defends the use of money as the basis of law and commerce: all levels of society need her, less for basic physical needs than to maintain law, order, and social dignity in relation to those below them, from the king down to the craftsman (265–83). The king in passus 3 accepts the portrait of Conscience without demur, or at least, for the moment, he finds the fundamental claim that Meed is universally needed a convincing proof that Meed is "worthy . . . þe maistrye to haue" (285).

226–28 (B 180–82, A 167–69): Wel thow wost, weye . . . grypen my gold and gyue hit wher þe liked: Meed treats Conscience as the historical figure the king has introduced, a powerful "knyght" at the king's court (147); yet she addresses him with the familiar pronoun, as he has addressed her (she addresses the king in the respectful plural). The events Meed accuses Conscience of being involved in through this section may be loosely identifiable with those of the Black Prince, Gaunt, and the king during the French campaigns leading up to the treaty of Brétigny (see below, B 189–200nn). The actions of dispensing gold fit so generally with the crown's military operations of mercenaries, ransoms, and wages that it is prudent to take the Conscience Meed describes as a personification of the king's entire military leadership and council members; that is, of central royal military counsel and power. This identification is clear in Meed's charge (in C only) that Conscience has counseled the king "a kyndom to sulle" (244n). So identifying and defining him is a bold strategem: it shapes him into an entity that necessarily requires money. For Conscience's own redefinitions of what "meed" is, see below, B 231–51n.

hanged on my half enleuene tymes: "Clung to my side (i.e. party) many a time."

231–32 (B 184–85, A 171–72): y may . . . maynteyne thi manhede more then thow knowest: One sense of **manhede** is "chivalric dignity," and this sense bespeaks the ethos of epic chivalry (see also 250, 268). But the **manhede** Meed supports more specifically implies "manpower" in terms of military numbers, hence the "meyne" to which lords offered maintenance (see the one possible instance of this sense, MED 3f). Meed is coolly reminding Conscience that, as royal policy, in matters like the wars with France he relies on her to keep his armies strong and contented. For the phrasing, and the underlying sense of military might, compare *William of Palerne* (ed. Bunt 1985), "Forþi, alle my bolde burnes, I biseche and preie, / for love þat ȝe owe to þe Lord þat let ȝou be fourmed, / meyntenes ȝit ȝoure manchip manli a while" (lines 2674–76).

233 (B 187, A 174): For kulde y neuere no kyng ne conseilede so to done: Meed answers Conscience's most serious complaint: regicide (164). There may be a veiled counter-attack in her slight elaboration of his original charge, **ne conseilede so to done**: Conscience, as an embodiment of the higher courtiers or, again, of nation-shaping policy, carries some taint of the deposition and murder of Edward II by the higher nobility; many of their descendants were allowed under Edward III to retain prominent positions at court (see Holmes 1966:124).

B 189–200 (A 176–87): In Normandie was he noȝt noyed for my sake . . . And dide hem hoppe for hope to haue me at wille: In A and B, Meed aggressively seeks to disgrace Conscience by recalling the series of raised and dashed military, political and financial hopes leading up to the treaty of Brétigny of 1360, which marked a disappointing close to the first, successful stretch of the war with France, whose crown Edward had claimed in 1337, on the grounds that the right came to him through his mother Isabella of France and on the grounds that the French king (to whom Edward had earlier made allegiance as a vassal of Gascony) were illegally aiding the Scots, and then had illegally confiscated Gascony (McKisack 1959[1991]:121–26). A series of promising assaults on France began with John of Gaunt's and the Black Prince's successful campaigns in 1355 through Normandy and Gascony, culminating in the Black Prince's bold capture of the French king John at Poitiers in 1356, widely seen as a humiliation for the French (and leading several French writers to attack the failures of the French nobility; see Barber 1996:146–47, and generally Barber 1996:113–69). A series of efforts to ransom John followed, beginning with a demand for four million florins as well as restoration to English sovereignty of Aquitaine and Ponthieu, but the French nobles refused this vast ransom, and they did so again when King John negotiated a second and larger ransom and grants of more territories in France. In response, Edward III departed again on campaign in 1359, but was stalled outside Rheims in harsh January weather with low provisions, and after more setbacks settled for a ransom of 200,000 gold moutons for King John, payable by Easter 1361, in return for the English surrender of the castle of Flavigny and a three-years' truce.

Only part of the ransom was ever received. Edward III continued his military assault but was finally forced to give up its military plans in April after a devastating storm, on a day that one fifteenth-century chronicler calls "black Monday, and wolle be longe time here affter" (Barber 1996:166; McKisack 1959[1991]:137–42; Waugh 1991:17–18). The disappointing treaty of Brétigny that resulted is alluded to in lines that C retained and expanded (below, C 242–57n).

What Meed implies by her oblique allusions to this sequence is that Conscience, as royal policy, was properly focused on gaining as much money as possible, and held considerable promise of doing so **In Normandie** as the English moved in toward Poitiers, but that he failed to achieve the money the English wanted because of the difficulties, which themselves show his need for her.

B 191–94 (A 178–81): Crope into a Cabane . . . And hastedest þee homward for hunger of þi wombe: As Bennett notes, the most obvious candidate for a storm in the campaign of 1356–59 was that which beset Edward III outside Rheims on 13 April 1359, during a siege that had begun in January (**Wendest þat wynter wolde han ylasted euere**), and which was noted by all English and French chroniclers. A **dym cloude** surely evokes the name "black Monday" that chroniclers call the day (see above B 189–200n). Most chroniclers of the campaign of 1356–59 mark the missed opportunity in this outcome to the Normandy campaign but lack any reference to English "dread" (e.g., *Anonimalle Chronicle*, ed. Galbraith 1927:46–47). Froissart, however, may be thought to hint that fear from the storm led to the king's vow for a truce:

It seemed truly as if the world must end, for it rained from the air hailstones so large that they killed men and horses, and even the strongest were entirely struck down. And then the king of England looked toward the church of Notre Dame of Chartres and he devoutly prayed to Our Lady, promising, as he said and confessed afterwards, that he would agree to a truce. (Froissart, Bk. 1, part 2, chap. 126; quoted by Bennett 1943a:569)

The prose *Brut* similarly describes "suche a storme & tempest þat non of our nacioun herd ne sawe neuere non such; thurght þe whiche, þousandeȝ of our men & of here horses in here iourneyng (as it were þorugh vangeaunce), sodenly were slayn & perisshed." The *Brut* adds, perhaps obliquely registering views like Meed's, that "þe which tempestes ful mich ferid not þe Kyng, ne myche of his peple, þat þey ne wenden forth in her viage þat þey had begunne" (ed. Brie 1908:311).

Cabane: Here, specifically a tent used in military camps; *Wynnere and Wastoure* describes an elaborate "caban" from which the king emerges, "alle raylede with rede the rofe and the sydes / With Ynglysse besantes full brighte betyn of golde" (ed. Trigg 1990, lines 60–61). A.12.35–36 (the John But section) mentions one with a small door. The word is sometimes flexibly used to indicate any small house or room (e.g., by Trevisa to translate Latin *cellula*, "booth" [for the Roman theater], *casa*, "hut" [for the earliest houses of human beings], and *mansiunculae*, "little rooms" [for the Ark]; see the *Polychronicon*, ed. Babington 1865, 1.221; 2.226, 2.233, 2.235), but its currency in *Wynnere and Wastoure*, a poem likely alluding to the Black Prince and his chief administrator, Sir John Wingfield, who accompanied the Black Prince on his campaigns in Normandy, suggests an authentic detail from the period Meed is describing (for Wingfield, see Barber 1996:127–28; but note the cautious views of Trigg 1990:xxii–xxiv, and her notes to line 117).

B 195–200 (A 182–87): Wiþouten pite, Pilour, pouere men þow robbedest . . . dide hem hoppe for hope to haue me at wille: Meed contrasts Conscience's depraved means of journeying out to gain wealth with her comfort and offering of hope to the king's men that they will get *her*—that is, still more wealth. The historical allusion in Conscience's pillaging is somewhat obscure, and perhaps no single campaign is meant; but it is bracketed by the evident following reference to the mourning for Queen Philippa, who died in 1369 (the reference to the king's own **mournyng** in A is tempered and generalized to the court as a whole in B). Bennett's suggestion (1943a:570) that **pouere men þow robbedest / And bere hire bras at þi bak to Caleis to selle** refers to Gaunt's massively destructive series of forays out from Calais in the same year is apt, although depredations by the English in France were common, and Calais, as one of the few continental positions the English still held after Brétigny, was perennially an entrepôt for all transactions between the two countries (see Wallace 2004:22–90). The *Anonimalle Chronicle* lengthily documents the continuous attacks by Gaunt as well as several other English earls and their armies, "burning and devastating the country around," in one foray alone of which were captured "more than four score and ten towns and castles and fortresses" (ed. Galbraith 1927:60); Henry Knighton's *Chronicle* similarly describes the lucrative profits of Sir Robert Knollys' depredations of Auxerre in 1358 (ed. Martin 1995:164–65).

Meed's account of her efforts to comfort and encourage the mourning king and his followers while Conscience is on his journeys resembles some chroniclers' juxtaposition of Queen Philippa's death with the military campaigns out of Calais; the chronicler Thomas Walsingham reports that Alice Perrers "placated" Edward III while he was in mourning for the queen's death (*Chronicon Angliae*, ed. Thomson 1874:95–98. This is perhaps the most plausible instance where Meed directly if briefly evokes Perrers (see Bennett 1943a:566). But Meed's claim to have led all of Edward's **meynee** to **hoppe for**

hope to haue me at wille shows her own emphasis on her abstract status as money. As a charge against Conscience, in the context of the French wars this likely reflects the hope for a vast ransom from the capture of King John (see above B 189–200n), and secondarily from general pillaging during the war, or indeed any war, for the hope for profit from war remains salient through the century and beyond.

234–41: Ac y haue saued myselue sixty thousand lyues . . . as his wyrdus were ordeyned at þe wille of oure lorde: Only this section in C replaces B 195–200; the following new section in C, 242–57, amplifies and anticipates the section on the "selling" of the English claim to France following that, when the three versions again coincide (see 258–64n). The point of the present new section is similar to B 195–200 in contrasting Conscience's military influence to Meed's, but instead of a depredating "Pilour," Conscience is now one who has fearfully restrained (**arwed**) the heroic actions praised by alliterative heroic poetry, whose diction is here parodically invoked: **To berne and to bruttene, to bete adoun strenghtes** (compare *Sir Gawain and the Green Knight*, ed. Andrew and Waldron 1996, lines 1–10). The change confirms that B 195–200 appeared to the C-reviser in terms of Gaunt's long, destructive campaign of 1369, with the English "destroying and burning all the country," for the section recasts the portrait of Conscience directly in opposition to such campaigns, perhaps implying some pity for the French (in contrast to this, however, Huppé [1939:42] thought it unlikely that L would allow "pity for the French poor" in Meed's speech at B 195–200 and thus ruled out an allusion to campaigning in France in those lines). Meed's military influence is changed from inciting desire and expectation for war booty (B 195–200n) to providing ransoms, a major source of income in late medieval wars; the argument is incomplete, since the **sixty thousand lyues** (234) she has **saued** are lives that were put at risk largely by their pursuit of her.

240–41: fortune; wyrdus: In one sermon on the battle of Crécy, Thomas Bradwardine denounced belief in fortune or fates as the cause of victory (Oberman and Weisheipl 1958). Such emphasis on **fortune** bespeaks an outlook conducive to military adventuring, which Meed with her imperial appetites partly embodies; it also aligns her with Lady Philosophy's antagonist in the long tradition of Boethius (see *De consolatione Philosophiae*, 2, ed. and trans. Stewart, Rand, and Tester 1973).

B 201: Hadde I ben Marshal of his men: See below, 256–57n.

242–57: Caytifliche thow, Consience . . . Ne be Marschal ouer my men there y moste fyhte: Meed continues to invoke an ethos of knightly honor that Conscience's restraint or cowardice has violated: now he is the mercenary figure, unwilling to reward loyal service with the kind of generosity appropriate for **þe kynde of a kyng**. Above, 130, the king, also in C only, speaks courteously "as his kynde wolde." At 1.67, another C only passage, Holy Church similarly explains Lucifer's actions by his "kynde." The terms may point to a late stratum of the poet's language or view of human (or superhuman) nature.

The lines almost certainly allude to the treaty of Brétigny, when Edward III yielded his claim to the title of king of France in exchange for a promise of 3,000,000 écus (£667,000); they start by virtually repeating, then greatly expand on, three lines of B, still left below as two lines in C: "Cowardly þow, Conscience, . . . þe richeste Reaume þat reyn ouerhoueþ" (B 206–8; cp. C 263–64). C's clarification of B confirms the allusion: **leten / In his enemyes handes his heritage of Fraunce** (242–43). The treaty did not in fact turn out well; see above, B 189–200n. **Vnconnynge** (244) may raise the implication, beyond her intentional chiding, that any strategic errors that were made in that or other efforts at peace were the result of ignorance about the final outcome. But "ignorant" is no praise for royal policy.

244: a kyndom to sulle: Meed continues to criticize the treaty of Brétigny, in which Edward III for a time gave up his larger claims to the French crown. But the phrase also evokes more literally a rumor appearing in many chroniclers under the year 1387 as one of the bases for the rising of the Lords Appellant against the king. As the *Westminster Chronicle* says, "There were reports at this time that prompted by some of the counselors who surrounded him, the king of England proposed to relinquish to the king of the French, for a lump sum to be mutually agreed, all his overseas castles, towns, and other possessions, except Aquitaine, for which he would willingly do homage to the French king provided that he was freely allowed to hold it in his own hand as peaceably and quietly as his predecessors had done in the past" (ed. and trans. Hector and Harvey 1982:204–5). Other writers describe outrage about this (Froissart, trans. Brereton 1978:425; Walsingham repeatedly mentions and more vividly elaborates the rumor, *Chronicon Angliae*, ed. Thomson 1874:383, 385; *Historia Anglicana*, ed. Riley 1864, 2.170). The rumor was evidently groundless, part of the pro-Appellant propaganda; it does not appear in later charges against Richard (*Westminster Chronicle*, ed. Hector and Harvey 1982:lxi-lxii). Since this date is near the outside limit for C (but not impossible; see Hanna 1993:16), possibly the rumor had earlier incarnations as well, as indeed it could have had at any point from the disappointing ransom of King John through the treaty of Brétigny. For possible topical relevance to 1388 in the C additions here, see also below, 407–11n, 408n.

256–57: sholde neuere Consience be my constable . . . Ne be Marschal: constable is the king's chief household officer, **Marschal**, the king's chief military commander, and the two together are the king's two principal military officers, whose joint responsibility for military discipline and martial law led to the Court of Chivalry, where disputes between private gentlemen on matters concerning their honor were settled (McKisack 1959:265). Meed's comment might imply that Conscience in fact does represent such figures and institutions, part of her point that if he speaks for royal policy, he must seek effective and honorable ways to carry that out militarily. In 1379 the reliance on civil rather than common law by the Court of Chivalry led to complaints in Parliament against the constable and marshall (Rot. Parl. 3.65); since Conscience is generally identified with equity (see Prol.95–135n), and thus with a trend of finding other options than common law, this association might be behind Meed's complaints.

Specific topical identifications are inappropriate, but the holders of these offices comprised the kind of aristocratic royal policy makers and users of civil law with whom Meed loosely aligns Conscience. The office of constable (*constabularius*), deemed higher than that of marshall, was held by the Bohuns, earls of Hereford from the twelfth century; after the last earl of Bohun died in 1373 the office passed by an elder daughter's marriage to Thomas of Woodstock, duke of Gloucester, until his murder in 1397, when it went to the husband of the younger Bohun daughter, Henry, earl of Derby (Henry IV). The office of marshall (*magister marescallus*) followed a much more contested path; it was held first by the family that took the name Marshall, then after several shifts with the extinctions of male issue Edward III granted it for life only to William de Montagu, earl of Salisbury. Then at the Court of Claims at Richard II's coronation, it was unsuccessfully sought by Margaret "Marshall," countess of Norfolk; after this extraordinary claim by a woman to hold the position failed, in 1380 Richard gave it to his half-brother Thomas, earl of Kent, for life, but Richard then took it from him in 1385 and gave it for life to Thomas Mowbray, earl of Nottingham, the heir-apparent of Margaret, countess of Norfolk (although she remained alive until 1400). When Mowbray was banished in 1398, his dukedom was considered forfeit, and in 1399 Henry IV granted the office to the earl of Westmoreland for life (Cokayne 1910–59, vol. 2.603–14; see also Cokayne 1910–59, vol. 10.91–99).

258–64 (B 201–8, A 188–95): Ac hadde y, mede, ben marchel of his men in Fraunce . . . his lordschipe for a litel mone: This initial passage on the treaty of Brétigny (see above B 189–200n, 242–57n) is stridently ironic; **To lete so his lordschipe for a litel mone** (C 264 [B 207]) is as demeaning of the English agreement as "dym cloude" is about their supposed dread at the storm of

April 1359 (B 191–94n). Prsl observes that "the possibility cannot be excluded that the reference is to . . . some more petty truce," but there is little doubt that the presentation of the Brétigny treaty in C's new lines returns to the same topic as the B passage, signalled by the near-repetition of the key phrase, **Vnconnyngliche [B, A: Cowardly] þow, Consience, conseiledest hym / To lete so his lordschipe** (263 [B 206]) at the beginning of the section inserted in C (above, 242–43). Richard's efforts in the 1380s to find some peace in France would maintain the topicality of any remarks on such actions of diplomacy; Froissart puts similar opinions about royal pusillanimity in the mouth of Thomas of Woodstock, duke of Gloucester, criticizing in the late 1390s Richard's past French policies (tran. Brereton 1978:421–23).

By calling the royal policies **Cowardly** in B and A Meed daringly claims that the true potential for military bravado by the English would be unleashed by her "command" (i.e., her values and principles). Heroic diction again fleetingly surfaces to describe the king's power, **He sholde haue ben lord of þat lond alenghe and abrede**, and sustained by encouragment of kingly generosity for loyal followers: **The leeste brolle of his blod a Barones pere** (C 260–62 [B 203–5]; with the reading "lond" for "blod," the B manuscripts R and F witness a B sub-archetypal reading that frames this as an even more broadly general egalitarianism). A similar phrase appears in Henry Knighton's chronicle when describing the great rewards gained from Robert Knollys' *chivauchée* in France in 1358, perhaps similarly seen nostalgically in light of the later setbacks: "ipsi abstulerunt, rapuerunt, et asportauerunt bona innumera, et ibi diuites sunt nimis. Et non erat ibi Anglus tam pauper, quin de auro et argento et aliis iocalibus, et preciosis, ad plenum ditatus est" ("and [the English] took away, seized, and carried off uncounted goods; for there people are exceedingly rich. And there was no Englishman there so poor but that with gold and silver and other jewels and precious things he was made a wealthy man": ed. Martin 1995:164–65 [translation mine]). Meed's endorsement is more warmly chivalric, and actually less focused on money.

258 (B 201, A 188): Hadde I ben Marchal of his men: The statement might have topical interest at the time of B, because of the failed but remarkable claim to hold the office of marshall by Margaret, countess of Norfolk, made in the Court of Claims at Richard's coronation in 1376, a period suited to many of B's, but also some of C's topical possibilities; see above, 256–57n, and below, 367–70n.

265–81 (B 209–26, A 196–213): Hit bycometh for a kyng þat shal kepe a reume . . . Marchaundise and mede mot nede go togedere: All of these uses of money are in themselves acceptable, even laudable or pious (e.g. the mass-pence of line 279), except that they are generalized into the whole system of society with no room for other ethical or social bases or motives. For the basis in Aristotle, see above 221–83n. But seeing society as defined chiefly by and for income and reward is a different matter from the Aristotelean statement about exchange value as a basic foundation for justice and civic communication. By presenting the estates and professions one by one as focused not on duty to the commonweal or commitment to traditional vocation—the ideals behind most medieval social theory, including a widely disseminated sermon by Thomas Wimbledon in the 1380s, *Redde Rationem Villicationis Tue* (ed. Knight 1967; see Prol.22–94n)—but on payment, the list presents self-interest as an ideal for the entire social hierarchy, an implied, miniature estates satire in its purest form. To some extent, the view of social estates was drifting toward distinctions by income rather than traditional status: in the Statute and Ordinance of Laborers of 1349 and again 1388, and the sumptuary ordinance of 1363, social ranks appear defined as much by income as by estate (see Galloway 2000:25–26). Meed's view sharpens this possibility to an extreme point. So too, the view that a king should be generous is typical and uncontroversial, if tending toward quantifiable "gratitude" (even down, by Henry VIII's time, to calling taxes "benevolences" to indicate subjects' "fondness" for the king; see Galloway 1994:383). But Meed's claim that money **maketh hym byloued and for a man yholde** (268; see also 231, 250), is again an extreme view of the transactional nature of loyalty and of "manhede," and, especially in the context of the preceding discussion of the brutality and violence Meed would unleash (238), it implies constant aggression.

Meed's views of society as based on self-interested transactions are, in sum, not parodic or specious, and may even be prescient. Thomas Norton's *Ordinal of Alchemy* (c. 1470; ed. Reidy 1975) presents a similar description of the universal desire for money that should be considered an important part of the reception history of Lady Meed: his introduction declares that "euery state which is within mankynde" seeks to know alchemy "Only for appetite of lucour and richesse," and this leads him to list how every social estate desires wealth:

As popis with cardynales of dignitee,
Archbissopis & bissoppis of hye degree,
with abbottis & priours of religion,
with freris, heremites & prestis many on,
And kingis, with princis, lordis grete of blode,
For euery estate desirith after goode;
And merchantis al-so which dwelle in fyre
Of brennyng couetise haue therto desire . . .

He continues listing those whose "brennyng couetise" leads them to pursue alchemy, noting that "comon workmen . . . as wel as lordis . . . loue þis noble craft," and mentioning goldsmiths, freemasons, tanners, parish clerks, stainers, glazers, and tinkers who all bend their efforts in pursuit of wealth and his abstruse art of alchemy. But for Norton, writing in the late fifteenth century, this survey of universal self-interest and monetary greed is not grounds for moral condemnation but only for a better and more readable guide like his that might help such seekers after wealth, who are only to be pitied for wasting their efforts in "hasty credence to fume a-wai theire thrifte" (Prohemium, lines 18–46).

282–83 (cp. B 227, A 214): Is no lede þat leueth þat he ne loueth mede / And glad for to grype here, gret lord oþer pore [B, A: No wiȝt, as I wene, wiþouten Mede may libbe]: The basic phrase recalls the proverb, recorded in *Havelok* and elsewhere, that "He was ful wis þat first yaf mede!" (ed. Smithers 1987, line 1636, where some analogues are cited). The argumentative use of the idea in Meed's own (apparently novel) proverb is more subtle yet also more self-indicting. In B and A, Meed's concluding thesis is modest; in C her conclusion draws attention to a desire for Meed that may easily be aligned with the trust in worldly goods on which Lucifer relies (see 1.67n). The avaricious "love" and "gladness" **for to grype here** suggests cupidinous desire (for the same earthy phrase, see Meed's remark to Conscience that he has "grypen my gold" [above, 228; see also Conscience's retort, B 250]). This focus on the intention and outlook of users of money is the opening that C's more than B's version of Conscience's rebuttal takes, since in C more than B Conscience emphasizes the importance of faith and obedience to God's will in both human and divine rewards.

285 (B 229, A 216): "Mede is worthy . . . þe maistrye to haue": Claiming **maistrye to haue** (i.e., 'win a victory'; MED) is a traditional, militaristic way to describe the outcome of a debate: cp. the debate with the pagans in *Life of St. Katherine* where Katherine's "witti & wis . . . wordes . . . mot meistre[n] us alle" (ed. d'Ardenne 1961:27). The repeated variations on "maistrye" and "maistre" throughout the scene charge the situation with the sense of a battle (see also 215 [B 169], 443 [B 290], also 4.132 [B.4.135]), a common way to define debate (see Enders 1992:129–61).

Conscience's rebuttal: the B and A texts

B 231–51 (A 218–30): "Ther are two manere of Medes . . . Shal abien it bittre or þe book lieþ": Conscience's rebuttal ignores the charges of pusillanimity and the focus on military and royal power, and changes the style of the debate from Meed's flyting to a preacher's elucidation of multiple meanings in words. The tone and genre of the debate shift from her highly secular range of values to his highly clerical range, an effect increased substantially in the C text by the addition of 286–412.

Conscience's rebuttal in B and A seeks to answer by two tactics Meed's final claim in those texts, that meed is necessary to uphold the kingdom and its social ties. First (B 231–51), he distinguishes between two kinds of meed, only one of which is indeed profitable and legitimate because it is the reward that God gives **To hem þat werchen wel while þei ben here** (B 233). The other subverts and destroys because it brings down God's wrath on individuals as well as kingdoms, the latter instanced below by the "vengeaunce" that "fel on Saul and on his children," a passage where the versions again coincide (B 259–77; see below, 407–32n). Thus far from helping kings rule (as Meed has claimed: B 209: see above, 265–81n), improper elevation of meed above trust in God leads to the ruin of kingdoms. So too, the proper kind of meed, God's reward, is far beyond Meed's claims for herself. Conscience's strategy here is to broaden the scope of the terms beyond the social field that Meed has presented. As Adams points out about the entire section in B, the shift in defining heavenly meed to a context of just and equitable divine reward risks implying a "semi-Pelagian" point of view, where "the hallmark of God's grace is its correlation with the previous good deeds and merit of the recipient" (Adams 1988a:219). It should be noted, however, that God's rewarding of those who **werchen wel** is made not on the basis of the absolute merit of good deeds, but out **of [God's] grace . . . in his blisse** (B 232). This is what late medieval theologians would call "merit *de congruo*," which is not the same as Pelagianism, since it involves God's freely self-imposed obligation to infuse his grace in everyone who has done his best, *facientibus in se quod est, Deus non denegat gratiam* ("to those doing what is in them, God will not deny grace"), repaying good works with his grace, but only "as if" such good works were worthy. A universe of Pelagian exchange of works for grace is thus allowed, but maintained only by God's free choice to do so, not because of any real equity between the terms involved (see Coleman 1981; Oberman 1983:131–45; Adams 1988a:230n13 [although there claiming that nothing "so technical is intended" by the poet]; Adams 1983; Adams 1988b; Courtenay 1987:307–24; Lawler 2000:124). For further commentary on the issue, see below, B 248n, C 348–51n, and 352–54n.

Just as Meed has redefined Conscience as "royal policy" and thus necessarily in need of her (see above, 226–28n), so Conscience redefines Meed as essentially not the kinds of reward that are good both on earth or in heaven:

he removes from her whole parts of the identity that she has claimed. Thus, having distinguished two kinds of reward, measured and unmeasured, Conscience's second tactic (B 255–58) is to exclude altogether from the term "meed" the payment to laborers and to merchants for goods, the instances of "necessary meed" on which Meed had closed her argument (above, B 225–26 = C 280–81). Thus as Mitchell says, "the point that Conscience is trying to make is not that there are good sorts of reward and bad sorts of reward, but rather that there are only two things that deserve to be called by the name of Meed, reward, at all, namely the heavenly reward of God and the rewards given to wrongdoers" (1956 [1969]:183). Since Meed is not the first kind of reward, she is left simply embodying "bad reward," a drastically narrowed meaning of the allegorical figure before us, whose lineage and status even Theology was willing to find redeemable (2.123n, 124n, 125n). In so detaching major notions of "reward" from her identity, namely, wages for honest work and divine reward for good deeds, Conscience strives to shrink the meaning of the vibrant entity that has for so extended a section dominated the poem. Such a strategy has special power when dealing with an allegorical personification. Indeed, after his redefinition of her, her role in the poem loses its dramatic proportions, even though she remains present through the following passus. For further discussion of the logic of Conscience's argument, see below, B 255–58n.

**B 234a, 237a, 241a (A 221a): *Domine, quis habitabit in tabernaculo tuo?*; *Qui ingreditur sine macula & operatur Iusticiam*; *Qui pecuniam suam non dedit ad vsuram et munera super innocentem &c:* "Lord, who will dwell in your tabernacle?"; "He who walks without blemish and works justice"; "He who has not put his money out to usury [nor taken] bribes against the innocent": all quotations from Psalm 14 (lines 1, 2, and 5), used to define the first "manere" of meed, admittance into God's grace. On the importance of this psalm in the poem, already used by Holy Church to define the saved, see especially 2.39–42n, also Prol.15n.

Conscience is here answering Meed not by logic but by authority. Yet there is an implied argument in the use of the psalm: the psalm, defining the reward of God's grace as excluding those with ill-gotten rewards, allows Conscience to introduce the notions of "justice" and "innocence" to show that Meed's presentation of herself and of reward excludes any moral scope.

B 236–37: þis askeþ Dauid. / And Dauid assoileþ it hymself: On such awareness of the rhetorical structure of Psalm 14, see 2.39n, 41n.

B 242–44 / A 222–24: B: And alle þat helpen þe Innocent and holden with þe riȝtfulle, / Wiþouten Mede doþ hem good . . . shul haue þis firste Mede / A: Tak no mede, my lord, of men þat ben trewe . . . Godis mede & his mercy þerwiþ miȝte þou wynne: Many of the English lines appearing next to the Latin can be matched to lines in Psalm 14 or seen as summarizing its point; an apparent exception, however, is the claim—in the only passage in this section which is found in different forms in A and B—that one should not take money from the innocent for one's services, **Wiþouten Mede doþ hem good**, a view directed to the king in A and recast to **alle** in B. The basis for the claim is the deliberate and consistent construing of the Vulgate *munera super innocentem non accepit* as "He [who] does not take money from the innocent" rather than (its literally correct meaning, which the poet likely knew), "He [who] does not take bribes against the innocent": see 2.39–42n. Thus there is no reason to take the English lines in B as a reference to Luke 6:35, "Do good, and lend to one another, expecting nothing in return" (so Bnt). Conscience's point is quite different from the Lucan passage. B's use of Psalm 14 line 5 in the Pardon passus shows the same forced construal of *super* as "from, of" rather than "against": "For þe Sauter saueþ hem noȝt, *swiche as take ȝiftes*, / And nameliche *of Innocentȝ . . . / Super innocentem munera non accipies*" (B.7.41–42a; emphasis added). That C drops all these passages does not necessarily show a full rejection of this construal, as 2.38 shows, but it may show a retreat from emphasizing that eccentric interpretation of the psalm's monetary ethics.

B 246: Ther is a Mede mesurelees þat maistres desireþ: Added in B, this more clearly distinguishes the second meed than does A (see above, B 231–52n). The claim is that a reward is bad when one cannot determine how much it "should" be for the specific thing or labor purchased, but the reward is accepted nonetheless as a binding contract for the thing or labor. It is in effect a contract without an extrinsic, fixed reference point of value. This is the center of Conscience's argument against her in both B and C. His basic claim echoes Thomistic thought about money and its abuses, especially usury. Money, Aquinas says quoting Aristotle (*Ethics* 5.5 and *Politics* 1.5, 6), was "devised primarily for the purpose of effecting exchanges; and so the proper and principal use of money is the consumption or alienation (*distractio*) of it, whereby it is expended in making purchases. Therefore, in itself, it is unlawful to receive a price for the use of money lent, which is called usury" (*Summa Theologiae* IIa IIae, qu. 78, art. 1, resp). Aquinas accordingly (like Conscience offering two definitions of meed) distinguishes two kinds of exchange: the first is of completely equal value, without gain, and is "natural and necessary, by means of which one thing is exchanged for another, or things for money to meet the needs of life," and this is "praiseworthy, because it serves natural needs." The second kind of exchange is "money for money or of things for money, not to meet the needs of life, but to acquire gain," and this is "justly condemned, because, in itself, it serves the desire for gain, which knows no limit but extends to infinity" (*Summa Theologiae*, IIa IIae, qu. 77, art. IV, resp.). Conscience's definitions of Meed as measureless seem in part to be a case of a transferred epithet: as Thomas, in his second kind, describes desire for gain as extending to infinity, so Conscience describes Meed herself as extending to infinity, measureless. The position was common enough in medieval economic thought, and often used to insist on a fixed market price and the need to avoid usury, but by the fourteenth century it was used to allow less commensurability between monetary value and a good's isolated value; profit was increasingly justified within the "equivalence" scheme by claiming that including merchants' skill, labor, and risk as "worth" the profits they earned (see Kaye 1998:137–40). The problem of measurable and unmeasurable entities preoccupied other intellectual realms in the period. For a contemporary exposition of how incommensurability defines some aspects of the movements of planets and thus God's creation, see Nicholas Oresme's *De commensurabilitate*, the third book of which is a dialogue in which Mathematics (arguing for commensurability) debates Geometry (arguing for incommensurability of the heavens); the dialogue ends by the narrator awakening without Apollo, who is presiding, rendering a judgment (ed. Grant 1971; see also Kaye 1998:214).

When Conscience merges such a claim with ideas of God's rewards, this also leads to some paradoxes. As Adams notes, condemning "measureless" rewards suggests that good, heavenly reward is in contrast measured, implicitly in accord to one's merit. But this is a heretical position since it grants merit real "buying power" over salvation. Adams argues that the need to qualify this heretically "Pelagian" theology in response to a more rigorously Augustinian position (revived in the fourteenth century by Thomas Bradwardine among others) "that divine grace has *no relationship whatsoever* to preceding human 'good works' or merits" (Adams 1988a:219–20), was a chief reason for C's alteration of Conscience's rebuttal to Meed. Yet even in B, Conscience does not explicitly draw the corollary implication about divine reward as "measured"; this silence allows him to keep in divine reward an element of contingency and gratuity in God's recognition of merit ("god of his grace gyueþ in his blisse" [B 232; see B 231–51n]), while still using the implications of divine measure in Psalm 14 to generate the contrasting category of the "measureless" meed of bribery and maintenance. Below, the story of Saul presents several instances of *un*measured divine punishment, when God threatens to destroy Agag "and al his peple after . . . for a dede þat doon hadde hire eldres" (B 262–3 = C 415–16), and Saul "And al his seed" (B 277 = C 430).

B 249 (A 228): *In quorum manibus iniquitates sunt; dextra eorum repleta est muneribus*: "In whose hands are iniquities; their right hand is full of gifts": Psalm 25:10. The preceding notion of "mede mesurelees" (see note above) is supported by the reference to hands full of gifts, if one understands *repleta* as "overflowing," hence "measureless" rather than simply "full." In turn, the quotation informs Conscience's following statement about "he þat gripeþ hir giftes" (B 250), where "gripeþ" is 'obtaining' such rewards (MED *gripen* 2b) without implying thereby some precise measurement of them. In both the Latin and English statements, "gifts" invokes the uncertain relation between merit and payment that Conscience condemns. For Meed the word "gifts" signals a principle of social harmony (e.g., B 184, 211ff., etc. = C 230, 267ff., etc.); for Conscience it invariably signals a principle of social destruction and moral anxiety, chiefly, bribes (e.g., B 126 = C 163). See the transferred position of this line to the narrator's interpolation at C 118–18a, above (see note).

B 252–54a (A 231–33a): Preestes and persons þat plesynge desireþ . . . *Amen amen Receperunt mercedem suam*: The point answers Meed's argument that priests take meed (B 223–24 = C 278–79), as Conscience moves through her closing sequence of instances of 'necessary meed.' "Amen, Amen, they have received their reward": Mt 6:5, in the context of hypocrites who pray in public in order to be seen as pious, and whose reward is earthly honor (only): that the clerks here desire **plesynge** follows the scriptural context. A's reading, **Shal haue mede on þis molde þat matthew haþ grauntid**, adopted for B by KD-B, is more metrical than archetypal B (as in Schm: "Taken hire mede here as Matthew us techeth").

B 255–58 (A 234–37): That laborers and lowe lewede folk . . . a penyworþ for anoþer: For the traditional argument that money should effect an exactly equal exchange, see above, B 246n. Finishing here his reply to Meed's instances of "necessary meed," Conscience segregates labor and merchandise from **Mede** altogether, making "meed" in sum now a concept for what is not **mesurable hire**, not a **permutacion** of exchangeable value, i.e., Meed is neither fair wages or equitable exchange: hence implicitly she is only the evil, measureless forms of meed (or *munera*) that he described above.

It is worth reviewing the logic by which Conscience has achieved this progressive shrinking or caging of the definition or identity of Meed. His rebuttal in B has progressively cordoned off possible meanings of her: he asserts in B that her identity is in fact neither "divine reward" nor "due earthly payment for labor and goods." Conscience's ability to carry this dual restriction forward depends on some slender distinctions between kinds of meed that are Meed and kinds of meed that are not, and between kinds of measureless rewards that are bad, and kinds of measureless rewards that are good. He first defines Meed as a bad form of "mesurelees" (246) reward (i.e., presumably a reward driven by the "infinite" desire for gain, and opposed to the virtue of moderation as well as equivalency in exchanges; see 1.33n); she is thus not to be identified with a transaction between strict equivalents, "a penyworþ for anoþer" (258), in the Aristotelean phrase. In the level of the allegory, she always offers something more than strict equivalence, in the desire for infinite gain she solicits— figured preeminently in the "ravishment" that she induces upon the narrator and most others who view her and use her. Yet at nearly the same time Conscience defines salvation as an altogether different kind of unmeasurable reward ("þis firste Mede / Of god . . . whan þei gon hennes" [B 244–45]). He then identifies her with simoniacal payments to "Preestes and persons" "for masses þat þei syngeþ" (252–53)—and this time he puts her on the side of inappropriately "measured" value, since by the definition of simony, the priests and parsons are condemned for appraising, and selling, at worldly prices an infinite good of spiritual value (*Summa Theologiae* IIa IIae qu. 100 art. 1, resp.).

Conscience's definition of her in B denies her a claim on fulfilling the justice that both the divine and the earthly kinds of reward he uses as references otherwise possess. She is left defined as measureless and measurable in all the wrong ways. Yet Conscience's accomplishment has relied on extracting just those wrong elements of "reward" from the whole range of earthly and spiritual transactions, and thus he is left with an energetic display of his analytic powers but with no essential control of just when Meed, as he has defined her, enters into either kind of transaction. He cannot indeed marry her since he sees her so pejoratively, but neither can he protect himself or others from her, since his argument has shown that to define her presence precisely in any given transaction is an arduous matter, and that the effort to define her once and for all, in order that everyone might see her immediately in every transaction she might enter, is impossible.

Conscience's rebuttal: the C text

286–412: "Nay," quod Consience to þe kyng, "clerkes witeth þe sothe . . . and ȝaf the kyndom to his knaue þat kept shep and lambren": Conscience's final terms in B for what is *not* "meed," **mesurable hire** and **permutacion**, offer relatively sophisticated analytical distinctions of reward in the vernacular (see above esp. B 246n, B 255–58n). C's revision offers an ambitious expansion of the intellectual possibilities of vernacular poetry (see below, 343n). As in Holy Church's speech, puns and word-play are crucial to Conscience's logic in C (see Overstreet 1984). Much of what is elaborated here, however, has a general fidelity to the ideal of labor, faith, and payment presented in the claims by Piers Plowman himself about his wages from Truth, in the first appearance of the plowman in the poem, and present from the A text on (see 7.182–99 [B.5.537–55, A.6.25–42]; and see below, 348–51n).

The section as a whole is no longer a closely argued attack against Lady Meed's points but a rhetorical tour-de-force of its own; no answer to Conscience's claims is offered or seems expected. Whether as the poet's attempt to present a "lower profile" to "those heresy hunters eager to sniff out any sentimental suggestion of a correlation between natural merit and divine reward" (Adams 1988a:220), or as the poet's indulgence in his verbal and intellectual sophistication for its own sake, or both, the speech causes the debate to lose much of the tempo it had in B. As a poetic achievement, its new nuances of thought and rhetorical elaborations must be balanced against the loss of confrontational excitement that the lengthy and complex speech allows. But dramatic tension remains a significant element throughout the C revisions, here and elsewhere, as the notes on 47–49, 52, 66, 77–127, 118–18a, 343, 363–73, 367–70, and 485–88 variously suggest.

Reversing the order of B's and A's section, the new presentation first develops reward in human spheres (291–351), then introduces terms that suggest reward in spiritual and divine senses. The direction of development is not linear; the definition of religious reward (good and bad, salvation and damnation) turns rapidly back to secular circumstances as metaphors, whose tenors imply further elements of proper reward in secular life (labor; inheritance; marriage; royal privileges). The weaving together of the religious and secular constitutes the section's subtlest achievement, although the pattern linking these is the most disputed section of the passage: the exposition of an analogy from grammar.

In this analogy, the argument, as Smith points out, is centrally preoccupied with defining not just remuneration but **relacioun**, the circumstantial nature of which subtends any exchange and reward, and the poem's treatments can be compared to philosophical as well as grammatical contexts (Smith 1994, and 2001:157–70). The concept is clearly linked to the allegorical plot at the beginning and end of the speech in C: Conscience begins by declaring that Meed has an ongoing and corrupt relationship with Guile (**euermore**

a mayntenour of Gyle, 287), and Conscience concludes the passus, in C only, by stating that whoever accepts Meed is guilty of being a receiver of Guile (**rescetour of Gyle**, 500). Meed's *relations* to evil, and human beings to her, frame the discussion. Meed does not consistently appear to be an intrinsically evil figure; instead, as the grammatical analogy suggests more clearly than the arguments in B, she is the principle of indirect relation and indirect reward that produces evil by her relation to her user.

Indirect relations are elsewhere condemned in similarly grammatical and theological terms in Alan of Lille's twelfth-century *De planctu Naturae*, where Nature occupies an unreliable mediating role between God and human beings, and thus where Nature draws sexuality into forms presented as dangerous and perverse, which are similarly defined in grammatical terms. Meed is like Alan's Nature in this sense, and the twelfth-century work is one of the likely backgrounds to the section (no definitive echoes have been identified, but see Schmidt 1987:58–59 et passim). Other uses of grammar to define theology and cosmology appear throughout medieval writing, but usually in fragmentary rather than sustained forms (see the surveys in Alford 1982 and Brinkmann 1980:21–51); whether L elaborated any one of these—such as the brief grammatical consideration of the word *credo* in the Nicene Creed found in numerous places from the fourth century on (see below 356–60n)—into Conscience's large structure of thought, or whether he used Alan's sustained but quite different use of the grammatical analogy as direct inspiration, remains uncertain. More even than most of PP, this section draws on varied and often to us obscure poetic models and rhetorical inspirations.

288–90: As þe sauhter sayth by such . . . hauen large handes / To ȝeue men mede: Recalls Psalm 25:10, already (partially) quoted by Meed herself (above, 118–18a and n). Meed has flatteringly paraphrased the phrase *dextra eorum repleta* ("their right hand is full") as having "riche handes"; Conscience's paraphrase **large handes** is grotesquely unflattering (with an ironic reminder in the second sense of **large**, 'lavish,' of the proper kind of **handes** to have).

291–332: Ac ther is mede and mercede . . . And efte haue hit aȝeyne of hem þat don ylle: Instead of two kinds of "meed" (only one of which turns out to be Meed herself) as in B (see above, B 231–51n), Conscience now clarifies with two distinct terms, both rewards (**A desert for som doynge**). The section first defines **Mede** (293–303) then, shifting mid-line, **mercede** (303–32). (For controversy about that point of division, see below, 315–32n.) **Mede** is now defined as payment **bifore þe doynge** (293) and *pre manibus* (300n): a measureless reward, because the prepayment may not be the full price, as in the case of usury, where a "gift" is often presented at the point of borrowing the money, and the money and perhaps still more must be returned later (for some discussion of the manipulation of such "gifts" see *Dives and Pauper*, 7.25; ed. Barnum 1980:199). Prepayment also characterizes bribes and transactions with trades that are not protected by civic laws (such as prostitutes or doctors: 301). In general, prepayment is seen as either a presumptuous claim on future time itself (296–97) or a deceit, if one never intends to fulfill the **doynge** in question, as with a "gift" advanced in usury. Both cases lack a basis of real merit that, in Conscience's view, must precede reward. On the general clerical concern with usury as "selling" time, see Le Goff 1980:29–42.

Conscience's view seems less concerned with selling time as such, than with the merit of a **doynge**, an ethic of committed labor that is keyed to the central issue of the poem, doing well, and against which everything, from writing poetry to speculation in money or ideas, must be measured and usually falls short. In its assessments, the poem is much less focused on intention than, for example, *Dives and Pauper*, where the mechanisms of usury, simony, etc. are all less important than the intention and knowledge of those making the transactions (ed. Barnum 1980, e.g., 178–80, 198–99). As throughout this section, the focus is on the laborer or professional claiming the reward or money, rather than the lord or the client delivering it. But the ethics of doing and being rewarded emerge in this passage as requiring a broad context of mutual faith; see below note to 333–406a. Ultimately, prepayment includes receiving honor and reward on earth as opposed to salvation later in heaven: as Patience later says (most succinctly and explicitly in B), "god is of a wonder wille, by þat kyne wit sheweþ, / To ȝyue many men his mercymonye er he it haue deserued. / Riȝt so fareþ god by som riche; ruþe me it þynkeþ, / For þei han hir hire heer and heuene as it were" (B.14.126–29; cp. C.15.295–306a). When Truth does pay Piers Plowman, however, "He is þe presteste payere þat eny pore man knoweth; / He withhalt non hewe his huyre ouer euen" (7.195–96 [B.5.551–52, A.6.38–39]). But the work must go unrewarded until the "euen," that is, in terms of salvation, at death. For a further display in PP of payments offered before the doing, see above, 38–67n; note also the sequence of payment and service for lawyers at 2.160–66n, and the same issue at 9.44–45 (C only), where it defines the reason that lawyers do not get pardoned.

mercede, due reward paid **at þe ende** rather than first (303), seems to be L's neologism, an anglicized form of the Latin *merces* (accusative *mercedem*), which is the word used throughout the Latin Vulgate for wages, rewards, and sometimes the reward of eternal life (Overstreet 1984:284n87; Adams 1988a:218). Usually *merces* is translated as "mede" in the Wycliffite Bible (ed. Forshall and Madden 1850); L's distinctive term is an effort to produce a new, self-evident entity, perhaps, like all coinages of nomenclature, in order to establish it as a concept not needing long explication and continual nuancing as Conscience's definitions of two *kinds* of meed required in B. (If so, the purpose failed.) The term may have occurred to L from the Latin quotation of Mt. 5:6, cited at different points in each of the three versions (A 63–64a, B 252–54a, C 311–12; see notes on these), and surely not from any prior English use. A few scattered uses of **mercede** appear from the late sixteenth century to mean 'a gift' (see OED), which is not Conscience's sense, although possibly these spring from some common source. But **mercede** also seems confusingly close to Middle English "mercyede," 'repaid,' from "mercien," used above in the pejorative sense 'bribed' at 21. Why Conscience coins a word for good reward so close to a pejorative one is unclear. The medieval penchant for seeing words (especially Latin ones) as intimately and inextricably tied to realities here achieves both a strong assertion but a strained demonstration.

294–95: And þat is nother resoun ne ryhte . . . That eny man Mede toke but he hit myhte deserue: The term **Mede** instead of "mercede" fleetingly used for a just payment seems to confuse the categories just presented, requiring the positing of a momentary loosening of Conscience's tight control over his diction (Adams 1988a:224). A zealous effort at rationalization might be productive: the payment in question is illicit "meed" in the circumstance described by the clause, **That eny man Mede toke**; it only *becomes* "mercede" when it enters the condition defined by the next clause, **but he hit myhte deserue**.

300: *pre manibus*: "Before-hand"; found in this form or in the Anglo-Norman "avaunt la mayn" in legal records describing advance payments, "often associated with usurious or unethical agreements" (Alford, *Gloss.*, citing examples). See above, 38–67n, 291–332n, and other passages cited there. Payment for illegal activities (e.g., prostitution, quackery) was demanded in advance of the service or product because there was no legal basis if the client or purchaser refused to pay later; usury often involved a valuable advance security (amounting to the usurious interest) for the same reason. Aquinas offers a more subtle connection between usury and advance payments below the just price for goods: "if a buyer wishes to buy for less than the just price, on the ground that he pays the money before the thing can be delivered to him, it is a sin of usury, because that paying of money in advance has the character of a loan, the price of which is the amount deducted from the just price of the thing bought" (*Summa Theologiae* IIa IIae, qu. 78, art. 2, resp.). See also above, 291–332n. But L's phrase also appears describing the common practice of lawyers, 9.44–45.

308a: *Non morabitur opus mersenarii &c:* "The wages of him [that has been hired by you] shall not abide [with you until the morning]": Lev 19:13. A proof-text in canon law for prompt payment (Alford, *Quot.*). See Piers Plowman's comment on Truth's payment before "euen" (as noted above, 291–332n).

309–10: And ther is resoun as a reue . . . and the laborer be leely yserued: Briefly approaching the B text again, the miniature manorial allegory recasts the B reply to Meed concerning laborers, above B 255–58n; the relationship between the laborer and his lord is now kept (tacitly this time) from the category of "meed" because (**That** = "so that") it is mediated by proper accounting (**resoun**), just as the accounts between lords and laborers are mediated by reeves.

311–12: The mede þat many prestes . . . *Mercedem suam receperunt:* See above, B 252–54a and note, and A 63–64a and note.

313–14: In Marchandise is no mede . . . on peneworth for another: C's only completely intact preservation of a stretch of B until the end of the inserted section; see B 246n, and B 255–58n. The traditional point that proper economic exchanges must be "equivalent" remains crucial to Conscience's argument in C.

315–32: And thow the kyng of his cortesye, Cayser or pope . . . And efte haue hit aȝeyne of hem þat don ylle: An exception to exact exchange is a gift; this is rendered ethical by declaring the basis for the gift in love, and the possession of the gift as conditional on deserving the love. Conscience's effort to define good gifts is not so much an answer to Meed as an answer to his own B text condemnation of all gifts, by which he typically means payments for maintenance and bribes (see e.g., B 250). Here, the gift carries a contract in it, which obtains only so long as the loyalty persists. The gift also seems potentially inexhaustible; Conscience seems to imagine a king who is a conqueror (like William I), and who could make "large giftes" without concern for the short supply of available lands to give, always a concern when later medieval kings wished to reward followers. Landlordship was rarely so efficacious; for most landholders, themselves tenants, complex legal machinery was necessary to make any changes in tenancy (see Waugh 1991:100–1). But English kings gave to the followers they chose lands or incomes from lands that had been confiscated to the crown (e.g. due to lack of heirs), and from the thirteenth century on, they could and often did freely remove tenants (*per voluntatem*), in spite of Magna Carta's claim that the king could disseise only by legal process, a product of baronial wishful thinking never corresponding to practice (see Milsom 1976:24–25).

There is considerable debate about what term the feudal examples define, and thus whether the definition of "mercede" has in fact yet begun. Two studies argue that the enfeoffment of lines 314–31 is "meed," not "mercede"; both studies must assume that Conscience has added a "good" kind of "meed" to his taxonomy of rewards. Amassian and Sadowsky, who split Conscience's terms to argue that he is presenting a good "Meed-prompted-by-love" whenever love is mentioned, in contrast to, but not in lower value from, a good "Mercede-prompted-by-justice" whenever justice is implied, see the king's and pope's grant of lands and gifts as an instance of the "good meed" (Amassian and Sadowsky 1971:460–61). Overstreet, on the basis of the parallel between Conscience's mention of royal ȝeftes in the discussion of feudal entitlements and Meed's mention of ȝeftes the king should give to aliens and others in order to be "byloued and for a man yholde" (above, 265–68), similarly considers Conscience's examples here to be a form of "meed," although one redeemed by a shift of cause and effect: Conscience argues, Overstreet says, "that this rightful, kingly use of meed, far from being a principal cause of love, proceeds from an existing relationship of love" (1984:269). The consequence of both readings, however, is still that the relationship in question is legitimate, which seems all that Conscience ultimately requires to define a reward that is not Meed. Overstreet allows us to see that Conscience's focus here develops the notion of "mercede" as not simply post facto reward, but a form of positive relationship of reason and loyalty that undergirds all specific remunerations.

Finally, Adams argues that the pregranting yet the permanent conditional status of the examples here denies them from being either "meed" or "mercede" (1988a:221). Yet Conscience's discussion of a reward enjoyed so long as one has not **don ylle** (332) and hence so long as **loue** is sustained, is to the contrary a display of how "mercede" is part of the theological realm, as the summary of Solomon's fall from wealth and success after apostasy in 3 Kings 11 shows. As Overstreet points out, the materially economic relation between the king, caesar, or pope and his man has a moral substrate more important than the precise amount of rent the tenant pays or how much service he does: he does what he is able in following his lord's will, because a loving agreement that this will yield a sufficient reward underpins his efforts, like the theological formulation *facientibus in se quod est, Deus non denegat gratiam* (see above B 231–51n). This much in Conscience's argument has not changed between B and C (Adams 1988a:232).

Supported by comparison to B's version and by its own terms, the structure of the C passage here seems best taken as a treatment of "meed" first, "mercede" second. The shift of terms to **mercede**, then, occurs at 303a, is made explicit at 305, and is continued until 332.

324–28: For god gaf salomon grace . . . y leue he be in helle: A gift that is conditional, and contractual, continuing the focus on a lord's bestowing of dominion in a contractual manner. For the view, see also 11.209–13a (B.10.384–87, A.11.265–69). Solomon's fate was a debated topic by the later Middle Ages, as witnessed by the tract *De damnatione Salomonis* by Philip of Harveng in the later twelfth century (PL 203:621–66), where summary and references to the opinions of the Fathers are conveniently collected (and where, as in Conscience's view, judgment is given that he is damned). Jerome and especially Ambrose had seen him as saved (even, Ambrose declared, *sanctus*); Augustine, Bede, and others had described him as or implied he was damned.

329: god gyueth no grace þat *si* ne is the glose: "If": the customary indication of a condition. The explanation of Solomon's damnation shows that the feudal metaphor is perceived in textual terms, of contract and gloss; for the encroachment of textual contract in relations between lords and retainers, see Waugh 1986; for the "documentary" mode of religious transactions, see Steiner 2003:193–228 et passim. The terms of fealty are also of course those of the Covenant, which in the Pentateuch becomes increasingly contractual (e.g., Leviticus 26:3, "if you walk in my precepts . . ."), and is further transformed in Paul's Epistle to the Romans, where a complex sequence of "if . . . then" clauses appear.

In context, the line appears to declare that human merit is necessary for the gift of grace, thus making this line a hint to the "right" kind of gift, one that is in direct relation to merit. But the relevant passages in Romans raise further and complex implications about that relation, and the function of the example of Solomon. Paul says, "if you confess with your mouth the Lord Jesus and believe in your heart that God has raised him up from the dead, you shall be saved" (Rom. 10:9); but then he says, "there is a remnant saved according to the election of grace. And if by grace, it is not now by works; otherwise grace is no more grace" (Rom. 11:6). Thereafter in Romans 11, Paul presents a series of conditional statements concerning the spiritual potential of the chosen Gentiles who live by faith, imagined by analogy with the "remnant" of the righteous Jews who lived by works, from Israel on. Solomon is part of that lineage, and in the terms of Romans 11, he is an example of a Jew justified by works but also sinning in works, who is thus a metaphor and a warning for those Christians who are more fully justified by faith: "if some of the branches [i.e., the Jews] be broken, and thou, being a wild olive, art ingrafted in them . . . boast not against the branches . . . because of unbelief they were broken off . . . if God has not spared the natural branches, fear lest perhaps also he spare not you. See, then, the goodness and the severity of God; towards them indeed that are fallen, the severity; but towards you, the goodness of God, if you abide in goodness. Otherwise, you also shall be cut off. And they also, if they abide not still in unbelief, shall be grafted in" (Romans 11:17–23). The terms of Romans 10–11 seem also to govern the following lines, especially 348–51 and 355–62, both "if" presentations (see notes on these below).

333–406a: Thus is mede and mercede as two maner relacions . . . *Nominatiuo, pater & filius & spiritus sanctus*: The two basic terms developed so far, **mede and mercede**, are now pursued as parallels or equivalencies to two other terms, "rect and indirect relacions." These are notoriously elusive, in part because of doubts about the structure of the argument presenting them. Only **rect relacion** in fact links its terms by fundamental likenesses, figured as grammatical agreement between adjectives and their nouns. And only **rect relacion** receives extensive treatment via grammatical simile (in this PP reverses the asymmetry of Alan of Lille's *De planctu naturae*, where only perverse sexual relations are extensively discussed in grammatical terms). But the basic point is that a given transaction can be assessed only in terms of its context and background, the relation between those carrying it out, not the single moment of the exchange. This marks a major advance over the apparent endeavor in B to distinguish particular transactions in some ideally self-evident way (as one or another kind of "meed"; or as "meed" or "mercede").

The emphasis on relationships presents a theory of transactions that demands scrutiny of a wider range of social, motivational, and chronological settings, and the results of such scrutiny must thus be immensely complex, even if their ultimate outcome is decisive in the way that the Pardon is decisive: those who do well, gain eternal life; those who do evil, gain eternal damnation. The Pardon haunts this section as fully as any in the poem (see generally Lawler 2000).

Rect is a strongly positive word, implying secular and religious righteousness and adherence to law; the grammatical sense of its Latin forms is common (*recte scribere, recte scripta pronunciaciare, recte pronunciata intelligere*, etc. [see Miner 1990:151]), but it is attested only here in Middle English, where it is charged with the ideals of worldly and divine law. **Rect relacion** and **indirect relacion** are both less transactions in themselves than the terms that define transaction. **Rect relacion** is a properly grammatical structure, whose terms of fidelity, loyalty, humility, and self-denying piety establish the terms for an equitable transaction that lacks any connection to the infinite desire for gain, or to an illicit surplus that might result from such a desire. **Rect** also has a specific legal sense, 'rightful'; the word appears in this form in the "law French" of the Yearbooks in this period (see A-ND *rect*). Like "mercede," the gifts of right relation spring from immeasurable love and lead to the immeasurable rewards of salvation; the basis it implies for all transactions is a scrupulous fidelity to a dominant but beneficent lord. **Rect relacion** offers not a prepayment, as do the transactions that Conscience spurns (see 38–67n, 291–332n, 300n and other passages cited there), but instead a preexisting reassurance of some kind of aid and comfort no matter what, which functions more powerfully than a particular prepayment might. Such reassurance—specified in the case of a lord and laborer below as **pay hym yf he parforme and haue pite yf he faileth** (see 348–51n), and echoing the reassuring theological dictum *facientibus in se quod est, Deus non denegat gratiam* (see B 231–51n)—posits a larger contract by which particular contracts are premised. Ultimately, such a contract allows the terms of salvation to include not just doing well and evil, but also doing evil but repenting, as what Lawler calls the "third term" of the Pardon present throughout the poem (Lawler 2000). For a more menacing context in the late fourteenth century in which "pity" serves as an "implied social contract" to express the king's omnipotence, see Galloway 2002. The metaphors here for this prevailing contract, beyond proper grammatical agreement between noun and adjective (336–40a, 344–47) and thus human beings with the grammar of the Incarnate Word (352–62, 394–406a), are of a dutiful agrarian laborer and a giving lord (348–51), and an obedient people and a principled and just king (374–82).

   Relacion indirect or **Indirect thyng** is defined less by grammar than by desire: **Alle kyn kynde to knowe and to folowe** (363–64), recalling the Thomistic "infinite desire for gain" that may have inspired the two kinds of "meed" in B (see Headnote, B 255–58n, and below 363–73n). Its social metaphors are of sons who abandon the obligations passed down by their fathers and bridegrooms who do not accept the debts of their brides (367–72); a rebelliously self-serving people who ignore the costs to the greater community of their own pursuits of gain (383–87); and, finally, self-serving professional lawyers who profit at others' earthly and spiritual expense (388–93).

333–34: mede and mercede as two maner relacions, / Rect and indirect: The pairs of terms cannot be parallel, since Conscience has defined **mede** as an improper relation to reward and **mercede** as a proper relation, but clearly defines **rect** as proper and **indirect** as improper. The superficially balanced phrases, where a short word is followed by a longer one, most likely generates a chiasm. This may be because of euphony (Amassian and Sadowsky 1971:465, although they interpret the phrase as introducing two manner of relations for both **mede** and **mercede**, not the two pairs meed/indirect, mercede/rect); because of stylistic carelessness (Adams 1988a:223); or conceivably because the poet (or Conscience) wished to challenge the reader (and listeners) to find a "right relation" between the terms so teasingly linked once and once only. The nature of the exposition, however, makes it clear when Conscience is discussing "rect" and when "indirect" relation.

334–35: reninde bothe / On a sad and a siker semblable to hemsuluen: Even though language was not generally seen as corresponding directly to the things to which it referred, grammar offered many medieval writers powerfully authoritative ("serious and certain") explanations for theology, cognition, and cosmology (see Alford 1982). By the mid-thirteenth century, "it had become common to call grammatical properties of words 'modes of signifying,' and a distinction had been introduced between a word's 'general' (lexical) signification and the 'special signification' due to its grammatical form . . . . It was assumed that the structure of human language reflected a correct understanding of the structure of external reality" (Ebbesen 1998:394). **semblable**: Only "meed" presents grammatical relations with inherent features of "likeness." But in another sense of **semblable**, both "meed" and "mercede" are readily productive of similes, likenesses, poetic analogies (which this comment seems to license in abundance).

336–39: Ac adiectif and sustantif vnite asken . . . to alle lele lyuynge: Conscience begins his first description of "relacioun rect," which concludes at 362: much of his effort is an expansion, instigated by the king's demand, of his initial, tersely expressed proposition here about grammar as a tool for assessing the context and thus the meaning of payment or gain. Again, the point throughout this section is that a given transaction, earthly or divine, must be assessed in terms of its background and context, and the fundamental relationship (of some hierarchical subordination yet also of unity) between the parties carrying out the transaction. The **vnite** that grammatically accurate endings of nouns and their modifiers display is an emblem of the principles of loyalty and desire for a collective good. **kynde** means grammatical "gender" throughout this section, in a usage rarely attested elsewhere, although a common translation of Latin *genus*, which has "gender" among its meanings, is *kynde*. The root meaning *genus* later allows Conscience to include the broader sense too

(356). When case, number, and gender are all in concord, they all contribute to the resulting phrase's combined expressive power (**ayther is otheres helpe**). With this grammatical comment the speech unexpectedly turns to heavenly rewards, using the latinate term **retribucoun**, a positive term for "reward" (the word lacked the dark meaning it now possesses). Just how heavenly reward is related to grammatical concord is not yet clear, although this will emerge when the grammatical metaphor is more directly linked to Christian theology. But the connection here between the mutual "help" of the various parts of speech in grammatical concord, and the heavenly reward, may suggest Galatians 6:2: "Bear ye one another's burdens; and so you shall fulfill the law of Christ." The social meanings are considerably clearer, in the latent metaphor of loyal and subservient labor for a common good, and a lord's **gyft** made generally for such **lele lyuynge** (339). On the idea of "the common good," see Prol.169n.

340–40a: Grace of good ende . . . *Retribuere dignare domine deus &c*: "Deign, O Lord God, to reward [with eternal life all who us do good]": part of a Latin grace said after dinner (Alford, *Quot.*); for some of these see *The Babees Boke*, ed. Furnivall 1868:382–85 (so Prsl). The application here is that transactions take place across time and their meanings and values are assessed in terms of what comes before and what comes after. The notion is clearly part of the complex of terms used in the Pardon, here the first term; see Lawler 2000:125. For the C-text's distinctive use of **good ende** to identify that term, see Prol.29n.

343: adiectyf and sustantyf: Ancient grammar treated both nouns and adjectives as *nomina* (nouns), either "adjectival" or "substantive." The influential early sixth-century grammarian, Priscian, distinguished adjectives as what is "added to" nouns or proper nouns to reveal their qualities (see below, 345–46n).

343: englisch was it neuere: Grammatical guides in fact frequently presented in English information about Latin cases and agreement; in such contexts, a statement that a student must turn either from Latin into English or the reverse was called a *vulgare* (see Orme 1989:93–112); for one such phrase demonstrably used in these books, see 2.220–22n. The courtly and literary context and the theological uses of such materials constitute the real innovation here; the posture of analyzing momentous social and religious issues by means of such grammatical pedantry, and before a marvelling and intellectually curious English king, frames the exercise with as much drama as the materials perhaps allow. The request resembles Hawkin's remark that he "can nat construe al this," and Patience's reply that such a matter "propreliche to tell . . . / In engelysch is ful hard," before venturing further in the topic of poverty (C.16.117–19 [B.14.277–78]). At both points the sense of "things unattempted yet in prose or rhyme" adds drama to these teachers' efforts. See also 4.140–45n.

The king's interruption notes the novelty and positions him as a willing student on behalf of all other English-only speakers: "knowen y wolde," in an example of a ruler's ideal humility before a learned guide, the configuration imagined by the many works in the "mirrors for princes" tradition (see Ferster 1996). Compare the posture in C of the knight learning from Piers: "on þe teeme treuely ytauhte was y neuere. / Y wolde y couthe . . ." (8.20–21; A/B's knight [B.6.34–36] does not mention an interest in learning). Other demands by teachers or speakers that their audiences should or need to "construe it on englisch" (4.142; 9.282 [B.7.108]) are aggressive challenges or patronizing insults to those who do not know Latin, and thus emphasize a posture of exacerbating rather than trying to overcome the difference between the learned elite and the laity. The debate between Conscience and Meed in all versions of the present passus ends with a portrayal of a poorly instructed lay-woman, and the issue of the laity's need if not desire for authoritative instruction is a theme throughout the poem (see, e.g., in addition to Patience's comments to Hawkin, Study's speech at 11.1–80 [B.10.1–139], and Imaginative's at 13.218–14.217 [B.11.410–12.297]). See below, 489–500n and 493n.

344a: *Quia antelate rei recordatiuum est*: "Because it calls to mind what has gone before": a formula commonly found in Latin grammars to explain grammatical relation, usually of a relative pronoun to its antecedent (Alford, *Quot.*; Smith 1994:135n; Smith 2001:161). Conscience's word-play provides an etymology for *relatio*: as *rei* which is "placed" (*late*) "before" (*ante*), that is, *rei-late*. The grammar of retribution as throughout this section emphasizes that any transaction must be considered in terms of background or motive or basis, what comes *ante* the event itself. Meed lacks such connections to historical or motivational depth in the promiscuous exchanges she enables. Just as her own lineage is unclear (see 2.24n, 25–26n), so the lineage and grammar of the transactions she allows are obscure.

345–46: Folowynge and fyndynge out . . . to strenghe þe fundement: Conscience's definition of a "relacioun rect" folds his answer to the first part of the king's question into an answer about adjectives and substantives, the second part of the king's question. Adjectives and substantives demonstrate right relation when the adjective correctly reveals a noun's case, number or gender (for **fyndynge out** as 'reveal, discover,' see MED *finden* 7). Compare Priscian, *Institutiones*, 2.25: "adiectiva autem ideo vocantur, quod aliis appellativis, quae substantiam significant, vel etiam propriis adici solent ad manifestandam eorum qualitatem vel quantitatem, quae augeri vel minui sine substantiae consumptione possunt, ut 'bonum animal,' 'magnus homo,' 'sapiens grammaticus,' 'magnus Homerus'" ("they are therefore called adjectives, since they are commonly 'added to' other 'appellatives' [i.e., nouns other than proper nouns] or to proper nouns, in order to reveal their quality or quantity, which are able to be increased or diminished without using up the substance, such as 'good animal,' 'great man,' wise grammarian,' 'great Homer'"; ed. Keil 1857–80, vol. 2.58).

The chiastic phrase **þe fundement of a strenghe** and **to strenghe þe fundement** suggests the mutual action of reinforcement. A **strenghe** may refer to the grammatical term *vis*, a word's "force," which allows it to "rule" other words, a sense often analogized to social relations (see the materials in Kaske 1969:235–36; Bland 1988; the connection to this word is made by Martin 1993:170–71). The playfully changing grammatical nature of the words **fundement** and **strenghe** in the two lines demonstrates the need for grammatical understanding to differentiate between, say, **strenghe** as noun and as verb. But the language also pulls the lines into describing a legal inquiry: "a record of treuthe" (344) describes the court record; **Folowynge** can describe pursuing a legal suit (see MED *folwer* 3 and MED *folwen* 5a); **fyndynge out þe fundement of a strenghe** can describe discovering the foundation of legal validity (MED *strenghe* 14a). Many of the following examples evoke significant legal issues in the period: labor laws, inheritance laws, marital laws.

348–51: As a leel laborer . . . al þat treuthe wolde: The laborer is analogous to the adjectival noun, the master to the substantival noun (see preceding note): in a "relacioun rect," they are in concord, allowing the laborer not only fair pay for fair work, but pity (and some implied alms) if he cannot accomplish his task. But neither pay nor pity will be forthcoming until the **trauaile** has been undertaken, whatever the outcome (see above, 291–332n). Such labor here involves and is underpinned by the laborer's belief in the lord: **byleueth with his maister,** and with the lord's reassurance that he will repay the laborer as his labor warrants (see also note to 333–406a, B 231–51n). The analogy, a central one to this section, develops ultimately from (because, as a C addition, written later than) the presentation Piers Plowman makes about his own **hardy relacoun** to Truth, and includes all these elements of wages, faith, and continuous and committed labor (see 7.182–99 [B.5.537–55, A.6.25–42]).

The grammatical complexity of the Latin word for believing, *credo*, is possibly pertinent here as well as below (see 356–60n): the uncertainty and importance of how *credo* is syntactically attached to its object accounts for the surprising preposition after **byleueth** that RK-C correctly amend in the copy-text, **with**. As for other examples of a "relacioun rect," the fundamental faith and **hope** ('hope' but also 'expectation') undergirding the exchange mean that no penalty results even **yf he faileth**. Both that and **pay hym yf he parforme** are instances where *si* (**yf**) is the gloss of a lord's grace (see above 329n); as noted above, the conditions turn out to be safety nets rather than traps, and they also turn out to show the necessity of having a lord, in social and spiritual domains, to establish a broadly supportive contract of success or failure within which any particular contracts occur.

The lines underscore the value of unalterably hierarchical society, with lordship and laborers, and in this sense support the spirit of the labor statutes of 1352 and 1388 (see Middleton 1997; also Palmer 1993), which require wages to remain at the level that they had held before the Black Death, and remaining with the same employer. A suspicious scrutiny of the laborer's actions and demands rather than the lord's characterizes the grammatical analogy generally. But the lines here imply a foundation of mutual support, a traditional ideal whose scope far exceeds the fourteenth-century labor legislation.

352–54: So of hol herte . . . a graciouse antecedent: A comma might be inserted after **hope** to indicate more clearly that **hardy relacoun** is the subject of the following verbs in **Seketh and seweth his sustantif sauacioun**. But the momentary ambiguity by which **hardy relacoun** is instead another subject of **cometh**, and thus a further product of the **hol herte**, is not infelicitous, since **hope** is the basis for a **hardy relacoun** between the true laborer and the perfect master God.

In Priscian's terms, **relacoun** is the "adjectival" noun, seeking its **sustantif sauacioun, / That is god . . . a graciouse antecedent**. See the passage from the *Institutiones* quoted above, 345–46n (also Amassian and Sadowsky 1971:463–64; Overstreet 1984:265; Adams 1988a:222–23). The dependent or "adjectival" noun "man," who seeks his **sustantif sauacioun**, moves toward that goal by a series of crucial further adjectives: a **hol** heart, and a **hardy** relation. To call God **the ground of al** uses a phrase usually associated with grammar itself (see Isidore *Etymologiae* 1.5.1: "Grammatica est . . . origo et fundamentum liberalium litterarum" ["grammar is the ground and foundation of philosophical writings": ed. Lindsay 1911]; partly quoted at PP 17.108 [B.15.372]).

356–60: He accordeth with crist in kynde . . . as oure crede vs kenneth with crist withouten ende: The first description of right relation concludes by drawing various examples of concordant gender, case, and number between God and human beings, as analogies for how these may have a proper or "rect" relationship as the basis for a "mercede" or properly framed reward. The relation is clearest in that between a faithful laborer and a remunerative and pitying lord; the relation of proper "reward" and its conditions summed up in the dictum that to those doing what they can, God (or any good lord) will not deny grace (see B 231–51n, B 248n, and C 348–51n, 356–60n). The analogies derive from central elements of the Nicene Creed: belief in the Incarnation, in the church, and in the resurrection of the flesh at the second coming. The points chosen from the Creed are not, however, arranged in the Creed's order. It is a bravura finale to a definition of proper reward (which thereby, more implicitly than in A/B, excludes Meed), but it sometimes suggests the problems of Conscience's venture of offering so elaborate a lesson. For all the examples bear further intricate meaning and allusiveness, but all at some level rely on ambiguity, or inscrutability. The proper relation between God and human beings necessary for any particular reward remains very difficult to define.

Numerous commentaries exist on the Nicene Creed and other creeds; Alan of Lille in the twelfth century wrote at least four, plus one apparently compiled from student notes (see *Plaint of Nature*, ed. Sheridan 1980:16–19; de Lage 1943; Häring 1974a, 1974b, 1974c, 1975). Alan's treatises have only one specific parallel to the points Conscience develops, with the treatment of *credere* (a widely explicated issue; see below), but his commentaries suggest a generic model for Conscience's development here.

verbum caro factum est: "the word was made flesh" (John 1:14). "The verse stands for an article ('Et homo factus est') of the Nicene Creed, recited in the Ordinary of the Mass" (Alford, *Quot.*). Repentance also cites the verse (7.140a) and glosses it as describing Jesus' appearance "in oure sekte"—that is, our "clothing," our body (B's corresponding "in oure armes" [5.500] suggests a similar metaphorical reference to human bodily existence). Here again **kynde** means "gender" in the grammatical sense (see 336–37n, 347), but also "nature, kind" (Latin *genus*), based on John's terse description of the Incarnation. The vernacular ambiguity of the English word here serves Conscience's purpose admirably.

In case, *credere in ecclesia*, in holy kyrke to bileue: "to believe in the church," as immediately translated; the phrase partly follows the Nicene Creed's "credo in . . . unam sanctam catholicam et apostolicam Ecclesiam." *credere* aptly exemplifies case because from the patristic era on, theologians had used the word to discuss "belief" in terms of grammatical case. Augustine and many followers, including Peter Lombard in the *Sentences* (Lib. III, d. xxiii, cap. iv), distinguish different relations between the believer and the believed on the basis of *credere* and the case of its object *Deus*. *Credere Deum* meant to believe that God exists, *credere Deo* that what God says is true, and *credere in Deum* that one had faith in God. In the present line from the Creed, the use of *in* plus the accusative (*credere in . . . ecclesiam*) was sometimes thought to require special explanation in treating belief or faith in the church (see Overstreet 1984:258–59). The verb's grammar was fertile ground for subtle theological and rhetorical (even literary) exposition. Alan of Lille, in one of his commentaries on the Creed, notes that the phrase *Credo in unum deum* in the Creed of the Mass is offered "not in propria persona, but in the persona of the church," thus a preacher in a state of deadly sin is not lying to utter the first-person verbs of the Creed. Alan also suggests that we may take the phrase loosely as "I have faith about God, whether it is precise or inchoate faith" (Häring 1974b:290–91; see also what are possibly Alan's lectures in which he notes, following Augustine, the complexities of case with *credere*, in de Lage 1943:332). Conscience may be creating a new category of faith in the church by inventing a new combination for *credere*, with *in* plus the ablative, perhaps suggesting a belief that combines the absolute faith reserved for God with the belief that what the church says is true. It is possible that a simple macron marking a final 'm,' making **ecclesia** accusative as in the Creed, was omitted early in the textual transmission, but there is no manuscript support for such a view.

In nombre, Rotye and aryse and remissioun to haue, . . . And lyue as oure crede vs kenneth with crist withouten ende: The lines make explicit the allusions to the Nicene Creed, which ends "I look for the resurrection of the dead and the life of the world to come." The emphasis on **remissioun** and being **with crist**, also part of the Creed, suggests that the **nombre** is "one." The concept is that of "Atonement," itself from the Middle English adverbial phrase, *at one*, which is attested from the early fourteenth century. The use of the noun *atonement* to indicate the reconciliation of humanity with God (see 2 Cor. 5:19, "Deus erat in Christo mundum reconcilians sibi") is one of the few theological terms in modern English to derive from wholly English origins. But the noun is not attested before the sixteenth century. The adverbial phrase *at one*, however, likely shapes the poet's thought here. See also Gal. 3:27–28: "For as many of you as have been baptized in Christ have put on Christ. There is neither Jew nor Greek; there is neither bond nor free; there is neither male nor female. For you are all one in Christ Jesus [*omnes enim vos unus estis in Christo Iesu*]."

In spite of the promise of clarification of legal and social ethics in all of this, the grammar of divinity in Conscience's examples is full of ambiguity, perhaps deliberately leaving room for the reader's further association and reflection, rather than definitive understanding and, thus, immediate practical application. The ablative plus *in* renders the meaning of the case of *ecclesia* mysterious; the "gender" that the Incarnate God adopts may be either feminine (*caro*), neuter (*verbum . . . factum*), masculine (*homo*), or some universal combination as in Galatians, "non est masculus et femina" (perhaps corresponding to *hic et haec homo*; see below, 405n); if the number in the final example refers to humanity's reconcilation with God, that is a **nombre** beyond rational comprehension, as in Galatians' "vos unus estis."

363–73: Indirect thyng . . . and alle kyn trauayle: "An indirect situation is when anyone covets to know and adhere to all manner of natures . . ." Having completed a first run at "relacoun rect," Conscience turns briefly to a definition of **Indirect thyng**. This is an indiscriminate coveting, recalling the comments above about Meed's promiscuity (169 [B 132, A 121]), and similar to Thomas Aquinas' definition of an improper exchange as predicated on "the desire for gain, which knows no limit but extends to infinity" (see Headnote above, and references there). The definition emphasizes a circumstance applying to anyone with excessive desire (**hoso coueytede**), a condition defined by the grammatical metaphor here as words' blind desire for adhering to other words regardless of grammatical agreement. As above, "adjective" can refer to a noun that is "thrown on," defined by its relation to a more "essential" noun. All the key elements of grammatical agreement between nouns, pronouns, and "adjectival nouns"—**kynde, case, nombres**—swiftly appear, displaying a blind desire for attachment to the world and other people. Compare Alan of Lille's description of the "grammar" of homosexuality in the *De planctu Naturae*, a playful poetic elaboration of the problems of case that occupied Alan in his academic lectures and commentaries on the Creeds: "Of those men who subscribe to Venus' procedures in grammar, some closely embrace those of masculine gender only, others, those of feminine gender, others, those of common, or epicene gender. Some, indeed, as though belonging to the heteroclite class, show variations in deviation by reclining with those of female gender in Winter and those of masculine gender in Summer. There are some, who in the disputations in Venus' school of logic, in their conclusions reach a law of interchangeability of subject and predicate. There are those who take the part of the subject and cannot function as predicate. There are some who function as predicates only but have no desire to have the subject term duly submit to them . . ." (*De planctu* 8 pr. 4; trans. Sheridan 1980:136–37). But the perverse desires in PP here are more broadly social than sexual. The grammatical metaphor is also now overlayered with puns on legal terms, suggesting the crucial role of professional law in furthering such desires: **thyng** can mean 'contract' or 'stipulation in a legal document' (MED 11); **withoute case** can mean both 'lacking grammatical case' and 'lacking a valid suit at law.' The legal implications are pursued in the examples: a **sone** suing at a court of law for a father's patrimony, and a father enfeoffing his son-in-law with his daughter's reckoning of goods (evidently including her debts or less desirable goods). As Alford observes, L's shift from grammar into legal materials distinguishes his usage from the many other examples of grammatical metaphor (Alford 1982:758). Even in the recondite realms of such analogy the poet redefines his genre.

367–70: Þat is nat resonable ne rect to refuse my syre name . . . here foule taylende: The point of both examples is that pursuing a legal claim requires a willingness to accept full legal responsibility of the resulting contract or ownership (as Mitchell 1969:185). Both examples of cases involve property law, and suggest the complexity of transmitting property in the late fourteenth and fifteenth centuries, when traditions of common law were supplemented and to some extent circumvented by various other legal mechanisms (see Bellamy 1989:34–56; Biancalana 2001). Both brief instances are dense and complicated by legal possibilities, wordplay, and presumably unintended ambiguities. Yet they clearly present symmetrical cases, of a son and a daughter, as inheritors of property as well as obligations, that is, of lineages of which they must take account.

Neither case is immediately easy to grasp; both are couched in terms meant for insiders to fairly technical late medieval legal conventions and exceptions. Indeed, the more deeply both are probed, the more specific the range of technical knowledge appears to be, escaping the range that some of the scribes could understand. In **to refuse my syre name**, the case concerning a son, **syre name** may be either "my father's name," or "my surname" (see MED). RK-C evidently view the common alternate reading "syre sirname" (printed by Schm) as a scribal effort to resolve an ambiguous original. Surnames are not generally inherited or even present features in England before the fourteenth century, when greater legal enrollments of property, more complex inheritance possibilities, and greater concentrations of population in cities had made them more widely necessary. Middleton notes that surnames in this period might be based not on the father's name but on the particular landholdings that were or would be inherited by a given son (1990:64–65); thus the name "Langland" rather than "de Rokayle" (as in the memorandum in Trinity College, MS. 212, stating that the poet's father was Stacy de Rokayle [Hanna 1993:25–26]) might have been given because of a particular property passed to

him, in this case one that was named, suggestively, after the term for a strip of
land that a plowman plows (Middleton 1990:64–65, 50). Middleton speculates
that refusals of surnames, or a desire to confect them, might be advantageous
in the period of the poll taxes of 1377, 1379, and 1380, which taxed individuals,
and whose severe and novel impositions partly led to the Rising of 1381; for
similar reasons of avoiding the law, fictive surnames were indeed paraded by
at least some of the most visible of the rebels (Middleton 1990:66–73).

But the line needs a less topical reason for making the refusal of a surname, or a father's name, a strong instance of not being **rect**, which carries a
clear legal import (see note to 333–46a). So too **refuse** has often a technical
legal sense. What can the line precisely mean? Coleman, one of the few to
attempt to interpret it directly in legal terms, suggests it has a simple sense
drawn from civil law: "according to civil law, you cannot reject the surname
of your father if you thereafter expect to inherit his rights and privileges. Similarly, if you reject the expectations of the covenant and do not fulfil the contract of the *lex christi*, how can you then expect eternal reward?" (1981:95). The
terse clarification is attractive, but she cites no basis for it in civil law (that is,
Roman law), used on the Continent but not in England except for ecclesiastical property matters. Justinian's *Institutes* (ed. and trans. Birks, McLeod, and
Krueger 1987) does not discussion the status of a *cognomen* in any inheritance
issues; the *Digest*, under the discussion of disinheritance (*Digest*, trans. Watson
1998; 28.5), includes Ulpian's brief attention to the question of whether a person being disinherited "by name" must be named by *nomen, praenomen*, and
cognomen (the Roman system of personal and familiar names), but the *Digest*
swiftly determines that any one of these is enough—or even simply "my son"
if there is only one son. Subsequent discussions in the *Digest* of the name of
heirs of whatever sort leave the matter at that. Civil law, indeed, had no place
in English secular property law, which was governed by common law (Ullman
notes that "a . . . reason for the dearth of [explicit political theory] in England
was that the main legal system which nourished so much political ideology on
the Continent—the Roman law—had virtually no practical significance here"
[1975:300], although Ullman finds traces of civil or Roman law in Richard II's
efforts to define kingship's absolute powers, and in some other legislation that
the king proposed [1975:300n1]). More important to understanding the point,
however, is the problem of why one would want to reject a father's surname.
How could this be related to temptations of "indirect relation" and covetousness, the immediate context of the line?

The possibilities for explaining the line are somewhat complicated by the
manuscripts' nearly balanced division between **Sethe y, his sone and his seruant, sewe for his ryhte**, which RK-C print along with punctuation that shows

that **sewe** is the finite verb, and "Sethe y am his sone and his seruant sewe for his rhyte," printed by Prsl and, with different preceding punctuation, by Schm. In the second form, "sewe" is either an adjectival infinitive modifying "seruant": "since I am his son and his servant, and also suing for his right," or, as Schm more clearly implies with his punctuation for these lines, **sewe** is an infinitive dependent on "ne rect" and parallel with "to refuse": as Schm prints this, "þat is nat resonable ne rect—to refuse my syre sirename, / Sethe Y am his sone and his seruant, sewe for his ryhte": "that is not reasonable or right—to refuse my sire's surname (since I am his son and his servant) [and also] to sue for his right." Taking "sone" and "seruant" as two entities, a third option, impossibly confuses the sense (see Overstreet 1984:270n48, who wisely rejects the last, and offers one of the few direct considerations of the syntactic problems of the line's two readings).

If the line is taken as "since I, his son and servant, sue for my father's property," what is implied here appears to be a refusal of warranty, in a case where warranty (which a lord's son inherits with his father's lordship) would mean protecting a grant of land made by the father. The distinction between lordship (**syres name**) and property (**ryhte**) in common law particularly vexed lawyers and commentators in the thirteenth and fourteenth centuries: if a son's father, a lord, granted land to someone else and his heirs, the son on his father's death would inherit the lordship, but with lordship came "warranty," the obligation to protect the grants made by his father, so that he could not recover the land even if it passed, by the death of whomever his father had granted it to, to a remotely collateral heir of that grantee. The rules of warranty were made (and from the thirteenth century enforced) in order to protect the continuity of grants made outside the family; but these rules raised many problems for grants made within families: if a younger son were granted land and died, the father could not give it then to the eldest son, since when he inherited lordship he would inherit the warranty that obliged him not to be both lord and heir. Land granted carried the obligation of the grantor, so the father himself could also not recover the land that he had himself granted, since he was the present lord and therefore had the obligation of warranty over his own grant. The result might be that the father's brother or other more distant male relative, rather than the father's own elder son, would by common law be automatically next in line for a grant made to a youngest son—a mechanical thwarting of the effort to keep a father's land within a family and passed down to an eldest son (see Biancalana 2001:14–15).

A legal historian can describe the legal solution that evolved to this in relatively simple terms, as the emergence of "fee tail," in which further condi-

tions for land transfers could be spelled out, including reversion to the grantor
(who could then, unencumbered by common law of fee simple, decide where
he wished it to go, e.g., to an elder son if the younger son died). But in practice
this would depend on a father's legal care in constructing a fee entail, and thus
the forces of fee simple and warranty would still often prevail. An heir's
response might be not to uphold or "vouch to" warranty; and in turn a distant
relative who stood to benefit might try to force an heir to acknowledge his
warranty (as heir to his father) and thus yield claims to land that could be
shown to have been somehow gained by a grant from his father or more distant ancestor to some ancestor of the one wishing to claim the land. The procedure of summoning an heir to do so was known as "vouching to warranty"
(*voucher au garantie*, or *voucher a garant*), and by it a complainant could call
an heir into court either to uphold the grant or (as more often) to make some
other compensation. The Year Books of Edward III describe cases in which,
e.g., an infant is vouched to warranty (*vocha a garrantie*) in order to gain a
dower promised a woman (ed. Horwood 1883:90–93). Warranty might even be
extended to collateral warranty, a more complex notion that could be used to
bar those who were not first-born and their heirs from property on the
grounds of warranty (Biancalana 2001:212–42). Refusals of warranty under
these terms were not uncommon (for a writ of vouching to warranty, and its
refusal, see Palmer 1984:57–59; see also Harding 1973:70; and see also the other
examples of vouching to warranty cited in A-ND s.vv. *vouché, vouchable,
voucher [a garant], voucheresce, voucheur*). Heirs might choose to acquire
property as a purchaser rather than an heir, and with this, dissolve altogether
the obligations of traditional lordship passed down with land (ed. Horwood
1883:64–67). Therein lies the connection to the "indirect relations" fostered by
Lady Meed.

   The language of these lines in PP, and some of the principles behind their
point, are similar to the discussions of "vouching to warranty" in a source
that was influenced by civil law, partly confirming Coleman's assumption that
traditions from Roman law might be pertinent here. Vouching to warranty
could be avoided by claiming an error in the name, says "Bracton," the name
given to the thirteenth-century work attributed to Henry of Bracton (or Bratton), *De legibus et consuetudinibus Angliae*, which seeks to codify the "unwrit-
ten law and custom" of common law that (the author says) only England relies
on, resulting in a summary and reshaping of procedures for writs and various
points of legal status and property that was at least known to most judges if
not followed (trans. and ed. Thorne and Woodbine 1968; on some aspects of
the influence of civil or Roman law on Bracton, and its influence and uses, see
generally Hyams 1980). Writs in general must have proper surnames, Bracton

says: "if there is error in a syllable, as where he names another 'Henry of Brothton' where he ought to name him 'of Bratton.' And so of a letter, by naming him 'Henry of Bretton' when he ought to name him 'Henry of Bratton'" (trans. and ed. Thorne and Woodbine 1968, vol. 3.79). Elsewhere, Bracton mentions possible strategies by which claiming (or showing) that a name was in error might be useful for blocking warranty of a deceased lord; for example, a tenant of property might prevent a widow of the owner of the property from taking it to a new lord as a dower if she remarried, if the tenant could argue that her name was wrong in the documents supporting her action—although Bracton says that in the case of a widow, the point would not need to apply to the *cognomen* (surname), since she would simply be "the wife of N." But the principle he presents would apply to other exceptions of vouching a warrantor where a male surname was given: "When the tenant, a stranger or the heir himself, is in possession, and does not wish to vouch a warrantor against the woman claiming dower, he may except against her in many ways . . . The woman shows in her *intentio* and in the evidence on which it is founded by what right the action of dower belongs to her. It is put thus: 'Such a woman N.' Thus we must first see that there is no error in the name, as above, [*interpolated*: in the given name], because for the surname it is enough to say 'such a one who was the wife of such a one etc'" (ed. and trans. Thorne and Woodbine 1968, vol. 3.370). Bracton, as often, may not determine legal principles but nonetheless reflects the language and forms of thought in the English legal world (see, e.g., Hyams 1980:82–124).

The general point in Conscience's legal example is that acceptance of warranty should prevail over any pecuniary interests: the good faith of warranty in the traditional sense should be maintained in tandem with being the lord's **sone and . . . servant.** Conscience's concern seems to be the "grammatical" linkage between legal categories that had become variously misjoined in the period, and thus he supports a fundamental solidity in legal identity and **ryhte,** even while he exists in a culture where such identity was complexly composite, and indeed he elaborates the terms that make it so. In these terms, a topical connection is possible: in 1376, the commons petitioned Parliament to extend the Statute of Gloucester (from 1276) to collateral warranty. This statute had restricted the extent to which warranty might bar an heir, and the 1376 petition suggests concern with how the rules of collateral warranty might be similarly encumbering. The petition presents an extreme case: it notes that it would be possible for a collateral ancestor of a heir to warrant someone who in fact disseised (that is, unlawfully occupied the property of) that heir (SR 2.334, no. 77; see Biancalana 2001:236–37).

If the 1376 petition presents an extreme case against the force of warranty,

Conscience presents a rather extreme insistence in favor of it, possibly in direct response to that parliamentary petition (for the poem's close connections to Parliament, see Giancarlo 2003, and 4.45n). If so, this represents one of the few internal indications of a date distinctive to the C text, although it does not assist in the dating of that version since B has evident indications of a date after 1378 (see Prol., Headnote); nor does it help or complicate the case for dating C sometime after 1388, a view that depends on seeing C.5.1–105 as alluding to the Parliament at Cambridge that year (see Hanna 1993:16; Middleton 1997; but cp. Clopper 1992, and Scase 1987). By invoking a discussion from parliamentary contexts, Conscience would be living up to his dramatic circumstance in the debate at Westminster (for the suggestion that the whole scene is before full Parliament, see Giancarlo 2003). But for more daring implications in such a setting if C is after 1388, see below, 407–11n, and 408n.

feffe hym with here fayre and with here foule taylende: The second instance of "rect," concerning property passed to a son-in-law, chooses a similarly tenuous means of property transfer, focusing on entailment, this time for a daughter. In the previous example, the point of view was the son's in relation to his father; in this it is the father's in relation to his daughter and her family. **feffe** (enfeoff) is to put a person (or institution) in legal possession of property, but to *taillen* (entail) land is to "settle a substantial estate on a son (or daughter), who was not the heir by primogeniture, which he (or she) could not alienate until after the third heir had entered" (Bellamy 1989:37; Biancalana, however, notes that after the middle of the fourteenth century the restrictions in entails were often much longer, or even indefinite [2001:126]). The **foule taylende** would be in this sense the debts or other inconveniences of such conditional ownership—as well as the more obvious sexual pun on "tail end" (as at Chaucer's Shipman's Tale, line 434). The pairing of "fair" and "foul" moreover recalls the marriage contract, "for better for worse" (Mitchell 1956 [1969]:185); and indeed, the entailment here is a marriage settlement, from the bride's father to the groom, but it is not free of obligations as would be a *maritagium* (see 2.75n). For the popularity in the fourteenth and fifteenth centuries of using a fee tail in marriage settlements, with the consequent restrictions and obligations, over a *maritagium*, with no obligatory fines, see Biancalana 2001:182.

In both legal instances Conscience seems to have given himself a stiff challenge: the rectitude of both cases is made difficult by their being points in property law that allowed complex disjunctions between rights and property. Both examples are also challenging in terms of the threads of the argument. The definition of "indirect thyng" was an indiscriminate reaching for something "In whiche ben gode and nat gode" (366); yet both of these cases extoll

seeking elements that are "nat gode" as well as "gode." Indeed, Amassian and
Sadowsky suggest that what is extolled in these examples is a *good* kind of
"relacoun indirect," which they see as implied (but only in a textual "lacuna")
by the entire speech and by this section in particular (1971:469). However,
whenever "relacoun indirect" is named in the text, it is roundly condemned,
as it is both before and after these examples; the examples of a son spurning
his warranty while suing for his property, and of a spouse spurning the foul
and just taking the fair, are clearly "nat resonable ne rect," offering no room
for a category that is both "resonable and indirect" (see also above 315–32n).
It is "direct" and "rect" to accept full responsibility in both cases; it is "indirect" to want only the personally enriching aspects of a father's patrimony and
not the obligations or the entailed land and not the debts or other conditions.

The lack of discrimination being criticized in these cases of relations
(which confusingly involve greedy discriminations, in wishing to take only the
good and leave the onerous) is in not sufficiently distinguishing one's own
motives, e.g., those that are selfish and those more charitable ones that lead to
various mutual bonds. When a lord takes on a laborer who has belief in him,
the lord is obligated to "pay hym yf he parforme and haue pite yf he faileth"
(see 348–51n), that is, to accept the fair and the foul; and if the lord is God, the
lord will not deny grace to those who do what they can, even if they fail (as
they must in that case) at an adequate achievement for such a reward (see B
231–51n). God will take the good and the less good if underpinned by the right
offer of faith; and Conscience has found legal instances, balanced symmetri-
cally between a son and a daughter, where the same applies.

371–73: inlyche to coueyte . . . and alle kyn trauayle: inlyche should be
defined (as usual) as "entirely," or even "indiscriminately," with the paradox
that such overwhelming and indiscriminate desire is founded on an effort at
self-interested discrimination, in seeking to gain **Withouten coest and care
and alle kyn trauayle**; see above note. Since the grammatical terms **kynde**
(gender) and **nombre** are mentioned, it is possible that "case" is evoked by
coest and care. The line, echoing 363–66, closes off in a ring-structure the brief
definition of the "indirect" relation as a preexisting condition for any transaction of infinite desire for gain and only gain, i.e., falling prey to Meed's continual promise of personal gain without any corresponding solicitation of
responsibilities (right relations) for penalty, loss, and sacrifice for the greater
good. The same point is emphasized below at 383–85 when the definition of
"indirect" is again presented and exemplified.

374–82: Ac relacoun rect . . . for a trewe marke: In a quickening tempo, for
the rest of his speech Conscience moves between the two definitions he has

advanced, as if seeking to contain the terms of the entire debate within his own discourse. His focus shifts from law to political theory, although law remains a constant metaphoric base and social association. Now the definition of **rela-coun rect** is sought in the proper relation between king and people—a topic with obvious pertinence to the royal setting, and forming a belated further answer to Meed's argument for meed's importance in proper kingship and all harmonious social hierarchy (above 265–81 [B 209–26, A 196–213]). A **rela-coun rect** between king and people is such that allows the king **to clayme the comune at his wille** (375), including supporting him with subsidies and other taxes (**to fynde hym**), and in turn allows the people to "claim" from the king his law and loyalty as well as love, and above all his removal from party politics, a sensitive issue throughout the Ricardian decades. **So comune claymeth of a kyng** is a correlative notion to what the king claims: "And so too in the same way, the people may demand from the king in return . . . ."

The terms echo and elaborate the contract between king and people in B.Prol.121–22, omitted from C perhaps in tandem to the insertion here (see also B.Prol.139–45n). As there, the emphasis on a contract between king and people corresponds to an important constitutional development of the later Middle Ages and early modern period (see Black 1993; Kean 1969). **standynge as a stake that stikede in a mere**: The king establishes the realm's interior boundaries, as a condition of "rect relacion" for the kind of beneficent transactions described by "mercede." Again property law is the central metaphor and social focus, here a boundary marker resolving disputes in order for "eche lif to knowe his owene" in an unambiguous sense of 'his own property' (cp. B.Prol.122n).

379: Lawe, loue and lewete: lewete is, from earlier stages of the poem's composition, a clear version of "relacoun rect": see Prol.149–51n, and 2.51–52n; see generally Kean 1969:147–51. Love, less often discussed, is another instance of social as well as spiritual rectitude throughout the poem, occasionally, though not here, a faint allegorical personification, first glimpsed in B and C at Prol.130 (B.Prol.102) (see Prol.130n, Prol.128–33n; and especially 1.153–58n). As was made clear first in the B text Prologue, these are needed to modify the severity, but equal rectitude, of Law (see Prol.153–59n). Thus Kean takes the formulation here in C to express the central political and social ideal of PP in all versions, comparable to Thomas Aquinas' and Aristotle's notion of justice as "the sum of all virtues," and thus a supremely moral view of politics as a social contract for the right way to live according to Truth (Kean 1969). Clearly this is a key combination of terms in the poet's later thought, and it is precisely what is missing from Meed's formulation of the self-interested desires that unify society in the common pursuit of reward (above, 265–81n).

Meed's challenge seems to be the fruitful occasion for enunciating this point; otherwise only rarely, and mostly in C, does the ideal emerge as a clear trinity. Love is linked with Leaute on numerous other occasions without "law," as (first in sequence of composition) below at A 267 (see 444n); see also 4.36n, 10.172 (C only), B.11.167 (B only), etc. Love is also linked with Law, without Leaute, on several occasions: B.7.63 (A.8.65) (and paraphrastically at the corresponding C passage, 9.59), etc. For all three again together, see 7.260, also C only, a description of the kind of "church" to establish in the "hole herte"; and the slightly varied "onlyche loue and leaute as in my lawes demynge" (12.80 [B.11.145]), in Trajan's expression of his own set of guiding ethics.

384: For they wilnen and wolden as beste were for hemsulue: The definition of "indirect" relation continues with the political theory defining the king's relation to his people, and having exemplified the king's ideal role as the epitome of "relacoun rect," proceeds to have the king's subjects exemplify the opposite of "relacoun rect" as well as the counterpart to any ideal. In spite of its appearance of balance, the argument here is tendentiously flattering the king and blaming his subjects, as does the C version of the Rat Parliament (see Prol.167–219 [B 146–208] and notes). The people, it seems, not the crown, create the conditions for lawyers (see following note). Implicitly, it is thus heavily the king's responsibility to create a "relation" between himself and his people leading to less self-interested transactions.

387–93: for hem lakketh case . . . How þat cliauntes acorde acounteth mede litel: The metaphoric focus and linguistic doublemeanings specify lawyers as epitomizing those "inparfit peple" who are "puyr indirect." **hem lakketh case** "leads us directly into the courtroom, and the terminology of grammar—for example, case, parties, number, accord—suddenly becomes the terminology of the law" (Alford 1982:758). The general criticism of "þe moste partie of peple" (383) thereby is mitigated by greater criticism of those lawyers who profit from the conflicts of **parties** (390), now used in the legal sense. The simple criticism of lawyers here is that they are happy to stir up conflicts where they do not really have a "case" and from which they alone profit; compare *The Simonie*, "Attourneis in cuntre, þeih geten siluer for noht. / Þeih maken men biginne þat þei neuere hadden þouht" (ed. Embree and Urquhart 1991, A 349–50). A late fourteenth-century sermon—which also uses the text from Matthew (6:2) that appears throughout this scene in all versions—declares that even if a legal case is just, its lawyers' motive for profit removes any spiritual reward for themselves: "ʒif [þise ryche men] plete for a man and is quarell be trewe, anone þei wene þat þei haue getton heven for here mede, but for god [good] þat is aftur þat þer loue is sett. For and þei do itt principally to resceyve grett ӡeftes, þer, trewly, þan, þei haue resceyved hur mede and no rewarde in heven" (ed. Ross 1940:201–2). Such concerns both for the clients' souls and the lawyers' might be aligned with the increasing interest in motives in discussions of legal contracts (the "doctrine of consideration": A. W. B. Simpson 1975:316–26), and generally the increasing emphasis on "conscience" in legal decisions (see above, Headnote, 367–70 and notes, and Prol.95–135n). Criticism of lawyers and judges is general in the poem; see Prol. 160–66n.

399–400: And coueyte þe case . . . soffre harde penaunce: The proper kind of "case" to covet is that in the "court of conscience," where sins will be revealed and penance sought (see Prol.95–135n). The distinction is from the kind of self-gratifying coveting described above in lines 363–65, 371–72, and 384.

402a: *Deus homo*: "God [and] man [are made one Christ]": echoing the Athanasian Creed "Ita Deus et homo unus est Christus" (Alford, *Quot.*). The following English line also appears to draw on the source behind this line. At this point, the focus and metaphoric vehicle pull away from a grammar of law and shift to a grammar of theology. In the latter terms, as Amassian and Sadowsky point out, identifying God and human beings as one in the Incarnation allows Conscience to define *homo* as a "substantival noun" seeking God as its proper adjective, as below in 405, rather than as an "adjectival noun" that "Seketh and seweth his sustantif sauacioun / That is god," as at 353–54 (Amassian and Sadowsky 1971:473–74).

403a: *Qui in caritate manet . . . in eo*: "he that abides in charity abides in God, and God in him": 1 John 4:16, said in the daily grace (Alford, *Quot.*). The passage is a favored one in the poem; see also Prol.82n, and B.5.486b and B.9.65a. Since a unity of human beings and God is effected by a single unifying charity, the "noumbre" of humanity into which God is drawn is both numerous and single.

405–6: As *hic & hec homo* askyng an adiectyf / Of thre trewe termisonus, *trinitas vnus deus*: "This [male] and this [female] person": the alliterative phrase is evidently based on *hic et haec sacerdos* (this male and female priest) used in Donatus and its commentaries, translations, and adaptations to illustrate demonstrative pronouns (see Alford, *Quot.*); see also Isidore, *Etymologiae* 1.7.28 (ed. Lindsay 1911), where "hic et haec canis" ("this male and this female dog") illustrates a "common noun" (what Alan of Lille calls "heteroclite" nouns, that "show variations in deviation by reclining with those of female gender in Winter and those of masculine gender in Summer" [*De planctu*, 8, pr. 4, trans. Sheridan 1980:136]). The context of unity with God suggests again that the phrase is shaped by Gal. 3:28, "there is neither male nor female. For you are all one in Christ Jesus." The "masculine and feminine human being" is **askyng** in the sense of "praying" as well as "requiring" three **trewe termisonus**, the last a word attested only here but whose sense, "final sounds" or "grammatical endings," is clear. But the details of the sense here are still obscure. **hic & hec homo** seem not yet to have "three true terminsons" because they present endings with different final sounds, rather than the *–s* endings of **trinitas vnus deus**, "Trinity and one God" (as in the Athanasian Creed [Alford, *Quot.*]). The paradox of the Trinity informs the complexities here. Since **homo** is a "common noun" of both genders, it asks for only one adjective, but with three endings. Possibly the one adjective needed by **homo** is *deus*, as in *deus homo*, at 402a. The following line offers three different "termisons" for the Trinity, but in the present line, the Trinity's unity is emphasized by the layered repetitions of 'tr' and 'us.'

406a: *Nominatiuo, pater & filius & spiritus sanctus*: "In the nominative, the Father and Son and Holy Spirit," with an allusion to the formula "In nomine Patris et Filii et Spiritus Sancti" (Alford, *Quot.*, who speculates that it may be a grammarbook example). The benedictional allusion makes a formal conclusion to Conscience's "grammatical" lesson, which ends with this line. The turn towards this homiletic style may reflect how medieval Parliaments often opened with a sermon, but the gesture is a general one.

Conscience's conclusion

407–83 (B 259–330; A 238–76): Ac hoso rat of *regum* . . . For *melius est bonum nomen quam diuicie multe*: The texts rejoin for the balance of the passus to present Conscience's conclusion, which builds from a directly political criticism of the use of Meed by the powerful to a view of apocalyptic renovation of rule, justice, and reward. At this climax, offering a warning to the present-day rulers, lawyers, and judges in the scene, A breaks off; B and C continue with a final exchange between Conscience and Meed about her selective style of reading Scripture. The discussion in all the versions rehearses the books of Kings (*regum*), especially the story of Saul's fall. The basic account is summarized up to 433 (B 280, A 258) more or less literally and directly, oriented to the moral declared by the prophet Samuel in the text (1 Kings 15:22–23): when Saul, told by God to destroy Amalec utterly, spares its king Agag and "the best of the flocks of sheep and of the herds, and the garments and the rams, and all that was beautiful," Samuel tells him that God will punish him for his disobedience, idolatry, and rebellion, even though Saul's people make a burnt offering of the goods and cattle. The application to an association with Meed is not difficult, but it is unusual to warn kings of avarice in this way. For an interpretation of Saul as alienated from God on account of greed, *propter avaritiam*, see Paul of Aquina, *Exhortatio* (PL 99:226).

In the terms Conscience has been using in C, the example of Saul shows a king allowing an inordinate, "indirect" desire to trump an intrinsic desire for his antecedent, God. The shift at 437 (B 284, A 260) to an anagogic reading of the situation in Kings, where the triumph of David and Samuel over Saul is described as a future, apocalyptic event, draws on a long tradition of seeing David as the type of Christ (e.g., Bede, *In primam partem Samuhelis libri iv*, ed. Hurst, 1962, where lines from the Kings text are systematically intercalated with parallel details in the gospel to show the fulfillment of David in Christ).

407–11: hoso rat of *regum* . . . kept shep and lambren: C fills in more of the text from 1 Kings 15–16, more directly summarizing the downfall of Saul and the exaltation of David, a mere shepherd (1 Kings [Vulg.] 16:11–12). The expansion of these details in C might offer some additionally sharpened warnings to King Richard, who according to some accounts was briefly deposed in 1387, then reinstated when the Lords Appellant could not agree which of them they would make king in his stead; they went on to appeal, condemn, and execute many of his closest supporters (see Goodman 1971; Taylor 1987:87–88; Galloway 2002). The emphasis in this courtly setting on the overthrow of a king and the rise of a shepherd king, however familiar, is bold no matter what the date of C, but quite dangerous if after 1388.

408: How he absoloun to hangynge brouhte: "He" is Meed (the southwestern form of the feminine pronoun, vulgarly clarified in MS. F, "How þat hore"). See 2 Kings (Vulg.) 14–18. C's insertion of this later part of David's own tragedy identifies Absalom also as a victim of greed, evidently because Absolom sought royal power. The emphasis on Meed's agency rather than Absalom's recalls Holy Church's presentation of Wrong (see 1.63–64n). The executions of the royal favorites in 1388 by the Lords Appellant, especially Simon Burley, would be a possible association from the C insertion for readers after that date, and just possibly part of the poet's emphasis; see note above.

413 (cp. B 259, A 238): As me ret in *regum* of þe reuthe of kynges [Ac reddestow neuere *Regum*]: See 1 Kings (Vulg.) 15–16. In C Conscience continues with an impersonal, and less aggressive, construction, "one (**me**) reads"; he is less the prosecuting attorney of Meed that he is in A and B, and more a teacher or preacher of the court as a whole, and particularly the king, who is pointedly offered the parallel of Saul's downfall. C's addition of the death of David's own sometime favorite, Absalom (above 408n), to the story of Saul's and Agag's downfalls justifies C's general comment on "the sorrows of kings." The C revision of passus 4 ends with still more direct and unusual advice to a king, completing the pattern of the "mirror of princes"; see below, 4.191–94n.

433 (B 280, A 258): The *culorum* of this kaes: The "ending," taken by MED as based on the final syllables of *in secula seculorum* ("for ever and ever"), the typical ending of a prayer, just before "Amen"; similarly at 11.246 (B.10.415). Perhaps the sense is influenced by Anglo-Norman *coleure*, 'strained material,' 'pulp,' thus 'gist.' The warning is a general one to those in power, presumably modeled on Samuel's comments to Saul at 1 Kings (Vulg.) 15:22–26 but specifically emphasizing avarice.

436 (B 283): he þat sayth men sothes is sonnest yblamed: Inserted in B, the lines parallel the thrust of the various truth-telling royal counselors added in the B.Prol. In the context of a date after 1388 for C, however, they would possess a new urgency (see notes to lines above from 407–11 on). The phrase is a variant of the proverb, "who sayth soth he shal be shent" (made the refrain of a lyric in the Vernon MS., f. 408b: ed. Brown 1957, no. 103; for the proverb, see, e.g., Pantin 1930:109, no. 16). John Bromyard, under "*veritas*," has in his *Summa praedicantium* a Latin paraphrase, "Tempora mutantur, homines deteriorantur, et qui vult dicere ueritatem, frangitur sibi caput" ("the times are changed and men are the worse, and whoever wishes to say the truth has his head broken": 1485:420, quoted in Wawn 1983:273n9, who surveys the Middle English literary tradition emphasizing this notion). The lines here make clear that Conscience's summary of Saul's downfall is focused not on Meed herself but on the powerful who use her; like the narrator in the Prologue, Conscience draws attention to his dangerous soothsaying by declaring that he will not say it (see also 3.363–73n, and the Prologue narrator's similar posture, Prol.138n; Prol.220–21n).

437–82a (B 284–330, cp. A 260–76): I, Consience, knowe this . . . *quam diuicie multe*: The A text's conclusion of the passus at **suche loue shal aryse** (C 453/B 300, refashioned by B into the first part of a "such . . . That" clause) moves to an ideal renovation of law and social order, by which an ideal monarch will rule without Meed or lawyers. The scope of the claims and the likely date of the A text make unlikely Skeat's conviction that the closing section refers primarily to the proclamation of a jubilee in 1376, the last year of Edward III's reign, his fiftieth (as support, Skt notes the prophetic temper of "John of Bridlington's" [c. 1377] mention of the jubilee: "Pacis erunt dies, belli terrore remoto . . .": "there will be days of peace, with the terror of war removed" [ed. Wright 1861, bk. 3 cap. 8], but the preceding lines have stressed the sorrows of kings). It seems likelier that the late 1380s contributed to a sense of political crises and the prospect that Richard II might not reign long, leading to general anxieties about the social governance and order on which Conscience's speech builds. As Skeat puts it, "the poet . . . prophesies that certain rather unlikely events will first happen [before the new era of perfect peace], thus revealing his fear that no such good time was at hand" (Skt 2.51). The passage, especially as extended in B and C following A's conclusion at C 453 (B 300), suggests the apocalyptic tradition somewhat like "Thomas of Erceldoune's Prophecy" (ed. Robbins 1959:29), used as a rhetorical climax like Reason's *impossibilia* speeches at 4.108–45 (B.4.113–48, A.4.100–31) and 5.168–79 (cp. B.10.322–32).

Like Reason's speeches, Conscience's examples of that time are more socially reformist than "Thomas of Erceldoune's Prophecy," and evoke more Christian images of judgment. Thus as, for example, the *Holkham Bible Picture Book* presents in its conclusion a Day of Judgment that will be heralded by the resistance to judgment of the powerful ("le grant pouple") and the widespread uprisings of the common people ("le commoune gent"; ed. Pickering 1971), so Conscience's vision likewise involves massive disruption of social class, in his case the levelling or near levelling of all to a state of labor and penance. And as the *Holkham Bible*, like all visions of Christian apocalypse, stresses that the Son of God will convene all in a universal judgment, so Conscience concludes by declaring that **Al shal be but o couert and o buyrne be Iustice** (474/B 321).

438 (B 285, A 261): resoun shal regne: Conscience's new world recalls Holy Church's interpretation of Matthew 22:21 (1.48–53n); Conscience here suggests that Holy Church's ideal principles can be and will be political realities in some apocalyptic future. So too the comments against those who "taketh aȝeyn treuthe" (446; and even more closely B/A's "trespaseþ to truþe" [B 293, A 268]) make into an apocalyptic future Holy Church's declaration that "Kynges and knyghtes" should punish "*transgressores*" "Til treuthe hadde termyned here trespas to þe ende" (1.93 [B1.97, A1.95]). The A text's passus ending here is well formed, since here what Holy Church has declared ought to be so among the powerful, Conscience declares someday *will* be so. His apocalyptic recasting of Holy Church's ideals emphasizes that they, as yet, are far from fulfilled but all the more bear reemphasizing.

442 (B 289, A 265): o cristene kyng: For this important ideal, close to the universal absolutism of Dante's *De monarchia*, see the apocalyptic context of 21/B.20.427 (see 21.424–27n).

444 (B 291, A 267): loue and lownesse and lewete togyderes: In sequence of composition, this is the first place where Love joins Leaute (A 267); C joins those figures at 379 above (see n).

448–49 (B 295–96, cp. A 270–71): a selk houe / Ne no pelure in his panelon [A: Ne no ray robe wiþ riche pelure]: Sergeants at law wore close, tied head-pieces and robes with banded (**ray**) sleeves in red and green or blue-green; see the illustration of these figures at the Court of Chancery, from a fifteenth-century manuscript, in Fisher (1965), frontispiece. Gower, in a passage criticizing lawyers, though less absolutely, describes them as dressed in red and blue with "raye mance" ("banded sleeves"; *Mirour de l'Omme*; ed. Macaulay 1899), line 21774; see also "Sinners Beware," lines 133–38; ed. Morris 1872:76). For particular critical attention in PP to sergeants at law, see Prol.160–66n, Prol.161–62n, 2.39–42n. **panelon** is unattested elsewhere in Middle English, but see *pan(e)*, 'cloak,' *panel*, cloth piece (esp. saddle cloth), and, closer, Anglo-Norman *pan-elloun*, 'piece' (of tapestry, horse-cloth, etc.). The variant reading *pavillion* means 'tent' everywhere else, so the sense 'coif' for that word here only (so Bnt) is doubtful; more likely this is from scribal confusion between "n" and "u/v" (MED 2).

452 (B 299, cp. A 275): B/C kynde loue; A kynde wyt: The A text, at this climactic point in Conscience's utopian future, brings in Kind Wit as Conscience's help in refashioning society; the voice, which now names Conscience as well as Kind Wit and so can no longer be simply Conscience speaking, shifts into that of an objective voice of prophecy or apocalypse.

Since Kind Wit's role is advanced in B and C to the Prologue, and altered to become a primary agent in history's original (rather than final) pattern of social creation and division (see Prol.141–47n, 1.51n), B and C introduce here for the present different purposes a new figure, **kynde loue**. Thus, in B and C, Kind Wit is shown founding society in its first form, and Kind Love will remake it under a new dispensation. The latter entity recalls other significant references in C/B only (or B only) to the elusive entity **loue**; see above, 379n. But Kind Love is evidently a different force or entity from these, or a different instantiation for a specific historical role at the end of time. The apocalyptic vision of PP is often compared with Joachim of Flora's notion of the "age of the Holy Ghost" in the final phase of history, aligned with Paul's discussion of "charity" (see Bloomfield 1962:65–66, 111–12). But a general sense of meeting God obtains in mentions of "charity" in PP that does not require the Joachimite connection (see 1.37n).

kynde loue is specifically identified as *Caritas* (charity) at 14.14 (C only), evidently based on B's presentation of **kynde loue** as what "coueiteþ noȝt no catel but speche" (B.13.150), in the riddling passage on the "half a laumpe lyne." The Latin gloss later in that B section, "*Caritas nichil timet*" (B.13.163a), shows that **kynde loue** there also is a translation of *Caritas*, the central Christian ideal of spiritual love (as in 1 Cor. 13). **kynde loue** or *Caritas* is thus distinct from the more capacious "lele loue," one of the incarnations Liberum Arbitrium (Anima in B) claims for herself, since she defines this specifically as "in latyn Amor" (16.196 [B.15.34]). The ideal social contract present or future is based on faith, love, and fidelity, as other presentations of **loue** show (see e.g. above, 444n); thus the remaking of society that Conscience in B/C imagines at the present passage looks toward a spirit of sacred reconciliation with no need for the intellectual labors of lawyers, leaving them to apply themselves to "truer" labor (implicitly, plowing, as below 462 [B 309]).

457 (B 303): Moyses or Messie: That is, the future Christ will fulfill his type, Moses; the Jews will rejoice at a **Messie** (messiah) who seems a mere variation, even in his name, on their **Moyses**.

454–83 (B 301–30): And such pees . . . *quam diuicie multe*: Conscience's ideal of reformation is extended to all of society, perhaps prompted by the invocation here of Isaiah 2:4 with its reference to "Gentiles," to include the non-Christian world of **iewes** and **saresines**. The Jews are converted at least in part by the (uncharacteristic) spectacle of the reformed Christians: **þat men ben so trewe** (457 [B 304]; see Galloway 1995:90). The social estates will collapse into a minimalist form of society lacking the accoutrements of "pride" displayed in the Prologue and elsewhere (see Prol.25–26n), and thus compressing the differences into those who labor and those who pray: the aristocratic, military estate will become plowmen and laborers, as will the lawyers ("maky of lawe a laborer" [453 (B 300)]), and the clerical estates will be strictly limited to prayer. Implicitly, aristocratic women are similarly reduced to **Spynne oþer speke of god** (463 [cp. B 310]), just as Piers will later order them to (8.9–14 [B.6.10–14, cp. A.7.10–13]). The reduction of the military estate follows Isaiah 2:4; see note below and at 477a; the reduction of other estates appears to extend that conception elsewhere.

458–63 (B 305–10): For alle þat bereth baslard . . . and spille no tyme: Following the lawyers, the reduction of the aristocracy to laborers plays off Isaiah

2:4, **Conflabunt gladios suos in vomeres & lancias suas in falces**, "And they shall turn their swords into plowshares and their spears into sickles." The passage is continued at 477a (B 324a), where it is applied to the craftsman rather than the user.

464–67 (B 311–14): Prestes and persones *placebo* **and** *dirige . . .* **and his lyf parauntur:** *Placebo* is the first word of the antiphon that begins the Office of the Dead at vespers: "Placebo Domino in regione vivorum," "I will please the Lord in the land of the living," based on Psalm 114:9; *Dirige* begins the Office of the Dead at matins, based on Psalm 5:9: "Dirige Domine Deus meus in conspectu tuo viam meam," "Direct my path O my Lord in your sight" (Alford, *Quot.*). **here seuene psalmes** refers to the seven "penitential" psalms: 6, 31, 37, 50, 101, 129, 142 (= AV 6, 32, 38, 51, 102, 130, 143). In the later fourteenth century the Carmelite friar Richard Maidstone wrote rhymed alliterative elaborations of each line of these (ed. Edden 1990). These are also Will's "lomes" ('tools'; C.5.45–47).

B 311: wiþ *Placebo* **to hunte:** B allows a metaphorical "hunting" for priests like that implied at B.5.417–18. The metaphor is elaborated in a sermon by Thomas of Chobham in the thirteenth century: the devil and the flesh are vicious hunters of our souls, but what we should truly be hunting is what we can rightly enjoy, i.e., God (sermo 6, ed. Morenzoni 1993). A closer parallel to PP's pungent phrasing and point, however, is the early eleventh-century Old English *Canons of Edgar*, attributed to Archbishop Wulfstan: "We læraþ þæt preost ne beo hunta ne hafecere ne tæflere, ac plegge on his bocum swa his hade gebirað" ("we teach that a priest should not be a hunter or a hawker or a gambler, but should play on his books as his calling demands": sec. 65, ed. Fowler 1972:14; Bethurum 1957:92 notes the parallel).

466–67 (B 313–14): Haukyng or huntyng yf eny of hem hit vse / Shal lese þerfore his lyflode: Canon law initially discouraged, then directly prohibited priests from hunting. For discouragement, see above, B 311n (Wulfstan); for prohibition, see the Fourth Lateran Council, Constitutio 15 (ed. Alberigo 1973:243): "Venationem et aucupationem universis clericis interdicimus unde nec canes nec aves ad aucupandum habere praesumant": "We prohibit hunting and fowling to all clerics, wherefore they should not presume to possess hounds, or birds for fowling." The satirical tradition is rich with assertions that this was violated; see 5.156–62 (B.10.311–16), 7.32–34 (B.5.417–19), and Chaucer, General Prologue I.165–207.

B 312: dyngen vpon Dauid: The priest's day-long "pounding away on David" is another way that an estate is reduced to basic labor, as in B.6.141, "dyngen vpon sheues"; compare the lyric "I donke upon David til my tonge talmes," Sisam and Sisam 1970:186. The same phrase appears in *The Papelard Priest*, c. 1349, to refer to what seems to the reluctant priest who narrates that poem as the drudgery of menial spiritual work that pulls him away from sitting and eating pears, when the bell tower calls him to deliver a service: "þen mot I nede parten and passen from my perus / to dyngen opon dauyd wyt a dirige" (ed. Smith 1951, line 55–56).

470 (B 317): Ne potte hem in panele to do hem plihte here treuthe: panele is originally a paper or board on which names of jurors were written, thence the jury itself (and thence too the verb "empanellen"). Alford, *Quot.* s.v. *panel* provides a series of examples indicating complaints about sheriffs and bailiffs oppressing people by summoning excessive numbers of lower status men to duty on a jury panel with the intention of oppressing them or taking bribes from them; Alford notes that the statute *De ponendis in assisis* (1306), which established a substantial minimum income for jury duty, was formed to correct such abuses. See also the materials presented at 2.60–63n. The offense here is the extraction of a vow (**plihte here treuthe**) under compulsion or bribery. Making a false vow was a deadly sin; see Prol.69n.

471 (cp. B 318): the doom shal record [B: oon doom shal rewarde] / Mercy or no mercy: C's **record** is a more technical term for announcing officially the proceedings of a trial (see Alford, *Gloss.*); B's **rewarde** simply means "grant." A judgment of **mercy** refers to a remission of punishment granted before any sentence has been imposed (see Alford, *Gloss.*).

473 (B 320): Kyngus Court and comune Court; constorie and chapitre: The variety of secular and religious law courts, which began proliferating after William I divided "Christian" and "royal" courts, meant that cases might be judged with different results in different courts, and that the results of justice were fissured into sometimes irreconcilable outcomes and processes (which plaintiffs might manipulate, e.g., appealing a case in one court that had not been settled in another). The broad theme of irreconcilable modes of legal existence is soon expressed in the complaint of Peace in the next passus. To mention these courts is to make "a careful differentiation among four contemporary courts" (Kirk 1933:326), even while those are imagined as collapsed into one. **Kyngus Court and comune Court** refer to King's Bench and Common Pleas, the first handling more significant and select matters, the second handling the vast numbers of cases by the wider populace; **constorie and chapitre** are, respectively, the high ecclesiastical court (analogous to the King's Bench; see Prol. 126–27n) and the rural chapter, responsible for dealing with "the resident parochial clergy and the peasantry who constituted nine tenths of the Church's subjects" (Scammell 1971:1).

For the apocalyptic ideal of political unity in general, compare John 10:16, "other sheep I have that are not of this fold; them also I must bring. And they shall hear my voice; and there shall be one fold and one shepherd"; also Matt. 25:31–46, where "all nations shall be gathered together before" God, and Isaiah 2:4, where "he shall judge the Gentiles and rebuke many people."

475 (B 322): trewe-tonge: Perhaps the same figure appears again as a servant at Reason's household; see 4.18–19.

477a (B 324a): *Non leuabit gens contra gentem gladium nec excercebuntur ultra ad prelium*: "Nation shall not lift up sword against nation: neither shall they be exercised any more to war" (Isaiah 2:4), in B continuing the quotation begun at 308a above, and implied throughout this section. This quotation directly provides the basis for transforming the military, and by extension other, social estates to focus strictly on prayer and labor; see above 454–83n.

479–80 (B 326–27): Be sixe sonnes and a ship and half a shef of Arwes; / And the myddell of a mone shal make þe iewes turne: This prophetic statement has not been explained, and the leads so far proposed for doing so are not promising. The context of the quotation from Isaiah 2:4 points to a future moment hidden from present view, and perhaps a date is implied in the first line: **ship** has been interpreted on the grounds of the shape of a medieval vessel as an "x" (i.e., ten; so Bnt), and a sheaf of arrows usually carried twenty-four arrows (Bnt); also, the appearance of multiple suns is a commonplace of dire portents (Bnt). Bloomfield drew attention to passages of the Malmesbury chronicle called the *Eulogium historiarum sive temporis* (Bloomfield 1962:88): under 8 October 1366, the chronicler notes that "burning torches were seen passing to and fro in the firmament, extending from the sphere of the moon down to the earth, some to a thickness of a human leg and extending three cubits, some to six, some to twelve, with very sharp points like spears and widening toward the base, in the manner of wax candles but a hundredfold larger, displaying a great length"; under 22 October, the chronicle mentions a similar phenomenon, this time comparing the extensions of flame to *ignita jacula*, which Bloomfield suggests are like "arrows of fire" but properly are (as under 8 October) "burning spears" (Haydon 1863:240–41). The connection seems dubious. If a dating clause is meant like those in the prophecies of "John of Bridlington," it is not changed between B and C. The Jews, it was said, would be converted in the last days; here, the prophecy of the conversion of the Jews is linked to the enigmatic **myddell of a mone**; possibly this relies on the *Elucidarium* 3.50 which says that the Last Judgment will take place at midnight (Bloomfield 1962:211–12). Or **myddell of a mone** may refer to a graphic riddle, which is more certainly the case for the C replacement of the same phrase at 15.157–61 (cp. B.13.151–57). In that case, the phrase refers to the letter "C," the first part of a graphic riddle spelling "COR," "heart," as the solution to "what God demands from you"; in the Latin riddle, the riddling phrase equivalent to **myddell of a mone** is "Lune dimidium" ("half of a moon"; see Galloway 1995, and other studies cited there). This points toward the notion of "kynde loue" that will rule the world. The connection to the general apocalyptic tradition that Bloomfield outlined remains evident (see especially Bloomfield 1962:98–126). Reason's closing speech in the next passus ends on a similarly challenging, and silencing, riddle (see 4.140–45n).

481 (cp. B 328): sarisines . . . *Credo in spiritum sanctum* [B: *Gloria in excelsis &*]: In B, the Saracens offer a hymn, the Gloria of the Mass ("Glory in the highest . . ."; see Alford, *Quot.*); in C, they sing the Apostles' Creed ("I believe in the holy spirit"). The change may be a way of uniting the passage with the earlier references to the Creed in Conscience's grammar lesson (above, 356–60 and 402a and notes), or of emphasizing the need for doctrinal reformation (i.e., belief in the Trinity) by the infidel rather than simply praise for a single God by those who are already monotheists: see B.15.393–96. The turn to Saracens continues to follow the reference to God judging "the Gentiles" at Isaiah 2:4.

483 (B 330): *melius est bonum nomen quam diuicie multe*: Prov. 22:1, with word order slightly varied: "a good name is better than great riches." Good repute in general social contexts is not the intended sense in this apocalyptic context, nor was it generally in explicit medieval interpretations of this proverb. Exegetes, however, felt some pressure from the literal sense of mere "fame" that appears here; Bede, for example, says that "nomen bonum dicit non quod a turbis vulgi imperiti sed quod fidelium quamuis paucorum testimonio laudetur" ("he [Solomon] calls a good name that which may be praised by the testimony of the faithful, however few, not the hordes of ignorant rabble"; Book 2, cap. 22; ed. Hurst 1983). In subtler senses the quotation may have particular resonances with Conscience's overall speech: the proper defining of the term "meed," redeeming its "good name," hence showing the impropriety of Meed's own name, has exercised him for much of his presentation. The issue of a "good name" in other senses has pointed others of his arguments too, as at C 367 and C 402. But Meed takes the quotation in its most direct sense; see following note.

The final exchange

485–88 (B 333–36): "Loo what salamon sayth . . . *Honorem adquiret qui dat munera*: Meed begins responding by answering Conscience's quotation regarding the importance of a "good name" in Proverbs 22:1 by presenting another statement in the same chapter of Proverbs about honor which extolls her own role in granting that: "He that makes presents shall purchase victory and honor" (Prov. 22:9). Her citation of that verse from Proverbs 22 is significantly incomplete, as Conscience goes on to emphasize in dramatic fashion (see following note); but it is effective in challenging the unity of values and meanings of Proverbs 22 as a whole. Since a "good name" in the first proverb of Proverbs 22 that Conscience has quoted means "honor," should we not seek the means to gain that? Can Conscience's criticism of earthly "reward" as mere honor on earth, using Matthew 6:2, be reconciled with his use of Proverbs 22:1 (see B 252–54a and C 311–12)? Meed's exegetical abilities here are shrewder than Conscience acknowledges in his following denunciation of her unskilled reading. The finding of difficulties in Proverbs was itself an ancient tradition of interpretive effort; Davlin 1988 compares the entire poem to that tradition. Here again, Meed's ingenuity forces Conscience to a further elaborate effort. **in *sapiense* in þe bible:** The term used throughout the poem for the book of Proverbs (see, e.g., below 496, B.6.235, C.11.209, etc.).

489–500 (B 337–53): "I leue the, lady . . . rescetour of Gyle": Conscience avoids the question of what exactly a "good name" means in Proverbs 22:1, and instead brings the focus to the proper manner of reading in context, using as example the two-clause, paratactic structure of many biblical sententiae. In formal terms, Conscience displays his mastery of both scripture and rhetorical form by first offering as a simile for Meed's partial reading another biblical verse whose first clause is strongly qualified by its second; then, completing a chiasm, Conscience presents the second part of the line Meed has quoted. His example in the simile is not arbitrary: **omnia probate . . . Quod bonum est tenete**, "prove all things, hold fast to that which is good" (1 Thess. 5:21), returns to the motif Holy Church brought in of *trying* treasures, but Conscience emphasizes the choosing (see 1.81–204n). The idea is a fundamental principle in the poem's presentation of authentic understanding and wisdom, perhaps as a fullscale remoralizing of the same point in the *Roman de la Rose* (see 1.77–78n, and Prologue, Headnote). Meed, Conscience shows, has left out the part about judgment in such gains: the rest of Proverbs 22:9, **Animam autem aufert Accipiencium,** "but he carries away the souls of the receivers." The "trying" of Meed, and the trial of Meed, concludes with an emphasis on human choosing and divine judgment.

490 (B 338): Thow art lyk a lady þat a lessoun radde: For the phrasing and diction, compare *William of Palerne*, "ful wel him liked þe lessun þat þe lady radde" (ed. Bunt 1985, line 4442). The sense of the formula for "a woman speaking a message" is here used for a more literally bookish point, both in "reading" and in "a lesson."

493 (cp. B 347): Ac hadde she loked in þe luft half [B: Ac yow failed a konnynge clerk]: The simile in C no longer asserts that the problem was a lack of a **konnynge clerk** as assistant; instead, the scene of a lady reading alone is left to imply that ladies should know how to read properly on their own. Women's private devotional reading, increasingly evident in the fourteenth and fifteenth centuries (see Clanchy 1993:189–96, 251–52; Clanchy 2004), is thereby in C not regarded as an anomaly but acknowledged to carry its own responsibility for basic interpretive integrity. This change in C is accompanied, however, by more emphatic examples of laypersons desiring proper instruction (see 343n).

499–500: Worschipe a wynneth . . . here is rescetour of Gyle: C's restatement of Proverbs 22:9 ("He who wishes to give meed wins worship") is syntactically more elliptical than B's, and returns to the technical legal language near the end of C's earlier expansion in the grammatical analogy: **resceyueth or recetteth** evokes a common legal formula for harboring a criminal or wrongdoer; and a **rescetour** is one who so harbors (see Alford, *Gloss.*). With **rescetour of Gyle** Conscience closes by implying Meed's continued connection to Guile, whom the king has already sentenced to death (2.216 [B.2.202, A.2.163]) and who has fled to hide in the depths of the city. If Meed is a companion to Guile, then to accept her is to harbor a criminal's abettor. There is perhaps a return to the issue of friars accepting donations of ill-gotten money, what Lawler identifies as "miswinning" (Lawler 2005). Conscience thus adds a pressingly topical legal meaning to the sense of Proverbs 22:9, the final turn in the closing interpretive puzzles made of that text, as well as anticipating the C text's emphasis on some legal detention of Meed at the end of the next passus.

C Passus 4; B Passus 4; A Passus 4

Headnote

The first vision ends with another marked shift of genre, literally a dramatic one: from a debate to a trial, propelled forward and animated by a series of figures whose interactions and characters are pursued in distinct, sometimes comic, and thematically implicated detail. The transition from the previous passus—occasioned by the king's brusque interruption of the debate and Peace's unexpected arrival to lodge a petition against Wrong, who turns out to be there along with some others of Meed's retinue who now emerge from the shadows—appears more circumstantial and abrupt than most of the transitions between genres of the first vision. But initially unexplained entrances are common in the poem (see Prol.139–47n). Moreover, the debate of passus 3 already had become more of a trial of Meed than a pursuit of whom she had married or ought to marry: a trial was imminent throughout the previous passus as soon as Conscience, the accuser, arrived (see 3.147n). More broadly, the theme of "making trial" of something, and of passing judgment on it, has been present explicitly from Holy Church's speech on: the theme of her sermon, "When alle tresores ben tried treuthe is þe beste" (1.81–204n) has led logically to the "trying" of Lady Meed and her followers by the narrator himself, as well as the other entities in passūs 2 and 3 seeking to define or marry or arrest her, then to Conscience's declaration of the principle of *omnia probate, quod bonum est tenete* (3.489–500n; see also 1.77–78n, and Prologue, Headnote). This theme now culminates literally, with an official "trial" of her and the social relations that she generates; the "holding" of the good is displayed in the king's condemnation of Wrong, and in his counselors' efforts at the court's reformation. Yet the distinction between the Tower on the Toft and the deep dale below is shown at the end of the scene, in Reason's speech, as far broader than the king's punishments and judgments, whose success here remains qualified, and which thus leaves his laws, like the entire human world, themselves on trial.

  Indeed, in much of the trial here not Meed herself but the social world that uses her is put on trial, in the form of Wrong and his attorneys and the mode of facile monetary reconciliation or "amends" they offer. Arbitration to settle complaints about property outside official courtrooms and legal procedures was very common in late medieval England, probably less a sign of social chaos than one of a long tradition of favoring reconciliation in the most flexible and local way (Powell 1989:93–107). Even mayhem and homicide could be settled out of court, and the nature of the settlements could be suited to repairing the social consequences of the crime or event (Rawcliffe 1984:44–45). One might then wonder why the effort at reconciliation here is so vilified, indeed increasingly so across the three versions. The ideal of a "loveday" (*dies amoris*), a name given to a wide range of kinds of settlements from the least formal to officially sanctioned and formal events, tapped into the most sacred notions of Christian and other social reconciliation on matters of social conflict; but a handful of moralists and satirists in the later fourteenth century, chiefly Wycliffite writers, perhaps obliquely Chaucer, but perhaps most clearly and categorically of all, Langland—seem to condemn such arrangements as unruly, extortionary, or otherwise illicit (Josephine Bennett 1958; see 3.196–97n). The basis for the concern—which by no means was universal, nor was the name "loveday" commonly opprobrious—seems to be the lack of official oversight in such arrangements, a sense of illicit forgiveness that evades justice and the proper hierarchy of authority. For a Wycliffite writer, the problem with making ad hoc amends seems related to an excessive ease in offering absolution of sin as well as crime, that is, in a matter concerning a higher authority than those involved in the reconciliation: "And þus louedayes of manus damage ben comunely aȝenus þis gospel [Matth. 18:15, 'if your brother shall offend against you, go and rebuke him between you and him alone'], for man shulde forȝyue frely þe harm þat is don aȝenus hym, and entirmete not of Goddis iniurie, for God onely may forȝyue þis" (Ferial Sermon 3 in the third week of Lent; ed. Gradon and Hudson 1983–96, vol. 3.111). As a practical matter, to be deemed fair, settlements usually required some form of judge or "umpire" above the participants; in PP, even a tavern game over a hood has a "noun-pere" (6.388 [B.5.330, A.5.179]; see Rawcliffe 1984:40–41). The absence of this is one of several ways in which the effort at reconciliation here is satirically evil, exacerbated by the sense of a degree of sin that cannot be settled by a monetary payment. The poem's continual and, comparing B with C, increasing concern with the king as the governing principle of authority (see, e.g., Prol.139–47n) may be related to the degree of satire on this point. Perhaps the very closeness of such easy reconciliation here to the most important ideals of society and religion in the poem, culminating with the Atonement or God's reconciliation itself, renders the effort to make amends here, right under the king's nose, particularly heinous. Like Meed herself, who evokes a central aspect of the poem's religious and social ideals—true reward—reconciliation, "amends," must be explored in its evil forms in order to understand its good ones.

Peace's petition, and first Wrong's, then the king's party's response, fall in the center of questions about rendering authoritative judgment and the question of just what sphere of authority is pertinent. The drama hinges on a central point of ambiguity in late medieval law and culture: private injury can merit private compensation and reconciliation, but a crime demands public judgment (or public pardon). Peace cannot make a settlement because his injury is not his own, but the king's. Peace's bill parades signs of both kinds of legal status, and, as himself both a hapless personal plaintiff and a personification of the principle of "the king's peace," he stands as a literary paradox of these issues, and to some extent a victim either way.

The point of Peace's legal status might seem technical, and like various aspects of the poem it assumes that at least part of its audience would be familiar with such matters (see further at Prol.85–94n, and 3.3n). But the trial's energetic drama does not linger in explicit debate about legal procedures: instead, it simply enacts one of the largest problems of defining an adequate authority for justice on earth in a world where private reconciliation was as common as public, royal determinations, and where even the latter might be resented or openly criticized. As the warning to the king in the Prologue suggests (see Prol.153–59n), and as the end of the trial here shows (see below 166–75n), a king's judgment must reside in principles and forces higher than himself. If, as in C, such a power is the king's own "conscience" and "reason," this allows him some freedom from the commons, but in this passus in C, the commons themselves can communicate to Conscience (see 151–59n).

If the first vision may be seen as a narrative unit (however self-sufficiently it was originally conceived), climaxing that unit with a trial follows a range of literary traditions. A trial often serves to fashion a climax in medieval romance and chanson de geste, from the *Chanson de Roland* through *Tristan* and beyond (see the index of Alford and Seniff 1984, s.v. *trial*). In Middle English, both *Havelok* and *Beves of Hampton* climax with trials before the king's council; religious drama and poetry likewise frequently end with trials, often of a more intricately legalistic kind, concerning the salvation of human beings or a particular human being; the paradigmatic English example is the *Castle of Perseverance* (c. 1425) where the trial of the soul of Genus Humanum completes the long spectacle, and may usefully exemplify a long Latin tradition of climactic trials between Jesus and the Devil, and between the Four Daughters of God (Peace, Righteousness, Justice, and Mercy), concerning the legitimacy of the Atonement or the salvation of a particular soul (see Traver 1907, 1925 and see notes to 20.271–346 [B.18.263–424]). And the form of climaxing a work with a trial governs PP itself in its revised versions: passus 4 explores a worldly and in part satirical version of the conflict between reconciliation and justice that occupies the later debate in the poem between the Four Daughters of God. But nothing quite like the tonal range of passus 4 can be found in these various models. What was generally high style in the debate of passus 3 becomes, in B and A at least, sometimes nearly farcical or comedic (in the style of twelfth-century Latin "comoedia" like *Geta*; see below, 27–31n) in the intrigues of and postures struck by Wrong's legal counsel, the hapless victimizing of Peace, and the final shaming of Lady Meed; the style also becomes prophetic tirade in Reason's final denunciation, in a combination with the farce that is difficult to parallel. Some similarities to this appear in the satirical allegory of a battle between Droit ("Right") and Tort ("Wrong") in Huon de Méri's mid-thirteenth-century *Torneiment Anticrist*, where Tort is punningly said to "joustify"—for in this context, the French verb suggests both 'rides against' and 'makes just'—Droit and his mother, Justice ("Vi contre Droit chevauchier Tort / Pur justisier Droit, e Justice, / Le mere Droit": "I saw Wrong charge against Right to joust with Right, and Justice, the mother of Right": ed. Bender 1976, lines 723–25). Tort, who cannot ride straight or "rightly" ("ne siet chevauchier droit" [line 728]) because his lazy horse uses only three legs, carries a huge shield emblazoned with Disloyalty, Falsity, and Treason and tongues drawn from lawyers' throats.

The three versions of the passus vary only in a set of limited passages. The differences, however, while numerically slight, are significant for the emphases of the allegory in its character development, social specificity, and moral tone. The particular balance of these in each version varies considerably: B greatly elaborates the comic potential present in A, while C more sternly enforces the rigor of the criticism. But all three define a mode of dramatic action and interaction, with a staging that is complex and thematically meaningful, a theatrical style and genre captured only intermittently elsewhere in the poem, most notably in the Banquet scene (15 [B.13]) and, more fully, the Crucifixion and the final three dreams of the poem (20–22 [B.18–20]). As in those cases, so here the theatrical mode is realistically intimate at times and at times cosmically encompassing. A's description of the opening journey of Reason with Conscience to the court is elaborated in B, and subsequently recompressed in C, with little loss of the new dramatic content that B had introduced but addition of more evident and sinister criminality.

C also expands slightly but significantly the wrongs that Peace has experienced from Wrong; here, the legal issue, of whether Peace is suing for personal trespass or presenting a complaint of criminal action, shifts decisively to felony, helping explain why the king will not allow Peace to settle his own damages. C compresses the description of Wrong's lawyers, especially of Sir Warren Wisdom, who appears most fully and even sympathetically in B. B expands, and C further expands, Reason's speech concerning the (impossible) terms on which he would pardon Wrong, in answer to those who appeal for mercy on Wrong's behalf; C alone notes Meed's quiet but legally enigmatic departure, adding at least this touch of literal drama. C also expands Reason's and the King's agreement from the agreement in A and B of "lyue we togi-deres" (B 195, A 158) to make Reason and Conscience specific court officers, respectively, Reason as Chancellor in the Exchequer and Parliament, and Con-science as King's Justice. Finally, just as in C Reason is granted a specific administrative job, so he responds there with a more detailed and specific set of conditions for accepting this arrangement.

C's changes (especially the compression of B's flamboyant Sir Warren Wisdom) thus make room at several points for more literal social particulars in the allegory and starker moral insistence, whereby Wrong is more emphati-cally and even satanically wrong. In keeping with both emphases, in C the dreamer awakens at the end of the passus hearing Conscience and Reason being given their royal commissions; in C he must immediately in the next passus face them himself and account for his lack of everyday social productiv-ity and his own hopes for reward or at least avoidance of prosecution. In A and B the dream persists to the end of the passus and slightly beyond, and in those versions the awakening, when it occurs early in the next passus, is a more whimsical, innocent, and fleeting hiatus than the long C awakening and inter-rogation inserted there (see 5.1–103). In A and B, the first vision climaxes with the generic potpourri of the trial here; in C, the larger importance of the trial is somewhat diminished and the pacing shifted, both by the major expansion of Conscience's speech in passus 3 and by the following "trial" of the narrator himself.

The king's suspended judgment and Reason's journey to court

1–5: "Cesseth . . . rather wol y dey": Debate poems frequently present mixed or suspended results; the closest parallel to the king's first effort to settle things here is the end of *Wynnere and Wastoure* (incomplete though its single manu-script is), when the king sends the two debaters to reside in parts of the world that best suit them (Cheapside and Rome). But here the king's initial, rough, and (as is apparent almost immediately from Conscience's despairing flight from court for assistance) inadequate resolution to the debate merely reveals the limitations of a superficial and imposed reconciliation of warring principles and parties; compare the spontaneous and mutual embrace and kiss resolving the debate between the Four Daughters of God (20.460 [B.18.417]). The king's demand for a kiss of reconciliation is the prerogative of a lord officiating over a quarrel, legal or personal, like Chaucer's Knight's order that the Host kiss the Pardoner after they have argued (*Canterbury Tales*, VI.963–67). But here the king is not chiefly concerned with their mutual love; instead, he reacts from his own exasperation at the labor of picking between their two arguments (**y soffre ȝow no lengore**). The king's first reaction is perhaps more fitting for a real marriage case, but altogether unsuitable here, as Conscience and then Reason will point out, because of the vast social issues crystallized in the debate, including the status of reconciliation, with which the king will soon be confronted in terms directly pertinent to his interests. It is probable that through the king's reaction the poet wryly acknowledges the fatigue that even some medieval readers must have felt at the increasingly lengthy distinctions Conscience has offered (note Skt's comment, "barely intelligible, and very dull" [2.50]).

Such reconciliation would be a victory for Meed, who is, briefly, assured royal protection provided she agree to **serue** him (and since she agrees to serve everyone who asks, her answer is predetermined). The prospect of it deals a severe blow to Conscience, who has expended so much effort on an increasingly complex lesson about their irreconcilability. Conscience's promise (or desperate asseveration) that he will only obey the king if Reason agrees opens the passus to more basic claims of right and law (and wrong and lawlessness) rather than the fine splitting of language in which Conscience is engaged. (RK-C has here a typographical error in the text in line 2, which should read "ȝe shal sauhtene.")

5–7 (B 5–7, A 5–7): "But resoun rede me þertyl . . ." ". . . Rape the to ryde and resoun þat thow fecche": Conscience's comment is a commonplace of phrasing in the parliamentary records, where the king routinely responds to queries and complaints by promising to do as *loi et raison* or *droit et reson* demand (e.g., Rot. Parl. 2.94 [1335], 2.192 [1347], and others in A-ND *raisun*); compare, e.g., Prol.184 (B.Prol.167), and see further at 1.50n. Immediately, however, the "it" becomes a "he," and Conscience's wish to receive some counsel from reason becomes an action and a literal consultation with Reason; the king's command allows the habitual expression to take life before our eyes. Compare the process of generating personifications like False at 1.5–9n, and Do Well at 10.75 ff. (B.8.77 ff., A.9.68 ff.).

resoun: The notion in many medieval contexts expresses supreme order, right, and, especially, law (Alford 1988b). That Conscience is the one appealing to Reason's authority follows the pattern of some medieval facultative and theological schemes. In one such scheme, Aquinas', Conscience is the impulse of choosing the good, a process or action rather than a faculty; Reason is the wider faculty comprehending the bases for such choices. Thus Conscience needs Reason for fuller authority, and indeed Reason's authoritative governance is noticeably higher in rank than Conscience's throughout the poem (see Whitworth 1972). But in general understanding Conscience and Reason belong together as fundamental medieval judicial principles, a view more precisely explaining their joint roles here. "Law is reason" (*lex est ratio*) is a recurrent medieval maxim, ultimately deriving from Cicero, widely available to medieval culture through Isidore of Seville (Alford 1988b). Anima later defines the roles of Conscience and Reason in terms closely suited to their judicial roles here: Anima defines Conscience by accusing or not accusing ("when y chalenge or chalenge nat"; see also Prol.95–135n), and Anima defines Reason as rendering judgments, relying on the highest principle of justice, truth ("when y deme domus and do as treuthe techeth") (16.191 [B.15.31], 16.187 [B.15.27]).

The pairing of Reason and Conscience also suggests the emergence of equity procedures and courts, which rapidly became more established in the early fifteenth century and which often explicitly relied on these principles to pass judgments rather than on the patterns and formulae of common law. Such equity procedures appeared first before the king's council, then before the Chancellor, who was already receiving petitions for this by the mid-fourteenth century and whose court of Chancery developed in the fifteenth century specifically for such a purpose (see Jones 1967:9–14; Avery 1969; Harding 1973:100–102). A general attention to the possibilities of equity in legal decisions seems to pervade the poem (see Prol.95–135n, 2.151n, 2.155n, 3.256–57n, 3.473n, and 20.386–87n, 20.395n, and below, 45–63n; see also Birnes 1975).

6–12: "And y comaunde the . . . lered and lewed": The king accepts Conscience's appeal without hesitation, and goes on to announce Reason's preeminence over all his other counselors, indeed all his subjects. **acounte with the . . . How thow ledest my peple** evokes the Latin *redde rationem vilicationis tuae* of Luke 16:2, "Give an account of your stewardship" (quoted directly, in part, at C.9.273). The statement is not a direct command (as in the Bible), but a statement of what Reason will do on behalf of Conscience before the king. The instructions, and the biblical echo, indicate that the king approves of Conscience's consultation with Reason but also that the king expects Conscience still to answer to himself, and to use Reason to help mitigate any disfavor Conscience has gained by not marrying Meed or any other lapses in leading the people. Reason is thus further defined as, in the best sense, a rationalizer. The speech indicates that although the king appeared exasperated with both debaters, he acknowledges Conscience's public role in leading **my peple**. This role of "royal policy" for which Conscience is responsible is precisely what left Conscience open to Meed's insistence that he needs her (see passus 3 Headnote, 3.147n, 3.231–32n, B.3.189–200n). The present passus confirms (and indeed in C especially strengthens) this role, but it still leaves unsettled the problem of how Conscience in such a role can define a clear relationship to the worldly goods and rewards that the king must maintain (see below, 169n, 176–78n). Reason is only somewhat more helpful in the same effort (see 179–86n, but cp. 195–96n, in C only).

17–23 (A 17–21, B 17–23): And kalde Catoun his knaue . . . "with peynted wittes" [B (A): ". . . For he wol make wehee twies er we be þere"]: Conscience can rely on Reason to uphold his opinions about Meed, for Reason treats him as a close associate (note the familiar "the," line 16), although Conscience addresses Reason more respectfully (note "syre resoun," line 34). Reason is depicted as a great lord (possibly another glimpse of John of Gaunt, whose manor of the Savoy was within a short ride from Westminster, although not all images of great lords in the period must be thought of as Gaunt's doubles): he receives Conscience with lordly politeness, allowing him to rest while his own rather august servants prepare themselves and him for the short journey to judge Meed. The bestirred household does not, surprisingly, equip Reason for (allegorical) battle or with (allegorical) weapons, as might be expected in the psychomachia tradition from Prudentius; instead of weapons against others, each member of the household equips himself or is equipped with various means for self-restraint, especially discipline in speech. **Catoun his knaue**, in A Reason's only (quasi-)human servant, represents not the severe senator from republican Rome, but the author of a collection of the *Disticha Catonis*, the late imperial poem so widely read, glossed, and translated in the Middle Ages, often as part of school texts (see Orme 1973:102–4; Galloway 1987). In PP the distichs are often quoted and Cato's name occasionally cited, especially in the B text, most notably in Dame Study's worry about the divergence from Christian ethics of Cato's statement, *sic ars deluditur arte*, "thus craft is deceived by craft" (B.10.185–202), and in Will's defense in the B text of writing poetry (B.12.20–23) with *Interpone tuis interdum gaudia curis*, "interpose your cares with joys at times" (see Milton's *Lycidas*, "so to interpose a little ease / Let our frail thoughts dally with false surmise"; lines 152–53). Both those uses of Cato in PP (and Milton) justify rhetorical or artisanal endeavors, and consistent with this is calling Reason's servant Cato **Corteys of speche**, that is, "respectful and well-mannered in speech," a power that Reason will need to win over the audience at the court (which he does, with a powerful display of eloquence: see below 108–45nn).

And also thomme trewe-tonge . . . "with peynted wittes" [B (A): ". . . For he wol make wehee twies er we be þere"]: Reason's second servant, introduced in B perhaps at 3.475, is an even more careful speaker and listener. Tommy's job is to load Reason's horse with a multiplicity of further self-inflicted restraints, in effect building up for the horse an allegorical identity as heavy with safeguards as his own. In A, Cato is given this task; perhaps B's change registers a sense that making Cato a stable-boy (even for Reason) was too demeaning. The same figure may be cited by Conscience in his conclusion to his previous argument, also first introduced in B; see 3.475 (B.3.322). **Thomme** is a laborer's name; Gower uses it among others to metonymize the sorts of people who thronged to Wat Tyler's rebellion in 1381, satirically inserting its English form into his Latin verse ("Watte vocat, cui Thomme venit . . ." ["Wat calls, to whom Tommy comes . . ."]: *Vox Clamantis* 1.783, ed. Macaulay 1902). Yet **Thomme** is, in contrast to the 1381 rebellious laborers, almost a parodically exemplary servant, whose name takes nearly as long to summon as the orders Reason gives him. Other such sententious names appear in Piers' itinerary to Truth (7.213–44.[A.6.53–83, B.5.566–96]), and, a closer parallel, the names of Piers' wife, daughter, and especially son, whose name in C equals, and in A and B far exceeds, Tommy's in length and moral burden (8.80–83 [A.7.70–74, B.6.78–82]). Young men evidently need especially elaborate self-discipline; but Tommy is not restrained from any youthful physical impulses so much as from jests and fables.

Finally, Reason's horse is loaded with even more restraints, a need explained in A and B by his sexual energies (which the **wehee** signifies; see B.7.92, A.8.74; Burrow 1990:140–41; compare Chaucer's Reeve's Tale, I.4064–66), and in C by **þe wone of wil to wynse and to kyke**, that is, the will's general impulse to be rebellious (MED *kiken* vb. 1; see also Acts 9:5). His trappings assume a powerful and energetic horse: in all versions he is saddled and well warroked (girded up, presumably with the saddle-girth, A's and B's **witful gerþes**); in A and B he is hung with **þe heuy bridel**, while in C he is more elegantly but no less burdensomely "peytreled," furnished with a poitrel (a heavy, decorative harness; an elaborate instance is that of Lord Geoffrey Luttrell's horse in the "Luttrell Psalter," fol. 202ᵛ [see Camille 1998:49–50, plate 29]), and then "polled," attested only here, which appears to mean fitted with a strap between the reins and saddle-girth to prevent him from raising his head or rearing (MED *pollen* 3).

C: with peynted wittes: Prsl emends C's additional phrase to "with peynted withes," for the sense "painted withies," bands made from tough flexible fibers, which might conceivably be used as the means to **pole** him; this sense is likely behind the reading *withtes* in the C manuscript M. Prsl notes that the phrase with the reading **wittes** could take **with** as "against" and mean "against temptations exerted by specious shows of reason." A pun on the two senses that Prsl proposes, keeping the RK-C reading, is attractive in the duplicitous significations of an allegorical context: the horse is being harnessed "with" various things, while the allegory of wisdom is being protected "against" various things.

The sexual impulses of the horse in A and B evoke the common motif of the horse as body, but C shifts to a different scheme with the passing assimilation of the horse to the will (see Burrow 1990). Calling the horse this, apparently in addition to calling him **soffre-tyl-y-se-my-tyme**, seems to explain better the need to restrain him at all. Indeed, as Burrow notes, a textual tradition in C that includes RK-C's copytext (manuscripts XYJ, partly joined by UD) makes the horse's name Will only; in this tradition the lines read (with Burrow's suggestion for capitalization),

And lat warrokye Wil with auyse-þe-byfore;
For hit is þe wone of Wil to wynse and to kyke
Lat peytrele Wil and pol hym with peynted wittes.

Burrow observes that this removes a basic contradiction of the allegory here in A, B and the rest of the C tradition, where a horse named **soffre-tyl-y-se-my-tyme** must nonetheless be restrained in so many ways; instead, Burrow suggests, the saddle bears the name **soffre-tyl-y-se-my-tyme**, with **upon** as an adverb, as common in Middle English, and the horse Will thus more logically requires all such restraining moral equipment. The suggestion is persuasive and in keeping with elaborate allegories like the *Char d'Orgeuil*. Yet keeping RK-C's readings, the horse may be considered a dynamic not static allegory: the horse is at once a repository of sexual and other rebellious energies, and also proleptically named as "endurance," with the identity he will have only after he is equipped as Tommy (or Cato) equips him. The horse's name **soffre-tyl-y-se-my-tyme** is not inconsistent with the horse having a rebellious **wil**, because the horse's name only comes into full force when the equipment which is an inherent part of its allegorical meaning is assembled. Having the name **soffre-tyl-y-se-my-tyme** does not mean he is not pure "suffrance"; instead, the meaning of "suffrance" involves having a will that must be checked and disciplined.

26 (cp. B 26): Whiche a maistre mede was [B: Whiche maistries Mede makeþ]: C's small but significant elevation of Meed's direct status and power in Conscience's and Reason's private conversation—where she now is herself a **maistre**—sums up C's view of her personal power and thus responsibility for the damage she does. C's line echoes C.3.215; see also 3.285n. Other subtle signs of C's emphasis on Meed's individual responsibility are at C.3.490 (cp. B.3.347), and below at 162–68, where she is personally addressed, condemned, and imprisoned by the king (in B her fate is not mentioned).

27–31 (cp. B 27–31, A 24–28): Ooen wareyn wiseman and wilyman his felawe . . . and wareyne wrynglawe [B, A: Oon waryn wisdom and witty his feere . . . to saue hemseluen from shame and from harmes]: A subplot of legal corruption breaks into the action, presenting figures whose identities and clarity of motives change slightly with each version, and with varying degrees of consistency and control. Some degree of chaotic inconsistency of marginal characters accompanies the satire in all versions, and perhaps contributes to the surreal style of satire here as with whatever sins or satiric types appear around Meed (see 2.25–26n). A/B name them Waryn Wisdom and Witty, but only B (followed by C) explains immediately why Conscience and Reason ride so fast away from them (see below, 32–41n). B at 67 reverses parts of their names to "Wisdom" and "Warren Witty," but otherwise keeps their identities consistent. C first changes those names to Wareyn Wiseman and Wilyman, then at once expands (and confuses) their identities further to include **wilyman and wittyman and wareyne wrynglawe**. C then reverts to the name "Wisdom" (66) for one of them, and this, perhaps by proverbial or formulaic association, subsequently seems to change the name of the other to "Wit" (C 72). Critical appreciation for the style here has depended on what version the critic is concerned with, and with what views of revision. Lawler, examining B's revision of A (and arguing that the reverse sequence is impossible), sees what is "so vague in A" as being clarified throughout by B, as in the introduction of the moral status and the motives of the Wareyn Wisdom and Witty figures (Lawler 1996:159–62). But he finds the lack of moral explanation in A attractively enigmatic ("I rather miss the last glimpse of Wisdom and Wit standing staring in A, but that has been replaced in part by this speech [B 155–56; see below] and more directly by the assizer, summoner, and sheriff's clerk who flock to Meed even in her defeat" at B 167–70; Lawler 1996:162). Donaldson, examining C's revision of B (and arguing that the same writer was responsible for both), says that if we try to follow the literal sense of C's presentation we would decide that "C's negligence amounts to downright incompetence," but he suggests instead that, like the blurring of the names of Meed's companions, "all these *w-* and *f*-alliterating personages are of exactly the same sort, indistinguishable in their common desire to make money by misuse of the law. They are the Rosencrantzes and Guildensterns *de petites affaires*" (1966:70).

In all versions, those trying to overtake Reason and Conscience before they arrive at court are involved in legal actions at Westminster and enter the story by importuning the two authoritative figures to manipulate the outcomes of their particular cases. Such a narrative technique has no obvious parallels in other literary or theological trials, but it is consistent generally with the disruptive style of the poem (see the Headnote to the Prologue). Compare also the arrival of Chaucer's Canon's Yeoman into the Canterbury pilgrimage (*Canterbury Tales* VIII.554–86), or the abrupt appearances and disappearances of figures in some farcical medieval Latin materials, such as the verse dialogue or drama the *Geta*, the twelfth-century adaptation of Plautus' *Amphytruo* by Vitalis of Blois, extant in over one hundred manuscripts (ed. Bate 1976). From whatever basis the use of dramatic surprise and interruption of Conscience's plans derives, the encounter here artfully turns the passus in a new way toward its general focus: the force of Meed pervading and perverting law and society.

In B and A, the newcomers seek Reason's help to avoid **shame** and **harmes**, a translation of the "law French" *damage e huntage* or the Latin *dampnum et pudor*, formulas used in civil (as opposed to criminal) actions. In these versions, they are lower legal denizens frequenting the Exchequer and Chancery to seek some sort of release from legal contracts (**thynges**; see MED *thing* 11). The Exchequer was notorious as the court that imposed distraint, the confiscation of property, on those sued for injury and damage; the property would be confiscated even before the outcome of the suit, and this power was subject to abuse. "No complaint of the time is more often repeated than that against excessive distraints, by which for a petty debt to the king or another a party might in a moment be deprived of all or much of his property" (Leadam and Baldwin 1918:liv). Cases show that distraint could be manipulated by those invoking the Exchequer's jurisdiction, in order to force their opponents to compromise in a dispute. Whether the figures here represent defendants in such a case or, as Alford suggests, themselves plaintiffs, seeking compensation for "insult and injury supposedly done to them," is not certain (see Alford, *Gloss.* s.v. *harm and shame*). In A and B they appear also as legal advisors to Wrong, and in that role they move throughout the passus as comic side-figures, somewhat like the scheming servant figures of Roman comedy but far less competent.

In C their role is reduced to the cameo here, but the point of their accosting of Reason is more sinister and specific: they hope to influence his verdict in a criminal case against those whom they represent, whose names blur and who indeed may include themselves. They are now clearly advocates or members of a criminal group, and of a sinister kind, as the new name given to one in their party, **wareyne wrynglawe**, suggests. As their dramatic role diminishes from B to C, the scale of their own or their clients' criminality increases. The concern in A/B about *damage e huntage* could apply to any trespass suit concerning material loss or defamation (see Helmholz 1985:li; Kiralfy 1951:12–14), but concern about a complaint from the commons as in C suggests a much larger issue, namely, a criminal charge against them, not a personal trespass suit they are seeking damages for or lodging to gain remedies for. It is not clear if, in C, **þe comune**'s complaint is the general public outcry against them, or a parliamentary petition from the commons, as found frequently from the mid-fourteenth century on (Waugh 1991:202–3). In C the criminal group is on horseback (**faste ryden aftur** [28]), and the reason the commons of whatever sort are involved in the case may be that their case involves a gang, presumably (because of the horses) from the gentry, a relatively common phenomenon in the century (see "Foluyles lawes" at 21.247n [B.19.247]; also Waugh 1991:161–69). The efforts by the more menacing group in C to interfere with justice by accosting and trying to bribe Reason are typical of the sorts of extortion and corruption of justice stereotypically associated in this period with high social rank (see Hanawalt 1975; Stones 1957; but see Hicks 1995:1129–36; see also 21.302–7n). Whatever the truth of such images, they are common in the parliamentary rolls (see, e.g., Green 1985:73–74n24).

29–30: þat recorde sholde / Byfore þe kyng and Consience: A new duty of Reason in C is to **recorde**, i.e., present orally before the king and Conscience the particulars of what had previously happened in court, a role that would also include citing from memory the relevant law and making other official pronouncements; thus Reason is later said to "recorde" the law concerning the Fall, with Christ as judge (B.18.330–32 [C.20.373–75]; see Alford, *Gloss.*). The task is consistent with Reason's role in C as chancellor (see below, 184–86n), even though he is not officially made that until the end of the passus, because the chancellor would hear complaints, verbally examine the witnesses, declare indictments in Parliament, and express judgment on behalf of the king, as Michael de la Pole did by indicting the Bishop of Norwich in 1383 and, later, declaring to the king's steward and justices the king's judgment of London officials indicted in 1384 (see Harding 1973:99–100; *Westminster Chronicle*, ed. Hector and Harvey 1982:52, 96).

32–41 (cp. B 32–43): Ac Consience knewe hem wel . . . dede as Consience hym kennede til he þe kyng mette: The B version first introduces this early clarification for why Reason and Conscience flee Waryn Wisedom and Witty; the passage offers the first stage of the moral darkening of the lawyers in each successive revision. Lawler (1996:161) suggests that the poet clarified this outlook, and inserted it into B, only after writing the later, more directly homiletic sections of the poem, such as A.11.17–22 (kept as B.10.17–22 and C.11.15–20), "Wisdom and wyt now is not worþ a risshe / But it be cardit wiþ coueitise . . .". The passage explains why, in all versions, Conscience urges Reason to ride to court ahead of these figures, and not allow the figures to gain any claims on Reason himself, or perhaps even to get up on Reason's horse: as he says in B 40, **Forþi, Reson, lat hem ride þo riche by hemselue**. The expansion of Conscience's role in B here from A is a notable deepening and clarifying of the scene's overall moral significance and clarity.

The metaphor of sins "riding" various figures carries over from passus 2, and perhaps the effort of Waryn Wisdom and Witty, who are on foot in A/B, chasing Reason and Conscience, who are mounted on horseback (in all versions), is to be understood as a stray extension of the other sins' earlier mounted expedition to Westminster. These figures want mounts too, though, with the incompetence that they display throughout the passus, they have chosen the wrong entities to provide those. But the motif does not receive any further development in the present passus, and C drops all effort to suggest it, omitting Conscience's statement in B 40 that Waryn and Witty should go "ride the rich alone," and now giving them their own horses ("faste ryden aftur": C 28).

34, 43, 154: syre resoun: In C both Conscience and the narrator refer to Reason as a great lord, a particularly authoritative figure who easily associates with the king and guides his endeavors and actions, just as Conscience usually expresses public policy and deals with the "commons" more broadly; see also 187–90n.

36 (B 36): loue and leutee: B inserts an early mention of Love, who appears in A later to taunt Meed after Reason's speech (A 139); B also adds Leaute as a heckler there. B introduces the two together at the outset here as opponents of Warren Wiseman and the other petitioners to Reason and Conscience; for Love and Leaute as linked entities and as representative of major principles of social fairness and justice, see 3.379n. Their presence darkens the status of Warren and his companions from the outset of the trial, and dramatically increases the public humiliation of Meed at its conclusion (see below, 151–59n). Introducing them here allows some anticipation that there will be a vigorous crowd interaction with the debate and the principal parties.

36a (B 36a–37a): *Contricio & infelicitas . . . eorum*: "Destruction and unhappiness in their ways; and the way of peace they have not known: there is no fear of God before their eyes" (Psalm 13:3, also quoted in Rom. 3:16–18). The reference to the "way of peace" has specific application to the following case in court. The psalm quoted is the same referred to satirically by the Priest speaking to Piers (*Dixit insipiens*); see B.7.141. As perhaps another kind of satirical comment using the psalm that begins "The fool said . . . ," the names of all those Conscience refers to include "wit" or "wisdom," although the abuse of knowledge is a topos of satire against lawyers (see Yunck 1988).

43 (B 45, A 32): bytwene hymsulue and his sone: The reference to the king's **sone** supports the common view that A was composed before the Black Prince's death in 1376; its retention in the later versions, however, shows that the king was never meant to be thought of as historically specific. The ideal of kingship, as the tableau suggests here, inherently involves hereditary prospects.

Peace's bill against Wrong

45–63 (B 47–60, A 34–47): Thanne com pees into þe parlement . . . "vnneþe to loke": As often with sudden arrivals, the reader is left for some time to grope for meaning in the new situation (see Prol.139–47n). Peace's case seems at first wholly unrelated to the proceedings about Meed's marriage and status. This, the third interruption of the passus (the king's interruption of the debate being the first), continues the sense of proliferating and colliding actions and characters. If the scene is imagined as a full parliament (see below, 45n), then a major disruption of the case before Parliament has occurred. If the scene is imagined as another kind of court session before the king, then the effect may be evocative of the simultaneous legal actions that frequently occupied a medieval session of court at Westminster, where in the same vast hall several different courts would be simultaneously held: Common Pleas on the west side, the Exchequer just outside, and at the top and south end the court of King's Bench and that of Chancery, divided by the raised dais in the center on which stood a marble table nineteen feet in length and approached by steps (see Baker 2000:247–62).

The thematic connection of Peace's intrusion emerges more fully only when Meed, invoked by Wrong's counselors Warren and Witty, involves herself in Peace's case and shows her ability to help injustice evade royal justice, even in front of the king (below 90–93n). Peace and Wrong have a long formal relationship in medieval legal terminology. "Peace" was originally the protection that any lord could possess, grant, and collect compensation for if someone broke it; between the ninth century and the Constitutions of Clarendon (1164), the king's peace gradually became the exclusive category, absorbing responsibility for justice in all serious matters (see Harding 1973:14–15, 44–49). By the later Middle Ages, it was a powerful expression of the king's control and the nation's harmonious unity; to Richard II, it became almost a doctrine of absolutism (see Saul 1997:387–88), and the generally stronger support for the principle in the C version of passus 4, by the king's insistence on its being a peace that is his to defend against any smaller-scale local arbitration (see below 99–104n) is to be compared to the changes toward absolutism in the C Prologue (see Prol.139–47n).

Wrong has as long a tradition, in its Latin and French forms: *iniuria* or *vis et arma*, and *tort et force*, which became simply *tort* (see Harding 1973:15, 76–77; Alford, *Gloss.* s.v. *wrong*). Earlier in the first vision Wrong presents a broad principle of evil expressed in a variety of ways (see 1.59–60n); here, the sense is a particular instantiation from legal concepts: whatever was involved in breaking the king's peace. In the late Middle Ages, the paired terms, acting *vi et armis* or by *tort* "against the king's peace" (*contra pacem domini regis*), were formulae to define "trespass," a general category of a wide range of civil injuries, from personal assault to breach of contract, both of which Wrong has committed here; but his wrongs tilt toward felonies, especially in C (see below, 46–48n).

Peace and Wrong are suggestive of recognizable social types. In A/B especially, but also still in C, Wrong resembles a corrupt royal purveyor, who requisitions goods from local landowners with no payment but tallies of debt at best (61: **taketh me but a tayle for ten quarteres otes**), and violent seizure at worst (60: **breketh vp my berne dores and bereth awey my whete**); in all versions he displays general rapacity in sexual and economic contexts. On purveyance, see 2.60–63n, and 21.258–60n. In C, Wrong assumes a wider range of forms: the range of victims he rapes increases, and he is more explicitly a highwayman (51–54). Peace embodies an equally wide range of entities served by the maintenance of the king's Peace, but especially small landowners and merchants. Baldwin notes, "Peace is . . . an allegorisation of the law and order for which the king was directly responsible. His presence before the king now [before the king's own Privy Council] demonstrates that the king has failed to protect the Peace through his own courts of Common Law" (1981:43). But, since Peace cannot in fact prevail in his personal suit before the king either, his efforts to seek personal compensation and reconciliation in this setting also display a fundamental tension in late medieval law between self-interest and the public good, impulses that such human law cannot perfectly reconcile, as his own embodiment of both personal and public interests shows; see also next note.

For just as Wrong is a varied, earthly personification of the principle of Wrong that Holy Church mentions (1.59–60n), so Peace is a varied, earthly personification of the principle that Peace the Daughter of God later presents (see notes to 20.271–346 [B.18.263–424]; and Stokes 1984:139–40). There seems little continuity of identity here between these various "peaces" (but cp. Schm at B 47), for Peace combines human desires for compensation with human vulnerabilities to trespass and damage. But just as the Daughter of God debates Righteousness, so here Peace's motives come in conflict with the king's demands for justice (see below, 99–104n). Thus Peace differs from the Daughter of God chiefly in incarnating on a human and social scale the same essential motives. He is readily moved to reconciliation rather than victory, and so he is more obviously linked to the fatally pliable Peace of 22.342 (B.20.342), as Schm notes (at B 47). Compare too the Doctor of Divinity's dismissal of peace in the realm of international politics (15.170–73 [B.14.171–76]).

45 (B 47, A 44): into þe parlement and putte vp a bille: A written petition, one of the poem's several positive presentations of public legal instruments, in contrast to the earlier destructive documents of the first vision (see Prol.67, 71n; notes to 2.80a-118; Steiner 2003:93–142). But the **bille** is a focus of some ambiguity in terms of the kinds of wrong committed it presents, and thus in terms of whether Peace's "own" case or the king's case (with calculated paradox, on behalf of the king's peace) can or should be pursued, and in what combination. In contrast to a writ—that is, a form of official indictment or action that might follow from a bill or from justice's own summoning—a bill is the plaintiff's own presentation of wrongs done (even though it might well be fashioned with legal help), often mixing civil and criminal elements together, sometimes in careful calculation to arrive at the right mixture of public remedy for private injuries (see Harding 1975:74–77). The complaints Peace offers include elements that might be used for writs of trespass primarily to seek damages for personal injury: the stealing of geese and lack of payment for a borrowed horse, for example; in this period, trespass was increasingly being used to accommodate suits of damages (see Kiralfy 1951; Harding 1973:76–77; and below, 50–61n). But many other elements of Peace's bill would trigger prosecution for felony; see below, 46–48n. Peace, who is persuaded to take private compensation only (see below 90–93n), seems not to wish to be in a publicly representative role, as a complaint that felony and even minor injury could require, although his allegorical identity demands this role.

The awkwardness developing in this issue of private and public justice through Peace's trial can indeed be paralleled by the developments wrought in the fourteenth century because of the torrent of bills brought before the King's Bench (initially brought there rather than to justices in eyre because of general social disruption in the early fourteenth century), in which a large range of civil injuries (claims for damages from personal assault, trespass on another's land, defamation, fraud, breach of contract, etc.) were built into the writ of trespass against the king's peace (Harding 1973:76). As Harding explains some of the dimensions of this complex development,

The bills of ordinary people naturally went to the local justices of the peace. In the course of the fourteenth century, the J.P.'s were barred from hearing suits of the party [i.e., lawsuits for private injuries]. Defendants were therefore always tried at the king's suit, and their trespasses were recognised as a second category of crimes, below felonies, to which a later generation of lawyers gave the name of misdemeanour. In the complaint of trespass the citizen first used the concept of public wrongfulness to get redress for private injuries, so creating the category of tort; and then the king used the complaint of private injury by bill of trespass as a way of bringing new types of offender to prosecution, so creating the category of indictable trespass or misdemeanour. Both processes rested on the basic principle of the double suit which had first come to the surface in the appeal of felony, the principle that a violent injury which was the subject of a private complaint was also a trespass against the king's peace which the king must prosecute *ex officio suo*. (Harding 1975:77)

For an historical example of a case where a sheriff had to remind someone pursuing a lawsuit that "the indytement longyth to the Kyng and not to yow," and where the sheriff faced the question of whether the king or the principles in the lawsuit had the greater authority for telling him how to choose his jurors, see 2.60–63n.

The allegorical construct of Peace partly follows from this structural development. Like all plaintiffs in the position Harding describes, he is the subject of discordant legal identities. As Harding's summary suggests, the legal status of ordinary plaintiffs imposed a dual identity on their own wrongs; they all necessarily became versions of Peace, representatives of the king's suit, yet were in court to pursue their own injuries. As the trial ultimately shows, if Peace's presence demonstrates the failure of common law to give him recourse, his presence before the king cannot gain him satisfaction either. He embodies the problem of human justice as separated into irreconcilable categories, like the disjunction between mismatching "case" and "kind" that Conscience in the previous passus elaborates in the "grammatical analogy." His dilemma more particularly suggests the basis for the apocalyptic ideal of unifying all "courts" that Conscience presents at the end of the last passus, a solution for justice in a world of fragmentary concepts that can answer to personal as well as collective demands, and earthly as well as religious law, but which Conscience shows will be available only at the end of time (see 3.473n).

parlement: Peace's petition is made in the first instance before clerks, earls, lawyers, and the King's Privy Council, comprised of Conscience and Reason (see 3.152n); Baldwin presents evidence that in the fourteenth century, the Privy Council sat as a court, one of the several "prerogative" courts over which the king had direct control; and Baldwin shows that such courts were sometimes called "parliaments," which thus need not mean full Parliament (1981:41). The term was a fluid one in the thirteenth century, in politics and literature (see, e.g., the mid-thirteenth-century French *Gui de Warewic*, "Mult s'aturnerent a grant honur / Li noble barun de la cité. / Al parlement se sunt alé / Li quons Alberi e Terri sun fiz . . . Od els cinc cent chevalers"; "the noble lords of the city readied themselves with great formality; to the parliament went Earl Albert and his son Terri . . . along with five hundred knights": line 5694–99; ed. Ewert 1932). But after 1275, in political contexts and presumably literary works closely informed by those, "the term gained greater specificity" (Waugh 2003:214). There is therefore no reason not to consider a full parliament for the occasion of a marriage to a royal kinswoman and a major breach of the peace, as Giancarlo argues (2003). No oath was required of plaintiffs, defendants, or even witnesses in most cases before the king's council (see Leadam and Baldwin 1918:xliii), or indeed at Parliament; in either case Peace begins his complaint without preamble. His evidence of "his heued and his panne blody" (74) serve as sufficient proof of his words.

46–48 (cp. B 48–50, A 35–38): How wrong wilfully . . . And how . . . by nyhte . . . as he mette here late [B, A: ayeins his wille . . . Reignaldes looue . . . maugree hire chekes]: The status of the wrongs against Peace is varied; some are more or less clearly felonious, thus more clearly the king's suit, and those are amplified in C's version. But C also emphasizes others where Peace seems to be seeking compensation for private losses (see below, 50–61n). From the thirteenth century on, an appeal of felony would mean that the plaintiff automatically could not gain compensation for the injuries to himself as a private person (Harding 1973:57). A distinction between less and more serious felonies was stealth, implying premeditation; in the late fourteenth and fifteenth centuries the appeal (that is, an accusation of felony) often specifically emphasizes that an action was done "at night" (see Harding 1973:96, and examples). In A and B, Peace implicitly presents some of Wrong's actions as felonies, since they include rape and imply malice aforethought ("He maynteneþ hise men to murþere myne hewen"; B 55, A 42)—although there merely the aforethought is evident, not actual murder. An appeal against Wrong for felony could be drawn out of Peace's petition, but it would require some studied evaluation. C more directly formulates Wrong's wrongs using the terms of art for serious felony, imposing a graver dilemma on Peace himself. C's account of Wrong's rapes declare that Wrong **wilfully** raped Peace's wife (46); he ravished Rose **by nyhte** (47), and he raped Margaret **as he mette here late** (48).

Clearly evil in A and B, Wrong's character in C is more desperate, his crimes, already heinous, more clearly picked out as entirely felonious because of their nighttime stealth and their "willful" violation of women. C's new emphasis may in part aim criticism against royal pardons of felons on various grounds, which the commons frequently complained of, as petitions in the parliamentary rolls from the 1340s on show (e.g., see Green 1985:73–74n24; e.g., Rot. Parl. 2.253b [1353]). Sentiment against such pardons was longstanding, and from 1380 clear efforts were made to limit the proliferation of royal pardons, so that pardons from this period usually had a clause pardoning for "all felonies" except "treason, murder, and rape" (see Green 1985:75; see also Galloway 2002). C's date is not clear, although 1380 falls conservatively within the range considered viable (see Hanna 1993:14–17), and some C passages in passus 3 would have particular daring if published after 1387 (see 3.244n, 3.407–11n, 3.408n). C's strengthened language describing Wrong's wrongs would make any effort at pardon seem particularly corrupt, thus issuing an oblique condemnation of the royal court's own efforts at corrupt reconciliation.

50–61 (cp. B 52–58, A 39–45): Y dar nat for his felawschipe . . . for ten quarteres otes [cp. B, A: I dar noȝt for fere of hym . . . ten quarters Otes]: Not all the economic losses in Peace's bill are serious enough to be more than private injuries; thus his pursuit of these suggest his wish for just compensation as a private suitor. The usual threshold for felony was loss of 12d or more, but losses greater than 12d were sometimes presented as trespasses (as above, 45n; see also Green 1985:60). But since Peace's bill as a whole amounts to something the king could hardly countenance—the very principle of violating his own peace—no private suit can proceed from these matters, whatever Peace's own wishes. The list of economic injuries lengthens in C's bill, compounding the paradox of Peace's immediate self-interested motives and his public status. In all versions, his motives are now generally clear as seeking restitution for personal injuries, not public judgment against a felon. As Warren Wiseman and his companions sought to make a private deal with Reason and Conscience on behalf of public felons, even including (in C) an effort at bribing Reason (40, see above, 27–31n), so Peace will soon be shown engaged in a more innocent version of the same thing. Reconciliation, pardon, and restitution in human terms are, in this passus, figured as irreconcilable with justice—the very dilemma that obtains in more cosmic terms in the debate between the Four Daughters of God in the third to last vision of the poem (20.271–346 [B.18.263–424]).

50–54: Y dar nat . . . to ruyfle me yf y ryde softe: C's most specific addition to Peace's travails, here showing him en route to purchase goods at the Winchester fair of St. Giles. This major market was originally held on just three days around the feast of St. Giles in late August, but was extended to sixteen days by the mid-thirteenth century (Moore 1985:17–21). Fairs throughout England lost much international trade through the later fourteenth century but remained viable for local trade; indeed, Edward III expanded the rights of the fair of St. Giles in 1349 (see Moore 1985). C's insertion probably springs from the A/B reference to Peace's own "fayres" (59n). Covetise will later describe how he learned his sharp practices at the same Winchester fair (see 6.211ff. (B.5.202ff., A.5.119ff.).

yf y ryde softe: A thickly wooded stretch of road between London and Winchester, near Alton, was notoriously dangerous for merchants traveling to the St. Giles fair. From the thirteenth century, the bishop of Winchester's justices appointed up to twelve horse guards and ten foot guards to patrol the road while the fair was on (Moore 1985:160). **softe** here means 'slowly' (MED adv. 6a), as it does also in the same sense, and with a related connotation of a slow, easy target, at 16.52 (B.14.211), where "þe ryche hath moche to rykene and riht softe walketh."

57 (B 54, 41): no ferthyng for nouhte y couthe plede: plede is strictly technical, "pursued law suits." Peace has evidently tried before to gain compensation from Wrong for the horse that he took. The complaint suggests he sees his present "pleading" in similar terms, as indeed many petitioners to the King's Bench and other royal justices did (see Harding 1975:77).

59 (B 56, A 43): Forstalleth my fayres and fyhteth in my chepynge: Forestalling is the practice of buying a commodity before it reached its official market (that is, 'before' its 'stall') to create a scarcity and drive up price; this might involve buying foodstuffs just outside fair grounds for resale at higher rates in the fair (see Moore 1985:131; Hilton 1992:80). Buying up goods for resale elsewhere, for example to avoid customs, was a separate but related offense known as "regrating" (see 6.225ff. [B.5.217ff., A.5.133ff.]). Forestalling and regrating had clear public dimensions: civic court records are full of references to both practices, and civic authorities imposed very severe penalties, on the grounds of the resulting scarcity and rise in prices (Hilton 1992:79–80). Forestalling might even be claimed in disputes between whole towns over their respective merchants' rights during fairs, as in a case of 1378–80 before the king's council (Leadam and Baldwin 1918:xcvi, 66, 69). Peace's slightly odd use of possessives for large public entities, *my* **fayres**; *my* **chepynge**, imply his large allegorical identity as well as his sense of a private right that is his own to manage and adjudicate. For the public sense, compare, e.g., the royal charter establishing the St. Giles fair at Winchester, where King Henry I specifies that "all who come to the fair, remain at it, and return from it, have my firm peace" (Moore 1985:157–58). In historical practice, responsibility for the "peace of the fair" would not reside in one person but was divided between the king and the local fair owner: the king's constabulary governed only serious crimes, such as felony and murder, at annual fairs and regular urban marketplaces (*chepynges*), leaving general peace-keeping and law-enforcement to the local owner. Thus merchants often found it useful to obtain special safe-conducts from the king to transact their business, even though the king's peace in theory protected them automatically (Moore 1985:159).

The lines define Wrong's social and geographical identity as a shadow of Peace's: where Peace is a member of the country gentry, Wrong appears as a rural figure; where Peace is a merchant, Wrong is a highwayman and ruffian. In any form, Peace does not condemn him on the grounds of the public good. Peace's outlook thus presents some of the same paradoxes as the perspective of the sins, who are told they must confess (see passūs 6–7 [B.5, A.6]).

The response by Wrong's party

66–68 (cp. B 62, 74–75; A 49, 60–61): Tho was wrong afered and wisdom a souhte . . . handy dandy payde [cp. B 74–47, A 60–61: Thanne wowede wrong . . . handy dandy payed]: The first line is in all versions; C, however, using a passage a few lines later in A/B, expands what **wisdom** means quite literally: **men of lawe** who will serve anyone for the right price. The expansion is consonant with the view of lawyers as "sellers of knowledge" expressed throughout the first vision (see Prol.160–66n, and some further references there), though the theme, for all the vehemence it possesses in this vision, does not explicitly reappear after this vision. So too at the end of the passus, in B the king glowers at "lawe" but in C at "men of lawe" (B 174, C 168). C's shifting of the instant of payment from *after* to *before* Wisdom's answer may correspond to the *pre*payment that lawyers in the Prologue are said to demand before speaking ("til"): "Thow myghtest betre meten myst on maluerne hulles / Than gete a Mum of here mouth til moneye be shewed" (Prol.165–66 [B.Prol.215–16,

A.Prol.88–89]). In the last passus Conscience has vigorously condemned pre-payment; see 3.38–67n, 291–332n, 300n.

B 62: a wikked luft: **luft** (or "lift," 'left'), is a rare substantive form of the adjective, denoting 'an evil person' (see MED *luft* adj. 3b). For the association of evil and deceit with the "left half," see 2.5, 8n; but the odd phrase has a colloquial tone that suggests a more light-hearted condemnation than C's "wykked man."

68 (cp. B 64, A 50): for to haue here helpe [B, A: To maken his pees with hise pens]: C's line knits two half-lines remaining after C removed a passage describing consultation between Wrong and his attorneys; see below, B 67–75n. The change here is further touched up to alter Wrong's motives when seeking Wisdom's help: A/B suggest that Wisdom might be acting, or Wrong might be asking him to act, in the spirit of earnest reconciliation. The change removes the wittily paradoxical contradiction of Wrong seeking **To maken his pees** with Peace, on Wrong's (monetary) terms. The result of the change is a blunter severity in the portrayal of Wrong and Wisdom, removing a sympathetic touch found in the earlier versions.

68 (B 75, A 61): handy dandy: as noun or adverb, conveying a bribe or the secret manner of that action, presumably because holding something in a closed hand, since much later the phrase is attested as referring to a children's game of guessing which hand is holding something (OED; Skt extensively quotes modern sources describing this). But only here is the sense 'bribe' or 'in a bribing manner' attested at any date. The casually witty technical usage bespeaks an established idiom, hence OED's assertion that the sense of a children's game attested only later must have preceded the sense of bribery that L alone uses. L's easy usage also bespeaks a professional legal world where the phrase might well have circulated, possibly in law French.

B 67–75 (A 53–61): Tho wan Wisdom and sire waryn þe wity . . . handy dandy payed: In A and B there are several quiet side-conversations in the scene, a display of dramatic specificity and realism, here a negotiation sub rosa. The portrayal of Wrong's party in A and B shows them as at least superficially well-meaning rogues, solicitous of their client if carefully self-serving in being the means to transmit his money. The side-conversation divides the action into two simultaneous stages: their hushed deal-making and Peace's public presentation, which climaxes while Wrong's advocates plan their response. The wry image of Wrong's solicitors is answered by an equally playful depiction of Wrong's constant desperate efforts to be reconciled with Peace, urged on by Wisdom who wishes him **To maken his pees wiþ his pens**, a phrase repeated in B from B 64. This impulse makes Wrong and Wisdom, at this point in the poem, seem proponents of arbitration rather than of the justice of the king's and Reason's absolute measures (see Galloway 2001b; for arbitration, see above, Headnote). Irony and satire remain in Wrong's and Wisdom's confusion of **pees** in the more usual sense—achieved by **pens**, but still a real cessation of conflict—with Peace in the sense of the king's peace, which involves an assertion of the authority of abstract principles and of the king's equally abstract claims on the entire "folk." But the realm of Wrong and Wisdom in A/B is at least partly the realm of arbitration rather than simply diabolic depravity. Because of these touches, the drama in A/B allows a more social and "everyday" perspective on the king's and Reason's justice, so that it appears in part an unreasonable imposition of central power on individual relations. This appearance is belied in turn, however, by the marks of serious felony in Peace's writ, even in A and B, and by the repeated statement in A, and the single statement in B, that the king knows that Wrong is wicked (A 47–48, A only; B 61–62 [A 66–67]; for the rearrangements here, see below, 76n). In C, which deletes all of Wrong's efforts at reconciliation at B 67–75 (A 53–61) and adds instead Wrong's contempt for Peace (below, 69–70n), the king's use of justice holds an almost unqualified claim on moral supremacy, apart from the paradox that Peace's own personal motives are left unsatisfied.

B 67–69 (A 53–55): Tho wan Wisdom . . . And warnede wrong þo with swich a wis tale: The singular verbs and pronouns show that only Wisdom speaks, or else that he and Warren Witty have collapsed into a single force of legal corruption; his (or their) "advice" to Wrong to use Meed also slyly requests payment for himself (or themselves). The intransitive sense of **wan**, 'made his way forward' (OED *win* 12) is relatively common in Middle English, especially in alliterative poetry (e.g., *Sir Gawain and the Green Knight*, ed. Andrew and Waldron 1996, line 461, etc.), but elsewhere the word is more often 'gained, earned,' or 'struggled,' and scholars have supported all of these, as pertinent verbs for Wisdom's and Witty's action here. Skt and Schm take the sense to be 'strove'; in this view, the verb is complete in the first line. Also seeking to make the sense of the verb in line 67 complete, Fowler (1954) compares **wan** here to *Troilus and Criseyde* 1.390, "And gan loude on his sorwe for to wynne," where "wynne" (he argues) seems to mean 'to overcome,' but, by way of a sense of 'struggle,' is shifting toward 'complain.' Thus Fowler takes **wan** here as 'remonstrated,' as a unique attestation in Middle English of the Old English *winnan* in the sense 'contend with words' (itself a rare basis, only in *Genesis A*

2237–52). Probably as scribal clarification, however, almost all manuscripts here present "wente," rejected by KD-B (presumably as an easier reading).

Most likely, the sense of the verb involves all three lines, "went [. . . to warn . . .]." The interruptive **For þat wrong . . .** is best taken as explaining Wisdom's and Warren Witty's **wan . . . and warnede wrong** although the action is not fully described until after the explanation. The **swich a wis tale** refers to the following advice, whose point is not true self-restraint of the will (like Cato's horse) but rather advice to use subterfuge to avoid punishment.

B 73 (A 59): "boþe þi life and þi lond": Wrong's legal counsel offer some tough choices, since no other motivation might move Wrong: pay up or you will be given the maximum sentence. But their advice in B/A is, or should be, itself a misjudgment of the law, the first sign of their serious incompetence, suggested from the outset. Deprivation of life and land was the standard punishment for felony (with the land held in fee being returned to the felon's lord after the king took its profits for a year), and if indeed Wrong is convicted of that crime, there should be no hope of monetary reconciliation (see Harding 1973:57). One A manuscript here, MS. Harley 875 (= H), reads "lyf and lyme," the formula simply for death, not death and deprivation of all property for one's family; but "lif and lim" is a common poetic formula (MED *lif* 1c [a]), so the change is probably simply an easier reading, not an effort to keep Wrong's lawyers from seeming to admit he is liable for felony even while they claim he can buy his way out. "Lif and lond" appears rarely in poetry (but note in the Middle English romance *Richard Coeur de Lyon* the king's threatened punishment using this phrase to Saracens who might want to stay in the land he had conquered; ed. Brunner 1913, line 257). Yet Wrong's lawyers are not wholly wrong about the king in A/B, who seems to leave open the possibility of a pardon (see below 104n). In fact the king's council rarely inflicted bodily punishment in its sentences (Leadam and Baldwin 1918:xlv). The point is thus in part against the leniency of even royal justice, which was criticized in the mid- and later fourteenth century for too readily dispensing pardons to felons (see above, 46–48n).

69–70: Hadde y loue of my lord lytel wolde y reche . . . thow he pleyne euere: C adds a comment that shows Wrong arrogantly dismissing Peace's concerns; he hopes only for the king's pardon (**my lord**). The hope is dashed, but it redefines his lawyers' immediately preceding advice as more clearly for bribing the king or his officials for a pardon, rather than becoming reconciled with Peace (compare B 67–75n).

74–75 [B 78–79, A 64–65]: ȝut pees put forth his heued . . . "gat y this scathe": Peace climaxes his bill with a display of his injuries, a traditional part of complaints of assault, codified in legal theory by the maxim *res ipsa loquitur* ["the facts speak for themselves"]; see 2.39, 41n. The display of his bloody head as much as the speech makes Peace's presentation instantly effective in persuading the king to imprison Wrong; he offers a display of injured innocence. Presenting evidence in a criminal trial was the responsibility of the victim (or, if dead, of kin or a coroner), not lawyers or the judge (although the last might prompt a victim to present the most damning evidence; see Green 1985:135). In the early seventeenth century, Sir Edward Coke declared that "in case of life [i.e., a capital crime], the evidence to convic[t] [the accused] should be so manifest, as it could not be contradicted" (Coke 1644:137). The theatrical moment is an example of how readily dramatic realization and legal process can merge (see also Enders 1992). (RK-C's initial "Þut" here and in line 55 above are typographical errors for "ȝut.")

76 (cp. B 80, cp. A 66–67): "Consience knoweth hit wel" [B: Conscience and þe commune kn[e]wen wel þe soþe; A: Consience & þe king kneuȝ . . . wrong was a shrewe euere]: RK-C keeps C's majority reading **knoweth** (which is also the majority reading in B), so that this line is part of Peace's speech. But KD-B changes B's similar majority to match A's past tense, making the line the narrator's description. The emendation of B is possible but unfounded. The past tense in the A line here is necessary since it is the narrator's comment, completed in a following line, **And wisten wel þat wrong was a shrewe euere** (A 67), a line confirming the king's knowledge that was shifted in the other versions to an earlier point (C 65 [B 62; corresponding to a point after A 48]). The moment of revision that shifted A 67 to those earlier points would also quite likely have been the moment when (as the majority of B and C copies indeed present it) the tense of the remaining single line was changed.

Whether the line is taken as Peace's thought or the narrator's, C's and B's versions here and following both associate Conscience with the Commons, a validating of "the commons" along the lines of *vox populi vox dei*; see also Prol.95 (see Prol.95–135n).

82 (B 85, A 73): see his feet [ones]: Most C manuscripts end the line with "ne handes," accepted by Schm but rejected by RK-C as "more emphatic scribal substitution" (105). The king's punishment of Wrong emphasizes in all versions that he is evil incarnate, nearly the same as Lucifer, who is called Wrong in passus 1 (see 1.59–60n) and bound "with chaynes" in the Harrowing of Hell (20.446 [B.18.403]; see also 1.121). Leg irons were not unusual, since prisons were not fully secure. The 1430 ordinances for Newgate declare that the keeper "shall not put any freeman or woman in irons if imprisoned for a debt of less than 100s" (Rickert 1948:34). The darkness of the cell here (the reason for not seeing feet, or hands) completes the parallel with hell, the "merke dale" (1.1).

83–98 (B 87–103, A 74–90): "Yet he amendes . . . And amende . . . to amende . . . hath made my mendes": The defense of Wrong, raised in a chorus until Peace yields to it and climaxes the chorus, pivots on the intrinsic value of Meed's mother, Amends (see 2.125n, 2.126n). The intensity of this public pressure for clemency, matched below (160–61) by calls for condemnation, is probably indicative of medieval courtroom settings; compare the calls for mercy in Chaucer's Wife of Bath's Tale, III.894–96, Melibee VII.1834–74, Knight's Tale, I.1748–60 (not a court, but like one), and the resounding call for "Pite" for the narrator of Gower's *Confessio Amantis* by the lovers from ages past in the court of Venus (ed. Macaulay 1900, 8:2728–32). Those calls for mercy or pity prevail. Below at 19.285–87 (B.17.305–7), however, the Samaritan notes that such mercy is rare for a criminal "þer alle resoun hym dampneth." For the anxieties about pity in legal and political spheres in the period, and for some effects of this on literature, see Galloway 2002.

83 (B 87, A 74): wysdom: All C manuscripts read "a wys oen" (so Prsl, Schm) or variants on that; RK-C emends here to conform to A and B, and to maintain consistent identities in the scene, and presumably also because of the easy loss of the *d* in the corrupt B archetype used for revision. But it is possible that in the C revision the poet, more intent on other matters of revision, was not particular about the clarity of these names and that this should be allowed; see above, 27–31n.

84–85 (B 88–89, A 75–76): maynprise, borw, bote: Wisdom's appeal for release on bail, in which full responsibility would fall on the *mainpernor* (see below, 107n), partly allegorizes **maynprise** as an entity who will be Wrong's **borw**, his guarantor, and purchase his **bote,** or compensation. **maynprise** is the subject of the list of actions that Wisdom proposes; Schm's capitalizing of "Maynprise" responds to this, although all the instruments of monetary warranty are given a kind of confused life here. The king had earlier insisted that no bail would be offered for False and the rest of Meed's retinue (see 2.207–19n), a hint that the present request is likely to fail.

88–89 (B 92–93, A 79–80): "Betere is . . . neuer þe betere": "It is better for compensation to overcome harm, than for harm [i.e., the wrongdoer] to be punished and compensation [i.e., the one seeking compensation] not any the better for it." Taking his turn, Wit speaks up for **bote** in a witty and apparently original elaboration of a proverb, in which **bale** and **bote** both change meaning, from objective, abstract notions to the subjects and agents whose actions or efforts seek those abstractions: the miniature process of personification, which has already begun with "maynprise" (84), parallels the larger emergence of Peace and Wrong from notions into characters via a similar dramatic interaction. The typical proverb using the terms "bote" and "bale" is of the sort that "when bote is highest then bale is nearest" (e.g., *Owl and Nightingale*, ed. Cartlidge 2001, line 688; see MED *bote* 2e for other examples). Wit's hyperalliterative chiastic proverb, however, has a completely different meaning, based loosely on proverbs of the sort of "mercy surpasses justice" (Whiting and Whiting 1968, M508 as in, e.g., Chaucer, *Troilus and Criseyde* 3.1282), but generating from this general notion a specific approval of recompense to the victim rather than punishment of a criminal. Huppé notes that "the pattern of the 'tongue-twister' . . . serves to suggest the verbal trickery of Wit" (1950:166–67). On the surface Wit seems to have a weak case; he is arguing that compensation to the victim and punishment of the wrong-doing are mutually irreconcilable. In fact, they often were; a felony appeal would categorically disallow the plaintiff from seeking any personal compensation (see above 46–48n). Wit's argument puts some pressure on this doctrine of felony, which indeed was part of the impetus for the complex development of distinctions between criminal and civil law throughout the fourteenth century (Harding 1973:57). Reason rebuts this quasi-proverb with an equally brief metaphor or miniature allegory based on another proverb; see below 140–45n.

90–93 (B 94–97, A 81–84): Then gan mede to meken here . . . "do so no mare": Meed, performing the first action in this chorus, directly offers Peace a golden coin by which she will **wage** (that is, offer a pledge) on Wrong's behalf. To have Meed alone act in this chorus, finally offering the money as amends that the others have promised or argued for, allows a blurring of her mode of existence, a sign that action and commentary on the action are transposable throughout this allegorical scene.

94–98 (B 98–102, A 85–90): Pitousliche pees tho . . . "by so þe kyng assente": Peace climaxes this appeal to the king with his assertion that **alle my claymes ben quyt**, that is, he would take a "quitclaim," "a release or acquittance given to one man by another, in respect of any action the he has or might have against him" (Black; quoted in Alford, *Gloss.* s.v. *quiten*). Having opened the proceedings with one very efficacious document, his "bille," he now seeks to close things down with another. But the problem for Peace is that, as "the king's peace," once he has made the claims, they are not strictly "his" but the king's (see above, 45n); moreover, as noted, his claims even if made by ordinary plaintiffs open the likelihood of an appeal of felony (see above 46–48n). C's shift of the concession **by so þe kyng assente** from the middle (as in A/B) to the final position in this small speech emphasizes the warning that Peace will not be allowed any "bote" at all. Peace's bill is, then, another example of setting in motion a powerful process that the individual initiator cannot control; see 3.90–107n.

Throughout the chorus, Amends' claims to authority are far greater than mere bribery, since making amends draws on the value of reconciliation present in all these legal actions and instruments (for Amends, see 1.125n, 1.126n); but at the same time, in this chorus Wrong's advocates are simply trying to fulfill their plan "To ouercome þe kyng with catel yf they myhte" (78). The trial has succeeded in putting not just Meed on trial, but her mother as well: the status and the king's judgment of 'amends' in these terms becomes the point of conflict.

B 101 (A 88): I forgyue hym þat gilt wiþ a good wille: Peace offers the spirit of reconciliation incarnate here; but as a Wycliffite attack on "lovedays" points out, human beings cannot forgive what has injured God, namely, sin (see above, Headnote), a problem analogous to the king's claims on crimes (**gilt** indicates both). The line is dropped from C, avoiding the challenge to a reader who would approve of Peace's impulse here.

The judgments by the king and his councilors

99–104 (B 104–9, A 91–96): "Nay, by crist! . . . for his luther werkes": Although the advice to the king in the Prologue was to clothe justice with pity (Prol.153–59n), the king here does not even address Wisdom's, Wit's, Meed's and even Peace's arguments for reconciliation, but simply dismisses them, leaving Peace with no compensation and Wrong's party subject to punishment to be carried out on Wrong immediately, who will be put **in þe stokkes** (here, constraints or fetters worn in prison, not in a public display [MED *stok* n. 1 (4)]). The king's dismissal of the appeals for pity is made on legitimate grounds (see above, 46–48n). His judgment is, moreover, not cruel but focused on protecting his **hewes**, a concern that contrasts with Peace's willingness to accept compensation only on his own behalf and allowing to be forgotten the assaults on his own servants (also called "hewes" [58]) and household. Peace does not need a technical understanding of the distinctions between felony, trespass, and more private (or minor) injury to seem unethically weak here; his joining with the requests of Wrong's party suggests that he has become more like them in other ways.

In contrast, the king is unwilling to consider a pardon—indeed, less willing in each version (see 104n). The king does make his sentence hold **ar y wete more** (C 100 [B 105, A 92]), and allows it to be subject to the (intrinsically impossible) event of Reason having **reuth** on Wrong. In fourteenth-century practice, a defendant might be imprisoned for several years awaiting trial (Leadam and Baldwin 1918:xl). But Wrong is not simply held over for trial; he has been, by the king's words, sentenced to prison **as long as y lyue** (C 104 [B 109, A 96]). This is a more than usually stringent version of the typical closing formula in sentencing (e.g., *Court Baron*: "He shall be put in the stocks . . . until he hath the grace of his lord" [103]; other such formulae appear at B.18.392 and above, 82). Such indeterminate imprisonments were typical of the king's council, whose sentences often ended "until it is otherwise ordered" (Leadam and Baldwin 1918:xlv).

104: "for his luther werkes" / B 109: "but lowenesse hym borwe" / A 99: "but more loue it make": A's and B's final half-lines offer decreasingly promising hints of later royal pardon; C's removes hope altogether. A's **"but more loue it make"** ("unless [the king's] greater love causes this to change") more directly implies royal pardon than B's **"but lowenesse hym borwe"** ("unless [Wrong's] humility stands bail for him"), although there too the hint remains. C's roundly critical replacement for those half-line concessions offers no possibility for mitigating Wrong's punishment apart from Reason's unlikely mercy. As elsewhere, C's change might be a way of more strictly refusing to countenance royal pardons for felonies and murders, a view found throughout the 1380s and 90s; see above 46–48n; also, C here as elsewhere confronts the impossibility of a "right wrong": see below 108–45n. The king's severity in C also particularly contrasts with the historical king's council, which was rarely severe because of the high social rank of most of its defendants. The king's reference in C to Reason as the only principle that might spare Wrong shows how clearly C has established a hierarchy of authority for justice and rule in the passus.

105–6 (cp. B 110–11, A 97–98): Summe radden resoun . . . on Consience thei lokede [B, A: Summe radde Reson . . to counseille þe kyng and Conscience boþe]: C here slightly elevates Conscience's status on the king's bench by having **summe** (presumably to be imagined as lordly members of the parliamentary court) "look to" Conscience along with Reason to counsel the king, an indication of how Conscience has been recast in C as a (or the) king's justice, given duties over "alle my Courtes" (C 186; see below, 184–86n), and also a subtle instance of how Conscience's role, especially his authority to speak *to* authority, expands throughout C (see, e.g., Prol.95–135, 3.286–412). In A/B here, with Reason the sole addressee of **summe** and the sole counselor of both Conscience and the king, Conscience's role is still secondary.

107 (B 112, A 99): That mede myhte be maynpernour: A larger audience now joins the chorus appealing to the king, echoing Meed's earlier offer that she "wage" or be a "wedde" for Wrong (see above, 84–85n, 90–93n). To make her a **maynpernour** (lit. 'taker in hand,' Fr. *main-preneur*, Lat. *manucaptor*) in theory would increase her responsibility beyond "waging" for Wrong, not just binding her with a contract to give huge sums of money if the defendant was not presented, but also *corps pur corps*, that is, liable to the fines and even imprisonment levied on the defendant. But the distinction between these notions is particularly elusive in Meed's case: her *corps* is also the money she would wage. At any rate, Meed's own offer was appropriately made before the king had passed judgment; this later group's proposal ignores or implicitly protests the king's sentence against Wrong (above, 99–104n). No bond of release should by law now be possible. As a petition to Reason, the embodiment of law, the request is particularly ill-judged. It incites Reason to an explosive denunciation of all manner of moral transgressions, but, curiously, of very few illegal ones like those of which Peace has complained (see next note). The assumptions that have led to the request by "summe" (105) speak to a pervasive moral temporizing and corruption, which Reason assails at its root.

108–45 (B 113–48, A 100–131): "Rede me nat . . . as the leef lyketh": To this point, Reason's obvious authority has mainly been expressed in social terms: as a figure of high social status and confidence, a baron who, like John of Gaunt, is not far from court (above, 17–23n). However, as suddenly becomes clear now, in all versions, Reason's authority exceeds any social terms. He now emerges more clearly as a general principle of law and justice, and he speaks a language of social leveling rather than of lordly privilege. If Peace and the king are Wrong's antagonists and opponents in the social and legal frame of reference in which the passus has opened, especially in A/B, now that frame shifts to a broader one of moral absolutes, in which Reason emerges as the comprehensive antagonist and opposite of Wrong, embodying the self-sufficient principle of right and law (see above, 5–7n). His terms for Wrong's release are "implacable . . . as by definition [Reason] must be" (Alford 1988b:207). For the first time in A and B, and to a greater degree than earlier in C, Wrong is thereby more clearly revealed as an absolute moral evil.

Reason's first long speech is not necessarily a series of impossibles (see Prsl at 113n), 'till rivers run backward,' but a utopian vision. The difference is important, because he seeks to carry out his vision. Like many of the social lists in the poem, his has elements of estates satire (Alford 1988b:207–8). Indeed, it offers a thoroughgoing reversal of Meed's earlier reductive presentation of how all social groups need and desire money (see 3.265–81n), and to some extent offers an ideal revision of the estates surveyed in the Prologue. Reason's portrayal of estates follows such severe social and moral principles that the very bases of those estates, especially in the later portions of the speech, tend to dissolve under the pressures of an ideal of poverty's spiritual sanctity and a condemnation of elitism and the self-indulgence of the wealthy. In pointing directly away from material reward as a principle of society, and thus gesturing toward a dissolution of the upper tiers of the social hierarchy, Reason's speech is closely akin to the climax of Conscience's speech near the end of the preceding passus (3.436–83). The early fourteenth-century "prophecy" by Thomas of Erceldoune preserved in Harley MS. 2253 offers a rhetorical precedent in Middle English for a utopian future (in that case when the wars with Scotland will end) "nouþer in þine tyme ne in myne, ah comen & gon [but will come and go] wiþinne twenty wynter ant on" (ed. Robbins 1959:29, lines 17–18). But "Thomas of Erceldoune's Prophecy" presents generally frightening prospects (e.g., "When ryþt ant Wrong ascenteþ togedere"), not the ideal or reformist images that Reason offers. More closely related in some poetic strategies might be the surreal early fourteenth-century Anglo-Irish *Land of Cockaygne* (ed. Bennett and Smithers 1974:138–44), although there the point is the effortless fulfillment of appetite with all manner of food; here, the sometimes equally surreal imagery serves nearly the opposite goal, of reimagining the social world in terms of universal conditions of strict justice and physical austerity.

Reason's speech broadly moves from the nobility to the clerical orders, ending, like the sequence of estates in the Prologue, with a rag-tag of more socially subordinate figures, granting the poorest—whether sick, in (debtors'?) prisons, or humble cottagers—a special claim on sanctity, before returning all the more severely to condemn lawyers corrupted by money. The underlying connection, therefore, answers Meed's earlier definition of the good society by showing the corrupting influence not just of money but of worldly goods on all segments of society. Several of the points reappear in what, in B and C, becomes Reason's general sermon, 5.114–200 (Conscience's sermon in A); their elaboration there displays the poet's typical modes of repeating and extending an idea.

109 (B 114, A 101): Til lordes and ladies louen alle treuthe: Reason begins with a declaration of the fundamental moral term, **treuthe** (see Prol.15n), but he indicates the particular need for the higher social orders to sustain this. His moral hierarchy inverts his social one.

110 (B 115; cp. A 106): And hatien alle harlotrie: In a formula used elsewhere (B.15.106 [C.16.260]), B's addition reconfigures A's preceding line (from "be curteis of here mouþes" to "louen alle truþe") to make it the first part of a new dichotomy "louen . . . hatien"; this display of formal rhetoric is used without irony to inveigh against sins of the tongue. B's change also shifts the focus strictly to secular orders (A's "clerkis & kniȝtes" are now "lordes and ladies"), part of B's clarifying of the estates in Reason's sermon. The clergy will be treated separately below (see 114–15n, 116n, 117n). Given its dichotomous opposition to "treuthe" here, **Harlotrie** here may mean more than its sense in Chaucer, of a popularly performed and wholly unedifying story such as a fabliau (as at *Canterbury Tales* I.560, 3145, 3184); rather, it is presented as any speech opposed to "treuthe" and thus all manner of verbal deceit and fraud, though it clearly includes scurrilous entertainment (see 7.22 [B.5.406]). For the stern focus on the last, see Prol.35–38n, B.Prol.33–37n; and 7.89–95 (B.13.429–35).

110 (B 116, A 102): Tyl purnele porfiel be putte in here whicche: C's **purnele** is genitive singular (without the "s" as often in proper names), and **porfiel** is her fur-lined clothing to be folded up in her clothes chest. Latin "Petronilla," like its derivative "Purnele" (Old French and Middle English), was often a type-name for a woman who was a sexual object, especially a prostitute or priest's concubine, as at 6.135 (B.5.160) (MED *Pernele*; see Mustanoja 1970:74–75); for an instance of the Latin form, see the *Lamentationes* of Matheolus (e.g., Latin lines 553–80, ed. van Hamel 1892–1905). In PP the name, doubtless because of its handy alliteration with "purfil," often designates a woman wearing comfortable and "proud" if not luxurious clothing, as again at 5.128–29 (B.5.26–27, A.5.26–27), and Wrath mentions Dame Purnele the priest's mistress ("dame purnele a prestis fyle": 6.136 [B.5.160]). But Proud Purnele does penance with a hair shirt and confession at 6.3–11 (B.5.62–70, A.5.45–53), and Piers mentions St. Pernele (also Petronilla; B.6.275 [A.7.259]; C.8.296 has "seynt Poul"). A similar range appears in the elaborations of "Robert the Robber" (see Prol.45n). L's scope of real women's names is narrow, partly a result of the language of exemplum and homily: he uses one to serve for nearly all, developing differences as variations on the narrow theme of a woman with finery. **Porfiel:** a type-name for luxury garments; for Meed's similar outfit, see

2.10–15n. Here the figure seems less socially elevated, so perhaps she would be liable to the fines from the sumptuary statute of 1363 (see 2.10–15n). A late fourteenth-century London ordinance also focused primarily on brewsters, nurses, servants, and prostitutes wearing furs outside of the home (see Hanawalt 1998:27). Reason's concern, like the London ordinance, is with an ethics of public display and, if the repetition of the idea at 5.128–29 (B.5.26–27, A.5.26–27) glosses this passage, of economic thrift.

112 (B 117, A 103): chyldren chersyng: chyldren is genitive plural: "until the spoiling of children is [itself] chastized with rods." Reason repeats and elaborates this point in his next sermon (5.136–39a [B.5.34–40, A.5.32–33]).

113 (cp. B 118, A 104): harlotes holynesse be an heye ferie [(B)A: be holden for an heþyng]: Prsl suggests "And the holiness of worthless scoundrels be (an occasion for) a high feast-day," but he notes that **harlotes holynesse** could also be "the superficial piety of *harlotes* as they are now and not as they will be, reformed, in which case it should be a matter of derision" (taking **holden for an heþyng** as 'considered absurd'). But that gloss renders the poet's revision implausibly radical: it assumes that the reading accepted for A/B by K and KD-B (see further below), **be holden for an heþyng,** points toward the second sense of **harlotes holynesse,** as "the superficial piety of *harlotes* as they are now," while C's new phrase **be an heye ferie** takes **harlotes holynesse** in the other sense, as "the [actual] holiness of worthless scoundrels," at the very moment at which, still more confusingly, they will in fact no longer be **harlotes** (that is, male scoundrels as in Old French, not promiscuous women, for which the earliest attestation is fifteenth century; see MED *harlot* 3b). The contrast between the two options Prsl proposes, and thus between A/B and C, is even sharper than Prsl's gloss suggests, for "holden for an hething" is often not simply "consider absurd" but "consider grossly immoral or sacrilegious" (as in the early fifteenth-century Townley Play of the Conspiracy and Capture, where Caiphas says of Jesus not keeping the Sabbath, "This hold I great hethyng"; ed. Stevens and Cawley 1994:231, line 143; see further, MED *hething* 2(c)).

A better solution is offered by Lawler (2005): he takes **harlotes holynesse** in a more specific form of the ironic sense: "absolution for miswinning [illicit gain by whatever means] in exchange for a donation," like what the friar offers Meed in 3.38–67 (see n), and **be an heye ferie** as "be as rare as high feast days" (a sense supported by Haukyn's B-text character as "slothful" by which "Ech day is halyday with hym or an heiȝ ferye" [B.13.414]). Thus Lawler shows that the shift from A/B to C is consistent in substance though not emphasis: "In B the emphasis falls on the clergy: in the new society, such payments will be scorned, that is, refused. In C the emphasis falls on the harlot: the attempt to make such payments will be as rare as high feast days." **harlotes holynesse** is thus a nonce-term for any piously cloaked sin that, in the utopian world Reason looks toward, will be either considered grossly immoral or be exceedingly rare. A possible model for the phrase in those terms is "pope holy" (created from French *papelard*, 'hypocrite'), found also in Haukyn's B-text character, transferred in C to Pride's confession (B.13.283; C.6.37).

RK-C include C's revision to **be an heye ferie** among those where the reviser encountered a stretch in the copy of B he used to revise that was so corrupt that he made numerous small changes in what he found in his corrupt B, "some merely tinkering, some—allowing for the limited scale—quite radical. The rewriting may restore lost meaning, or add to the meaning of B, or substitute new meaning for that of B" (RK-C 73). Their grounds for thinking that C made a radical departure here lie at least in part in the Athlone editors' own radical editing of the line in A and B: for all B and nearly all A manuscripts (followed by Schm) read "hyne" not **heþyng**: a single A manuscript, Liverpool University Library MS. F.4.8 (Ch), provides both K-A's and KD-B's reading here, accepted, Kane says, because of its greater difficulty than "hyne" and because MS. Ch does not otherwise archaize the poem's diction (K-A pp. 161–62). But Rigg and Brewer, editing the "Z text" where "hyne" also appears, correctly note that "hyne" is the less common word in the sense here (*hine*: 'a servant,' so the phrase "holden f. a. h." is presumed, by this instance only, to be 'consider worthless,' as Donaldson also translates the line in his 1990 translation [MED *hine* 2(c)]; see Rigg and Brewer at Z.4.106n, ed. 1983:74). The phrase **holden for an heþyng** is for its part commonly attested in late fourteenth- and fifteenth-century instances, although it has a stronger presence earlier, reaching back to the twelfth century (MED *hething* 2(c)). Choosing for A/B the reading **heþyng** rather than "hyne" does not have any simple justification, but is probably correct. The C-reviser's change leaves a secondary resonance of sanctity in the line, which, as before, chimes complexly with the ironic sense of sanctity in the nonce-phrase of **harlotes holynesse**. As often, the Athlone emendations are not amenable to proof, but the A/B reading **heþyng**, with its sense 'blasphemy' (as in Caiaphas' usage) offers a clearer sense than "hyne" of the ironic resonance of sanctity that permeates the line. The pressure for a spiritually governed world that moves throughout Reason's speech, even transmitted through such ironies, lifts and warps the line in C even more powerfully than its predecessors, both authorial and scribal.

114–15 (cp. B 119): "Til Clerkene Coueytise be cloth for þe pore . . . and here palfrayes pore menne lyflode" [B: "Til clerkene coueitise be to cloþe þe

pouere and fede"]: B's first insertion into A's sermon earns its place by defining an ideal clerical desire to social charity by pivoting **coueitise** between the two senses 'avarice' (MED 1) and 'strong desire' (good or bad; MED 3: e.g. *Ayenbite* 137: "Þer is an holy coueytise . . ."). C's further expansion of the point emphasizes clerical use of wealth for the poor as necessary for such social charity; the argument tends toward other proposals for disendowment (see Scase 1989:102–12; Aston 1984), but remains short of that; see also 5.168–79 / B.10.322–35. C's expansion turns B's language into metonymy or allegory; compare the "new clothing" that, in a further C expansion of the theme below, clerics and the church will someday wear (see 5.178–79).

116 [cp. B 120]: And religious outryderes be reclused in here Cloistres [B: Religiouse Romeris *Recordare* in hir cloistres]: The C revision simplifies a difficult and allusive line in B, in a pattern of several such efforts here. In B, the line presumably means 'And [until] religious roamers say 'Remember' in their cloisters,' using the imperative form for the deponent verb *Recordare*. A mass to prevent sudden death in the widespread Sarum Use begins, "Recordare, Domine, testamenti tui, et dic angelo percutienti, cesset jam manus tua" ("remember, Lord, your covenant, and say to your angel striking a blow, Let your hand hold back"; Dickinson 1969:*886]). The Latin word suggests a pun on "recalling their *cor*," their "heart," to their enclosed way of life. Perhaps it also hints that instead of being "recorders" in court and other secular offices, clerics should be saying masses in fear of imminent death in their cloisters (for *recorden* in the legal sense, see above, 29–30n). **Romeris** points critically to gyrovagi religious; C's **outryderes** clarifies the implication (for a sharp satiric portrayal, see C.5.156–62 [B.10.311–16]; for a bland satiric portrayal, see Chaucer, General Prologue, lines 165–207).

117 (cp. B 121): be as Benet hem bad, dominik [B: Bernard] and fraunceys: The Benedictine order of monks, and the Dominican and Franciscan orders of friars, are all criticized as not living up to their ideals, an example of the pervasive "new anticlericalism" in the poem by which all orders of clergy are condemned on various grounds, from what Scase defines as some elusive supra-clerical ethical point of view that the poem often occupies (see Scase 1989). B's **Bernard** indicts the Cistercian reformers as well; and B's following line against "prechours," dropped from C, evidently speaks against the Dominicans (called the "Friars Preacher"). C's replacement of Bernard with Dominic is thus merely a compression, not a shift in the view of Dominicans or Cistercians (for a parallel of the poem's materials with those known by at least one Cistercian, see Galloway 1992b and 1995; Clopper 1997 presents a general comparison of the poem with Franciscan outlooks, in spite of its antifraternal satire). The perspective is indeed radical in regard to religious orders: as Conscience at the end of passus 3 has envisioned a reduction of social standing of estates to labor and prayer, so Reason argues that the original founders of the religious orders envisioned humble, emphatically stable, and utterly lay lives for their followers, down to the levels of "Breweres and taylours" (C 120). For a similar nostalgia for Francis and Dominic, see 16.355–56 (B.15.230–31), 22.256 (B.20.256).

119 (B 123): til þe kynges consayl be alle comune profit: A surprisingly direct criticism of the venue in which this is occurring. Reason's speech seems, though, to move outside the literal drama as his identity here moves outside the lordly figure he resembled toward spiritual governance of all earthly matters. For the ideal of the **comune profit**, see Prol.169n.

B 124: Til Bisshopes Bayardes ben beggeris Chaumbres: That is, until churchmen's luxurious possessions will be made housing for the poor. **Bayardes** are horses, and so the image is surreal, a small climax of impossibility in Reason's speech. Its image somewhat parallels the much paler phrase in "Thomas of Erceldoune's Prophecy," "When mon makes stables of kyrkes" (ed. Robbins 1959:29, line 6); but the differences suggest PP's greater poetic boldness. Note also the peculiar anti-clerical taunt in the Anglo-Norman prose *Fouke le Fitz Waryn* (ed. Hathaway et al. 1975:29/32–33): "veiz cy un moygne gros e grant, et si ad le ventre bien large a herbiger deus galons de chens" ("see here a huge fat monk, who has a belly big enough to house two gallons of dogs"; the most recent editors defend the manuscript reading here [137n]).

Beyond the surreal images of horses made into houses, the line may also allude to a major religious house. The Dominicans had their large London house on the former site of Baynard's Castle, London, which had been built at the Conquest on the riverbank at the far western edge of the city wall but was destroyed by King John because of its owner's association with the rebel barons (the Dominican house in turn was destroyed later, leaving its name to Blackfriars). The area was given by the Archbishop of Canterbury in 1272 to the Dominicans to build their London house (Besant 1893:184–86, 133–34; Brooke 1975:214–15). The name "Baynard" remained associated with the area (the Thames side south of St. Paul's) as Baynard Castle Ward, including its parish church, St. Andrew's of Baynard Castle (Brooke 1975:123–24). A London house owned there by the prior of Okebourne "in the lane of Baynard Castle" was sold in 1352 to the Dominicans to enlarge their own house to the north; it was returned to the prior of Okebourne sometime before 1406, when the king took possession of it, but during the period of PP the Dominicans had a particularly dominant presence among the other great houses in Baynard Castle Ward (Honeybourne 1965:35). Possibly **Bisshopes Bayardes** refers punningly (and sardonically) to the Dominicans' dwellings there, as grand houses for false beggars living in luxury which should rightly be made **Chaumbres** for true beggars. **Bisshopes** may recall that the land was originally granted by the archbishop, and to distinguish the Black Friars' house from the "other" Baynard Castle, the name given to the local great house that had been built sometime in the 1330s near the site of the original castle, and which was later owned by the dukes of York, then given by Henry VIII to each of his wives in turn; it was destroyed in the Great Fire of London (Honeybourne 1965:35, 38; Besant 1893:186). For the grandeur of Franciscan and Dominican houses, an antifraternal topos, see 3.38–67n, 3.64–76n.

122–24 (cp. B 126–27, A 109–10): And til saynt Iames be souhte there pore sykke lyggen [B, A: þere I shal assigne] . . . but yf he go for euere: Pilgrimages to St. James of Compostella in Galicia were common, as were the claims for resulting religious merit and, among an increasing group of reformist voices, criticisms against such literal pilgrimages: see notes to Prol.47–50 (B.Prol.46–49, A.Prol.46–49). B/A's **þere I shal assigne** implies the metaphorical or spiritual "pilgrimage" by good deeds that C's **there pore sykke lyggen** exemplifies; James should be "visited" through the "works of charity specified in his own definition of 'religion clean and undefiled . . . to visit the fatherless and widows'" (Schm, quoting James 1:27). **but yf he go for euere** may imply a final pilgrimage to make a good death (Bnt; see also Dimier 1955).

125 (B 128, A 111): Rome rennares: **Rome rennares** presents a pejorative term found well through the sixteenth century to refer to those who journey to the papal court carrying money to confirm or influence elections to clerical office; see OED. But the papacy was in Avignon from 1308 to 1377, except between October 1367 and September 1370 when Urban V established his papal seat briefly in Rome. Thus Bennett (1943a) used the appearance of the phrase here in A to argue that that version must have been written between October 1367 and September 1370, since the other allusions in A (as well as the presumed order of composing A, B, and C) seemed to prevent it from being dated after 1377. For Bennett, the preservation of the phrase in B dated that version by a similar principle, to after 1377: "priests would carry money to Rome only when the papal court was functioning there" (1943b:60). Bloomfield, however, first emphasized that **Rome** was a set term for the papal curia with no value for narrow dating (1962:89), and parliamentary records 1307–67 bear this out (see passus 2 Headnote). The phrase must considerably predate L to mean simply "those who travel to the pope" (wherever he might be). A seemingly derivative phrase in *The Awntyrs off Arthure*, from probably the early fifteenth century, "remus orerennus" (ed. Shepherd 1995:219–43, line 262), 'realm over-runners,' suggests how widespread versions of such a phrase likely were (see also *Patience*, ed. Andrew and Waldron 1996, line 52).

125–28 (cp. B 128–31, A 111–16): for ruyflares in Fraunce [B/A: for Robberes of biyonde] . . . Vp forfeture of þat fee, ho fyndeth hym ouerward [B/A: who fynt hym at Douere]: "Because of robbers in France [B/A: overseas] . . . on forfeiture of the fee from whoever has financed his journey abroad." The concern is loss of English coinage by travelers abroad, but the **ruyflares** may be corrupt moneychangers rather than outright thieves. Laws prohibiting the export of sterling were passed in 1363 and 1365, on the latter occasion on the grounds that merchants secretly profited from the exchange rates and pilgrims lost much of the king's coinage, and including the grounds that "clerics for the sake of seeking and obtaining various church benefices have consumed much money arguing in the papal court" ("clerici quoque ob varia beneficia ecclesiastica impetranda et obtinenda in curia litigantes plurima consumpserunt": recorded by John of Reading, ed. Tait 1914:164, quoted in Bennett 1943a:567; the same view is found in a Wycliffite tract titled "Whi pore prestis han none benefice"; ed. Matthew 1902:245). Special royal license could allow such transportation of English currency "for necessary expenses," but no attested acts exempted the travelers specified here and variously elaborated in the three versions (see Bnt).

    ho fyndeth hym ouerward [A/B: at Douere]: The penalty is confiscation of the stake-money put up by whoever financed the journey, here of some illegitimate sort not covered by the exceptions that follow, i.e., currency exchange for a profit rather than the legitimate travels of merchants and their documented agents or documented pilgrims, all of whom had to carry letters when traveling abroad. The laws against exporting currency required pilgrims to pass through Dover; A/B's **at Douere** suggests that the stake-supplier arranges the plan using pilgrims at Dover about to depart, while C clarifies that anyone caught sending an agent overseas for this purpose will have his stake-money confiscated. The list of legitimate figures in the immediately following lines who may be sent overseas with proper papers, and thus exempted from the penalty of confiscation (an instance from the Plea and Memoranda rolls would be the merchant's apprentice John Colshull, who in 1383 claimed that he had power of attorney to receive his master's debts, give acquittances, trade with his goods, and enter into bonds for payments while he was traveling on his master's behalf through Italy and the Low Countries; ed. Thomas 1932:32–33). Reason's thought moves quickly and precisely into statute law and even into the exemptions offered there without breaking its moral intensity, bespeaking considerable familiarity with the law in question, and, as often, law in general.

140–45 (B 143–48, A 126–31): For *nullum malum* þe man . . . as the leef lyketh: For marks the lines as a rhetorical climax of Reason's denunciation of courtly and ecclesiastical abuse of wealth and privilege, with a warning about spiritual consequences that is only slightly obscured by the personified or parable macaronic form. Reason's parable-like maxim is offered to the king's friar-confessor in the terms of an arcane challenge equal to other difficult Latin materials—**construe this in englische** (for other instances of this challenge in the poem, see 3.343n)—yet the proverb that Reason alludes to and adapts is very widely attested from the twelfth century, especially in penitential contexts, "*nullum malum inpunitum, nullum bonum irremuneratum*": "no evil [will be] unpunished, no good unrewarded" (Walther 1982–86, no. 39079c). In several ways it is also a long-withheld reply to Wit. As Wit refashioned a proverb to suit his case for compensation rather than punishment of wrong-doing (above 88–89n), so Reason produces a personified allusion to a maxim that offers the firmest possible declaration of the principle of just reward and punishment. Appearances of it in penitential and confessional materials include Innocent III's *De miseria humanae conditionis* (3:14); see also Paul of Hungary's *De confessione* (23); Hostiensis' *Summa Aurea* (5); Peter the Cantor's *Summa de sacramentis et animae consiliis* (2:92); and Alan of Lille's *Liber poenitentialis* (2.7; but not in the PL edition), and others (for these see Gray 1986:55–56; see also Alford, *Quot.*). It also appears in collections of maxims, such as John of Fonte's late thirteenth-century florilegium (ed. Hamesse 1974:sent.58), and it is in casual clerical usage from the twelfth century on (e.g., John of Salisbury, ed. Millor et al. 1979:446). It is well established in the Middle English penitential tradition too; it appears in the twelfth-century "Moral Ode," "Ne schal non vuel beon vn-bouht. ne no god vn-vor-gulde," a poem that goes on to make a sharp division, like the later Pardon in PP, between "Heo þat habbeþ wel idon" who "To heoveriche . . . schulle vare" and "Heo þat habbeþ feondes werk idon" and "schulle fare forþ myd him in-to helle grunde" (ed. Morris 1872:60, lines 62, 175–78). It appears as well in the thirteenth-century lyric "Worldes Blis," which has a clear connection to the "Moral Ode" (ed. Brown 1932:82). Among L's contemporaries, John Mirk (c. 1390) uses it in his homily collection: "God . . . woll þat yche man haue his good dedes rewardud, and þat yche synne be yponysched" (ed. Erbe 1905:79).

Against all these instances and the weight of penitential traditions that they represent, Reason's version, however, does demand special attention for its literary and dramatic properties. It is fundamentally bilingual; its precise effect and point depend on its mixture of languages. Reason's **nullum malum** does not refer to evil that will be punished (as the fully Latin or fully translated English versions of the proverb demand), nor even to "the good," directly conceived, but to an entity "No Evil" who meets with the figure "Not Punished" and requests that "No Good" not be rewarded (or even that No Good *become* yet another entity, "Not Rewarded"). Such personified negations recall the word-play in a tradition of Latin satires on "Nemo" ("No One"): this man, according to Scripture, has accomplished many wondrous things: "Nemo deum vidit" ("'No One' has seen God"), etc. (ed. Bayless 1996:259–310). Reason's maxim displays the principle, ultimately deriving from such Latin wordplay, of creating character features and "identity" from negative concepts; this recalls the early strokes of character-portrayal of the narrator as "vnholy of werkes" (see Prol.3n) and, in a broader sense, the identities of the Sins presented in the next vision, whose very existence depends upon their continued negation of the "confessing" and contrition that Repentance demands of them (see passūs 6–7 [B.5, A.5]).

The ethic of merited punishment and merited "meed" is deeply engrained in medieval culture, and Reason's instruction for the king's **Confessour** (who would be a friar) and all the other "Clerkes þat were confessours" to **construe this in englische** serves, in the first instance, simply to remind them of what should be a mainstay of their professional advice at court: that eternal damnation will fall upon those who do evil, and eternal reward on those who do good. In this sense, Reason's phrase is a version of the Pardon (see Lawler 2000). The **confessours'** consultation among themselves to **construe this clause, kyndeliche what it meneth**, implies (like the reaction of the Priest reading the Pardon; 9.289–92 [B.7.115–18; A.8.97–100]) an unnecessarily fine parsing of a simple point, and perhaps some self-interested effort to find some grounds for leniency in what passes for confession in their hands (compare the corrupt "confession" of Lady Meed that the "confessour ycoped as a frere" carries out, 3.38 [B.3.35, A.3.34]).

But Reason's maxim does not present the directness of the Pardon, or of the penitential point expressed by the maxim elsewhere. By its nature, in its netherworld of neither pure English nor pure Latin, his wordplay in its literal terms evades any direct claim of reward or punishment; it can only argue for negations of those things, and therefore it suggests a fundamental uncertainty about the reward and punishment that may come, and to whom those may come: perhaps reward will be a lack of punishment, and the reverse as well; perhaps good will be a lack of evil, and the reverse of that too. His personification of negations suggests that direct knowledge of justice, reward, goodness, and punishment is difficult or impossible. Even in the simply schematic way that the personifications allow, moral values are shown to be approachable only by their opposites, a point central to the principle of *omnia probate*, encompassing in the poem even God's need to learn both sorrow and joy by their opposites (see 1.81–204n).

In the Crucifixion passus, Jesus directly cites the maxim *nullum malum impunitum* (C.20.431 [B.18.390a]) in a context of declaring he will "do mercy of my rihtwysnesse," and in B only he adds that his punishment for those who have done ill will be purgatory to "cleanse" them, as if no punishment were eternal (B.18.390–96). The omission of that last passage from C, and a new emphasis there that *nullum malum impunitum* means "þat y be wreke of hem þat wrouhte ille" (20.432), leaves this hope less clear, but the poem insists throughout and in all versions on an ultimate uncertainty of divine judgment: "hit lith in my grace / Where [whether] they deye or dey nat, dede they neuere so ille" (20.428–29 [B.18.386–87]).

148–50 (cp. B 152–53): Mede in the mothalle tho on men of lawe gan wynke . . . þat myhte resoun stoppe [B: And þei lauȝynge lope to hire and lefte Reson manye]: B's line provides the reason for Warren Wisdom and the others to gather around Meed; C's revision shows her isolated even from the lawyers in court, and merely hoping in vain for their support. In C, public opinion shifts universally away from Meed (see below 151–59n).

B 154–56: Waryn wisdom wynked . . . "and faile speche ofte": B and A grant Waryn Wisdom (and in A also Witty) a final appearance: in A, their reaction is put in the spotlight after the judgment (see below, A 141–43n); in B, Waryn Wisdom alone makes a final effort to defend Meed but manages only a comically incoherent speech, declaring his incoherence, the failure of his legal efforts, but his promise of continued loyalty. As Meed has winked to the lawyers in court and so that they "lope to hire and lefte Reson manye" (B 153), her follower Waryn winks back in continued conspiracy, as presumably he must since he is farther away speaking before the king: but this wink turns out to be all he can communicate clearly on her behalf. His sputtering incapacity is only slightly less profound than his and Witty's final bovine stares in A (141–43). **I falle in floryns** is, Kane suggests (1989:97), the symptom of "an illness

with which a clever lawyer is afflicted, which makes him speak hypocritically";
for the basis, see MED *fallen* 24c. But the condition of "falling in florins" is an
explanation now not of his (previous) hypocrisy but of his present inability to
say more; it signifies "both that he has a way of coming upon money and that
he is so up to his neck in it that he trips over it and is choked by it" (Lawler
1996:162). The indication of a disease or condition is apt. Images of avarice
personified, in manuscripts and sculpture, often show a figure with a huge
mouth, indicating consuming not speaking, and holding large bags; sometimes
the figure is vomiting or defecating coins (see Little 1971). For another personification in PP of **floryns**, as a streetcrowd of retainers too thickly packed for
Faith to move through, see 3.193–95n. In the *Roman de Fauvel*, the pope is
portrayed as fishing for florins with a huge net, which is so full of florins that
his boat swamps and shatters (ed. Långfors 1914–19, lines 553–62). The sense
of money as a physical obstacle to spiritual goals or forces is clear in Holy
Church's speech (e.g., 2.38n).

The king's second judgment of Meed, and the compact with Reason [and
with Conscience]

**151–97 (cp. B 157–95, cp. A 134–58): al ryhtful recordede þat resoun treuthe
sayde . . . And receyue tho that resoun louede; and riht with þat y wakede
[B: Alle riȝtfulle recordede . . . " . . . lyue we togideres"; A: Ac whanne
resoun among þise renkis . . . ". . . libbe we togideris"]**: The debate ends with
an increasingly elaborated judgment. The three versions present progressive
refinements on how the popular judgment of the debate filters up to those in
power, and varying degrees of emphasis on the king's responsibility and ability
to represent and enforce the popular approval of Reason. The king's role
increases in the three versions, but so too do those of Reason and Conscience
as his counselors and mentors, along with the indications of the authority of
the common judgment. A model of moral governance is implicitly explored
by the court's processes of rendering, communicating, and imposing judgment
on the debate; and in varying ways it is shown to fall short of Reason's ideals.

Yet in spite of an increasing focus on the unfinished and larger problems
in the model of governance here displayed, its mechanisms are elaborated
through the versions with increasing detail, institutional realism, and signs of
effort to repair any practical or ethical shortcomings. While the subplot of
Waryn Wisdom and Witty has considerable wit, satire, and surrealism (though
much diminished in C), the resolution of the debate does not allow wit, satire,
surrealism, or absurdity to become ends in themselves, as sometimes at the

end of allegorical debates. Nor does the ending of the first vision rest by simply affirming the principles of justice and reason that the common opinion here endorses. Instead, the most basic problems of just governance that the king faces are brought to the fore and examined with renewed religious idealism as well as social practicality. The effort to come to a serious resolution to the problems raised here and throughout the first vision is remarkable in relation to the irreconcilable tones as well as conflicting principles in passus 4. The complexity of the resolution virtually demands that the poem cannot close with this vision, and also bespeaks an ongoing commitment to testing rigorous religious ethics against practice that helps explain the impulse for repeatedly revising the poem as a whole. Driven by this, which bespeaks the poet's ethical as well as poetic commitments, the ending of every vision in the poem confronts formidable challenges in coming to a resolution; but perhaps at no other point does the poem strive so clearly to make governance and the institutions of justice the focal point of such extraordinary literary and intellectual demands.

151–59 (cp. B 157–66, cp. A 134–40): Ac al ryhtful recordede . . . called hire an hore: In A and B, the popular view of the outcome is colloquial and blunt affirmation of Reason's case and, even more, of Meed's depravity, framed in terms of her sexual promiscuity; in C, the decorum is elevated but her promiscuity remains emphasized. The poem thus rejoins the original question of the validity of Meed's marriage, from which each version has departed in an increasingly wide compass. The essential paradoxical conceit remains, that it is impossible to marry Meed except **for welthe of here goodes** since indeed she is only that, however **welthe** and **goodes** are defined (the impetus for the widening scope of the revisions). The vignette here of Meed shamed (B followed by C adds the commons' insult) has a farcical or comedic style, e.g., as at the end of the twelfth-century Latin *Geta*, when Alcmena is discovered having (unknowingly) been an adulteress. But the spectacle of public humiliation here more likely evokes civic punishments of women, including "rough music": the *Liber Albus* declares that a prostitute would be taken from prison to Aldgate "with a hood of ray [striped cloth] and a white wand in her hand," then "openly be brought, with minstrels, from prison until the thew [i.e., the pining stool; see 3.79n] and there set on" while the cause was read aloud, whereupon she would be led "through Chepe and Newgate to Cokkeslane where she was to take up her abode" (quoted in Hanawalt 1998:26–27).

Seeing a topical portrait here of Alice Perrers humiliated in the Good Parliament would require a later date for A than is commonly allowed (see passus 2 Headnote), but A does focus more on the lawyers' failure than on Meed's

downfall (see below A 141–43n), and it is quite possible that B's shift to emphasize Meed's downfall at the scene's climax responds to or capitalizes on the
events of 1376 (see, e.g., Giancarlo 2003:157–60). Likely enough, however, the
shaming of notable and eloquent women in court preceded and followed Alice
Perrers' downfall, and in any case, A's attention to Waryn Wisdom and Witty
is a distraction (though one of several in all of the versions) from the plot with
which the trial began.

    In spite of the crudeness of the judgment against Meed, the three versions
present an increasing authority, efficaciousness, and social scope in the common audience as it responds to Reason's speech and the entire preceding
debate. As Giancarlo says, the "speech has taken place in a law court, but also
in the court of public opinion, so to speak, and Langland seems at pains to
stress this public aspect" (2003:156). In A, they think Meed a **muche wrecche**
(A 136); in B **a mansed sherewe** (B 160); in neither does this common audience
have a way to announce its views directly to any of the presiding officials, but
in B, the populace of **Alle riȝtfulle recordede** (B 157) the legitimacy of Reason's
speech, using **recordede** in the sense of its Latin root, "take to heart," recalling
B 120 above (see C 116n), with a further play on "record" in the sense of a
courtroom pronouncement (which the repetition of the verb for the king
makes clearer at B 172; C advances this verb to 27–31; see note). B's terms of
riȝtfulle and **recordede** thus grant the common opinion both ethical and legal
or constitutional authority. B also adds **Kynde wit** as a member of the listening
court (B 158), and his presence further ratifies the validity of the judgment
of **Alle riȝfulle**: their "native moral sense" is thus explicit (for Kind Wit, see
Prol.141–47n).

    In A and B, the common views are published in equally crude terms by
Love and, in B, seconded by Leaute, whom Sothness overhears and whose
defamatory words Sothness presumably spreads further (indeed, all manuscripts of B read not **soþnesse it herde** [B 162] but "al þe halle it herde": KD
emend properly *causa metri* here, but the archetypal error may have suggested
to the poet, using a corrupt B manuscript, the fuller publicity he presents in
C). These roles are consistent with elements of these figures elsewhere, especially as they develop in B: for Leaute's role in such publishing of satire, see
2.51–52n; for Love's association with Leaute, see 3.379n; for Sothness' role in
purveying truth, see 2.24n. These figures' denunciation of Meed at court contrasts with Meed's denunciation of Leaute at the pope's court, which Holy
Church has mentioned (2.20–21n), but even more, they provide a model for
how a poem might be both bawdily defamatory and ethically useful; the
importance of defamation and gossip here might be a model of the rapidity

and invasiveness with which the condemnation of Meed might be spread by the poem, rendering it to the status of "news."

As noted, the A version here goes on to climax this scene of popular judgment with a focus on the figures of the stymied and stunned lawyers for Wrong, which is thus offered as the chief result of the public verdict (141–43n); B concludes instead with a steady focus on Meed's **heuy chere / For þe comune calde here queynte comune hore** (165–66), responding to Love's and Leaute's slander but also recalling Conscience's at 3.169 (see n), in what Giancarlo calls "an almost irresistible pun" on the parliamentary style of "common clamor" (2003:157), in his view a further indication of the parliamentary venue that the scene invokes.

The C version keeps all of B's enhancements of the listening commons' authority, and further ratifies Reason's speech by having **kynde wit** and, now, **Consience** thank Reason for it **corteysliche** (152), although this new realistic touch of social decorum slightly reduces the scale of Reason's presence to more literal dimensions of a courtroom or parliamentary appearance. But C more capaciously defines **al ryhtful** as **ryche and pore**, emphasizing the social range of those approving of Reason's denunciation of Meed, as if the trial and the scene were witnessed not just by the king's council, or even by a full parliament, but by the entire 'field full of folk,' "þe mene and þe riche" (Prol.20n). In C, the crowd is no longer simply reduced to murmuring and cat-calls but can express its views to Reason directly, and in respectful terms (**"syre resoun"** [154]); this sign of decorousness and protocol, like Kind Wit's and Conscience's public thanks to Reason for his eloquence, establishes the audience's public authority more and overwrites the crudity of public judgments in the earlier versions. C keeps, however, Love's and Leaute's colloquial condemnation of Meed for her promiscuity, but now this is what these figures **cryede to Consience, the kyng myhte hit here** (157), completing the path of the common opinion up to the king directly. The address to him is oblique, indicating that he should also listen to Conscience and Reason, and serving to emphasize his responsibility for further action, as well as, perhaps, indicating the poem's own aspirations for status as a kind of "rule of princes" (for the Middle English versions of the genre, see Ferster 1996).

162–65 (cp. B 167–70): A sysour and a somnour . . . "*capias* mede / *Et saluo custodias set non cum carceratis*" [B: Ac a Sisour and a Somonour . . . "þe worþ of a risshe"]: The A text has no reference to what happens to Meed after her disgrace by the court's general lambasting. B suggests she departs followed by an assizer and a summoner, with an exit speech by an embittered sheriff's clerk who can get gifts by no other means (on these typical targets of satire, see 2.60–63n and 2.65–66n). But B then has the king glare at her, suggesting the departure was not successful. C makes this explicit and makes the sheriff's clerk into the king's agent, who cries out—except for the final clause—a standard order for her arrest: "Let you seize her, and let you take custody of her safely, but not among those imprisoned." Alford finds no precedent for the final qualification instead of the usual *in prisona nostra*, but he notes that this does not mean the modification was the poet's original shaping of the form, since writs appear in many forms (Alford, *Quot.*). The flexibility of writ forms could, however, be used to hypothesize the poet's meaningful manipulation of the formula. Here, the king's agent seems to declare that Meed's treatment will be gentler than the king has demanded; she remains a favored figure in the hands of the king's corrupt servants. Thus the C king's initial threat to imprison her in the "Castel of Corf . . . / Or in a wel wors, wone ther as an ancre" (3.141–42n), fails at the last. But her nature demands such leniency: those in prison do not have money, so Meed will not remain there.

A 141–43: Waryn wisdom þo . . . stariden for stodyenge and stoden as bestis: The A text focuses attention at the end not on Meed but on the lawyers helping Meed and Wrong; B first shifts the final focus to Meed (see above, e.g., B 167–70; see 162–65n). To *stonden and studien* is a common phrase for 'to be perplexed' (MED *studien* 3d), but the simile **as bestis** makes the phrase more literal than usual. Such bestial stupidity contrasts with the powers of speech and wit by which they live; a similar connotation lies in the next use of **bestis** in the A text (A.6.2; the present lines are dropped but that line is kept in B and C: B.5.514, C.7.159). Lawler finds some literary charm in the last view of them here in A (1996:162), but he notes that this leaves their maneuvering, as throughout A, not as clearly "exposed or condemned" as in the other versions (1996:159).

166–75 (cp. B 171–81): The kyng to consayl tho toek Consience . . . ". . . my lawe shal be demed": The king's need for governance by proper counselors and high principles is emphasized here as it is in the Prologue; as there, C emphasizes the king making Conscience his literal councilor, perhaps a way to claim freedom from the control of other kinds of social entities such as Parliament or the "commons" (see Prol.152n; but see also above, 151–59n). The moment of the Prologue's appearance of the king and the founding of the commonwealth is revisited here deliberately and in a reforming spirit: a powerful effort is made to establish the king's authority to fix what is wrong with the kingdom. But the king's first declarations reveal the seriousness of his problems. Although B and C omit A's final comic view of Wrong's corrupt lawyers (A 141–43), the efforts in B and C of some minor county officials to help Meed (above, 162–65n) are followed by the king's direct wrath against lawyers as the heaviest abusers of Meed (for the tradition, see Yunck 1988). He declares emphatic principles of just rule: in B the king affirms that **wrong shal be demed** (B 181), C shifts to imply that corrupt judges might be removed: **by lele and by lyfholy** [sc. judges] **my lawe shal be demed** (C 175). The question of removing royal judges appeared both in the Good Parliament of 1376 (when the commons impeached some royal justices) and in 1387, when Richard II posed a series of infamously leading "questions" to the royal judges about the legitimacy of the commons having done this (recorded in, e.g., the *Westminster Chronicle*, ed. and trans. Hector and Harvey 1982:196–203), although those "questions" could be presented as a request from the king for clarification of the law, i.e., as seeking not autocracy but the explicit rule of law. Whatever the atmosphere of this issue in the decades of the B and C texts, a warning for the king to have just judges may more tactfully appear in the king's own mouth than in his critics'.

169 (B 175): Thorw ȝoure lawe, as y leue, y lese many chetes: The king's need to receive **chetes** ('escheats,' that is, the lands or goods coming into his possession, because of failure of heirs, or for convictions of felony) was recognized by the commons as necessary to keep him from imposing additional taxes on his subjects (see Stokes 1984:152–53). In May 1382, the Commons presented the king a petition demanding essentially what the C king here wants: "that he should be able to live honorably and regally off his own revenues," including escheats, so that he will not burden the Commons further (Rot. Parl. 3.139). The view was traditional, and B would likely not have been late enough for this. A sense of the national importance of the king's fiscal solvency continued to be expressed in the period, in parliamentary petitions that were often surrounded by grave political tensions. In 1385 a bill was presented by nine lords arguing that Richard II should increase his escheats as well as other sources of income and refrain from his impulsive gifts, a complaint that set the terms for the impeachment of the chancellor Michael de la Pole in 1386 (Roskell 1984:61–63; see also below, 184–86n). Under 1386, the Westminster Chronicler echoes this complaint: "sic enim suis aliis erogatis communitatem de necessitate opprimere est compulsus; unde pauperes super hoc graviter conqueruntur, assertens se tale onus diu sustinere non posse. Utinam rex disponeret eosdem in aliquo alleviare; et profecto comodum inde non modicum, ut estimo, reportaret" ("Having thus handed out his own substance to others, he had perforce to come down on the commons, with the result that the poor are loud in their complaints and declare that they cannot go on supporting the burden. If only the king would arrange matters so as to give them some relief! He would, I think, reap no small benefit by doing so"; ed. and trans. Hector and Harvey 1982:162–63). As with the lines above, placing such views in the mouth of the king cleverly avoids aligning the poem with any of the voices or parties in conflict with the king on this point, and allows the poem's king to speak the lessons that the historical English king was perceived to need.

The phrase carries special emphasis in the king's declarations of his new moral order. Given this, and given the widespread concern with the issue in the period, the line is probably not ironic. Yet it presents the king declaring his need for monetary reward in the act of trying to send Meed to prison, and this at least displays some complexity in his position as supreme temporal ruler. He must find a way to gain, use and direct the use and ownership of "þe moneye of þis molde" (1.42 [B.144, A.1.42]), since this is his responsibility as king, but to do so without capitulating to Meed's view that no values other than desire for monetary reward move and bind society. He has initially tried to match Meed (his kinswoman) with Conscience precisely because of his complex position, in needing to offer rewards (one of the traditional ideals of a medieval king) but to avoid illicit ones. The need for a just economy has motivated the poem from the satire of the many corrupt economic systems in the Prologue, through the statement that the help of the king, knighthood, and clergy (or in C, Kind Wit and Conscience) can help the commons "here comunes fynde" (see Prol.139–47 [B.Prol.112–21] and n), through Holy Church's declaration that Reason should be the guardian of treasure (see 1.42–53 [B.1.43–57, A.1.41–55] and n), through Conscience's endeavor to define a faithful relation between servant and master (see 3.348–51n).

The focus continues throughout the poem, in the individual lives and choices of the narrator and all other figures. But the broadest social and spiritual consequences of a just or unjust economy, and the heaviest responsibility for pursuing either, devolve upon the king, the kingdom's most important owner of the "þe moneye of þis molde." In A/B, his emphatic concern with gaining enough **chetes** right after dismissing Meed is not explored further, but in C's final coda the issue of his relation to the treasure of this earth is further pursued after the agreement between the king, Reason, and Conscience (see below 184–86n).

176–78 (B 182–84, cp. A 146–47): "withoute þe comune helpe . . . to lede thus euene" [A: "Ac it is wel hard, by my hed . . . to lede þus euene"]: The concerns expressed about enlisting the common's help and reforming the king's higher **lege ledes** to just governance (**to lede thus euene**) shift from the mouth of the king in A, to that of Conscience in B/C, who thereby asserts his importance as a cautionary counselor. Burrow notes that the following vision immediately turns to this problem of reforming **þe comune** (1965[1969]:210–11). The revisions in this section increase the king's claims to power but also his responsibilities and difficulties. The need for the commons to assent to the royal prerogative is clear already from B.Prol.121–22, B.Prol.139–45, and C.3.374–82 (see notes on these passages); only the present passage revisiting this issue, however, directly confronts the problem of whether the commons will in fact do so.

179–86 (cp. B 185–95, A 148–58): "By hym þat rauhte on þe rode . . . And Consience in alle my Courtes be as kynges Iustice" [B, A: . . . "Als longe as I lyue lyue we togideres"]: After Conscience has raised doubts about the outcome of any endeavor of national reform, Reason responds by vowing to put the whole kingdom under his rule, on pain of his own mutilation in various horrific forms through the three versions (**rende out my ribbes** [A], **rende out my guttes** [B], **reueth me my syhte** [C]). Reason's offer is contractual (see Fowler 1995), and the terms are not entirely empty figures of speech. The king must be obedient to Reason (or "law"), and must continue to obey Conscience, whereas if Reason fails, he will thereby have been destroyed by the kingdom. The punishments Reason proposes for himself suggest the more painful parts of the penalties for treason, including disemboweling and blinding; these literalize Reason's vulnerability to the people of the kingdom who "torture" reason by their lawlessness.

The contract of making a court here is a new social contract, analogous to a robustly celebrated marriage: **For as longe as I lyue lete þee I nelle** (B 191, A 154); as Fowler notes (1995), in spite of the traces of such an analogy, the scene elides the female figure who generated the need for such an arrangement. But that female figure remains a part of the new relationship insofar as she remains among or available to the people whom the king and his counselors try to govern; thus she is not in fact truly omitted from the relationship. As Reason's sermon has revised the Prologue's survey of estates, so the remaking of the court offers a return to the Prologue's founding of the commonwealth (see Prol.139–59n), but in terms of preparing to engage serious challenges. Apart from Reason's and Conscience's interrogation of the vagrant narrator in the next passus in C only, however, the poem does not persist in trying to use royal power to reform the kingdom; in following visions, the true guides for the people come from unexpected walks of life.

All three versions of the end of the passus, and of the vision, focus on the conciliar oversight of the king; this was an issue both in the period of Richard's minority, from 1376-c. 1381, and again from 1386–87 when Richard had a "great and continual" council supervising his expenditures and pardons (Saul 1997:24–111, 148–75). The king's agreement in A/B has the stipulation that his council of **clerkes and of Erles** be included; Reason and Conscience are additional counselors for the king, to whom he pledges his undying loyalty. In C, the existing courtly community is ignored, and the king makes Reason and Conscience themselves his chief and perhaps only counselors, and councilors, a dismissal that is followed by the further dismissal of all of Conscience's officers (C 195). The political solution in A/B is to commit the king and his entire council to a venture to reform the kingdom, or let Reason be tortured and mutilated in the attempt. The ending of A/B's vision on this note carries some effort at communal joviality, although the assent of the actual "commons" to this remains deeply uncertain. That question, and thus the question of any moral reform on political or social grounds, thus both lies open for a long further pursuit and testing, and is already framed in terms that suggest the quixotic nature of such a quest. The vows made are hedged with provisions and caveats; in A/B, there is no certainty even that the king's **clerkes** and **Erles** will assent to this new order, much less that the broader social world of the commons will do so.

The political solution in C is more royalist (no other earthly power can confine or obligate the king), and also considerably more idealist in its plan. Perhaps this registers the inevitability of failure to accomplish a moral reform by political or social means, and perhaps also anticipates and authorizes the poem's failure for more than short stretches even to attempt reform (anticipating and accommodating, for example, the Doctor of Divinity's flat skepticism about such political idealism [15.170 (B.13.172)]).

184–86: "Forthy, resoun . . . as kynges Iustice": For the germ of the promotion of these figures to official status, see 2.205n. The king's definition, in C only, of Reason's new position as **cheef Chaunceller in Cheker and in parlement** may not mean "lord chancellor," since there were many chancellors. But Reason's role suggests the scope of what a lord chancellor's powers had become by the mid-fourteenth century (see Jones 1967:7–8; Harding 1973:99–100); for other indications of this new role, see above, 5–7n, 29–30n. The chancellor's authority, as keeper of the Great Seal, was theoretically a direct extension of the king's will, but during Richard's reign the distance between the king and chancery grew, in the simplest terms measured by the successive other seals that Richard (along with other late medieval kings) created to establish his own authority outside that of the chancellor (see Galbraith 1963:25–34). In the later fourteenth century the position of chancellor became a point of keen struggle in the savage conflicts that took place between Richard II and the higher nobility. Richard le Scrope, a retainer of John of Gaunt, was lord chancellor from 1378–82 but with frequent interruptions from political crises: in 1380 Scrope resigned from the "continual council" overseeing Richard (increasingly against Richard's will), whereby Scrope was briefly replaced by Archbishop Courtenay until Scrope was reinstalled (Saul 1997:45, 81); in July 1382 the king dismissed Scrope when he resisted some of Richard's grants to petitioners, and Richard then installed Michael de la Pole, another close supporter, as chancellor. But de la Pole was impeached by the higher nobility in the "Wonderful Parliament" in 1386, and they replaced him with Thomas Arundel (then bishop of Ely). In 1388 Scrope was condemned to death by the group of lords who appealed and condemned to death many of Richard's followers, but by then Scrope had fled the realm (Saul 1997:111, 161–93). Arundel held the post from 1386 until May of 1389, when Richard dismissed the key ministers of chancellor and treasurer that the Lords Appellant had imposed on him, replacing Arundel with the aged William Wyckham, bishop of Winchester, and replacing the treasurer that the Appellants had imposed on him, John Gilbert, bishop of Hereford, with the also very aged Thomas Brantingham, bishop of Exeter (Saul 1997:126, 158, 162–63, 202–3). Given the broader political conflicts expressed through many of these appointments and dismissals during the period of the C text, the delegation of Reason to this office appears a political utopia. But even here there are minor conflicts with the king (see next note).

Conscience's appointment in C **in alle my Courtes** to be **as kynges Iustice** (186) adds another significantly utopian claim about royal justices, who in the century were often attacked, especially after Richard II's use of the highest judges in 1387 to declare treasonous the impeachment of de la Pole and other actions against Richard's followers (see Harding 1984; Galloway 2001a:10; and see above 105–6n). Fittingly for his allegory, Conscience is not simply "a" king's justice; he *is* **kynges Iustice**: the lack of an indefinite article here allows the full sense of the abstraction (as well as being idiomatic for an administrative position).

The likeliest detailed topical resonance for these aspects of C's ending to passus 4 is in the commission appointed in 1381 "to survey and reform the king's household" (Saul 1997:81), which it was agreed would be led by "two senior lords . . . appointed to reside perpetually in the household 'to counsel and govern' the king": for this the earl of Arundel was selected, and Michael de la Pole, at the moment of reappointment to chancellor. Just as the C king wishes Reason to be **cheef Chaunceller in Cheker and in parlement**, a supervisory position over those venues, so in 1381 were passed in parliament a series of measures to reform and streamline the Exchequer (see Rot. Parl. 3.100–2). The terms of C's conclusion may well derive from the events and plans for political and financial reform bruited in Parliament 1382–83.

But the ideal of constraining the king by advisors was perennial and acute throughout medieval kingship, and certainly through Richard's reign. Reason warms to this role in the final lines, in C only (187–96), shifting from the polite "ye" (**ʒowsulue, ʒoure**) to the familiar "thow" (191, 192, 193), thus finally standing in the position of the Goliard as tutoying adviser for the king (see B.Prol.139–45 and nn), or indeed above the Goliard since Reason selects the king's officers (C 197). Although C has removed from the Prologue the king's unexpected advisors, and reduced the Rats and Mice to positions of self-acknowledging subservience, it has consolidated the political authority and confidence of Reason and Conscience. This might be seen as freeing the monarchy from the contractual constraints of the commons (see Baldwin), but might also be seen as locating those complaints in more authoritative voices, abstracted into broader thematic rather than locally specific forms. This second possibility is more evident at this end of the first vision than at the beginning.

187–90: by so ʒowsulue yhere / *Audiatis alteram partem* . . . vnsittynge suffraunce . . . supersedias: C's Reason accepts his new role only with a series of stipulations (analogous to the "if" clauses emphasized in C.3.329; see n). He first stipulates "Let you hear the other side," a maxim of Roman law and a principle of natural justice; this demands that the king allow political participation by urban officials and citizens (**aldremen and comeneres**), allowing cities to confront the king (as London unsuccessfully did in 1392, too late for PP but a looming problem in the period: see Saul 1997:258–61). The warning against **vnsittynge suffraunce** cautions the king from improper indulgence of fraud or other crime, using a phrase elsewhere inserted into C (see 3.203–10n, also Prol.124n), and here perhaps especially related to his power to pardon crimes since transmitted via his **priue lettres**; such autocratic pardons were a pressing issue during the later decades of Richard's reign (see above, 46–48n). So too, Reason stipulates that **supersedias** (*sic* for *supersedeas*)—writs that stayed or put an end to a proceeding (Alford, *Gloss.*)—must not be doled out by the king on his own whim but passed through Reason's hands (see also 2.190–92n). The advice registers complaints made throughout Richard's rule; the tone of a "mirror for princes" is at its closest here, but these suggestions are precise and informed in ways that that heavily formulaic didactic tradition rarely is, although it can convey topicality in coded ways (see Ferster 1996).

191–94: And y dar lege my lyf þat loue wol lene þe seluer .. by lone as iewes:
In C, Reason persists in his utopian idealism, now one that approaches Matt.
6:25–34, "be not solicitous for your life, what you shall eat, nor for your body,
what you shall put on," so far implied only in the Prologue (35–38n, 41–46n)
but soon to be a central issue in the narrator's own pious, or slothful, mendicant vagrancy (5.1–106, in C only). If the king adheres to all of Reason's stipulations, Love will be his moneylender, not Lombards or Jews (who were of
course important sources of royal capital). Thus C's Reason, even in the act of
accepting a position in a new regime of government and rule, proposes an
apostolic ideal of kingship, one approaching the most ascetic mendicant ideal.
But this, Reason claims, will be the result if the king follows principles of just
governance; he will not seek to be a hermit, but to be *as* a hermit, applying the
ideal of the apostolic life in the form in which his estate allows. The focus is
consistent with emphases on the "mixed life" and the instruction for the piety
of laymen in the period, to be pious and detached within while they led secular
lives (see Pantin 1955:252–61; he cites the instance of the late fourteenth-century *Abbey of The Holy Ghost*; see ed. Blake 1972:88–102, available in many late
medieval copies including the Vernon Manuscript, Bodleian Library, Oxford,
MS. Eng. poet. a.1, which includes an A text of PP).

But C's coda for the passus presents a larger version of the "mixed life"
than such treatises. Reason now presents a full royal economic policy in terms
of a mendicant ideal, an issue whose practical applications are dubious even
on the individual level of the poem. The advice is, perhaps, Reason's oblique
rebuke to the king for claiming above that he must get rid of Meed because he
needs more meed (above, 169n). But the continued idealism of the plan and
its further fruits shows just how demanding it is to have Reason as royal councilor, as it has already been shown how hard it is to have Conscience as chief
courtier. Both counselors have sought to convey to him ways of conducting
government in order to allow all individual transactions to be "mercedes," as
in Conscience's speech at 3.374–82 (see n). But the king's hopes for reform are
thereby placed all the more firmly in those who follow him: the principle of
not being solicitous for the morrow is one of relinquishing control fully over
his subjects and his financial affairs. All he can do is summon his followers,
although here too he must narrow the field to those who are fit for such service.

**195–96: The kyng comaundede Consience tho to congeye alle his offeceres /
And receyue tho that resoun louede; and riht with þat y wakede:** C's addition to passus 4 ends with the king's dismissal of all his courtly officers, offering a political purge in response to the satire of corrupt figures at court

throughout the vision. Only those who are truly lawful (who loved Reason or whom Reason loved and, as lord chancellor, selected) will be kept. The division of the just and unjust is severe, but in keeping with the principles of Reason's proverb (above, 140–45n). But the uncertainties of who these are and how they are known also reflect the principles of Reason's proverb, and of the poem's long exploration of "truth" and justice in general. The quasi-mendicant ethics that Reason in C proposes for the king's economic practices (above 191–94n) is followed by an ascetic stripping of courtly personnel, remaking the king's household as Reason would remake the kingdom.

receuye tho that resoun louede recalls the principle *quod bonum est tenete*, the outcome of the process of "trying and holding the good" that pervades the vision, and in many ways the poem as a whole (see, e.g., 1.81–204n). As with Jesus' selection from hell "which hym luste" and dismissal of the rest (20.449 [B.18.406]; see 20.414n, 20.449n), the identity of that number is invisible to the narrator and to the poem's readers, a blank that the dreamer's reemergence at just this moment into the waking world of London or Malvern renders still less certain.

Works Cited

Multiple authors are listed only under the first author or editor.

Abrahams, P. "The Mercator-Scenes in Mediaeval French Passion-Plays." *Medium Ævum* 3 (1934): 112–23.

Adams, Robert. "Piers' Pardon and Langland's Semi-Pelagianism." *Traditio* 39 (1983): 367–418.

———. "The Reliability of the Rubrics in the B-Text of *Piers Plowman*." *Medium Ævum* 54 (1985): 208–31.

———. "Mede and Mercede: The Evolution of the Economics of Grace in the *Piers Plowman* B and C Versions." In *Medieval English Studies Presented to George Kane*, ed. Edward Donald Kennedy, Ronald Waldron, and Joseph S. Wittig. Woodbridge, Suffolk: D.S. Brewer, 1988. 217–32. = 1988a

———. "Langland's Theology." In *A Companion to Piers Plowman*, ed. John A. Alford. Berkeley: University of California Press, 1988. 87–114. =1988b

———. "Editing and the Limitations of *Durior Lectio*." *Yearbook of Langland Studies* 5 (1991): 7–15.

———. "Langland's *Ordinatio*: The *Visio* and the *Vita* Once More." *Yearbook of Langland Studies* 8 (1994): 51–84.

Aers, David. *Piers Plowman and Christian Allegory*. London: Edward Arnold, 1975.

———. "Reflections on the 'Allegory of the Theologians,' Ideology and *Piers Plowman*." In his *Medieval Literature: Criticism, Ideology and History*. Brighton: Harvester Press, 1986. 58–73.

———. *Sanctifying Signs: Making Christian Tradition in Late Medieval England*. Notre Dame, Ind.: University of Notre Dame Press, 2004.

Alberigo, J., J. A. Dossetti, P. P. Joannou, C. Leonardi, P. Prodi, with H. Jedin, eds. *Conciliorum Oecumenicorum Decreta*. 3rd ed. Bologna: Istituto per le scienze religiose, 1973.

Albumazar (Abū Maʿshar). *Introductorium in astronomiam*, trans. Adelard of Bath. Venice: Mechio Sessa, 1506.

Alford, John A. "The Grammatical Metaphor: A Survey of Its Use in the Middle Ages." *Speculum* 57 (1982): 728–60.

———. "The Design of the Poem." In *A Companion to Piers Plowman*, ed. John A. Alford. Berkeley: University of California Press, 1988. 32–39. =1988a

———. "The Idea of Reason in Piers Plowman." In *Medieval English Studies Presented to George Kane*, ed. Edward Donald Kennedy, Ronald Waldron, and Joseph S. Wittig. Wolfeboro, N.H.: D.S. Brewer, 1988. 199–215. = 1988b

Alford, John A. and Dennis P. Seniff. *Literature and Law in the Middle Ages: A Bibliography of Scholarship*. New York: Garland, 1984.

Allen, D. C. "*Paradise Lost*, I, 254–55." *Modern Language Notes* 71 (1956): 324–26.

Allen, Hope Emily, ed. *English Writings of Richard Rolle, Hermit of Hampole*. Oxford: Clarendon, 1931; repr. St. Clair Shores, Mich.: Scholarly Press, 1971.

Amassian, Margaret and J. Sadowsky. "Mede and Mercede: A Study of the Grammatical Metaphor in *Piers Plowman* C: IV:335–409." *Neuphilologische Mitteilungen* 72 (1971): 457–76.

Amelia (Klenke), M., ed. *Three Saints' Lives by Nicholas Bozon*. St. Bonaventure, N.Y.: Franciscan Institute, 1947.

Andrew, Malcolm and Ronald Waldron, eds. *The Poems of the Pearl Manuscript*. Exeter: University of Exeter Press, 1996.

Apperson, G. L. *English Proverbs and Proverbial Phrases; A Historical Dictionary*. London: J.M. Dent, 1929.

Aquinas, St. Thomas. *Opera omnia iussa impensaque Leonis XIII P. M. edita*. 50 vols. Rome: Typographia Polyglotta S. C. de Propaganda Fide, 1882–2000.

Armitage-Smith, Sydney. *John of Gaunt*. Westminster: Archibald Constable and Co., 1904.

Armstrong, Regis J., J. A. Wayne Hellman, and William Short, eds. and trans. *Francis of Assisi, Early Documents*, vol. 1, *The Saint*. New York: New City Press, 1999.

Arnold, Thomas, ed. *Select English Works of John Wyclif*. 3 vols. Oxford: Oxford University Press, 1869–71.

Aston, Margaret. "'Caim's Castles': Poverty, Politics, and Disendowment." In *The Church, Politics and Patronage in the Fifteenth Century*, ed. Barrie Dobson. Gloucester: Alan Sutton, 1984. 45–81.

———. "Wyclif and the Vernacular." In *From Ockham to Wyclif*, ed. Anne Hudson and Michael Wilks. Studies in Church History Subsidia 5. Oxford: Blackwell, 1987. 281–300.

———. "Segregation in Church." In *Women in the Church*, ed. W. J. Sheils and Diana Wood. Studies in Church History 27. Oxford, Blackwell, 1990. 237–94.

Aston, Margaret and Colin Richmond, eds. *Lollardy and the Gentry in the Later Middle Ages*. Stroud: Sutton, 1997.

Avenare (Abraham Ben Meïr Ibn Ezra). *Introductorium quod dicitur principium sapientie*. Venice: Petrus Liechtenstein, 1521.

Avery, Margaret E. "The History of the Equitable Jurisdiction of Chancery Before 1460." *Bulletin of the Institute of Historical Research* 42 (1969): 129–44.

Babington, Churchill and Joseph Lumby, eds. *Polychronicon Ranulphi Higden monachi Cestrensis: Together with the English Translations of John Trevisa and of an Unknown Writer of the Fifteenth Century*. Rolls Series 41. 9 vols. London: Longmans, 1865–86.

Badel, Pierre-Yves. *Le Roman de la Rose au XIVe siècle: étude de la réception de l'œvre*. Geneva: Droz, 1980.

Baker, John Hamilton. *The Common Law Tradition: Lawyers, Books and the Law*. London: Hambledon, 2000.

———. *The Order of Serjeants at Law*. London: Selden Society, 1984.

Baker, John Hamilton and S. F. C. Milsom, eds. and trans. *Sources of English Legal History: Private Law to 1750*. London: Butterworths, 1986.

Balbus, Johannes. *Catholicon*. Lyon: Boniface, 1496.

Baldwin, Anna. *The Theme of Government in Piers Plowman*. Woodbridge, Suffolk: D.S. Brewer, 1981.

Baldwin, James Fosdick. *The King's Council in England During the Middle Ages.* Oxford: Clarendon Press, 1913.

Barber, Richard. *Edward, Prince of Wales and Aquitaine.* Woodbridge, Suffolk: Boydell, 1996.

Barney, Stephen A. "The Plowshare of the Tongue: The Progress of a Symbol from the Bible to *Piers Plowman.*" *Mediaeval Studies* 35 (1973): 261–93.

———. *Allegories of History, Allegories of Love.* New Haven, Conn.: Archon, 1979.

———. "Chaucer's Lists." In *The Wisdom of Poetry: Essays in Early English Literature in Honor of Morton W. Bloomfield,* ed. Larry D. Benson and Siegfried Wenzel. Kalamazoo, Mich.: Medieval Institute, 1982. 189–223.

———. "Allegorical Visions." In *A Companion to Piers Plowman,* ed. John A. Alford. Berkeley: University of California Press, 1988. 117–33.

———. "Langland's Prosody: The State of Study." In *The Endless Knot: Essays on Old and Middle English in Honor of Marie Borroff,* ed. M. Teresa Tavormina and R. F. Yeager. Cambridge: D.S. Brewer, 1995. 65–85. = 1995a

———. "Response to John Alford's 'Langland's Learning.'" *Yearbook of Langland Studies* 9 (1995): 8–10. = 1995b

———. "Langland's Mighty Line." In *William Langland's Piers Plowman: A Book of Essays,* ed. Kathleen Hewett-Smith. New York: Routledge, 2001. 103–17.

Barnum, Priscilla Heath, ed. *Dives and Pauper.* Parts 1 and 2. Early English Text Society 275, 280. London: Oxford University Press, 1976, 1980.

Barr, Helen. *Socioliterary Practice in Late Medieval England.* Oxford: Oxford University Press, 2001.

———, ed. *The Piers Plowman Tradition.* London: J.M. Dent, 1993.

Barratt, Alexandra. "The Characters 'Civil' and 'Theology' in *Piers Plowman.*" *Traditio* 38 (1982): 352–64.

Barron, Caroline. "The Parish Fraternities of Medieval London." In *The Church in Pre-Reformation Society,* ed. C. M. Barron and C. Harper-Bill. Woodbridge, Suffolk: D.S. Brewer, 1985. 13–37.

———. "William Langland: A London Poet." In *Chaucer's England: Literature in Historical Context,* ed. Barbara A. Hanawalt. Medieval Studies at Minnesota 4. Minneapolis: University of Minnesota Press, 1992. 91–109.

———. "Richard II and London." In *Richard II: The Art of Kingship,* ed. A. Goodman and J. Gillespie. Oxford: Oxford University Press, 1999. 129–54.

———. "London, 1300–1540." In *The Cambridge Urban History of Britain, vol. 1, 600–1540,* ed. D. M. Palliser. Cambridge: Cambridge University Press, 2000. 395–440.

———. *London in the Later Middle Ages: Government and People, 1200–1500.* Oxford: Oxford University Press, 2004.

Bate, Keith, ed. *Three Latin Comedies.* Toronto: Pontifical Institute of Mediaeval Studies, 1976.

Bayless, Martha. *Parody in the Middle Ages: The Latin Tradition.* Ann Arbor: University of Michigan Press, 1996.

Bayot, Alphonse, ed. *Le Poème moral.* Publications de l'Académie Royale de Langue et de Littérature françaises de Belgique; Textes anciens 1. Paris: Éditions Albert, [1929].

Beadle, Richard, ed. *The York Plays.* London: Edward Arnold, 1982.

Beck, Sigisberti, Ivvamen Praestante, R. De Kegel, eds. *Frowinus de Monte Angelorum.*

Explanatio dominicae orationis; additus Tractatus de veritate. Corpus Christian-orum, Continuatio Mediaevalis 134. Turnhout: Brepols, 2004.

Beilby, Mark. "The Profits of Expertise: The Rise of the Civil Lawyers and Chancery Equity." In *Profit, Piety and the Professions in Later Medieval England*, ed. Michael Hicks. Gloucester: Alan Sutton, 1990. 72–90.

Bellamy, J. G. *Bastard Feudalism and the Law.* London: Routledge, 1989.

Bender, Margaret O., ed. *Le Torneiment Anticrist by Huon de Méri: A Critical Edition.* Romance Monographs 17. University, Miss.: Romance Monographs, 1976.

Bennett, J. A. W. "The Date of the A-Text of *Piers Plowman.*" *Publications of the Modern Language Association* 58 (1943): 566–72. = 1943a

———. "The Date of the B-Text of *Piers Plowman.*" *Medium Ævum* 12 (1943): 55–64. = 1943b

———. *The Parlement of Foules: An Interpretation.* Oxford: Oxford University Press, 1957.

Bennett, J. A. W. and G. V. Smithers, eds. *Early Middle English Verse and Prose.* With glossary by Norman Davis. 2nd ed. rev. Oxford: Clarendon Press, 1974.

Bennett, Josephine Waters. "The Mediaeval Loveday." *Speculum* 33 (1958): 351–70.

Benson, C. David. "The Function of Lady Meed in *Piers Plowman.*" *English Studies* 61 (1980): 193–205.

———. *Public Piers Plowman: Modern Scholarship and Late Medieval English Culture.* University Park: Pennsylvania State University Press, 2004.

Benson, C. David and Lynne S. Blanchfield. *The Manuscripts of Piers Plowman: The B Version.* Woodbridge, Suffolk: D.S. Brewer, 1997.

Benson, Larry D. "The Occasion of *The Parliament of Fowls.*" In *Contradictions: From Beowulf to Chaucer.* Ed. Theodore M. Andersson and Stephen A. Barney. Aldershot, Hants: Scolar Press, 1995. 175–97.

———, ed., rev. ed. Edward E. Foster. *King Arthur's Death: The Middle English Stanzaic Morte Arthur and Alliterative Morte Arthure.* Kalamazoo, Mich.: Medieval Institute Publications, 1994.

Besant, Walter. *London.* Vol. 1. Leipzig, 1893.

Bestul, Thomas H., ed. *Walter Hilton: The Scale of Perfection.* Kalamazoo, Mich.: Medieval Institute Publications, 2000.

Bethurum, Dorothy, ed. *The Homilies of Wulfstan.* Oxford: Clarendon Press, 1957.

Beveridge, Erskine, ed. *Fergusson's Scottish Proverbs from the Original Print of 1641.* Scottish Text Society 15. Edinburgh: Blackwood and Sons, 1924.

Bevington, David, ed. *Medieval Drama.* Boston: Houghton Mifflin, 1975.

Biancalana, Joseph. *The Fee Tail and the Common Recovery in Medieval England, 1176–1502.* Cambridge: Cambridge University Press, 2001.

Binski, Paul. *Westminster Abbey and the Plantagenets: Kingship and the Representation of Power, 1200–1400.* New Haven, Conn.: Yale University Press, 1995.

Birch, Debra J. "Jacques de Vitry and the Ideology of Pilgrimage." In *Pilgrimage Explored*, ed. J. Stopford. York: York Medieval Press, 1999. 79–93.

Birks, Peter, Grant McLeod (trans.), and Paul Kreuger (Latin text). *Justinian's Institutes.* Ithaca, N.Y.: Cornell University Press, 1987.

Birnes, William J. "Christ as Advocate: The Legal Metaphor of *Piers Plowman.*" *Annuale Medievale* 16 (1975): 71–93.

Black, Antony. "The Individual and Society." In *The Cambridge History of Medieval*

Political Thought, c. 350-c.1450, ed. J. H. Burns. Cambridge: Cambridge University Press, 1988. 588–606.

———. *Political Thought in Europe, 1250–1450*. Cambridge: Cambridge University Press, 1992.

———. "The Juristic Origins of Social Contract Theory." *History of Political Thought* 14 (1993): 57–76.

Blake, N. F. *Caxton and his World*. Elmsford, N.Y.: London House and Maxwell, 1969. = 1969a

———. "Rhythmical Alliteration." *Modern Philology* 67 (1969): 118–24. = 1969b

———, ed. *Middle English Religious Prose*. Evanston, Ill.: Northwestern University Press, 1972.

Blamires, Alcuin. *The Case for Women in Medieval Culture*. Oxford: Clarendon Press, 1997.

Blamires, Alcuin, ed., with Karen Pratt and C. W. Marx. *Woman Defamed and Woman Defended: An Anthology of Medieval Texts*. Oxford: Clarendon Press, 1992.

Bland, Cynthia Renée. "Langland's Use of the Term *Ex vi transicionis*." *Yearbook of Langland Studies* 2 (1988): 125–35.

Bloomfield, Morton W. *Piers Plowman as a Fourteenth-Century Apocalypse*. New Brunswick, N.J.: Rutgers University Press, n.d. [1962].

Blyth, Charles, ed. *Thomas Hoccleve: The Regiment of Princes*. Kalamazoo, Mich.: Medieval Institute Publications, 1999.

Bossuat, R, ed. *Alain de Lille, Anticlaudianus*. Paris: Librairie Philosophique J. Vrin, 1955.

Bowers, John M. *The Crisis of Will in Piers Plowman*. Washington, D.C.: Catholic University of America Press, 1986.

———. "Piers Plowman and the Police: Notes Toward a History of the Wycliffite Langland." *Yearbook of Langland Studies* 6 (1992): 1–50.

Bowers, R. H. "A Middle English Poem on Lovedays." *Modern Language Review* 47 (1952): 374–75.

Boyle, Leonard E. "The Fourth Lateran Council and Manuals of Popular Theology." In *The Popular Literature of Medieval England*, ed. Thomas J. Heffernan. Tennessee Studies in Literature 28. Knoxville: University of Tennessee Press, 1985. 30–43.

Braddy, Haldeen. "Chaucer and Dame Alice Perrers." *Speculum* 21 (1946): 222–28.

———. "Chaucer, Alice Perrers, and Cecily Chaumpaigne." *Speculum* 52 (1977): 902–11.

Brand, Paul. *The Making of the Common Law*. London: Hambledon Press, 1992.

Bremmer, Rolf H., Jr., ed. *The Fyve Wyttes: A Late Middle English Devotional Treatise*. Costerus n. s. 65. Amsterdam: Rodopi, 1987.

Brereton, Geoffrey, trans. and ed. *Froissart: Chronicles*. London: Penguin, 1978.

Brereton, Georgine and Janet M. Ferrier, eds. *Le Menagier de Paris*. Oxford: Clarendon Press, 1981.

Breymann, Hermann, ed. *La Dime de Penitance . . . von Jehan von Journi*. Bibliothek des litterarischen Vereins in Stuttgart 120. Tübingen: Litterarischer Verein in Stuttgart, 1874.

Brie, Friedrich W. D., ed. *The Brut*. Early English Text Society o.s. 131, 136. London: Oxford University Press, 1906, 1908.

Bright, Allan H. *New Light on Piers Plowman*. London: Oxford University Press, 1928.

Brinkmann, Hennig. *Mittelalterliche Hermeneutik*. Tübingen: Max Niemeyer, 1980.

Britnell, Richard H. *The Commercialisation of English Society, 1000–1500*. Manchester: Manchester University Press, 1996.

Bromyard, John. *Summa praedicantium*. 2 vols. Basel 1484.

Brook, G. L., ed. *The Harley Lyrics: The Middle English Lyrics of MS. Harley 2253*. Manchester: Manchester University Press, 1948; 1964.

Brook, G. L. and R. F. Leslie, eds. *Laȝamon: Brut*. Early English Text Society 250, 277. London: Oxford University Press, 1963, 1977.

Brooke, Christopher N. L. *London 800–1216: The Shaping of a City*. Berkeley: University of California Press, 1975.

Brown, Beatrice Daw. "A Thirteenth-Century Chaucerian Analogue." *Modern Language Notes* 52 (1937): 28–31.

Brown, Carleton, ed. *English Lyrics of the XIIIth Century*. Oxford: Clarendon Press, 1932.

———. *Religious Lyrics of the XIVth Century*. 2nd ed. rev. G. V. Smithers. Oxford: Clarendon Press, 1957.

Brown, Roger and Albert Gilman. "The Pronouns of Power and Solidarity." In *Style in Language*, ed. Thomas A. Sebeok. Cambridge, Mass.: Technology Press of MIT, 1960. 253–77.

Brundage, James A. *Law, Sex, and Christian Society in Medieval Europe*. Chicago: University of Chicago Press, 1987.

Brunner, Karl, ed. *Richard Coeur de Lyon*. Wiener Beiträge zur englische Philologie 42. Vienna: W. Braumüller, 1913.

Bunt, G. H. V., ed. *William of Palerne: An Alliterative Romance*. Groningen: Bouma's Boekhuis, 1985.

Burnley, J. D. "Christine de Pizan and the So-Called *Style Clergial*." *Modern Language Review* 81 (1986): 1–6.

———. "Langland's Clergial Lunatic." In *Langland, the Mystics and the Medieval English Religious Tradition: Essays in Honour of S. S. Hussey*, ed. Helen Phillips. Cambridge: Cambridge University Press, 1990. 31–38.

———. *Courtliness and Literature in Medieval England*. London: Longman, 1998.

Burrow, J. A. "The Action of Langland's Second Vision." In *Essays in Criticism* 15 (1965), 247–68; repr. in *Style and Symbolism in Piers Plowman: A Modern Critical Anthology*, ed. Robert J. Blanch. Knoxville: University of Tennessee Press, 1969. 209–27.

———. "The Audience of *Piers Plowman*." *Anglia* 75 (1957), 373–84; repr. with addenda in his *Essays on Medieval Literature*. Oxford: Clarendon Press, 1984. 106–16.

———. "Reason's Horse." *Yearbook of Langland Studies* 4 (1990): 139–44.

———. *Langland's Fictions*. Oxford: Clarendon Press, 1993.

———. "Gestures and Looks in *Piers Plowman*." *Yearbook of Langland Studies* 14 (2000): 75–83.

———. *Gestures and Looks in Medieval Narrative*. Cambridge: Cambridge University Press, 2002.

———. "Wasting Time, Wasting Words in *Piers Plowman* B and C." *Yearbook of Langland Studies* 17 (2003): 191–202.

Cam, Helen. *Law-Finder and Law-Makers in Medieval England: Collected Studies in Legal and Constitutional History*. New York: Barnes and Noble, 1963.

Camille, Michael. *Mirror in Parchment: The Luttrell Psalter and the Making of Medieval England*. Chicago: University of Chicago Press, 1998.

Campbell, James. "Power and Authority 600–1300." In *The Cambridge Urban History of Britain*, vol. 1, *600–1540*, ed. D. M. Palliser. Cambridge: Cambridge University Press, 2000. 51–78.

Cannon, Debbie. "London Pride: Citizenship and the Fourteenth-Century Custumals of the City of London." In *Learning and Literacy in Medieval England and Abroad*, ed. Sarah Rees Jones. Utrecht Studies in Medieval Literacy 3. Turnhout: Brepols, 2003. 179–98.

Cargill, Oscar. "The Date of the A-Text of *Piers Plowman*." *Publications of the Modern Language Association* 47 (1932): 354–62.

Carlson, David, ed., with A. G. Rigg, trans. *Richard Maidstone: Concordia*. Kalamazoo, Mich.: Medieval Institute Publications, 2003.

Carmody, Francis J., ed. *Li livres dou Tresor*. Berkeley: University of California Press, 1948.

Carruthers, Mary. *The Search for St. Truth: A Study of Meaning in Piers Plowman*. Evanston, Illinois: Northwestern University Press, 1973.

Cartlidge, Neil, ed. *The Owl and the Nightingale: Text and Translation*. Exeter Medieval English Texts and Studies. Exeter: University of Exeter Press, 2001.

Cassidy, Frederic G. "The Merit of Malkyn." *Modern Language Notes* 63 (1948): 52–53.

Catto, J. I. "Religion and the English Nobility in the Later Fourteenth Century." In *History and Imagination: Essays in Honor of H. R. Trevor-Roper*, ed. Hugh Lloyd-Jones, Valerie Pearl, and Blair Worden. London and New York: Holmes and Meier, 1982. 43–55.

Chambers, R.W. "The Authorship of *Piers Plowman*." *Modern Language Review* 5 (1910): 1–25.

———. "Long Will, Dante, and the Righteous Heathen." In *Essays and Studies*, ed. W. P. Ker. Vol. 9. Oxford: Clarendon Press, 1924.

Chambers, R. W. and J. H. G. Grattan. "The Text of *Piers Plowman*." *Modern Language Review* 26 (1931): 1–51.

Chambers, R. W. and Marjorie Daunt, eds. *A Book of London English, 1384–1425*. Oxford: Clarendon Press, 1931.

Charland, Thomas. *Artes praedicandi; contribution à l'histoire de la rhétorique au moyen âge*. Paris: J. Vrin, 1936.

Cheney, C. R. "Rules for the Observance of Feast-Days in Medieval England." *Bulletin of the Institute of Historical Research, University of London* 34 (1961): 117–49; repr. in his *The English Church and its Laws, 12th-14th Centuries*. London: Variorum Reprints, 1982.

———. *Notaries Public in England in the Thirteenth and Fourteenth Centuries*. Oxford: Clarendon Press, 1972.

Chiapelli, Fredi, ed. *Dante Alghieri: Tutte le opere*. Milan: Mursia, 1965.

Childs, Wendy R. and John Taylor, eds. and trans. *The Anonimalle Chronicle, 1307 to 1334: from Brotherton Collection MS 29*. Leeds: Yorkshire Archaeological Society, 1991.

Cigman, Gloria, ed. *Lollard Sermons*. Early English Text Society 294. Oxford: Oxford University Press, 1989.

Clanchy, M. T. "Did Henry III Have a Policy?" *History* n.s. 53 (1968): 203–16.

————. *From Memory to Written Record: England 1066–1307.* 2nd ed. Oxford: Blackwell, 1993.

————. "Images of Ladies with Prayer Books: What Do They Signify?" In *The Church and the Book*, ed. R. N. Swanson. Studies in Church History 38. Woodbridge, Suffolk: Boydell Press, 2004. 106–22.

Clark, Elaine. "The Decision to Marry in Thirteenth- and Early Fourteenth-Century Norfolk." *Mediaeval Studies* 49 (1987): 496–516.

Clay, Rotha Mary. *The Hermits and Anchorites of England.* London: Methuen, 1914.

Clifton, Linda J. "Struggling with Will: Jangling, Sloth, and Thinking in *Piers Plowman* B." In *Suche Werkis to Werche: Essays on Piers Plowman In Honor of David C. Fowler*, ed. Míčeál F. Vaughan. East Lansing, Mich.: Colleagues Press, 1993. 29–52.

Clifton, Nicole. "The Romance Convention of the Disguised Duel and the Climax of Piers Plowman." *Yearbook of Langland Studies* 7 (1993): 123–28.

Clopper, Lawrence M. "Langland's Markings for the Structure of *Piers Plowman*." *Modern Philology* 85 (1988): 245–55.

————. "Need Men and Women Labor? Langland's Wanderer and the Labor Ordinances." In *Chaucer's England: Literature in Historical Context*, ed. Barbara Hanawalt. Minneapolis: University of Minnesota Press, 1992. 110–32.

————. "A Response to Robert Adams, 'Langland's *Ordinatio*'." *Yearbook of Langland Studies* 9 (1995): 141–46.

————. *"Songes of Rechelesnesse": Langland and the Franciscans.* Ann Arbor: University of Michigan Press, 1997.

————. "Franciscans, Lollards, and Reform." In *Lollards and their Influence in Late Medieval England*, ed. Fiona Somerset, Jill C. Havens, and Derrick G. Pitard. Suffolk, Woodbridge: Boydell, 2003. 177–96.

Cokayne, G. E. *The Complete Peerage of England, Scotland, Ireland, Great Britain, and the United Kingdom*, rev. Vicary Gibbs. 14 vols. London: St. Catherine Press, 1910–59.

Coke, Edward. *The Third Part of the Institutes of the Laws of England: Concerning High Treason, and other Pleas of the Crown, and Criminal Causes.* London: Rawlins, 1644.

Cole, Andrew. "William Langland and the Invention of Lollardy." In *Lollards and their Influence in Late Medieval England*, ed. Fiona Somerset, Jill C. Havens, and Derrick G. Pitard. Suffolk, Woodbridge: Boydell, 2003. 37–58.

Coleman, Janet. *Piers Plowman and the Moderni.* Rome: Edizione di Storia e Letteratura, 1981.

————. "Property and Poverty." In *The Cambridge History of Medieval Political Thought, c. 350–c.1450*, ed. J. H. Burns. Cambridge: Cambridge University Press, 1988. 607–48.

Colledge, Edmund, and Noel Chadwick, eds. "'Remedies Against Temptations': The Third English Version of William Flete." *Archivio Italiano per la Storia della Pietà* 5 (1968): 203–40.

Collins, A. Jefferies, ed. *Manuale ad Vsum Percelebris Ecclesie Sarisburiensis.* Henry Bradshaw Society, 91. Chichester: Moore and Tillyer, 1960 (for 1958).

Conlee, John. *Middle English Debate Poetry: A Critical Anthology.* East Lansing, Mich.: Colleagues Press, 1991.

Cooper, Helen. "Langland's and Chaucer's Prologues." *Yearbook of Langland Studies* 1 (1987): 71–81.

Cornelius, Roberta D. *The Figurative Castle: A Study of the Mediaeval Allegory of the Edifice with Especial Reference to Religious Writings.* Published dissertation. Bryn Mawr, Penn.: Bryn Mawr College, 1930.

———. "*Piers Plowman* and the *Roman de Fauvel.*" *Publications of the Modern Language Association* 47 (1932): 363–67.

Corrie, Marilyn. "Kings and Kingship in British Library MS Harley 2253." In *Medieval and Early Modern Miscellanies and Anthologies*, ed. Phillipa Hardman. *Yearbook of English Studies* 33 (2003): 64–79.

Courtenay, William J. *Schools and Scholars in Fourteenth-Century England.* Princeton, N.J.: Princeton University Press, 1987.

Craun, Edwin. *Lies, Slander, Obscenity in Medieval English Literature: Pastoral Rhetoric and the Deviant Speaker.* Cambridge: Cambridge University Press, 1997.

———. "'Ȝe, by Peter and by Poul!': Lewte and the Practice of Fraternal Correction." *Yearbook of Langland Studies* 15 (2001): 15–25.

Crimes, S. B. and A. L. Brown, eds. *Select Documents of English Constitutional History, 1307–1485.* London: Adam and Charles Black, 1961.

Cropsey, Joseph, ed. *Thomas Hobbes: A Dialogue Between a Philosopher and a Student of the Common Laws of England.* Chicago: University of Chicago Press, 1971.

Crow, Martin M. and Clair C. Olson, ed. *Chaucer Life Records.* [np]: University of Texas Press, 1966.

Dahlberg, Charles, trans. *The Romance of the Rose: Guillaume de Lorris and Jean de Meun.* Hanover, N.H.: University Press of New England, 1986.

Daniélou, J. "Terre et paradis chez les pères de l'église." *Eranos Jahrbuch* 22 (1953): 433–72.

d'Ardenne, S. T. R. O., ed. *Þe Liflade and te Passiun of Seinte Juliene.* Early English Text Society 248. Oxford: Oxford University Press, 1961.

d'Ardenne, S. T. R. O. and E. J. Dobson, eds. *Seinte Katerine.* Early English Text Society s.s. 7. Oxford: Oxford University Press, 1981.

Daur, K.-D., ed. *Augustinus Hipponensis: De uera religione.* Corpus Christianorum Series Latina 32. Turnholt: Brepols, 1962. 187–260.

Day, Mabel. "The Revisions of *Piers Plowman.*" *Modern Language Review* 23 (1928): 1–27.

Day, Sebastian J. *Intuitive Cognition: A Key to the Significance of the Later Scholastics.* St. Bonaventure, N.Y.: Franciscan Institute, 1947.

Davenport, W. A. "Patterns in Middle English Dialogues." In *Medieval English Studies Presented to George Kane*, ed. Edward Donald Kennedy, Ronald Waldron, and Joseph S. Wittig. Woodbridge, Suffolk: D.S. Brewer, 1988. 127–45.

Davies, Rees. "The Life, Travels, and Library of an Early Reader of *Piers Plowman.*" *Yearbook of Langland Studies* 13 (1999): 49–64.

Davis, Norman, ed. *Non-Cycle Plays and Fragments.* Early English Text Society, Supplementary Text No. 1. London: Oxford University Press, 1970.

———, ed. *Paston Letters and Papers of the Fifteenth Century.* 2 vols. Oxford: Oxford University Press, 1971, 1976. Repr. with corrections, Early English Text Society s.s. 20, 21. Oxford: Oxford University Press, 2004, 2005.

Davis, Virginia. "The Rule of Saint Paul, The First Hermit, in Late Medieval England." In *Monks, Hermits and the Ascetic Tradition*, ed. W. J. Sheils. *Studies in Church History* 22 (1985): 203–14.

Davlin, Sister Mary Clemente. "*Kynde Knowyng* as a Major Theme in *Piers Plowman* B." *Review of English Studies* n.s. 22 (1971): 1–19.

———. "*Kynde Knowyng* As a Middle English Equivalent for 'Wisdom' in *Piers Plowman* B." *Medium Ævum* 50 (1981): 5–17.

———. "*Piers Plowman* and the Books of Wisdom." *Yearbook of Langland Studies* 2 (1988): 23–33.

———. *A Game of Heaven: Word Play and the Meaning of Piers Plowman B*. Cambridge: D.S. Brewer, 1989.

———. "*Piers Plowman* and the Gospel and First Epistle of John." *Yearbook of Langland Studies* 10 (1996): 89–127.

Dean, James M., ed. *Medieval English Political Writings*. Kalamazoo: Medieval Institute Publications, Western Michigan University, 1996.

———, ed. *Richard the Redeless and Mum and the Sothsegger*. Kalamazoo: Medieval Institute Publications, Western Michigan University 2000.

de Labriolle, Pierre, ed. and trans. *Soliloquia*. In *Œvres de Saint Augustin: 1re série: Opuscules: V: Dialogues philosophiques: II: Dieu et l'âme*. [n.p.]: Desclée, de Brouwer, et Cie, 1939. 24–163.

de Lage, Raynaud. "Deux questions sur la foi, inspirées d'Alain de Lille." *Archives d'histoire doctrinaire et littéraire du moyen âge* 18 (1943): 323–36.

Delahaye, Hippolyte. "Les lettres d'indulgence collectives." *Analecta Bollandiana* 44 (1926): 342–79; 45 (1927): 97–123, 323–44; 46 (1928): 148–57, 287–343.

de Man, Paul, ed. *Selected Poetry of Keats*. New York: Signet, 1966.

D'Evelyn, Charlotte and Anna J. Mill, eds. *The South English Legendary*. 3 vols. Early English Text Society 235, 236, 244. London: Oxford University Press, 1956, 1959; repr. 1967, 1969.

Devlin, Sister Mary Aquinas, ed. *The Sermons of Thomas Brinton, Bishop of Rochester (1373–1389)*. 2 vols. Camden Society, 3rd Ser. 55–56. London: Offices of the Royal Historical Society, 1954.

Dickinson, Francis H., ed. *Missale ad Usum insignis et praeclarae ecclesi;ae Sarum*. Oxford: J. Parker, 1861–63; repr. 1969.

Diekstra, F. N. M., ed. *The Middle English Weye of Paradys and the Middle French Voie de Paradis: A Parallel-Text Edition*. Leiden: Brill, 1991.

Dimier, M. A. "Mourir à Clairvaux!" *Collectanea ordinis Cisterciensium reformatorum* 17 (1955): 272–85.

Dobbie, Elliott van Kirk, ed. *The Anglo-Saxon Minor Poems*. The Anglo-Saxon Poetic Records 6. New York: Columbia University Press, 1942.

Dobson, E. J. "The Etymology and Meaning of *Boy*." *Medium Ævum* 9 (1940): 121–54.

Dobson, R. B. *The Peasants' Revolt of 1381*. London: Macmillan, 1970.

Dolan, T. P. "Shame on Meed." In *Suche Werkis to Werche: Essays on Piers Plowman In Honor of David C. Fowler*, ed. Míċeál F. Vaughan. East Lansing, Mich.: Colleagues Press, 1993. 81–88.

Dolbeau, F., ed. *Augustin d'Hippone: Vingt-six sermons au peuple d'Afrique, retrouvés à Mayence*. Paris: Institut d'études augustiniennes, 1996.

Donaldson, E. Talbot. *Piers Plowman: The C-Text and its Poet*. New Haven, Conn.: Yale University Press, 1949, repr. London: Frank Cass and Co., 1966.

———. "Chaucer the Pilgrim." *Publications of the Modern Language Association* 60 (1954): 928–36; repr. in his *Speaking of Chaucer*. London: Athlone Press, 1970.

————. "Patristic Exegesis in the Criticism of Medieval Literature: The Opposition." In *Critical Approaches to Medieval Literature: Selected Papers from the English Institute, 1958–59,* ed. Dorothy Bethurum. New York: Columbia University Press, 1960. 3–26; repr. in his *Speaking of Chaucer.* London: Athlone Press, 1970.

————. *William Langland, Piers Plowman: An Alliterative Verse Translation.* New York: Norton, 1990.

Donatelli, Joseph M.P., ed. *Death and Liffe.* Cambridge, Mass.: Medieval Academy of America, 1989.

Duby, Georges. *The Three Orders: Feudal Society Imagined,* trans. Arthur Goldhammer. Chicago: University of Chicago Press, 1980.

Dudash, Susan J. "Christine de Pizan and the 'menu peuple.'" *Speculum* 78 (2003): 788–832.

Duff, J. Wright and Arnold M. Duff. *Minor Latin Poets.* Vol. 2. Cambridge, Mass.: Harvard University Press, 1982.

Duffy, Eamon. *The Stripping of the Altars: Traditional Religion in England c. 1400-c.1580.* New Haven, Conn.: Yale University Press, 1992.

Duggan, Hoyt N. "Langland's Dialect and Final –*e.*" *Studies in the Age of Chaucer* 12 (1990): 157–91.

Duggan, Hoyt N. and Thorlac Turville-Petre, eds. *The Wars of Alexander.* Early English Text Society s.s. 10. Oxford: Oxford University Press, 1989.

Duncan, A. A. M., ed. and trans. *John Barbour: The Bruce.* Edinburgh: Canongate, 1999.

Dunning, T. P. *Piers Plowman: An Interpretation of the A-Text.* London: Longmans, Green, 1937. 2nd ed. rev. by T. P. Dolan, Oxford: Clarendon Press, 1980.

Dyas, Dee. "A Pilgrim in Sheep's Clothing? The Nature of Wandering in *Piers Plowman.*" *English Language Notes* 39 (2002): 1–12.

Dyboski, R. and Arend, Z. M., eds. *Knyghthode and Bataile.* Early English Text Society 201. London: Oxford University Press, 1936 (for 1935).

Dyer, Christopher. *Standards of Living in the Later Middle Ages: Social Change in England c. 1200–1520.* Cambridge: Cambridge University Press, 1989.

Ebbesen, Sten. "Language, Medieval Theories of." In *Routledge Encyclopedia of Philosophy,* ed. E. Craig. London: Routledge, 1998. Vol. 5.389–404.

Eccles, Mark, ed. *The Macro Plays.* Early English Text Society o.s. 262. London: Oxford University Press, 1969.

Edden, Valerie, ed. *Richard Maidstone's Penitential Psalms.* Heidelberg: Carl Winter Universitätsverlag, 1990.

Embree, Dan. *The Chronicles of Rome: An Edition of the Middle English Chronicles of Popes and Emperors and the Lollard Chronicle.* Woodbridge, Suffolk: Boydell, 1999.

Embree, Dan and Elizabeth Urquhart, eds. *The Simonie: A Parallel-Text Edition.* Heidelberg: Carl Winter Universitätsverlag, 1991.

Emden, A. B. *A Biographical Register of the University of Oxford to 1500.* 3 vols. Oxford: Oxford University Press, 1959.

Emerton, Ephraim, trans. *The Correspondence of Pope Gregory VII: Selected Letters from the Registrum.* New York: Columbia University Press, 1932.

Emmerson, Richard K. "'Coveitise to Konne,' 'Goddes Pryvetee,' and Will's Ambiguous Dream Experience in Piers Plowman." In *Suche Werkis to Werche: Essays on Piers Plowman In Honor of David C. Fowler,* ed. Míċeál F. Vaughan. East Lansing, Mich.: Colleagues Press, 1993. 89–122.

Enders, Jody. *Rhetoric and the Origins of Medieval Drama*. Ithaca, N.Y.: Cornell University Press, 1992.

Epstein, Steven. *Wage Labor and Guilds in Medieval Europe*. Chapel Hill: University of North Carolina Press, 1991.

Erbe, Theodore, ed. *Mirk, John. Mirk's Festial: A Collection of Homilies*. Part 1. Early English Text Society 96. London: Kegan Paul, Trench, Trübner, 1905.

Evans, G. Blakemore, gen. ed. *The Riverside Shakespeare*. Boston: Houghton Mifflin, 1974.

Evans, G. R. "Exegesis and Authority in the Thirteenth Century." In *Ad litteram: Authoritative Texts and Their Medieval Readers*, ed. Mark D. Jordan and Kent Emery. Notre Dame, Ind.: University of Notre Dame Press, 1992.

Evans, Joan. *Art in Mediaeval France, 987–1498*. London: Oxford University Press, 1952.

Ewert, Alfred, ed. *Gui de Warewic, roman du XIIIe siècle*. 2 vols. Paris: Librairie ancienne Édouard Champion, 1932.

Faral, E. and J. Bastin, eds. *Oeuvres complètes de Rutebeuf*. 2 vols. Paris: Picard, 1959–60.

Farmer, Hugh, ed.; trans. anon. *The Monk of Farne; the Meditations of a Fourteenth Century Monk*. Baltimore: Helicon Press, 1961.

Ferguson, George. *Signs and Symbols in Christian Art*. New York: Oxford University Press, 1966.

Ferster, Judith. *Fictions of Advice: The Literature and Politics of Counsel in Late Medieval England*. Philadelphia: University of Pennsylvania Press, 1996.

Finlayson, J. "*The Simonie*: Two Authors?" *Archiv für das Studium der neueren Sprachen und Literaturen* 226 (1989): 39–51.

Finucane, Ronald C. *Miracles and Pilgrims: Popular Beliefs in Medieval England*. London: J.M. Dent, 1977.

Fisher, John H. *John Gower: Moral Philospher and Friend of Chaucer*. London: Methuen, 1965.

Fisher, John H., Malcolm Richardson, and Jane L. Fisher. *An Anthology of Chancery English*. Knoxville: University of Tennessee Press, 1984.

Fleming, John V. *An Introduction to the Franciscan Literature of the Middle Ages*. Chicago: Franciscan Herald Press, 1977.

———. "Chaucer and Erasmus on the Pilgrimage to Canterbury: An Iconographical Speculation." In *The Popular Literature of Medieval England*, ed. Thomas J. Heffernan. Tennessee Studies in Literature 28. Knoxville: University of Tennessee Press, 1985. 148–66.

———. *Reason and the Lover*. Princeton, N. J.: Princeton University Press, 1984.

Fletcher, Alan J. "Line 30 of the Man of Law's Tale and the Medieval Malkyn." *English Language Notes* 24 (1986): 15–20.

———. "A Simoniacal Moment in *Piers Plowman*." *Yearbook of Langland Studies* 4 (1990): 135–38.

———. "The Essential (Ephemeral) William Langland: Textual Revision as Ethical Process in *Piers Plowman*." *Yearbook of Langland Studies* 15 (2001): 61–84.

Forshall, J. and F. Madden, ed. *The Holy Bible . . . by John Wycliffe and His Followers*. 4 vols. Oxford: Oxford University Press, 1850.

Fowler, Alastair, ed. *Milton: Paradise Lost*. London: Longman, 1968, 1980.

Fowler, David C. "An Unusual Meaning of 'Win' in Chaucer's *Troilus and Criseyde*." *Modern Language Notes* 69 (1954): 313–15.

Fowler, Elizabeth. "Civil Death and the Maiden: Agency and the Conditions of Contract in *Piers Plowman*." *Speculum* 70 (1995): 760–92.

Fowler, Roger. *Wulfstan's Canons of Edgar*. Early English Text Society 266. London: Oxford University Press, 1972.

Fraipont, J., ed. *Bede: De die iudicii*. In *Bedae Venerabilis opera pars III-IV*. Corpus Christianorum Series Latina 122. Turnhout: Brepols, 1955. 439–44.

———, ed. *Bede: De locis sanctis*. In *Itineraria et alia geographica*. Corpus Christianorum Series Latina 175. Turnhout: Brepols, 1965.

Francis, W. Nelson, ed. *The Book of Vices and Virtues; A Fourteenth Century English Translation of the Somme le Roi of Lorens d'Orléans*. Early English Text Society o.s. 217. London: Oxford University Press, 1942.

Freccero, John. *Dante and the Poetics of Conversion*. Cambridge, Mass.: Harvard University Press, 1986.

Friedberg, Aemilius, ed. *Corpus Iuris Canonici*. Leipzig: Tauchnitz, 1879. Repr. Graz: Akademische Druck- und Verlagsanstatt, 1959.

Friedman, John B. "The Friar Portrait in Bodleian Library MS. Douce 104: Contemporary Satire?" *Yearbook of Langland Studies* 8 (1994): 177–85.

Furnivall, Frederick J. *The Babees Book*. Early English Text Society 32. London: Trübner, 1868.

Furnivall, Frederick J. and Katherine B. Locock, ed. *The Pilgrimage of the Life of Man, Englisht by John Lydgate*. Early English Text Society e.s. 77, 83, 92. London: Kegan Paul, Trench, Trübner, 1899–1904.

Gabrielson, Arvid, ed. *Le Sermon de Guischard de Beaulieu*. Skrifter utgifna af K. Humanistiska Vetenskaps-Samfundet i Uppsala 12, no. 5. Uppsala: A-B. Akademiska Bokhandeln, 1909.

Gairdner, J., ed. *Gregory's Chronicle*. Camden Society n.s. 17. London, 1876.

Galbraith, V. H. *The Anonimalle Chronicle, 1333–1381*. London: Manchester University Press, 1927.

———. *An Introduction to the Use of the Public Records*. Oxford: Clarendon Press, 1934; 1963.

Galloway, Andrew. "Two Notes on Langland's Cato: *Piers Plowman* B I.88–91; IV.20–23." *English Language Notes* 25 (1987): 9–12.

———. Rev. of Nicholas Orme, *Education and Society in Medieval and Renaissance England*. *Yearbook of Langland Studies* 4 (1990): 170–76.

———. "Marriage Sermons, Polemical Sermons, and the *Wife of Bath's Prologue*: A Generic Excursus." *Studies in the Age of Chaucer* 14 (1992): 3–30. = 1992a

———. "*Piers Plowman* and the Schools." *Yearbook of Langland Studies* 6 (1992): 89–107. = 1992b

———. "The Making of a Social Ethic in Late-Medieval England: From *Gratitudo* to 'Kyndenesse.'" *Journal of the History of Ideas* 55 (1994): 365–83.

———. "The Rhetoric of Riddling in Late Medieval England: The 'Oxford' Riddles, the *Secretum philosophorum*, and the Riddles in *Piers Plowman*." *Speculum* 70 (1995): 68–105.

———. "Chaucer's *Former Age* and the Fourteenth-Century Anthropology of Craft: The Social Logic of a Premodernist Lyric." *English Literary History* 63 (1996): 535–53.

———. "Private Selves and the Intellectual Marketplace in Late Fourteenth-Century England: The Case of the Two Usks." *New Literary History* 28 (1997): 291–318.

———— "Intellectual Pregnancy, Metaphysical Femininity, and the Social Doctrine of the Trinity in *Piers Plowman*." *Yearbook of Langland Studies* 12 (1998): 118–52. = 1998a

————. "Gender and *Piers Plowman*: Introduction to Special Section." *Yearbook of Langland Studies* 12 (1998): 1–4. = 1998b

————. "Uncharacterizable Entities: The Poetics of Middle English Scribal Culture and the Definitive *Piers Plowman*." *Studies in Bibliography* 52 (1999): 59–87.

————. "Authority." In *The Blackwell Companion to Chaucer*, ed. Peter Brown. Oxford: Blackwell, 2000. 23–39.

————. "Making History Legal: *Piers Plowman* and the Rebels of Fourteenth-Century England." In *William Langland's Piers Plowman: A Book of Essays*, ed. Kathleen Hewett-Smith. New York: Routledge, 2001. 7–39. = 2001a

————. "*Piers Plowman* and the Subject of the Law." *Yearbook of Langland Studies* 15 (2001): 117–28. = 2001b

————. "The Literature of 1388 and the Politics of Pity in Gower's *Confessio Amantis*." In *The Letter of the Law: Legal Practice and Literary Production in Medieval England*, ed. Emily Steiner and Candace Barrington. Ithaca, N.Y.: Cornell University Press, 2002. 67–104.

————. "Latin England." In *Imagining a Medieval English Nation*, ed. Kathy Lavezzo. Minneapolis: University of Minnesota Press, 2004. 41–95. = 2004a

————. "Reading *Piers Plowman* in the Fifteenth and the Twenty-First Centuries: Notes on Manuscripts F and W in the *Piers Plowman Electronic Archive*." *Journal of English and Germanic Philology* 103 (2004): 247–67. = 2004b

————. "Middle English Prologues." In *Readings in Medieval Texts*, ed. David Johnson and Elaine Treharne. Oxford: Oxford University Press, 2005. 288–305.

————. "Chaucer's Quarrel with Gower, and the Origins of Bourgeois Didacticism in Fourteenth-Century London Poetry." In *Calliope's Workshop: Didactic Poetry from Antiquity to the Renaissance*, ed. Annette Harder, Geritt Reinink, and Alasdair MacDonald. Forthcoming.

Garnier, Annette, ed. *Gautier de Coinci, Le Miracle de Théophile*. Paris: Honoré Champion, 1998.

Giancarlo, Matthew. "*Piers Plowman*, Parliament, and the Public Voice." *Yearbook of Langland Studies* 17 (2003): 135–74.

Gierke, Otto. *Political Theories of the Middle Age*, trans. Frederic William Maitland. Cambridge: Cambridge University Press, 1900; repr. Boston: Beacon, 1958.

Gilbert, Beverly Brian. "'Civil' and the Notaries in *Piers Plowman*." *Medium Ævum* 50 (1981): 49–63.

Given-Wilson, Chris. *The Royal Household and the King's Affinity: Service, Politics, and Finance in England 1360–1413*. New Haven, Conn.: Yale University Press, 1986.

————, ed. and trans. *The Chronicle of Adam Usk, 1377–1421*. Oxford: Clarendon Press, 1997.

Glorieux, P., ed. *Jean Gerson: Oeuvres complètes*. Vol. 9. Paris: Desclée, 1973.

Glossa Ordinaria. Biblia Latina cum Glossa Ordinaria. Facsimile Reprint of the Editio Princeps. Adolph Rusch of Strassburg 1480/81. Intro. by Karlfried Froelich and Margaret T. Gibson. 4 vols. Turnhout: Brepols, 1992.

Godden, Malcolm. "Ælfric and Anglo-Saxon Kingship." *English Historical Review* 102 (1987): 911–15.

———. *The Making of Piers Plowman.* London: Longman, 1990.

Goldberg, P. J. P. *Women, Work, and Life Cycle in a Medieval Economy: Women in York and Yorkshire, c. 1300–1520.* Oxford: Clarendon Press, 1992.

———, trans. and ed. *Women in England, c. 1275–1525: Documentary Sources.* Manchester: Manchester University Press, 1995.

Goldin, Frederick, ed. and trans. *Lyrics of the Troubadours and Trouvères; An Anthology and a History.* Garden City, N.Y.: Anchor, 1973.

Goodman, Anthony. *The Loyal Conspiracy: The Lords Appellant under Richard II.* London: Routledge and Kegan Paul, 1971.

Gorski, Richard. *The Fourteenth-Century Sheriff: English Local Administration in the Late Middle Ages.* Woodbridge, Suffolk: Boydell, 2003.

Gradon, Pamela. "Langland and the Ideology of Dissent." *Proceedings of the British Academy* 66 (1980): 179–205.

Gradon, Pamela and Anne Hudson, eds. *English Wycliffite Sermons.* 5 vols. Oxford: Clarendon Press, 1983–1996.

Grady, Frank. "Chaucer Reading Langland: The House of Fame." *Studies in the Age of Chaucer* 18 (1996): 3–23.

Graesse, Th., ed. *Jacobi a Voragine: Legenda Aurea.* Dresden: Arnold, 1846. 3rd ed., 1890.

Grant, Edward, ed. and trans. *Nicole Oresme and the Kinematics of Circular Motion: Tractatus de commensurabilitate vel incommensurabilitate motuum celi.* Madison: University of Wisconsin, 1971.

Gray, Douglas, ed. *English Medieval Religious Lyrics.* Exeter: University of Exeter Press, 1975.

Gray, Nick. "Langland's Quotations from the Penitential Tradition." *Modern Philology* 84 (1986): 53–60.

Green, Richard Firth. *Poets and Princepleasers: Literature and the English Court in the Late Middle Ages.* Toronto: University of Toronto Press, 1980.

———. "John Ball's Letters: Literary History and Historical Literature." In *Chaucer's England: Literature in Historical Context,* ed. Barbara Hanawalt. Minneapolis: University of Minnesota Press, 1992. 176–200.

———. "Friar William Appleton and the Date of Langland's B Text." *Yearbook of Langland Studies* 11 (1997): 87–96.

———. *A Crisis of Truth: Literature and Law in Ricardian England.* Philadelphia: University of Pennsylvania Press, 1999.

Green, Thomas Andrew. *Verdict According to Conscience: Perspectives on the English Criminal Trial Jury, 1200–1800.* Chicago: University of Chicago Press, 1985.

Greene, Richard Leighton. *The Early English Carols.* 2nd ed. Oxford: Clarendon Press, 1977.

Greenhill, Eleanor Simmons. "The Child in the Tree." *Traditio* 10 (1954): 323–71.

Greenia, M. Conrad, trans. *Bernard of Clairvaux: In Praise of the New Knighthood.* Kalamazoo, Mich.: Cistercian Publications, 2000.

Grenville, Jane. *Medieval Housing.* London: Leicester University Press, 1997.

Griffiths, Lavinia. *Personification in Piers Plowman.* Cambridge: D.S. Brewer, 1985.

Gurevich, Aaron. "Heresy and Literacy: Evidence of the Thirteenth-Century 'Exempla.'" In *Heresy and Literacy, 1000–1530,* ed. Peter Biller and Anne Hudson. Cambridge: Cambridge University Press, 1994. 104–11.

Gwynn, A. *The English Austin Friars in the Time of Wyclif.* London: Oxford University Press, Humphrey Milford, 1940.

———. "The Date of the B-Text of *Piers Plowman*." *Review of English Studies* 19 (1943): 1–24.

Hall, Theophilus D. "Was Langland the Author of the C-Text of *The Vision of Piers Plowman?*" *Modern Language Review* 4 (1908): 1–13.

Hamand, L. A. *The Ancient Windows of Gt. Malvern Priory Church*. 3rd ed. Upton on Severn, Worcestershire: Severnside Press, 1995.

Hamelius, P., ed. *Mandeville's Travels . . . Edited from MS. Cotton Titus c.XVI*. 2 vols. Early English Text Society 153, 154. London: Oxford University Press, 1919, 1923.

Hamesse, J., ed. *Les Auctoritates Aristotelis: un florilège médiéval: étude historique et édition critique*. Louvain: Publications universitaires, 1974.

Hanawalt, Barbara. "Fur-Collar Crime: The Pattern of Crime Among the Fourteenth-Century English Nobility." *Journal of Social History* 8 (1975): 1–17.

———. *"Of Good and Ill Repute": Gender and Social Control in Medieval England*. New York: Oxford University Press, 1998.

Hanna, Ralph. "Sir Thomas Berkeley and His Patronage." *Speculum* 64 (1989): 878–916.

———. *"Piers Plowman* A.5.155: 'Pyenye.'" *Yearbook of Langland Studies* 4 (1990): 145–49. =1990a

———. "The Difficulty of Ricardian Prose Translation: The Case of the Lollards." *Modern Language Quarterly* 51 (1990): 319–40. =1990b

———. *William Langland*. Aldershot, Hants.: Ashgate, 1993.

———. "'Meddling with Makings' and Will's Work." In *Late-Medieval Religious Texts and their Transmission*, ed. A. J. Minnis. Cambridge: D.S. Brewer, 1994. 85–94.

———. *Pursuing History: Middle English Manuscripts and Their Texts*. Stanford, Calif.: Stanford University Press, 1996.

———. "Will's Work." In *Written Work: Langland, Labor, and Authorship*, ed. Steven Justice and Kathryn Kerby-Fulton. Philadelphia: University of Pennsylvania Press, 1997. 23–66.

———. "Two New (?) Lost *Piers* Manuscripts (?)." *Yearbook of Langland Studies* 16 (2002): 169–77.

———. *London Literature, c. 1310–1380*. Cambridge: Cambridge University Press, 2005.

Hanna, Ralph and David Lawton, eds. *The Siege of Jerusalem*. Early English Text Society o.s. 320. Oxford: Oxford University Press, 2003.

Hanska, Jussi. "Reconstructing the Mental Calendar of Medieval Preaching: A Method and Its Limits—An Analysis of Sunday Sermons." In *Preacher, Sermon and Audience in the Middle Ages*, ed. Carolyn Muessig. Leiden: Brill, 2002. 293–315.

Harding, Alan. *The Law Courts of Medieval England*. London: George Allen and Unwin, 1973.

——— "Plaints and Bills in the History of English Law, Mainly in the Period 1250–1350." In *Legal History Studies 1972: Papers Presented to the Legal History Conference, Abserystwyth, 18–21 July 1972*, ed. Dafydd Jenkins. Cardiff: University of Wales Press, 1975. 65–86.

——— "The Revolt Against the Justices." In *The English Rising of 1381*, ed. R. H. Hilton and T. H. Aston. Cambridge: Cambridge University Press, 1984. 165–93.

———. *England in the Thirteenth Century*. Cambridge: Cambridge University Press, 1993.

Häring, Nikolaus. "A Commentary on the Apostles' Creed by Alan of Lille (O. Cist.)." *Analecta Cisterciensia* 30 (1974): 7–45. = 1974a

———. "A Commentary on the Creed of the Mass by Alan of Lille (O. Cist.)." *Analecta Cisterciensia* 30 (1974): 281–303. = 1974b

———. "A Poem by Alan of Lille on the Pseudo-Athanasian Creed." *Revue d'histoire des textes* 4 (1974): 225–38. =1974c

———. "A Commentary on the Our Father by Alan of Lille." *Analecta Cisterciensia* 31 (1975): 149–77.

Harvey, Margaret. *Solutions to the Schism: A Study of Some English Attitudes, 1378 to 1409.* St. Ottilien: EOS Verlag, 1983.

Harwood, Britten J. "Langland's *Kynde Wit.*" *Journal of English and Germanic Philology* 75 (1976): 330–36.

———. *Piers Plowman and the Problem of Belief.* Toronto: University of Toronto Press, 1992.

Hathaway, E. J., P. T. Ricketts, C. A. Robson and A. D. Wilshere, eds. *Fouke le Fitz Waryn.* Anglo-Norman Text Society 26–28. Oxford: Blackwell, 1975.

Haydon, Frank Scott, ed. *Eulogium historiarum sive temporis.* Rolls Series 9:3. London: Longman, Green, 1863.

Heath, Peter. *The English Parish Clergy on the Eve of the Reformation.* London: Routledge, 1969.

Hector, L. C. and Barbara F. Harvey, eds. and trans. *The Westminster Chronicle 1381–94.* Oxford: Clarendon Press, 1982.

Helmholz, R. H. *Marriage Litigation in Medieval England.* Cambridge: Cambridge University Press, 1974.

———. *Select Cases of Defamation to 1600.* Selden Society 101. London: The Society, 1985.

Herlihy, David. *The Black Death and the Transformation of the West.* Ed. Samuel K. Cohn, Jr. Cambridge, Mass.: Harvard University Press, 1997.

Hervieux, Léopold, ed. *Les fabulistes latins depuis le siècle d'Auguste jusqu'à la fin du moyen âge.* 5 vols. Paris: Firmin-Didot, 1884–99.

Hewett-Smith, Kathleen M. " 'Nede ne hath no lawe': Poverty and the De-stabilization of Allegory in the Final Visions of *Piers Plowman.*" In *William Langland's Piers Plowman: A Book of Essays,* ed. Kathleen Hewett-Smith. New York: Routledge Press, 2001. 233–53.

Heyworth, P. L., ed. *Jack Upland, Friar Daw's Reply, and Upland's Rejoinder.* Oxford: Oxford University Press, 1968.

Hicks, Michael. *Bastard Feudalism.* London: Longman, 1995.

———. *English Political Culture in the Fifteenth Century.* London: Routledge, 2002.

Hill, Rosalind. " 'A Chaunterie For Soules': London Chantries in the Reign of Richard II." In *The Reign of Richard II: Essays in Honour of May McKisack,* ed. F. R. H. du Boulay and Caroline M. Barron. London: Athlone, 1971. 242–55.

Hill, Thomas D. "Two Notes on Exegetical Allusion in Langland: *Piers Plowman* XI, 161–67, and B, I, 115–24." *Neuphilologische Mitteilungen* 75 (1974): 92–97.

———. " 'Dumb David': Silence and Zeal in Lady Church's Speech, *Piers Plowman* C.2.30–40." *Yearbook of Langland Studies* 15 (2001): 203–11. = 2001a

———. "The Problem of Synecdochic Flesh: *Piers Plowman* B.9.49–50." *Yearbook of Langland Studies* 15 (2001): 213–18. =2001b

———. "*Consilium et Auxilium* and the Lament for Æschere: A Lordship Formula in *Beowulf.*" *Haskins Society Journal* 12 (2002): 71–82.

Hilton, Rodney. *Class Conflict and the Crisis of Feudalism*. Rev. ed. London: Verso, 1990.

———. *English and French Towns in Feudal Society: A Comparative Study*. Cambridge: Cambridge University Press, 1992.

Hitchcock, Elsie Vaughan, ed. *The Donet*. Early English Text Society o.s. 156. London: Oxford University Press, 1921.

Hodgson, Phyllis. "*Ignorancia Sacerdotum*: A Fifteenth-Century Discourse on the Lambeth Constitutions." *Review of English Studies* 24 (1948): 1–11.

Holaday, Allan, ed. *Thomas Heywood's The Rape of Lucrece*. Urbana: University of Illinois Press, 1950.

Holloway, John. *A London Childhood*. New York: Charles Scribner, 1996.

Holmes, George. *The Good Parliament*. Oxford: Clarendon Press, 1975.

———. *The Later Middle Ages, 1272–1485*. New York: W. W. Norton, 1966.

Holt, James C. *Magna Carta and the Idea of Liberty*. New York: John Wiley, 1972.

Holthausen, Ferd., ed. *Vices and Virtues, Being a Soul's Confession of its Sins, with Reason's Description of the Virtues: A Middle-English Dialogue of About 1200 A. D.* Early English Text Society 89, 159 (bound as one volume). London: Trübner, 1888, 1921.

Honeybourne, Margorie B. "The Reconstructed Map of London under Richard II." *London Topographical Record* 22 (1965): 29–76.

Horowitz, Maryanne Cline. *Seeds of Virtue and Knowledge*. Princeton, N.J.: Princeton University Press, 1998.

Horwood, Alfred J., ed. and trans. *Year Books of the Reign of King Edward the Third, Years XI and XII*. Rolls Series 31:6. London: Longman, 1883.

House, Roy Temple, ed. *L'Ordene de chevalerie; An Old French Poem*. University of Oklahoma Bulletin n.s. 162, extension series 48. Norman, Okla., 1919.

Houser, R. E., trans. *The Cardinal Virtues: Aquinas, Albert, and Philip the Chancellor*. Medieval Sources in Translation 39; Studies in Medieval Moral Teaching 4. Toronto: Pontifical Institute of Mediaeval Studies, 2004.

Hudson, Anne. "Wyclif and the English Language." In *Wyclif in His Times*, ed. A. Kenney. Oxford: Oxford University Press, 1986. 85–103.

———. *The Premature Reformation: Wycliffite Texts and Lollard History*. Oxford: Clarendon Press, 1988. =1988a

———. "Epilogue: The Legacy of *Piers Plowman*." In *A Companion to Piers Plowman*, ed. John A. Alford. Berkeley: University of California Press, 1988. 251–66. =1988b

———. "*Laicus litteratus*: The Paradox of Lollardy." In *Heresy and Literacy, 1000–1530*, ed. Peter Biller and Anne Hudson. Cambridge: Cambridge University Press, 1994. 222–36.

———, ed. *Selections from English Wycliffite Writings*. Cambridge: Cambridge University Press, 1978.

———, ed. *Two Wycliffite Texts: The Sermon of William Taylor 1406, the Testimony of William Thorpe 1407*. Early English Text Society 301. Oxford: Oxford University Press, 1993.

Hughes, M. E. J. "'The feffement that Fals hath ymaked': A Study of the Image of the Document in *Piers Plowman* and Some Literary Analogues." *Neuphilologische Mitteilungen* 93 (1992): 125–33.

Huot, Sylvia. *The Romance of the Rose and its Medieval Readers: Interpretation, Reception, Manuscript Transmission*. Cambridge: Cambridge University Press, 1993.

Huppé, Bernard F. "The A-Text of *Piers Plowman* and the Norman Wars." *Publications of the Modern Language Association* 54 (1939): 37–64.

———. "The Date of the B-Text of *Piers Plowman*." *Studies in Philology* 38 (1941): 34–44.

———. "The Authorship of the A and B Texts of *Piers Plowman*." *Speculum* 22 (1947): 578–620.

———. "*Petrus id est Christus*: Word Play in *Piers Plowman*." *English Literary History* 17 (1950): 163–90.

Hurst, D. ed. *Beda Uenerabilis: In primam partem Samuhelis libri iv*. Corpus Christianorum Series Latina 119. Turnholt: Brepols, 1962. 5–287.

———, ed. *Beda Uenerabilis: In prouerbia Salomonis libri iii*. Corpus Christianorum Series Latina 119B. Turnholt: Brepols, 1983. 23–163.

Huygens, R. B. C., ed. *Commentum in Theodolum (1076–1099): Bernard d'Utrecht*. Biblioteca degli *Studi medievali* 8. Leiden: Brill, 1977.

Hyams, Paul. *King, Lords and Peasants in Medieval England: The Common Law of Villeinage in the Twelfth and Thirteenth Centuries*. Oxford: Clarendon Press, 1980.

Jacobs, John C., trans. *The Fables of Odo of Cheriton*. Syracuse, N.Y: Syracuse University Press, 1985.

Jeffrey, David L. and Brian J. Levy. *The Anglo-Norman Lyric: An Anthology*. Studies and Texts 93. Toronto: Pontifical Institute of Mediaeval Studies, 1990.

Jennings, Margaret, ed. *The Ars Componendi Sermones of Ranulph Higden, O. S. B*. Davis Medieval Texts and Studies 6. Leiden: Brill, 1991.

Johnson, John, trans. *A Collection of the Laws and Canons of the Church of England*. 2 vols. Oxford: John Henry Parker, 1851.

Johnston, Alexandra F. and Margaret Rogerson, eds. *Records of Early English Drama: York*. 2 vols. Toronto: University of Toronto Press, 1979.

Jones, W. J. *The Elizabethan Court of Chancery*. Oxford: Clarendon Press, 1967.

Jusserand, J. J. "*Piers Plowman*: The Work of One or Five." *Modern Philology* 6 (1909): 271–329.

———. "*Piers Plowman*, the Work of One or of Five: A Reply." *Modern Philology* 7 (1910): 288–326.

———. *English Wayfaring Life in the Middle Ages*, trans. Lucy Toulmin Smith. London: 1889; repr. London: Metheun, 1961.

———. *Piers Plowman: A Contribution to the History of English Mysticism*, trans. M.E.R. London: Unwin, 1894; repr. New York: Russell and Russell, 1965.

Justice, Steven. "The Genres of *Piers Plowman*." *Viator* 19 (1988): 291–306.

———. *Writing and Rebellion: England in 1381*. Berkeley: University of California Press, 1994.

Kaeuper, Richard W. and Elspeth Kennedy, eds. and trans. *The Book of Chivalry of Geoffroi de Charny*. Philadelphia: University of Pennsylvania Press, 1996.

Kane, George. *The Autobiographical Fallacy in Chaucer and Langland Studies*. The Chambers Memorial Lecture. University College, London: H. K. Lewis, 1965.

———. *The Liberating Truth: The Concept of Integrity in Chaucer's Writings*. London: Athlone, 1980.

———. *Chaucer and Langland: Historical and Textual Approaches*. Berkeley: University of California Press, 1989.

Kaske, R. E. "*Sapientia et Fortitudo* as the Controlling Theme of *Beowulf*." *Studies in*

Philology 55(1958): 423–56; repr. in *An Anthology of Beowulf Criticism*, ed. Lewis E. Nicholson. Notre Dame, Ind.: Notre Dame University Press, 1963. 269–310.

———. "Patristic Exegesis in the Criticism of Medieval Literature: The Defense." In *Critical Approaches to Medieval Literature: Selected Papers from the English Institute, 1958–59*, ed. Dorothy Bethurum. New York: Columbia University Press, 1960. 27–60.

———. "*Ex vi transicionis* and Its Passage in *Piers Plowman*." In *Style and Symbolism in Piers Plowman: A Modern Critical Anthology*, ed. Robert J. Blanch. Knoxville: University of Tennessee Press, 1969. 228–63.

———. "Holy Church's Speech and the Structure of *Piers Plowman*." In *Chaucer and Middle English Studies in Honour of Rossell Hope Robbins*, ed. Beryl Rowland. London: George Allen and Unwin, 1974. 320–27.

Kaulbach, Ernest N. *Imaginative Prophecy in the B-Text of Piers Plowman*. Piers Plowman Studies 8. Cambridge: D.S. Brewer, 1993.

Kaye, Joel. *Economy and Nature in the Fourteenth Century: Money, Market Exchange, and the Emergence of Scientific Thought*. Cambridge: Cambridge University Press, 1998.

Kean, P. M. "Love, Law, and *Lewte* in *Piers Plowman*." *Review of English Studies* n.s. 15 (1964): 241–61; repr. in *Style and Symbolism in Piers Plowman: A Modern Critical Anthology*, ed. Robert J. Blanch. Knoxville: University of Tennessee Press, 1969. 132–55.

Keen, Maurice. *Chivalry*. New Haven, Conn.: Yale University Press, 1984.

———. *English Society in the Later Middle Ages, 1348–1500*. London: Penguin, 1990.

Keene, Derek. "London from the post-Roman Period to 1300." In *The Cambridge Urban History of Britain*, vol. 1, *600–1540*, ed. D. M. Palliser. Cambridge: Cambridge University Press, 2000. 187–216.

Keil, Heinrich, ed. *Grammatici latini*. 7 vols. Leipzig: Teubner, 1857–80.

Kellogg, Alfred L. "Langland and Two Scriptural Texts." *Traditio* 14 (1958): 385–98.

———. *Chaucer, Langland, Arthur: Essays in Middle English Literature*. New Brunswick, N.J.: Rutgers University Press, 1972.

Kenny, Anthony. *Wyclif*. Oxford: Oxford University Press, 1985.

Kerby-Fulton, Kathryn. *Reformist Apocalypticism and Piers Plowman*. Cambridge: Cambridge University Press, 1990.

Kerby-Fulton, Kathryn and Steven Justice. "Langlandian Reading Circles and the Civil Service in London and Dublin, 1380–1427." In *New Medieval Literatures*, vol. I, ed. Wendy Scase, Rita Copeland, and David Lawton. Oxford: Oxford University Press, 1997.

Kermode, Jenny. *Medieval Merchants: York, Beverley, and Hull in the Later Middle Ages*. Cambridge: Cambridge University Press, 1998.

———. "The Greater Towns." In *The Cambridge Urban History of Britain*, vol. 1, *600–1540*, ed. D. M. Palliser. Cambridge: Cambridge University Press, 2000. 441–65.

Kim, Margaret. "Hunger, Need, and the Politics of Poverty in *Piers Plowman*." *Yearbook of Langland Studies* 16 (2002): 131–68.

Kinsley, James, ed. *William Dunbar: Poems*. Exeter: University of Exeter Press, 1989.

Kipling, Gordon. *Enter the King: Theatre, Liturgy, and Ritual in the Medieval Civic Triumph*. Oxford: Clarendon Press, 1998.

Kiralfy, A. K. *The Action on the Case*. London: Sweet and Maxwell, 1951.

Kirk, Rudolf. "References to the Law in *Piers the Plowman.*" *Publications of the Modern Language Association* 48 (1933): 322–27.

Klibansky, Raymond, Erwin Panofsky, and Fritz Saxl. *Saturn and Melancholy: Studies in the History of Natural Philosophy, Religion, and Art.* London: Thomas Nelson and Sons, 1964; repr. Nendeln: Kraus-Thomson Organization Ltd., 1979.

Knight, Ione Kemp, ed. *Wimbledon's Sermon "Redde Rationem Villicationis Tue."* Pittsburgh: Duquesne University Press, 1967.

Koldeweij, A. M. "Lifting the Veil on Pilgrim Badges." In *Pilgrimage Explored*, ed. J. Stopford. York: York Medieval Press, 1999. 161–88.

Krapp, George Philip, ed. *The Vercelli Book.* The Anglo-Saxon Poetic Records 2. New York: Columbia University Press, 1932.

Krapp, George Philip and Elliott van Kirk Dobbie, eds. *The Exeter Book.* The Anglo-Saxon Poetic Records 3. New York: Columbia University Press, 1961.

Kreider, Alan. *English Chantries: The Road to Dissolution.* Cambridge, Mass.: Harvard University Press, 1979.

Kruger, Steven F. *Dreaming in the Middle Ages.* Cambridge: Cambridge University Press, 1992.

Kuttner, Stephen. "Cardinalis: The History of a Canonical Concept." *Traditio* 3 (1945): 129–214.

Laehr, Gerhard. *Die konstantinischen Schenkung in der abendländischen Literatur des Mittelalters bis zur Mitte des 14. Jahrhunderts.* Historische Studien 166. Berlin: E. Ebering, 1926.

Lamond, Elizabeth, ed. and trans. *Walter of Henley's Husbandry.* London: Longmans, Green, 1890.

Lander, J. R. *Government and Community: England 1450–1509.* Cambridge, Mass.: Harvard University Press, 1980.

Långfors, Arthur, ed. *Le Roman de Fauvel par Gervais du Bus.* Paris: Librairie de Firmin Didot, 1914–19.

Langholm, Odd. *Economics in the Medieval Schools: Wealth, Exchange, Value, Money, and Usury According to the Paris Theological Tradition, 1200–1350.* Leiden: Brill, 1992.

Lawler, Traugott. "The Gracious Imagining of Redemption in *Piers Plowman.*" *English* 28 (1979): 203–16.

———. *The One and the Many in the Canterbury Tales.* Hamden, Conn.: Archon, 1980.

———. "A Reply to Jill Mann, Reaffirming the Traditional Relation between the A and B Versions of *Piers Plowman.*" *Yearbook of Langland Studies* 10 (1996): 145–80.

———. "The Pardon Formula in *Piers Plowman*: Its Ubiquity, Its Binary Shape, Its Silent Middle Term." *Yearbook of Langland Studies* 14 (2000): 117–52.

———. "The Secular Clergy in *Piers Plowman.*" *Yearbook of Langland Studies* 16 (2002): 85–117.

———. "Harlots' Holiness: the System of Absolution for Miswinning as a Major Theme in *Piers Plowman.*" *Yearbook of Langland Studies* 19 (2005).

———. "The Secular Clergy (Again): A Brief Rejoinder to Míceál Vaughan's Response." *Yearbook of Langland Studies* 17 (2003): 203–7.

Lawton, David A. "The Unity of Middle English Alliterative Poetry." *Speculum* 58 (1983): 72–94.

———. "The Subject of *Piers Plowman.*" *Yearbook of Langland Studies* 1 (1987): 1–30.

———. "Alliterative Style." In *A Companion to Piers Plowman*, ed. John A. Alford. Berkeley: University of California Press, 1988. 223–49.

Leadam, I. S., ed. *Select Cases in the Court of Requests*. Selden Society. Cambridge, Mass.: The Society, 1898.

Leadam, I. S. and J. F. Baldwin, eds. *Select Cases before the King's Council, 1243–1482*. Selden Society 35. Cambridge, Mass.: The Society, 1918.

Lees, Clare A. "Gender and Exchange in *Piers Plowman*." In *Class and Gender in Early English Literature: Intersections*. Ed. Britton J. Harwood and Gillian R. Overing. Bloomington and Indianapolis: Indiana University Press, 1994. 112–30.

Le Goff, Jacques. *Time, Work, and Culture in the Middle Ages*. Trans. Arthur Goldhammer. Chicago: University of Chicago Press, 1980.

Lester, Geoffrey, ed. *The Earliest English Translation of Vegetius's De Re Militari*. Middle English Texts 21. Heidelberg: Carl Winter Universitätsverlag, 1988.

Levett, Ada Elizabeth. *Studies in Manorial History*, ed. H. M. Cam, M. Coate, and L. S. Sutherland. New York: Barnes and Noble, 1963.

Levy, Brian J. *Nine Verse Sermons by Nicholas Bozon: The Art of an Anglo-Norman Poet and Preacher*. Medium Ævum Monographs n. s. 11. Oxford: Society for the Study of Medi;aeval Languages and Literature, 1981.

Lewis, Robert E., ed. and trans. *Lotario dei Segni (Pope Innocent III): De Condicionis Humanae*. Athens: University of Georgia Press, 1978.

Liebermann, F., ed. *Die Gesetze der Angelsachsen*. 3 vols. Halle: Niemeyer, 1903–16.

Lindberg, Conrad. *The Middle English Bible: Prefatory Epistles of St. Jerome*. Oslo: Universitetsforlaget, 1978.

Lindsay, W.M., ed. *Isidori Hispalensis Episcopi Etymologiarum . . . Libri XX*. 2 vols., paginated separately in recent issues. Oxford: Clarendon Press, 1911.

Little, Lester. "Pride Goes Before Avarice: Social Change and the Vices in Latin Christendom." *American Historical Review* 76 (1971): 16–49.

———. *Religious Poverty and the Profit Economy in Medieval Europe*. Ithaca, N.Y.: Cornell University Press, 1978.

Lombard, Peter. *Sententiae in IV Libris Distinctae*. 2 vols. Rome: Colegius S. Bonaventurae ad Claras Aquas, 1981.

Lord, Evelyn. *The Knights Templar in Britain*. London: Longman, 2002.

Loserth, Iohann, ed. *Iohannis Wyclif: Tractatus de Ecclesia*. London: Trübner, 1886.

Louis, Cameron. "Proverbs, Precepts, and Monitory Pieces." In *A Manual of the Writings in Middle English, 1050–1500*, vol. 9, ed. Albert Hartung. New Haven: Connecticut Academy of Arts and Sciences, 1993. 2957–3048, 3349–3404.

Lucas, Angela M., ed. *Anglo-Irish Poems of the Middle Ages*. Dublin: Columba Press, 1995.

Lumby, Joseph R., ed. *Henry Knighton: Chronicon*. Rolls Series 92. London: Eyre and Spottiswoode, 1889–95.

Lynch, Kathryn L. *The High Medieval Dream Vision: Poetry, Philosophy, and Literary Form*. Stanford, Calif.: Stanford University Press, 1988.

Macaulay, G. C., ed. *The Works of John Gower*. Vol. 1 (*The French Works*); Vol. 4 (*The Latin Works*). Oxford: Clarendon, 1899; 1902. *The English Works*. 2 vols. Early English Text Society e.s. 81, 82. Oxford: 1900, 1901.

MacCracken, Henry Noble, ed. *The Minor Poems of John Lydgate*. 2 vols. Early English Text Society 107, 192. London: Oxford University Press, 1911, 1934.

Macrae-Gibson, O. D., ed. *Of Arthour and of Merlin*. Early English Text Society 268, 279. London: Oxford University Press, 1973, 1979.

Magoun, F. P., Jr., ed. *The Gests of King Alexander of Macedon*. Cambridge, Mass.: Harvard University Press, 1929.

Maniates, Maria Rika and Richard Freedman. "Street Cries." In *The New Grove Dictionary of Music and Musicians*, ed. Stanley Sadie. 2nd ed. London: Macmillan, 2001.

Manly, John M. "The Lost Leaf of *Piers the Plowman*." *Modern Philology* 3 (1906): 359–66.

———. "*Piers the Plowman* and Its Sequence." In *The Cambridge History of English Literature*, Vol. 2, *The End of the Middle Ages*, ed. Sir A. W. Ward and A. R. Waller. Cambridge: Cambridge University Press, 1908. 1–42.

———. "The Authorship of *Piers Plowman*." *Modern Philology* 7 (1909–10): 83–144.

Mann, Jill. *Chaucer and Medieval Estates Satire*. Cambridge: Cambridge University Press, 1973.

———. "Eating and Drinking in *Piers Plowman*." *Essays and Studies* 32 (1979): 26–43.

———. "Satiric Subject and Satiric Object in Goliardic Literature." *Mittellateinisches Jahrbuch: Internationale Zeitschrift für Mediavistik* 15 (1980): 63–86.

———. *Apologies to Women*. Cambridge: Cambridge University Press, 1991.

———. "The Power of the Alphabet: A Reassessment of the Relation between the A and B Versions of *Piers Plowman*." *Yearbook of Langland Studies* 8 (1994): 21–50.

Manzalaoui, M. A., ed. *Secretum secretorum: Nine English Versions*. Early English Text Society 276. Oxford: Oxford University Press, 1977.

Marsh, Christopher. "The Sound of Print in Early Modern England: The Broadside Ballad as Song." In *The Uses of Script and Print, 1300–1700*, ed. Julia Crick and Alexandra Walsham. Cambridge: Cambridge University Press, 2004. 171–90.

Martin, G. H., ed. and trans. *Knighton's Chronicle: 1337–1396*. Oxford: Clarendon Press, 1995.

Martin, Priscilla. "*Piers Plowman*: Indirect Relations and the Record of Truth." In *Suche Werkis to Werche: Essays on Piers Plowman In Honor of David C. Fowler*, ed. Míceál F. Vaughan. East Lansing, Mich.: Colleagues Press, 1993. 89–122.

Matthew, F. D., ed. *The English Works of Wyclif Hitherto Unprinted*. Early English Text Society 74. Oxford: Oxford University Press, 1880; 2nd rev. ed. 1902.

Maxwell, Clark. "Some Letters of Confraternity." *Archaeologia* 75 (1926), 19–60, and 79 (1929), 176–216.

McDonough, C. J., ed. *The Oxford Poems of Hugh Primas and the Arundel Lyrics*. Toronto: Pontifical Institute of Mediaeval Studies, 1984.

McFarlane, K. B. *The Nobility of Later Medieval England*. Oxford: Clarendon Press, 1973.

McHardy, A. K. "The Churchmen of Chaucer's London: The Seculars." *Medieval Prosopography* 16 (1995): 57–87.

———, ed. *Royal Writs Addressed to John Buckingham, Bishop of Lincoln, 1363–1398*. The Canterbury and York Society and the Lincoln Record Society 86. Woodbridge, Suffolk: Boydell, 1997.

McKisack, May. *The Fourteenth Century: 1307–1399*. Oxford History of England. Oxford: Clarendon Press, 1959; repr. 1991.

Meech, Sanford Brown and Hope Emily Allen, eds. *The Book of Margery Kempe*. Early English Text Society o.s. 212. London: Oxford University Press, 1940, repr. 1961.

Meredith, Peter, ed. *The Mary Play from the N. Town Manuscript.* Exeter: University of Exeter Press, 1997.

Menut, Albert D. *Maistre Nicole Oresme: Le Livre de Ethiques D'Aristote.* New York: G.E. Stechert, 1940.

Meyer, Wilhelm, ed. *Vita Adae et Evae. Abhandlungen der bayerischen Akademie, philos.-philol. Kl.* 14 no. 10 (Munich, 1878): 185–220.

Middleton, Anne. "The Idea of Public Poetry in the Reign of Richard II." *Speculum* 53 (1978): 94–114.

———. "Narration and the Invention of Experience: Episodic Form in *Piers Plowman.*" In *The Wisdom of Poetry: Essays in Early English Literature in Honor of Morton W. Bloomfield,* ed. Larry D. Benson and Siegfried Wenzel. Kalamazoo, Mich.: Medieval Institute, 1982. 91–122, 280–83. = 1982a

———. "The Audience and Public of *Piers Plowman.*" In *Middle English Alliterative Poetry and its Literary Background,* ed. David A. Lawton. Suffolk: D.S. Brewer, 1982. 101–23, 147–54. = 1982b

———. "Introduction: The Critical Heritage." In *A Companion to Piers Plowman,* ed. John A. Alford. Berkeley: University of California Press, 1988. 1–25.

———. "William Langland's 'Kynde Name': Authorial Signature and Social Identity in Late Fourteenth-Century England." In *Literary Practice and Social Change in Britain, 1380–1530,* ed. Lee Patterson. Berkeley: University of California Press, 1990. 15–82.

———. "Acts of Vagrancy: The C Version 'Autobiography' and the Statute of 1388." In *Written Work: Langland, Labor, and Authorship,* ed. Steven Justice and Kathryn Kerby-Fulton. Philadelphia: University of Pennsylvania Press, 1997. 208–317.

Mihm, Madelyn Timmel, ed. *The Songe d'Enfer of Raoul de Houdenc: An Edition Based on All the Extant Manuscripts.* Tübingen: Max Niemeyer, 1984.

Millett, Bella and Jocelyn Wogan-Browne, ed. *Medieval English Prose for Women: Selections from the Katherine Group and Ancrene Wisse.* Oxford: Clarendon Press, 1990.

Millor, W. J., H. E. Butler, and C. N. L. Brooke, eds. *Epistularium Iohannis Sarisberiensis: Epistulae Iohannis et quorundam aliorum contemporaneorum.* Oxford: Oxford University Press, 1979.

Mills, M., ed. *Lybeaus Desconus.* Early English Text Society 261. London and New York: Oxford University Press, 1969.

Milsom, S. F. C. *The Legal Framework of English Feudalism.* Cambridge: Cambridge University Press, 1976.

Miner, John N. *The Grammar Schools of Medieval England: A. F. Leach in Historiographical Perspective.* Montreal: McGill-Queen's University Press, 1990.

Minnis, A. J. *Medieval Theory of Authorship: Scholastic Literary Attitudes in the Later Middle Ages.* London: Scolar Press, 1984.

———. "Reclaiming the Pardoners." *Journal of Medieval and Early Modern Studies* 33 (2003): 311–34.

Mitchell, A. G. "Lady Meed and the Art of *Piers Plowman.*" In *Style and Symbolism in Piers Plowman: A Modern Critical Anthology,* ed. Robert J. Blanch. Knoxville: University of Tennessee Press, 1969. 174–93.

Modesto, Christine. *Studien zur Cena Cypriani und zu deren Rezeption.* Classica Monacensia 3. Tübingen: Gunter Narr, 1992.

Mohl, Ruth. *The Three Estates in Medieval and Renaissance Literature.* New York: F. Ungar, 1933.

Monroe, Arthur Eli. *Early Economic Thought: Selections from Economic Literature Prior to Adam Smith*. Cambridge, Mass.: Harvard University Press, 1948.

Montaiglon, Anatole de, and Gaston Raynaud, eds. *Recueil general et complet des fabliaux des XIIIe et XIVe siècles*. 6 vols. Paris: Librairie des Bibliophiles, 1872–90.

Moore, Arthur K. "'Somer' and 'Lenten' as Terms for Spring." *Notes and Queries* 194 (1949): 82–83.

Moore, Ellen Wedemeyer. *The Fairs of Medieval England: An Introductory Study*. Toronto Studies and Texts 72. Toronto: Pontifical Institute, 1985.

Moorman, John R. H. *A History of the Franciscan Order from its Origins to the Year 1517*. Oxford: Clarendon Press, 1968.

Morenzoni, Franco, ed. *Thomas de Chobham: Sermones*. Corpus Christianorum Continuatio Medievalis 82A. Turnholt: Brepols, 1993.

Morgan, Gerald. "The Meaning of Kind Wit, Conscience, and Reason in the First Vision of *Piers Plowman*." *Modern Philology* 85 (1987): 351–58.

Morley, Henry, ed. *John Stow: A Survey of London*. London: Routledge, 1908.

Morris, Colin. "The Commissary of the Bishop of the Diocese of Lincoln." *Journal of Ecclesiastical History* 10 (1959): 50–65.

———. "A Consistory Court in the Middle Ages." *Journal of Ecclesiastical History* 14 (1963): 150–59.

———. "*Equestris ordo*: Chivalry as a Vocation in the Twelfth Century." *Studies in Church History* 15 (1978): 87–96.

Morris, Richard, ed. *Cursor Mundi*. Early English Text Society (London: Oxford University Press): o.s. 57: Part 1, ll. 1–4954, 1874, repr. 1961; o.s. 59: Part 2, ll. 4955–12558, 1875, repr. 1966; os 62: Part 3, ll. 12559–19300, 1876, repr. 1966; o.s. 66: Part 4, ll. 19301–23826, 1877, repr. 1966; o.s. 68: Part 5, ll. 23827-end, 1878, repr. 1966; os 99: Part 6, Pref., Notes, Gloss., 1892, repr. 1962; o.s. 101, essay by H. Hupe (disowned by Morris), Part 7, 1893, repr. 1962.

———, ed. *The Pricke of Conscience*. Berlin: A. Asher, 1863.

———, ed. *Old English Miscellany, Containing A Bestiary, Kentish Sermons, Proverbs of Alfred, Religious Poems of the Thirteenth Century*. Early English Text Society 49. London: Trübner 1872.

Morrison, Susan Signe. *Women Pilgrims in Late Medieval England: Private Piety as Public Performance*. London: Routledge, 2000.

Muessig, Carolyn. "Audience and Preacher: *Ad Status* Sermons and Social Classification." In *Preacher, Sermon and Audience in the Middle Ages*, ed. Carolyn Muessig. Leiden: Brill, 2002. 255–76.

Murdoch, Brian, and J. A. Tasioulas, ed. *The Apocryphal Lives of Adam and Eve*. Exeter: University of Exeter Press, 2002.

Murphy, Colette. "Lady Holy Church and Meed the Maid: Re-envisioning Female Personifications in *Piers Plowman*." In *Feminist Readings in Middle English Literature: The Wife of Bath and All Her Sect*, ed. Ruth Evans and Lesley Johnson. London: Routledge, 1994. 140–64.

Muscatine, Charles. *Poetry and Crisis in the Age of Chaucer*. Notre Dame, Ind.: University of Notre Dame Press, 1972; repr. in his *Medieval Literature, Style, and Culture*. Columbia: University of South Carolina Press, 1999. 65–163.

Musson, Anthony, and W. M. Ormrod. *The Evolution of English Justice: Law, Politics and Society in the Fourteenth Century*. Houndmills, Basingstoke, Hampshire: MacMillan, 1999.

Mustanoja, Tauno F. *A Middle English Syntax, Part I.* Mémoires de la Société Néophilo-logique de Helsinki 23. Helsinki: Société Néophilologique, 1960.

———. "The Suggestive Use of Christian Names in Middle English Poetry." In *Medieval Literature and Folklore Studies in Honor of Francis Lee Utley*, ed. Jerome Mandel and Bruce A. Rosenberg. New Brunswick, N.J.: Rutgers University Press, 1970. 51–76.

———, ed. *The Good Wife Taught her Daughter; The Good Wyfe Wold a Pylgremage; The Thewis of Gud Women.* Helsinki: Academia Scientiarum Fennica, 1948.

Myers, A. R. *London in the Age of Chaucer.* Norman: University of Oklahoma Press, [1972].

Narin van Court, Elisa. "The Hermeneutics of Supersession: The Revision of the Jews from the B to the C Text of *Piers Plowman.*" *Yearbook of Langland Studies* 10 (1996): 43–87.

Nederman, Cary J., "The Royal Will and the Baronial Bridle: The Place of the *Addicio de cartis* in Bractonian Political Thought." *History of Political Thought* 9 (1988): 415–29.

———, ed. and trans. *Political Thought in Early Fourteenth-Century England: Treatises by Walter of Milemete, William of Pagula, and William of Ockham.* Tempe: Arizona Center for Medieval and Renaissance Studies, in collaboration with Brepols, 2002.

Nelson, Alan H. "Mechanical Wheels of Fortune, 1100–1547." *Journal of the Warburg and Courtauld Institutes* 58 (1980): 227–33.

Nelson, Janet. "The Earliest Royal *Ordo.*" In *Authority and Power: Studies on Medieval Law and Government Presented to Walter Ullmann on his seventieth Birthday*, ed. B. Tierney and P. Linehan. Cambridge: Cambridge University Press, 1980. 29–48.

———. "The Rites of the Conqueror." In *Proceedings of the Battle Conference on Anglo-Norman Studies* 4 (1981), ed. R. Allen Brown. Woodbridge, Suffolk: Boydell and Brewer, 1982. 117–32.

Nelson, William, ed. *A Fifteenth Century School Book.* Oxford: Clarendon Press, 1956.

Nevanlinna, Saara. "The Adjective *weary* in Middle English Structures: A Syntactic-Semantic Study." In *Placing Middle English in Context*, ed. Irma Taavitsainen, Terttu Nevalainen, Päivi Pahta, and Matti Rissanen. Topics in English Linguistics 35. Berlin: Mouton de Gruyter, 2000. 339–53.

Newhauser, Richard G. *The Early History of Greed: The Sin of Avarice in Early Medieval Thought and Literature.* Cambridge: Cambridge University Press, 2000.

Newton, Stella May. *Fashion in the Age of the Black Prince.* Woodbridge, Suffolk: Boydell Press, 1980.

Niermeyer, J. F. *Mediae Latinitatis Lexicon Minus.* Rev. ed. C. van de Kieft. Leiden: Brill, 1997.

Nilson, Benjamin John. *Cathedral Shrines of Medieval England.* Woodbridge, Suffolk: Boydell, 1998.

———. "The Medieval Experience at the Shrine." In *Pilgrimage Explored*, ed. J. Stopford. York: York Medieval Press, 1999. 95–122.

Nohl, Johannes. *The Black Death: A Chronicle of the Plague Compiled from Contemporary Sources.* Trans. C. H. Clarke. London: Unwin, 1926, 1971.

Nolan, Maura. *John Lydgate and the Making of Public Culture.* Cambridge: Cambridge University Press, 2005.

Noonan, John T. *The Scholastic Analysis of Usury*. Cambridge, Mass.: Harvard University Press, 1957.

———. "Power to Choose." *Viator* 4 (1973): 419–34.

———. *Bribes*. London: Macmillan, 1984.

Nummenmaa, Liisa. *The Uses of So, Al So, and As in Early Middle English*. Mémoires de la Société Néophilologique de Helsinki 39. Helsinki, 1973.

Oakden, J. P. *Alliterative Poetry in Middle English: Part I: The Dialectical and Metrical Survey*. Publications of the University of Manchester 205; English Series 18. Manchester: Manchester University Press, 1930.

Oakden, J. P. with Elizabeth R. Innes. *Alliterative Poetry in Middle English: Part II: A Survey of the Traditions*. Publications of the University of Manchester 236; English Series 22. Manchester: Manchester University Press, 1935.

Oberman, Heiko Augustinus. *The Harvest of Medieval Theology: Gabriel Biel and Late Medieval Nominalism*. Durham, N.C.: Labyrinth Press, 1983.

Oberman, Heiko Augustinus and J. A. Weisheipl. "The *Sermo Epinicius* ascribed to Thomas Bradwardine (1346)." *Archives d'histoire doctrinale et littéraire du moyen âge* 33 (1958): 295–329.

Offord, M. Y., ed. *The Parlement of the Thre Ages*. Early English Text Society 246. London: Oxford University Press, 1959.

Ogilvie-Thomson, S.J., ed. *Richard Rolle: Prose and Verse*. Early English Text Society o.s. 293. Oxford: Oxford University Press, 1988.

Olson, Paul A. "*The Parliament of Foules*: Aristotle's *Politics* and the Foundation of Human Society." *Studies in the Age of Chaucer* 2 (1980): 53–69.

Önnerfors, Alf, ed. *P. Flavii Vegeti Renati Epitoma Re Militaris*. Stuttgart: Teubner, 1995.

Orme, Nicholas. *English Schools in the Middle Ages*. London, Methuen, 1973.

———. *Education and Society in Medieval and Renaissance England*. London: Hambledon, 1989.

Ormrod, W.M. "The English Government and the Black Death of 1348–49." In *England in the Fourteenth Century*, ed. W. M. Ormrod. Woodbridge, Suffolk: Boydell, 1986. 175–88.

———. *The Reign of Edward III*. New Haven, Conn.: Yale University Press, 1990.

Oschinsky, Dorothea, ed. *Walter of Henley and Other Treatises on Estate Management and Accounting*. Oxford: Clarendon Press, 1971.

Overstreet, Samuel A. "'Grammaticus Ludens': Theological Aspects of Langland's Grammatical Allegory." *Traditio* 40 (1984): 251–96.

Owen, Dorothy. *Piers Plowman: A Comparison with Some Earlier and Contemporary French Allegories*. London: University of London Press, 1912.

Owst, G. R. "The 'Angel' and the 'Goliardeys' of Langland's Prologue." *Modern Language Review* 20 (1925): 270–79.

———. *Literature and Pulpit in Medieval England*. Cambridge: Cambridge University Press, 1933.

Paley Baildon, W. "The Trousseaux of Princess Philippa, Wife of Eric, King of Denmark, Norway, and Sweden." *Archaeologia* 67 (1915–16): 163–88.

Palliser, D. M., T. R. Slater and E. Patricia Dennison. "The Topography of Towns 600–1300." In *The Cambridge Urban History of Britain*, vol. 1, *600–1540*, ed. D. M. Palliser. Cambridge: Cambridge University Press, 2000. 153–86.

Palmer, R. Barton, ed. and tr. *Guillaume de Machaut: La fonteinne amoureuse, and Two Other Love Vision Poems*. New York: Garland, 1993.

Palmer, Robert C. *The County Courts of Medieval England, 1150–1350.* Princeton, N.J.: Princeton University Press, 1982.

———. *The Whilton Dispute, 1264–1380.* Princeton, N.J.: Princeton University Press, 1984.

———. *English Law in the Age of the Black Death, 1348–1381: A Transformation of Governance and Law.* Chapel Hill: University of North Carolina Press, 1993.

Pantin, W. A. "A Medieval Collection of Latin and English Proverbs and Riddles, from the Rylands Latin MS 394." *Bulletin of the John Rylands Library* 14 (1930): 81–114.

———. "The Monk-Solitary of Farne: A Fourteenth Century English Mystic." *English Historical Review* 59 (1944): 162–86.

———. *The English Church in the Fourteenth Century.* London: Cambridge University Press, 1955.

Panton, G. A. and D. Donaldson, eds. *The "Gest Hystoriale" of the Destruction of Troy.* Early English Text Society 39, 56 (repr. as one vol.). Oxford: Oxford University Press, 1968.

Parker, John, trans. *The Works of Dionysius the Areopagite: Part II: The Heavenly Hierarchy.* Repr., Merrick, N.Y.: Richwood, 1976.

Patterson, Lee. *Chaucer and the Subject of History.* Madison: University of Wisconsin Press, 1991.

Payen, Jean Charles. *Le motif du repentir dans la littérature française médiévale.* Geneva: Droz, 1967.

Pearcy, Roy J. "Langland's *Fair Feld.*" *Yearbook of Langland Studies* 11 (1997): 39–48.

Pearsall, Derek. "The Ilchester Manuscript of *Piers Plowman.*" *Neuphilologische Mitteilungen* 82 (1981): 181–93.

———. "The Alliterative Revival: Origins and Social Backgrounds." In *Middle English Alliterative Poetry and its Literary Background,* ed. David A. Lawton. Woodbridge, Suffolk: D.S. Brewer, 1982. 34–53.

———. "Poverty and Poor People in *Piers Plowman.*" In *Medieval English Studies Presented to George Kane,* ed. Donald Kennedy, Ronald Waldron, and Joseph S. Wittig. Wolfeboro, N.H.: D.S. Brewer, 1988. 167–85.

———. "Langland's London." In *Written Work: Langland, Labor, and Authorship,* ed. Steven Justice and Kathryn Kerby-Fulton. Philadelphia: University of Pennsylvania Press, 1997. 185–207.

———. "Langland and Lollardy: From B to C." *Yearbook of Langland Studies* 17 (2003): 7–23.

Pedersen, Frederik. *Marriage Disputes in Medieval England.* London: Hambledon and London, 2000.

Pecham, John. *Determinationes Quaestionum circa Regulam Fratrum Minorum.* In *S. Bonaventurae Opera Omnia.* Vol. 8. Florence: Collegium S. Bonaventurae, 1898. 336–74.

Pennington, Kenneth. *The Prince and the Law, 1200–1600: Sovereignty and Rights in the Western Legal Tradition.* Berkeley and Los Angeles: University of California Press, 1993.

Perryman, Judith, ed. *The King of Tars.* Heidelberg: Carl Winter Universitätsverlag, 1980.

Pfaff, R. W. *New Liturgical Feasts in Later Medieval England.* Oxford: Clarendon, 1970.

Phillips, Helen, ed. *Langland, the Mystics and the Medieval English Religious Tradition: Essays in Honour of S. S. Hussey.* Cambridge: Cambridge University Press, 1990.

Pickering, F. P., ed. *The Anglo-Norman Text of the Holkham Bible Picture Book.* Anglo-Norman Texts 23. Oxford: Basil Blackwell, 1971.

Piehler, Paul. *The Visionary Landscape: A Study in Medieval Allegory.* London: Edward Arnold, 1971.

Poirion, Daniel, ed. *Le Roman de la Rose.* Paris: Garnier-Flammarion, 1974.

Pollock, Frederick, and Frederick William Maitland. *The History of English Law Before the Time of Edward I.* 2 vols. 2nd ed. Cambridge: Cambridge University Press, 1952.

Porter, Mary Louise. "Richard Rolle's Latin Commentary on the Psalms, To Which Is Prefixed a Study of Rolle's Life and Works." Ph.D. dissertation, Cornell University, 1929.

Post, Gaines, Kimon Giocarnis, and Richard Kay. "The Medieval Heritage of a Humanistic Ideal: 'Scientia Donum Dei Est, Unde Vendi Non Potest.'" *Traditio* 11 (1955): 195–234.

Potts, Timothy C. *Conscience in Medieval Philosophy.* Cambridge: Cambridge University Press, 1980.

———. "Conscience." In *The Cambridge History of Later Medieval Philosophy,* ed. Norman Kretzmann, Anthony Kenny, and Jan Pinborg; assoc. ed. Eleanore Stump. Cambridge: Cambridge University Press, 1982, 1988. 687–704.

Powell, Edward. *Kingship, Law, and Society: Criminal Justice in the Reign of Henry V.* Oxford: Clarendon Press, 1989.

Powell, Sue. "The Transmission and Circulation of *The Lay Folks' Catechism.*" In *Late-Medieval Religious Texts and their Transmission,* ed. A. J. Minnis. Cambridge: D.S. Brewer, 1994. 67–84.

Powicke, F. M. and C. R. Cheney, eds. *Councils and Synods with Other Documents Relating to the English Church.* Vol. 2, Part 2, 1265–1313. Oxford: Clarendon Press, 1964.

Pugh, R. B. *Imprisonment in Medieval England.* Cambridge: Cambridge University Press, 1968.

Purdie, Rhiannon, ed. *Ipomadon.* Early English Text Society o.s. 316. Oxford: Oxford University Press, 2001.

Putnam, Bertha Haven. *The Enforcement of the Statutes of Labourers During the First Decade after the Black Death, 1349–1359.* New York: [no pub.], 1908.

———. *The Place in Legal History of Sir William Shareshull.* Cambridge: Cambridge University Press, 1950.

Quillet, Jeannine. "Community, Counsel and Representation." In *The Cambridge History of Medieval Political Thought, c. 350-c.1450,* ed. J. H. Burns. Cambridge: Cambridge University Press, 1988. 520–72.

Quirk, Randolf. "Langland's Use of *Kind Wit* and *Inwit.*" *Journal of English and Germanic Philology* 52 (1953): 182–88.

Raabe, Pamela. *Imitating God: The Allegory of Faith in Piers Plowman B.* Athens: University of Georgia Press, 1990.

Raby, R. J. E. "*Turris Alithie* and the *Ecloga Theoduli.*" *Medium Ævum* 34 (1965): 226–29.

Ramsey, Nigel. "Retained Legal Counsel, c. 1275–1475." *Transactions of the Royal Historical Society* 5th ser. 35 (1985): 95–112.

———. "Scriveners and Notaries as Legal Intermediaries in Later Medieval England."

In *Enterprise and Individuals in Fifteenth-Century England*, ed. Jennifer Kermode. Stroud: Alan Sutton, 1991. 118–31.

Ratcliff, S. C., ed. *Elton Manorial Records, 1279–1351*, trans. D. M. Gregory. Cambridge: Cambridge University Press, 1946.

Rawcliffe, Carole. "The Great Lord as Peacekeeper: Arbitration by English Noblemen and their Councils in the Later Middle Ages." In *Law and Social Change in British History*, ed. J. A. Guy and H. G. Beale. London: Royal Historical Society, 1984. 34–53.

Raymo, Richard R. "Works of Religious and Philosophical Instruction." In *A Manual of the Writings in Middle English, 1050–1500*, vol. 7, ed. Albert Hartung. New Haven, Conn.: Connecticut Academy of Arts and Sciences, 1986. 2255–372, 2470–577.

Reidy, John, ed. *Thomas Norton's Ordinal of Alchemy*. Early English Text Society 272. London: Oxford University Press, 1975.

Reinsch, Robert, ed. *Le Bestiaire of Guillaume le Clerc: Das Thierbuch des normannischen Dichters Guillaume le Clerc*. Leipzig: Fues's Verlag, 1890.

Rex, Richard. *The Lollards*. Houndmills, Basingstoke, Hampshire: Palgrave, 2002.

Rickert, Edith. *Chaucer's World*. Ed. Clair C. Olson and Martin M. Crow. New York: Columbia University Press, 1948.

Rigby, S. H. *English Society in the Later Middle Ages: Class, Status, and Gender*. New York: St. Martin's Press, 1995.

Rigg, A. G. *Gawain on Marriage: The Textual Tradition of the De coniuge non ducenda with Critical Edition and Translation*. Toronto: Pontifical Institute of Mediaeval Studies, 1986.

Rigg, A. G. and Charlotte Brewer, eds. *Piers Plowman: The Z Version*. Toronto: Pontifical Institute of Mediaeval Studies, 1983.

Riley, Henry Thomas, ed. *Liber Albus. Munimenta Gildhallæ Londoniensis*. Vol. 1. London: Longman, Brown, 1859. Repr. Nendeln: Kraus, 1968.

———, ed. *Liber Custumarum*. Rolls Series 12:2. London: Longman, 1860.

———, ed. *Thomas Walsingham: Historia Anglicana*. 2 vols. Rolls Series 28. London: Longman, 1863, 1864.

———, ed. *Memorials of London and London Life in the XIIIth, XIVth, and Xvth Centuries*. 2 vols., continuously paginated. London: Longmans, 1868.

Risse, Robert. "The Augustinian Paraphrase of Isaiah 14:13–14 in *Piers Plowman* and the Commentary on the Fables of Avianus." *Philological Quarterly* 45 (1966): 712–17.

Robert, Ulysse, ed. *L'art de chevalerie; traduction du De re militari par Jean de Meun*. Paris: Firmin Didot, 1897.

Roberts, Jane. "*Robbares and reuares þat ryche men despoilen*: Some Competing Forms." In *Placing Middle English in Context*, ed. Irma Taavitsainen, Terttu Nevalainen, Päivi Pahta, and Matti Rissanen. Topics in English Linguistics 35. Berlin: Mouton de Gruyter, 2000. 235–53.

Robertson, D. W. *Chaucer's London*. New York: John Wiley, 1968.

Robertson, D. W. and Bernard F. Huppé. *Piers Plowman and Scriptural Tradition*. Princeton, N.J.: Princeton University Press, 1951.

Robbins, Rossell Hope, ed. *Secular Lyrics of the XIVth and XVth Centuries*. Oxford: Clarendon Press, 1952.

———, ed. *Historical Poems of the XIVth and XVth Centuries*. New York: Columbia University Press, 1959.

Robinson, I. S. "Church and Papacy." In *The Cambridge History of Medieval Political Thought, c. 350-c.1450*, ed. J. H. Burns. Cambridge: Cambridge University Press, 1988. 252–305.

Rogers, William Elford. *Interpretation in Piers Plowman*. Washington, D.C.: Catholic University of America Press, 2002.

Roney, Lois. "Winner and Waster's 'Wyse Wordes': Teaching Economics and Nationalism in Fourteenth-Century England." *Speculum* 69 (1994): 1070–100.

Rosenthal, Joel T. *Patriarchy and Families of Privilege in Fifteenth-Century England* Philadelphia: University of Pennsylvania Press, 1991.

Roskell, J. S. *The Impeachment of Michael de la Pole, Earl of Suffolk, 1386, in the Context of the Reign of Richard II*. Manchester: Manchester University Press, 1984.

Ross, Woodburn O., ed. *Middle English Sermons*. Early English Text Society o.s. 149. London: Oxford University Press, 1940 (for 1938).

Rothwell, W. "The Trilingual England of Geoffrey Chaucer." *Studies in the Age of Chaucer* 16 (1994): 45–67.

Russell, George. "'As They Read It': Some Notes on Early Responses to the C-Version of *Piers Plowman*." *Leeds Studies in English* 20 (1989): 173–89.

Ryan, W. Granger and Helmut Ripperges, trans. *The Golden Legend of Jacobus de Voragine*. New York: Longmans, Green, 1941. Expanded ed., trans. Ryan. 2 vols. Princeton, N.J.: Princeton University Press, 1993.

Saenger, Paul. *Space Between Words: The Origins of Silent Reading*. Stanford, Calif.: Stanford University Press, 1997.

Salter, Elizabeth. "*Piers Plowman* and *The Simonie*." *Archiv für das Studium der neueren Sprachen und Literaturen* 203 (1967): 241–54.

———. "Alliterative Modes and Affiliations in the Fourteenth Century." *Neuphilologische Mitteilungen* 79 (1978):25–35.

———. *Fourteenth-Century English Poetry: Contexts and Readings*. Oxford: Oxford University Press, 1983.

——— and Derek Pearsall, ed. *Piers Plowman: Selections from the C-Text*. London: Edward Arnold, 1967.

Samuels, M. L. "Langland's Dialect." *Medium Ævum* 54 (1985): 232–47.

———. "Dialect and Grammar." In *A Companion to Piers Plowman*, ed. John A. Alford. Berkeley: University of California Press, 1988. 201–21.

Sandison, Helen. *The "Chanson d'Aventure" in Middle English*. Bryn Mawr College Monographs 12. Bryn Mawr, Penn., 1913.

Saul, Nigel. "'Forget-Me-Nots': Patronage in Gothic England." In *Age of Chivalry: Art and Society in Late Medieval England*, ed. Nigel Saul. N.p.: Brockhampton Press, 1992. 36–47.

———. *Richard II*. New Haven, Conn.: Yale University Press, 1997.

———. "The Kingship of Richard II." In *Richard II: The Art of Kingship*, ed. Anthony Goodman and James Gillespie. Oxford: Clarendon Press, 1999. 37–57.

Sayles, George O. *The Functions of the Medieval Parliament of England*. London: Hambledon Press, 1988.

Scammell, Jean. "The Rural Chapter in England from the Eleventh to the Fourteenth Century." *English Historical Review* 86 (1971): 1–21.

Scase, Wendy. "Two *Piers Plowman* C-Text Interpolations: Evidence for a Second Textual Tradition." *Notes and Queries* 232 (1987): 456–63.

————. *Piers Plowman and the New Anticlericalism*. Cambridge: Cambridge University Press, 1989.

Schmidt, A. V. C. "The Inner Dreams in *Piers Plowman*." *Medium Ævum* 55 (1986): 24–40.

————. *The Clerkly Maker: Langland's Poetic Art*. Cambridge: D.S. Brewer, 1987.

————. "Langland's Visions and Revisions." *Yearbook of Langland Studies* 14 (2000): 5–27.

Scott, Anne M. "'Nevere noon so nedy ne poverer deide': *Piers Plowman* and the Value of Poverty." *Yearbook of Langland Studies* 15 (2001): 141–53.

————. *Piers Plowman and the Poor*. Dublin: Four Courts Press, 2004.

Scott, Kathleen, with an introduction by Derek Pearsall. *Piers Plowman : a facsimile of Bodleian Library, Oxford, MS Douce 104*. Woodbridge, Suffolk: D. S. Brewer, 1992.

Scragg, D. G., ed. *The Vercelli Homilies and Related Texts*. Early English Text Society o.s. 300. Oxford: Oxford University Press, 1992.

Selzer, John L. "Topical Allegory in *Piers Plowman*: Lady Meed's B-Text Debate with Conscience." *Philological Quarterly* 59 (1980): 257–67.

Seymour, M. C., ed. *The Bodley Version of Mandeville's Travels*. Early English Text Society 253. London: Oxford University Press, 1963.

———— gen. ed. *On the Properties of Things: John Trevisa's Translation of Bartholomæus Anglicus, De proprietatibus rerum*. 3 vols. Oxford: Clarendon Press, 1975–88.

Sharpe, Reginald R., ed. *Calendar of Letter-Books . . . of the City of London: Letter-Book E, ca. A.D. 1314–1337*. London: John Edward Francis, 1903.

————, ed. *Calendar of Letter-Books . . . of the City of London: Letter-Book H, ca. A.D. 1375–1399*. London: John Edward Francis, 1907.

Shaw, Judith. "The Influence of Canonical and Episcopal Reform on Popular Books of Instruction." In *The Popular Literature of Medieval England*, ed. Thomas J. Heffernan. Tennessee Studies in Literature 28. Knoxville: University of Tennessee Press, 1985. 44–60.

Shepherd, Geoffrey. "Poverty in Piers Plowman." In *Social Relations and Ideas: Essays in Honour of R. H. Hilton*, ed. T. H. Aston et al. Cambridge: Cambridge University Press, 1983. 169–89.

Shepherd, H. A. Stephen. "Langland's Romances." In *William Langland's Piers Plowman: A Book of Essays*, ed. Kathleen Hewett-Smith. New York: Routledge, 2001. 69–82.

————, ed. *Middle English Romances*. New York: Norton, 1995.

Sheridan, James J., trans. *Alan of Lille: Anticlaudianus or The Good and Perfect Man*. Toronto: Pontifical Institute of Mediaeval Studies, 1973.

————, trans. *Alan of Lille: The Plaint of Nature*. Toronto: Pontifical Institute of Mediaeval Studies, 1980.

Shoaf, R. Allen, ed. *Thomas Usk: The Testament of Love*. Kalamazoo, Mich.: Medieval Institute Publications, 1998.

Simmons, T. F. and H. E. Nolloth, eds. *John Thoresby: The Lay Folks' Catechism*. Early English Text Society o.s. 118. London: Oxford University Press, 1901.

Simpson, A. W. B. *A History of the Common Law of Contract: The Rise of the Action of Assumpsit*. Oxford: Clarendon Press, 1975.

Simpson, James. "The Transformation of Meaning: A Figure of Thought in *Piers Plowman*." *Review of English Studies* n.s. 37 (1986): 161–83.

————. "Spirituality and Economics in Passus 1–7 of the B Text." *Yearbook of Langland Studies* 1 (1987): 83–103.

————. "The Constraints of Satire in *Piers Plowman* and *Mum and the Sothsegger*." In *Langland, the Mystics and the Medieval English Religious Tradition: Essays in Honour of S. S. Hussey*, ed. Helen Phillips. Cambridge: D.S. Brewer, 1990. 11–30. = 1990a

————. *Piers Plowman: An Introduction to the B-Text*. London: Longman, 1990. = 1990b

————. "The Power of Impropriety: Authorial Naming in *Piers Plowman*." In *William Langland's Piers Plowman: A Book of Essays*, ed. Kathleen Hewett-Smith. New York: Routledge, 2001. 145–65.

Singer, Samuel, ed. *Thesaurus proverbiorum medii aevi = Lexikon der Sprichwörter des romanisch-germanischen Mittelalters*. 13 vols. Berlin: W. de Gruyter, 1995–2002.

Sisam, Celia and Kenneth, ed. *Oxford Book of Medieval English Verse*. Oxford: Clarendon Press, 1970.

Skeat, Walter W., ed. *The vision of William concerning Piers Plowman. Part 1 (A Text)*. Early English Text Society 28. London: Trübner, 1867.

————, ed. *The Vision of William Concerning Piers the Plowman. Part 3 (C Text)*. Early English Text Society 54. London: Oxford University Press, 1873.

————, ed. *Alexander and Dindimus: or, The Letters of Alexander to Dindimus, King of the Brahmans*. Early English Text Society 31. London: Trübner, 1878.

Smith, A. H., ed. "The Middle English Lyrics in Additional MS. 45896." *London Mediaeval Studies* 2 (1951): 33–49.

Smith, Ben H. *Traditional Imagery of Charity in Piers Plowman*. The Hague: Mouton, 1966.

Smith, D. Vance. "The Labors of Reward: Meed, Mercede, and the Beginning of Salvation." *Yearbook of Langland Studies* 8 (1994): 127–54.

————. *The Book of the Incipit: Beginnings in the Fourteenth Century*. Medieval Cultures 28. Minneapolis: University of Minnesota Press, 2001.

————. "*Piers Plowman* and the National Noetic of Edward III." In *Imagining a Medieval English Nation*, ed. Kathy Lavezzo. Minneapolis: University of Minnesota Press, 2004. 234–60.

Smith, Lucy Toulmin and Paul Meyer, eds. *Les Contes moralisés de Nicole Bozon*. Paris: Firmin-Didot, 1889.

Smithers, G. V., ed. *Havelok*. Oxford: Clarendon Press, 1987.

Somerset, Fiona. "Expanding the Langlandian Canon: Radical Latin and the Stylistics of Reform." *Yearbook of Langland Studies* 17 (2003): 73–92.

Southern, Richard. *The Medieval Theatre in the Round; A Study of the Staging of The Castle of Perseverance, and Related Matters*. London: Faber and Faber, 1957.

Southern, Sir Richard. *Western Society and the Church in the Middle Ages*. Pelican History of the Church 2. Harmondsworth, Middlesex: Penguin, 1970.

Southworth, John. *The English Medieval Minstrel*. Woodbridge, Suffolk: Boydell Press, 1989.

Spearing, A. C. "The Development of a Theme in *Piers Plowman*." *Review of English Studies* 11 (1960): 241–53.

————. *Medieval Dream Poetry*. Cambridge: Cambridge University Press, 1976.

Spencer, H. Leith. *English Preaching in the Late Middle Ages*. Oxford: Clarendon, 1993.

Spufford, Peter. *Money and its Use in Medieval Europe.* Cambridge: Cambridge University Press, 1988.

Stahl, Harvey and Robert Johnson, with E. L. Burge. *Martianus Capella and the Seven Liberal Arts.* Vol. 2, trans, *The Marriage of Philology and Mercury.* New York: Columbia University Press, 1977.

Steiner, Emily. *Documentary Culture and the Making of Medieval English Literature.* Cambridge: Cambridge University Press, 2003.

Stelten, Leo F., ed. and trans. *Flavius Vegetius Renatus: Epitoma Rei Militaris.* New York: Peter Lang, 1990.

Stevens, Martin, and A. C. Cawley, eds. *The Towneley Plays.* 2 vols. Early English Text Society s.s. 13, 14. Oxford: Oxford University Press, 1994.

Stevenson, Joseph, ed. *Letters and Papers Illustrative of the Wars of the English in France during the Reign of Henry the Sixth.* Rolls Series 22. Vol. 2, part 2. London: Longman, Green, Longman, Roberts, and Green, 1864.

Stewart, H. F., E. K. Rand, and S. J. Tester, eds. and trans. *Boethius: The Theological Tractates and The Consolation of Philosophy.* Cambridge, Mass.: Harvard University Press, 1978.

Stockton, Eric W., trans. *The Major Latin Works of John Gower.* Seattle: University of Washington Press, 1962.

Stokes, Myra. *Justice and Mercy in Piers Plowman: A Reading of the B Text Visio.* London: Croom Helm, 1984.

Stones, E. L. G. "The Folvilles of Ashby-Folville, Leicestershire, and Their Associates in Crime, 1326–47." *Transactions of the Royal Historical Society* 5th series, 7 (1957): 117–36.

Strohm, Paul. "The Literature of Livery." In his *Hochon's Arrow: The Social Imagination of Fourteenth-Century Texts.* Princeton, N.J.: Princeton University Press, 1992. 179–85.

Struder, Paul and Joan Evans, eds. *Anglo-Norman Lapidaries.* Paris: Librairie ancienne Édouard Champion, 1924.

Stürzinger, J. J., ed. *Le Pelerinage de Vie Humaine de Guillaume de Deguileville.* Roxburghe Club. London: Nichols and Sons, 1893.

———, ed. *Le Pelerinage de l'ame de Guillaume de Deguileville.* Roxburghe Club. London: Nichols and Sons, 1895.

———, ed. *Le Pelerinage Jhesucrist de Guillaume de Deguileville.* Roxburghe Club. London: Nichols and Sons, 1897.

Suchier, Walther, ed. *Zwei altfranzösische Reimpredigten (Grant mal fist Adam, Deu le omnipotent).* Bibliotheca Normannica 1. Halle: Niemeyer, 1949.

———, ed. *Das mittellateinische Gespräch Adrian und Epictitus nebst verwandten Texten (Joca Monachorum).* Tübingen: M. Niemeyer, 1955.

Sullens, Idelle, ed. *Robert Mannyng of Brunne: Handlyng Synne.* Binghamton, N.Y.: Medieval and Renaissance Texts and Studies, 1983.

———, ed. *Robert Mannyng of Brunne: The Chronicle.* Binghamton, N.Y.: Medieval and Renaissance Texts and Studies, 1996.

Sumption, Jonathan. *Pilgrimage: An Image of Medieval Religion.* Totowa, N.J.: Rowman and Littlefield, 1975.

Swanson, R. N. *Church and Society in Late Medieval England.* Oxford: Blackwell, 1989.

———. "Literacy, Heresy, History and Orthodoxy." In *Heresy and Literacy, 1000–1530,* ed. Peter Biller and Anne Hudson. Cambridge: Cambridge University Press, 1994. 279–93.

———. *Religion and Devotion in Europe, c. 1215-c.1515.* Cambridge: Cambridge University Press, 1995.

———. "Letters of Confraternity and Indulgence in Late Medieval England." *Archives* 25 (2000): 40–57.

———. "Mendicants and Confraternity." In *The Religious Orders in Pre-Reformation England*, ed. James Clark. Woodbridge, Suffolk: Boydell, 2002. 121–41.

Swinburn, Lilian M. *The Lanterne of Liȝt.* Early English Text Society o.s. 151. London: Kegan Paul, 1917 for 1915.

Szittya, Penn R. *The Antifraternal Tradition in Medieval Literature.* Princeton, N.J.: Princeton University Press, 1986.

Tait, James. *The Medieval English Borough: Studies on its Origins and Constitutional History.* Manchester: Manchester University Press, 1936.

———, ed. *Johannis de Reading et Anonymi Cantuariensis, 1346–67.* Manchester: Manchester University Press, 1914.

Taitt, Peter. "In Defence of Lot." *Notes and Queries* 216 (1971): 284–85.

Tanquerey, Frédéric Joseph. *Recueil de lettres anglo-françaises (1265–1399).* Paris: É. Champion, 1916.

Tavormina, M. Teresa. "*Piers Plowman* and the Liturgy of St. Lawrence: Composition and Revision in Langland's Poetry." *Studies in Philology* 84 (1987): 245–71.

———. *Kindly Similitude: Marriage and Family in Piers Plowman.* Cambridge: D.S. Brewer, 1995.

Taylor, John. *English Historical Literature in the Fourteenth Century.* Oxford: Clarendon Press, 1987.

Thomas, A. H., ed. *Calendar of Select Pleas and Memoranda of the City of London . . . 1381–1412.* Cambridge: Cambridge University Press, 1932.

Thompson, Craig R., trans. *Ten Colloquies of Erasmus.* New York: The Liberal Arts Press, 1957.

Thompson, W. Meredith, ed. *Þe Wohunge of Ure Lauerd.* Early English Text Society 241. London: Oxford University Press, 1958.

Thomson, Edward Maunde, ed. *Thomas Walsingham: Chronicon Angliae.* Rolls Series 64. London: Longman, 1874.

Thomson, H. J., ed. and trans. *Prudentius.* 2 vols. Cambridge, Mass.: Harvard University Press, 1949, 1953.

Thomson, J. A. F. "Piety and Charity in Late Medieval London." *Journal of Ecclesiastical History* 16 (1965): 178–95.

Thorne, Samuel, trans.; George Woodbine, ed. *De legibus et consuetudinibus Angliae: On the laws and customs of England.* 4 vols. Cambridge, Mass.: Harvard University Press, 1968.

Thorpe, Lewis, trans. *Geoffrey of Monmouth: The History of the Kings of Britain.* London: Penguin, 1966.

Thrupp, Sylvia L. *The Merchant Class of Medieval London.* Ann Arbor: Univerity of Michigan Press, 1948, 1989.

———. "The Grocers of London: A Study of Distributive Trade." In *Studies in English Trade in the Fifteenth Century*, ed. Eileen Power and M. M. Postan. New York: Barnes and Noble, 1966. 247–92.

Tierney, Brian. *Medieval Poor Law.* Berkeley: University of California Press, 1959.

———. *Origins of Papal Infallibility, 1150–1350: A Study on the Concepts of Infallibility, Sovereignty, and Tradition in the Middle Ages.* Leiden: Brill, 1972.

Todd, James Henthorn, ed. *The Last Age of the Church.* Dublin: University Press, 1840.

Tout, T. F. *Chapters in the Administrative History of Mediaeval England.* 6 vols. Manchester: Manchester University Press, 1920–33.

———. "The Captivity and Death of Edward of Carnarvon." In *The Collected Papers of Thomas Frederick Tout.* 3 vols. Manchester: Manchester University Press, 1932–34. 3.145–90.

Traver, Hope. *The Four Daughters of God: A Study of the Versions of this Allegory with Special Reference to those in Latin, French, and English.* Bryn Mawr College Monographs, Vol. 6. Bryn Mawr, Penn.: Bryn Mawr College, 1907.

———. "The Four Daughters of God: A Mirror of Changing Doctrine." *Publications of the Modern Language Association* 40 (1925): 44–92.

Trigg, Stephanie. "The Traffic in Medieval Women: Alice Perrers, Feminist Criticism and *Piers Plowman.*" *Yearbook of Langland Studies* 12 (1998): 5–29.

———, ed. *Wynnere and Wastoure.* Early English Text Society 297. Oxford: Oxford University Press, 1990.

Trower, Katherine Bache. "Temporal Tensions in the *Visio* of *Piers Plowman.*" *Mediaeval Studies* 35 (1973): 389–412.

Tuck, Anthony. *Richard II and the English Nobility.* New York: St. Martin's, 1974.

Turner, Ralph V. "England: Kingship and the Political Community, c. 1100–1272." In *A Companion to Britain in the Later Middle Ages,* ed. S. H. Rigby. Oxford: Blackwell, 2003. 183–207.

Turville-Petre, Thorlac. *The Alliterative Revival.* Cambridge: D.S. Brewer, 1977.

———. "Politics and Poetry in the Early Fourteenth Century: The Case of Robert Mannyng's *Chronicle.*" *Review of English Studies* n.s. 39 (1988): 1–28.

———, ed. *Alliterative Poetry of the Later Middle Ages: An Anthology.* Washington, D.C.: Catholic University of America Press, 1989.

Twinch, Carol. *In Search of St. Walstan: East Anglia's Enduring Legend.* Lavenham, Suffolk: Lavenham Press, 1995.

Ullmann, Walter. *Law and Politics in the Middle Ages: An Introduction to the Sources of Medieval Political Ideas.* Bristol: Sources of History Ltd., 1975.

Utley, Francis Lee. "Dialogues, Debates, and Catechisms." In *A Manual of the Writings in Middle English, 1050–1500,* vol. 3, ed. Albert E. Hartung. New Haven: Connecticut Academy of Arts and Sciences, 1972. 669–745, 829–908.

Vale, Malcolm. *War and Chivalry.* London: Duckworth, 1981.

Vale, Juliet and Malcolm Vale. "Knightly Codes and Piety." In *Age of Chivalry: Art and Society in Late Medieval England,* ed. Nigel Saul. N.p.: Brockhampton Press, 1992. 24–35.

Van Hamel, A. G., ed. *Les Lamentations de Matheolus et le Livre de leesce de Jehan Le Fèvre, de Resson.* 2 vols. in 1. Paris: É. Bouillon, 1892–1905.

———, ed. *Renclus de Moilliens Barthélemy: Li Romans de Carité.* Paris: Vieweg, 1885.

van Kluyve, Robert A., ed. *Thomae Walsingham de archana* [sic] *deorum.* Durham, N.C.: Duke University Press, 1968.

Vasta, Edward. *The Spiritual Basis of Piers Plowman.* The Hague: Mouton, 1965.

Vising, Johan, ed. *Deux Poemes de Nicholas Bozon: Le Char d'Orgueil; La Lettre de*

L'Empereur Orgueil. Göteborgs Högskolas Årsskrift 3. Göteborg: Wettergen and Kerber, 1919.

Wailes, Stephen L. *Medieval Allegories of Jesus' Parables.* Berkeley: University of California Press, 1987.

Waldron, Ronald A. "Oral-Formulaic Technique and Middle English Alliterative Poetry." *Speculum* 32 (1957): 792–804.

Walker, Simon. *The Lancastrian Affinity, 1361–1399.* Oxford: Clarendon Press, 1990.

Wallace, David. "Chaucer and the Absent City." In *Chaucer's England: Literature in Historical Context,* ed. Barbara Hanawalt. Minneapolis: University of Minnesota Press, 1992. 59–90.

———. *Premodern Places: Calais to Surinam, Chaucer to Aphra Behn.* Malden, Mass.: Blackwell, 2004.

Wallner, Björn, ed. *An Exposition of Qui Habitat and Bonum Est in English.* Lund Studies in English 23. Lund: Gleerup, 1954.

Walther, Hans. *Das Streitgedicht in der lateinischen Literatur des Mittelalters.* München: C.H. and Oscar Beck, 1920.

———. *Proverbia sententiaeque Latinitatis Medii ac recentioris aevi. Nova series = Lateinische Sprichwörter und Sentenzen des Mittelalters und der frühen Neuzeit in alphabetischer Anordnung. Neue Reihe,* ed. Gerhard Schmidt. 3 vols. Göttingen: Vandenhoeck and Ruprecht, 1982–86.

Warner, G. F., ed. *Gerald of Wales, De Principis Instructione.* Rolls Series 21:8 London: Longman, 1891.

——— ed. *Queen Mary's Psalter: Miniatures and Drawings, by an English Artist of the 14th century, Reproduced from Royal Ms. 2 B. VII in the British Museum.* London: Trustees of the British Museum, 1912.

Warner, Lawrence. "The Ur-B *Piers Plowman* and the Earliest Production of C and B." *Yearbook of Langland Studies* 16 (2002): 3–39.

———. "Langland and the Problem of *William of Palerne.*" *Viator* 37 (2006).

Warren, Ann. *Anchorites and their Patrons in Medieval England.* Berkeley: University of California Press, 1985.

Watts, William, ed. and trans. *Augustine: Confessions.* 2 vols. Cambridge, Mass.: Harvard University Press, 1999.

Watson, Alan, trans. *The Digest of Justinian.* Rev. ed. 2 vols. Philadelphia: University of Pennsylvania Press, 1998.

Watson, Nicholas. *Richard Rolle and the Invention of Authority.* New York: Cambridge University Press, 1991.

Waugh, Scott L. "Tenure to Contract: Lordship and Clientage in Thirteenth-Century England." *English Historical Review* 101 (1986): 811–39.

———. *England in the Reign of Edward III.* New York: Cambridge University Press, 1991.

———. "England: Kingship and the Political Community, 1272–1377." In *A Companion to Britain in the Later Middle Ages,* ed. S. H. Rigby. Oxford: Blackwell, 2003. 208–23.

Wawn, Andrew. "Truth-Telling and the Tradition of *Mum and the Sothsegger.*" *Yearbook of English Studies* 13 (1983): 270–87.

Weatherly, Edward H., ed. *Speculum Sacerdotale.* Early English Text Society 200. Oxford: Oxford University Press, 1936.

Webb, Diana. *Pilgrimage in Medieval England*. London: Hambledon and London, 2000.

Weldon, James F. G. "The Structure of Dream Visions in *Piers Plowman*." *Mediaeval Studies* 49 (1987): 254–81.

———. "Gesture of Perception: The Pattern of Kneeling in *Piers Plowman* B.18–19." *Yearbook of Langland Studies* 3 (1989): 49–66.

———. "*Ordinatio* and Genre in MS CCC 201: A Mediaeval Reading of the B-Text of *Piers Plowman*." *Florilegium* 12 (1993): 159–75.

Wenzel, Siegfried. "The Pilgrimage of Life as a Late Medieval Genre." *Mediaeval Studies* 35 (1973): 370–88.

———. "Medieval Sermons." In *A Companion to Piers Plowman*, ed. John A. Alford. Berkeley: University of California Press, 1988. 155–72.

———. "Eli and His Sons." *Yearbook of Langland Studies* 13 (1999): 137–52.

———. *Verses in Sermons: "Fasciculus Morum" and Its Middle English Poems*. Cambridge, Mass.: Mediaeval Academy of America, 1978.

———, ed. *Summa virtutum de remediis anime*. Chaucer Library. Athens, Georgia: University of Georgia Press, 1984.

Wesling, Donald. "Eschatology and the Language of Satire in *Piers Plowman*." *Criticism* 10 (1968): 277–89.

Wetherbee, Winthrop. *Platonism and Poetry in the Twelfth Century: The Literary Influence of the School of Chartres*. Princeton, N.J.: Princeton University Press, 1972.

———, trans. *The Cosmographia of Bernardus Silvestris*. New York: Columbia University Press, 1973.

Whitaker, Thomas Dunham, ed. *Robert Langland: Visio Willi de Petro Plouhman, Item Visiones ejusdem de Dowel, Dobet, et Dobest*. London: John Murray, 1813.

Whittaker, William Joseph, ed. *The Mirror of Justices*. [By Andrew Horne.] Selden Society 7. London: Bernard Quaritch, 1895.

White, Hugh. *Nature and Salvation in Piers Plowman*. Cambridge: D.S. Brewer, 1988.

Whiting, Bartlett Jere, with Helen Wescott Whiting. *Proverbs, Sentences, and Proverbial Phrases from English Writings Mainly Before 1500*. Cambridge, Mass.: Harvard University Press, 1968.

Whiting, Ella Keats, ed. *The Poems of John Audelay*. Early English Text Society o.s. 184. London: Oxford University Press, 1931.

Whitworth, Charles W., Jr. "Changes in the Roles of Reason and Conscience in the Revisions of *Piers Plowman*." *Notes and Queries* 217, n.s. 19 (January, 1972): 4–7.

Wilkins, David, ed. *Concilia Magnae Britanniae et Hiberniae a . . . CCCCXLVI ad . . . MDCCXVII*. 4 vols. Vols. 2 and 3, London: R. Gosling et al., 1737; repr. Brussels: Culture et Civilisation, 1964.

Wilks, Michael. "Predestination, Property, and Power: Wyclif's Theory of Dominion and Grace." *Studies in Church History* 2 (1965): 220–36.

Willard, James Field. "Inland Transportation in England During the Fourteenth Century." *Speculum* 1 (1926): 361–74.

Willems, R., ed. *Sancti Aurelii Augustini In Johannis Evangelium Tractatus CXXIV*. Corpus Christianorum Series Latina 36. Turnhout: Brepols, 1954.

Williams, Arnold. "Relations Between the Mendicant Friars and the Secular Clergy in England in the Later Fourteenth Century." *Annuale Medievale* 1 (1960): 22–95.

Wilmart, A. *Auteurs spirituels et textes dévots du moyen âge latin*. Paris: Librairie Bloud et Gay, 1932.

Wilson, Edward. *A Descriptive Index of the English Lyrics in John of Grimestone's Preaching Book.* Medium Ævum Monographs n.s. 2. Oxford: Blackwell, 1973.

Wilson, F. P., ed. *Oxford Dictionary of English Proverbs.* 3rd ed. Oxford: Clarendon Press, 1970.

Wilson, William Burton, trans. *John Gower: Mirour de l'Omme.* Rev. by Nancy Wilson Van Baak. East Lansing, Mich.: Colleagues Press, 1992.

Wine, M. L., ed. *Drama of the English Renaissance.* New York: Modern Library, 1969.

Wittig, Joseph S. "*Piers Plowman* B IX-XII: Elements in the Design of the Inward Journey." *Traditio* 28 (1972): 211–80.

———. "The Dramatic and Rhetorical Development of Long Will's Pilgrimage." *Neuphilologische Mitteilungen* 76 (1975): 52–76.

———. "The Middle English 'Absolute Infinitive' and 'The Speech of Book.'" In *Magister Regis: Studies in Honor of Robert Earl Kaske,* ed. Arthur Groos et al. New York: Fordham University Press, 1986. 217–40.

———. *Piers Plowman: Concordance.* London and New York: Athlone, 2001.

Wood, Robert A. "A Fourteenth-Century London Owner of *Piers Plowman.*" *Medium Ævum* 53 (1984): 83–90.

Woods, Marjorie Curry and Rita Copeland. "Classroom and Confession." In *The Cambridge History of Medieval English Literature,* ed. David Wallace. Cambridge: Cambridge University Press, 2002. 376–406.

Woodward, David. "Medieval *Mappaemundi.*" In *Cartography in Prehistoric, Ancient, and Medieval Europe and the Mediterranean,* ed. J. B. Harley and David Woodward. The History of Cartography 1. Chicago: University of Chicago Press, 1987. 286–370.

Woolf, Rosemary. "The Tearing of the Pardon." In *Piers Plowman: Critical Approaches,* ed. S. S. Hussey. London: Methuen, 1969. 50–75.

Woolgar, C. M. *The Great Household in Late Medieval England.* New Haven, Conn.: Yale University Press, 1999.

Workman, H. B. *John Wyclif: A Study of the English Medieval Church.* 2 vols. Oxford: Oxford University Press, 1926.

Wright, Thomas, ed. *Political Songs of England.* Camden Society 6. London: J. B. Nichols, 1839.

———, ed. *The Latin Poems Commonly Attributed to Walter Mapes.* Camden Society 17. London: Camden Society, 1841.

———, ed. *Political Poems and Songs Relating to English History.* 2 vols. Rolls Series. London: Longman, Green, Longman, and Roberts, 1859, 1861.

Wullff, F. and E. Walberg, eds. *Vers de la Mort.* Paris: Firmin Didot, 1905.

Yunck, John A. *The Lineage of Lady Meed: The Development of Mediaeval Venality Satire.* South Bend, Ind.: University of Notre Dame Press, 1963.

———. "Satire." In *A Companion to Piers Plowman,* ed. John A. Alford. Berkeley: University of California Press, 1988. 135–54.

Zacher, Christian. *Curiosity and Pilgrimage: The Literature of Discovery in Fourteenth-Century England.* Baltimore: Johns Hopkins University Press, 1976.

Zumthor, Paul. *Toward a Medieval Poetics,* trans. Philip Bennett. Minneapolis: University of Minnesota Press, 1992.

Zutshi, P. N. R. "Some Inedited Papal Documents Relating to the University of Cambridge in the Fourteenth Century." *Archivum historiae pontificiae* 26 (1988): 393–409.

———. "Collective Indulgences from Rome and Avignon in English Collections." In *Medieval Ecclesiastical Studies in Honour of Dorothy M. Owen*, ed. M. J. Franklin and Christopher Harper-Bill. Woodbridge, Suffolk: Boydell, 1995. 281–97.

Index of Historical and Modern Works, Authors, Persons, and Topics

Literary works by known authors are listed under the authors' names, anonymous works under the names of the works. References to characters and personages in *Piers Plowman*, and in the Bible, are included (but are not exhaustive for sections where those figures are continually present), but not those in other works. Central discussions of figures or central ideas in *Piers Plowman* are indicated in bold. All modern scholars are included (except simply as editors of primary texts), using initials only of first names; all other writers, historical and modern, are given with full names. References to the commentaries in Pearsall (Prsl), Schmidt (Schm), and Bennett (Bnt), and to the two handbooks by John A. Alford (Alford, *Gloss.* and Alford, *Quot.*), are not included since they are ubiquitous, but references to other works by those scholars are included, as are references to comments by Skeat in his edition (Skt). The topics included are chiefly restricted to literary, historical, and social materials mentioned in the commentary, such as literary traditions, genres, historical events, and some basic issues in the poem and its contexts (e.g., "Latin satire"; "law"; "kingship"). References to mentions of a small number of more abstract themes recurrent in the poem are also collected here, but they are meant to be suggestive and are certainly not comprehensive. References to discussion of editorial or textual issues are gathered under "textual cruces"; references to manuscripts under "manuscripts"; references to particular statutes and ordinances under "statutes and ordinances."

Index of Passages and Notes Mentioned in the Commentary

Citations do not include those made within the passages' own lemmata. As in the commentary, references to notes ("n") by passage refer to notes that often include discussion of all the other parallel versions.